The Queer Encyclopedia of Music, Dance & Musical Theater

The Queer Encyclopedia of Music, Dance & Musical Theater

Claude J. Summers

Editor

Published in the United States by Cleis Press Inc.,
P.O. Box 14697, San Francisco, California 94114.
Printed in the United States.
Cover design: Scott Idleman
Cover photograph: Vaslav Nijinski rehearsing "La Danse Siamoise" (from *Les Orientales*) taken Sunday, June 19, 1910, by Eugène Druet. © Bibliothèque Nationale de France.
Book design: Karen Quigg
Cleis Press logo art: Juana Alicia
First Edition.
10 9 8 7 6 5 4 3 2 1

Many organizations and individuals have been indispensable in providing access to the images that illustrate *The Queer Encyclopedia of Music, Dance & Musical Theater*. These deserve particular thanks. Blackheart Records for providing the image on page 135. Cleis Press for providing the images on pages 141 and 187. Clipart.com for providing the image on page 79 (Copyright © 2002–2004, Clipart.com). Dreamworks Records for providing the image on page 282. Marc Geller for providing the image on page 222. Les Ballets Trockadero de Monte Carlo for providing the image on page 17. The Library of Congress Prints and Photographs Division for providing the images on pages 1, 4, 18, 25, 29, 92, 114, 117, 167, 168, 209, 214, 217, 227, 230, 237, 246, 253, 255, and 256. The Mark Morris Dance Group and Cleis Press for providing the image on page 177. Miller Wright and Associates, Inc. for providing the image on page 103. Holly Near for providing the image on page 186. NewsCom for providing the images on pages 68, 223, 241, and 267. NewsCom/INFGoff.com for providing the image on page 137. NewsCom/Notimex for providing the image on page 262. NewsCom/UPPA for providing the image on page 244. Northwestern University Library Art Collection for providing access to the image on page 144. The office of Tom Robinson for providing the image on page 218. Righteous Babe Records for providing the image on page 80. Rude Girl Publishing for providing the image on page 128. Sacks and Company for providing the image on 156. Snap/Zuma/NewsCom for providing the images on pages 108 and 159. Wolf Moon, Inc. for providing the image on page 274. Zuma Press/NewsCom for providing the image on page 162.

LIBRARY OF CONGRESS CATALOGING-IN-PUBLICATION DATA

The queer encyclopedia of music, dance, and musical theater / Claude J. Summers, editor.—1st ed.
    p. cm.
    Includes bibliographical references and indexes.
    ISBN 1-57344-198-8 (pbk. : alk. paper)
1. Homosexuality and music—Encyclopedias. 2. Homosexuality and dance—Encyclopedias. 3. Music—Encyclopedias. 4. Dance—Encyclopedias. 5. Musicals—Encyclopedias. I. Summers, Claude J.
    ML100.Q44 2004
    791'.08664'03—dc22
                2004021689

For Ted, again;

and for Wik, the "onlie begetter,"

and for Albert Carey and George Koschel

CONTENTS

ACKNOWLEDGMENTS

A collaborative project of the scope of *The Queer Encyclopedia of Music, Dance & Musical Theater* necessarily depends on the kindness and cooperation of numerous individuals, including especially the authors of the articles.

I owe most to Andrew "Wik" Wikholm, President of glbtq, Inc., whose vision and commitment and enthusiasm have made this book possible. Ted-Larry Pebworth has been a supportive partner and collaborator in many ways beyond the indexing and copyediting skills that he has deployed in this project. Linda Rapp, friend and assistant, has generously contributed her time, energy, and expertise.

I am grateful to all those who offered advice and made suggestions, especially as to topics and contributors. Patricia Juliana Smith and Thomas Riis have been especially helpful as members of the www.glbtq.com advisory board, as was Douglas Turnbaugh. Michael Tanimura, production manager at glbtq, discovered a number of inconsistencies and errors and knew how to correct them. Betsy Greco, glbtq project administrator, has been unfailingly efficient and cheerful. The sharp-eyed and informed editorial staff at Cleis Press has been a joy to work with. I am especially grateful to Mark Rhynsburger.

Work on this project has been sustained by the support of numerous friends, including Albert Carey, Raymond Frontain, Robert Herndon, and George Koschel.

Introduction

*T*HE QUEER ENCYCLOPEDIA OF MUSIC, DANCE & *Musical Theater* introduces a remarkably rich cultural achievement. It surveys the contributions of gay, lesbian, bisexual, transgender, and queer people to popular and classical music, modern dance and ballet, and musical theater and opera, and also their representation in and sometimes vexed relationship to these varied arts. That is, this work is interested in glbtq individuals not only as composers, choreographers, lyricists, and performers, but also as subjects and objects and consumers of music, dance, and musical theater.

Presenting some 170 articles on individuals, artistic movements, musical genres, and topics such as Music and AIDS, Women's Music, and Cabarets and Revues, *The Queer Encyclopedia of Music, Dance & Musical Theater* offers a revisionist history of these arts by seeing them through a queer lens. It places the achievements of gay, lesbian, bisexual, transgender, and queer composers, musicians, and performers in historical contexts and privileges the representation of subjects that have traditionally been censored or marginalized.

Celebrating the richness and variety of queer contributions to the musical arts, this book presents that achievement as an invaluable cultural legacy to be celebrated and treasured. This legacy includes accomplishments as diverse as the protean and transforming vision of Sergei Diaghilev and the iconoclasm of John Cage; the contributions of composers as different but equally seminal as George Frideric Handel, Cole Porter, and Billy Strayhorn; the vital work of blues artists as redoubtable as "Ma" Rainey and Bessie Smith; the accomplishments of performers as distinct as Joan Baez, Ray Bourbon, Liberace, Janis Joplin, Peter Pears, Charles Pierce, and the Indigo Girls; and the community-building efforts of gay and lesbian choruses and bands and women's music festivals.

It would be hard to imagine twentieth-century classical music without the presence of such gay or bisexual composers as Aaron Copland, Samuel Barber, Leonard Bernstein, Benjamin Britten, Manuel de Falla, or Karol Szymanowski, or to appreciate opera without understanding the phenomena of castrati, opera queens, and diva worship. But glbtq performers and composers have also influenced musical genres as apparently "nongay" as hard rock and even as reputedly "antigay" as jazz and country music, even as they have also pioneered in creating genres particularly associated with modern lesbian and gay culture, such as women's music, drag performance, and disco and dance music. Moreover, certain performers—Judy Garland, Mabel Mercer, and Chavela Vargas, for example—and certain genres—opera and musical theater, most obviously—have had a particular resonance with glbtq audiences.

The queer presence in the musical arts is so various and pervasive that it resists neat summary. Indeed, it is an integral part of humanity's artistic expression, and as diverse as humanity itself. It can scarcely be divorced from "mainstream music and dance," for so many of the world's most prominent composers, choreographers, and performers have in fact been of alternative sexualities. One could not write a history of world music and dance without acknowledging the pivotal contributions of individuals whose sexual interests or gender expression varied from the orthodox (though, of course, many histories have been written that suppress the sexualities of those individuals).

Yet there is real value in isolating queer contributions to music and dance in order to see them in their own terms as expressions of a multifaceted queer artistic impulse and as documentations of the variety of queer experience. That these contributions have often been made in the face of rejection and prejudice, and at the expense of denial and invisibility, make them even more remarkable.

Not only have gay men and lesbians made enormous contributions to musical theater, cabaret, dance, and opera, but these art forms have enjoyed particular favor with glbtq audiences. Hence, the relationship of queer audiences to particular forms of music and dance is also a recurrent subject of this book.

Queer art has so often been denigrated, suppressed, or robbed of its specificity and roots in efforts to render it "universal," that it has very infrequently been seen whole and in the contexts that gave it life. The aim of *The Queer Encyclopedia of Music, Dance & Musical Theater* is to help remedy the effects of an old but still active, homophobic project of exclusion and denial, by in fact presenting queer music and dance whole and in the multiple contexts that helped shape it. Doing so yields new insight into the creation of art and increases our understanding of a wide range of artistic achievements.

Recovering and Reclaiming Our Artistic Heritage

Recovering our cultural heritage is a crucially important endeavor for everyone, but it is especially significant for gay men, lesbians, and others who have grown up in families and societies in which their sexual identities or gender expressions have been ignored, concealed, or condemned. They often come to a realization of their difference with little or no understanding of alternative sexualities beyond the negative stereotypes that pervade contemporary society, and they usually feel isolated and frightened at the very time they most need reassurance and encouragement.

Not surprisingly, a staple of the gay and lesbian coming-out story is the trip to the local library, where the young homosexual, desperate for the most basic information, is usually utterly confused or bitterly disappointed by what he or she discovers, for even now our society does not make it easy for young people to find accurate information about alternative sexualities. Only later is the radical loneliness of young people who have accepted their sexual identity assuaged by the discovery of a large and varied cultural heritage, one that speaks directly to the experience of contemporary men and women in the West but that also reflects other forms of same-sex love and desire in different times and places.

This volume is at once a documentation and reclamation of that cultural legacy and also a contribution to it. It participates in a long endeavor by queer men and women to recover a social and cultural history that has frequently been deliberately distorted and censored.

For centuries, educated and literate homosexuals living in eras that condemned homosexuality have looked to other ages and other societies in order to find cultural permission for homosexual behavior, to experience some relief from the incessant attacks on their self-esteem, and to penetrate the barriers of censorship that precluded open discussion of the love that dared not speak its name. Such attempts range from the ubiquitous lists of famous homosexuals in history to more elaborate and sophisticated historical research, such as that of Jeremy Bentham in the eighteenth century and of Edward Carpenter and John Addington Symonds at the end of the nineteenth century, as well as the recurrent attempts by gay and lesbian artists and writers to discover traditions and languages through which to express themselves.

Too often, however, attempts to document the gay and lesbian cultural legacy paid little attention to historical differences and tended to make few distinctions between different kinds of homosexualities, equating the emergent homosexual of the nineteenth century with the ancient Greek pederast, the medieval sodomite, and the Native North American *berdache*, for example, as though all four phenomena were merely minor variations on the same pattern.

The Queer Encyclopedia of Music, Dance & Musical Theater is motivated by the same impulse to understand the past and to recover the (often suppressed or disguised) artistic expressions of same-sex love that propelled earlier projects. But as the beneficiary of a more open climate and a recent explosion of knowledge about homosexuality in history, it is in a far better position to discover a usable past. The new understanding of sexuality in history and culture that emerged in the 1980s and 1990s has in fact enabled this particular enterprise. Without the gay, lesbian, and queer studies movement, this volume would not have been possible.

Gay, Lesbian, Queer Studies Movement

In entering the academic mainstream, gay, lesbian, and queer studies have enlarged our understanding of the meaning of sexual identities, both in our own culture and in other times and places. They have challenged naive, uninformed, and prejudiced views, and, perhaps most important, have discovered and recovered significant artifacts and neglected artists.

Queer studies in music and dance have also reclaimed established and celebrated composers and performers, revealing the pertinence and centrality of (frequently disguised or previously misinterpreted) same-sex relationships and queer experience to understanding canonical works. They have viewed celebrated achievements through a queer lens, in the process discovering aspects of the world's artistic heritage that either had not been noticed or had been suppressed.

But although gay, lesbian, and queer studies have enriched the academic study of history and culture, they still tend to be ghettoized in elite universities, often in women's studies programs that are themselves frequently isolated. Meanwhile, standard cultural histories continue all too often to omit or discount gay and lesbian representations, fail to supply relevant biographical information about gay, lesbian, bisexual, and transgender artists, and foster the grievously mistaken impression that the world's artistic traditions are almost exclusively heterosexual.

The Queer Encyclopedia of Music, Dance & Musical Theater aims to redress these deficiencies. It seeks to place portrayals of same-sex desire in historical context, to provide accurate biographical information about artists who have contributed to queer artistic traditions, and to explore important questions about the presence of homoeroticism in the world's artistic legacy.

How does the homosexuality of an artist affect his or her work even when that work has nothing specifically to do with homosexuality? How does one decipher the "coding" of works in which the homosexual import is disguised? Is there such a thing as a gay sensibility? Are some musical genres more amenable to homoeroticism than others? Why have gay men been especially enthralled by ballet, opera, and musical theater? Why have folk music traditions been so important in the creation of women's music? Why is Judy Garland such an icon of gay men of a certain age? Why is drag performance so important a feature of gay male and (more recently) lesbian culture? Why have so few gay conductors been able to be open about their sexuality? These are some of the questions asked and variously answered in this book.

Theoretical Issues

The study of the representation of alternative sexualities in culture must inevitably confront a variety of vexed issues, including basic conceptual questions of definition and identity. Who, exactly, is a homosexual? What constitutes sexual identity? To what extent is sexuality the product of broadly defined social forces? To what degree do sexual object-choices manifest a biological or psychological essence within the desiring individual? These questions not only are problematic for the historical study of homosexuality and of queer art, but also reflect current controversies about contemporary and historical sexual roles and categories, and they resist glib answers.

Although contemporary North Americans and Western Europeans typically think in terms of a dichotomy between homosexuality and heterosexuality, and between the homosexual and the heterosexual, with vague compartments for bisexuality and bisexuals, such a conception is a historically contingent cultural construct, more revealing of our own age's sexual ideology than of actual erotic practices even today. The range of human sexual response is considerably less restricted than these artificial classifications suggest, and different ages and cultures have interpreted (and regulated) sexual behavior differently.

Because human sexual behavior and emotions are fluid and various rather than static or exclusive, the sexologist Alfred Kinsey and others have argued that the terms *homosexual* and *heterosexual* should more properly be used as adjectives rather than nouns, referring to acts and emotions but not to people. Moreover, the conception of homosexuality and heterosexuality as essential and exclusive categories has historically operated as a form of social control, defining the person who responds erotically to individuals of his or her own sex as the "Other," or, more particularly, as *queer* or *unnatural*.

But though it may be tempting to conclude that there are no such entities as homosexuals or heterosexuals or bisexuals, this view, which so attractively stresses the commonality of human beings and minimizes the significance of sexual object-choices, poses its own dangers. Human sexuality is simply not as plastic as some theorists assert, and to deny the existence of homosexuals, bisexuals, and heterosexuals—or the pertinence of such categories—is to deny the genuineness of the personal identities and forms of erotic life that exist today. It is, indeed, to engage in a process of denial and erasure, rendering invisible a group that has had to struggle for recognition and visibility.

For most people, sexual orientation is not merely a matter of choice or preference but a classification that reflects a deep-seated internal, as well as social, reality. However arbitrary, subjective, inexact, and culture-bound the labels may be, they are impossible to escape and they affect individuals—especially those in the minority categories—in profound and manifold ways.

The most painful and destructive injustice visited upon people of alternative sexuality has been their separation from the normal and the natural, their stigmatization as *queer*. Yet the internalization of this stigma has also been their greatest strength and, indeed, the core of their identity in societies that regularly assign individuals to ostensibly exclusive categories of sexual desire. The consciousness of difference both spurred and made possible the recent creation of a homosexual minority—a gay and lesbian community—in the Western democracies, a process that involved transforming the conception of homosexuality from a "social problem" and personal failing to an individual and collective identity.

Quite apart from the fact that it facilitates identity politics, however, an acceptance of otherness, whether defined as lesbian, gay, bisexual, transgender, or the umbrella term *queer*, is also often personally empowering. Fostering qualities of introspection and encouraging social analysis, it enables people who feel excluded from some of the core assumptions and rituals of their society to evaluate themselves and their society from an ambiguous and often revealing perspective.

Homoerotic desire and behavior have been documented in every conceivable kind of society. What varies are the meanings that they are accorded from era to era and place to place. In some societies, homosexuality is tolerated and even institutionalized, whereas in others it is vilified and persecuted. In every society, there are undoubtedly individuals who are predominantly attracted to members of their own sex or who do not conform easily to gender expectations, but the extent to which that sexual attraction or gender nonconformity functions as a defining characteristic of these individuals' personal and social identities varies considerably from culture to culture.

Thus, any transhistorical and transcultural exploration of the queer artistic heritage must guard against the risk of anachronism, of inappropriately imposing contemporary culture-bound conceptions of homosexuality on earlier ages and different societies. Sexual categories are always historically and culturally specific rather than universal and invariant.

On the other hand, however, the recognition of cultural specificity in regard to sexual attitudes need not estrange the past or obscure connections and continuities between historical periods and between sexual ideologies. For instance, modern North American and Western European male homosexuality, which is predominantly androphilic (that is, between adult men), egalitarian, and socially disdained, is in many crucial respects quite different from ancient Greek male homosexuality, which was predominantly—though by no means exclusively—pederastic, asymmetrical in power, and socially valorized; but awareness of those differences does not obviate the similarities that link the two distinct historical constructs.

Neither does the acknowledgment of the distinctions between ancient Greek homosexuality and modern homosexuality entail the dismissal of the enormous influence that classical Greek attitudes toward same-sex love exerted on the formation of modern Western attitudes toward homosexuality. For many individuals in the early modern and modern eras, ancient Greek literature, philosophy, and art helped counter the negative attitudes toward same-sex eroticism fostered by Christian culture. Ancient Greek literature and art have provided readers, writers, and artists of subsequent centuries a pantheon of heroes, a catalogue of images, and a set of references by which same-sex desire could be encoded into their own representations and through which they could interpret their own experiences.

Nor should our sensitivity to the cultural specificity of sexual attitudes cause us to rob individual artists of individual perspectives or to condescend toward the past. All artists exist in relation to their time and must necessarily create from within their world views, or, as philosopher Michel Foucault would say, the *epistemes* of their ages. But the fact that artists are embedded in their cultures does not mean that they lack agency and individuality.

Artists tend to be more independent than their contemporaries, not less; and though they may express the tendencies and suppositions of their societies, they also frequently challenge them, even if those challenges are themselves facilitated and contained by societal beliefs. Hence, it is a mistake to assume that artists of earlier ages, before the general emergence of a modern homosexual identity, could not share important aspects of that consciousness, including a subjective awareness of difference and a sense of alienation from society. One of the rewards of studying the queer artistic heritage is, in fact, the discovery of a queer subjectivity in the past and of the affinities as well as differences between earlier and later homosexualities.

A Beginning, Not an End

For all its considerable heft, *The Queer Encyclopedia of Music, Dance & Musical Theater* has no pretensions to comprehensiveness. There are some notable omissions of topics and artists, due variously to lack of space, an absence of available information and research, a difficulty in finding qualified contributors, and a continuing fearfulness on the part of many performers and artists to acknowledge their sexuality, even in fields such as opera or musical theater that would seem to be queer friendly. Moreover, *The Queer Encyclopedia of Music, Dance & Musical Theater* is undoubtedly biased in favor of European and American musical traditions, even as it also provides a great deal of information about other traditions and cultures.

The point that needs emphasis, however, is that as the first comprehensive work of its kind, this encyclopedia is an important beginning, not an end. It introduces readers to a wealth of achievement in the areas of music and dance, making accessible the fruits of the intense study that has recently been focused on queer culture.

How to Use *The Queer Encyclopedia of Music, Dance & Musical Theater*

S IR FRANCIS BACON DIVIDED BOOKS INTO THREE TYPES. "Some books are to be tasted, others to be swallowed, and some few to be chewed and digested: that is, some books are to be read only in parts; others to be read, but cursorily; and some few to be read wholly and with diligence and attention." This book aspires to all three categories.

We certainly believe that *The Queer Encyclopedia of Music, Dance & Musical Theater* is inviting and rewarding enough to entice readers into diligent and attentive study. At the same time, however, we hope that the book will also invite browsers, who will dip into it repeatedly over time for pleasure and enlightenment. In addition, we hope that it will serve as a valuable reference tool for readers who need to find particular information quickly.

The essays in the *Encyclopedia* are presented alphabetically, an arrangement that should encourage browsing. They are generally of three types: overviews of musical and dance genres, essays on topics or movements of particular significance for the queer musical and dance traditions, and entries on individual artists important to the queer musical and dance heritage. The A-to-Z List of Entries provides a convenient, alphabetical guide to the entries.

The entries on individual artists are diverse, varying from succinct accounts to in-depth critical analyses of major figures. The most important criterion in determining whether an artist was assigned an entry is his or her contribution to the queer musical and dance tradition. The lack of an individual entry for a composer or

dancer or performer does not, however, mean that the individual is not significant to the glbtq heritage or is not discussed in the volume. For example, there are no entries for Francesca Caccini, often credited as the first woman opera composer, or for the contemporary choreographer Matthew Bourne, who has staged some spectacularly homoerotic dances, but both can be found in the volume. Discussions of artists who are not accorded individual author entries can most conveniently be found via the Index of Names.

The frequent cross-references should be helpful for readers interested in related topics or in finding further discussions of particular authors. At the end of nearly all the articles, readers are urged to "see also" other entries.

Each article is followed by a brief bibliography. With some exceptions, the bibliographies emphasize secondary rather than primary material, pointing the reader to other studies of the topic or artist.

Finally, the volume's two indexes should be of help in maneuvering through this large collection. The Topical Index conveniently groups entries that are related to each other in various ways, such as sharing the same musical genre or profession. One can tell at a glance, for example, what entries discuss popular music or classical music or musical theater or dance or composers or choreographers, and so on. The Index of Names should be especially valuable in enabling readers to discover discussions of individual artists or other figures, some of whom are discussed in several entries in addition to—or in lieu of—their own entries.

A-to-Z List of Entries

Topical Index

Ailey, Alvin (1931–1989)

As a dancer, Alvin Ailey was noted for his sexual charisma. Lena Horne famously described him as "like a young lion and yet like an earth man." But he achieved international acclaim as a choreographer. His company has performed before an estimated fifteen million people in forty-eight states and forty-five countries.

Ailey was born on January 5, 1931, in direst poverty in the Brazos Valley of Texas. His father abandoned him and his mother three months later.

At various stages of his life Ailey had to contend with racism, homophobia, issues of political correctness, exploitative sexual partners, and venal management. In the face of all these obstacles, he triumphed as a creative genius. But homophobia, especially that of his mother, undermined his sense of worth as a man and helped make his personal life a tragedy.

When Ailey was a child, he moved with his mother to Los Angeles, where she secured work in an aircraft factory. School was a haven for him. He spent long hours in the library, reading and writing poetry. The large, solidly built boy who looked like fullback material managed to avoid contact sports—and avoid being stigmatized as a sissy—by taking up gymnastics.

At the age of eighteen, Ailey caught the eye of Lester Horton, a white dancer, teacher, and choreographer who had created in Los Angeles the first multiracial dance company in the United States. With Horton, Ailey found an emotional home and quickly learned dance styles and

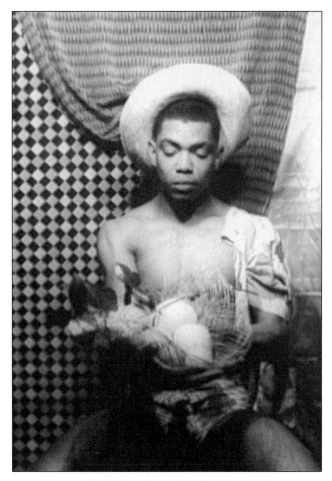

Alvin Ailey, photographed by Carl Van Vechten in 1955.

techniques from classical ballet to Native American dance. He performed in Horton's company and found work in Hollywood films, eventually succeeding Horton as director upon the latter's death in 1953.

For the first two years that Ailey danced with the Lester Horton company, he kept his life in dance a secret from his mother. When she first came to his dressing room and saw him in stage makeup, she slapped his face.

Ailey moved to New York in 1954 to dance on Broadway. He appeared in *House of Flowers* (1954), with Harry Belafonte in *Sing, Man, Sing* (1956), and with Lena Horne in *Jamaica* (1957). He also studied with teachers such as Martha Graham, Hanya Holm, and Karel Shook, while beginning to choreograph pieces of his own.

In 1957, Ailey formed his own group, which presented its inaugural concert on March 30, 1958. Among the dances premiered in that concert was his *Blues Suite,* a work deriving from blues songs that expresses the pain and anger felt by African Americans. With its combination of ballet, modern dance, jazz, and black dance techniques, plus flamboyant theatricality and intense emotional appeal, *Blues Suite* was an instant success and defined Ailey's particular genius.

In 1960, for his company's third season, Ailey created his masterpiece, *Revelations.* Based on African American spirituals and gospel music, it is perhaps the most popular ballet created in the twentieth century.

While Ailey continued to choreograph for his own company, he created dances for other companies as well. For example, in 1973 he created *Ariadne* for the Harkness Ballet, with Maria Tallchief in the title role; and in 1983 he devised *Precipice* for the Paris Opera Ballet.

Ailey was proud that his company was multiracial. On the one hand, he wanted to give black dancers, who had often been discriminated against by other dance companies, an opportunity to dance; but he also wanted to transcend the issue of *negritude*—what in later years would be called black pride. His company employed dancers, composers, and choreographers of all hues based entirely on their artistic talent.

While Ailey was pleased that the U.S. State Department sponsored his company's first overseas tour in 1962, he suspected that the sponsors' motives were propagandistic rather than altruistic, as they wanted to demonstrate that "a modern Negro dance group" could flourish in the United States.

Ailey was profoundly honored when American Ballet Theatre commissioned *The River* (1970), to music of Duke Ellington. He looked upon the commission as an opportunity to work with some of the best ballet dancers in the world, particularly the great dramatic ballerina Sally Wilson. However, he was deeply disappointed when ABT insisted that the leading male role be danced by the only black man in the company, who was a conspicuously mediocre dancer.

Although his company was sometimes described as patriarchal, with male dancers the center of attention, Ailey was also known for fostering the careers of several important female dancers, most notably Judith Jamison, who debuted with the company in 1965 and who spoke of Ailey as a great teacher. One of Ailey's major successes was *Cry* (1971), which he dedicated to his mother and to black women everywhere and which became a signature piece for Jamison.

Ailey was a loving man, who was adored by many devoted friends and who functioned as a father figure to his dancers. However, his personal and professional lives were dogged with problems. Abused by lovers, he seemed in later life to enjoy the company of street hustlers. Similarly, he entrusted management and money matters to people who victimized him.

The Alvin Ailey American Dance Theater did not secure a permanent home and stable management until 1979, when the company and school moved into splendid facilities in the Broadway theater district of Manhattan. But by this time, Ailey had become erratic. He was addicted to cocaine, increasingly crippled by arthritis, and dependent on lithium as a mood regulator.

Like many men of his generation, including Jerome Robbins, for example, Ailey was deeply ashamed of his homosexuality. For years, he refused to consider writing an autobiography because "my mother wouldn't like it." When he finally did collaborate on an autobiography, it was sexually sanitized, notwithstanding the fact that it was to be published posthumously. To spare his mother the social stigma of his death of AIDS in 1989, Ailey asked his doctor to announce that he had died of terminal blood dyscrasia.

Although the choreographer could sincerely dance to the words "I've been 'buked and I've been scorned," he nevertheless managed to celebrate the beauty of his heritage and translate his pain into art. His ballets embody his aspirations for all-encompassing love and compassion. They still rock the soul of a worldwide audience.

—*Douglas Blair Turnbaugh*

BIBLIOGRAPHY

Ailey, Alvin, with A. Peter Bailey. *Revelations. The Autobiography of Alvin Ailey.* New York: Birch Lane Press; Secaucus, N.J.: Carol Publishing Group, 1995.

Craine, Debra, and Judith Mackrell. "Alvin Ailey." *The Oxford Dictionary of Dance.* New York: Oxford University Press, 2000. 5–6.

Dunning, Jennifer. *A Life in Dance.* Reading, Mass.: Addison-Wesley, 1996.

Marie, Jacquelyn. "Alvin Ailey." *Gay & Lesbian Biography.* Michael J. Tyrkus, ed. Detroit: St. James Press, 1997. 8–10.

Mitchell, Jack. *Alvin Ailey American Dance Theater: Jack Mitchell Photographs.* Judith Jamison, foreword; Richard Philp, introduction. Kansas City: Andrews and McMeel, 1994.

SEE ALSO

Dance; Ballet; Robbins, Jerome

Allan, Maud   *(1873–1956)*

IN THE EARLY YEARS OF THE TWENTIETH CENTURY, Maud Allan achieved worldwide renown as "the Salome Dancer" for her stunning performances of the best-known piece in her repertoire, *The Vision of Salome.* She is also remembered for a lawsuit that she brought against a newspaper publisher for alleging that she was a lesbian. Although it was Allan who charged libel, in court her opponent tried to put both her and Oscar Wilde's play *Salome* on trial.

Early Life and Education

Born Beulah Maud Durrant in 1873 in Toronto, Allan was the daughter of William Allan Durrant, a shoemaker, and Isa (also known as Isabella) Matilda Hutchinson. Three years after her birth, William Durrant moved to San Francisco, where he bounced from job to job, mainly in the shoe manufacturing industry. In 1879, Isabella Durrant followed with their two children, Maud and her brother William Henry Theodore (usually known as Theo).

As a youngster Allan excelled at arts and crafts—carving, clay modeling, sketching, and sewing. She also showed talent for music and studied to be a concert pianist. It may be that the dream of a career for Allan on the concert stage was at least as much her mother's as her own, but the young woman showed sufficient promise that her teacher, Eugene Bonelli of the San Francisco Grand Academy of Music, advised her to go to Germany to complete her musical studies.

In February 1895, Allan set off for Berlin, where she was admitted to the Hochschule für Musik. Hardly had she begun her studies, however, when she received the shocking news that her brother had been arrested for murder.

In April 1895, the bodies of two young women were discovered in San Francisco's Emmanuel Baptist Church, where Theo Durrant was the assistant Sunday School superintendent. The grisly murders, which were compared to the crimes of Jack the Ripper, received sensational and sometimes speculative coverage in the California press. Over 3,600 potential jurors needed to be examined before twelve could be chosen to hear the case.

On November 1, the jury found Durrant guilty of first-degree murder. He was sentenced to be put to death on February 21, 1896, but appeals of the case delayed the execution three times. Durrant was finally hanged for murder on January 7, 1898.

Throughout this entire period, Maud Allan, at her brother's request, remained in Europe. The siblings, who had always been extremely close, kept in frequent contact by letter. Allan held out hope for a reprieve until the very end, and she never stopped asserting her belief in her brother's innocence.

With little money coming from her family in America, Allan needed to work while pursuing her studies. She sometimes gave English lessons but earned little in this way. She had greater success when she joined with several other people in a corset-making business. (Allan designed, sewed, and even modeled the product.) On one occasion she put her drawing skills to use, illustrating a sex manual for women, *Illustriertes Konversations-Lexikon der Frau* (1900).

Dancing Career

Although Allan continued her piano studies as her mother wished, she had become intrigued with the idea of "dancing as an art of poetical and musical expression." A pivotal point in her career came when she met the Belgian musician and critic Marcel Rémy, who encouraged her to explore and develop her thoughts on dance and who wrote the music for *The Vision of Salome,* the performance piece for which Allan would become famous.

Allan would always emphasize that she had never taken a dancing lesson and insist that her style of dancing was entirely her own creation. What rankled her especially was to be compared to Isadora Duncan, whom she strongly disliked. While Allan's claims of complete originality were overstated, she did show great imagination and creativity. These, combined with her unconventional costumes (which she designed and sometimes sewed herself), lent uniqueness to her art. Her musicality and natural grace allowed her to suit her movements to music most effectively. As one reviewer put it, "She simply alchemized a piece of music for you."

Although Allan's repertoire consisted of a wide variety of pieces, including Mendelssohn's *Spring Song,* Schubert's *Ave Maria,* and Chopin's *Marche funèbre,* it was Rémy's *The Vision of Salome* that made her reputation and earned her the nickname "the Salome Dancer." Her interpretation of the piece was all the more powerful because Rémy had caused her to associate the execution of John the Baptist with that of her own brother, thus evoking an especially passionate performance of this work.

In 1908, Allan went to London and took the city by storm, giving more than 250 performances that year. As a result of her fame, she received the patronage of members of royalty and of Prime Minister Herbert Asquith and his wife Margot. Allan developed a close friendship with Margot Asquith, who for many years paid the rent for Allan's luxurious living quarters in the west wing of Holford House, a villa overlooking Regent's Park.

In 1910, Allan left Europe and toured extensively for several years, performing in America, Africa, Asia, and Australia. In 1915, she went to California to spend time with her parents. During that sojourn she played the title role in a silent film called *The Rugmaker's Daughter*. It featured excerpts of three of her dances, including *The Vision of Salome*. Unfortunately, no copies of this film are known to survive.

"The Cult of the Clitoris" Libel Case

In 1916, Allan returned to England in hopes of reviving her faltering career. In 1918, she became involved in a bizarre court case resulting from her performance in a production of Oscar Wilde's *Salome*. The case was a tangled thicket of personal and political animosity as well as homophobia, anti-Semitism, and wartime hysteria.

Allan sued for libel against an Independent Member of Parliament, Noel Pemberton Billing. In addition to his political career, Billing ran a newspaper called the *Imperialist*, later renamed the *Vigilante*, which he used to promulgate his views that Germany was a thoroughly degenerate country owing to the power of Jews and homosexuals there and that German agents were attempting to weaken the moral fabric of Britain by luring its citizens into vice.

In the January 26, 1918, issue of the *Imperialist*, Billing claimed that the Germans had a "Black Book" containing the names of 47,000 British men and women who were vulnerable to blackmail or had betrayed state secrets because of their "sexual peculiarities." His source for this claim was Captain Harold Spencer, who had been invalided out of the British Army and British Secret Service for "delusional insanity."

Billing invited a lawsuit from Allan by printing an item in the February 16, 1918, issue of the *Vigilante* headlined "The Cult of the Clitoris." In the brief article he suggested that subscribers to Allan's upcoming private performance of Wilde's *Salome* were likely to be among the 47,000 listed in the "Black Book."

The use of the word *clitoris* was a calculated one by Billing and Spencer. The latter testified that, in the course of searching for a headline "that would only be understood by those whom it should be understood by," he had elicited the word from a village doctor, who had informed him that the clitoris was an "organ that, when unduly excited...possessed the most dreadful influence on any woman...." Allan's acknowledgment that she knew the word was presented as evidence of sexual perversion.

Billing further used innuendo by introducing the fact that Allan was the sister of a convicted murderer. His argument was that murder showed evidence of sadism (defined, in the testimony of Spencer, as "the lust for dead bodies"), which Billing alleged was hereditary. He discussed various perversions that he claimed to find in Wilde's *Salome*, implying that a performer willing to depict these might well practice them herself. He also tried to insinuate that Allan had an unusually close friendship with Margot Asquith.

Another witness, Eileen Villiers-Stuart, who claimed to have seen the "Black Book," testified that the names of both Herbert and Margot Asquith were in it (along with that of Charles Darling, the judge presiding in the case).

On the final day of the trial, Billing suddenly claimed that he had never suggested that Allan was a lesbian, only that "she was pandering to those who practised unnatural vice by her performance."

Following long and rather confusing instructions from the judge, the jury deliberated for less than an hour and a half before returning a verdict in Billing's favor.

Maude Allan, photographed by Arnold Genthe in 1916.

Later Years

After the trial, Allan resumed her career, but her popularity soon waned.

For at least ten years, from the late 1920s to 1938, Allan shared the west wing of Holford House with Verna Aldrich, her secretary, who became her lover.

Allan lived out her final years in California. A film loosely based on her life, *Salome, Where She Danced*, was directed by Charles Lamont and produced by Walter Wanger in 1951.

Allan died on October 7, 1956, at the age of eighty-four.

—*Linda Rapp*

BIBLIOGRAPHY

Bland, Lucy. "Allan, Maud." *Lesbian Histories and Cultures.* Bonnie Zimmerman, ed. New York: Garland, 2000. 24–25.

Cherniavsky, Felix. *The Salome Dancer: The Life and Times of Maud Allan.* Toronto: McClelland & Stewart, 1991.

Hoare, Philip. *Wilde's Last Stand: Decadence, Conspiracy, and the First World War.* London: Duckworth, 1997.

Travis, Jennifer. "Clits in Court: Salome, Sodomy, and the Lesbian 'Sadist.'" *Lesbian Erotics.* Karla Jay, ed. New York: New York University Press, 1995. 147–163.

SEE ALSO

Dance; Duncan, Isadora; Schubert, Franz

Allen, Peter   (1944–1992)

CAMPY AND FLAMBOYANT, PETER ALLEN WAS THE supreme gay performer, a song-and-dance man with flash, romance, and a sense of humor about himself. A lifelong entertainer and award-winning songwriter, Allen won fame first as Judy Garland's protégé and Liza Minnelli's husband, then as a semicloseted gay artist whose scandalous affairs were whispered loudly around the entertainment world.

Although some critics sneered that Allen's success was due less to talent than to his relentless self-promotion, his rapid decline and death of AIDS in 1992 cut short a career that had been as irrepressible as Allen himself.

An Australian, Allen was born Peter Allen Woolnough in Tenterfield, New South Wales. When he was still a child, his father committed suicide, leaving Allen, his mother, and his sister to fend for themselves. Allen was a natural extrovert and took to the stage early, earning extra money for the family by singing in local pubs as early as age twelve. In 1959, he sought his fortune in the big city, moving to Sydney, where he met singer Chris Ball. Together they formed the popular Allen Brothers and sang rock and roll on television and in clubs around Australia and abroad.

On one of these tours, in 1964, while performing at the Hong Kong Hilton's Starlight Room, Allen met Judy Garland, who was attending the show with husband Mark Herron. Garland hired Allen's group to open for her, thus pushing Peter Allen further into the international limelight. Allen became close to Garland and her family. He married Garland's daughter Liza Minnelli in 1967 (they were divorced in 1970), and he had a relationship with Herron, Garland's soon-to-be-ex-husband.

After moving to the United States, Allen developed a campy cabaret act and pursued a fertile career as a songwriter. He wrote songs for fellow Australians Olivia Newton-John and Helen Reddy, including Newton-John's chart-topping hit "I Honestly Love You" (1974). He won a Grammy and an Oscar for his 1981 collaboration with Burt Bacharach, Christopher Cross, and Carole Bayer Sager on "Arthur's Theme" ("Best That You Can Do").

Allen also collaborated with Carole Bayer Sager on well-received tunes for Rita Coolidge and Melissa Manchester, as well as a touching tribute to Judy Garland called "Quiet Please, There's a Lady on the Stage" (1980). He teamed up with Australian songwriter Angry Anderson in 1979 to write the energetic rhythms of "I Go to Rio," which became his signature song.

But Allen was not content to remain behind the pen. His career was prolific and varied, even frenetic. During the 1980s, he performed to packed houses at Radio City Music Hall and created a long-running autobiographical musical titled "Up in One—More than a Concert." He remained popular in Australia; his "I Still Call Australia Home" (1972) has long been the advertising theme for Qantas Airways.

In 1988, he collaborated with Harvey Fierstein and Charles Suppon to create the ambitious Broadway musical flop *Legs Diamond*. Despite his disappointment at the musical's spectacular failure, Allen could not be defeated. At his last concert in Sydney, in January, 1992, he was still singing, dancing, and clowning before sold-out audiences.

While he was in Australia for that concert, Allen was bothered by a nagging sore throat. Trips to the doctor revealed that the pain in his throat was caused by Kaposi's sarcoma, an AIDS-related cancer. Allen died just five months later, on June 18, 1992, of AIDS-related complications.

Although his sexual orientation was widely known or suspected in the entertainment and gay communities, Allen was never publicly out as a gay man. However, his flamboyant persona and the subtexts of many of his songs, from the impossible romance of "I Honestly Love You" to the defiant raunch of "Honest Queen" (1971), clearly identified Allen to his gay fans.

Allen's life and music are the subject of the musical *The Boy from Oz*, featuring a book by playwright Martin Sherman and an acclaimed performance by Hugh Jackman as Allen. Despite mixed reviews, it scored a Broadway success in 2003. —*Tina Gianoulis*

BIBLIOGRAPHY

Flippo, Chet. "Peter Allen Has it All." *New York*, February 9, 1981, 31.

Goodman, Mark. "A Blazing Star Flickers Out." *People*, July 6, 1992, 49.

Rothstein, Mervyn. "Peter Allen Decides Life Is Not a Cabaret." *New York Times*, October 18, 1988.

Yahoo! Australia and New Zealand Music Website au.travel.yahoo.com/muze/performer/AllenPeter.html (May 7, 2000)

SEE ALSO

Popular Music; Cabarets and Revues; Faye, Frances; Garland, Judy

Ashman, Howard　　　　　(1950–1991)

AWARD-WINNING LYRICIST AND PLAYWRIGHT HOWARD Ashman collaborated with Alan Menken on projects as diverse as the stage musical *Little Shop of Horrors* and the animated Disney film *Beauty and the Beast*.

A native of Baltimore, born on May 17, 1950, Howard Elliott Ashman studied at Goddard College and Boston University and earned a Master of Fine Arts degree from Indiana University. The aspiring playwright moved to New York in 1974, taking an editing job at Grossett & Dunlap to earn a living while working at his craft.

Ashman's early plays include *'Cause Maggie's Afraid of the Dark*, *The Confirmation*, and *Dreamstuff*. The last, a musical version of Shakespeare's *The Tempest*, was presented at the WPA Theater in 1976. The theater closed shortly thereafter, but it reopened the following year with Ashman as its artistic director, a post he held until 1982.

During this time, Ashman began his musical collaboration with Alan Menken. Their first work, *God Bless You, Mr. Rosewater*, based on the Kurt Vonnegut Jr. novel of the same name, was produced in 1979, with Ashman directing. The play had moderate success, but greater things lay ahead.

Ashman wrote the book, and he and Menken the score, for *Little Shop of Horrors*, a musical based on Roger Corman's 1960 film. The play, which opened in 1982, was a spectacular success, becoming the highest-grossing off-Broadway musical to that time. The show earned the New York Drama Critics' Circle Award for Best Musical. The quirky story of flower-shop worker Seymour, his love-interest Audrey, and a monstrous man-eating plant became a movie musical in 1986. Frank Oz directed, and Ashman wrote the screenplay. Ashman and Menken received an Academy Award nomination for their music.

Ashman teamed with Marvin Hamlisch for *Smile* (1986), a musical stage version of Michael Ritchie's 1975 film spoofing beauty pageants. The show closed after a short run, but Ashman garnered a Tony nomination for Best Book.

Ashman reunited with Menken to write the music for John Musker and Ron Clements's Disney-animated feature film *The Little Mermaid* (1989). Their work earned them a Golden Globe Award, two Grammy Awards, and an Academy Award for the song "Under the Sea," a catchy calypso number.

In 1991, Ashman and Menken had another triumph with Gary Trousdale and Kirk Wise's *Beauty and the Beast*, another Disney production. The film, not originally conceived as a musical, gained direction when Ashman was brought on board as executive producer. It was he who encouraged the writers and producers to place the focus on the Beast's becoming a person, and to turn props—a candelabrum, a clock, and a teapot—into characters.

Ashman's contributions added considerably to the artistic richness of the film, elevating it from a mere cartoon to "what we used to see on Broadway," in the words of Angela Lansbury, who voiced Mrs. Potts, the teapot. *Beauty and the Beast* became the first fully-animated film to receive an Academy Award nomination as Best Picture.

Ashman worked on *Beauty and the Beast* when he was terminally ill with AIDS, a condition that he concealed even from Menken until after they had won the Oscar for *The Little Mermaid*. Tragically, Ashman was terrified of losing the opportunity to work and feared that "friends would be afraid to have their children sit on his lap, or to go out to dinner with him," according to Menken.

Ashman died on March 14, 1991. The following year, when the title song from *Beauty and the Beast* won the Oscar for Best Original Song, it was Ashman's life partner, architect William P. Lauch, who joined Menken in accepting the award. In a moving speech, Lauch proudly declared, "Howard and I shared a home and a life together." He went on to note that this was "the first Academy Award given to someone we've lost to AIDS." Later, he praised the Disney Company and the Motion Picture Academy for treating him as Ashman's survivor.

Beauty and the Beast bears a dedication to Ashman: "To our friend, Howard, who gave a mermaid her voice and a beast his soul, we will be forever grateful."

Until shortly before his death, Ashman had been collaborating with Menken on the score for another animated Disney feature, Musker and Clements's *Aladdin* (1992). One of their songs, "Friend Like Me," was nominated for an Oscar. When Ashman could no longer work, Tim Rice was brought in as lyricist to complete the score.

Menken stated that Ashman "was the best librettist of our generation" and praised his generous friendship, saying, "He was a tremendous support for a lot of people, including me."

Critics, impressed by the collaborative work of Ashman and Menken, saw in them the potential for taking a place among the great teams of musical theater. Their music ended too soon.   —*Linda Rapp*

BIBLIOGRAPHY

"'Beauty' Last Work by Lyricist Who Died of AIDS." *San Francisco Chronicle,* November 25, 1991.

Blau, Eleanor. "Howard Ashman Is Dead at 40; Writer of 'Little Shop of Horrors.'" *New York Times,* March 15, 1991.

Lipper, Hal. "Beauty in the Making." *St. Petersburg (Fla.) Times,* November 23, 1991.

Lyke, M. L. "Songwriting Team's Final Collaboration Beautifully Beastly." *Seattle Post-Intelligencer,* November 23, 1991.

Schaefer, Steven. "Composer Confronts 'Beast'; Partner's Death Haunts Menken." *Boston Herald,* November 21, 1991.

Weinraub, Bernard. "The Talk of Hollywood; 2 Titans Clash and All of Filmdom Feels Shock Waves." *New York Times,* April 13, 1992.

SEE ALSO

Musical Theater and Film

Ashton, Sir Frederick   (1904–1988)

S IR FREDERICK ASHTON MAY BE DESCRIBED AS THE choreographer who most fully defined British ballet in the twentieth century.

He was born on September 17, 1904, in Guayaquil, Ecuador, of English parents. In Lima, Peru, at the susceptible age of thirteen, he saw Anna Pavlova dance. In the great ballerina he recognized exquisite feminine qualities that he felt within himself. Pavlova became a template of the personality he was to become.

His father was repelled by Ashton's effeminacy. However, his siblings were not. "I was buggered by all of my brothers," Ashton recalled, adding that he "rather enjoyed it" with Charlie, the brother who later paid for his ballet lessons.

When he was fourteen, Ashton was sent to school in England. In London, he saw Sergei Diaghilev's Ballets Russes. He soon began to study dance with Léonide Massine, one of the Ballets Russes's leading choreographers.

After a brief career dancing with the Rubenstein Ballet in Paris, Ashton returned to England. Encouraged by Marie Rambert, he began creating ballets for her Ballet Club and the Camargo Society, as well as dances for revues and musical comedies.

Ashton's first great success, *Façade* (1931), still in active repertoire, epitomizes the combined qualities of wit, fantasy, elegance, and sophistication that distinguish him from all other choreographers. These qualities give Ashton a place in ballet akin to that of Oscar Wilde in literature.

In 1934, Ashton staged the Virgil Thomson-Gertrude Stein opera *Four Saints in Three Acts* in Hartford, Connecticut. The following year, Ninette de Valois invited him to join the Vic-Wells Ballet as dancer and choreographer.

Ashton remained with this company, which successively became the Sadler's Wells Ballet and then the Royal Ballet, for the next thirty-five years. He served as its artistic director from 1963 to 1970, the years of the company's greatest success. It was here that Ashton discovered in the ballerina Margot Fonteyn his alter ego. He would create leading roles for Fonteyn for twenty-five years.

Although he could not perform the ethereal roles for ballerina that he created for Fonteyn, Ashton did choreograph and perform great comic *travesti* roles, notably the Ugly Sisters in *Cinderella* (1948) and Widow Simone in *La Fille mal gardée* (1960). Ashton's hilarious performance as the older Ugly Sister, with Robert Helpman in a high-camp turn as the younger Ugly Sister, has become legendary, and these are now coveted roles.

Another of Ashton's great comic inventions is Bottom, the peasant weaver changed into an ass by naughty Puck in *The Dream* (1964, based on Shakespeare's *A Midsummer's Night's Dream*). Not only does the male dancer performing the role wear an ass mask, but he dances *en pointe* to give the effect of being hoofed.

Love is an essential theme and human relationships an important thread in all of Ashton's ballets, which are filled with tender moments. Although his oeuvre cannot be described as homoerotic, his creations are often the realization of a gay man's fantasy of being the goddess Pavlova, of being adored and lovingly partnered by a heterosexual man.

This subtext was not recognized by the general public, but it did reflect Ashton's own life. The choreographer's emotional life focused on the unattainable and the unsuitable, and it often wreaked havoc in his ballet company, as when, in the case of the heterosexual Michael Somes (Fonteyn's principal partner), Ashton's beloved enjoyed and exploited his favoritism to the point that other dancers signed a petition of protest.

Ashton, like so many other famous gay men of his epoch, including Cecil Beaton and Noël Coward, was necessarily discreet, but he was not closeted. The British high society in which he moved enjoyed the scintillating company of flamboyant gay artists.

Ashton was a member of the circle of gay men who surrounded Queen Elizabeth, the late Queen Mother, whom he taught to tango. When she heard that Ashton, a formidable mimic, did imitations of her, she retaliated by imitating his own queenly manners.

For services to British ballet, Ashton was created a C.B.E. (Commander of the Order of the British Empire) in 1950 and was knighted in 1962.

Ashton died in his sleep on August 19, 1988, aged 83.

Regarding his sex life, Ashton remarked, "I was always the loser." However, his true love was ballet, and his happy, lifelong affair with dance produced masterpieces that remain among the most popular ballets in the world.

—*Douglas Blair Turnbaugh*

BIBLIOGRAPHY

Bland, Alexander. *The Royal Ballet: The First Fifty Years*. London: Threshold Books, 1981.

Kavanagh, Julie. *Secret Muses: The Life of Frederick Ashton*. New York: Pantheon Books, 1996.

Vaughan, David. *Frederick Ashton and His Ballets*. New York: Alfred A. Knopf, 1977.

SEE ALSO

Dance; Ballet; Ballets Russes; Coward, Sir Noël; Diaghilev, Sergei; Kemp, Lindsay; Lifar, Serge; Thomson, Virgil

b

Baez, Joan

JOAN BAEZ IS NOTHING LESS THAN A LEGEND, BOTH AS a folk musician and as a catalyst for social change. A singer, guitarist, and songwriter with eight gold records and six Grammy nominations thus far, Baez has long been visible as a protest figure supporting civil rights, peace efforts, and human rights through her direct activism and numerous free concerts.

Born on January 9, 1941, in Staten Island, New York, to a Scottish mother and Mexican American father, Baez moved with her family to California when she was a small child. She lived in Baghdad from 1951 to 1952; there, confronted with rampant poverty and human suffering in the streets, she first realized her passion for social justice.

Baez stood out as an artistic nonconformist and peace activist in her high school in Palo Alto, California, and then at Boston University—where she remained for only a short time. She had begun playing at local coffeehouses and decided to drop out of school in 1958 to concentrate on her musical career.

Only a year after leaving Boston University, Baez started playing in clubs such as Gate of Horn, which belonged to the impresario (and Baez's future manager) Albert Grossman, and appearing with well-known musicians such as Pete Seeger. She gave a highly successful performance at the inaugural Newport Folk Festival in August of 1959.

In 1960, her first album, *Joan Baez*, was released to huge acclaim by Vanguard Recording Society. Gifted with an extraordinarily beautiful voice, she also brought an unusual intelligence to the interpretation of folk songs, both traditional and new.

As the 1960s progressed, Baez became increasingly involved with the civil rights movement, using her growing fame as a means of drawing attention to a cause she believed in deeply. She often shared the stage with Dr. Martin Luther King Jr.; Dr. King's speeches and Baez's singing were a staple of demonstrations and rallies during the turbulent 1960s.

Baez also became very active in promoting nonviolence. During the Vietnam War, she visited Hanoi for thirteen days to witness the horrors of war herself, and for ten years she withheld the percentage of her income taxes that would have been put toward military expenses. In 1967, she was arrested twice—and jailed for a month—for blocking the entrance of the Armed Forces Induction Center in Oakland, California.

All the while, she continued recording albums in her signature clear soprano, both writing her own material and performing classic songs of resistance such as "We Shall Overcome," "Oh, Freedom," and "Where Have All the Flowers Gone?"

She founded both the Institute for the Study of Nonviolence (now The Resource Center for Nonviolence) in California in 1965 and the Humanitas International Human Rights Committee, which she headed from 1979 until its demise thirteen years later.

In August 1975, she was honored with a Public Service Award at the first annual Rock Music Awards and with a "Joan Baez Day" in Atlanta.

Although she may be most famous for her activism on behalf of civil rights and peace, Baez has also been prominent in the struggle for gay and lesbian rights.

She has been open about the relationship she had with a woman in 1962; in an interview a decade later, she told a reporter that she basically considered herself bisexual, a statement she stood by despite the controversy it sparked. She married activist David Harris in 1968, and had their son Gabe in 1969; although the couple eventually divorced, Baez never again pursued a lesbian relationship.

Still, she has been visible in the gay community; in 1978, she performed at several benefit concerts to defeat Proposition 6 (the Briggs Initiative), which proposed banning all openly gay people from teaching in the public schools of California. Later that year, she participated in memorial marches for the assassinated San Francisco city supervisor, openly gay Harvey Milk.

Alongside Janis Ian, she played a benefit for the National Gay and Lesbian Task Force in 1994, and has performed numerous times with the lesbian duo Indigo Girls.

To date, Baez has recorded over forty albums—including several greatest hits records, compilations, live albums, and a boxed set. She has written two memoirs: the best-selling *Daybreak* (1968) and the more recent *And a Voice to Sing With* (1987).

Baez continues to pursue an active schedule of concerts and tours.

                                     —*Teresa Theophano*

BIBLIOGRAPHY

Baez, Joan. *And A Voice To Sing With.* New York: Summit Books, 1987.

————. *Daybreak.* New York: Dial Press, 1968.

www.joanbaez.com

SEE ALSO

Popular Music; Ian, Janis; Indigo Girls

Ballet

MEN IN TIGHTS ON THE FOOTBALL FIELD BATTLING each other with calculated brutality and jumping into each other's embrace with screams of orgiastic pleasure whenever a point is scored are presumed to be heterosexual models for American youth. On the other hand, men in tights on the stage romantically dancing with women, tenderly carrying them overhead in apparently effortless lifts, are presumed to be gay and, therefore, unmanly.

But the gauge for manliness has not always been brute force. In other times, virility was idealized through grace achieved by control and refinement of physical strength. And by that measure, ballet dancers are virile indeed.

Although it has sometimes proved embarrassing to those who periodically attempt to construct a macho image for ballet dancers, the enduring and persistent connection between ballet and male homosexuality is undeniable. This connection is undoubtedly related to ballet's remarkably masculine provenance. Unlike dance in general, which early on celebrated the fecundity of the female, the ballet was initially designed to celebrate male power.

Origins and Early Development of Ballet

The first ballet star was Louis XIV of France (1638–1715), the Sun King, who danced in extravagant *fêtes* with his court at Versailles. In 1661, Louis established the *Académie Royale de la Danse,* to teach his courtiers to dance and to train ballet masters and choreographers, who then disseminated this form throughout Europe.

Until 1681, boys danced the female roles in professional ballets. Moreover, the physical technique unique to the ballet is directly based on the elegant but physically demanding martial art of fencing with the *épée.* An element of this discipline is grace under pressure. To show any sign of strain or physical effort would be beneath the dignity of a nobleman, as it is even today for a *danseur noble.*

Ballet's floor patterns were based on social dances of the French court, such as minuets and gavottes, while the dancers' movements were based on the very high style of the king's courtiers, who were accomplished swordsmen. Bows, flexibility of the wrists, *épaulement* (or carriage of the torso, in fencing a device to protect the chest from the opponent's *épée*) and "turnout" (or twisting the leg in the hip socket so that the foot is turned sideways, in fencing a device to improve balance), are examples of the martial arts techniques that became integral to ballet.

These basic techniques allowed for revolutionary developments later, as, for example, the addition of *pirouettes* and *grands jetés,* the multiple turns and big jumps always so appreciated by audiences.

By the 1720s, professional ballets were being given in opera houses all over Europe and women began to emerge as stars, notably Marie Camargo and her rival Marie Sallé. Their theatrical costumes became lighter than the heavy court costumes, and high-heeled shoes were supplanted by soft slippers, allowing freer movement. An undergarment, the forerunner of tights, became standard stage wear as skirts were shortened to expose the legs. Over time, skirts went as high as they could go, ultimately culminating in the *tutu.*

Jean-Georges Noverre (1727–1810), a celebrated French choreographer, advanced the art of ballet through his ideas for the *ballet d'action*, or ballet with a plot and with mythological, heroic, or pastoral themes. Masks were discarded and spoken words were dispensed with, leaving the story to be told through movement, mime, and facial expression.

Noverre visited England, where he was dubbed "the Shakespeare of the dance." He became ballet master at the court of the Duke of Württemberg in Stuttgart and later worked in Vienna with the composer Gluck to create *Iphigenie en Tauris* (1779), and with Mozart, who wrote *Les Petits Riens* (1778) for him. He also taught ballet to Marie Antoinette; when she became Queen of France, he was appointed ballet master at the Paris Opera.

For three generations, men of the Vestris family were stars of the ballet stage, notably Gaetan (1729–1808), his son Auguste (1760–1842), and Auguste's son Armand (1787–1825). Auguste had great physical technique; the height of his jumps was tremendous and his *entrechats* and *pirouettes* exhibited new virtuosity.

Carlo Blasis (1803–1878), ballet master of Teatro alla Scala in Milan, invented the ballet position *attitude*, based on the statue of Mercury by Giovanni di Bologna. This statue is almost as famous in gay iconography as Michelangelo's *David*. Blasis also published the first textbook for ballet dancers and teachers.

All over Europe, ballet developed from court entertainments into professional theater. In Sweden, King Gustav III (1746–1792), who liked to appear on stage himself, engaged a French ballet master and dancer, Antoine Bournonville (1760–1843), and twenty-four dancers to found the Swedish Royal Ballet.

In Denmark, where court dance spectacles had flourished from the time of Frederick II (1559–1588), ballet was well established at the Royal Theatre by 1771. Auguste Bournonville (1806–1879), son of Antoine, administered Danish ballet for nearly fifty years and developed a distinctive technique that is still influential today.

Women became the dancing stars in the Romantic period. Ballerinas Maria Taglioni (1804–1884), Fanny Elssler (1810–1884), and Carlotta Grisi (1819–1899) became internationally famous. Elssler is also notable for introducing national folk dances into ballet choreography.

Tragic love, the Romantic motif *par excellence*, emphasized the fragility and ethereal spirit of maidens. The introduction of the "toeshoe," which gave support to the foot and toes, allowed the dancer to rise onto the tips of her toes, which helped to create the illusion of defying gravity.

In this period, male dancers became mere *porteurs*, hoisting the ladies into the air to give them the appearance of weightlessness. The epitome of the ballets of this period is *Giselle* (1841, music by Adolphe Adam; choreography by Jean Coralli and Jules Perrot). In Act 1, Giselle, a peasant girl, dies after being seduced and abandoned by a nobleman; and in Act 2, she is initiated by other victims of men into a conspicuously lesbian spirit world. *Giselle* remains a defining work for ballerinas today.

As the art of ballet in Western Europe declined in the second half of the nineteenth century, men disappeared from the stage altogether. Men's roles were danced *en travesti* by women. As several paintings by Degas illustrate, the opera houses' green rooms became a sexual marketplace where wealthy gentlemen could select physically fit mistresses.

Russian Ballet

In the nineteenth century in Russia, then practically unknown to the West, men dominated the ballet, which was supported by the court until the Revolution of 1917. In 1734, Empress Anna had engaged the Frenchman Jean Baptiste Landet to teach dancing to cadets at the Military School of Nobles and then to create a School of Ballet. Czar Paul I (1754–1801) studied ballet and danced in the Court Theatre.

In 1801, Charles Louis Didelot, a Swede who had been a pupil of Auguste Vestris in Paris, became ballet master at the Imperial Theatre. He was succeeded by two influential Frenchmen, Jules Perrot and Arthur Saint-Léon.

Another Frenchman, Marius Petipa, arrived in Russia in 1847. A choreographer as well as ballet master, he ruled over the St. Petersburg Imperial Theatre until 1903. Petipa established the "classic ballet," which is based on the tradition and the rules of composition and technique developed during the preceding two centuries. Petipa believed in the primacy of choreography over all other theatrical elements. Among his greatest and still popular ballets are *La Bayadère* (music by Leon Minkus), *The Sleeping Beauty,* and *Swan Lake* (both: music by Pyotr Ilich Tchaikovsky).

Choreographer Michel Fokine (1880–1942) challenged Petipa's insistence on the primacy of choreography and revolutionized ballet with his organic fusion of dance, music, and painting. Sergei Diaghilev invited him to create ballets for the proposed season of Russian ballet in Paris in 1909. This launched Fokine's career and gave the Ballets Russes its initial repertoire, including such works as *Cléopâtre, Schéhérazade* (both by Nikolai Rimsky-Korsakov), and *Pétrouchka* (Igor Stravinsky).

Performing in these sensational and erotically charged ballets was the great dancer Vaslav Nijinsky (1890–1950). He reestablished the primacy of the male dancer on the European ballet stage. Himself an innovative choreographer, Nijinsky created a completely new language of movement, one that abandoned classic ballet's courtly graces for a more primal, on-the-earth effect, as in his *L'Après-midi d'un Faune* (1912, music by Claude Debussy) and *Le Sacre du Printemps* (1913, music by Stravinsky).

Following in Diaghilev's footsteps, Rolf de Maré, a Swedish millionaire, created Les Ballets Suédois (1920–1925) to feature his lover, Jean Borlin, as *premier danseur* and choreographer. Borlin created many ballets in collaboration with leading composers and artists of the Parisian avant-garde.

Among the ways in which Diaghilev's Ballets Russes revolutionized ballet is the space it carved out for gay men, both as members of a cosmopolitan audience and as artists whose work was welcomed. Attracting a large audience of gay men in European capitals and in America, the Ballets Russes may be said to be among the earliest gay-identified multinational enterprises.

In the Ballets Russes, gay men, whatever their nationality, were highly visible and their influence extended outward from ballet into related art forms such as cinema, painting, music, and fashion.

Diaghilev's Ballets Russes was an unrivalled font of creativity. Many members of the company went on to teach and found ballet companies throughout the world. Choreographers Léonide Massine and Bronislava Nijinska worked internationally, while George Balanchine, Serge Lifar, and Ninette de Valois established ballet theaters in, respectively, the United States, France, and Great Britain.

During the Soviet period, ballet remained a popular form of entertainment, but socialist realism dictated the subject matter (with workers in love with their tractors, for example). Moreover, the Soviet bureaucrats held a prurient view of men in tights—for classical ballets, for the sake of modesty, men were required to wear a kind of bloomers. Male dancers literally lived in fear of their lives should they be accused of being gay.

Ballet in America

Ballet has always been popular in America, which has long been known as a place for dancers to make their fortunes. Elssler's visit in 1840 was extended from three months to two years. In 1916, Diaghilev and his company risked being torpedoed at sea to get to the United States during World War I, and then they toured by special train from coast to coast.

The immensely popular ballerina Anna Pavlova (1881–1931) toured the country for years with her own ballet company. Rudolph Nureyev, to many balletomanes a reincarnation of Nijinsky, became the God of Dance in America in the 1960s and 1970s. "I have danced in Champaign, Illinois," he told Dick Cavett.

Although many opera houses had corps de ballets, until relatively recently there were few independent ballet companies in the United States. A notable exception is the San Francisco Ballet, which was founded in 1933 as the San Francisco Opera Ballet and was brought to prominence by Willam Christensen, who arrived in 1938. In

1940, the company presented the first full-length *Swan Lake* to be produced in the United States.

A short-lived independent company was Ballet Caravan, for which Lew Christensen, brother of Willam, choreographed *Filling Station* (1938), one of the first ballets with a distinctly American scenario. Christensen's collaborators on *Filling Station* were prominent in the gay artistic world of the time: Virgil Thomson (music), Lincoln Kirstein (scenario), and Paul Cadmus (costumes).

Cadmus's daring costume for the filling-station attendant, Mac, used completely transparent material for the overalls. In performance, of course, the dancer's genitals were covered by his bikini-like "dance belt," but the photographer George Platt Lynes somehow persuaded self-proclaimed heterosexual dancer Jacques d'Amboise to pose nude in this costume. The show-all photograph is now in the collection of the Kinsey Institute.

The first large-scale, major American ballet companies were the Ballet Russe de Monte Carlo (1937–1962), American Ballet Theatre (1940 to the present), and the New York City Ballet (1948 to the present).

Originally formed in Monte Carlo after the death of Diaghilev and led by choreographer Léonide Massine, the Ballet Russe de Monte Carlo became the national ballet company of the United States by virtue of its transcontinental tours from 1940 until its demise in 1962.

Financed with American money and directed by Serge Denham, a Russian banker, the company strove to continue the great tradition of the original Ballets Russes. One of its distinctions is that it commissioned many ballets by a dozen women choreographers, most notably Agnes de Mille's *Rodeo* (1942, music by Aaron Copland).

The American Ballet Theatre, an outgrowth of Diaghilev star Mikhail Mordkin's Ballet, came into being in 1940 under the patronage and direction of Lucia Chase, herself a dancer. Incorporating classics as well as new work, great dancers and choreographers collaborated in creating perhaps the richest and most varied repertoire of any ballet company in the world.

Significant among the choreographers associated with the American Ballet Theatre are Antony Tudor (1909–1987) and Jerome Robbins (1918–1998). Of particular intellectual distinction is the work of the Englishman Tudor. Father of the psychological ballet, Tudor created dances concerned with the anguish of frustrated love, as exemplified by *Lilac Garden* (1936, music by Ernest Chausson), *Undertow* (1945, music by William Schuman), *Pillar of Fire* (1942, music by Arnold Schoenberg), and *Romeo and Juliet* (1943, music by Frederick Delius)—all featuring Tudor's lover, the dancer Hugh Laing.

Jerome Robbins, the most famous American choreographer both in the ballet and on Broadway, was also one of the most ferociously in-the-closet personalities in the dance world. Fearful of exposure if he failed to cooperate, he named many colleagues as Communist Party members under questioning by the U.S. Congress's House Un-American Activities Committee during its inquests of the early 1950s.

Robbins's first ballet for American Ballet Theatre, *Fancy Free* (1944, music by Leonard Bernstein), about three sailor buddies on leave in New York City, is still an audience favorite. Created for New York City Ballet, his masterpieces *Afternoon of a Faun* (1953, Debussy), an ode to narcissism, and *The Cage* (1951, Stravinsky), a fable about woman destroying man, are rarely revived, but his more humorous and less provocative work is still in the repertoire.

Despite its precarious position as a touring company with no home theater, American Ballet Theatre has survived for more than sixty years and currently features an unrivalled complement of male superstars, including José Manuel Carreño, Angel Corella, Julio Bocca, Ethan Stiefel, Vladimir Malakhov, and Maxim Belotserkovsky.

The New York City Ballet was created by an odd couple, Lincoln Kirstein (1907–1996), a wealthy, sometimes closeted gay man, and George Balanchine (1904–1983), the much-married, ostentatiously heterosexual choreographer. With a home theater provided by the City of New York and, later, a huge grant from the Ford Foundation, this alliance produced the most politically powerful ballet organization in the United States.

Balanchine, after his initial success with Diaghilev, was a failure in Europe, but he spectacularly revived his faltering career in New York City and came to dominate the ballet scene for nearly thirty years. Like Petipa, he believed in the primacy of choreography and insisted his ballets were "pure" movement, though he acknowledged the role of music as the source of choreography.

In Balanchine's ballets, the dancers' individuality was suppressed, their personalities subservient to the structure of his choreography. Nonetheless, two of his best-known ballets remain *Apollo* (1928) and *Prodigal Son* (1929), both specifically tailored to highlight the special talents of Diaghilev's lover, Serge Lifar. Typical of Balanchine's celebrated "abstract" ballets are *Theme and Variations* (1947) and *Agon* (1957).

Along with Fokine, Balanchine is one of the few major twentieth-century choreographers who is recognizably heterosexual. Uninterested in choreographing for male dancers, Balanchine's fixation on the female is remarkably misogynistic, conspicuously in his requirement that the *poitrines* of his *danseuses* be flat as a boy's. This dictum has made the anorexic look *de rigueur* for his women dancers, which creates a weird stage picture in contrast with the pumped-up bodies of today's male dancers.

Kirstein's preference for hunky, working-class, "straight" men (as personified in *Filling Station*) and his

abhorrence of "effeminacy" resulted, for many years, in the bloodless, corpselike look of his male dancers' faces on stage—they dared not put any color on their lips or cheeks. Formerly a leading dancer and currently the company director, the heterosexual Peter Martins is now choreographing ballets that more comfortably feature men and make them look good.

The Harkness Ballet (1964–1974) was founded by Rebekah Harkness (1915–1982). The remarkably gay-friendly Mrs. Harkness possessed such vast wealth that, in the manner of European sovereigns, she was the single patron of her company. A distinction of the Harkness Ballet was the excellence of the male dancers—and their often seminude costuming.

Most Harkness ballets were extremely sexy and many were suffused in homoeroticism, as, for example, the works of John Butler (1918–1993)—*A Season in Hell*, the story of Verlaine and Rimbaud, and *Sebastian* (1963, music by Gian Carlo Menotti). Also noteworthy are *Monument for a Dead Boy* (1966), choreographed by Rudi Van Dantzig (b. 1933) and *Gemini* (1972), by Vincente Nebrada (b. 1932).

The company mostly toured abroad, in the great theaters of Europe, to great acclaim, giving its dancers and choreographers a cosmopolitan experience unknown to their American colleagues.

The Joffrey Ballet, founded by Robert Joffrey (1930–1988), began as a small group touring in a station wagon. Support from Mrs. Harkness allowed it to grow into a major institution in American dance. It was famous for the youth and vivacity of its dancers.

Joffrey gave up his promising career as a choreographer—his ballet *Astarte* (1967) was the subject of a *Time* magazine cover story—to focus on building his company's repertoire, which featured the hyperkinetic ballets of his lover, Gerald Arpino (b. 1928), as well as reconstructions of masterpieces.

Among Arpino's ballets are *Viva Vivaldi!* (1965) and *Olympics* (1966); reconstructions from the Diaghilev repertoire included Nijinsky's *L'Après-midi d'un Faune* and *Le Sacre du Printemps*. Since Joffrey's death of AIDS in 1988, the company, directed by Arpino, has gone through several transformations and is now based in Chicago.

Other Major Choreographers

The work of several other major choreographers has enriched the art of twentieth-century ballet: Sir Frederick Ashton (1906–1988), Maurice Béjart (b. 1927), and Rudi Van Dantzig.

Celebrated for his gay wit and high style, Ashton first scored with the 1926 ballet *Tragedy of Fashion*. A pioneer in establishing British ballet as a notably gay workplace, Ashton was a member of the gay coterie of the late Queen

Elizabeth, the Queen Mother, whom he taught to tango. His relationships with men were not secret, particularly his relationship with dancer Michael Somes, whom he featured in many ballets, but homoeroticism was not an element in his work.

Ashton personally identified himself with women and delighted in creating roles for women, especially for his favorite ballerina, Margot Fonteyn. A virtuoso of his craft, Ashton worked in a wide range of styles.

Among his works are a ballet to the Virgil Thomson/Gertrude Stein opera *Four Saints in Three Acts* (1933–1934); abstract ballets such as *Monotones* (1965, music by Erik Satie); and full-length works such as *Cinderella* (1948, music by Sergei Prokofiev), in which he created a delightful role for himself as the Elder Ugly Sister, and *La Fille mal gardée* (1960, music by Hérold/Lanchbery), perhaps the wittiest ballet ever created. He was a founder and chief choreographer of London's Royal Ballet.

French-born Maurice Béjart studied classical ballet but early in his career established an individual style, which, new at the time, combined classic dance with modern jazz, and acrobatics with *musique concrète*, as in his *Symphonie pour un homme seul* (1955, music by Henry/Schaeffer). European based, his own company, under various names, became one of the world's foremost troupes, with continual international tours.

Often infused with mysticism and ritual, as in his ballet *Boléro* (1960, music by Maurice Ravel), or with sexual drama, as in *Nijinsky: Clown of God* (1971, music by Tchaikovsky), Béjart's total-spectacle ballets attracted huge, new, and young audiences that filled sports arenas, including New York's Madison Square Garden, as rock concerts do now.

Béjart created an autobiographical ballet in which he was featured as the Princess in *The Sleeping Beauty*. In this scenario, the evil fairy's curse on the baby Maurice was "You will be short."

Amsterdam-born choreographer Rudi Van Dantzig is a founder of the Dutch National Ballet and has created ballets for major companies throughout the world. He uses his personal experiences and feelings as a gay man as a source for his work, as in *Monument for a Dead Boy* (1965, music by Jan Boerman) and *The Ropes of Time* (1970, music by György Ligeti). His autobiographical novel *For a Lost Soldier*, the story of a twelve-year-old Dutch boy's love affair with one of the Canadian soldiers who liberated his village from the Germans, was made into a major motion picture in 1994.

Conclusion

Today, almost every major city in America has a ballet company in its cultural center. But although the ballet industry has always been a gay-friendly workplace, currently "Don't ask, don't tell" is the prudent policy.

As ballet companies are now big business, financed by sexophobic government agencies, conservative foundations, and cautious businesses, and with a concern for "family entertainment" (the annual *Nutcracker* for children is the greatest money-maker in the New York City Ballet repertoire), there is great emphasis on gymnastics, with an eye to breaking records in the manner of sports, at the expense of creative explorations of life and sexuality.

In the generally sterile atmosphere of institutionalized ballet today, a few joyous exceptions have been sighted, notably from England, such as Matthew Bourne's (b. 1960) fabulous *Swan Lake* (1996), in which the Prince is still in love with an enchanted swan—who happens to be a man—and David Bintley's (b. 1957) *Edward II* (1995) for the Birmingham Royal Ballet, an explicit account of Edward's passionate love for Piers Gaveston. These are evidence that the ballet can still be a medium for gay expression and provocative, thrilling theater.

—*Douglas Blair Turnbaugh*

BIBLIOGRAPHY

Baril, Jacques. *Dictionnaire de Danse*. Paris: Microcosme/Éditions du Seuil, 1964.

Chujoy, Anatole, and P. W. Manchester, comps. and eds. *The Dance Encyclopedia*. New York: Simon & Schuster, 1967.

Craine, Debora, and Judith Mackrell, eds. *The Oxford Dictionary of Dance*. New York: Oxford University Press, 2000.

Karsavina, Tamara. *Classical Ballet: The Flow of Movement*. London: Adam and Charles Black, 1962.

Koegler, Horst, ed. *The Concise Oxford Dictionary of Ballet*. London: Oxford University Press, 1977.

Tarasov, Nikolai Ivanovich. *Ballet Technique for the Male Dancer*. New York: Doubleday, 1985.

Vaganova, Agrippina. *Basic Principles of Classical Ballet: Russian Ballet Technique*. London: Adam and Charles Black, 1965.

Wilson, G. B. L. *A Dictionary of Ballet*. New York: Theatre Arts Books, 1974.

SEE ALSO

Dance; Ballets Russes; Ashton, Sir Frederick; Béjart, Maurice; Diaghilev, Sergei; Joffrey, Robert; Kirstein, Lincoln; Lifar, Serge; Menotti, Gian Carlo; Nijinsky, Vaslav; Nureyev, Rudolf; Robbins, Jerome; Thomson, Virgil; Van Dantzig, Rudi

Ballets Russes   *(1909–1962)*

ALTHOUGH *BALLETS RUSSES* MIGHT SOUND LIKE A generic term, meaning simply Russian ballets, it actually refers to the ballet company that is the hallmark of twentieth-century theatrical dance. The Ballets Russes represents not only a crucial turning point in dance history, but a milestone in gay history as well.

The brainchild of impresario Sergei Diaghilev (1872–1929), a gay Russian nobleman who fell in love with the nineteen-year-old Vaslav Nijinksy, a rising star in the Imperial Russian Ballet, the Ballets Russes might be seen as one of the earliest gay-identified multinational enterprises.

Although the first Ballets Russes company was not officially organized until 1911, it dates from 1909, when Diaghilev assembled a group of dancers from the Imperial theaters and charged a brilliant young choreographer, Michel Fokine, with creating a repertoire to spotlight Nijinsky's great talent.

Under the patronage of Czar Nicholas II, Diaghilev brought his Ballets Russes to Paris in May 1909. Its success was immediate and sensational. The brilliant artistry of the dancers, including Tamara Karsavina as well as Nijinsky, combined with erotic choreography, startlingly modern music, and strikingly original scene designs, altered the course of dance history, making the Ballets Russes the vanguard of distinctly twentieth-century art.

For the next twenty years, Diaghilev never failed to discover fresh genius, featuring the work of then uncelebrated composers such as Sergei Prokofiev and Igor Stravinsky and artists such as Jean Cocteau and Pablo Picasso. His company specialized in ballets of "total theater" in which all aspects of the production were important, though the Ballets Russes was especially noted for its superb male dancers.

After he fired Nijinsky in 1913 (when the dancer married a Hungarian admirer, Romola Pulszky), Diaghilev took as his lover the eighteen-year-old Léonide Massine, who was to serve as the company's principal dancer and choreographer for the next seven years. In 1924, Diaghilev met the last of his protégés and lovers, seventeen-year-old Serge Lifar, who became the company's *premier danseur* and later became director of the Paris Opera Ballet.

After the Russian Revolution, the Ballets Russes, which had never performed in Russia, was permanently cut off from its homeland. Diaghilev featured many Russian émigré dancers, but turned increasingly to French composers and painters as collaborators for his choreographers.

In the Ballets Russes, gay men, whatever their nationality, were highly visible and their influence extended outward from ballet into related art forms such as cinema, painting, music, and fashion.

At Diaghilev's untimely death in 1929, the original Ballets Russes, then based in Monte Carlo, dissolved. But in 1931 many of his dancers and choreographers were reunited in a company formed by Colonel Wassily de Basil, a former officer in the Russian army. The new company incorporated Diaghilev's repertoire, but also developed new stars—notably the celebrated "baby ballerinas," Irina Baronova, Tamara Toumanova, and Tatiana Riabouchinska—and new ballets.

Among the new works commissioned by de Basil's Ballets Russes was David Lichine's *Cain and Abel* (1946), perhaps the first overtly homoerotic ballet in history. The work features the two title dancers nearly nude in a sensual *pas de deux*.

Colonel de Basil's Ballets Russes toured extensively in South America and Australia and survived the terrible vicissitudes of World War II, but disbanded in 1952 after the Colonel's death.

In 1937, an artistic schism occurred within de Basil's company and dissenters, led by Léonide Massine, formed a rival company in Monaco. Financed with American money and directed by Serge Denham, a Russian banker, the new company was called the *Ballet Russe de Monte Carlo*. Massine strove to continue the great tradition of the original Ballets Russes.

With the outbreak of World War II, the new company relocated to the United States, where, by virtue of its transcontinental annual tours, it became the national ballet company of America. For more than twenty years, until its demise in 1962, it visited as many as 100 towns and cities in a season, astonishing audiences with its glamour and awakening in many isolated gay men the dazzling reality of a gay-friendly artistic milieu.

Some of these men first exposed to dance in this way searched out ballet studios and eventually had dance careers of their own.

Among the most important legacies of the Ballets Russes is its function as a nursery to other companies. Many dancers and others associated with the various Ballets Russes companies opened schools throughout the world. They produced dancers trained in the great tradition, as well as an audience prepared to support civic ballet companies.

Nearly all of the most prestigious international ballet companies descend directly or indirectly from the Ballets Russes. And without the Ballets Russes, we would not have its saucy offspring, Les Ballets Trockadero de Monte Carlo, the all-male American troupe triumphantly touring the world, *en pointe* and *en travesti*.

—*Douglas Blair Turnbaugh*

BIBLIOGRAPHY

Anderson, Jack. *The One and Only: The Ballet Russe de Monte Carlo.* New York: Dance Horizons, 1981.

Kodicek, Ann, ed. *Diaghilev: Creator of the Ballets Russes: Art-Music-Dance.* London: Barbican Art Gallery/Lund Humphries, 1996.

Macdonald, Nesta. *Diaghilev Observed by Critics in England and the United States 1911–1929.* New York: Dance Horizons, 1975.

Walker, Katherine Sorley. *De Basil's Ballets Russes.* London: Hutchinson, 1982.

Ballets Trockadero de Monte Carlo

COMPANY BALLET CLASS HAS ENDED AND TWENTY MALE dancers bound the stairs to their dressing room to prepare for this evening's performance. Some head for the showers, some brandish razors to tame five o'clock shadows, some grab a bite to eat, and others smoke.

The dressing room is a mayhem of activity as the men don pink tights and pointe shoes, affix flyswatter-sized eyelashes on their eyelids, and cajole wig hair into regulation ballet buns. A couple more pliés and leg extensions coax tired muscles into performance mode as the dancers ready themselves in the wings.

An announcer with a heavy Russian accent imperiously informs the audience, "Ladies and Gentleman, in accordance with the greatest traditions of Russian ballet, there *will* be a change in tonight's program...."

Tchaikovsky's famous overture to *Swan Lake* begins, and the curtain rises on another performance by Les Ballets Trockadero de Monte Carlo.

While the United States has been home to several all-male theatrical groups that employ performative gender illusion—from varsity clubs such as Harvard's Hasty Pudding Club and Princeton's Triangle Club to professional drag troupes such as San Francisco's Finocchio's (1937–1999) and the touring Jewel Box Revue (1944–1967)—the practice of combining ballet, cross-dressing, and comedy has belonged exclusively to the various companies known as the Trockadero.

Trockadero Gloxinia Ballet Company
In 1972, three members (Larry Ree, Richard Goldberger, and Lohr Wilson) of Charles Ludlam's Ridiculous Theatrical Company formed their own dance troupe, the Trockadero Gloxinia Ballet Company. Combining a psychosexual mixture of camp, drag, exaggeration, and Ludlum's respect for theatrical history, the aesthetic groundwork was laid for Ree and company to explore the world of dance *en travesti*.

Celebrating the operatic rather than the minimal, valuing artifice more than reality, and privileging the ridiculous over the conventional, the Gloxinia was primed to do with choreographic texts what the Ridiculous Theatrical Company was doing with verbal texts.

Performing in a succession of Greenwich Village lofts and small theaters, the Gloxinia attracted a growing audience base, enough to expand the company to a dozen

dancers. But their range was rather limited in that there were no male characters on stage (which made impossible a mainstay of classical ballet, the *pas de deux*) and the entire performance revolved around Madame Ekathrina Sobechanskaya, Ree's stage persona.

Les Ballets Trockadero de Monte Carlo
Wanting to focus more on choreographic satire than the cult of the drag ballerina, four members of Ree's troupe decided to form their own company in 1974. Thus was born Les Ballets Trockadero de Monte Carlo.

With better choreography, more technically trained dancers, and a triumvirate of artistic directors (Peter Anastos, Natch Taylor, and Anthony Bassae), the new troupe was stronger in many ways than its predecessor. While Ree's company continued to perform sporadically in small Village spaces until 1992, Les Ballets Trockadero de Monte Carlo—affectionately known as the Trocks—garnered the favorable attention of mainstream dance critics. By 1977, the company had performed on Broadway and on national television.

The bulk of the Trocks' repertoire comes from the classical ballet canon: *Swan Lake* Act II and *Pas de Quatre*, *Giselle* Act II, *Les Sylphides*, *The Dying Swan*, *Don Quixote*. As performed by the Trocks, these warhorses are informed by a unique combination of parody and satire. The Trocks not only demonstrate a thorough knowledge of the source material, but also celebrate a wickedly delicious wit. The humor is amplified by the outrageous, faux-Russian-ballerina stage names assumed by the dancers.

Original choreography performed by the Trocks pinpoints specific choreographers: Shawn Avrea's *Phaedra Monotonous #1148* aims a skewed eye at Martha Graham; Natch Taylor's *Gambol* takes Paul Taylor to task; Anastos's *Yes, Virginia, Another Piano Ballet* targets Jerome Robbins; Roy Fialkow's *I Wanted to Dance With You at the Cafe of Experience* dissects Pina Bausch; and Anastos's *Go for Barocco* and Robert La Fosse's *Stars & Stripes Forever* are deconstructions of George Balanchine.

Camp, Drag, and Dance
While early-1970s gay patrons no doubt reveled in the camp drag aspects of the Gloxinia and the Trocks, critics were far more interested in the choreographic mission of the latter than in the gender issues raised by men dancing as ballerinas.

From the beginning of the company's existence, when it performed on a makeshift stage at the Westside Discussion Group (a "homophile" organization on West 14th Street in New York City), General Director Eugene McDougle has held to the belief that after ten minutes the audience will have exhausted the thrill of seeing men dressed in drag, so the company must offer an evening of exemplary dance and witty physical comedy.

Reasons for the Trocks' Success

Much of the Trocks' success is attributable to their lean managerial structure. A nonprofit organization, the troupe has not burdened itself with expensive New York real estate or a large operating staff. Moreover, they have survived financially without private or government grants. Their complete dependence on box-office income is very unusual in the dance world. Indeed, the Trocks are the only professional comedic dance company that has achieved financial success.

Another factor in their success is that the identity of the company is not linked to one performer, choreographer, or artistic director. Bassae (Tamara Karpova) left the Trocks in 1976 to form his own company, Les Ballets Trockadero de La Karpova (1976–1983); Anastos (Olga Tchikaboumskaya) left in 1978 to pursue a career as a freelance choreographer; and Taylor (Alexis Ivanovitch

Lermontov and Suzina LaFuzziovitch) was voted out by the board in 1990. (Another spin-off company, Les Ballets Grandiva, was formed in 1996 by ex-Trocks Victor Trevino, Marcus Galante, Oswaldo Muniz, and Allen Dennis.)

Tory Dobrin, a dancer who joined the company in 1980, assumed responsibility for artistic matters of the Trocks as their Associate Director in 1991.

The Trocks Today

While parodying the world of dance has been the consistent mission of the Trocks since their founding in 1974, much has changed about the company. The Trocks have performed regularly at New York City's Joyce Theatre, and tour extensively in the United States and abroad.

Early members of the troupe were often better at acting like ballerinas than dancing like them, but later members of the company are accomplished dancers. Indeed, they often dance with other professional dance companies when not engaged by the Trocks.

The cast of Ballets Trockadero de Monte Carlo in a production of *The Humpback Horse*, photographed by Sasha Vaughan.

As *New York Times* columnist Jennifer Dunning notes, "One of the happier conundrums of dance today is how the Trocks have come to such a perfect balance of tribute and sendup."

—*Bud Coleman*

BIBLIOGRAPHY

Coleman, Bud. "Ballerinos on pointe: Les Ballets Trockadero de Monte Carlo." *Choreography and Dance: An International Journal* 5.1 (1998): 9–23.

Croce, Arlene. "The Two Trockaderos." *Afterimages.* New York: Vintage Books, 1979.

Dunning, Jennifer. "Russian Chestnuts Done to Nutty Perfection." *New York Times,* August 16, 2000.

www.trockadero.org

SEE ALSO

Dance; Ballet; Ballets Russes; Robbins, Jerome; Taylor, Paul; Tchaikovsky, Pyotr Ilich

Samuel Barber, photographed by Carl Van Vechten in 1944.

Barber, Samuel   *(1910–1981)*

AMERICAN COMPOSER SAMUEL BARBER MADE AN enduring contribution to the cultural life of the United States and the world, though he is also remembered for the spectacular failure of his opera *Antony and Cleopatra.*

Barber was born on March 9, 1910, in West Chester, Pennsylvania, to a musical family; his aunt was the prominent mezzo-soprano Louise Homer. He began composing at the age of seven, and at fourteen became one of the first students of the prestigious Curtis Institute of Music.

During his studies at Curtis (1924–1932), he met the young Italian composer Gian Carlo Menotti (b. 1911), a fellow student who became his life partner and occasional artistic collaborator. The two men traveled extensively in Europe during the 1930s, a period that saw the composition of Barber's best-known and most enduring work, the *Adagio for Strings* (1938). In 1943, Barber and Menotti bought a house in Mount Kisco, New York, which served for many years as their artistic retreat.

Although Virgil Thomson and Aaron Copland had blazed a trail in the creation of a characteristically "American" mode of orchestral and vocal music in earlier decades, by the 1950s Barber had achieved a level of mainstream recognition virtually unprecedented for an American composer of classical music working in a traditional European style.

With the end of World War II, he embarked on a succession of ambitious commissioned works, including the *Cello Concerto* (1947), the ballet *Medea* (1946) for Martha Graham, and the dance score *Souvenirs* (1952) for Lincoln Kirstein and the Ballet Society of New York.

This period also saw the composition of Barber's most memorable vocal music: *Knoxville: Summer of 1915* (1947), commissioned by soprano Eleanor Steber; *Hermit Songs* (1953), premiered by the young and then unknown Leontyne Price; and the choral work *Prayers of Kierkegaard* (1954).

This string of artistic and critical triumphs culminated in the opera *Vanessa* (1958), for which Menotti wrote the libretto. Commissioned by the Metropolitan Opera, *Vanessa* was acclaimed as the first American "grand" opera.

The leading role was originally offered to Maria Callas, who, preferring not to sing in English, declined; consequently Steber, long a champion of Barber's works, was chosen to be the first Vanessa. The opera won its composer the 1958 Pulitzer Prize for music.

Barber's *Piano Concerto* (1962) brought a second Pulitzer, but the stunning chain of successes came to a bitter end with, ironically, what should have been the crowning moment of his career. Following the acclaim that greeted *Vanessa*, Barber received a commission for a full-scale opera to mark the 1966 opening of the new Metropolitan Opera House at Lincoln Center. The result was *Antony and Cleopatra*, with a libretto by Franco Zeffirelli after Shakespeare's play, and the lead role sung by Leontyne Price.

The elaborate production, designed and executed by Zeffirelli, was marred by numerous technological disasters; it also overwhelmed and obscured Barber's music, which most critics faulted as uncharacteristically weak and unoriginal.

Distressed by the fiasco, Barber left the United States soon thereafter and spent a number of years in seclusion in Europe, a period also marked by his estrangement from Menotti.

Barber died on January 23, 1981, in New York City.

In recent years, a revised version of *Antony and Cleopatra*, for which Menotti provided collaborative assistance, has enjoyed some success. Despite the disappointments of his later years, Barber nevertheless remains a major figure in American classical music, as the oft-performed *Adagio for Strings* so amply attests.

—*Patricia Juliana Smith*

BIBLIOGRAPHY

Heyman, Barbara B. *Samuel Barber: The Composer and His Music.* New York: Oxford University Press, 1992.

SEE ALSO

Classical Music; Copland, Aaron; Kirstein, Lincoln; Menotti, Gian Carlo; Thomson, Virgil; Zeffirelli, Franco

Béjart, Maurice   (b. 1927)

PERHAPS THE PREEMINENT DESCENDANT OF SERGEI Diaghilev and Serge Lifar, Maurice Béjart has been a significant presence in late-twentieth-century dance as an innovator with a radical vision. Central to his reinvigoration of classical ballet has been his creation of palpably homoerotic dances that celebrate male beauty.

Born Maurice Jean Berger in Marseille, France, on January 1, 1927, Béjart in his youth was an ardent student and appeared to be following the strict example set by his father Gaston Berger, a hard-working university administrator and educator who was largely self-taught. Béjart was so fanatical a student, in fact, that at fourteen he had to be enrolled on doctor's orders in the ballet school of the Marseilles Opera for exercise to increase his physical vigor. That prescription has worked wonders for over sixty years.

Young Maurice also exhibited his father's trait for independent action when he abandoned academic schooling after graduating from the Lycée de Marseille and the Faculty of Philosophy in Aix-en-Provence in 1945. Breaking free on many levels at eighteen, he left home for Paris, where he studied ballet and soon dropped "Berger" to adopt the maiden name of Molière's wife.

After studying with Léo Staats, Lubov Egorova, and Madama Rousanne (Sarkissian) in Paris, he performed with Mona Inglesby's International Ballet and the Royal Swedish Ballet, sealing his reputation as an industrious and disciplined dancer before creating dances for his own pathbreaking companies.

Symphonie pour un homme seul (1955), with a score by Pierre Schaeffer and Pierre Henry—the first electronic score to accompany a ballet—established Béjart as an innovator with a radical vision. In 1959, at the Théâtre Royale de la Monnaie in Brussels, Béjart presented an electrifying interpretation of *The Rite of Spring* (set to the original Igor Stravinsky score) informed by myth, sexual heat, and stage flash.

In the same year and at the same theater, Béjart founded The Ballet of the Twentieth Century, a company that has had a major influence on the European Dance Theatre movement. Based in Brussels until 1987, Béjart developed his ideas of ballet as total theater to explore the complex forces buffeting the individual in contemporary society. His highly theatrical and often shocking productions, some on such a grand scale that they had to be staged in stadium-size arenas, have attracted new, youthful audiences in unprecedented numbers.

Béjart has said, "Choreography, like love, is made by couples. Since I began I've been perpetually creating the same ballet, journal of friendships, my loves, my discovery of the universe." *Nijinsky: Clown of God* (1971, set to a score combining music by Pyotr Ilich Tchaikovsky and Pierre Henry), a dreamlike meditation on Vaslav Nijinsky and his legacy, is only one prominent example of Béjart's personal identification and connection with his choreographic subjects.

Many times, that connection, as in *Nijinsky: Clown of God*, has been palpably homoerotic. In addition to reimagining, to spectacular effect, Ballets Russes classics such as *The Firebird* and *Pétrouchka* (both set to the original Stravinsky scores) and *The Specter of the Rose* (to a piano piece by Carl Maria von Weber, orchestrated by Hector Berlioz), Béjart has also derived inspiration from such classical gay icons as Prometheus, Dionysus, Orpheus, and Saint Sebastian.

Collaborating closely with many extraordinarily handsome men (the Argentine Jorge Donn and the Italian Paolo Bortoluzzi among them), Béjart has consistently created dances celebrating male beauty and eroticism, not the least of which is the all-male variant of his *Boléro* (1960, to the throbbing score by Maurice Ravel).

As far back as the early 1970s, Béjart's popular success and penchant for showcasing the virtuosity of his artists ruffled the feathers of many dance purists, including Arlene Croce, the influential dance critic for *The New Yorker,* who carped about his "cult of the dancer."

Undeterred by critical sniping at his vision for dance, the choreographer worked on, enticing ballet superstars such as Suzanne Farrell in the early 1970s and Sylvie Guillem in the 1990s to join his company and dazzle audiences in new ways.

An inveterate showman, a convert to Sufism, and a long-time student of Zen Buddhism, Béjart has integrated his diverse artistic, spiritual, and social interests by viewing dance as a religious rite available to all, not just to an elite.

By refusing to regard any aspect of life as profane, he celebrates the carnal without apology; his work, ever theatrical, can carry an unambiguously sexual charge that some congregations would protest loudly.

From his current base in Lausanne, Switzerland, Béjart could rest on his laurels and receive homages from his own spiritual heirs in the European Dance Theater movement (Pina Bausch, Boris Eifman, and Matthew Bourne, among others). Instead, he remains prolific and fully capable of stirring controversy.

Audiences and critics are either enthralled or enraged by recent offerings such as the celebratory *Ballet for Life* (1997, set to a score combining classical Mozart with pop-rock Queen), in response to the AIDS-related deaths of his friends Jorge Donn and Freddie Mercury of the rock group Queen; and *Bolero for Gianni* (1999, set to his all-time-favorite Ravel score), a tribute to the murdered Gianni Versace, who had designed the eye-popping costumes for *Ballet for Life.*

Such projects, as well as his many collaborations across classical and popular lines, have permitted Béjart not only to present his work to large theater audiences but also to record a remarkable number of performances on film and video for wider accessibility.   —*John McFarland*

BIBLIOGRAPHY

Christout, Marie-Françoise. "Maurice Béjart." *International Encyclopedia of Dance.* Vol. 1. New York: Oxford University Press, 1996. 403–407.

Clarke, Mary, and Clement Crisp. *The History of Dance.* New York: Crown, 1981.

Croce, Arlene. "Folies Béjart." *Afterimages.* New York: Alfred A. Knopf, 1997. 380–90.

Gruen, John. *The Private World of Ballet.* New York: Viking Press, 1975.

Masson, Colette, Jean-Louis Rousseau, and Pierre Faucheux, with handwritten comments by Maurice Béjart. *Béjart by Béjart.* New York: Congdon & Lattes, 1979.

Masson, Colette, and Gerard Mannoni. *Maurice Béjart.* Paris: Edition Plume, 1991.

"Maurice Béjart: A Journey of Initiation." *The UNESCO Courier* 1 (January 1996): 4–7.

Sayers, Lesley-Anne. "The Emperor's New Clothes: Maurice Béjart and Anna Teresa de Keersmaeker." *Dance Theatre Journal* 10.3 (Spring–Summer 1993): 42–46.

Whyte, Sally. "A Traveller through Dance." *Dance and Dancers* 49.3 (March 1990): 16–17.

SEE ALSO

Ballet; Dance; Ballets Russes; Diaghilev, Sergei; Lifar, Serge; Mercury, Freddie; Nijinsky, Vaslav; Ravel, Maurice; Tchaikovsky, Pyotr Ilich

Bell, Andy   *(b. 1964)*

FLAMBOYANT, OPENLY GAY ANDY BELL AND STAID, straight Vince Clarke have been called one of the oddest couples in music, but the chemistry works for them, and they have had a long and successful career as the synth-pop band Erasure.

Andy Bell, born on April 25, 1964, in Peterborough, England, moved to London at the age of nineteen. He was working as a mincer in a meat factory and playing in a band "going nowhere" when he responded to an ad placed by Clarke, a former member of Depeche Mode and Yazoo, seeking a musician to form a new band. Bell, the forty-first singer auditioned, was Clarke's choice, and Erasure was founded in 1985.

Their first album, *Wonderland* (1986), was not a success, but their second, *Circus* (1987), did somewhat better. When fans in Scandinavia embraced the single "Oh L'amour," British listeners began taking notice of the band. Erasure's third album, *The Innocents* (1988), went to the top of the album charts in the United Kingdom, as did *Wild!* (1989) and *Chorus* (1991).

Bell's singing voice contributes to Erasure's distinctive sound. Music critic Chuck Taylor praises his "rich, sultry vocals," while Glenn Gamboa calls them "sweet" and "swooning."

In addition to performing, Bell has written the lyrics for many of Erasure's songs, including "Hideaway," a coming-out song about a young man leaving home because he fears rejection by his family. Bell's lyrics advise "Don't be afraid" and offer the message that one need not hide if one feels different.

Hiding has never been Bell's style. One of the first openly gay rock musicians, he has always been candid about his sexual orientation.

Bell's performances onstage at Erasure concerts reflect his campy sense of humor. He has appeared in drag, in sequins, and in a variety of costumes from cowboy to spaceman.

Bell's positive attitude as a gay man has won Erasure many gay fans, but the group appeals to mainstream audiences as well. Michael Snyder of the *San Francisco*

Chronicle described a 1990 concert at which "there were some adult male couples…, yet they were easily outnumbered by the jubilant jocks and tight-skirted mall rats gyrating throughout the show." Their fans come in many nationalities as well; they have played successful concert tours in Europe, North America, and Asia.

In addition to performing original numbers, Erasure has occasionally covered other musicians, as on their 2003 album *Other People's Songs*. Taylor commented that with this album Erasure had "gone from hip to same-ole to retro, and now they actually sound fresh and fun."

Since the mid-1980s, Bell has been in a stable relationship with another man whom he identifies simply as Paul. The pair now make their home in Spain. Paul, who manages Bell's business affairs, suffered a serious stroke in 2000 in Los Angeles, where Erasure was in concert at the time. He has since recovered and is able to join the band for some of their tour dates. On these occasions, Bell serenades him with the romantic ballad "Goodnight," which he wrote for him.

Bell does not consider himself particularly political. In 1994, he commented on his role as a high-profile gay entertainer: "My real obligation to the world is to show people that I am a happy person who happens to be gay. To me, it comes down to how you feel deep down inside. You can't change the world if you're miserable and hate yourself."

— *Linda Rapp*

BIBLIOGRAPHY

Flick, Larry. "Andy Bell in the Public Eye; Mariah in the House." *Billboard*, June 25, 1994, 37.

Gamboa, Glenn. "Erasure Climbs Back Up the Charts with Remakes." *Ottawa Citizen*, March 15, 2003.

Snyder, Michael. "Erasure Aims to Wipe Out Prejudice." *San Francisco Chronicle*, March 9, 1990.

Swarbrick, Susan. "The Third Degree; Andy Bell: The Erasure Star Believes Passionately in Recycling—Sometimes in Surprising Ways." *Herald* (Glasgow), December 21, 2002.

Taylor, Chuck. "Erasure." *Billboard*, February 15, 2003, 30.

SEE ALSO

Popular Music; Rock Music

Bennett, Michael   *(1943–1987)*

THE CHARISMATIC BROADWAY DIRECTOR AND CHOREOGrapher Michael Bennett, creator of the landmark musical *A Chorus Line*, was notorious for producing strong reactions in his collaborators. James Kirkwood, coauthor of *A Chorus Line*, lashed out at him thus: "Michael would do anything—anything—to get a show

on. The cruelty was extensive. And not just in his professional life. He was amoral."

Bennett was a lover of men and women. His two primary heterosexual relationships were stormy, first with wife Donna McKechnie (wed December 1976, divorced four months later) and then with Sabine Cassel, whom he promised to wed but did not.

His relationships with men were less publicized, but they included long relationships with dancers Larry Fuller, Scott Pearson, Richard Christopher, and Gene Pruitt, his last lover.

Born Michael Bennett DiFiglia in Buffalo, New York, on April 8, 1943, young Mickey was a child prodigy of dance. He dropped out of high school at the age of sixteen to join a touring company of Jerome Robbins's *West Side Story*. Robbins was to become one of his principal influences.

Bennett made his Broadway debut as a dancer in *Subways Are for Sleeping* (1961), but he soon realized that he had a greater talent for choreography than for dancing. Bennett's first solo assignments as a choreographer were on *A Joyful Noise* (1966) and *Henry, Sweet Henry* (1967).

His first big hit was *Promises, Promises* (1968), which was followed by *Coco* (1969). Working with Harold Prince on Stephen Sondheim's *Company* (1970) and *Follies* (1971) led him to decide that he wanted to be a director as well as a choreographer.

Bennett's dream was realized when he was called in to save *Seesaw* (1973). He agreed to take over the show on the condition that he would have creative control of the production. He ultimately received credit (and Tony nominations) as librettist, director, and co-choreographer.

The process of taking over this ailing show on the road, just six months before it was scheduled to open, convinced Bennett that the standard way of developing musicals—rehearsals, out-of-town tryouts, previews, and then opening—was no longer efficient. He came up with a better plan.

Bennett decided to do a show about the lives of dancers, but rather than commission a script he let the story line evolve from the experiences of real dancers. After conducting hours of interviews with Broadway gypsies (or chorus dancers), Bennett began an unprecedented year of workshops at Joseph Papp's Public Theatre.

The result was *A Chorus Line* (1975). A risk all the way around, the show opened without stars and ran two hours and ten minutes without an intermission. Bennett received credit as director, coproducer, coauthor, and co-choreographer.

After a few months at the Public Theatre, *A Chorus Line* moved to Broadway on July 25, 1975, where it remained at the Schubert Theatre for the next fifteen years. The breakthrough musical won the New York

Drama Critics' Circle Award, the Tony Award, and the Pulitzer Prize, among many other honors. When the show closed on April 28, 1990, it had run for 6,137 performances, still a record for a Broadway musical written by Americans.

While *Applause* (1970) is considered the first Broadway musical to introduce an openly gay character, Bennett is responsible for the second and third appearances of homosexual characters. *Seesaw* features David, a gay choreographer, and *A Chorus Line* introduced audiences to Paul and Greg, gay dancers. Many have criticized the bisexual Bennett for the fact that neither Paul nor Greg is finally chosen for the chorus line, thus maintaining the myth that all working actors are heterosexual.

Winner of eight Tony Awards, Bennett's legacy to musical theater is undoubtedly his fluid, cinematic style of choreography and staging, which reached its ultimate realization in *Dreamgirls* (1981), where even the computerized towers of the set were choreographed into the action of the play. Like Robbins, he did more than choreograph steps; he put the entire show into motion.

Inadvertently, Bennett's other great benefaction was to provide the New York Shakespeare Festival with the bulk of its income for many years. As one of the producers of *A Chorus Line*, the Public Theatre earned approximately $37,800,000 from Bennett's landmark production.

In January 1985, Bennett abandoned the almost completed musical *Scandal*, which he had been developing through an extended series of workshops. Many observers felt this to be Bennett's strongest work, with few understanding the toll that alcohol, drugs, and a weakened immune system had taken on this genius of the theater.

When Michael Bennett died at the age of forty-four on July 2, 1987, of AIDS-related lymphoma, he left a sizable portion of his estate to funding research to fight the AIDS epidemic.   —*Bud Coleman*

BIBLIOGRAPHY

Flinn, Denny Martin. *What They Did for Love: The Untold Story Behind the Making of "A Chorus Line."* New York: Bantam Books, 1989.

Kelly, Kevin. *One Singular Sensation: The Michael Bennett Story.* New York: Zebra Books, 1990.

Mandelbaum, Ken. *"A Chorus Line" and the Musicals of Michael Bennett.* New York: St. Martin's Press, 1989.

Rothstein, Mervyn. *" 'A Chorus Line,' Broadway Giant, Closing at Age 15."* *New York Times,* February 22, 1990.

Viagas, Robert, Baayork Lee, and Thommie Walsh. *On the Line: The Creation of "A Chorus Line."* New York: William Morrow, 1990.

SEE ALSO

Musical Theater and Film; Dance; Robbins, Jerome; Sondheim, Stephen; Tune, Tommy

Bentley, Gladys   (1907–1960)

AFRICAN AMERICAN BLUES SINGER GLADYS BENTLEY openly flaunted her lesbianism in the 1920s and 1930s, but recanted in the 1950s in an attempt to salvage her career.

Bentley was born on August 12, 1907, the oldest of George L. Bentley and Mary C. Mote's four children. By Bentley's own account, her childhood in Philadelphia was not a happy one. She was a "problem child," feeling at odds with her peers, who taunted her for being overweight and a tomboy.

In an interview in *Ebony* magazine late in her life, Bentley remembered having crushes on women in her early childhood; these infatuations apparently alarmed her parents, who may have sought medical help for their daughter.

At the age of sixteen, Bentley left her parents' home and ran away to New York City. At first she made a meager living in Harlem as a pianist and singer, playing primarily for rent parties. She specialized in improvising indecent lyrics to the tunes of popular melodies of the day; one of her songs combined "Sweet Georgia Brown" and "Alice Blue Gown" into a bawdy ode to anal intercourse.

Bentley eventually secured herself a position as pianist at speakeasies such as the Mad House on 133rd Street, where she was paid $35 a week. When Bentley began to attract a white downtown audience, including writer Carl Van Vechten, her salary was raised to $100 a week.

As Eric Garber notes, Bentley's name came to be synonymous with "Hot Harlem" of the 1920s. The singer appeared at the Cotton Club and headlined at The Clam House for several years, where she performed in a white tuxedo and top hat. She cultivated her image as a "bulldagger," openly flaunting her lesbianism not only in performance but also in public. In a much publicized ceremony, she even married her white lesbian lover.

In 1928, at the height of her fame, Bentley made a number of recordings for Okeh records. She issued other records in the 1940s and 1950s. While she never became a popular recording artist, her records, which do not make an issue of her sexual orientation or include her filthy lyrics, do reveal her as a strong, independent woman.

"How Much Can I Stand," featured on Rosetta Records' compilation of early blues recordings, *Mean Mothers: Independent Women's Blues, Vol. 1* (1992), perfectly captures Bentley's gravelly alto. Accompanied by the white guitarist Eddie Lang, Bentley sings a slow blues, answering the guitar with vocal imitations of trumpet frills that are reminiscent of Louis Armstrong.

During the 1920s and later, Bentley was frequently the subject of gossip columns. She also made an indelible impression on a number of writers and memoirists. In 1945, Langston Hughes, in his autobiography *The Big*

Sea, remembered her as "an amazing exhibition of musical energy—a large, dark, masculine lady, whose feet pounded the floor while her fingers pounded the keyboard—a perfect piece of African sculpture, animated by her own rhythm."

She was probably the model for Sybil, the lesbian piano player in Blair Niles's gay novel *Strange Brother* (1931). Garber notes that she also makes "unnamed but unmistakable" appearances in Carl Van Vechten's *Parties* (1930) and Clement Wood's *Deep River* (1934).

The stock-market crash of 1929 dealt a severe blow to Harlem's night life, but Bentley managed to prolong her career into the 1930s. In this decade Bentley was featured at the Ubangi Club on 133rd Street, a gay club with a chorus of female impersonators.

In 1937, Bentley abandoned Harlem for Los Angeles, where, with some difficulty, she managed to secure club dates, but where she was harassed by police for her cross-dressing. During World War II, Bentley increasingly relied on night spots catering to a homosexual clientele for her bookings.

In the 1950s, Bentley's trademark lesbian act became a liability as McCarthyism swept the United States. In an effort to save her career and maintain her livelihood, Bentley cleaned up her act and began to perform in dresses.

During this period, she wrote the autobiographical piece "I am a Woman Again," which was published in *Ebony* in 1952. In this article Bentley repudiated her former life, claiming to have "lived in a personal hell" of unhappiness and loneliness until she found the love of a good man and sought medical treatment to cure her of what she described as deviation.

Eric Garber notes that "numerous elements of this autobiographical account ring false." These include the medical treatment she claims she sought, her alleged marriage, which was later denied by the supposed husband, and details of her childhood—for example, she claimed that her mother had longed for a son throughout her pregnancy. Garber views this article as Bentley's last-ditch attempt to salvage her career at a time when her livelihood was threatened.

Bentley's strategy seems to have worked, but she never regained her popularity of the 1920s and 1930s. She was briefly married to a man in 1952, and at the end of her life sought solace in the church, becoming a devoted member of the Temple of Love in Christ, Inc. Bentley died on January 18, 1960, of influenza.   —*Gillian Rodger*

BIBLIOGRAPHY

Bentley, Gladys. "I am a Woman Again." *Ebony,* August 1952, 92.

_____. "How Much Can I Stand." *Mean Mothers: Independent Women's Blues,* Vol. 1. Sound recording. New York: Rosetta Records (RR1300), 1992.

Chauncey, George. *Gay New York: Gender, Culture, and the Making of the Gay Male World, 1890–1940.* New York: Basic Books, 1994.

Faderman, Lillian. 1992. *Odd Girls and Twilight Lovers: A History of Lesbian Life in Twentieth-Century America.* New York: Penguin Books, 1992.

Garber, Eric. "Gladys Bentley: The Bulldagger Who Sang the Blues." *OUTLook: National Lesbian & Gay Quarterly* 1 (Spring 1998): 52–61.

SEE ALSO

Blues Music; Drag Shows: Drag Kings and Male Impersonators; Jazz; Cabarets and Revues

Berners, Baron Gerald Hugh Tyrwhitt-Wilson
(1883–1950)

GERALD HUGH TYRWHITT-WILSON, THE FOURTEENTH Baron Berners, was, as his friend Osbert Sitwell reflected, a dilettante, but a dilettante in the best sense of the word. A composer, painter, and novelist, he was, first and foremost, a genuine British aristocratic eccentric whose life was, in a sense, a grand performance.

He was born on September 18, 1883, at Apley Park, Shropshire, to a family with a long, noble pedigree. A shy and effeminate boy, he was discouraged from pursuing his love of art and music by his pious and conventional mother, who felt such inclinations unbecoming a young man of his class.

Berners was educated at Eton and, in 1899, entered the diplomatic service, despite failing its written examinations. He was first posted as an honorary attaché to Constantinople, where he met Harold Nicolson, later the husband of Vita Sackville-West. Subsequently, he was posted to Rome, where he became a friend of Ronald Firbank, who was his major literary influence, and Igor Stravinsky, who admired his musical compositions.

In 1918, he inherited his uncle's title, fortune, and properties. Consequently, he left the diplomatic service and retired to the family estate at Faringdon, Oxfordshire, in order to devote his life entirely to the pursuit of his pastimes and pleasures. As Lord Berners, he cultivated a considerable reputation as an eccentric.

He was known for such antics as dyeing the doves on his estate various colors, arranging color-coordinated meals, and traveling through Europe with a spinet piano in the rear seat of his Rolls-Royce. He also frequented many of the literary and artistic circles of his day, and numbered Evelyn Waugh, the Mitford sisters, and the Sitwells among his friends and guests.

Even while entertaining extravagantly, Berners still found time to pursue his various artistic careers. As a composer, he was largely self-taught; nonetheless, he produced an impressive number of compositions that could be deemed lighthearted "serious" music, influenced by contemporary French composers. He wrote a considerable number of songs and pieces for solo piano.

His best-known and most enduring works, however, are his ballets, particularly *The Triumph of Neptune* (produced by Diaghilev, choreographed by Balanchine, 1926), as well as *Luna Park* (1930) and *A Wedding Bouquet* (with words by Gertrude Stein, 1936). He also commissioned Stein to write an opera libretto, *Doctor Faustus Lights the Lights,* but he never actually composed the music for it.

Berners also achieved some success as a writer. His published work includes three volumes of amusing autobiography, including *First Childhood* (1934), *A Distant Prospect* (1945), and the recently discovered *The Château de Résenlieu* (published in 2000).

In addition, he wrote a number of short, campy Firbankian novels, including *The Girls of Radcliff Hall* (1934), a roman à clef (published under the pseudonym "Adela Quebec"). This fiction is set in a girls' school (the name of which alludes to the lesbian author of *The Well of Loneliness*) in which all the "girls" are disguised portraits of his various gay male acquaintances. The volume has become rare, as several of those portrayed, particularly Cecil Beaton, were offended and thus bought and destroyed many of the copies.

In the 1930s, Berners enjoyed a brief vogue as a painter as well; his landscapes, though not terribly original, sold for extraordinary prices.

For over twenty years, Berners lived openly with a much younger man, the equally eccentric Robert Heber-Percy (1911–1986). In 1934, Berners had a "folly" tower, perhaps the last such structure built in England, erected on his estate as a birthday present for the "Mad Boy." Despite Heber-Percy's short-lived wartime marriage to a woman, Berners left him his estate and fortune upon his death on April 19, 1950.   —*Patricia Juliana Smith*

BIBLIOGRAPHY

Amory, Mark. *Lord Berners: The Last Eccentric.* London: Chatto and Windus, 1998.

Berners, Gerald Hugh Tyrwhitt-Wilson, Lord. *The Château de Résenlieu.* Chappaqua, N.Y.: Turtle Point Press, 2000.

_____. *A Distant Prospect.* Chappaqua, N.Y.: Turtle Point Press, 1998.

_____. *First Childhood.* Chappaqua, N.Y.: Turtle Point Press, 1998.

SEE ALSO

Classical Music; Ballet; Diaghilev, Sergei

Bernstein, Leonard   (1918–1990)

THROUGHOUT THE 1960s, LEONARD BERNSTEIN WAS undoubtedly the most visible proponent of classical music in American culture. Through his outgoing personality and resourceful uses of the media, particularly television, Bernstein introduced "highbrow" culture into the homes of middle America, while also defending rock and roll as "real" music and espousing radical causes.

Given his overwhelming celebrity and acclaim as a composer, conductor, pianist, and lecturer, the meteoric career of this son of Russian Jewish immigrants would seem to exemplify the all-American success story; yet, for most of his life, the specter of the closet lurked threateningly behind the glamorous and often brash public image of Leonard Bernstein.

Born in Lawrence, Massachusetts, on August 25, 1918, Bernstein studied at Harvard University, the Curtis Institute, and the Berkshire Music Center at Tanglewood, where he came to the attention of maestro Serge Koussevitzky, who mentored the early stages of his career.

In 1944, the twenty-six-year-old Bernstein was called on at the last minute to replace maestro Bruno Walter in conducting the New York Philharmonic Orchestra. The public notice and acclaim that resulted from this performance thrust the young musician into the limelight, and he was soon in demand as a conductor and teacher throughout the United States and Europe.

In 1958, Bernstein was appointed musical director and chief conductor of the New York Philharmonic, a post he retained until 1969, and he remained conductor laureate until his death.

In 1959, at the height of the Cold War, he traveled with the Philharmonic to the Soviet Union, where the orchestra performed his Second Symphony, entitled *The Age of Anxiety* after the W. H. Auden poem that inspired it, an apt work for the given historical moment.

Bernstein was also a noted (if, at times, controversial) opera conductor as well, and is remembered for his performances and recordings with the Vienna State Opera, the Metropolitan Opera, and La Scala. In the latter venue, Bernstein scored a significant triumph when, in December 1953, he made his house debut on short notice, conducting Maria Callas in what would become one of her signature roles, the title character in Luigi Cherubini's *Medea*.

Bernstein simultaneously pursued a very diverse career as a composer, creating "serious" pieces, including three symphonies, three ballets, the choral work *Chichester Psalms* (1965), and *Mass* (1971), a theater piece commissioned for the opening of the Kennedy Center for the Performing Arts in Washington, D.C.

His best-known works, however, are those he wrote for the Broadway musical stage, including *On the Town* (1944), *Wonderful Town* (1953), *Candide* (1956; revised as an opera, 1982), and the highly popular *West Side Story* (1957).

Bernstein's respect for popular music is also evinced by the fact that his classical compositions frequently attempt to synthesize jazz and pop themes into more traditional classical styles.

By the early 1960s, Bernstein was one of the most prominent cultural figures in American society. Through his association with the Kennedy family and his media appearances, he exerted a tremendous influence in presenting the fine arts to the American public in a manner free from the social snobbery with which they are so often associated.

He was one of the first orchestral conductors to utilize the relatively new medium of television, and his frequent appearances familiarized the general public with his flamboyant style and extravagant gestures at the podium, mannerisms that infuriated many "purists" but established him as a familiar figure in many American living rooms.

Through his televised educational series of Young People's Concerts (1958–1972), he demonstrated that classical music was not just accessible to the masses but that it could even be *fun.*

Unlike most classical musicians, Bernstein was outspoken in his political views, particularly on the Vietnam War and civil rights issues. His *Mass* disturbed many critics and listeners with its unambiguous antiwar sentiments. So did some of his well-intentioned but nonetheless eccentric gestures, such as inviting members of the Black Panther party, a radical group of African American militants, to his cocktail parties to mingle with socialites and other representatives of the cultural elite.

As a result, he was exposed to barbs and ridicule in the press (satirist Tom Wolfe labeled Bernstein and his actions as paradigms of "radical chic") and occasionally to booing from New York Philharmonic audiences. His advocacy of rock and roll drew derision from classical and rock camps alike.

In spite of Bernstein's public avowal of unpopular causes, he was, for much of his career, unwilling to risk exposure of his homosexuality. Indeed, the social mores of the 1950s and 1960s were such that a revelation of homosexuality would undoubtedly have destroyed the celebrity and influence he had attained.

In 1951, Bernstein married the Chilean actress Felicia Montealegre, with whom he had three children. Bernstein nonetheless engaged in a number of homosexual relationships over the years. In the mid-1970s, the couple separated, and Bernstein attempted to live an openly gay life with Tom Cochran, who had been his lover since 1971. A year later, he returned to his wife, who was by this time terminally ill.

After Montealegre's death in 1978, Bernstein became increasingly open about his gayness; even so, as his daugh-

Leonard Bernstein, photographed by Fred Polumbo in 1945.

ter Nina observed after his death, his need for a "middle-class sensibility" kept him from living a completely gay life.

Bernstein's final major composition, the opera *A Quiet Place* (1983), positions a bisexual male character, who functions as the mediator between the other, more conflicted characters, at the center of the action. The opera's message is one of reconciliation and acceptance among all people.

Although increasingly in ill health in his final years, Bernstein continued to perform and record until his death of a heart attack on October 14, 1990.

As a conductor, he had a vast repertoire and recorded frequently, often in collaboration with the greatest singers and solo musicians of the postwar era. As a result, he has left an extensive and remarkable legacy of recordings and video performances that will ensure his reputation as an intelligent and enthusiastic conductor, composer, and musician for generations to come.

—*Patricia Juliana Smith*

BIBLIOGRAPHY

Burton, Humphrey. *Leonard Bernstein.* New York: Doubleday, 1994.

Burton, Willi Westbrook, ed. *Conversations about Bernstein.* New York: Oxford University Press, 1995.

Myers, Paul. *Leonard Bernstein*. London: Phaidon, 1998.

Peyser, Joan. *Bernstein: A Biography*. Rev. ed. New York: Billboard Books, 1998.

Secrest, Meryle. *Leonard Bernstein: A Life*. New York: Knopf, 1994.

SEE ALSO

Classical Music; Musical Theater and Film; Conductors; Blitzstein, Marc; Britten, Benjamin; Copland, Aaron; Poulenc, Francis; Robbins, Jerome; Rorem, Ned; Sondheim, Stephen

Blitzstein, Marc   (1905–1964)

AMERICAN COMPOSER MARC BLITZSTEIN COMPOSED in a variety of forms, but is best known today for his opera scores, especially *The Cradle Will Rock* (1936). Although none of his operas is in the standard repertory or often performed, he had a major influence on other composers who aspired to blend classical and popular forms, especially Leonard Bernstein and Stephen Sondheim.

Blitzstein was born in Philadelphia on March 2, 1905, into an affluent Jewish banking family. He began playing piano at the age of three and began composing when he was seven. He attended the University of Pennsylvania briefly. He studied privately in New York City, enrolled in the Curtis Institute of Music in Philadelphia upon its founding in 1924, and then studied with Arnold Schoenberg in Berlin and Nadia Boulanger in Paris.

Upon returning to the United States, he performed his own *Piano Sonata* (1927) in New York in 1928. He began work as a music critic for *Modern Music* at this time, and eventually wrote for *Musical Quarterly* and *New Masses* as well.

Although he originally followed the "art for art's sake" doctrine prevalent in America, writing intellectually challenging music for a select elite, as he adopted more radical political positions (and joined the Communist Party) he came to espouse the doctrines of Kurt Weill, Bertolt Brecht, and Hanns Eisler, who were responsible for creating socially conscious, popular theater in Germany.

Blitzstein thus began to embrace the philosophy of "music for the people," the immediate result of which was the opera *The Cradle Will Rock* (1936), a politically charged work about labor unionism.

The first production was directed by Orson Welles at the Mary Elliott Theater in New York and produced by John Houseman under the auspices of the Federal Theater Project (FTP). Its legendary first performance was a sensation, in part because the Works Progress Administration (WPA), which administered the FTP, was under attack by the U.S. government for its pro-labor

stance. The WPA had its budget cut just before the premiere of the opera. The show went on without orchestra, sets, costumes, lights, or union actors, staged in a theater that had been procured the evening of the performance.

The success (and notoriety) of the impromptu production made Blitzstein famous as a leading exponent of politically committed musical theater. Leonard Bernstein, who saw a 1938 production of the opera on Broadway, produced it at Harvard and became a friend and protégé of the composer.

Other important Blitzstein works include his *Symphony: The Airborne* (1946), written while the composer was stationed in Great Britain during World War II and first performed in New York under the baton of Leonard Bernstein; his ambitious opera *Regina* (1949), based on Lillian Hellmann's play *The Little Foxes*; an influential and altogether successful adaptation and translation of Weill and Brecht's *The Threepenny Opera* (1952); and the opera *Juno* (1959), based on Sean O'Casey's play *Juno and the Paycock*.

Although necessarily publicly closeted, Blitzstein was honest about his homosexuality with his friends and colleagues. Nevertheless, in 1933, he married the critic and writer Eva Goldbeck (1901–1936), who seems to have been aware of his homosexuality; they had a deep relationship until her death three years later.

Subsequently, his erotic life seems to have been exclusively homosexual. His homosexuality probably inspired the sympathy for outsiders that motivated his political activism.

Blitzstein's death came in Martinique, where he was wintering in 1963. He apparently made sexual advances to three Portuguese sailors whom he had picked up. What exactly happened next is unclear, but Blitzstein was robbed, beaten, and stripped. Found the next morning, he was immediately taken to a hospital, where he died of internal bleeding on January 22, 1964.

Although interest in Blitzstein and his work declined in the 1960s and 1970s, more recently he has come to be recognized as a significant figure in the history of American musical theater. Renewed attention to Blitzstein has also resulted from Tim Robbins's film *Cradle Will Rock* (1999), which took as its subject the creation of *The Cradle Will Rock*.

—*Robert Kellerman*

BIBLIOGRAPHY

Burton, Peter. "Blitzstein, Marc." *Gay and Lesbian Biography*. Michael J. Tyrkus, ed. Detroit: St. James Press, 1997. 75–77.

Gordon, Eric A. *Mark the Music: The Life and Work of Marc Blitzstein*. New York: St. Martin's Press, 1989.

Kushner, David Z. "Blitzstein, Marc." *The New Grove Dictionary of Music and Musicians*. Stanley Satie, ed. Second ed. 29 vols. London: Macmillan, 2001. 3:702–704.

The Marc Blitzstein website. www.marcblitzstein.com

Blues Music

BLUES MUSIC AS IT FLOURISHED IN THE 1920S WAS women's music. Although it grew out of African American spirituals and a tradition of itinerant male singers in the rural South, female performers defined and popularized the genre, originally through performances on the black vaudeville and minstrel show circuits.

Most black performers traveled on the Theater Owner's Booking Association, or T.O.B.A., circuit, establishing an avid loyal following with black audiences and building up solid reputations before the advent of recording. Although most of these theaters were in the South, New York and especially Chicago became essential centers for blues performers and their audiences.

Early Recordings

In 1920, Mamie Smith became the first woman of color to make an audio recording; the first vocal blues record was her "Crazy Blues." Written by Perry Bradford, it was a tremendous success on the Okeh label, selling more than 100 thousand copies in its first month of release and officially ushering in the era of "race records"—records marketed expressly at black consumers—and the popularity of the blues.

Publishers rushed to capitalize on this previously unconsidered market, quickly employing popular club singers such as Alberta Hunter to make recordings to meet the burgeoning demand for blues music. Singers were paid a one-time fee for each usable "side" and the early artists were generally chosen for their vocal appeal to a crossover audience.

Hence, Bessie Smith's (no relation to Mamie) first attempt at recording was rejected as "too rough," but in 1923 her version of Hunter's "Down-Hearted Blues" would sell more than three-quarters of a million copies in less than six months, establishing Bessie Smith as the undisputed "Empress of the Blues."

"Ma" Rainey

If Bessie Smith was the "Empress" or sometimes "Queen" of the blues, then Gertrude ("Ma") Rainey, a veteran traveling show performer who gave Smith her professional start, was the "Mother of the Blues." Rainey was the first popular woman blues singer, performing and traveling with her husband, William "Pa" Rainey, in tent shows.

Having performed on the road for more than twenty-five years, Rainey received a recording contract in 1923 and made more than 100 recordings in just six years. In 1984, forty-five years after her death, she became the subject of August Wilson's award-winning Broadway play, *Ma Rainey's Black Bottom,* a fictional account of a recording session titled for one of her well-known songs.

Among the other blues "royalty" was Clara Smith, dubbed "Queen of the Moaners." Bessie and Clara were two of the "five blues-singing Smiths," as they were called, which also included Mamie, Laura, and Trixie, though none of the women were related. Bessie and Clara, however, occasionally claimed to be sisters. They recorded several duets, an unusual arrangement for Bessie, who generally would not allow another blues singer on the same bill as herself.

While men wrote many blues compositions, Rainey, Bessie Smith, and Hunter, along with Ida Cox, pianist Lovie Austin, and other women composed the music and lyrics for many of the songs they performed and recorded. Typically, however, these early artists did not retain copyright to their compositions, though in later years Hunter fought to gain control over the material she had written.

Sexuality in Blues Music

The most persistent theme in blues lyrics revolved around man—and sometimes woman—troubles, but other recurrent themes included poverty; drinking and drug use; violence and criminal behavior, particularly passion killing; prostitution; traveling, usually by train; and political protest.

Sexuality played a significant role in blues music. Colorful metaphors such as "jelly rolls," "peach trees," "handy men," and others were widely used to veil frank talk of sexual desire and satisfaction. The emphasis on sexual satisfaction for women was itself radical in the 1920s.

Although blues lyricists were masters of double entendres regarding sexuality, contemporary audiences recognized and accepted these references, including allusions to homosexuality.

Rainey's composition "Prove It on Me Blues" is perhaps the best-known explicit statement of lesbianism and transvestism in a blues song:

> They said I do it, ain't nobody caught me
> Sure got to prove it on me
> Went out last night with a crowd of my friends
> They must've been women, 'cause I don't like no men
> It's true I wear a collar and a tie...
> Talk to the gals just like any old man...

Similarly, Rainey's "Sissy Blues" plainly describes losing her man to another man, or "sissy," named "Kate." Tellingly, it lacks any moralizing tone.

Another singer, Lucille Bogan, also known as Bessie Jackson, was famous for her extremely risqué material. As Jackson, Bogan recorded "B.D. [Bull-Dykers] Woman's Blues" in 1935. Bull-daggers, Bogan insists, "can lay their jive just like a natural man / B.D. women sure is rough; they drink up many a whiskey and sure can strut their stuff."

Bisexual and Lesbian Performers

Such explicit material was commonplace in early blues songs, and many early blues performers, including Rainey, Smith, Hunter, and Gladys Bentley were openly bisexual or lesbian.

In 1925, Rainey was arrested for indecency after being caught naked with a group of women at a private party; still undressed, she fell down the stairs trying to get away. Bessie Smith bailed her out, and they would often joke afterward about the awkward yet humorous incident.

Smith, though also married, likewise made no secret of her numerous affairs with women. Bentley, described by Langston Hughes as "a large, dark masculine lady," was acclaimed for her bull-dagger image and gender performance.

Other renowned blues singers of the era included Sippie Wallace and Ethel Waters. Called "Sweet Mama Stringbean," Waters went on to a successful, Oscar-nominated film career.

Later Blues Singers

Vaudeville and blues music began to fall out of fashion around the time of the Great Depression, giving way to the rising popularity of motion pictures and the more upbeat jazz music. Male performers such as Muddy Waters and B.B. King who are today more readily associated with the genre did not emerge in popularity until the 1950s.

In the 1950s, female singers such as Ruth Brown, Koko Taylor, Dinah Washington, and Big Mama Thornton revived the tradition of the remarkably gutsy, pioneering female performers. Thornton, a powerful performer who frequently dressed in masculine clothing, released "Hound Dog" in 1953, three years before Elvis Presley's rendition.

Classic women's blues music experienced a resurgence of popularity in the 1960s and 1970s with the rerelease of Bessie Smith's catalog, as well as the spectacular reemergence of Hunter in 1977 following a twenty-year career hiatus.

—*Carla Williams*

Bibliography

Broer, Lawrence R., and John D. Walther, eds. *Dancing Fools and Weary Blues: The Great Escape of the Twenties.* Bowling Green, Oh.: Bowling Green State University Popular Press, 1990.

Davis, Angela Y. *Blues Legacies and Black Feminism: Gertrude 'Ma' Rainey, Bessie Smith and Billie Holiday.* New York: Pantheon Books, 1998.

Harrison, Daphne Duval. *Black Pearls: Blues Queens of the 1920s.* New Brunswick, N.J.: Rutgers University Press, 1988.

Oliver, Paul. *Aspects of the Blues Tradition.* New York: Oak Publications, 1968.

_____. *Blues Fell This Morning: Meaning in the Blues.* Cambridge: Cambridge University Press, 1994.

Sullivan, Tom. "Remember Ma Rainey." www.lambda.net/~maximum/rainey.html

See also

Popular Music; Bentley, Gladys; Hunter, Alberta; Rainey, Gertrude ("Ma"); Smith, Bessie; Waters, Ethel

Boulanger, Nadia   (1887–1979)

PERHAPS THE GREATEST TEACHER OF MUSICAL COMposition in the twentieth century, Nadia Boulanger greatly influenced modern classical music. One of very few women in a male-dominated field, she was nonetheless a significant presence in the careers of many of the best-known twentieth-century European and American composers.

Forsaking her own career as a composer because she predicted that it would be undistinguished (though her cantata *La Siréna* won second prize in the Prix de Rome in 1908), Boulanger devoted her life to teaching the principles of motion, harmony, and rhythm to the hundreds of students who came to her tiny Paris studio.

Born on September 16, 1877, of a French father and Russian mother, Boulanger was suited to a life dedicated to music, by virtue of her heritage. Her father's father had been a composer and his mother a singer with the Opéra Comique. Ernest Boulanger had been a composer and music professor himself when he met and married Nadia's mother, Raissa.

Although Ernest was sixty-three when Nadia was born, he and Raissa imparted the family love of music to Nadia and her sister Lili, who became a well-known composer but who died at the age of twenty-four. Throughout her life, Nadia remained devoted to her mother and sister. She held annual memorial masses for them after their deaths and tirelessly promoted her sister's music.

Boulanger entered the Paris Conservatory at the age of ten and won several prizes for her compositions. From 1908 to 1918, she was a teacher of harmony at the Conservatory. In 1921, she was appointed professor of harmony, counterpoint, and composition at the American Conservatory of Music in Fontainebleau. She continued these teaching duties until her death, becoming Director of the American Conservatory in 1950. She also taught at the École normale de musique in Paris and at the Paris Conservatory.

Nadia Boulanger.

Boulanger's roster of students included many who would later become internationally famous, from Philip Glass to Burt Bacharach. She taught so many prominent American composers that her influence on modern American music has been tremendous.

Among her students were many prominent gay composers who have helped define modern American classical music, such as Aaron Copland, Virgil Thomson, Leonard Bernstein, Marc Blitzstein, Gian Carlo Menotti, and Ned Rorem.

Among her female students were Ruth Anderson, Cécile Armagnac, Marion Bauer, Suzanne Bloch, Peggy Glanville-Hicks, Helen Hosmer, Thea Musgrave, and Louise Talma.

Along with the famous classes she taught in her Paris studio, Boulanger also toured energetically to lecture and conduct. During her 1939 American tour, she gave 102 lectures in 118 days, and also became the first woman to conduct the Boston Symphony, the New York Philharmonic, and the Philadelphia Orchestra.

She grew impatient with public amazement over what she had accomplished despite being a woman. She snapped at one reporter, "I've been a woman for a little over fifty years and have gotten over my initial astonishment."

Fiercely self-sufficient, Boulanger defied tradition to live an independent life. She created an opening for women in what had formerly been a male domain.

It is not certain that Boulanger was a lesbian, but it is likely that she was. She was protective of her privacy and a practicing Catholic, so she may have had conflicting emotions about sexuality in general. Although she allegedly avoided Gertrude Stein's salon because of its "flagrant homosexuality," she did frequent the more discreet salon of Princess de Polignac (Winaretta Singer), whose lesbianism was also well known.

Boulanger continued to preside over her exacting yet gentle lessons until her death on October 22, 1979, aged 92. Her principal heirs were her former student Cécile Armagnac and her longtime personal assistant, Annette Dieudonné.

Boulanger's attitude toward her craft is perhaps best expressed in a quotation of hers from Alan Kendall's biography: "The art of music is so deep and profound that to approach it very seriously only is not enough. One must approach music with a serious rigor and, at the same time, with a great, affectionate joy."   —*Tina Gianoulis*

BIBLIOGRAPHY

Kendall, Alan. *The Tender Tyrant: Nadia Boulanger, a Life Devoted to Music.* Chicago: Lyceum Books, 1977.

Mockus, Martha. "Music, Classical." *Lesbian Histories and Cultures.* Bonnie Zimmerman, ed. New York: Garland, 2000. 514–517.

Monsaingeon, Bruno. *Mademoiselle: Conversations with Nadia Boulanger.* Manchester, England: Carcanet, 1985.

Rosenstiel, Leonie. *Nadia Boulanger: A Life in Music.* New York: Norton, 1998.

Shawn. Allen "Nadia Boulanger's Lessons." *Atlantic Monthly,* March 1983, 78.

SEE ALSO

Classical Music; Conductors; Bernstein, Leonard; Blitzstein, Marc; Copland, Aaron; Landowska, Wanda; Menotti, Gian Carlo; Rorem, Ned; Stein, Gertrude; Thomson, Virgil

Bourbon, Ray   *(1892?–1971)*

L EGENDARY DRAG PERFORMER AND RECORDING ARTIST Ray (or Rae) Bourbon appeared in silent movies, vaudeville acts, Broadway plays, and, from the 1930s through the 1960s, performed across the United States in a gay nightclub circuit. Often arrested by the police for his "indecent" performances and for dressing in drag, Bourbon was ultimately convicted of conspiracy to commit murder and died in prison.

Bourbon deliberately obscured his origins, sometimes even claiming that he was "the last of the Hapsburg

Bourbons," but he was probably born Hal Waddell in Texarkana, Texas, sometime around 1892.

In the early 1920s, Bourbon worked as a stuntman in Hollywood and appeared in several silent films, sometimes in drag. He then teamed up with Bert Sherry in a successful vaudeville act, "Bourbon and Sherry," in which Sherry played the straight man to Bourbon's flamboyant drag persona.

He soon attracted the attention of Mae West, who in 1927 cast him in two of her plays—*Sex* and *Pleasure Man.* Both were raided by police who were attempting to "clean up" Broadway. Bourbon later appeared as an extra in West's movies and in supporting roles in productions of her plays.

In the early 1930s, Bourbon recorded the first of his many risqué records. He also began to appear in the "pansy clubs" that sprouted in Hollywood in an attempt to capitalize on the "pansy craze" in New York during the late 1920s. Bourbon created and starred in a drag revue called "Boys Will Be Girls." After the police shut down the Los Angeles establishments, he moved his show to San Francisco.

In the late 1930s and early 1940s, Bourbon managed his own club, The Rendezvous, in Los Angeles. His revue "Don't Call Me Madam" attracted celebrities such as Bob Hope and Bing Crosby. In addition, Bourbon also headlined at such venues as Finocchio's in San Francisco and continued to record albums issued by small record companies.

In 1934, Bourbon met the songwriting team Bob Wright and Chet Forrest. The young men, who would later write *Kismet* (1953) and *Grand Hotel* (1957), became lifelong friends of Bourbon and often served as his accompanists and wrote songs for his shows.

In the 1940s, Bourbon appeared in a Los Angeles stage production of his own revue *Insults of 1944,* and then with Mae West in New York and in touring productions of her plays *Diamond Lil* and *Catherine the Great.* During this period, he also gained attention with a solo recital at New York's Carnegie Hall that attracted a sold-out audience of "very spectacular characters," as the reviewer for the *New York Daily News* noted.

From the late 1940s through the 1950s, Bourbon released a series of albums on the UTC (for Under the Counter) label. Many of these albums feature explicitly gay content, including one about a police raid of a gay wedding in a Chicago church. These albums, with titles such as *The Wedding, You're Stepping on My Eyelashes,* and *Around the World in 80 Ways,* were distributed as "party" or "adult" records, often by mail order or sold at Bourbon's appearances.

What is most remarkable about Bourbon's performances on these albums is not his raunchy humor and double entendres, but his air of defiance and his satirical gibes at the hypocrisy of the dominant culture, as well as his ability to laugh at himself. Moreover, though UTC records were by necessity distributed *sub rosa* or "under the counter," their production over such a long period indicates a continuing demand for them and the development and growth of a market for gay material.

One of Bourbon's UTC albums of the mid-1950s, entitled *Take a Look at My Operation,* was ostensibly about his own sex-change operation, which he claimed to have undergone in Mexico. The claim was undoubtedly a publicity stunt to capitalize on the widespread media attention aroused by Christine Jorgensen's sex-reassignment surgery in 1954, but it also may have been inspired by a real operation for cancer.

Another of the 1950s albums was entitled *One on the Aisle: An Intimate View of Grand Opera.* The album features spoofs of operas by Wagner, Bizet, and Verdi, among others.

In the 1950s and 1960s, Bourbon was a popular performer on a gay nightclub circuit that spanned the country. He also toured with the famous racially mixed group of drag performers, the Jewel Box Revue.

Among the many clubs, bars, and theaters in which Bourbon appeared were such large and small venues as Albuquerque's Silver Slipper; Idaho Falls's Cheerio Club; Central City, Colorado's, Glory Hole; New Orleans's Dixie's Bar of Music; Atlanta's Imperial Lounge; Seattle's The Garden of Allah; Baltimore's Stacy's Bar; Portland's Clover Club; and St. Louis's Gaiety Theater.

The long list of gay clubs at which Bourbon appeared, and their impressive geographic diversity, is an instructive reminder that post–World War II gay culture flowered not merely in such cities as New York, Chicago, Los Angeles, and San Francisco, but also in medium-sized cities throughout the country.

Bourbon was noted particularly for his comic timing and camp humor, his deep Southern drawl, and his infectious, cackling laugh, as well as his inventive and witty ad libs. In his drag act, he did not impersonate divas. Rather, he created his own flamboyant (but not glamorous) persona, described by one audience member as "doyen drag." One of his most touching characterizations was that of a foul-mouthed cleaning lady.

The final years of Bourbon's life were sad ones. With the stirrings of a gay rights movement, Bourbon's career floundered. His humor may have seemed dated and retrograde. Certainly, his act, which at one time had seemed so daring, must in the 1960s have come to seem rather tame.

In early 1969, Bourbon was arrested and charged with hiring an accomplice to murder a kennel owner in Big Springs, Texas. Because Bourbon could not pay for the upkeep of dogs that he had boarded with the kennel owner in the summer of 1968, the latter had sold the animals to a research facility. Although Bourbon denied the charge, he was convicted and sentenced to life in prison.

Bourbon died in prison of a heart attack in July 1971. While in prison, he began an autobiography entitled "Daddy Was a Lady." The manuscript was lost for many years, but it has recently resurfaced and may soon be published.

Although Bourbon has been largely forgotten, there has recently been a resurgence of interest in his "sad and crazy life," as measured both by renewed interest in his albums and the appearance of an excellent website devoted to him. In many ways, his life and career are revealing of the status of gay culture in some crucial decades. He deserves recognition as an enormously talented comedian and a pioneering, openly gay entertainer.

—*Claude J. Summers*

BIBLIOGRAPHY

Newlin, Jon. "Rae Bourbon...Tells All! Memoirs of the Greatest Female Impersonator." *Wavelength* (New Orleans) (July 1988): 8–9.

"Rae Bourbon, A Protege of Mae West, Dead at 78." *New York Times,* July 22, 1971.

Riddle, Randy A. *"Don't Call Me Madam": The Sad and Crazy Life of Ray Bourbon.* www.coolcatdaddy.com/bourbon.html

Sears, James T. *Lonely Hunters: An Oral History of Lesbian and Gay Southern Life, 1948–1968.* Boulder, Colo.: Westview Press, 1997.

SEE ALSO

Drag Shows: Drag Queens and Female Impersonators; Cabarets and Revues; Variety and Vaudeville; Jorgensen, Christine; Wright, Robert, and George "Chet" Forrest

Bowery, Leigh   (*1961–1994*)

CLUB HOST, FASHION DESIGNER, FACE ABOUT TOWN, and artists' muse, Leigh Bowery transformed his body into the centerpiece of his performance art.

Bowery was born on March 26, 1961, in the Melbourne suburb of Sunshine. In October 1980, he moved to London, drawn to the city by the articles he read about London's punk scene and club nightlife. He quickly established a name for himself on the London club scene and was soon himself frequently featured in the "style" press that he had read in Sunshine.

In 1983, after a sojourn in New York, where he was involved in a series of fashion shows that promoted British fashion design, he began to concentrate on making himself into the product of his own designs, using the nightclub as his stage.

In 1985, Bowery was invited by club entrepreneur Tony Gordon to host a new club night, Taboo. The club became notorious for its outrageousness, and Bowery

infamous as the most outrageous fixture on the London nightclub scene.

Bowery had always been open about his sexuality. He was a constant face on London's gay club scene, using his increasingly bizarre and distorted looks to challenge the conformity of dress and body image that was becoming increasingly prevalent among gay men.

Attracted to Bowery's nonconformist appearance, the *enfant terrible* of the dance world, gay British dancer and choreographer Michael Clark, invited Bowery to design costumes for one of his ballets in 1984. This collaboration was the beginning of a long and productive relationship in which Bowery became not only costume designer but also performer in many of Clark's pieces.

By 1988, Bowery had come to think of his performances as a form of art as much as a form of entertainment. The result was a show at the d'Offay Gallery in London and a subsequent series of performances in which Bowery "disfigured" and revealed his body.

Leigh Bowery constantly reinvented himself by distorting his body shape and changing the proportions of his body. While many people use their clothes to hide physical defects or blemishes, Bowery embellished his, transforming them into the centerpiece of his art. Bowery used his "looks" to become something other than himself.

Bowery's performances became increasingly extreme as they played with notions of sexuality and aspects of sadism and masochism. In 1993, he played the role of "Madame Garbo" in Copi (Raul Damonte)'s 1971 play *The Homosexual (or the Difficulty of Sexpressing Oneself).*

In 1988, the artist Lucien Freud saw and was impressed by Bowery's performances at the d'Offay Gallery. In 1990, Bowery began to model for Freud.

Freud painted Bowery, whom he believed to be "perfectly beautiful," completely naked. The paintings celebrated Bowery's massive physical frame. Posing nude for Freud provided Bowery an opportunity to examine what he had made of himself in his distortions and alterations of his body, as well as to assess how his body actually looked without artificial distortions.

In 1988, Bowery discovered that he was HIV-positive, a fact he kept secret for a number of years from everyone except one friend. Although Bowery had never hidden his homosexuality and had frequently regaled his friends with tales of his sexual encounters, in May 1994, just six months before his death, he married his longtime friend, lover, and collaborator, Nicola Bateman.

Bowery died of AIDS-related meningitis in November 1994.

—*Shaun Cole*

BIBLIOGRAPHY

Dougary, Ginny. "Leigh Bowery: Soon to Be Revealed as a Man." *Independent,* September 19, 1991.

Sharkey, Alix. "Bowery Power." *i-D* 48 (June 1987): 58–63.

Tilley, Sue. *Leigh Bowery: The Life and Times of an Icon*. London: Hodder and Stoughton, 1997.

Violette, Robert, ed. *Leigh Bowery*. London: Violette Editions, 1998.

SEE ALSO

Boy George (George O'Dowd); Kemp, Lindsay

Bowie, David   (b. 1947)

DAVID BOWIE, ALSO KNOWN AS "THE DAME," BECAME a leading light in 1970s glam rock, going on to enjoy international superstar status.

Bowie's career has a longevity matched only by such grand old men as the Rolling Stones, and his status as media icon is unmatched by any of his contemporaries. The 1974 "Omnibus" documentary film *Cracked Actor*, exploring the relationship between Bowie and his stage personae, was the first of its kind; his fiftieth birthday was celebrated to international press and media interest; and in 2000 the BBC released a remastered CD of early studio sessions, which had acquired archival status. In the same year he headlined the equally iconic Glastonbury music festival, taking easy precedence over a younger generation of musicians.

Bowie was born David Robert Jones in the Brixton section of London on January 8, 1947, the son of a working-class family who soon moved to Beckenham, a conservative town in Kent, where he grew up. A fan of Little Richard and jazz, Bowie began playing music at age twelve, when his parents bought him a saxophone. He performed in a series of small-time groups while in high school, and then attended technical school, where he earned a degree in art. In 1965, he adopted the name David Bowie to avoid confusion with actor Davy Jones, who later became the "singer" for the made-for-TV band The Monkees.

Bowie's significance for queer culture is deeply contradictory, since his claims to be gay or bisexual were almost certainly never anything other than a publicity-seeking gambit. As a performer, Bowie adopted a seemingly endless string of personae, from Major Tom to Ziggy Stardust and the Thin White Duke, and his theatrical stage presence owed much to early collaboration with gay mime artist Lindsay Kemp. Wearing elements of drag and heavy makeup was an intrinsic part of this theatricality, rather than the expression of any inner queerness.

It seems to have been Bowie's then manager, Ken Pitt, who decided to play the gay card. He arranged for *Jeremy*, the only gay publication in Britain at the time, to publish an article about Bowie in January 1970. This was followed in 1972 by an interview for *Melody Maker* in which the singer stated, "Yes, of course I'm gay, and always have been." In a 1976 *Playboy* interview he declared himself bisexual rather than gay.

Such published statements were combined with onstage antics such as fellating Mick Ronson's guitar and some very public homoerotic partying with Mick Jagger, Lou Reed, and Iggy Pop. But Bowie's appropriation of a gay persona always existed alongside explicit warnings from the star himself that nothing he said was to be believed. In 1971, he cautioned, "My songwriting is certainly not an accurate picture of how I think at all." This is just as well, since close analysis of Bowie's "gay" lyrics reveals little gay pride. Lady Stardust sings "songs of darkness and disgrace"; the gay seducer in "Aladdin Sane" has a "tongue swollen with devil's love," and after he "smelt the burning pit of fear" (you don't need to be Freud to spot an anal metaphor here!), the protagonist knows he will never "go down to the Gods again."

It is an indication of the repressive invisibility of gayness in 1970s Britain that, however cynical and (arguably) homophobic Bowie's flirtation with queer sexuality, it is remembered as liberating and exhilarating by many gay men in both the United Kingdom and the United States. In the words of Tom Robinson, "For gay musicians, Bowie was seismic. To hell with whether he disowned us later."

—*Tamsin Wilton*

BIBLIOGRAPHY

Gill, John. *Queer Noises: Male and Female Homosexuality in Twentieth-Century Music*. London: Cassell, 1995.

Reynolds, Simon, and Joy Press. *The Sex Revolts: Gender, Rebellion and Rock 'n' Roll*. London: Serpent's Tail, 1995.

Rock, Mick. *Ziggy Stardust: Bowie 1972/1973*. London: St Martin's Press, 1984.

Simpson, Mark. *It's a Queer World*. London: Vintage, 1996.

SEE ALSO

Popular Music; Rock Music; Boy George (George O'Dowd); Kemp, Lindsay; Little Richard (Richard Penniman); Mercury, Freddie; Reed, Lou; Robinson, Tom

Boy George (George O'Dowd)   (b. 1961)

BOY GEORGE IS, LIKE MANY MIDDLE-AGED QUEERS, A survivor. And, like many pop icons, one of the main trials he has had to survive is his own fame.

The Boy George persona, which came to international attention with the success of the band Culture Club in the early 1980s, threatened to overshadow completely Boy George the performer. However, George's talent, resilience, and genuine affability have seen him through his band's breakup, his own drug addiction, an unexpected solo comeback, and a 1998 reunion with Culture Club. Retaining his sense of style and eclecticism throughout, George has proved he is not merely a stage persona, but also a real original and a gay pioneer.

Born in Bexleyheath, a cheerless section of South London, on June 14, 1961, George Alan O'Dowd was the third of six children born to working-class Irish parents. His father, a builder and boxing coach, and his mother, who worked in a nursing home, had little attention to spare to give emotional support to their children, especially little George, who showed signs of being "different" from a very early age.

He often showed up at church in outlandish hats and platform shoes. Indeed, the eccentric clothes he wore to school got him assigned to a class for incorrigibles. He soon dropped out and began to seek kindred spirits.

Perhaps tellingly, the first live concert Boy George attended featured gender-bender David Bowie. Flamboyantly dressed and wildly made up, George and his friends were regulars at hip London clubs, where George frequently attracted the attention of photographers. The photos in turn attracted the attention of band manager Malcolm McLaren (Sex Pistols) and bassist Mikey Craig, who approached George about forming a band. Soon, George was fronting Culture Club (named for the cultural mix of its members: the Jamaican Craig on bass, the Irish George on vocals, the Jewish Jon Moss on drums, and the English Roy Hay on keyboards).

Culture Club's pop-reggae-soul fusion made the group's first two albums, *Kissing to be Clever* (1982) and *Colour by Numbers* (1983), major hits. George's rich, soulful voice anchored the band, but it was his appearance, in braids and dresses or ornate geisha drag, with elaborate makeup that often took hours to apply, that made Culture Club notorious.

While fans loved the rebellious kitsch of George's effeminate look, his look was known to provoke homophobic reactions, as when a Detroit radio station distributed blindfolds at a concert so that listeners would not have to look at the offending "she-male."

George took the criticism in stride, though he downplayed his gayness in the early years, saying he had experimented with all kinds of sex. In fact, the early years of Culture Club were intensified by a relationship between George and bisexual drummer Jon Moss.

Success, however, took its toll, and soon George was using a variety of drugs, eventually becoming addicted to heroin. After a string of hits, including the singles "Do You Really Want to Hurt Me" (1982) and "Karma Chameleon" (1983), Culture Club broke up in 1986. George managed to quit heroin, and in 1987 he made his solo debut with the album *Sold*.

Since then, Boy George has remained in the peripheral vision of the public eye. A true music lover, he no longer seeks the kind of publicity that overwhelmed him in the 1980s, but neither does he accept the has-been status of "former icon." After another popularity surge in the mid-1990s, when he sang the title song from the 1995 film *The Crying Game*, he reunited with Culture Club for the 1998 Big Rewind Tour.

His most recent passion is deejaying, for which he has become newly famous in England, specializing in unlikely mixes of genres and artists, with hip and campy results. Spinning discs gives George a chance to step back from the spotlight while keeping both hands on the music he loves.

He has also recently scored a success in *Taboo*, a musical centered on the 1980s performance artist and fashion designer Leigh Bowery, for which he wrote the score and also appeared as himself. The show's 2003 transition from London, where it was received warmly, to New York, where it was produced by Rosie O'Donnell, was not easy, bedeviled as it was by rumors of artistic disagreements between management and cast members. Despite mostly negative reviews, *Taboo* ran for 100 performances before closing on February 8, 2004.   —*Tina Gianoulis*

BIBLIOGRAPHY

Bonisteel, James. "Interview with Boy George." *Rational Alternative Digital Cyberzine Website.* www.radcyberzine.com/text/interviews/boygeorge.int.3g.html.

Bono, Chastity. "Boy's life." *Advocate*, November 14, 1995, 68.

Boy George. *Take It Like a Man.* New York: HarperTrade, 1995.

Collins, Nancy. "Boy George: He Wears the Pants in Culture Club." *Rolling Stone*, June 7, 1984, 13.

Galvin, Peter. "Boy Will Be Boy." *Advocate*, June 23, 1998, 103.

SEE ALSO

Popular Music; Rock Music; Music Video; Bowery, Leigh; Bowie, David; Pet Shop Boys

Britten, Benjamin   *(1913–1976)*

BENJAMIN BRITTEN WAS THE MOST PROMINENT AND highly honored British composer of the twentieth century, perhaps the most acclaimed of his countrymen in classical music since Henry Purcell in the seventeenth century. Such recognition is not, however, without considerable irony; many of Britten's greatest works were inspired by his longtime personal and professional relationship with his lover, tenor Peter Pears, and created within the context of a society in which homosexual acts were criminal.

Edward Benjamin Britten (later Baron Britten of Aldeburgh) was born on November 22, 1913, in Lowestoft, Suffolk. Although his boyhood was by all accounts ordinary, he showed a prodigious aptitude for music and began playing the piano and composing pieces while still a small child.

He had already completed a number of works when, at age thirteen, he presented them to the composer Frank Bridge, whom he met at a local concert performance. Bridge was suitably impressed by Britten's work to accept the boy as a private student. As a childless couple, Bridge and his wife came to regard Britten as a sort of adopted son, and one of the young composer's early notable works, *Variations on a Theme of Frank Bridge* (1937), is a tribute to his mentor.

In 1930, Britten entered the Royal College of Music, where he studied composition and piano. When the RCM denied him permission to study with Alban Berg in Vienna, he left without completing a degree. In the same year, his choral work *A Boy Was Born* was chosen for a performance by the BBC singers. It was on this occasion that he first met, albeit briefly, Peter Pears, a member of the ensemble at that time.

The two were not actually acquainted until 1936, but within the following year they began a personal and professional collaboration that would endure for nearly forty years, until Britten's death. A considerable number of Britten's subsequent works feature the tenor voice and were written with Pears as the intended interpreter.

During the mid-to-late-1930s, Britten began writing music for stage and film, and he also worked collaboratively with W. H. Auden, whose poems he set to music in two song cycles, *Our Hunting Fathers* (1936) and *On This Island* (1937).

In May 1939, as World War II became inevitable, Britten and Pears left England, following fellow pacifists Auden and Christopher Isherwood to the United States, which was still officially a neutral nation. They settled first in New York, where Auden maintained a bohemian ménage, and subsequently in Southern California, where Isherwood also relocated.

While in New York, Britten collaborated with Auden on *Paul Bunyan* (1941), an operetta based on the American folklore character. The sojourn in America saw the composition of two song cycles for tenor voice that were settings of works by homosexual poets, Arthur Rimbaud's *Les illuminations* (for voice and strings, 1939) and *Seven Sonnets of Michelangelo* (for tenor and piano, 1940), as well as *Sinfonia da Requiem* (1940), in memory of the composer's parents.

While in California in 1941, Britten read E. M. Forster's essay about British poet George Crabbe, whose lengthy verse narrative *The Borough* (1810) detailed the hardships of life in a small fishing port. Crabbe, like Britten,

was a native of Suffolk. One of the episodes in *The Borough* relates the misfortunes of a visionary social outcast, a fisherman named Peter Grimes, who is accused of causing the deaths of two young apprentices—a matter with significant homoerotic undertones. The story served as the inspiration for Britten's first full-scale opera.

In 1942, after the United States had entered the war, Britten and Pears returned to Britain, working on *Peter Grimes* during their passage across the war-ravaged North Atlantic. They declared themselves conscientious objectors upon their return, a stand that entailed considerable social ostracism during the war years.

Peter Grimes was first performed on June 7, 1945, by Sadler's Wells Opera Company, London, with Pears in the title role. The following year marked its American premiere at the Tanglewood Music Festival, where it was conducted by the young Leonard Bernstein.

In the wake of *Peter Grimes*, opera became the genre with which Britten was most closely associated, and virtually all his operas featured Pears either in the lead or in a secondary role.

Albert Herring (1947), in which Pears created the role of the sexually repressed title character, was the first opera produced by the English Opera Group, a company Britten and Pears founded. Britten and Pears settled permanently in Aldeburgh, the Suffolk fishing village in which *Peter Grimes* was set, in 1948, the same year they established the annual Aldeburgh Festival, which continues to the present day.

Throughout the 1950s and 1960s, though he was engaged in administration of the festival, Britten nonetheless continued to compose prodigiously and was simultaneously active as conductor, with a varied repertoire of his own works as well as those of other composers.

The opera *Billy Budd*, with libretto by E. M. Forster and Eric Crozier after Herman Melville's novella, premiered at Covent Garden, London, in December 1951. The opera, which is unique in having an all-male cast, presents a story, however circumspect, of shipboard homosexual panic.

Attracted to the handsome Billy, the villainous master-at-arms Claggart enacts his desires by systematically attempting to destroy the young sailor. After Billy accidentally kills his nemesis, he is hanged for his murder, despite the affection that Captain Vere, the ship's commander, and the other sailors feel for the young man.

Because the slightly built Pears lacked the physique to play the title role, the character Billy was written (implausibly, according to some critics) for baritone voice, and the part of Captain Vere, which was assigned to Pears, was made more prominent than it was in Melville's text.

Britten's next opera, *Gloriana* (1953) was written for the celebrations on the occasion of the coronation of Queen Elizabeth II. Its libretto was by William Plomer, after Lytton Strachey's *Elizabeth and Essex*. Britten was subsequently awarded the title of Companion of Honour, but the opera did not prove a critical success.

Plomer, however, continued to collaborate with Britten, and provided the libretti for the composer's three "Parables for Church Performance," *Curlew River* (1964), *The Burning Fiery Furnace* (1966), and *The Prodigal Son* (1968).

Britten also composed two operas based on works by Henry James, *The Turn of the Screw* (1954) and *Owen Wingrave* (1970), and also set William Shakespeare's *A Midsummer's Night's Dream* (1960) as an opera.

During this highly productive period, Britten composed a number of major nonoperatic works as well. As befits Britten's pacifist beliefs, his *War Requiem*, arguably his greatest choral work, combines elements of the traditional Latin mass with passages from the antiwar poetry of Wilfred Owen. This moving piece was first performed in 1962, at the dedication of the new Coventry Cathedral, built on the site of the venerable medieval edifice that was completely destroyed by a German air raid in 1940.

Also notable is the *Symphony in D Major for Cello and Orchestra* (1963), which he wrote for his friend, Russian cellist and conductor Mstislav Rostropovich.

Britten was appointed to the Order of Merit by Queen Elizabeth in 1965.

Britten's last great operatic triumph was *Death in Venice* (1973), based on Thomas Mann's novella. The work delineates the decline of the middle-aged critic Aschenbach (a role created by Pears) as he becomes increasingly obsessed with Tadzio, a young boy he loves from afar.

Earlier in 1973, Britten had undergone open-heart surgery to replace a defective cardiac valve. The surgery left him an invalid for the remainder of his life, yet he recovered sufficiently to attend the first performance of his final opera.

In 1976, Britten was awarded a life peerage by the Queen and given the title Baron Britten of Aldeburgh. His poor health made it impossible for him ever to take his seat in the House of Lords. He died of heart failure on December 4, 1976, in the arms of Peter Pears, at their home in Aldeburgh.

Britten left an extensive body of compositions comprising operas, choral works, symphonies, song cycles, concerti for piano and for violin, chamber music, and numerous miscellaneous pieces.

Among the better known are the *Simple Symphony* (1925), *Hymn to St. Cecilia* (1942), *Serenade* (for tenor, horn, and strings, 1943), and *The Young Person's Guide to the Orchestra* (1945). His last major work, *Phaedra*, a song cycle composed for contralto Dame Janet Baker, had its first performance shortly before his death.

—*Patricia Juliana Smith*

BIBLIOGRAPHY

Blyth, Alan. *Remembering Britten.* London: Hutchinson, 1981.

Brett, Philip, ed. *Benjamin Britten: Peter Grimes.* Cambridge: Cambridge University Press, 1987.

Britten, Beth. *My Brother Benjamin.* Bourne End, England: Kensal Press, 1986.

Carpenter, Humphrey. *Benjamin Britten: A Biography.* London: Faber and Faber, 1992.

Cooke, Mervyn, ed. *The Cambridge Companion to Benjamin Britten.* Cambridge: Cambridge University Press, 1999.

———, and Philip Reed, eds. *Benjamin Britten: Billy Budd.* Cambridge: Cambridge University Press, 1993.

Evans, Peter. *The Music of Benjamin Britten.* London: Dent, 1989.

———, Philip Reed, and Paul Wilson, eds. *A Britten Source Book.* Aldeburgh, England: The Britten-Pears Library, 1987.

Headington, Christopher. *Britten.* London: Omnibus, 1996.

Kennedy, Michael. *Britten.* London: Dent, 1993.

Mitchell, Donald, ed. *Benjamin Britten: Death in Venice.* Cambridge: Cambridge University Press, 1987.

———. *Britten and Auden in the Thirties.* London: Faber and Faber, 1981.

———, and John Evans, eds. *Benjamin Britten, 1913–1976: A Pictorial Biography.* London: Faber and Faber, 1978.

———, and Philip Reed, eds. *Letters from a Life: Selected Letters and Diaries of Benjamin Britten, 1913–1976.* 2 vols. London: Faber and Faber, 1991.

Oliver, Michael. *Benjamin Britten.* London: Phaidon, 1996.

Palmer, Christopher, ed. *The Britten Companion.* London: Faber and Faber, 1984.

White, Eric Walter. *Benjamin Britten: His Life and Operas.* London: Faber and Faber, 1983.

SEE ALSO

Classical Music; Opera; Conductors; Bernstein, Leonard; Doone, Rupert; Pears, Peter; Poulenc, Francis

Bruhn, Erik   *(1928–1986)*

ERIK BRUHN WAS THE PREMIER MALE DANCER OF THE 1950s and epitomized the ethereally handsome prince and cavalier on the international ballet stage of the decade. Combining flawless technique with an understanding of modern, conflicted psychology, he set the standard by which the next generation of dancers, including Rudolf Nureyev, Mikhail Baryshnikov, Peter Schaufuss, and Peter Martins, measured their success.

Born on October 3, 1928, in Copenhagen, Bruhn was the fourth child of Ellen Evers Bruhn, the owner of a successful hair salon. After the departure of his father when Erik was five years old, he was the sole male in a household with six women, five of them his senior.

An introspective child who was his mother's favorite, Erik was enrolled in dance classes at the age of six in part to counter signs of social withdrawal. He took to dance like a duck to water; three years later he auditioned for the Royal Danish Ballet School, where he studied from 1937 to 1947.

With his classic Nordic good looks, agility, and musicality, Bruhn seemed made for the Auguste Bournonville technique taught at the school. He worked obsessively to master the technique's purity of line, lightness of jump, and clean footwork.

Although Bruhn performed the works of the Royal Danish Ballet to perfection without any apparent effort, he yearned to reach beyond mere technique. In 1947, he accepted an invitation to perform with London's Metropolitan Ballet. This experience would be the first step in his lifelong quest for growth as a dancer.

For the next decade, his career would be divided between starring with the Royal Danish Ballet and dancing as a guest artist with such leading companies as American Ballet Theatre, the Australian Ballet, and the Stuttgart Ballet.

On May 1, 1955, Bruhn partnered British ballerina Alicia Markova at the old Metropolitan Opera House in New York in his stunning debut as Albrecht in the Ballet Theatre production of *Giselle* (1884, choreography by Marius Petipa after Coralli and Perrot; score by Adolphe Adam).

A landmark ballet experience for audience members such as William Como of *Dance Magazine* and dance critic John Martin of the *New York Times*, this single performance elevated Bruhn to superstardom. From then on, he was the reigning prince in the world of ballet and was instrumental in changing the role of men in classical dance.

Bruhn's self-critical and brooding personality, however, kept him from enjoying his triumphs. Everyone may have

Erik Bruhn (second from left) visits backstage with (left to right) Diana Adams, Violette Verdy, Sonia Arova, and Rudolf Nureyev. Photograph by Fred Fehl.

loved him, but he loved no one—including himself. His reserve and tendency to overanalyze had been his burden and limitation as a child and shadowed his adulthood and maturity as well.

In May 1961, Bruhn was celebrated in a major article in *Time* and acclaimed for recent performances as different as Jean the Valet in Birgit Cullberg's *Miss Julie* (1950; score by Ture Rangström) and Don José in Roland Petit's *Carmen* (1949; score by Georges Bizet).

By this time, he virtually owned the roles of Albrecht in *Giselle*, James in *La Sylphide* (1836, choreography by Auguste Bournonville; score by Herman Severin von Løvenskjold), and Prince Siegfried in *Swan Lake* (1895, choreography by Lev Ivanov and Marius Petipa; score by Pyotr Ilich Tchaikovsky).

At age thirty-two, Bruhn was at the peak of his career, yet he felt stalled personally and artistically. He was desperate for renewal of some kind. This renewal came in the form of Rudolf Nureyev, a twenty-three-year-old Russian, who on June 17, 1961, announced his presence on the international dance scene by defecting from the Soviet Union in a headline-grabbing leap to freedom in Paris. Nureyev, all ambition and animal charisma, had said that of all the dancers in the world only Bruhn had something to teach him.

In a few short weeks, Nureyev found his way to Copenhagen to learn whatever Bruhn could teach him; ironically, Maria Tallchief, with whom Bruhn had had a brief affair and dancing partnership, engineered the introduction that would bring her own claim on Bruhn to an abrupt end.

As fate would have it, Bruhn and Nureyev, as different as Apollo and Dionysus, were fiercely attracted to one another. Although neither had had any previous serious romantic attachments to men (Bruhn had been engaged to Bulgarian ballerina Sonia Arova for about five years before his affair with Tallchief), they formed an intense, turbulent, and profoundly transformative relationship that Bruhn later referred to as "pure Strindberg."

Until their dying days, each regarded the other as the love of his life, despite the collapse of the sexual dimensions of their relationship by the mid-1960s.

In 1963, Bruhn began to experience severe stomach pain that repeated medical examinations failed to explain. Attributing the problem to psychosomatic causes, he decided to retire in late 1971 to reduce the stress in his life. Even after retirement, however, the pains continued and grew so critical that in 1973 he underwent emergency surgery that revealed a perforated ulcer.

In 1974, restored to health at age 46, Bruhn returned to dancing, but not as a regal prince. In a production of *Giselle* featuring ex-lover Nureyev in Bruhn's former signature role of Albrecht, Bruhn scored an astounding success as Madge, the evil witch.

This triumph signaled the start of the second phase of Bruhn's dancing career. His versatility and acting skill enabled him to make a graceful transition from dancing Prince Ideal to performing vividly realized character parts such as Dr. Coppelius in *Coppélia* (1975, choreography by Bruhn after the 1884 Petipa original; score by Leo Délibes), the Moor in *The Moor's Pavane* (1949, choreography by José Limón; score by Henry Purcell), and the title role in *Rasputin—The Holy Devil* (1978, choreography by James Clouser; score by St. Elmo's Fire Band).

The dancer's later triumphs brought renewed recognition of his uniqueness in ballet: his ability to combine flawless technique, intense character study, and total commitment to create stage performances that remained indelible to audiences.

Bruhn was appointed Artistic Director of the National Ballet of Canada in 1983, a position that he fulfilled admirably. By this time, he had cemented a stable and fulfilling relationship with the dancer and choreographer Constantin Patsalas, while Nureyev, his great but impossible love, remained a close friend.

Bruhn died of lung cancer in Toronto on April 1, 1986.

—*John McFarland*

BIBLIOGRAPHY

Aschengreen, Erik. "Erik Bruhn." *International Encyclopedia of Dance.* Selma Jeanne Cohen, ed. New York: Oxford University Press, 1998. 2:2–5.

Bland, Alexander, and John Percival. *Men Dancing: Performers and Performances.* New York: Macmillan, 1984.

Como, William. "The Dancer's Dancer: A Tribute to Erik Bruhn." *Dance Magazine*, May 1981, 36.

Gruen, John. *Erik Bruhn: Danseur Noble.* New York: Viking Press, 1979.

Maynard, Olga. "Erik Bruhn Talks to Olga Maynard." *Dance Magazine*, January 1966, 22.

Palatsky, Eugene. "Bruhn, Bournonville and Ballet." *Dance Magazine*, February 1962, 38.

_____, and Lillian Moore. *Bournonville and Ballet Technique: Studies and Comments on Auguste Bournonville's "Etudes Choreographiques."* London: A. & C. Black, 1961.

Pasborg, Lennart, director. *Erik Bruhn—I Am the Same, Only More.* Copenhagen: Steen Herdel, 2000.

Solway, Diane. *Nureyev: His Life.* New York: William Morrow, 1998.

Stuart, Otis. *Perpetual Motion: The Public and Private Lives of Rudolf Nureyev.* New York: Simon & Schuster, 1995.

SEE ALSO

Ballet; Dance; Nureyev, Rudolf; Tchaikovsky, Pyotr Ilich

Bussotti, Sylvano (b. 1931)

ITALIAN COMPOSER AND ARTIST SYLVANO BUSSOTTI HAS created the most dramatic and unusual graphic scores of the post–World War II avant-garde. He is also among the most important artists to bring a polymorphous sexuality onto the operatic and concert stage.

Born into an artistic, cosmopolitan family in Florence on October 1, 1931, Bussotti was encouraged to express himself from an early age. He studied violin from the age of five and enrolled at the Cherubini Conservatory when he was nine, then audaciously abandoned the Conservatory at the age of thirteen for independent study in composition. In 1956, he traveled to Paris to study with composer Max Deutsch, a student of Schoenberg. There he met Pierre Boulez, already notorious for his early compositions, among other notable musicians and artists.

In 1957, Bussotti met Heinz-Klaus Metzger, philosopher Theodor Adorno's most brilliant music student, and within a year they were lovers. Metzger's intellectual and political aesthetics were major influences on Bussotti's early works, until some years after their breakup at Christmas 1963.

Metzger brought Bussotti to the famous Darmstadt summer courses in new music in 1958, where he met the composer John Cage, among many others. At Darmstadt, Bussotti wrote his first mature works, including *due voci* (1958), the score of which was "corrected" by Boulez.

Bussotti triumphed at Karlheinz Stockhausen's seminar on music and graphics in 1959 with the *five piano pieces for david tudor*, excerpted from his homoerotic song cycle *pièces de chair II* (1958–1960). Works of this period, including *sette fogli* (1959) and *siciliano* (1962) for twelve male voices, represent an attack on formalism through beautifully drawn deconstructions of notation and linearity.

Bussotti's flamboyant behavior evidently created discomfort in Darmstadt among closeted gay composers such as Boulez and straight ones such as Stockhausen and Luigi Nono. His work emphasized the contrasts between the highly structured techniques of serialism and the freedom of indeterminacy; he thus helped intensify the already competitive atmosphere of the Darmstadt courses into one of hostility, and contributed to the divisions that followed in European avant-garde music in the early 1960s. Bussotti himself left the courses in late 1961 after a quarrel over fees and never returned.

Bussotti continued to build on his notoriety in the 1960s, and also on his relationships with musicians. The controversial and self-consciously decadent *la passion selon Sade* (1964) joined music, theater, lighting, and costumes in a tangle of symbolic seductions. The work was constructed around Cathy Berberian, not only as vocalist (who plays Justine, Juliette, and Pauline Réage's masochistic O all at once), but possibly also in reflection of her then ended relationship with composer Luciano Berio.

After *the rara requiem* of 1969–1970, Bussotti's works, including the operas *Lorenzaccio* (1972), *Le Racine* (1980), and *L'Ispirazione* (1988), were more traditionally composed and notated, though often based on erotic or campy subjects. Ballets such as *Bergkristall* (1974) frequently featured his lover, the dancer Romeo Amidei.

Bussotti became known for his grand-opera productions. His extravagant costumes and sets emphasize rich fabrics and beautiful bodies. He was artistic director of La Fenice from 1975 to 1983; his reputation in avant-garde circles declined, but he became an Italian celebrity. He became music director of the Venice Biennale in the late 1980s; he staged a flashy resignation in 1991, bringing in a famous prostitute to give the keynote speech.

Erotic activity abounds in Bussotti's works, but with little distinction between gay and straight. A polymorphous expression of sensuality is his chief tool in dissolving the rigidity of modernism.

—*Paul Attinello*

BIBLIOGRAPHY

Bucci, Moreno. *L'opera di Sylvano Bussotti: musica, segno, immagine, progetto, il teatro, le scene, i costumi gli attrezzi ed i capricci dagli anni quaranta al Bussottioperaballet* Exhibition catalog. Milano: Electa, 1988.

Bussotti, Sylvano. *I miei teatri: diario segreto, diario pubblico, alcuni saggi.* Palermo: Edizioni Novecento, 1982.

Morini, Luciano. *Mode et Musique dans les costumes de Sylvano Bussotti.* Paris: Dessain et Tolra, 1986.

SEE ALSO

Classical Music; Opera; Cage, John

Cabarets and Revues

HOMOSEXUALS HAVE BEEN ATTRACTED TO CABARETS, nightclubs, and coffeehouse performances throughout modern history, even when the acts presented may seem resolutely heterosexual. This may be explained, at least in part, by the fact that theatrical presentations do not contain a fixed set of signs allowing for only one interpretation.

Even though many revues, nightclub acts, and cabaret performances were not created or performed by homosexuals, gay patrons have often found in them a preferable alternative to the "legitimate" theater. Historically, cabarets and revues have been much more likely to mention (or imply) same-sex desire than the "legitimate" theater; perhaps, more importantly, same-sex desire has been less frequently condemned or criticized in cabarets and revues than in most mainstream plays.

In the public mind, homosexuality is often linked with bohemian artistic and theatrical circles. While there is nothing inherently queer about the performative, it is plausible that cabaret and other theatrical entertainments appeal to gay men and lesbians because most of them have been performing much of their lives: convincing people that they are "straight." Having a keen appreciation for performance as a form, many homosexuals have at various times in modern history found a supportive atmosphere in the many theaters, pubs, and cafés located in most major cities.

Variety Shows, Music Hall Entertainment, and Dance Halls

Early in the nineteenth century, many British taverns had a "music room" adjacent to the bar in which entertainment was performed. These variety shows presented singers, dancers, and comedians. In 1850, these entertainment lounges were separated from taverns to appeal to more middle-class, family audiences.

Despite the move, British music hall entertainment still had much to offer nonheterosexual patrons, for it often featured a "best boy" (a woman in a breeches role) and the "dame" (played by a man in drag). The fact that men were playing men, women playing women, men playing women, and women playing men on the same stage allowed for numerous double entendres, comic misconceptions, and sexual layerings.

These same conventions were employed in British pantomime, which began in the 1870s and continues to this day in the form of the English Christmas pantomime.

While the famous dance halls of Paris—such as the Folies Bergères (est. 1869) and the Moulin Rouge (est. 1889)—might seem wholly dedicated to heterosexual titillation, most of the Montmartre halls did their part to expand the sexual continuum. Nude showgirls did not appear until 1910, but female impersonators had been part of the bill since the beginning.

One of the most famous was Barbette (Vander Clyde, 1904–1973), an American acrobat who wowed audiences in the 1920s and 1930s as the "jazz-age Botticelli."

American Minstrel Shows

American theatrical sites of same-sex desire in the nineteenth century were also found in unlikely quarters: minstrel shows. As minstrelsy evolved from a solo act to an evening-length work in the early 1840s, the all-male, Caucasian cast members not only performed caricatures of African Americans, some of the men also played female roles. When actresses joined minstrelsy troupes in the 1890s, they were often called upon to play male roles.

Unlike European revues, American minstrelsy added the topic of race and racialized desire to the performance of gender. While it is true that many of the race and gender illusionists of these various British, French, and American entertainments resorted to the most demeaning and freakish of portrayals, it is also true that these performances put same-sexed bodies in romantic situations and occasionally pointed up the cultural construction of gender and race as well.

Revues

Given the loose structure of a revue, it is much easier (than in a book musical) to insert a same-sex allusion, or even a homosexual character, because such allusions or characters do not have to contribute to the development of an evening-long plot.

For example, Noël Coward's revue *Words and Music* (1932) contained the song "Mad About the Boy," in which a cockney woman, a schoolgirl, a prostitute, and a society lady sing about a handsome male movie star. For the New York production of this revue, Coward added a stanza sung by a businessman describing how he had "vexing dreams" about the boy in question.

In the 1920s and 1930s, queer allusions became a staple of the revues in New York and London. The critic Percy Hammond noted that *The Ritz Revue* (1924) contained so "many references...to topics so disorderly that one suspects Kraft-Ebbings [sic] to be hidden among the librettists."

In the West End, *The Gate Revue* (1939) featured the song "All Smart Women Must"—sung by two effeminate men and one lesbian—which warned women that "fairy" fashion designers conspired to make women unattractive to men.

In 1958, an official from the Lord Chamberlain's Office was sent to reassess a drag revue, *We're No Ladies*, appearing in a small London theater. While the script had received a license, the officer found that the audience was "familiar with the phraseology of the perverted" and suggested closing the show, as the venue was likely to become a "focal point for pederasts."

Similarly, due to the oppressive tactics of the police and citizen groups such as the Society for Suppression of Vice, theatrical presentations that ventured into same-sex desire in New York City were routinely closed during the period from 1870 to 1940.

Drag Revues

The most successful gay-themed revues, those that managed to avoid legal entanglements and were financially lucrative, were those featuring drag and theoretically aimed at a heterosexual audience. Notable examples include Finocchio's nightclub, the Jewel Box Revue, and military shows.

Located on Lower Broadway, the West 42nd Street of San Francisco, Finocchio's opened in 1936 with a performing company of sixteen. Run by Marjorie and Joseph Finocchio, it remained a family-owned business for sixty-three years until rising rents forced its closure in 1999. Headliners included twenty-seven-year veteran Lucian Phelps (a Sophie Tucker expert), drag legend Rae Bourbon, and Don McLean (also known as Lori Shannon), the 6-foot-6 comic who played Archie Bunker's drag queen friend on "All in the Family."

Other famous clubs featuring drag revues were the Queen Mary in Los Angeles, San Francisco's Black Cat Café (where José Sarria performed camp operas for over forty years, beginning in 1958), New Orleans's My Oh My Club, Miami's Gayla, Seattle's Garden of Allah, Minneapolis's Paradise Club, Hollywood's Garden of Eden, and New York City's Moroccan Village and Club 82 (open until 1978).

The Jewel Box Revue was not only the longest-running gay touring entertainment company (performing continually in the United States, Mexico, and Canada from 1942 to 1975), it also was one of the few racially integrated entertainments in the 1950s.

Begun in 1939 in a Miami gay bar (the Jewel Box), the revue, fashioned by lovers Danny Brown and Doc Benner, was an elaborate entertainment with comic sketches, musical numbers, lavish production numbers, fabulous costumes, but absolutely no lip sync. Eventually playing heterosexual nightclubs, the revue—featuring "Twenty-five Men and a Girl," as it billed itself—introduced many patrons to female impersonation (both comic and serious) for over thirty years.

Another genre of the drag revue that escaped police harassment was the cross-dressing entertainments common in British and American military units. So popular were they during World War II that they moved to legitimate theaters and continued to play for ten years after the end of the war.

Although it can be argued that these revues, with names such as *Misleading Ladies, Boys Will Be Girls, Forces in Petticoats*, and *Soldiers in Skirts*, were not wholly affirming of same-sex desire, they were nevertheless a far cry from "Don't ask, don't tell."

Without the elaborate sets and costumes that were the hallmark of the Jewel Box Revue, British Music Hall, Parisian girlie shows, and Broadway revues, intimate revues in bars and clubs often slipped around decency laws since they lacked the visibility of their more opulent sisters.

Nevertheless, it should not be forgotten that New York (and many other states) had laws that prohibited homosexuals from congregating in licensed public establishments, which meant that nightspots often paid off the police to remain safe spaces for their gay clientele. In many municipalities these laws were on the books until the 1970s.

Cabarets and Nightclubs

In the 1880s, cabarets that featured solo performers or small revues began to appear in Paris, and by 1900 in Berlin. A showcase for emerging artists, these revues frequently were critical of political and social repression, resulting in a satirical style immortalized in Christopher Isherwood's *Berlin Stories* (which were the source material for the 1966 Kander and Ebb musical *Cabaret*).

Early in the twentieth century, cabarets began to open in New York's Bowery, Greenwich Village, and Harlem districts. Typically, the audience was gayer than the material presented on stage. Historian George Chauncey cites a report in 1920 that "most of the patrons paid more attention to the action of the fairies [in the audience] than to the cabaret performance" onstage at the Hotel Koenig (East 4th Street near First Avenue).

Prohibition (1920–1933) radically transformed nightclubs and cabarets, as club owners sought out ever more outlandish acts in order to draw patrons to their now alcohol-less environments. Beginning in Greenwich Village as gay-oriented entertainment for a gay audience, "pansy shows" moved to Times Square nightspots, attracting heterosexual tourists and locals intrigued with homosexual exotica.

While some of the entertainers were gay, others were straight and performed the gender equivalent of blackface, coarsely broadening what they perceived to be the low camp and effeminacy that epitomized the gay male.

Nightspots in Harlem between the wars were a vital component of the Harlem Renaissance as African American writers and performers energized each other while exploring the possibilities of being black in America. These journeys were often led by lesbians, gay men, and bisexual performers such as Phil Black, Mabel Hampton, George Hanna, Alberta Hunter, Bessie Jackson, Frankie "Half Pint" Jaxon, Jackie "Moms" Mabley, Bessie Smith, and Gertrude "Ma" Rainey.

Among the most famous lesbian entertainers to emerge was Gladys Bentley, a large, masculine, dark-skinned woman who performed in a white tuxedo and top hat at Harlem's Clam House and Edmond's Cellar.

White patrons not only "slummed" in Harlem clubs to experience hot jazz, impassioned singing, and sensuous dancing, but also to participate in interracial drag costume balls at the Savoy Ballroom and the Manhattan Casino.

Gay-themed entertainment also found a supportive home in speakeasies, the private clubs that appeared during Prohibition—quasi-legal places where alcohol could be served because they were ostensibly membership-only establishments. Undoubtedly, the transgressive aura of homosexuality was seen as an acceptable element in the netherworld in which speakeasies operated.

Small Bars and Intimate Cabarets

With the repeal of Prohibition and the influx of military personnel to large urban areas during World War II, an enormous number of small bars and cabarets sprang up. The standard bill of fare in a bar or nightclub that provided live entertainment was the female singer. Accompanied by a single piano player or small combo, her material might be all comic, all cry-in-your-beer ballads, or a mixture of the two.

From chic nightclubs to the rankest coffeehouse, the intimate cabaret (fewer than 100 seats) also permitted a wide class range to attend, since admission was often covered by the price of a single drink. Famous New York nightspots that attracted gay customers include the Blue Angel (1943–1964) and the Mafia-owned Bon Soir at 40 West 8th Street, which ruled New York City's cabaret circuit from 1949 to 1967.

While female impressionists Lynne Carter, T. C. (Thomas Craig) Jones, and Charles Pierce were staples on the cabaret circuit during the 1950s and 1960s, many American cities had ordinances against cross-dressing, which obviously had a direct impact on the inclusion of *travesti* in revues and cabaret acts.

Thus, openly gay performers who performed flagrantly (or even veiled) gay material were often censored by nervous cabaret owners or through police intervention. Instead of hiring outrageous performers such as Gladys Bentley, post–World War II clubs most often featured a glamorous chanteuse whose set consisted of standards from the golden age of movie musicals.

The absence of gay performers or gay material did not mean that gay audiences abandoned nightclubs, however. Indeed, several performers were particularly known for attracting gay audiences despite the absence of overtly gay material. As the maître d' at New York City's Upstairs at the Downstairs told author James Gavin, "I mean, who could have a gayer following than Mabel Mercer? Every old queen with four days to live came to see her."

When Ben Bagley arrived at the same club in 1962, he was told he had free rein to create the types of revues he wanted, with the exception of hiring Kaye Ballard, since, according to owner Irving Haber, "she brings in the fags."

The 1960s

With increasing competition from television, and uncertain how to incorporate the new sexual frankness of the 1960s, many clubs that featured live entertainment began to close. Two women who appeared in the 1960s extended the life of cabaret, not only as a result of their extraordinary talent, but also because of the support of their gay fans.

When Barbra Streisand made her cabaret debut in 1961, the nineteen-year-old performer dealt a death knell to the icy café chanteuse. From 1961 to 1963, she alternated among New York City's Bon Soir and Blue Angel, Chicago's Mister Kelly's, and San Francisco's hungry i.

Bette Midler played at the Downstairs in 1967, and then, in a pathbreaking move that cemented her fame to a gay following, Midler and Barry Manilow played the Continental Baths in 1971.

With eclectic repertoires and undeniably rich voices, these unique women—the "S&M of Cabaret"—revitalized the nightclub act by discarding Hollywood/Vegas glamour for thrift-store clothes. Neither performer was classically beautiful and both were Jewish (Midler channeled her Jewishness via Hawaii and Streisand via Brooklyn), with a brazen chutzpah that found support from gay patrons looking for their own liberation in the midst of the 1960s sexual revolution.

Midler was perhaps the first mainstream performer not only to embrace her gay audience, but also consciously to tailor her act for them. As she told *Newsweek* in 1973, "I was playing to people who are always on the outside looking in."

Post-Stonewall Entertainments

Despite their popularity, the "S&M of Cabaret" could not save the genre. James Gavin estimates that in New York City between 1972 and 1982 almost forty nightclubs and cabarets opened and closed. Arthur Bell of the *Village Voice* dubbed many of them part of "the K-Y Circuit," since they depended upon a predominantly gay clientele.

Post-Stonewall entertainments basically divided into three groups: the drag lip-sync revues that became popular in many gay bars, now augmented by drag king shows in some women's bars; comedy clubs; and the return of upscale cabarets.

While stand-up comedians have been around since minstrelsy and vaudeville, nightspots dedicated completely to standup are a recent occurrence. After Jose's Cabaret and Juice Joint inaugurated Gay Comedy Open

Mike Nights in 1990 in San Francisco, other comedy clubs began to open their doors to gay comics.

Openly queer performers such as Rick Burd, Charles Busch, Kate Clinton, Sara Cytron, Frank DeCaro, Ellen DeGeneres, Lea Delaria, Maxine Feldman, Emmett Foster, Marga Gomez, Lisa Kron, Sabrina Matthews, Frank Maya, Steve Moore, Bob Smith, Robin Tyler, Suzanne Westenhoffer, and Karen Williams found humorous ways to incorporate their sexual identity into their acts.

The traditional nightclub refashioned itself in the 1980s and 1990s in elegant (and expensive) rooms such as Café Carlyle, which became a home to Bobby Short and Barbara Cook; joined by the Algonquin Club, the Rainbow Room, and Michael Feinstein's at the Regency, which all sought to return to the swank of legendary New York City nightclubs.

This trend was mirrored on the West Coast, at San Francisco's Plush Room (York Hotel) and at Los Angeles's Cinegrill (Hollywood Roosevelt Hotel) and Jazz Bakery.

Although frequented by a gay clientele, these clubs are in many ways a return to the 1940s, with their emphasis on female singers and revues featuring Broadway show tunes. With the rise of gay visibility in film, mainstream theater, television, and print media, cabarets are no longer among the rare venues where homosexuals can safely meet outside of private homes.

—*Bud Coleman*

BIBLIOGRAPHY

Chauncey, George. *Gay New York: Gender, Urban Culture, and the Making of the Gay Male World, 1890–1940.* New York: Basic Books, 1994.

Clum, John M. *Something for the Boys: Musical Theatre and Gay Culture.* New York: St. Martin's Press, 1999.

Gavin, James. *Intimate Nights: The Golden Age of New York Cabaret.* New York: Grove Weidenfeld, 1991.

Kaiser, Charles. *The Gay Metropolis: 1940–1996.* New York: Houghton Mifflin, 1997.

Kirk, Chris, and Ed Heath. *Men in Frocks.* London: Gay Men's Press, 1984.

Michener, Charles. "Bette Midler." *Newsweek,* December 17, 1973, 62.

Newton, Esther. *Mother Camp: Female Impersonators in America.* Chicago: University of Chicago Press, 1979.

Paulson, Don, with Roger Simpson. *An Evening at the Garden of Allah: A Gay Cabaret in Seattle.* New York: Columbia University Press, 1996.

Reballato, Dan. *1956 and All That: The Making of Modern British Drama.* London: Routledge, 1999.

Sinfield, Alan. *Out on Stage: Lesbian and Gay Theatre in the Twentieth Century.* New Haven: Yale University Press, 1999.

SEE ALSO

Variety and Vaudeville; Drag Shows: Drag Queens and Female Impersonators; Drag Shows: Drag Kings and Male Impersonators; Divas; Blues Music; Bentley, Gladys; Bourbon, Ray; Coward, Sir Noël; Feinstein, Michael; Kander, John, and Fred Ebb; Mercer, Mabel; Pierce, Charles; Rainey, Gertrude ("Ma"); Smith, Bessie; Waters, Ethel

Cage, John   *(1912–1992)*

ONE OF THE MOST INFLUENTIAL AND CONTROVERSIAL American composers of the twentieth century, John Cage is best known for his work utilizing chance as a factor in writing music.

Born in Los Angeles on September 5, 1912, the son of an inventor father and a writer mother, Cage developed musical interests early. After spending two years at Pomona College in Claremont, California, he spent two years in Europe, where he tried to compose music for the first time. After returning to the United States, he studied with Arnold Schoenberg and Henry Cowell.

In the mid-1930s, he began composing for percussion instruments and developing some of his ideas about sound and noise. He also married. Although Cage had had sexual affairs with young men, including the aspiring artist Don Sample, with whom he traveled in Europe, in 1935 he wed Xenia Andreevna Kashevaroff, the daughter of a Russian Orthodox priest.

Late in 1938, Cage and his wife moved to Seattle, where he gave percussion concerts and wrote his first piece utilizing electronic technology in composition, the *Imaginary Landscape No. 1.* Also in Seattle, he met a young student at the Cornish School for Performing and Visual Arts, the dancer Merce Cunningham, who was later to become his life partner and artistic collaborator.

In 1942, Cage and his wife moved to New York, where Cunningham was a member of the Martha Graham Dance Company. The composer and the dancer began developing dance programs. By 1945, Cage had divorced Xenia and acknowledged Cunningham as his personal as well as his professional partner.

The relationship with Cunningham would endure for the rest of Cage's life, which ended in New York City on August 12, 1992.

Cage and Cunningham produced pieces in which the music and dance were created independently but presented simultaneously. The two elements, neither related or unrelated, simply occurred in the same space and time. Their first great success was their ballet *The Seasons* (1947), which was commissioned by the Ballet Society of New York (later known as the New York City Ballet). After 1953, their preferred venue for their work was the Merce Cunningham Dance Company, which is still in existence.

Cage and Cunningham became part of a largely gay circle of New York avant-garde artists that included Robert Rauschenberg, Robert Motherwell, Jasper Johns, and Cy Twombly, who might be said to have anticipated postmodernism in their theories and practices.

Cage is best known for his theories de-emphasizing the role of personal expression in producing art. Inspired by Zen Buddhism, Cage sought to suppress his personal tastes and desires in favor of emulating nature's creative process through the use of chance operations and indeterminacy.

In 1951, Cage discovered the *I Ching*—the ancient Chinese *Book of Changes*, a system of divination based on the tossing of coins—and began using it to write music. He would assign musical value (pitch and duration) to all possible combinations of the three coins and write the music much as if he were taking dictation. The resulting compositions may in fact have emotional content but it is derived from the process and is not the result of the composer's intention (as is traditional in Western art).

These chance-derived pieces, once notated, were intended to be performed as written, and, barring the usual interpretive discrepancies, performances tended to be similar.

Cage later extended this thinking by writing music in which most or all pertinent decisions related to pitch and tempo were left to the performer, thus yielding radically different performances of the same piece.

Aria (1958), for example, uses a series of colored squiggles rather than conventional bar notation. The performer is instructed to assign a different vocal style to each color and follow the up-and-down direction of the line by singing higher or lower pitches.

Variations IV (1963) takes this approach to its logical conclusion by allowing the performers to employ any sound-making device or action for any length of time.

Another famous work is the *Imaginary Landscape No. 4* (1952), which uses twelve radios with two performers each, one controlling the tuning dial, the other the volume knob: the performance varies depending on what is being broadcast at any particular time.

Cage's practice of decentralizing the process of composition shifts the responsibility of creating meaning from the producer to the audience. Art is no longer solely in the hands of the artist but becomes an act of attentive observation and organization on the part of the viewer/listener/receiver. In this way, Cage's work follows the model of meditation.

Undoubtedly Cage's most famous (or notorious) example of this compositional process is the work entitled *4'33"* (1952), in which a pianist sits silently at a piano for precisely four minutes and thirty-three seconds. Inspired by Robert Rauschenberg's *White Painting*, Cage's work asks the listener to create a world of sound out of silence.

Cage introduced his ideas to an entire generation of artists through his teaching. In addition to numerous visiting appointments throughout the United States, he taught for extended periods at the School for Social Research in New York and at Black Mountain College in North Carolina. He encouraged students to look outside themselves for inspiration and to think of art not as self-expression but as self-alteration.

The abstract character of Cage's works does not present many opportunities to read them as "gay" works. Only a few pieces seem to have what might be considered autobiographical content, but his process does provide what might be considered a democratic attitude toward sound in which all sounds (including those generally considered noise) are valued equally. Silence itself is valued as much as any notes actually performed.

Art historian Jonathan D. Katz has suggested that Cage's ironic emphasis on the importance of silence in music reflects a political position related to the imposed silence of the closet prevalent in 1950s America.

—*Jeffery Byrd*

BIBLIOGRAPHY

Cage, John. *Silence*. Middletown, Conn.: Wesleyan University Press, 1961.

Katz, Jonathan D. "John Cage's Queer Silence or How to Avoid Making Matters Worse." *GLQ* 5.2 (1999): 231–252.

Perloff, Marjorie, and Charles Junkerman, eds. *John Cage: Composed in America*. Chicago: University of Chicago Press, 1994.

Pritchett, James. *The Music of John Cage*. Cambridge: Cambridge University Press, 1993.

Revill, David. *The Roaring Silence: John Cage: A Life*. London: Bloomsbury, 1992.

SEE ALSO

Classical Music; Dance; Cowell, Henry; Cunningham, Merce; McPhee, Colin

Castrati

CASTRATI (SINGULAR FORM: *CASTRATO*) WERE MALE singers who were castrated before they reached puberty so as to retain their high voices. This practice, while not exactly commonplace, persisted in Europe from the late sixteenth to the nineteenth century, and reached its height in the eighteenth century. It was, moreover, exploitative; castrati were usually poor boys, often orphans, and the operation itself was of dubious legality.

The justification for this extreme measure was the result of various dictates of the Catholic Church during the years following the Reformation. As certain scriptural passages called for women remaining silent in church, their voices were banned from choirs; therefore, in order to retain the four-part harmonies of polyphonic church music, the mutilation of young boys was deemed an acceptable sacrifice in the name of divine service.

As adults, castrati were capable of singing in the vocal range usual for female contraltos and, in some instances, sopranos, but with much stronger projection.

Castrati first entered papal service toward the end of the sixteenth century, and their numbers quickly increased. Simultaneously, they began to appear in opera, usually performing heroic male roles, such as Nerone in Claudio Monteverdi's *L'Incoronazione di Poppea* (1642), the title role in George Frideric Handel's *Giulio Cesare* (1724), and Orfeo in Christoph Willibald Gluck's *Orfeo ed Euridice* (1762). In regions where the Catholic Church banned women from performing on stage, castrati performed female roles as well.

Castrati reached the height of their popularity from the mid-seventeenth to the mid-eighteenth century. During this time, they were the major stars of the operatic stage and enjoyed the reputations and behaviors of latter-day female divas. They drew large fees for their performances, took fantastic stage names, were known for temperamental and capricious conduct on the stage and off, and, despite their mutilation, were said to engage in sexual intrigues of every sort with both sexes.

The most celebrated among them were Senesino (Francesco Bernardi, 1680–1750), Farinelli (Carlo Broschi, 1705–1782), and Caffarelli (Gaetano Majorano, 1710–1783).

Operatic roles for castrati continued to be written by major composers such as Mozart, Rossini, and Meyerbeer through the late eighteenth and early nineteenth century. But with the Napoleonic wars and the diminishing of papal powers, the practice of castration for musical purposes was more often seen as cruel and inhumane.

Women, moreover, had been seen and heard on the operatic stage with much greater frequency since the eighteenth century, and, with fewer castrati available, female contraltos in male attire took over their roles.

The last two known castrati were Domenico Mustafà (1829–1912), who was director of the pope's Sistine Choir from 1860 to 1898, and Alessandro Moreschi (1858–1922). In 1903, Pope Pius X banned castrati from papal choirs; Moreschi was, nonetheless, a member of the Sistine Choir until 1913.

Castrati were not necessarily homosexual, though many seem to have conducted affairs with either sex or both. They nevertheless occupy a "queer" space in cultural history, since their peculiar situation as emasculated men rendered them less than masculine according to societal norms, even as their performances made them objects of admiration and even envy.

Embodying the roles of women and male heroes alike, they blurred distinctions of sex and gender. Accordingly, these shape-shifters have retained a certain queer appeal—as evinced by their presence in such contemporary works as Anne Rice's novel *A Cry to Heaven* (1982) and Gérard Corbiau's film *Farinelli* (1994)—long after they have ceased to exist.

—*Patricia Juliana Smith*

BIBLIOGRAPHY

Garber, Marjorie. *Vested Interests: Cross-Dressing and Cultural Anxiety.* New York: Routledge, 1992.

Gilman, Todd S. "The Italian (Castrato) in London." *The Work of Opera: Genre, Nationhood, and Sexual Difference.* Richard Dellamora and Daniel Fischlin, eds. New York: Columbia University Press, 1997. 49–70.

Heriot, Angus. *The Castrati in Opera.* London: Calder and Boyars, 1975.

Miller, Felicia. "Farinelli's Electronic Hermaphrodite and the Contralto Tradition." *The Work of Opera: Genre, Nationhood, and Sexual Difference.* Richard Dellamora and Daniel Fischlin, eds. New York: Columbia University Press, 1997. 73–92.

Poizat, Michel. *The Angel's Cry: Beyond the Pleasure Principle in Opera.* Arthur Denner, trans. Ithaca, N.Y.: Cornell University Press, 1992.

Reynolds, Margaret. "Ruggiero's Deceptions, Cherubino's Distractions." *En Travesti: Women, Gender Subversion, Opera.* Corinne E. Blackmer and Patricia Juliana Smith, eds. New York: Columbia University Press, 1995. 132–151.

Rice, Anne. *A Cry to Heaven.* New York: Knopf, 1982.

Rosselli, John. *Singers of Italian Opera: The History of a Profession.* Cambridge: Cambridge University Press, 1992.

Straub, Kristina. *Sexual Suspects: Eighteenth-Century Players and Sexual Ideology.* Princeton, N.J.: Princeton University Press, 1992.

SEE ALSO

Opera; Classical Music; Handel, George Frideric

Cheung, Leslie   (1956–2003)

LESLIE CHEUNG FIRST GAINED LEGIONS OF FANS IN Asia as a pop singer. He went on to a successful career as an actor, appearing in sixty films, including the award-winning *Farewell My Concubine* (1993). Androgynously handsome, he sometimes played sexually ambiguous characters, as well as romantic leads in both gay- and heterosexually-themed films.

Leslie Cheung, born Cheung Kwok-Wing on September 12, 1956, was the tenth and youngest child of a Hong Kong tailor whose clients included Alfred Hitchcock and William Holden.

At the age of twelve, Cheung was sent to boarding school in England. There he adopted the English name Leslie, in part because he admired Leslie Howard in *Gone with the Wind*, but also because the name is "very unisex."

Cheung studied textiles at Leeds University, but when he returned to Hong Kong, he did not go into his father's profession. He entered a music talent contest on a Hong Kong television station and took second prize with his rendition of Don McLean's "American Pie."

His appearance in the contest led to acting roles in soap operas and drama series, and also launched his singing career. His first album, *The Wind Blows On* (1981), was a bestseller in Asia and established him as a rising star in the "Cantopop" style. He would eventually make over twenty albums in Cantonese and Mandarin.

Quickly gaining an enthusiastic fan following, Cheung played concerts in packed theaters, auditoriums, and stadiums. Although never as well known in North America, Cheung drew full houses for his concerts at Caesars Palace in Las Vegas in 2000, for which tickets cost as much as $238.

Beginning in the late 1970s, Cheung also pursued a movie career. His first film was the soft-porn *Erotic Dream of the Red Chamber* (1978).

In his next film, Patrick Tam's *Nomad* (1982), Cheung played a young man fixated on his mother. The initial version included a scene in which Cheung's character, clad only in underwear, fondled himself while talking on the telephone with his mother. Hong Kong censors objected, and the scene had to be reshot with Cheung in trousers.

Cheung had a featured role as a rookie policeman in John Woo's 1986 crime thriller *A Better Tomorrow*, one of the films that established the Hong Kong action genre. He also appeared in the movie's two sequels (1987 and 1989).

In 1989, Cheung was one of the stars of Stanley Kwan's *Rouge*, a stylish drama in which he played a young man who falls in love with a courtesan who is dressed as a man when he first encounters her. The young man reneges on a suicide pact with his sweetheart, whose ghost returns to visit him fifty years later.

Cheung also starred in Wong Kar-Wai's *Days of Being Wild* (1990), this time as a callous, womanizing playboy, a role that earned him the Best Actor Prize at the Hong Kong Film Awards.

Shortly after this success, Cheung announced his retirement from his singing career and moved to Vancouver, British Columbia, for a period.

The actor next went to China to make Chen Kaige's *Farewell My Concubine* (1993). The film won the Palme d'Or at the Cannes Film Festival and was nominated for an Academy Award for Best Foreign Film, but was banned in China because of its homosexual theme.

In *Farewell My Concubine*, Cheung played a young actor at the Peking Opera who specializes in women's roles. This was in accordance with the Opera's tradition that all characters, male and female, be portrayed by men. In preparation for his role, Cheung spent months studying the conventional movements and gestures used by the Opera's actors for such parts. He also learned the dialect of Beijing for the film.

Cheung's character in *Farewell My Concubine* is a boy who is made to chant "I am by nature a girl, not a boy" to prepare him for a career impersonating women. The youth is befriended by one of the Opera's leading men, of whom he becomes enamored. Critic Jay Carr called Cheung's performance the "most affecting and unceasingly fascinating" of the film.

Cheung next appeared in Peter Chan's gender-bending comedy *He's a Woman, She's a Man* (1995), playing a man who falls in love with a woman disguised as a man.

In Chen Kaige's *Temptress Moon* (1996), Cheung starred as an unsympathetic heterosexual character, a manipulative, blackmailing gigolo. Although the film was considered somewhat flawed, critic Stephen Holden described Cheung's performance as "arresting."

Cheung played one of a pair of gay lovers in Wong Kar-Wai's *Happy Together* (1997), an ironically titled piece because the couple, who make a trip to Argentina to rekindle their relationship, fail to find their longed-for happiness.

Cheung's personal situation was more fortunate. After making *Happy Together*, he came out publicly and acknowledged his lover, Tong Hock Tak, a banker. Speculation about Cheung's sexual orientation had been rife for some years, but he had always dodged questions, fearing that revealing his relationship might be deleterious to Tong's career. By this time, however, Cheung's fortune—skillfully managed by Tong—had grown to the point that Tong was able to retire from his job.

Still, coming out was not without risk for Cheung, since very few star Asian entertainers are openly gay. In Cheung's case, as the journalist Ronald Bergan reported, "the move did nothing to diminish his following; it only increased it."

In the late 1990s, Cheung resumed his singing career. His comeback album, *Legend* (1997), was a great success, and several more bestsellers followed. He returned to the concert stage as well, and in 2000 played a year-long "Passion" tour, described by Allan Hunter as "noted for the kind of spectacular costume changes and flamboyant attitude that would have made Liberace seem self-effacing." His onstage wardrobe featured eight outfits by Jean-Paul Gaultier, including a white tuxedo with angel wings, gold hot pants, and a "naughty skirt."

In reviving his singing career, Cheung made music videos, one of which featured a *pas de deux* with a Japanese male ballet dancer so sexy that it was banned by Hong Kong's top channel, TVB.

In his last film, Law Chi-Leung's *Inner Senses* (2002), Cheung played a psychiatrist tempted by evil spirits to kill himself.

Thus, fans who heard of Cheung's suicide on April 1, 2003, hoped at first that the story might be a macabre April Fool's Day joke. But soon they learned that Cheung had indeed taken his own life by jumping from a twenty-fourth-floor balcony at Hong Kong's Mandarin Oriental Hotel.

Cheung had long suffered from depression and reportedly had tried to commit suicide the previous year by taking an overdose of sleeping pills. He left a note in which he thanked Tong, his family, and his friends, but concluded poignantly, "I have not done one single bad thing in my life. Why is it like that?"

Disconsolate fans quickly created a shrine at the spot of Cheung's death. Their memorial offerings of flowers, notes, personal mementos, and photographs covered half a block. Admirers of all ages joined in paying tribute to the popular artist.

—*Linda Rapp*

BIBLIOGRAPHY

Bergan, Ronald. "Leslie Cheung: Asian Actor and Pop Star Famed for His Androgynous Performances on Stage and Screen." *Guardian* (London), April 5, 2003.

Carr, Jay. "'Farewell My Concubine' Holds an Unflattering Mirror to China." *Boston Globe*, October 29, 1993.

Corliss, Richard, and Stephen Short. "Forever Leslie." *Time* (International Edition), May 7, 2001, 44.

Goodman, Peter S. "Farewell to a Troubled Star and a City's High Times." *Washington Post*, April 5, 2003.

Hartl, John. "'Farewell My Concubine' Latest Film to Explore World of Sexual Ambiguity—a First for China." *Seattle Times*, October 24, 1993.

Holden, Stephen. "A 'Gone with the Wind' in China, without War." *New York Times*, October 5, 1996.

Hunter, Allan. "Leslie Cheung." *Scotsman*, April 3, 2003.

Mizui, Yoko. "Gender Bender from H.K." *Daily Yomiuri*, November 30, 1995.

Rayns, Tony. "Leslie Cheung; Pop singer and star of 'Farewell My Concubine.'" *Independent* (London), April 3, 2003.

Stuart, Jan. "Happy Together." *Advocate*, November 11, 1997, 67.

SEE ALSO

Liberace

Choruses and Bands

SINCE THEY WERE FIRST ESTABLISHED IN THE 1970S, lesbian and gay musical organizations have grown remarkably in number, size, and sophistication. Their many concerts, recordings, and events are among the most striking examples of communal expression within the gay and lesbian subculture.

Most medium and large North American cities boast gay and lesbian choruses, as do many cities in Europe and Oceania. These organizations have evolved to become much more than musical institutions. As representatives of gay and lesbian communities, they generate powerful political and social expression both for and between those communities, through texts and symbolism as well as through the sheer emotional power of music.

As alternatives to a bar/club culture, they are catalysts for the creation of solidarity and commonality among individuals often marginalized by the larger society.

Early Lesbian and Gay Musical Groups

Lesbian musical organizations began appearing in the 1970s. The earliest of these, called Women Like Me, was established by composer Roberta Kosse in 1971 in New York. The ensemble mostly performed Kosse's own works. It disbanded in 1980.

Hester Brown started the Victoria Woodhull All-Women's Marching Band in 1973 in New York. She named the group for a nineteenth-century feminist presidential candidate. The band played for the first Susan B. Anthony Day celebration and for three of the New York Gay Liberation Day parades. Although the Woodhull Band was not exclusively lesbian, its theme song was "When the Dykes Go Marching In."

Catherine Roma founded the oldest chorus still in operation, the Anna Crusis Women's Choir, in 1975 in Philadelphia. This group has since joined the Gay and Lesbian Association of Choruses (GALA), becoming its senior member.

On the West Coast, vocalist and conductor Sue Fink established the Los Angeles Community Women's Chorus in early 1976.

The Gotham Male Chorus was founded in New York in late 1977 by conductor Donald Rock, who wanted a chorus that would "dig music as well as each other." In 1980, this group added women to become the Stonewall Chorale, the first of the gay and lesbian mixed-voice ensembles.

The Legacy of Jon Sims

The San Francisco Gay Freedom Day Marching Band & Twirling Corps, the first such organization to declare a gay or lesbian identity by name, was founded in June 1978 by Jon Reed Sims (1947–1984). It made its first public appearance later that month at the city's Gay Pride Day parade.

After the establishment of the Band & Twirling Corps, Sims founded in rapid succession the San Francisco Gay Men's Chorus (November 1978, at the public memorial for slain City Supervisor Harvey Milk and Mayor George Moscone), Golden Gate Performing Arts (an administrative organization, March 1979), the orchestra Lambda Pro Musica, and the San Francisco Lesbian & Gay Men's Community Chorus.

Sims's work inspired a network of gay and lesbian instrumental and choral ensembles that came into existence with remarkable speed.

Choruses were soon founded in Los Angeles (July 1979), Seattle (September 1979), and Chicago (October 1979). A 1981 national tour by the San Francisco Gay Men's Chorus inspired the founding of choruses and bands in many other cities.

Sims directed the Band & Twirling Corps until January 1982. Under his leadership, the Corps presented concerts at such important San Francisco venues as the Louise Davies Symphony Hall, Grace Cathedral, and the famous disco Dreamland.

Sims died of AIDS in San Francisco on July 16, 1984. From the beginning, he intended to create a national network of gay and lesbian instrumental and choral ensembles. The success of that network, both during his lifetime and after, remains an astonishing legacy.

Sister Singers Network and GALA

In 1981, the Sister Singers Network was established among the women's and lesbian choruses. In 2002 it had forty-five choruses as members. It has produced a number of regional, national, and international women's choral festivals and encourages cooperation and sharing of resources among its members.

The first organizational meeting of what later became GALA (the Gay and Lesbian Association of Choruses) occurred in June 1981 in Chicago. That meeting involved a number of directors and founders of ensembles, including Jerry Carlson (Chicago Gay Men's Chorus, later the Los Angeles Gay Men's Chorus); Dennis Coleman (Seattle Men's Chorus); Richard Garrin (Chicago's Windy City Gay Chorus); Dick Kramer (San Francisco Gay Men's Chorus); Gary Miller (New York City Gay Men's Chorus); and Susan Schleef (Chicago's Artemis Singers).

In 1982 in San Francisco, at the first Gay Games, fourteen of the choruses met for the First West Coast Choral Festival. This meeting led to the establishment of the GALA Choruses Network that same year, with Jay Davidson of the San Francisco Gay Men's Chorus as its first President.

In addition to the choruses that belong to GALA, at least seventy other gay and lesbian choruses are in existence, including the members of the Sister Singers Network and a number of independent groups.

GALA Festivals

The first national GALA Festival, held in New York in 1983, was called COAST ("Come Out and Sing Together") and attracted twelve choruses with some 1,200 members. This event was followed by festivals in Minneapolis (1986), Seattle (1989), Denver (1992), Tampa (1996), and San Jose (2000). Each festival has shown a steady increase both in attendance and GALA membership.

In 2004, the GALA Festival was held in Montreal. This is the first festival to be hosted by a Canadian city.

Since 1995, GALA events have also included Small Ensemble Festivals, which showcase the numerous chamber and popular ensembles that have emerged from the larger choruses.

In addition to officially sponsored GALA festivals, member choruses are often involved in regional festivals, as well as guest appearances in each other's cities. For example, the New Orleans Gay Men's Chorus, founded in 1982 by Jerry Zachary, has in recent years scheduled joint concerts with choruses from Houston, St. Louis, Philadelphia, Chicago, and Berlin.

In 2002, GALA included 170 choruses with a total of about 8,000 individual members. These gay male, lesbian, and mixed-voice groups are scattered throughout North America, Europe, and Oceania.

GALA Activities

One of the most important functions of the GALA choruses has been the commissioning of new work by significant, mainly gay or lesbian, composers. Composers commissioned by the GALA choruses include Roger Bourland, David Conte, David Del Tredici, Janice Giteck, Libby Larsen, Holly Near, Ned Rorem, Robert Seeley, Conrad Susa, Gwyneth Walker, and Martin Wesley-Smith.

Many of these commissions have been subsequently published, some of them under the auspices of GALA. Often these works incorporate gay or lesbian issues and concerns, especially the creation of "family" within the community or, less often, specific political issues.

Performers who have appeared with GALA choruses include Maya Angelou, Natalie Cole, Michael Feinstein, Jerry Hadley, Marilyn Horne, Bobby McFerrin, Bette Midler, Liza Minnelli, Mark Morris, Holly Near, Bernadette Peters, Roberta Peters, Diane Schuur, and Frederica von Stade.

GALA choruses have received funding from the National Endowment for the Arts and from numerous state and municipal sources, as well as from private supporters and ticket sales. More than 600 thousand individuals purchase tickets to one or more GALA concerts per year. The combined audiences for GALA choruses—including community appearances and television and radio broadcasts—is said to be more than five million.

Repertoire

Although many of the choruses in the larger North American cities are large ensembles (thirty or more singers), most of the European choruses are smaller groups, often oriented toward chamber or cabaret productions.

The repertoire for the lesbian and gay choruses includes the traditional popular and classical choral music for women's and men's, as well as mixed, voices, in addition to many new compositions written for the choruses, as well as new arrangements of popular and classical works.

Instrumental Ensembles

Although they have not resulted in quite so large a network, instrumental ensembles such as concert and marching bands and orchestras have appeared in many cities. Perhaps the most notable of these is the Bay Area Women's Philharmonic of San Francisco.

The Lesbian & Gay Bands of America (LGBA) held its first meeting in Chicago on October 3, 1982. In 2002, it comprised twenty-five ensembles, including bands in North America and Australia. LGBA celebrated its tenth anniversary at the Gay Games in San Francisco in 1992. An ensemble of LGBA members performed at the Clinton Inaugural in 1993. Another celebration took place in Melbourne in 2002.

Programming

Programming concerts for lesbian and gay ensembles is a complex activity, since band and chorus music—especially as performed by same-sex choruses, with their limited pitch range—is not in itself a major attraction in the contemporary marketplace.

Gay and lesbian ensembles must target their communities carefully, presenting music that will appeal to a diverse audience and also further the communal and political aspirations of glbtq communities. This demands a great deal of flexibility in technique and repertoire, as many groups need to connect both with audiences interested in classical music and audiences who listen to a variety of genres of popular music.

Many ensembles find it useful to create traditions such as holiday concerts or yearly productions of stage shows to keep their audiences coming back. Choruses often form smaller ensembles that perform popular work in nontraditional venues such as gay and lesbian bars or cabarets.

Most groups also become a kind of community resource. In addition to their scheduled concerts, they often appear at local community events such as gay pride celebrations, scholarship fundraisers, PFLAG (Parents and Friends of Lesbians and Gays) receptions, and Human Rights Campaign dinners.

Organizational Structures

Lesbian and gay ensembles vary widely in their organizational structures. In the 1970s and early 1980s, many groups attempted to create structures that escaped the formal hierarchy of a conductor directing the activities of the group, or avoided the judgmental aspect of auditioning members.

In the long run, many groups found that a committee-based, partially democratic form of the traditional classical ensemble structure enabled them to achieve some continuity. The negotiations between organization and freedom remain an important aspect of the politics of each ensemble as well as an aspect of relations among ensembles.

These tensions sometimes produce conflicts between issues of musical presentation and sociopolitical status. Every lesbian and gay musical ensemble has at some time experienced the pull between the conflicting goals of musical excellence and community service. But despite these conflicts, many groups frequently manage to achieve high levels of musical professionalism.

The gay and lesbian choral movement has had a large impact, not only on gay and lesbian communities and their public image but also on the world of choral music, which has been greatly enlivened by its presence.

—*Paul Attinello*

Bibliography

Attinello, Paul. "Authority and Freedom: Toward a Sociology of the Gay Choruses." *Queering the Pitch: The New Gay and Lesbian Musicology.* Philip Brett, Elizabeth Wood, and Gary C. Thomas, eds. New York: Routledge, 1994. 315–346.

———. "Sims, John Reed." *Baker's Biographical Dictionary of Twentieth-Century Classical Musicians.* Laura Kuhn, ed. New York: Schirmer/Macmillan, 1997. 1263.

Boerger, Kristina. *Whose Music Is It Anyway?: Black Vocal Ensemble Traditions and the Feminist Choral Movement: Performance Practice as Politics.* D.M.A. diss., University of Illinois at Urbana-Champaign, 2000.

Gordon, Eric A. "GALA: The Lesbian and Gay Community of Song." *Choral Journal* 30.9 (1990): 25–32.

Roma, Catherine. "Choruses, Women's." *Lesbian Histories and Cultures: An Encyclopedia.* Bonnie Zimmerman, ed. New York: Garland, 2000. 166–167.

———. "Women's Choral Communities: Singing for Our Lives." *Hotwire* 8.1 (January 1992): 36.

Vukovich, Dyana. "The Anna Crusis Women's Choir." *Women and Performance: A Journal of Feminist Theory* 4.1, issue 7 (1986): 50–63.

Wise, Matthew. "Choruses and Marching Bands." *Gay Histories and Cultures: An Encyclopedia.* George E. Haggerty, ed. New York: Garland, 2000. 189–190.

See also

Classical Music; Popular Music; Conductors; Del Tredici, David; Feinstein, Michael; Morris, Mark; Near, Holly; Rorem, Ned; Susa, Conrad

Christian, Meg   *(b. 1946)*

A PIONEER IN WOMEN'S MUSIC, MEG CHRISTIAN WAS among the first to address lesbian and feminist issues in her songs. Her commitment to the empowerment of women also led her to become a founding member of Olivia Records, a woman-oriented company.

Christian was born and grew up in Lynchburg, Virginia. After graduating from the University of North Carolina with a double major in English and music, she briefly returned to her hometown but moved to Washington, D.C., in 1969 to perform in the city's nightclubs.

While there she had an epiphany. Watching an appearance by feminists Ti-Grace Atkinson and Robin Morgan on the *David Frost Show*, she was appalled by the host's disrespectful treatment of the women, which caused them to walk off the set. Christian was sufficiently incensed to write a letter to Frost, a move that she called "my first political act."

As a result of her newfound political consciousness Christian drastically changed her repertoire. She began to write her own music and to sing the songs of Cris Williamson in order to speak about women in "a loving, honest, positive way."

Her new focus made her show less commercially viable. Nightclub owners were uninterested in a performer who attracted a mostly female audience, especially an audience with a growing contingent of lesbian fans. Christian therefore took to appearing at alternative venues such as coffeehouses and women's centers.

Participating in the feminist movement gave Christian a sense of empowerment and inclusion. As she commented later, in a 1981 interview, "I certainly thought that I was 'the only one' in about 400 categories until I found the women's movement." During this period (the early 1970s), Christian embraced the idea of separatism. She joined a women's collective and preferred to play concerts before women-only audiences.

In 1973, she met and befriended Cris Williamson. Together with a group of others they founded an all-woman business, Olivia Records. The company's first album was Christian's *I Know You Know* (1975). Over the next decade she put out three more: *Face the Music* (1977), *Turning It Over* (1981), and *From the Heart* (1984). Olivia also released a compilation album, *The Best of Meg Christian*, in 1990.

After several years of operation in Washington, D.C., the collective moved Olivia to Oakland, California. The company did so well that in 1983 Stephen Holden of the *New York Times* dubbed it "one of the record industry's most solid success stories of the last decade."

Christian played an important role in Olivia's success. Her early hits such as "Ode to a Gym Teacher," which affirmed the value of a role model "who taught me being female meant you could still be strong," quickly won her fans, whose numbers just kept growing.

Other musicians were admirers as well, and many eagerly joined Christian on *Turning It Over*. In reviewing the album, Deborah Weiner commented on Christian's "impressive skills as a guitarist, singer, and songwriter" and also cited the "facility and expression of subtle shadings and dramatic textures" of her guitar technique. She praised Christian's contributions to lesbian music, writing, "we...need the intelligence, sensitivity, and humor" of Christian's work.

In addition to recording, Christian toured extensively, playing at music festivals and in concerts. She sometimes appeared with Holly Near, with whom she had a three-year love affair in the late 1970s. She also performed with Cris Williamson, notably at a Carnegie Hall concert to celebrate Olivia's tenth anniversary.

Christian put tremendous energy into working for both professional success and political causes, but she still felt that she "wasn't being good enough, that there was so much to be done." Under stress, she turned to alcohol. Eventually she recognized the need to get help and enrolled in several recovery programs. At the same time, she became interested in exploring spirituality and began studying Siddha Yoga.

In 1984, she decided to leave the music scene and devote herself entirely to the spiritual life. After traveling to ashrams (religious communities) throughout the world, Christian, who had adopted the first name Shambhavi, settled in one in upstate New York.

Through Siddha Yoga, Christian studied Indian music and instruments. As a result, she produced two CDs, *Fire of My Love* (1986) and *Songs of Ecstasy* (1995). The collections include both traditional religious songs and compositions by Christian.

Christian's departure from Olivia had been completely amicable, and she remained on excellent terms with the women there. She was reunited with the organization in 2002, when she performed on a cruise ship for Olivia, which now offers vacation packages for lesbians and their families and friends. Her first public performance in almost twenty years was warmly received. She has returned in subsequent years, giving delighted fans the opportunity once again to enjoy her artistry and her affirming voice for women.

—*Linda Rapp*

BIBLIOGRAPHY

Davenport, Katherine. "Meg Talks." *off our backs* 11 (March 31, 1981): 19.

Harper, Jorjet, and Toni Armstrong, Jr. "Meg Departs." *Hotwire* 5 (January 31, 1989): 21.

Harrington, Richard. "Heart of a Woman; Meg Christian's Music." *Washington Post*, November 3, 1981.

Holden, Stephen. "Olivia Records Is a Success in 'Women's Music.'" *New York Times*, November 4, 1983.

Near, Holly, and Derk Richardson. *Fire in the Rain...Singer in the Storm: An Autobiography.* New York: William Morrow and Company, 1990.

Weiner, Deborah. "Turning It Over." *off our backs* 11 (December 31, 1981): 26.

Classical Music

THE TERM *CLASSICAL MUSIC* IS A CONVENIENT SHORT-hand that refers to the body of Western art music, as distinguished from popular or folk music, composed from approximately 800 A.D. to the present.

Music history is generally divided into large stylistic periods. These periods and their approximate date ranges are: Medieval (prior to 1400), Renaissance (1400–1600), Baroque (1600–1750), Classical (1750–1820), Romantic (1820–1900), and Modern (1900–present). Many genres are represented in this long history, including chant, madrigal, motet, cantata, mass, requiem, concerto, quartet, symphony, opera, and song, to name only the most popular.

Although the terms *gay, lesbian, bisexual,* and *transsexual* are modern in origin and anachronistic when applied to premodern periods, in almost every era composers and musicians were known to be attracted to their own sex or wrote music that can now be understood as having particular interest for glbtq people. And one genre in particular, opera, has especially captured the hearts of gay men.

The presence in earlier musical eras of people we would now identify as gay or lesbian is apparent primarily through contextual clues rather than hard evidence or explicit documentation. Hence, the identification of individuals as evincing same-sex desire is sometimes highly controversial.

Pre-Baroque Music

As a result of its unfamiliar aesthetics, its largely ecclesiastical subject matter, and the predominance of vocal music, often in foreign languages, the music of periods prior to the Baroque is the least known and appreciated by modern listeners. A few works, however, have been used in movie soundtracks (such as the chant "Miserere," by Gregorio Allegri, which is used in Ismail Merchant and James Ivory's film of E. M. Forster's *Maurice*) or appear on novelty Christmas CDs (as in the popular *Chant Noël*).

The earlier the period, the slighter the surviving evidence as to the sexual orientation or affectional preference of composers or performers, and the more difficult it is to construct a case for same-sex attraction. However, much early music was composed within all-male or all-female subcultures, as in monasteries, priories, or convents, and homosocial elements may sometimes be discerned in the music, as, for example, in the texts and contexts of twelfth-century Notre Dame polyphony.

The strong emotional attachment of Hildegard von Bingen (1098–1179) to her disciple and assistant, Richardis von Stade, is well attested. Hildegard's liturgical cycle, the *Symphoniae,* which expresses physical and spiritual desire for the Virgin Mary, has frequently been regarded as homoerotic.

A thirteenth-century woman, Bieiris (or Bieris) de Romans, is credited as the author of the only surviving example of a secular lesbian love song, "Na Maria, pretz e fina valors."

Records exist of the Netherlands composer Nicholas Gombert (ca. 1490–ca. 1556) having violated a boy in the Holy Roman Emperor's service and being sentenced to the galleys for a period in exile on the high seas. This incident resulted in his removal as a priest (or canon) in the cathedral of Tournai, so we can infer homosexual interest (or at least pedophilia) on Gombert's part. Other Renaissance composers who were likely attracted to their own sex include the Burgundian Guillaume Dufay (ca. 1400–1474), the Netherlander Orlando di Lasso (1532–1594), and the Italian Madalena Casulana (ca. 1540–ca. 1590), the first published woman composer.

The Baroque Period

Baroque music is one of the most popular and well-known classical music styles today—thanks largely to Johann Sebastian Bach, Antonio Vivaldi, Georg Philipp Telemann, and George Frideric Handel. Baroque music features a clear harmonic structure with well-marked cadences, generally functional harmony (it sounds "right" to modern ears), and clear and memorable melodic lines.

One of the most famous of the Baroque composers is George Frideric Handel (1685–1759)—best known for *Messiah* and the *Music for the Royal Fireworks*. He left tantalizing clues suggesting his same-sex sexual orientation. Still a controversial claim, the gist of the argument is that Handel apparently never slept with women, so he must have slept with men.

Gary Thomas, in *Queering the Pitch*, the seminal collection of essays edited by Philip Brett, Elizabeth Wood, and Thomas, argues that the circumlocutions used by Handel's earliest biographers in an effort to avoid addressing this issue support the conclusion that they believed Handel must have been homosexual.

Thomas also discusses milieus in which Handel may have circulated with some impunity: molly houses (the eighteenth-century equivalent of a gay bar) and Italy; yet he leaves a final answer to the question open for further investigation.

In passing, Thomas also mentions the great likelihood that composer Arcangelo Corelli (1653–1713) was at least a Cardinal's kept boy in Rome. Other Baroque composers believed to be involved in homosexual liaisons are Jean-Baptiste Lully (1632–1687) and Johann Rosenmüller (ca. 1619–1684).

Francesca Caccini (1587–1641), a professional singer and composer of both sacred and secular music, and often credited as the first woman opera composer, apparently lived a woman-centered life. Her work, including the Florentine court opera *La liberazione di Ruggiero dall' isola d'Alcina* (1625), has been interpreted as strongly gynocentric. This opera, for example, uses the normative master plot reinforcing patriarchal monarchy to show how the female coregents of Florence might win by playing within the rules rather than lose by being perceived as too ambitious.

Sometimes, individual pieces by composers seem to be homophilic and thus subversive in nature. Or, conversely, composers sometimes alter their sources to disguise the homoeroticism that may have inspired their work. For example, Lydia Hamessley, in *Queering the Pitch*, argues that Henry Lawes deliberately misreads an erotic poem of attraction between women by Katherine Philips in his 1655 musical setting of the work to weaken the meaning of the text and reinforce the heterosexual norm. Playing against expected types in opera is also a means of exploring nonheterosexual ways of being.

The Classical and Romantic Periods

Music of the period of Mozart, Haydn, and (all but late) Beethoven is characterized by a slowing of harmonic rhythm (how rapidly the harmony changes), greater stability, an emphasis on gracefulness and balance, and a move from vocal toward instrumental compositions.

If the scholarly disagreements over Handel's alleged homosexuality are heated, even more contentious is the controversy over the strong likelihood that Franz Schubert (1797–1828) was also homosexual. Schubert is a transitional figure who bridges the end of the Classical period and the beginning of the Romantic period.

The Romantic style is characterized by a loosening of the harmonic and melodic rules, an increased emphasis on new harmonies, harmonic relationships, and dissonance (clashing or discordant sounds), a heightened emotional expressiveness, and the rise of the piano as a favored compositional medium.

Schubert chose to compose along a deliberately different path from that outlined by the aggressive and hypermasculine Beethoven, who was held up as the model and measure for composers until at least World War I.

Music historians have remarked on a studied, carefully planned and executed deviance in Schubert's choice of materials and, especially, his harmonies—in particular, the progression to keys related by the interval of a third rather than the more conventional dominant–tonic or fifth-related progression—and also in his creation of formal musical structures in sonata-allegro form, the traditional form of a first movement in the Classical and Romantic periods.

As a result of these tendencies, Schubert has often been dismissed as a "feminine" or weak composer, and this perceived femininity is sometimes related to his alleged homosexuality.

Much of the evidence for Schubert's homosexual orientation is circumstantial but nevertheless strong. It includes Schubert's own journal entries, accounts of him by his friends, and existing letters between Schubert and his friends. Schubert certainly moved in homophilic, if not actually homosexual, circles, and some of his close friends were jailed on morals charges; but the case for Schubert's own homosexuality, while very suggestive, is not yet considered conclusive among scholars.

Although the composer and critic Robert Schumann (1810–1856) once contrasted the "masculine" Beethoven (1770–1827) to the "feminine" Schubert, Beethoven's intense preoccupation with his own adopted nephew has invited speculation from some twentieth-century writers and filmmakers about his sexual orientation.

Similarly, the complicated, but apparently unconsummated, relationship between Schumann and Johannes Brahms has also been the subject of speculation.

More certain is the bisexuality of Frédéric Chopin (1810–1849).

The end of the Romantic period brought two further composers who were likely to have been homosexual: Pyotr Ilich Tchaikovsky (1840–1893) and the lesser-known Camille Saint-Saëns (1835–1921).

Tchaikovsky, well known for his ballets *Swan Lake, Nutcracker,* and *Sleeping Beauty,* his symphonies (especially the sixth, *Pathétique*), and the ever-popular *1812 Overture,* was alleged to have committed suicide because, so the story goes, his sexual involvement with a minor noble of the Russian Imperial Court was about to be revealed, creating a scandal that would have ruined him. The composer's death of cholera is reliably documented, but there is some question whether he knowingly drank untreated water, or was forced to do so.

Interestingly, Tchaikovsky is also the first documented case of "gay-bashing" among composers: Reviews of his works went from raves to scathing denunciations once the allegation of homosexuality became known. Perhaps for this reason, he has been a particular favorite among gay men, who have widely embraced the *Pathétique Symphony* as a musical sketch of unrequited homosexual love.

Best known for his *Carnival of the Animals* and Symphony no. 3 (*"Organ" Symphony),* Saint-Saëns was a prolific composer and mentor to the next generation of composers, including Gabriel Fauré, André Messager, and Eugène Gigout. Self-identified as a pederast, Saint-Saëns spent a great deal of time in North Africa, both to fulfill his desire for Arab boys and to absorb musical inspiration from the exotic locales.

Other lesser-known composers of the late Romantic period also thought to be homosexual are Reynaldo Hahn (1874–1947), a Frenchman who wrote miniature pieces and songs; Dame Ethel Smyth (1858–1944), whose sexuality is revealed in a close reading of her letters and diaries in conjunction with her compositions; Ernest Chausson (1855–1899), best known for his *Poème de l'amour et de la mer*; and Modeste Mussorgsky (1839–1881), composer of the popular *Pictures at an Exhibition* and *Night on Bald Mountain.*

Many of Smyth's compositions, including her *Songs of Sunrise,* were probably inspired by her passion for militant suffragist Emmeline Pankhurst.

Even Edward Elgar (1857–1934), heterosexually married and a stalwart Roman Catholic, and best known in the United States for his *Pomp and Circumstance March no. 1,* frequently used at commencement ceremonies, is thought by some to have had a homosexual affair with August Jaeger, the dedicatee of the Nimrod variation (no. 9) of the *"Enigma" Variations.*

The Twentieth Century to the Present

The common musical language recognizable from the Renaissance to the early part of the twentieth century was stretched to breaking and dissolution by the end of World War I.

New ideas about dissonance and its emancipation (that is, freeing dissonance from its traditional function as a momentary heightening of tension) were championed especially by the Viennese composer Arnold Schoenberg (1874–1951). These ideas led to freely atonal works (compositions not written in a traditional key) and twelve-tone, or dodecaphonic, music, but also opened the door for other experiments in classical music, including the incorporation of jazz and non-Western musical forms and instruments.

Gay and lesbian musicians, who are more easily identified in this period than in earlier ones, have been at the forefront of twentieth-century music. A short list of the great composers of the century who were gay would necessarily include such giants as Benjamin Britten (1913–1976) and Aaron Copland (1900–1990), plus a number of others both well known and beloved, including Karol Szymanowski, Samuel Barber, Leonard Bernstein, Gian Carlo Menotti, Francis Poulenc, Manuel de Falla, and Virgil Thomson. Similarly, many celebrated gay performers and conductors were active in twentieth-century music. Some closely related fields, such as ballet and modern dance, as well as opera, are also heavily populated by gay and lesbian artists.

Several famous lesbian salons, including those associated with Natalie Barney (1876–1972), Gertrude Stein (1874–1946), and the Princess de Polignac (1865–1943), emphasized classical music, among other arts. Nadia Boulanger (1887–1979), perhaps the greatest composition teacher of the century, not only frequented these circles, but numbered among her students such talented gay composers as Copland, Gian Carlo Menotti (b. 1911), Ned Rorem (b. 1923), and Virgil Thomson (1896–1989).

Gay men and lesbians also have often been among the most experimental musicians of the experimental twentieth century. For example, Francis Poulenc (1899–1963), Marc Blitzstein (1905–1964), and Leonard Bernstein (1918–1990) incorporated jazz rhythms, harmonies, new instruments, and melodic coloration into the classical language. The conductor and composer Dimitri Mitropoulos (1896–1960) introduced challenging music to classical music audiences all over the world, especially in Minneapolis and New York, though his tenure as music director of the New York Philharmonic was shortened as a result of rumors about his homosexuality.

Others, such as Copland, Thomson, Manuel de Falla (1876–1946), and Henry Cowell (1897–1965) explored the richness of folk music and dance traditions, expanding their musical idiom to include nontraditional types of harmony—for example, modal (based on Medieval church modes), quartal, and quintal (based on fourths and fifths instead of thirds).

Gay composer Lou Harrison (1917–2003) introduced Eastern influences and new instruments such as the Indonesian gamelan, or gong orchestra, into the common language.

Other gay composers achieved prominence in opera, including Britten, Menotti, Samuel Barber (1910–1981), and Hans Werner Henze (b. 1926). Composers such as Blitzstein and Bernstein often blurred the distinction between operatic music and more popular musical theater, a practice in which they were followed by David Del Tredici (b. 1937) and the most successful contemporary composer for the musical theater, Stephen Sondheim (b. 1930).

Perhaps the most experimental of all twentieth-century composers is John Cage (1912–1992), whose lover and collaborator was the pathbreaking choreographer Merce Cunningham (b. 1919). Cage broke all the rules of compositional control by including chance, or aleatoric, processes in his music. Among his most famous works is the piece entitled 4'33", which consists of four minutes and thirty-three seconds of silence.

Among the leading contemporary gay composers and conductors are the Pulitzer Prize– and Academy Award–winning composer John Corigliano, who has written moving music in response to the AIDS crisis; and Michael Tilson Thomas, who as music director of the San Francisco Symphony has commissioned music by openly gay composer David Del Tredici set to poems about gay life by authors such as Thom Gunn and Allen Ginsberg.

One could expand this list of gay and lesbian figures in classical music considerably—it is by no means exhaustive. What is not clear is whether there are more gay and lesbian composers today than in previous periods or we can simply recognize them more easily today. In any case, gay men and lesbians have had a sizable impact on the world of classical music and continue to shape its future.
—*Mario Champagne*

BIBLIOGRAPHY

Blackmer, Corinne E., and Patricia Juliana Smith, eds. E*n Travesti: Women, Gender Subversion, Opera.* Ithaca: Cornell University Press, 1995.

Brett, Philip, Elizabeth Wood, and Gary C. Thomas, eds. *Queering the Pitch: The New Gay and Lesbian Musicology.* New York and London: Routledge, 1994.

GLSG Newsletter. The Gay & Lesbian Study Group of the American Musicological Society (1991–).

Koestenbaum, Wayne. *The Queen's Throat: Opera, Homosexuality, and the Mystery of Desire.* New York: Vintage Books, 1993.

Kopelson, Kevin. *Beethoven's Kiss: Pianism, Perversion, and the Mastery of Desire.* Stanford: Stanford University Press, 1996.

Kramer, Lawrence, ed. "Schubert: Music, Sexuality, Culture." *Nineteenth-Century Music* 17.1 (Summer 1993).

Solie, Ruth, ed. *Musicology and Difference: Gender and Sexuality in Music Scholarship.* Berkeley: University of California Press, 1993.

SEE ALSO

Conductors; Opera; Barber, Samuel; Bernstein, Leonard; Blitzstein, Marc; Boulanger, Nadia; Britten, Benjamin; Cage, John; Copland, Aaron; Corelli, Arcangelo; Corigliano, John; Cowell, Henry; Cunningham, Merce; Del Tredici, David; Falla (y Matheu), Manuel de; Handel, George Frideric; Harrison, Lou; Henze, Hans Werner; Hildegard of Bingen; Lully, Jean-Baptiste; Menotti, Gian Carlo; Mitropoulos, Dimitri; Poulenc, Francis; Rorem, Ned; Rosenmüller, Johann; Saint-Saëns, Camille; Schubert, Franz; Smyth, Dame Ethel; Sondheim, Stephen; Szymanowski, Karol Maciej; Tchaikovsky, Pyotr Ilich; Thomson, Virgil

Cliburn, Van   (b. 1934)

THE YOUNG AMERICAN PIANIST VAN CLIBURN GAINED sudden worldwide fame in 1958 when, at the height of the Cold War, he won the inaugural International Tchaikovsky Piano Competition in Moscow. Critics praised his technique and virtuosity, and Americans hailed him as a hero. Cliburn embarked on an ambitious performing and recording career that garnered numerous awards and brought him international acclaim. Since 1962 he has sponsored a quadrennial International Piano Competition that bears his name. He retired from the stage in 1978 and resumed limited concert appearances only in 1989.

Harvey Lavan Cliburn, Jr. was born on July 12, 1934, in Shreveport, Louisiana, where his father, Harvey Lavan Cliburn, was working as a purchase and sales representative for an oil company. His mother, Rildia Bee O'Bryan Cliburn, was a piano teacher. She was to exert a major influence on the life and career of her only child.

Rildia Bee Cliburn was a serious and talented pianist. She attended the Cincinnati Conservatory of Music and then the New York School of Musical Art, where she studied with Arthur Friedheim, who had been a pupil of

Franz Liszt. The playing style that she learned and in turn taught to her son reflected the musical trends of the late nineteenth century.

Mrs. Cliburn hoped to be a concert pianist, but her parents considered such a career inappropriate for a woman, and so she went home to Texas and began giving piano lessons.

Van Cliburn started studying piano with her when he was three years old. By the age of four, he was performing with a children's church group.

In 1941, the Cliburn family moved to Kilgore, Texas. Cliburn performed at various venues in the area, earning a reputation as a prodigy. At twelve, he played Tchaikovsky's Piano Concerto no. 1 with the Houston Symphony Orchestra.

In 1951, Cliburn entered the Juilliard School, where he studied with Rosina Lhévinne. She brought a Russian romanticism to his style that was admirably suited to the repertoire he favored.

Cliburn's talent garnered him numerous awards. He won the Dealey Award and the Kosciuszko Foundation's Chopin Prize in 1952, and the Juilliard concerto competition the following year. In 1954, he won the Roeder Award and the Edgar M. Leventritt Foundation Award, the latter bringing him the opportunity to play with the New York Philharmonic Orchestra at Carnegie Hall. After graduating with honors later that year, Cliburn began touring as a solo performer.

The turning point in Cliburn's life came in 1958, when he won the International Tchaikovsky Piano Competition. His performance awed critics. Composer Aram Khachaturian declared Cliburn's rendition of Rachmaninoff's Piano Concerto no. 3 better than that of Rachmaninoff himself.

The response of the American public to Cliburn's triumph was based at least as much on politics as on aesthetics. Having been beaten at the space race when the Soviets launched Sputnik in 1957, Americans were eager for a victory of their own. Cliburn's success in Moscow gave them not only that but a classic American hero to boot. Tall, boyishly handsome, accomplished and charming yet modest, Cliburn was lionized by the press and embraced by the public.

Distrust between the superpowers was such that there were persistent rumors that Soviet officials had tried to pressure the judges to give the prize to a Russian, but that pianist Sviatoslav Richter had insisted that it go, deservedly, to Cliburn, and that Soviet premier Nikita Khrushchev himself had ratified the decision.

Cliburn was given a ticker-tape parade in New York upon his return from the competition and appeared on television shows such as *Person to Person*, *What's My Line?* and *The Tonight Show*. His recording of Tchaikovsky's Piano Concerto no. 1 shared the top of the LP charts with Johnny Mathis's *Greatest Hits* album and the soundtrack from *South Pacific*. It became the first classical music album to sell a million copies within two years.

Cliburn was much in demand on the concert tour. He gave almost a hundred performances a year. His appearances in 1960 included a tour of the Soviet Union, where he was an audience favorite.

By the mid-1960s, however, the adulatory reviews for Cliburn were becoming mixed. Critics complained that he had not expanded his repertoire much beyond the works that had brought him the Tchaikovsky prize and showed little interest in doing so. Although Cliburn's repertoire was in fact wider than such comments suggested, it is true that the core of his program changed little over time.

By the beginning of the 1970s, Cliburn's grueling concert schedule had taken a toll on him. His playing had become erratic, and critics continued to harp on his lack of musical growth. In 1974, Cliburn announced that after completing the concerts to which he was then committed he would take a respite from the stage. After September 1978, he did not perform publicly until 1989, when he began accepting a limited number of concert dates.

Cliburn retired to a lavish house in Fort Worth, Texas, and became prominent on the local music scene. Among the projects to which he devoted his time was the Van Cliburn International Piano Competition, which he founded in 1962 and which is held quadrennially in Fort Worth.

In 1996, Thomas E. Zaremba filed a palimony suit against Cliburn, claiming that due to "an oral and/or implied partnership agreement" he was entitled to a share of Cliburn's income and property. Zaremba asserted that he had assisted in the management of Cliburn's career and finances as well as performing domestic services such as helping Cliburn care for his aged mother. Zaremba further alleged that Cliburn may have exposed him to AIDS during their seventeen-year relationship, which lasted until around the end of 1994, after which Zaremba moved to Center Line, Michigan, where he found work as a mortician.

Cliburn called the accusations "salacious" but otherwise had little to say about the case. Indeed, though always described as gracious and polite, Cliburn is known to be notoriously difficult to interview. Music insiders had long been aware of his homosexuality, and he and Zaremba had appeared together at public functions in Fort Worth, but in Cliburn's thirty-plus years as a celebrity, the press had never linked him romantically with anyone.

The public's image of him was still that of an eleven-year-old American boy—he seemed almost frozen in time at the moment of his victory in Moscow. There is ample evidence in his habits for this image: He is a lifelong Baptist and a regular churchgoer, neither drinks nor smokes, lived with his mother until her death at 97, and begins his concerts with "The Star-Spangled Banner."

Zaremba's lawsuit was eventually dismissed due to the lack of a written agreement, which is required under Texas law.

In December 2001, Cliburn was among the artists feted at the Kennedy Center Honors. National Security Adviser Condoleezza Rice, herself a pianist, praised Cliburn's "grace and lyricism" and "the power of his music to build bridges across the cultural and political divide."

—*Linda Rapp*

BIBLIOGRAPHY

Douglas, Jack, and Wayne Lee Gay. "Man Sues Van Cliburn for Millions." *Fort Worth Star-Telegram*, April 30, 1996.

Horowitz, Joseph. "As Ever, Cliburn Does It His Way." *New York Times*, April 28, 1991.

Page, Tim. "For Van Cliburn, An Early Crescendo." *Washington Post*, December 2, 2001.

Recio, Maria. "Cliburn Saluted at Gala." *Fort Worth Star-Telegram*, December 3, 2001.

Reich, Howard. *Van Cliburn*. Nashville, Tenn.: Thomas Nelson Publishers, 1993.

Steinberg, Michael. "Cliburn, Van." *The New Grove Dictionary of Music and Musicians*. Stanley Sadie, ed. New York: Grove's Dictionaries, 2001. 16:55.

Teachout, Terry. "Two fallen stars." *Commentary* 106.1 (July 1998): 55–59.

SEE ALSO

Classical Music; Mathis, Johnny; Tchaikovsky, Pyotr Ilich

Conductors

In spite of the presence of many gay, lesbian, and bisexual figures in the field of classical music, it is difficult to identify more than a handful of self-identified, openly gay or lesbian conductors even in the early years of the twenty-first century. As well, it is difficult to find much explicit discussion of the relationship between homosexuality and conducting. Yet the invisibility of sexual minorities on the podium should in no way diminish their very real, if often overlooked, contributions to classical music.

As they gain a more secure place in the profession and more visibility, openly gay and lesbian conductors no longer fear explicit persecution, and a few have begun to enjoy a tentative and gradual acceptance. In the last twenty-five years, gay and lesbian conductors have used their success both to broaden classical music to speak to gay, lesbian, and bisexual people and to use music as an artistic activity around which to organize, strengthen, and heal glbtq communities.

The Rise of the Conductor

Conducting is a relatively new practice in the history of classical music. As the eighteenth century came to a close, a new role and public persona developed for music directors. Before the 1780s and 1790s, the terms *conductor* and *conducting* had little or no connection to music. Gradually, the meaning of the terms grew to encompass musical direction, and they acquired new nuances of meaning to coincide with the birth of the modern conductor.

Prior to this development, orchestral and choral directors existed, but they served more as timekeepers than interpreters and often played or sang in the ensembles they directed. Generally speaking, prior to the late eighteenth century, the job of the musical leader was to mark the beat and to maintain an even tempo.

The role was far from consistently fulfilled, and it involved a number of practices in the seventeenth and eighteenth centuries that appear quite foreign—and even humorous—to our notions of conducting. Musicians often rapped large wooden canes, waved handkerchiefs, or stomped loudly before the baton was introduced in the 1820s and became a standard conducting tool in the nineteenth and twentieth centuries.

In musical periods before the Romantic era (roughly 1820–1900), the composer typically found himself directing his own works, especially if he served as an official court or church musician. In this tradition, the *Kapellmeister* (literally "chapel master," or provincial conductor) served in many different musical capacities—composer, orchestral organizer, and conductor. Well-known composers such as Bach, Haydn, Mozart, and Beethoven often led performances of their music from the keyboard.

As the very structure of classical music began to change, both in terms of the music itself and how it was produced, the roles of composer and conductor grew apart, and the conductor began to take on new functions as interpreter of the score and performance coach of the orchestra and choir.

The need for a professional conductor grew in part from the rhythmic innovations of the music itself. Composers such as Mozart and particularly Haydn and Beethoven began to introduce rhythmic irregularity into their music, altering one of the chief characteristics of the prevailing Classical style. As composers experimented more with various ways of achieving rhythmic variety in a work, such as syncopation (the accenting of "off" beats) and *rubato* (flexibility of tempo), ensembles had greater need for a director not only to maintain an even tempo and steady beat but also to guide them through the new style of musical expression that such innovations required.

In the late eighteenth and early nineteenth centuries, musicians also began to rely less on the aristocracy and the church and more on public audiences and concerts for support. The new market for music created new professional and artistic independence from the previous system of patronage, but it also demanded higher standards for musicians and greater accountability. The conductor gradually assumed responsibility for the musicianship of the ensembles he directed. (*He*, that is, for until the latter part of the twentieth century almost all conductors were male.)

Over the course of the nineteenth century, the conductor became increasingly more influential and powerful. He grew into a celebrity in his own right. He was expected to be a charismatic leader who inspired the orchestra, interpreted the music, and attracted audiences to his ensemble's performances.

The Emergence of Gay Conductors

Prior to the consolidation of the role and identity of the conductor in the nineteenth century, many musicians who organized and directed choruses, orchestras, and smaller musical ensembles were also composers. Several of these composer-conductors were known for their involvement in same-sex sexual activity.

The clearest example of the type during this period may be Jean-Baptiste Lully (1632–1687), a central figure in French music in the late seventeenth century. In addition to being Louis XIV's royal composer, he is generally credited with primary responsibility for the development of French opera. Although he married Madeleine Lambert and fathered six children, he created a number of scandals because of his sexual relationships with men.

Scholars have much more easily identified conductors of the late nineteenth and early twentieth centuries who would now be classified as gay, lesbian, or bisexual, even though their sexuality often imperiled their conducting careers or required them to exercise great discretion.

The life and career of Dimitri Mitropoulos (1896–1960) highlights the difficulties gay conductors faced in the first half of the twentieth century. In the 1930s, he caused a sensation when he debuted at the helm of the Berlin Philharmonic Orchestra. His intensely physical conducting style, ability to conduct from memory without a score, and refusal to conduct with a baton marked him as an innovative and talented conductor. His assumed his first major position as conductor of the Minneapolis Symphony Orchestra; after twelve successful years there, he became the music director of the New York Philharmonic in 1950.

But Mitropoulos's tenure at the New York Philharmonic was troubled. In *The Maestro Myth*, Norman Lebrecht argues that not only did his critics dislike his musical tastes, they also despised him for his homosexuality, which was an open secret in the musical world. As Mitropoulos's popularity waned, critics used his bachelor status and implicit homosexual sensibility against him.

Mitropoulos was ultimately replaced by a man who more adeptly cultivated the proper masculine, heterosexual image that audiences required of their conductors. Ironically, that man was Leonard Bernstein, himself a deeply closeted homosexual.

Exposing the homophobia that pervades the conducting profession, Lebrecht argues that the world of classical music fiercely protects the virile, masculine, mysterious image of the conductor. "Gay conductors," he writes, "are advised to hide their presumed vice as timidly as any country vicar." Often gay conductors have been free to pursue their sexual inclinations in private, but they have been required to maintain the image of the powerful, heterosexual maestro.

If Aaron Copland (1900–1990) had a relatively easier time succeeding as a gay conductor than did Mitropoulos, it was probably due to the fact that he was a composer as well. Although better known as the "Dean of American Music," as he came to be called, Copland spent roughly the second half of his career actively conducting.

Early in his education, Copland studied conducting for a short period of time with Albert Wolff, but most of his training in conducting came informally through the opportunities he found to conduct his own early compositions.

During the 1950s, Copland began to pursue professional conducting more actively and expanded his repertoire to include works by other composers, mostly other twentieth-century figures. In January 1958, he conducted the New York Philharmonic; that performance led to an engagement shortly afterward with the London Symphony Orchestra, an ensemble he would work with over the next twenty-five years. From this point, Copland's career as a conductor took off, and he began an international career as a touring guest conductor.

Most critics agree that Copland accepted his homosexuality and was able to live his life in relative openness, even if he would not be regarded as publicly out by today's standards. Copland refrained from commenting explicitly on his sexuality and its relation to his work as a composer. Although the subject of the relationship of sexuality to music is now open to discussion, nothing has yet been written on Copland's sexuality in relation to his conducting.

Interestingly, critics generally tend to describe Copland's music as "masculine" and "manly," yet his presence on stage conveyed a different impression. As his biographer Howard Pollack notes, "For all his restraint, he cut a boyishly vigorous figure on the podium." Other critics have noted his "verve," "élan," and "zest" while conducting.

Given the difficulties Copland experienced in garnering respect from some of the American orchestras he worked with, it is tempting to speculate on the impact his sexuality—implicitly communicated or otherwise—may have had on his reception by the conservative classical music establishment.

Whereas Copland may have come to terms with his sexuality somewhat quietly and discreetly, it could be argued that Leonard Bernstein (1918–1990) never fully solved the puzzle that his homosexual desires presented him.

Married to the actress Felicia Montaleagre in 1951, Bernstein was well aware at that time of his sexual attraction to men. Unable to reconcile that attraction with his desire to be heterosexual, he remained committed to Montaleagre for most of his life, even as he pursued relationships with men. He remained conflicted over his homosexuality throughout his life.

If Bernstein's response to his sexuality was different from his one-time mentor Copland's, so, too, was his conducting career. Known for his dramatic presence in front of an orchestra, he was undeniably the most successful American conductor of the twentieth century (over the objections of critics who felt that his style was overly extravagant).

Bernstein's accomplishments were many. In succeeding Mitropoulos as music director of the New York Philharmonic in 1958, he became the first American-born conductor to lead one of the premier orchestras of the United States. Scholars credit him, along with other American composers and conductors, including Copland, with transforming classical music by creating a distinctly American idiom within a musical tradition that had been up to that time largely dominated by Europeans.

After assuming his role at the New York Philharmonic, Bernstein used his position as conductor to create innovative musical programs that emphasized the conductor's role as teacher. His mission, as he put it, was primarily educational. His televised series of Young People's Concerts was a landmark in bringing music appreciation to the masses. The recipient of numerous national music awards, he recorded prodigiously and reached a level of popularity and cultural visibility unprecedented for an American conductor.

Thomas Schippers (1930–1977) was a meteoric arrival on the American conducting scene until his untimely death at the age of forty-seven. Born in Kalamazoo, Michigan, he reportedly began studying piano at the age of four. At twenty, he made his Broadway debut conducting Gian Carlo Menotti's opera *The Consul*. At twenty-one, he became the youngest conductor to appear at the New York City Opera, and at twenty-five he became the second-youngest conductor to debut at the Metropolitan Opera.

In 1958, Schippers conducted the open-air concerts at the Spoleto Festival of Two Worlds, founded by his mentor, Menotti. He also conducted the ill-fated premiere of Samuel Barber's *Antony and Cleopatra* (1966), written to celebrate the opening of the Metropolitan

Opera's new home in Lincoln Center. In 1970, he became conductor of the Cincinnati Symphony Orchestra, a position he held until his death in 1977 of lung cancer.

Talented, stylish, youthful, and handsome, Schippers attracted admirers of both sexes. Although he married in 1965, he reportedly maintained a long relationship with Menotti.

The Overlooked History of Lesbian Conductors

Even though the history of conducting is almost entirely male dominated, there is also a history of lesbian conducting. In medieval and early modern Europe, convents were central sites of musicmaking for women. In these same-sex institutions women were responsible for all aspects of music, and from this rich history scholars have identified female musical directors who were likely involved in sexual relationships with other women.

Hildegard of Bingen (1098–1179), Madalena Casulana (ca. 1540–ca. 1590), Francesca Caccini (1587–1641?), and Isabella Leonarda (1620–1704) are women who composed and probably conducted works that invite lesbian interpretation and suggest the sexual interests of their composers.

The most prominent lesbian composer/conductor in the late nineteenth and early twentieth century in Britain was Dame Ethel Smyth (1858–1944). Best known for her compositions, especially in opera, she also conducted on occasion. Most of the critical work thus far on Smyth that considers her lesbianism relates it to her compositions rather than to her conducting. In addition to living openly as a lesbian, she was actively involved in the British suffrage movement and served a short sentence in prison for her radicalism.

Dutch Jewish lesbian Frieda Belinfante (1905–1995) was another pioneer. In Amsterdam just prior to World War II, she became the first woman to conduct her own orchestra. Belinfante began her musical career as a cellist, but the onset of the war postponed her career.

Active in the Dutch resistance and in helping other Jews escape the Netherlands, she was forced to flee after she participated in the attack on the Amsterdam population registry in 1943. After the war, she emigrated to the United States and settled in Orange County, California, where she founded and conducted the Orange County Philharmonic Orchestra.

Openly Gay Conductors

In the last twenty-five years, a few openly gay and lesbian conductors have been able to crack open the conducting closet and use their authority and experience to bolster the gay community and transform the heterosexism of the world of classical music.

Kay Gardner (b. 1941) entered the world of classical music as a flutist, but from a young age aspired to orchestral conducting. Keen to the challenges that women face in such a traditional field, she declared, "Conducting, especially orchestral conducting, is the last stronghold of the musical patriarchy."

Her early career involved researching and playing women's folk music, and, even though she married in 1960 and had two children, she remained interested in women's community and music, both folk and classical. In the late 1960s, Gardner formed her own chamber orchestra, and eventually left her husband to pursue her musical studies full-time at the State University of New York at Stony Brook.

In the early 1970s, she became active in Lavender Jane, a radical feminist music group, while she continued to work on her degree. In 1973, she helped produce the first openly lesbian classical LP, called *Lavender Jane Loves Women.*

In 1977, she decided to pursue her dream of conducting and moved to Denver, Colorado, to study under Maestra Antonia Brico. In 1978, she cofounded the New England Women's Symphony and became its principal conductor. The ensemble was in existence only briefly, but its commitment to showcasing and supporting women composers and conductors had a powerful impact on the growing role of women in classical music.

Since then, Gardner has grown less interested in conducting traditional classical music and has focused more on conducting her own work and using her influence as a conductor to support other female musicians.

Conductor, teacher, and administrator Jon Reed Sims (1947–1984) is best known for his work in founding a number of gay and lesbian music organizations in the late 1970s, including the San Francisco Gay Freedom Day Marching Band & Twirling Corps, the San Francisco Gay Men's Chorus, Golden Gate Performing Arts, the orchestra Lambda Pro Musica, and the San Francisco Lesbian and Gay Men's Community Chorus. His contributions to building gay and lesbian musical networks are regarded as fundamental to the creation of post-Stonewall gay communities in the United States.

Considered something of a maverick by the conservative faction of the music world, Michael Tilson Thomas (b. 1944) has had a notably successful international music career as pianist, conductor, and lately, composer. He became assistant conductor of the Boston Symphony Orchestra at twenty-five, in 1969. Subsequently, he held positions as music director of the Buffalo Philharmonic, principal guest conductor of the Los Angeles Philharmonic, and principal conductor of the London Symphony Orchestra.

In 1995, he assumed his current position as music director of the San Francisco Symphony. In this role, he has commissioned a number of important works by openly gay composers, including Lou Harrison and David Del Tredici.

Tilson Thomas's support of Del Tredici allowed the composer to create *Gay Life,* a series of pieces based on poems by Allen Ginsberg, Thom Gunn, and Paul Monette. In so doing, the composer and the conductor have helped broaden the range of classical music by allowing it to address explicitly gay issues and gay lives in music.

—*Geoffrey W. Bateman*

BIBLIOGRAPHY

Blackmer, Corinne E., and Patricia Juliana Smith, eds. *En Travesti: Women, Gender Subversion, Opera.* New York: Columbia University Press, 1995.

Brett, Phillip, Elizabeth Wood, and Gary C. Thomas, eds. *Queering the Pitch: The New Gay and Lesbian Musicology.* New York: Routledge, 1994.

Burton, Humphrey. *Leonard Bernstein.* New York: Doubleday, 1994.

But I Was a Girl (Maar Ik Was Een Meisje). Videotape. Dir. Toni Boumans. Interview with Frieda Belinfante by Klaus Müller. Frame Media Productions, 1999.

Galkin, Elliott W. *A History of Orchestral Conducting.* New York: Pendragon Press, 1988.

Holsinger, Bruce Wood. "The Flesh of the Voice: Embodiment and the Homoerotics of Devotion in the Music of Hildegard of Bingen (1098–1179)." *Signs: A Journal of Women in Culture and Society* 19 (1993): 91–125.

Jackson, Barbara Garvey. "Musical Women of the Seventeenth and Eighteenth Centuries." *Women and Music: A History.* Karin Pendle, ed. Bloomington: Indiana University Press, 1991. 54–94.

Lebrecht, Norman. *The Maestro Myth: Great Conductors in Pursuit of Power.* New York: Birch Lane Press, 1991.

LePage, Jane Weiner. "Kay Gardner." Women Composers, Conductors, and Musicians of the Twentieth Century. Metuchen, N.J.: Scarecrow Press, 1983. 92–117.

Pollack, Howard. *Aaron Copland: The Life and Work of an Uncommon Man.* New York: Henry Holt and Company, 1999.

Schuller, Gunther. *The Compleat Conductor.* New York: Oxford University Press, 1997.

Schwarz, Robert K. "Cracking the Classical Closet." *Advocate,* May 11, 1999, 48.

Secrest, Meryle. *Leonard Bernstein: A Life.* New York: Alfred A. Knopf, 1994.

"Sims, John." *Baker's Biographical Dictionary of Musicians.* New York: Schirmer/Macmillan, 1992. 1263.

Solie, Ruth A. *Musicology and Difference: Gender and Sexuality in Music Scholarship.* Berkeley: University of California Press, 1993.

Trotter, William. "Mitropoulos, Dmitri." *The New Grove Dictionary of Music and Musicians.* Second ed. Stanley Sadie, ed. New York: Macmillan, 2001. 16:764.

SEE ALSO

Classical Music; Opera; Women's Music; Choruses and Bands; Barber, Samuel; Bernstein, Leonard; Copland, Aaron; Del Tredici, David; Harrison, Lou; Hildegard of Bingen; Lully, Jean-Baptiste; Menotti, Gian Carlo; Mitropoulos, Dimitri; Smyth, Dame Ethel; Tilson Thomas, Michael

Copland, Aaron   (1900–1990)

IN THE COURSE OF A LONG LIFE THAT SPANNED NEARLY the entire twentieth century, Aaron Copland composed a significant number of frequently performed musical works that have become so ingrained in the American cultural consciousness that the mere hearing of them evokes for many the idea of American history, struggle, and courage.

Copland was born on November 14, 1900, to an impoverished Lithuanian Jewish immigrant family in Brooklyn, New York, and his early experiences were shaped by the urban "melting pot" of American culture. That he was also homosexual contributed to the outsider status that might be said to manifest itself in the celebration of the underdog, "the common man," that characterizes his music.

Like many other prominent twentieth-century American composers, Aaron Copland was trained in France by Nadia Boulanger. His music, however, is best known for its rejection of European, neo-Romantic forms and the creation of a uniquely American, modernist style in his orchestral works, particularly his ballets and film scores.

Upon his return from France in 1925, his *Symphony for Organ and Orchestra* had its premiere performance with the New York Symphony Orchestra, Boulanger playing the organ. This work established Copland's reputation in his own country, and by the late 1920s he had begun experimenting with a daringly modern style that incorporated elements of jazz, reflected most notably in his Piano Concerto (1927).

By the end of the 1930s, Copland had incorporated into his music elements suggesting a number of American popular motifs, particularly those of the American West (for example, the pioneering settlers, the cowboy, the outlaw), along with the influences of folk song and Hispanic culture.

These elements are present in Copland's most famous works written between the late 1930s and the early 1950s—the peak years of his career—particularly the ballets *Billy the Kid* (1938), *Rodeo* (1942), and *Appalachian Spring* (1944). The music from these ballets has, for over half a century, been appropriated for a wide variety of purposes in the media, whether as themes for television programs, in advertising, or, however ironically, in the soundtrack of Spike Lee's film *He Got Game* (1998).

So pervasive is his music in American culture that it is hardly an exaggeration to suppose that virtually every American, irrespective of any interest in classical music, has heard Copland's compositions somewhere.

Provocatively—perhaps subversively—his ballet pieces present traditionally "masculine" heroic roles and images in the supposedly "effeminate" (and, in many cases, homosexual) context of ballet and dance. Some critics, for instance, have seen a homoerotic element in the interactions of the title character and Sheriff Pat Garrett in *Billy the Kid*.

Rodeo presents an even more complex gender theme that many homosexuals, both then and now, can understand. Its heroine, a tomboy who is as adept as her male counterparts as a rodeo rider, is rejected and mocked for her efforts, and it is only when she puts on the garb and behavior of traditional femininity that she finds acceptance—and heterosexual romance. While more recent critics see the female protagonist's change as a capitulation to conformity, the ballet can also be interpreted as an ironic commentary on gender norms.

The success of these ballets notwithstanding, Copland's music reached an even larger audience, one outside the traditional sphere of "high culture," through his composition of scores for a number of now classic films addressing the American experience, including *Of Mice and Men* (1939), *Our Town* (1940), *The Red Pony* (1948), and *The Heiress* (1949).

Among his other famous compositions are *El Salón México* (1936), *A Lincoln Portrait* for narrator and orchestra (1942), and an opera, *The Tender Land* (1954), as well as the familiar *Fanfare for the Common Man* (1943).

It is ironic, considering the political climate rampant in the United States during the decade following World War II, that the composer whose music was so strongly identified with the American myth was not only a homosexual but a leftist. In 1953, despite (or perhaps because of) his public stature, Copland was called to testify before the House Un-American Activities Committee as an alleged Communist sympathizer, as he had—in his identification with the "common man"—supported socialist causes in the 1930s.

During the interrogation, Copland was a model of dignity and, in his answers, gave the committee no information that corroborated the Committee in its "witch hunts." Frustrated by this less than useful witness, the Committee dismissed Copland, but, as a result of his questioning, the performance of *A Lincoln Portrait* scheduled for President Dwight D. Eisenhower's inauguration a mere two weeks later was cancelled by government officials.

Despite this insult, only a decade later, in 1964, President Lyndon B. Johnson awarded Copland the Medal of Freedom for his contributions to American culture.

Unlike many gay men of his generation, Copland was neither ashamed of nor tortured by his sexuality. He apparently understood and accepted it from an early age, and throughout his life was involved in relationships with other men. In later years, his affairs were mostly with younger men, usually musicians or artists, whom he mentored, including composer Leonard Bernstein, dancer and artist Erik Johns (who wrote the libretto for *The Tender Land*), photographer Victor Kraft, and music critic Paul Moor.

Given the social prejudices of the times in which he lived, Copland was relatively open about his homosexuality, yet this seems not to have interfered with the acceptance of his music or with his status as a cultural figure. The likely explanation is that Copland conducted his personal life with the characteristic modesty, tactfulness, and serenity that marked his professional life as well.

In his later years, Copland was increasingly disabled with the advance of Alzheimer's disease. In spite of failing health, until his death at the age of ninety on December 2, 1990, he remained a participant in the advancement of American music and culture, not only as a composer but as a conductor, teacher, and author as well.

In the words of his recent biographer Howard Pollack, the accomplishments of this unlikely and unassuming cultural hero over the course of his long life made him truly an "Uncommon Man."   —*Patricia Juliana Smith*

BIBLIOGRAPHY

Berger, Arthur V. *Aaron Copland*. New York: Da Capo Press, 1990.

Butterworth, Neil. *The Music of Aaron Copland*. London: Toccata Press, 1986.

Copland, Aaron. *The New Music, 1900–1960*. New York: W. W. Norton, 1968.

Copland, Aaron, and Vivian Perlis. *Copland: 1900 through 1942*. New York: St. Martin's, 1984.

_____. *Copland: since 1943*. New York: St. Martin's, 1989.

Dobrin, Arnold. *Aaron Copland: His Life and Times*. New York: Crowell, 1967.

Peare, Catherine Owens. *Aaron Copland: His Life*. New York: Holt, Rinehart and Winston, 1969.

Pollack, Howard. *Aaron Copland: The Life and Work of an Uncommon Man*. New York: Henry Holt, 1999.

SEE ALSO

Classical Music; Conductors; Ballet; Bernstein, Leonard; Boulanger, Nadia; Del Tredici, David; Kirstein, Lincoln; Rorem, Ned

Corelli, Arcangelo   *(1653–1713)*

ARCANGELO CORELLI, BORN IN 1653 IN FUSIGNANO, an Italian village between Ravenna and Bologna, was one of the seventeenth century's most widely admired composers and performers. His music has lasting appeal largely due to its refined sense of poise, the balance of all the forces within each composition, and its modern sense of tonality. Some of his works are regarded as models of perfection, and Corelli himself has been called "a modern Orpheus."

Corelli's music is rigidly formal and simple in design, but nevertheless original. It achieves magnificent effects with a surprising economy of means. Corelli used intriguing sequential progressions and descending bass figurations that are typical of operatic laments. He helped achieve a new independent status for chamber forms such as the trio sonata that were formerly regarded as merely decorative.

After Corelli, the distinction between *musica da chiesa* (church music) and *musica da camera* (chamber or dance music) was increasingly blurred. His trio sonatas and *Concerti Grossi* (1714) were widely imitated all over Europe. Not only famous as a composer, he was also regarded as the foremost violinist of his day. In addition, he was admired for his skills as a music teacher.

Much of the information that exists about Corelli, especially about his early days as a student in Bologna, is unreliable. More particularly, a widely reported claim that he provoked the jealousy of French composer Jean-Baptiste Lully is almost certainly not true.

Corelli's personal life has been the subject of much speculation. Most scholars now believe him to have been discreetly homosexual. He never married and lived closely with male friends.

Corelli's rise to fame was meteoric, helped by the fact that music publishing began to proliferate in the early eighteenth century. His rise was also spurred by his influential patrons: Queen Christina of Sweden; Cardinal Pamphili, then the richest man in Rome; and the young and princely Cardinal Ottoboni, the nephew of Pope Alexander VIII. He thus enjoyed the patronage of the most influential people at a time when Rome became a flourishing center of music in Europe.

While many eighteenth-century descriptions of Corelli report on "the mildness of his temper and the modesty of his deportment," others note that his eyes sometimes bulged with anger. Corelli led a quiet, disciplined life, composing within the walls of Cardinal Pamphili's villa, where he shared rooms with fellow musicians Carlo Cignani and Carlo Marat.

He continued this kind of life after 1690, when he resided at the villa of Cardinal Ottoboni, La Cancelleria, which had the atmosphere of an exclusive academy of talented male artists.

While residing at Pamphili's villa, Corelli became utterly devoted to another of the cardinal's employees, the second violinist Matteo Fornari, whom he met in 1682. According to one source, the composer was never far from Matteo's side for almost twenty years after their first meeting. This long-standing intimacy is alluded to in the two fine trio sonatas dedicated to Corelli and Fornari by the younger composer Guiseppe Valentini. Fornari over-saw the publication of Corelli's op. VI concertos after the composer's death.

Corelli moved in the same circles as George Frideric Handel, now also widely believed to have been homo-sexual. Although Corelli's music influenced Handel's, Corelli claimed not to understand Handel's work, which was much fuller in texture and required more dynamic force than his own works. He said that he would be unable to play it correctly.

Corelli was admitted to the Academy in Rome, along with the composers Bernardo Pasquini and Alessandro Scarlatti, in 1706. Two years later, he retired from public life. He died in 1713, a wealthy and widely respected man. He was buried in the Pantheon, next to the painter Raphael.

Corelli's musical legacy and influence extends to the great figures of the succeeding generation of baroque composers, Handel, Bach, and Telemann, but also to Couperin and the enigmatic English composer John Ravenscroft. All of these composers have paid homage to Corelli's poised and elegant compositions.

—Kieron Devlin

BIBLIOGRAPHY

Allsop, Peter. *Corelli: New Orpheus of Our Times.* Oxford: Oxford University Press, 1999

Burrows, Donald. *Handel.* New York: Scribners, 1994.

Moroney, Davitt. "Corelli, Arcangelo." *Gay Histories and Cultures.* George E. Haggerty, ed. New York: Garland, 2000. 215.

Talbot, Michael. "Arcangelo Corelli." *The New Grove Dictionary of Music and Musicians.* Second ed. Stanley Sadie, ed. London and New York: Macmillan, 2001. 457–463.

SEE ALSO

Classical Music; Handel, George Frideric; Lully, Jean-Baptiste

Corigliano, John   (b. 1938)

AMERICAN COMPOSER OF SYMPHONIES, CHAMBER works, choral settings, operas, and film scores, John Corigliano has created some of the most moving music inspired by the AIDS epidemic.

Corigliano was born in New York on February 16, 1938, into a highly musical family. His father was a dis-tinguished violinist and the concertmaster of the New York Philharmonic from 1943 to 1966, while his mother was an accomplished pianist.

Corigliano trained at Columbia University and at the Manhattan School of Music, after which he worked as a music programmer for various New York radio stations

and as music director for the Morris Theatre in New Jersey. He has taught composition at the College of Church Musicians (Washington, D.C.), the Manhattan School, the Juilliard School, and Lehman College, City University of New York, where he holds the position of Distinguished Professor of Music.

Among Corigliano's works are a violin sonata (1964); a clarinet concerto (1977), a flute concerto (*Pied Piper Fantasy*, 1981), as well as various other concertos; a Grammy Award–winning string quartet (1996); the score to the film *Altered States* (1980), for which he was nominated for an Academy Award; and the *Dylan Thomas Trilogy* (1961–1976, settings of Thomas's poetry for chorus and orchestra).

He is perhaps best known for his score to the film *The Red Violin* (1997), for which he received an Academy Award; his music for the opera *The Ghosts of Versailles* (1991), which was commissioned and premiered by the Metropolitan Opera, New York; and his Symphony no. 1 (1990).

The Symphony no. 1 was inspired by the loss of many of Corigliano's friends to AIDS. Commissioned by Sir Georg Solti and the Chicago Symphony Orchestra, the symphony is notable for its large scale and dark mood. Although inspired by the devastation of AIDS, the symphony stands on its own on purely musical terms, without regard to a specific historical context.

Its third movement, "Giulio's Song," includes a cello solo based on a theme improvised by Corigliano and his cellist friend Giulio Sorrentino. This movement inspired the separate, briefer chaconne *Of Rage and Remembrance* (1993), which was commissioned by gay men's choruses in Seattle, New York City, and San Francisco.

Scored for chorus and soloists (mezzo-soprano, boy soprano, two tenors, and two baritones), this work is set to poetry about loss by the poet and playwright William Hoffmann (who also provided the libretto for *The Ghosts of Versailles*) and farewells to various friends lost to AIDS; the work concludes with a verse from Psalm 23, "Yea, though I walk through the valley of the shadow of death," sung in Hebrew by a boy soprano.

The vocal score explicitly names friends of Corigliano and Hoffmann who have died of AIDS, and directs the singers to name friends whom they have lost to AIDS as well. Thus, the work is not only an occasional piece but also a continuation of the venerable tradition of communal choral lament.

The year 2000 saw the premiere of *Vocalise*, scored for soprano, orchestra, and live electronics; a song cycle based on verses of Bob Dylan; the *Suite from The Ghosts of Versailles*; and the Symphony no. 2 for String Orches-tra, which was awarded the Pulitzer Prize for music in 2001. Corigliano continues to produce extraordinary compositions.

—Robert Kellerman

BIBLIOGRAPHY

Carman, Joseph. "Corigliano's Big Score." *Advocate,* May 9, 2000, 59.

Cockrell, Dale. "Corigliano, John." *The New Grove Dictionary of American Music.* H. Wiley Hancock and Stanley Sadie, eds. 4 vols. London: Macmillian, 1986. 1:511–512.

Corigliano, John. *Of Rage and Remembrance; Symphony no. 1.* St. Louis Symphony Orchestra, Leonard Slatkin, conductor. Sound recording. RCA Victor, 1996.

SEE ALSO

Classical Music; Music and AIDS; Opera

Country Music

Country music, like blues and jazz, is a peculiarly American musical form. With its roots in the folk ballads of England, Scotland, and Ireland, country music was born in the blend of the "hillbilly" music of the Appalachian mountains, the African American blues of the deep South, and the wailing twang of the cowboy music of the West.

But country music is more than a combination of various musical traditions. Lyrics give life to country music and those lyrics tell the real stories of ordinary people. Country music celebrates the trials and triumphs, loves and losses in the lives of small-town, rural, and, more recently, urban and mostly white working people.

Because of its focus on conservative social groups and old-fashioned values, country music has often been associated with bigotry, intolerance, and jingoistic patriotism. However, every kind of personal lifestyle, quirk, and foible is represented on the back roads and in the small towns of the United States, and country music has found room to discuss most of them frankly. Although country is in some ways one of the most conservative of musical genres, country songs cover a wider range of topics than almost any other type of popular music.

Gay and lesbian audiences are attracted to the country scene for several reasons. First, the sincerity of country's exploration of the emotions and experiences of working people draws many disenfranchised Americans to the genre. Then, there are the outfits. Ever since country left its simple hillbilly roots behind, the pageantry of bouffant hair and spangled cowboy shirts has been as much a part of the country-music scene as wailing fiddles and moaning slide guitars.

Many gay men, unable to resist a pageant, are drawn to the campy side of country, even as they also appreciate the directness of the music's emotional appeal. The adulation of gay men has been particularly important to the legends of such larger-than-life country-music performers as Patsy Cline and Dolly Parton. Moreover, many gay men have been attracted to country music by the recent advent of such "country hunks" as Dwight Yoakum, Alan Jackson, and Billy Ray Cyrus.

Lavender Country

In 2000, an unprecedented intersection of the gay community and country music occurred when the album *Lavender Country* by the band of the same name was inducted into the Country Music Hall of Fame in Nashville, Tennessee, as the first openly gay country-music album. Released in 1973 by a Seattle organization called Gay Community Social Services, *Lavender Country* was the direct result of the newly erupting gay liberation movement.

Patrick Haggerty, the founder of the band as well as its main songwriter, grew up working on his family's small dairy farm in Port Angeles, Washington. Country music had been the soundtrack of his childhood, and when he became a radical gay activist, country was the natural vehicle for him to express both the newly public emotional life of gay men and their desire for social change. Songs like "Back in the Closet Again" and "Singing These Cocksucking Blues" added a new dimension to country's traditional themes of heartbreak and hope.

Other Gay Country Singers

Lavender Country has been followed by other gay country-music singers, many of whom were also raised on the country sound. Doug Stevens, songwriter and front singer with the Outband grew up in Tupelo, Mississippi, and left his country roots behind to study classical music. When his lover left him after learning that Stevens was HIV-positive, however, he found that composing country songs best expressed his pain.

Other gay country singers such as Sid Spencer, Mark Weigle, Jeff Miller, and David Alan Mors find a welcoming venue at events sponsored by the International Gay Rodeo Association, founded in 1985 to unite more than twenty gay rodeo organizations in the United States and Canada. In 1998, the Lesbian and Gay Country Music Association was formed to support gay country musicians and to promote country music within the gay community.

Lesbians and Country Music

Lesbians have always been drawn to strong women, and lesbian interest in country was often expressed in the early 1970s by widespread crushes on such apparently straight country singers as tough-talking Tanya Tucker, deep-voiced Anne Murray, and down-to-earth glamour girl Dolly Parton.

Probably the best-known lesbian country singer is Canada's k.d. lang, whose rich, sophisticated voice practically seduced the country world to take her in. Although lang released three acclaimed country albums (*A Truly Western Experience* in 1984, *Angel with a Lariat* in 1987, and *Absolute Torch and Twang* in 1989) and delighted lesbian audiences with her overtly butch appearance on stage, she did not come out as a lesbian until 1992. Since then, lang has drifted away from country, becoming mostly a pop singer.

Other lesbian singers came from the folk tradition and thus were comfortable with a country song or two, but few were mainly identified as country. Since the birth of women's music in the early 1970s, Alix Dobkin, Woody Simmons, Robin Flower, Teresa Trull, and Barbara Higbie have demonstrated a definite country influence when they appear at women's coffeehouses, clubs, and festivals. Groups like the Reel World String Band, Deadly Nightshade, and Ranch Romance draw crowds of hooting, foot-stomping lesbians to concerts that rival any country hoedown.

Country Western Dancing

In the mid-1980s, another phenomenon gained popularity among both gay men and lesbians—country western dancing. Drawn to the flash and polish of country line dancing and two-step, gay men and lesbians from Dallas to New York City and from Los Angeles to Toronto flock to country-music dance clubs.

They dress in bolos and pointy-toed boots and learn the Texas two-step and line dances with names like "Achy Breaky Heart" and "Boot-Scootin' Boogie." On these dance floors those who grew up listening to the Grand Ole Opry (country music's venerable showcase of talent in Nashville) meet with those who grew up listening to rock and roll to dress in costume and move in the tightly controlled syncopation of the cowboy dance.

Political Attitudes

There are, however, many within the lesbian and gay communities who decry the increased popularity of country music, pointing out that country speaks to a straight, conservative, white society and that many fans of country music are homophobic and racist. In particular, gay men and lesbians of color have often felt alienated by the country craze, seeing it as the glorification of those who enforced segregation in the South and destroyed Native American society in the West.

Still, queer lovers of country music can point to such stars as multiple Grammy winner Garth Brooks, who has been publicly supportive of gay rights. Brooks even released a song, "We Shall Be Free," that includes in its definition of liberty the freedom to love whomever you choose. Even when it created a storm of controversy, Brooks stood behind his song, leading many gay and lesbian country fans to hope that country music can, indeed, find a place for everyone.

—*Tina Gianoulis*

BIBLIOGRAPHY

Dickinson, Chris. "Country Undetectable: Gay Artists in Country Music." *Journal of Country Music* 21.1 (1999): 28–39.

"Gay Ole Opry." *Advocate*, December 15, 1992), 75.

The International Association of Gay/Lesbian Country Western Dance Clubs: www.iaglcwdc.org.

The Official Lesbian and Gay Country Music Association: www.lgcma.com.

SEE ALSO

Popular Music; Women's Music; lang, k.d.

Coward, Sir Noël   *(1899–1973)*

Noël Coward occupies a unique place in twentieth-century theater. An accomplished playwright, actor, composer, and lyricist, he was also a singer and cabaret performer, as well as a writer of short stories and an accomplished amateur painter. Most of all, he was a consummate man of the theater, whose wit and sophistication belied his humble origins and helped define the role he played as heir to Oscar Wilde: a brilliant observer who both mirrored and satirized the dominant society that had, in a real sense, co-opted him.

After earning success at a very early age, he was both the epitome of upper-class English manners and a satirist who exposed the foibles and hypocrisies of his age, especially in regard to heterosexual courtship. Although he was a popular playwright whose intent was ostensibly merely to amuse and entertain, he nevertheless challenged surprisingly directly many of his society's assumptions about love and sex, imbuing his work with a camp sensibility that disdained conventional sexual morality as the product of small-minded individuals and groups.

For most of his life, homosexuality was a criminal offense in England; hence, it is not surprising that Coward was not openly gay. Yet his homosexuality was an open secret among the cognoscenti in the theater and in the café society where he held sway for five decades. Moreover, in his plays, particularly *Private Lives* (1930) and *Design for Living* (1933), he rejected normative sexual values, which are presented as stultifying and unsatisfying, in favor of more adventurous, unconventional arrangements; and in his songs and cabaret performances he often intimated, through double entendre and allusion, his own unconventional sexual preference.

Life and Career

Born Noël Pierce Coward on December 19, 1899, in Teddington, a village near London, he was the son of an ineffectual piano salesman and a doting mother.

Although his formal education consisted of only a few years at the Chapel Royal Choir School, he was a voracious reader who in effect educated himself. Near the end of his life, Coward mused, "How fortunate I was to have been born poor. If Mother had been able to send me to private school, Eton and Oxford or Cambridge, it would probably have set me back years. I have always distrusted too much education and intellectualism."

After participating in amateur and community theatricals, Coward launched his professional acting career at the age of twelve, debuting on the West End in 1911. Having appeared frequently in West End productions during his adolescence, he made his film debut in D. W. Griffith's *Hearts of the World* (1917), starring Lillian and Dorothy Gish.

He was introduced to high society as a fourteen-year-old protégé of artist Philip Streatfield, who died during World War I, but it was Coward's own wit and charm that bought him entrée to a world of upper-class privilege that would otherwise have snubbed him because of his lower-middle-class origins and rather suspect profession. Exposure to this society helped shape both his own persona as the cosmopolitan bon vivant and the settings and characters that he would employ in his plays. Coupled with his early absorption of the bohemian attitudes of the world of the theater, his experience in British upper-class society also helped free him from the bonds of middle-class sexual morality and manners.

Coward, who had a genius for friendship, would later count among his friends such members of the British aristocracy as the Duke of Kent (with whom he may have had an affair), Lord and Lady Mountbatten, and Queen Elizabeth, the Queen Mother. His close friendships in the theatrical community included Gertrude Lawrence, Beatrice Lillie, Lawrence Olivier, Vivien Leigh, Alfred Lunt, and Lynn Fontanne, all of whom appeared in his plays. Perhaps more surprisingly, he maintained a close friendship with novelist Radclyffe Hall and her partner Una, Lady Troubridge.

Enormously energetic and prolific, Coward dominated British theater between the two world wars. His first full-length play, *I Leave It to You* (1920), was produced when he was only twenty-one. He soon began writing songs for both his own shows and those of others. He alternated between producing and writing (and often starring in) musical revues and operettas, the genre pioneered by his friendly rival Ivor Novello, and writing (and sometimes appearing in) more serious comedies. Among the works of these decades are *The Vortex* (1924), *Hay Fever* (1925), *Bittersweet* (1929), *Private Lives* (1930), *Cavalcade* (1931), *Words and Music* (1932), *Design for Living* (1933), and *Tonight at 8:30* (1936). These works, which often featured Coward paired with actress Gertrude Lawrence, established the playwright

and actor as a leading figure among the younger generation of popular entertainers. Although from the vantage point of the twenty-first century, the works of this period may seem merely light and amusing, they were with some justification viewed by many of Coward's contemporaries as threatening. One reviewer protested that the characters of *Private Lives* were "four degenerates" and described the play as "a disgusting exhibition of moral and social decadence." Such a reaction is one indication that Coward succeeded in raising questions about his society's complacent morality and smug certainties.

In the politically charged 1930s, many intellectuals dismissed Coward's plays and musicals as breezy entertainments irrelevant to the momentous events that would culminate in social revolution and world war. But to see these works as completely nonpolitical is to miss their subversiveness.

In a manner similar to Wilde's comedies, Coward's plays amuse, but they also expose his society's often concealed tensions and anxieties, especially in regard to sexual matters. Moreover, given the censorship imposed on the popular stage during this time, particularly regarding sexual matters, Coward's penchant for pushing the envelope is remarkable.

During the years of World War II, Coward not only entertained British troops around the world, but he also produced such characteristic works as *Blithe Spirit* (1942) and *Present Laughter* (1942). He also produced, directed, wrote, and starred in the patriotic film *In Which We Serve* (1942). One of his one-act plays is the source of David Lean's acclaimed wartime film *Brief Encounter* (1945).

The years following World War II were difficult ones for Coward, at least as a playwright. To many theatergoers, he had come to seem old-fashioned, representative of a particular period—the years between the world wars—that was now long gone. His plays repeatedly failed in the West End. Moreover, when he relocated, first to Bermuda and then to Jamaica, to avoid crippling postwar taxes, he was regarded as unpatriotic. In addition, he was recovering from a personal crisis: Soon before the war, his longtime romantic relationship with American stockbroker and business manager Jack Wilson had come to an unhappy end.

In the postwar years, Coward both found his life partner and redirected his career. In 1945, he fell in love with South African actor Graham Payn, who had as a boy appeared in some of Coward's revues. Although Coward attempted to make a star of Payn, casting him in several shows, Payn, though talented, lacked his partner's charisma and ambition and never achieved the stardom that Coward sought for him. Nevertheless, theirs was a close and satisfying relationship that lasted the rest of Coward's life. Among their theatrical and society friends, they were accepted as a couple.

Although Coward continued to produce plays on the West End, he more and more oriented his career toward America, frequently appearing on American television and—at the suggestion of his friend Marlene Dietrich—launching a successful cabaret act that, rather improbably, took Las Vegas by storm. He also prepared successful screenplays for films of such earlier works as *The Astonished Heart* (1950) and *Tonight at 8:30* (1952), and acquired a large house at Les Avants in Switzerland.

In the late 1960s and early 1970s, Coward was in effect "rediscovered," with several major revivals of his work in New York and London, and a belated recognition of his achievement. During this time, he also wrote his most daring play on the subject of homosexuality, *Song at Twilight* (1966), a play that features a gay novelist, Hugh Latymer (perhaps based on Coward's old friend W. Somerset Maugham), who weighs the costs of coming out and decides to remain in the closet.

Coward himself made a decision not to come out publicly, even after homosexuality was decriminalized in England in 1967 and New York's Stonewall riots of 1969 ushered in the period of gay liberation. When friends urged him to come out, he refused, saying, not altogether facetiously, "There are still a few old ladies in Worthing who don't know." Perhaps the real reason he refused to declare his homosexuality is that he knew that such a declaration would preclude the knighthood that he richly deserved but that had been withheld from him for so long.

The knighthood was finally awarded in 1970. In 1971, Coward received a special Tony Award for Lifetime Achievement in the theater. In 1972, musical revues based on his songs and sketches began successful runs in both London (*Cowardly Custard*) and New York (*Oh Coward!*).

During this period of renewed appreciation, on March 26, 1973, Coward succumbed to a stroke. He was buried on the grounds of Firefly, his home in Jamaica. Later, a plaque in Westminster Abbey's Poet's Corner was erected in his honor.

On December 9, 1998, with Graham Payn at her side, Queen Elizabeth, the Queen Mother, unveiled a statue of her longtime friend in the foyer of Theatre Royal, Drury Lane, London.

Theater Music

Coward's contribution to musical theater is primarily that of songwriter. Although his fully realized musicals seem dated, his songs (often written for revues) have a life beyond their original contexts and continue to charm by virtue of their wit and sophistication.

Songs such as "A Room with a View" (1928), "If Love Were All" (1929), "Someday I'll Find You" (1930),

"Twentieth Century Blues" (1931), "Mad Dogs and Englishmen" (1932), "Mad about the Boy" (1932), "Mrs. Worthington, Don't Put Your Daughter on the Stage" (1935), "A Marvelous Party" (1939), "Matelot" (1945), and "Sail Away" (1950) have become standards.

Coward's songs are notable for their diversity, ranging as they do from comic patter songs rooted in the English music hall tradition to witty, often sardonic observations on twentieth-century life, to sophisticated, bittersweet ballads that express loss and longing and loneliness. Coward's signature as a songwriter is his peculiar balance of humor and pathos.

In an essay entitled "How I Write My Songs," Coward explained that, although he had very little formal training as a musician, he had "a perfect ear for pleasant sounds." In writing music, he generally worked with a professional musician who wrote down the notes for him.

But what is distinctive about a Coward song is not its melody, but its lyrics. As a lyricist, Coward ranks with such songwriters as Lorenz Hart, Cole Porter, and Stephen Sondheim. Since most of his songs were written for characters in musicals or sketches or operettas, they usually express emotions rooted in particular situations or plots, but they often transcend those situations to give voice to universal feelings.

Some of his songs have become particularly identified with Coward's own persona, though they were originally sung by women. For example, "Mad about the Boy," particularly when performed by Coward himself, captures the giddiness and hopelessness of an infatuation with an unobtainable object of desire. "It's pretty funny but I'm mad about the boy, / He has a gay appeal, that makes me feel, / There's maybe something sad about the boy." In songs such as this, Coward both reveals and conceals the desire that cannot be named openly.

Coward began writing songs for his own plays and, having a slight voice, he intentionally made them vocally undemanding. His style of singing—really dialogue with music—exerted considerable influence on American musical theater.

Indeed, Alan Jay Lerner and Frederick Loewe wrote the part of Henry Higgins in *My Fair Lady* (1956) with Coward in mind, tailoring the songs assigned to Higgins to Coward's style. Because Coward refused to make commitments of more than three months to any role, the part actually went to Rex Harrison. However, all of Higgins's songs, such as "Why Can't the English" and "A Hymn to Him" echo earlier Coward classics such as "Mad Dogs and Englishmen."

Ironically, Coward's later musicals, *Sail Away* (1960) and *The Girl Who Came to Supper* (1964), were criticized for sounding too much like *My Fair Lady*.

Cabaret Performer

Coward was a journeyman actor who frequently took roles in his own plays. He sometimes appeared in the works of others, such as a 1953 London revival of Shaw's *The Apple Cart* and Carol Reed's 1959 film of Graham Greene's *Our Man in Havana*. But his greatest role was always himself, the suave British sophisticate.

In the 1950s and 1960s, Coward often appeared on American television, usually in specials such as the show *Together with Music: Noël and Mary Martin* (1955), for which he wrote several new songs. But his paramount success as a performer may have been in his cabaret act.

Developed quickly for what was to have been a four-week booking at London's Café de Paris in 1951, the act was an unexpected success. It was revived many times during the 1950s, most famously in Las Vegas in 1955. For the Las Vegas opening, Frank Sinatra chartered a plane to bring such Hollywood celebrities as Judy Garland, Lauren Bacall, and Joseph Cotten. The cabaret act not only solved Coward's money problems, but also made him known in America as someone who—British sophistication notwithstanding—could entertain ordinary people.

The cabaret act presented him alone on stage with just a pianist, his only prop a lit cigarette extending from a long holder. In his persona of the slightly jaded, unabashedly queer, upper-class Englishman, he performed his songs, told stories, and reminisced. However, he never indulged in self-congratulatory comments on his long career. In one of his funniest songs, "Why Must the Show Go On?," he admonished against such a temptation, saying "Gallant old troupers / You've bored us all for years."

In a tribute to the American songwriter Cole Porter, he penned new—even more risqué—lyrics to Porter's classic, "Let's Do It," referring to such contemporary personalities as Tennessee Williams and Senator Joseph McCarthy.

In a prescient review of Coward's cabaret performance, Kenneth Tynan justly remarked that the success of the act depended less on the content of the show than on the qualities embodied in Coward himself. "In Coward's case star quality is the ability to project, without effort, the shape and essence of an unique personality, which had never existed before him in print or paint. Even the youngest of us will know, in fifty years' time, precisely what we mean by 'a very Noël Coward sort of person.'"

Coward's cabaret performances spawned such albums as *Noel Coward at Las Vegas* (1955) and *Noel Coward in New York* (1957).

Coward's plays are frequently produced all over the world. His musicals are seldom mounted, but his songs can be heard on many fine recordings and in compilation albums and revues such as *Oh Coward!*, *Cowardly Custard*, and *Noel and Gertie*.

—Claude J. Summers
—Albert J. Carey

BIBLIOGRAPHY

Castle, Terry. *Noël Coward and Radclyffe Hall: Kindred Spirits.* New York: Columbia University Press, 1996.

Clum, John. *Something for the Boys: Musical Theater and Gay Culture.* New York: St. Martin's Press, 1999.

Hoare, Philip. *Noël Coward: A Biography.* New York: Simon & Schuster, 1995.

Kenrick, John. "Noel Coward 101." www.musicals101.com/noel.htm

Lahr, John. *Coward the Playwright.* London: Methuen, 1982.

Lesley, Cole, Graham Payn, and Sheridan Morley. *Noel Coward and His Friends.* New York: William Morrow, 1979.

Mander, Raymond, and Joe Mitchenson. *Theatrical Companion to Coward: A Pictorial Record of the First Performances of the Theatrical Works of Coward.* New York: Macmillan, 1957.

Morley, Sheridan. *A Talent to Amuse: A Biography of Noel Coward.* Garden City, N.Y.: Doubleday, 1969.

Sinfield, Alan. "Private Lives/Public Theater: Noel Coward and the Politics of Homosexual Representation." *Representations* 36 (Fall 1991): 43–63.

SEE ALSO

Musical Theater and Film; Cabarets and Revues; Garland, Judy; Hart, Lorenz; Mercer, Mabel; Porter, Cole; Sondheim, Stephen

Cowell, Henry   *(1897–1965)*

AMERICAN COMPOSER, PIANIST, THEORIST, AND TEACHER Henry Dixon Cowell was an important musical innovator who sought to create an "ultramodern" style based on the synthesis of Western, Asian, and African music. His brilliant career as composer and performer was severely damaged when he was arrested at the age of thirty-nine for having sex with a seventeen-year-old male and subsequently imprisoned.

The circumstances of Cowell's upbringing were unusual and influenced his personal and musical perspectives throughout his life. He was born on March 11, 1897, in Menlo Park, California, then a rural area southeast of San Francisco. For many years, he made his primary residence in Menlo Park. Cowell's parents, who divorced in 1903, were writers of anarchist bent who provided him with home schooling.

As a boy, Cowell was better acquainted with Appalachian, Irish, Chinese, Japanese, and Tahitian music than with European concert forms. In 1910, he came to the attention of Stanford University's Lewis Terman, a pioneer of intelligence testing. Terman took note of the boy's erudition, facility in conversation, and limited academic skills. He observed, "Although the IQ is satisfactory, it is matched by scores of others...but there is only one Henry." Terman later diagnosed the composer as not a "true homosexual," but someone delayed in his heterosexual development.

From the start of his career as composer and performer, Cowell was a musical innovator. His piano composition *The Tides of Manaunaun* (1912) was the first to include tone clusters (adjacent notes sounded simultaneously, requiring that the keys be struck with the arm or hand). *Aeolian Harp* (1923) was one of Cowell's first pieces to require performers to manipulate the strings of a piano directly, a practice later associated with the "prepared piano" technique of Cowell's student, John Cage.

In 1931, Cowell collaborated with the Russian engineer and musical inventor Léon Thérémin to develop an electronic keyboard instrument called the Rhythmicon.

Although he composed twenty symphonies, Cowell's five *Hymns and Fuguing Tunes* (1941–1945), orchestral and choral works based on early American hymnody, remain his best-known works.

Cowell was an untiring advocate of contemporary music and frequently acted as mentor to other composers. As a teacher in California and New York, his students included Cage, Lou Harrison, George Gershwin, and Burt Bacharach.

In 1925, Cowell organized the New Music Society of California. In 1927, he founded the quarterly *New Music*, which grew to include a concert series and record label. During the late 1920s and early 1930s, Cowell guided the Pan-American Association of Composers. In 1930, he published *New Musical Resources*, a book he had worked on since 1919. Besides these efforts, he disseminated his views on music in countless articles and interviews, frequently championing other American composers, particularly Charles Ives.

In 1936, Cowell's career halted abruptly when he was arrested for having sexual relations with a seventeen-year-old youth. Hoping for a lenient sentence, Cowell pled guilty, confessing not only the incident with the boy but other homosexual contacts as well. Rather than leniency, he received a sentence of one to fifteen years in prison.

Beginning his term in San Quentin Penitentiary in 1937, Cowell continued to compose, teach, and write. Although he was vilified by much of the press, he received loyal support from his family and many colleagues, including dancer Martha Graham and composer Percy Grainger. Of his close friends, only Ives, whose work he had supported so faithfully, cut off relations with him.

In 1940, Cowell was paroled, and he moved to White Plains, New York, accepting work as an assistant to Grainger. In 1941, he married Sidney Hawkins Robertson, an ethnomusicologist who had lobbied for his release and with whom he was to collaborate on a study of Charles Ives. In 1942, he received a pardon that enabled him to become a Senior Music Editor in the Office of War Information.

In later years, until his death on December 10, 1965, Cowell continued to write, teach, and (though less frequently) perform. He was the recipient of many grants and honors. A prolific composer, he inspired contemporaries and younger musicians to embrace both world music and innovative techniques.

Many friends and music historians, however, believe that he never lived up to the promise he had shown before the disaster of his arrest and conviction, though some attribute the decline of his influence to his (idiosyncratic) interpretations of non-Western musical forms rather than to the trauma of his imprisonment.   —*Charles Krinsky*

BIBLIOGRAPHY

Cowell, Henry. *New Musical Resources*. New York: Knopf, 1930.

Hicks, Malcolm. "The Imprisonment of Henry Cowell." *Journal of the American Musicological Society* 44 (1991): 29–119.

Nicholls, David. "Cowell, Henry (Dixon)." *The New Grove Dictionary of Music and Musicians*. Second ed. Stanley Sadie, ed. 29 vols. New York: Grove, 2001. 6:620–630.

———, ed. *The Whole World of Music: A Henry Cowell Symposium*. Sydney: Harwood Academic Publishers, 1997.

Skinner, Graeme. "Cowell, Henry." *Who's Who in Gay and Lesbian History from Antiquity to World War II*. Robert Aldrich and Garry Wotherspoon, eds. London and New York: Routledge, 2000. 107–108.

SEE ALSO

Classical Music; Cage, John; Harrison, Lou

Cunningham, Merce   *(b. 1919)*

ONE OF THE TWENTIETH CENTURY'S MOST INFLUENTIAL dancers and choreographers, Merce Cunningham is known for his innovations and originality. Adapting the theories of his collaborator and partner, the composer John Cage, and of the French painter and art theorist Marcel Duchamp, Cunningham pioneered in his use of chance in the creation of dance pieces and in a nonhierarchical approach to movement and staging.

Cunningham was born on April 16, 1919, in Centralia, Washington, the second of three sons of a successful attorney and his wife. He began studying dance at an early age. He attended the University of Washington for a year, then studied at the Cornish School for Performing and Visual Arts in Seattle, where he met composer John Cage, who was working there as an accompanist. The two eventually became lifelong companions and artistic collaborators.

While studying in Seattle, Cunningham became acquainted with the choreography of Martha Graham. In 1939, while attending a summer of dance classes at

Merce Cunningham, photographed by J. J. Guillén in 2000.

to dominate the 1950s New York art scene, but also provided a model of alternative creative process that has become the hallmark of postmodern art.

Influenced by Cage's use of chance in music, Cunningham applied the same thinking to dance and devised methods whereby decisions about movement sequences would be determined randomly and unpredictably. Retaining the turnout of classical ballet and the fluid upper body of modern dance, Cunningham also utilized many "ordinary" movements such as walking and running.

Cunningham deconstructed the traditions of Western stagecraft by placing equal emphasis on all parts of the performance space. In Cunningham's work, each dancer is considered the center of the space he or she occupies; wherever the dancer faces is "front." Together, Cunningham and Cage developed an aesthetic based on democracy of space and form in which all elements are considered equal in value.

In the summer of 1948, and each summer thereafter until 1957, when the college closed, Cunningham and Cage taught at Black Mountain College in North Carolina, an arts school known for its spirit of innovation. In 1952, at Black Mountain, they staged what is arguably the first multimedia event in America.

This work, entitled *Theater Piece #1*, combined elements of movement, music, visual art, and poetry, all presented simultaneously, with no aspect dominating. This interdisciplinary approach became a hallmark of Cunningham's later work as he collaborated with luminaries from the worlds of visual art and music.

In 1953, Cunningham formed the Merce Cunningham Dance Company, which began touring nationally by 1955. For five decades, it has occupied a unique place in American dance. The company continues to perform both new and revived works.

Ever the innovator, Cunningham embraced technologies such as film and video in the 1970s, producing works that are not merely recorded documents of live performances but video dance pieces unto themselves. In the 1990s, Cunningham began working with a complex computer program called Life Forms, which provides new methods for generating movements to be performed by dancers and which also allows for the creation of images to be used as projections in live performances.

Cunningham's work does not reveal itself as queer in terms of its content. While other choreographers might employ same-sex duets to evoke such content, Cunningham does not, since the combination of dancers is often determined randomly. Indeed, Cunningham's work de-emphasizes gender altogether.

Insisting that his dances are not psychological or in any way "about" him, he eschews an overtly political stance in favor of a collaborative model that may be said to

Mills College in Oakland, California, he met Graham, who invited the young man to dance with her company in New York.

In the fall of 1939, Cunningham became only the second man to dance with Graham's company. He created several key roles in major pieces for her and became a soloist, but he eventually grew weary of her emphasis on narrative and psychological content. He wanted to explore movement through space in a more direct manner, without metaphoric overlay.

In 1942, Cage joined Cunningham in New York, and by 1944 they had begun presenting their own programs. In 1947, the Ballet Society of New York (later known as the New York City Ballet) commissioned their ballet *The Seasons*. This work, with costumes and sets by Isamu Noguchi, proved a great success and established them as significant figures on the American dance scene.

Along with painters Robert Rauschenberg and Jasper Johns, Cunningham and Cage became part of a circle of young gay artists whose ideas not only challenged the macho self-expressive Abstract Expressionists, who were represent a queering of the creative process. The creative artist is removed from the center of the artistic endeavor. All hierarchies are dismantled and all alternatives are considered equal.

Cunningham's relationship with Cage endured for fifty-four years, until Cage's death in 1992. The personal and professional collaborations between the two men have made them role models for several generations of gay men and lesbians.

Now recognized as a seminal figure in twentieth-century American culture, Merce Cunningham has received numerous prestigious awards and honors, including the National Medal of Arts and membership in the American Academy and the Institute of Arts and Letters.
                                                    —*Jeffery Byrd*

BIBLIOGRAPHY

Banes, Sally, intro. *Art Performs Life: Merce Cunningham/Meredith Monk/ Bill T. Jones.* Philippe Verge, Siri Engberg, and Kelli Jones, eds. Minneapolis: Walker Art Center, 1998.

Cunningham, Merce. *The Dancer and the Dance: Conversations with Jacqueline Lesschaeve.* New York: Marion Boyars, 1985.

Fitzpatrick, Laurie. "Merce Cunningham, 1919– ." *Gay and Lesbian Biography.* Michael J. Tyrkus, ed. Detroit: St. James Press, 1997. 139–140.

Jordan, John Bryce. "Cunningham, Merce (1919–)." *Gay Histories and Cultures.* George E. Haggerty, ed. New York: Garland, 2000. 231–232.

Sylvester, David, et al. *Cage, Cunningham, Johns: Dancers on a Plane.* New York: Knopf, 1990.

SEE ALSO

Ballet; Dance; Set and Costume Design; Cage, John; Goode, Joe

Curry, John   *(1949–1994)*

JOHN CURRY'S COMBINATION OF ATHLETICISM AND grace brought him enormous success in both figure skating and dance. A five-time champion in his native Britain, he also won gold medals in world and Olympic competition.

Although it was a potentially career-destroying move, Curry came out publicly as a gay man before the 1976 Winter Olympics, becoming one of the very few elite athletes to come out while still competing. Throughout his career, he consistently spoke candidly about his sexual orientation.

Curry was born on September 9, 1949, in Birmingham, England, where his father was an engineer and factory owner. As a small child, Curry became fascinated with dance, but his father considered dancing inappropriate

for boys and firmly vetoed the idea of dance lessons. He did, however, allow young Curry to take up figure skating at age seven.

With his natural aptitude and dedication, Curry won his first competition a year later. He continued to meet with success and went on to win the British junior title in 1967.

Although Curry's father had agreed to let the boy become a figure skater, he showed little enthusiasm for his son's athletic endeavors. Only twice did he see Curry skate.

After his father's death, Curry, then sixteen, moved to London, where he began taking the long-denied dance lessons and worked part-time to eke out enough money to pay for coaching for his skating.

Curry placed second in the 1968 and 1969 British championships and won the first of his five national titles in 1970.

Like his contemporary Toller Cranston of Canada, with whom he shared a number of traits including his sexuality, Curry suffered from the prejudice of judges against his skating style, which emphasized grace and artistry, and which some considered "feminine," even though Curry also demonstrated mastery in jumping and other physically demanding aspects of the sport.

Curry's glory year was 1976. After a narrow victory over Robin Cousins in the British championships, he went on to win gold medals in the European Championships, the Olympic Games, and the World Championships. Curry had the honor of carrying the British flag at the opening ceremony of the Olympics, and after his triumph at the games, he was awarded the Order of the British Empire. He was also named England's sporting personality of the year.

Curry had come out publicly as a gay man prior to the Olympics, and upon his return to Britain he spoke openly about his sexuality.

Curry turned professional after his win at the World Championships. Saying that he "never could see the point of spending twelve years training to go dress up in a Bugs Bunny suit," he turned down lucrative offers from established ice shows and formed his own company, one that emphasized dance.

His *Ice Dancing* show was a hit on Broadway as well as in London, Los Angeles, and San Francisco. In his production Curry sought to explore the relationship between skating and dance. Twyla Tharp was among the choreographers with whom he collaborated.

Curry also did choreography for the first show and took an increasing role in subsequent productions, choreographing fifteen of twenty-four numbers in the 1984 version of the show. These included Johann Strauss's *Skater's Waltz*, which Curry performed with JoJo Starbuck, and an ensemble piece to Aaron Copland's *Rodeo*.

In addition to his skating career, Curry appeared in a number of plays, including a 1980 Broadway production of Alan Jay Lerner and Frederick Loewe's *Brigadoon* that was choreographed by Agnes de Mille. Curry's performance of the "Sword Dance" was a highlight of the show.

Curry saw AIDS take a toll in the skating world. "It is hard to watch people in that situation, and it was frightening when people started to become ill," he said, adding, "You start to think 'When is it going to be my turn?'"

It was in late 1987 that Curry found out that he, too, was HIV-positive. The following year, he participated in *Skating for Life*, a show to help fund AIDS research. His final skating performance, in 1989, was part of another AIDS benefit.

Diagnosed with full-blown AIDS in 1991, Curry returned to England to spend his last years with his elderly mother. He died on April 15, 1994, in Binton, Warwickshire.

Curry was held in high regard by the skating community. World and Olympic champion Peggy Fleming described him as "totally devoted to the art of skating," and Olympic medalist Paul Wylie lauded him as "the ultimate skater." In recognition of his artistic interpretation of the music of classical composers, Curry has been called the "Nureyev of the ice."

He was also much admired for his candor and courage in coming out despite the potential risk to his athletic career. Curry was always forthright in this regard. In a 1992 interview, he stated, "I never pretended not to be homosexual, ever."

—*Linda Rapp*

BIBLIOGRAPHY

Bird, Dennis L. "John Curry." Obituary. *Independent* (London), April 16, 1994.

Draegin, Lois. "Dancing on a Knife-Edge." *Newsweek*, August 6, 1984, 73.

Longman, Jere. "John Curry, Figure Skater, Is Dead at 44." *New York Times*, April 16, 1994.

Malone, John. "Curry, John." *The Encyclopedia of Figure Skating.* New York: Facts on File, Inc., 1998. 43–44.

"Skater Who Was One Jump Ahead." *Manchester Guardian Weekly*, April 24, 1994, 31.

Springs, Sonja. "The End of an Ice Age." *Observer* (April 17, 1994): 15.

SEE ALSO

Dance; Nureyev, Rudolf

Dance

WHILE PROSTITUTION MAY BE THE OLDEST PROFES-sion, dance is almost certainly the oldest art. Worshipping and attempting to communicate with the unknown also seem to have been around forever. Over the years, these primal forces—sex, art, and spirituality—have intersected and sometimes happily merged, as when ancient temple dancers fornicated with devotees, guiding them via religious ritual toward divine resurrection of the flesh, while simultaneously raising funds to repair the altar.

During France's glittering Belle Epoque at the end of the nineteenth century, the foyer de la danse at L'Opéra was an exclusive showroom of danseuses available for hire. Similarly, troops of boy-dancer prostitutes were active in the Muslim world for centuries and as late as the 1960s. Even today, Japanese geishas may be considered among the most sophisticated of dancer-prostitutes.

The connection between sexuality and dance is apparent as well in contemporary venues such as discos and clubs, where music and recreational drugs animate dancers to lustful frenzy. Less obviously, even conventional theatrical dance strives to provide its more passive audiences a vicarious erotic encounter with exquisite nubile bodies.

In the twentieth century, artistic dance has proven to be a haven for glbtq people, who have made significant contributions in almost every area, including as choreographers, performers, and teachers. A number of gay choreographers have also included, with varying degrees of explicitness, homoerotic content in their dances.

Dance as Art

Dance is ephemeral. It generally leaves no artifacts for archaeologists. But it is clear that even prehistoric human beings danced from many of the same impulses and for similar ends that motivate human beings today: to release adrenalin, to celebrate or to mourn, to attract sexual partners, to express exuberance or despair, and to participate in religious rituals.

As a bonding agent, dance has been a factor in the creation of great civilizations as different as those of ancient Egypt and Greece and the Aztecs and the Incas. In contrast, Christianity, perhaps fearful of the sexual energy expressed in dance, excised it from its rituals.

Dance is at once a communal expression and a theatrical spectacle. The evolution of dance from communal ritual and individual self-expression to observed spectacle and choreographed movement is complex, but as dance developed into an art form requiring professional dancers who performed for spectators it became highly codified.

The rules that govern Indian dance, for example, were set out in the fifth century C.E. in the *Natya Sastra* of Bharata and the *Abhinaya Darpana* of Nandikesvara. The Western art of ballet was formally established in 1588, when a textbook of ballet steps was published by dancing master Thoinet Arbeau.

Ballet became Europe's international theatrical artistic dance, but by the late nineteenth century it had been reduced to a vitiated form of divertissement in opera, except in Russia. There, under the bountiful patronage of the czars, ballet remained a vital cultural force.

In 1909, the nobleman Sergei Diaghilev brought a company of Russian dancers, with choreographers, artists, theatrical designers, and composers, from the Imperial Theaters to Paris. Soon thereafter he formed an international touring company, the Ballets Russes, which dramatically influenced all areas of art in the twentieth century.

The gay presence in classical ballet in the twentieth century has been remarkable. Ballet may even be said to be the first multinational "gay industry," encompassing patrons as well as choreographers, dancers, designers, composers, and audience.

Even a short list of the most important gay contributors to twentieth-century ballet would have to include the following names: Diaghilev and his dancer lovers Vaslav Nijinsky, Léonide Massine, Boris Kochno, Anton Dolin, and Serge Lifar; Frederic Franklin and Leon Danelian of the Ballet Russe de Monte Carlo; Oliver Smith and Antony Tudor of Ballet Theatre; Edward M. M. Warburg and Lincoln Kirstein of the New York City Ballet, along with their coterie of gay artists such as Paul Cadmus and George Platt Lynes.

In addition, there are such figures as Marquis George de Cuevas and Roberto Ossorio, who supported their own ballet companies; Sir Frederick Ashton of the Royal Ballet; Maurice Béjart, choreographer of great homoerotic works such as *Nijinsky: Clown of God* (1971) and *Songs of a Wayfarer* (1971), created for Paolo Bortoluzzi and the greatest and gayest superstar of them all, Rudolph Nureyev; Robert Joffrey and Gerald Arpino; Rudi Van Dantzig; Lar Lubovitch; David Bintley, who created the homoerotic *Edward II* (1995) for the Stuttgart Ballet; Matthew Bourne, who created a *Swan Lake* (1995) with all male swans; and the sublime actor/dancer Erik Bruhn.

Modern Dance

While the Ballets Russes revitalized ballet as an artistic form early in the twentieth century, another important development in dance at the beginning of the twentieth century was the emergence of *modern dance*—a loose term basically referring to any nonballetic artistic dance. Among the most influential pioneers of modern dance were three American women, Ruth St. Denis, Isadora Duncan, and Martha Graham, as well as a German woman, Mary Wigman.

It was in the field of modern dance, pioneered by sexually uninhibited straight or bisexual women, who—like St. Denis, Duncan, and Graham—loved gay men, that gay creativity found its most accepting space. The fact that modern dance, unlike some other theatrical dance forms, was not "big business" allowed it to disregard many of the discriminatory practices of stage and screen, where "morals" clauses often kept performers, including dancers, deeply closeted.

St. Denis, Shawn, and Mumaw

Ruth St. Denis (1879–1968), who had worked as an actress and dancer in commercial theater, experienced a revelation in 1904 when she saw an exotic poster advertising Egyptian cigarettes. The Art Nouveau poster combined the erotic and the exotic (features also exploited by the Ballets Russes), and St. Denis seized on these to create a vibrant stage persona and repertoire for herself and the immensely popular touring company she formed.

In 1914, St. Denis married a twenty-two-year-old gay man, the ambitious and sexually charismatic Ted Shawn (1891–1972), who became her dance partner. Shawn appeared at any opportunity in the scantiest of costumes. In 1915, they founded the Denishawn Dance School in Los Angeles, which became a significant artistic center from which many creative dancers emerged, most notably Martha Graham.

Burton Mumaw (b. 1912), a student of Shawn's, first danced with the Denishawn company in 1931. Mumaw and Shawn soon became lovers and life companions. Shawn separated from St. Denis in 1933 and formed his Company of Male Dancers. Mumaw and Shawn were the leading soloists of the new company.

The repertoire allowed for maximum display of flesh, as, for example, with Native American warrior dances, and the company sometimes performed in the nude. Shawn claimed that his intention was to reestablish in the minds of Americans the right of men to dance. It is hard to imagine that the audience did not see the Company of Male Dancers as a gay group. It was disbanded with the coming of World War II.

After the war, at his farm in the Berkshire Hills near Lee, Massachusetts, Shawn established the Jacob's Pillow Dance Festival. It became a dance center of international renown.

Isadora Duncan

Isadora Duncan (1877–1927) studied ballet as a child in San Francisco, and it was in rebellion against its strictures that she discovered her own form of moving to music, which she vaguely described as the expression of an inner urge or impulse. Her inspiration was the art of ancient Greece, which she claimed was antithetical to the decadence of the ballet.

Hence, she danced in loose "Greek" gowns, without a corset and without a body stocking, making her bouncing breasts a conspicuous feature of her performance. She also danced in bare feet, which caused great scandal at the time.

Duncan achieved tremendous success in Europe, but received a frigid reception in the United States, not least because of her scandalous private life and leftist political beliefs. Not only did she bear children out of wedlock, but she was known for sexual affairs with both men and women.

She also avidly endorsed the Soviet Union and communism, and late in her life married a young, gay Russian poet, Sergei Esenin. Her death in a freak automobile accident—she was strangled when her long scarf became entangled in the spokes of a wheel—ended what had become in many ways a tragic life, especially after the loss of her children in a drowning accident.

Martha Graham

Martha Graham (1894–1991) may be described as the Shakespeare of dance. Like her predecessors, she found a way for herself to dance theatrically, but she went beyond them to create a new art form, a movement language with its own unique grammar and vocabulary, a language as formal and sophisticated as that of the classic ballet. Moreover, she created in that language choreographies that are now a major contribution to the world's cultural dance heritage.

Graham's technique is now integral to all theatrical dance and is also employed in contemporary ballet choreography. A student and member of the Denishawn company, Graham made her debut as a choreographer in 1926. She performed as a soloist and developed a company of women who were fiercely devoted to her.

The titles of her early works—*Lamentation* (1930) and *Primitive Mysteries* (1931), for example—reveal Freudian concerns. *Letter to the World* (1940), based on the life of Emily Dickinson, is often called the first modern dance ballet.

Graham was fearless in dealing with sexuality. Some of her greatest work, for example *Clytemnestra* (1958) and *Phaedra* (1962), was inspired by Greek myth and drama, but it is most significant for its frank expression of women's lust for men. This primal subject found expression in Graham's own life when she fell in love with Erick Hawkins, an intellectual, bisexual dancer and sexual athlete famous for his stamina and for the size of his penis.

Graham and Hawkins were briefly married. Many members of her conventlike troupe of women were disgusted by the new dynamic in Graham's choreography, its adoration of male virility. When asked how she, among all choreographers of either sex, so well understood and appreciated the male sex, Graham replied, "Well, dear, I like men."

Theatrical Dance

The movie industry and stage musicals during the twentieth century utilized the talents of uncounted gay male and lesbian dancers and choreographers, but fear of homophobic reaction caused most of them to hide their sexuality. The two great dancing stars of the Hollywood musicals—Fred Astaire and Gene Kelly—were self-consciously heterosexual.

Astaire (1899–1987) was a most unlikely masculine icon, with his reed-slim, white-tie-and-tails elegance and effete appearance; but his witty songs, wisecracks, and nimble tap dancing won the public. In collaboration with gay dance director Hermes Pan, Astaire created innovative choreography for the cinema.

Gene Kelly (1912–1996), a hoofer imported from Broadway almost as an antidote to Astaire, came to fame in the post–World War II years. Kelly had a short body and a limited dance vocabulary, but he compensated for these limitations by dancing with great physical vigor. His persona was the wisecracking, blue-collar, all-American man.

His worst effort was his unwise attempt to show himself the equal of ballet dancers, in the film *Invitation to the Dance* (1956). His greatest performance was his virtuoso solo in *Singin' in the Rain* (1952). Some of Kelly's films are marred by an element of homophobia, an ingredient no doubt added to reassure the public that not all male dancers were queer.

Even though the term *chorus boy* (like *hairdresser*) was almost synonymous with *gay male,* the New York stage also attempted to deny or minimize the gay presence in its ranks. Such was also the case with the many television shows that employed their own companies of dancers during the heyday of the musical. Indeed, dance professionals such as the choreographers Agnes de Mille and Jerome Robbins, the latter himself bisexual, often overtly expressed their homophobia.

Robbins was particularly unusual for his ability to shift gears from musical theater to concert dance and back again. Although he pursued sexual relationships with men and women alike, he was deeply closeted about his bisexuality. Nonetheless, in *The Goldberg Variations* (1971), he choreographed a stunning male–male duet.

Among other gay and bisexual choreographers who have made original contributions to the dance element in Broadway musicals are Michael Bennett and Tommy Tune, both of whom were dancers and directors as well.

Limón, Hawkins, Nikolais, and Louis

Many of the most significant dancers and choreographers of modern dance are aesthetic descendants of Martha Graham.

José Limón (1908–1972), for example, was a handsome Mexican American with a heroic presence. He danced with great masculine force but without macho brutality. He first danced with the Humphrey-Weidman Company, and then after serving in World War II formed his own company, for which he created his most famous ballet, *The Moor's Pavane* (1949), based on Shakespeare's *Othello*. The ballet is a masterpiece whose theme is homosexual jealousy. Another work with deep moral sensibility and homoerotic subtext is *The Traitor* (1954), based on Judas's betrayal of Christ.

Erick Hawkins (1909–1994), Martha Graham's lover and catalyst, formed his own company after the end of his marriage to Graham, but he never escaped her shadow. He developed an abstract style influenced by Greek and Asian art, and created a repertoire in close collaboration with composer Lucia Dlugoszewski, whom he also married. Despite his marriage, he continued to pursue gay sexual liaisons actively throughout his life.

Alwin Nikolais (1910–1993) studied with Graham and Doris Humphrey, among others, and after service in World War II became director of the Henry Street Playhouse in Manhattan, a center for experimental theater where he developed his own company. At that time, Murray Louis (b. 1926), also just out of the service, became his student, his lover, his colleague, and life partner.

Nikolais's innovation was to choreograph movement for dancers who were encased in flexible costumes that completely obscured their human form. He was also a great lighting designer. Thus, Nikolais created the first truly "abstract" choreography, movement shaped with no connection to reality, which seemed to float in colored space.

Louis formed his own company and choreographed work noted for its comic timing and humorous style. The Louis and Nikolais companies later merged. Murray Louis continues to create new work.

Cunningham, Taylor, Ailey, and Falco

Merce Cunningham (b. 1919) was a leading dancer for Martha Graham, who created many roles for him, most notably the self-flagellating hero of *El Penitente* (1940). In 1942, Cunningham began an enduring relationship with the composer John Cage (1912–1992), who began to write scores for Cunningham's ballets.

Forming his own company in 1953, Cunningham became a leading light in the avant-garde. Cunningham says that his choreography depends for inspiration on neither music nor design, but on chance. Still, his later work appears tightly composed to music and uses many elements of classical ballet.

Paul Taylor (b. 1930), one of the giants of American dance, trained as a swimmer and so was in great shape when he came to New York in 1952 to study modern dance with Graham, Limón, Cunningham, and Humphrey, and ballet with Antony Tudor and Margaret Craske. Taylor first danced in Cunningham's company and then as a leading dancer in Graham's. He founded his own company in 1954, working closely with artist Robert Rauschenberg, who designed all of Taylor's ballets of the 1950s.

Taylor's work is quite varied, but always well calculated for the effects it would create. In the early piece *Duet* (1957), which is typical of the avant-garde spirit of the era, literally nothing happens. To Cage's "non-score," Taylor and his pianist make no movements. This exercise in nothing, of course, gained him and his company much publicity and commentary.

Although openly gay, Taylor evinces no particularly gay sensibility in his choreography. Indeed, it occupies the opposite pole to Graham's: There is very little sexual passion in his work. Although he has explored psychological darkness, his work can be joyous and humorous, and it sometimes expresses great tenderness for human frailty. Like Graham, Taylor reshaped the parameters of dance and attracted a new audience for a new art form.

Alvin Ailey (1931–1989) also studied with Martha Graham, among other teachers. After dancing on Broadway, Ailey formed his own company in 1957. *Blues Suite* (1958), one of his earliest works, defines the choreographer's particular genius. Deriving from blues songs and expressing the pain and anger experienced by African Americans, the work combines ballet, modern dance, jazz, and black dance techniques, plus flamboyant theatricality and intense emotional appeal. Ailey's masterpiece is *Revelations* (1960), which is based on African American spirituals and gospel music. It may be the most popular ballet created in the twentieth century.

A student of Graham and a protégé of Limón, Louis Falco (1942–1993) danced with Limón's company. Ravishingly beautiful, with a great frizz of hair in the flowerchild mode, he began to choreograph when he formed his own company in 1967. His early work was abstract, but he increasingly used decors and props designed by avant-garde artists. Eventually, he moved from modern dance to ballet, creating works for the Netherlands Dance Theater, the Ballet Rambert, and La Scala Ballet. He was the choreographer for the film *Fame* (1980).

Contemporary Choreographers

A number of contemporary choreographers are openly gay and often quite explicit in their depiction of homoeroticism and in presenting homosexual themes. There are also a smaller number of lesbian choreographers, although they have not yet won the kind of national and international recognition that the gay male and bisexual choreographers have achieved. Among the rising stars in lesbian dance are such figures as Anne Blumenthal, Jill Togawa, and Krissy Keefer. Togawa is associated with the Purple Moon Dance Project, and Keefer is artistic director of the Bay Area's Dance Brigade.

In the vanguard of openly gay male choreographers are Bill T. Jones, Mark Morris, Joe Goode, Stephen Petronio, and Peter Pucci, all of whom came to prominence in the 1980s and established their own companies.

Bill T. Jones, Mark Morris, and Joe Goode

African American choreographer Bill T. Jones (b. 1952) discovered dance while on a sports scholarship at the State University of New York at Binghamton, where he met photographer Arnie Zane, who became his lover and collaborator. In 1973, they formed American Dance Asylum and then in 1982 the Bill T. Jones/Arnie Zane Dance Company. Their first big success was *Secret Pastures* (1984), which featured settings by gay artist Keith Haring. Zane died of AIDS in 1988 and Jones is HIV-positive; hence, disease and aging (as well as homosexuality and racism) have been important themes in Jones's works.

Jones has become a dominant figure on the contemporary dance scene and continues to work with major collaborators. His compassionate ballet about terminal illness, *Still/Here* (1994), became the center of controversy when the *New Yorker*'s dance critic Arlene Croce branded it "victim art" without even having seen it. The controversy served only to bring the work greater attention.

Another important figure in contemporary dance is Mark Morris (b. 1956), whose work typically mixes elements of Eastern and Western cultures and the traditional with the avant-garde. He sets dances to a wide range of musical styles, from classical to baroque to rock, and he frequently explores sexual ambiguities.

From 1988 to 1991, Morris served as Director of Dance for the Belgian National Opera in Brussels. He brought to European audiences dances with a distinctly American flair. In 2001, the Mark Morris Dance Center opened in Brooklyn, providing Morris and his company a permanent space in which to create, rehearse, and teach.

Joe Goode (b. 1951) often explores gay and gender issues in his work. Formed in 1986, the Joe Goode Performance Group quickly became a significant San Francisco cultural institution. Goode's work frequently challenges traditional assumptions about gender roles: The women may lift the men, and both sexes may appear strong as well as vulnerable. Goode also forthrightly approaches topics such as the plight of sex workers and the devastation wrought by AIDS.

—*Douglas Blair Turnbaugh*

BIBLIOGRAPHY

Anderson, Jack. *The World of Modern Dance.* Iowa City: University of Iowa Press, 1997.

Chujoy, Anatole, and P. W. Manchester, comps. and eds. *The Dance Encyclopedia.* New York: Simon & Schuster, 1997.

Cohen, Selma Jeanne, ed. *International Encyclopedia of Dance.* 6 vols. New York: Oxford University Press, 1998.

Craine, Debra, and Judith Mackrell, eds. *The Oxford Dictionary of Dance.* New York: Oxford University Press, 2000.

SEE ALSO

Ballet; Ballets Russes; Set and Costume Design; Ailey, Alvin; Ashton, Sir Frederick; Béjart, Maurice; Bennett, Michael; Bruhn, Erik; Cage, John; Cunningham, Merce; Diaghilev, Sergei; Duncan, Isadora; Goode, Joe; Jones, Bill T.; Kirstein, Lincoln; Lifar, Serge; Morris, Mark; Nijinsky, Vaslav; Nureyev, Rudolf; Robbins, Jerome; Taylor, Paul; Tune, Tommy; Van Dantzig, Rudi

Davies, Sir Peter Maxwell   (b. 1934)

SIR PETER MAXWELL DAVIES IS PERHAPS THE MOST renowned living British composer, and certainly one of the most prolific, having composed over three hundred works encompassing virtually every genre of classical music. His music, which often incorporates influences outside the Western musical tradition or pushes beyond the boundaries of established musical style, is regarded by some critics as iconoclastic. It is probably more accurate, however, to describe the "new music" Davies has created as a synthesis of many diverse musical forms.

"Max," as Davies is familiarly known, was born on September 8, 1934, in Salford (now part of Manchester) in the north of England. He studied piano as a child and began composing at an early age. At eight, he made his musical debut, playing a piano piece of his composition on a BBC radio program for children. As his school provided little in the way of music education, Davies independently sought out various sources of unfamiliar music, including scores from libraries and radio programs.

Davies began his formal musical studies when he was admitted simultaneously to the Royal Manchester College of Music and Manchester University. He earned a master's degree from the University in 1956, after completing a dissertation on Indian ragas. In the same year, he received a degree in composition from Royal Manchester.

While at the College of Music, Davies, along with fellow students Alexander Goehr, Harrison Birtwistle, Elgar Howarth, and John Ogdon, formed New Music Manchester, a performing ensemble dedicated to avant-garde music. Davies subsequently embarked on further studies in Rome and at Princeton.

From 1958 to 1961, Davies was the music headmaster at Cirencester Grammar School. His experiences in musical pedagogy had a profound effect on his composition style, which became more theatrical and less complicated as a result of teaching children.

While at Princeton, Davies began performing his first opera, *Taverner*, based on the life of sixteenth-century English composer John Taverner and incorporating many elements of the earlier composer's music. Davies worked on this ambitious composition, for which he also wrote the libretto, for over six years, then had to reconstruct portions of it after the manuscript score was partially destroyed by a fire.

By the time of the opera's debut in 1972, Davies was already known for his daring, edgy works, particularly in musical theater. Among the most notable of these is *Eight Songs for a Mad King* (1969), in which the vocalist, portraying King George III in his late, insane years, sings and talks to his birds, represented by various instruments.

Because Davies and his colleague Birtwistle were displeased with performances of their works by traditional ensembles, they formed, in 1967, the Pierrot Players (reconfigured and renamed the Fires of London in 1971), an experimental chamber group of instrumentalists and vocalists specializing in the intimate-scale musical theater pieces that the two composers produced during the 1960s.

In order to be surrounded by a natural silence in which to create his works, Davies moved to the Orkney Islands, in the North Sea off the coast of Scotland, in 1970. In this remote setting, his compositions became less severe, much clearer in their harmonies, softer, and—inspired by the folk traditions of the islands—more upbeat.

In the decade following relocation, Davies produced a prodigious number of works in various genres. Perhaps the most notable of these are the theatrical piece *Miss Donnithorne's Maggot* (1974), the chamber operas *The Martyrdom of St. Magnus* (1977) and *The Lighthouse* (1980), and his eight symphonies.

Although he continued to compose prolifically throughout the 1980s and 1990s, Davies has, since 1999, decided to compose less and focus primarily on works for chamber orchestra. His recent works include, nonetheless, an opera, *The Doctor of Myddfai* (1996), and the *Antarctic Symphony* (2001), the latter inspired by the composer's journey to the South Polar continent.

Davies was knighted by Queen Elizabeth II in 1987. While he is rather taciturn about his private life, he is quite open about being gay, and he is a patron of various gay causes, including the Lesbian and Gay Foundation (based in Manchester, his birthplace) and the Scottish Homosexual Rights Group.   —*Patricia Juliana Smith*

BIBLIOGRAPHY

Aldershot, Richard McGregor, ed. *Perspectives on Peter Maxwell Davies.* Burlington, Vt.: Ashgate, 2000.

Bayliss, Colin, ed. *The Music of Sir Peter Maxwell Davies: An Annotated Catalogue.* Beverley: Highgate, 1991.

Griffiths, Paul. *Peter Maxwell Davies.* London: Robson Books, 1982.

Seabrook, Mike. *Max: The Life and Music of Peter Maxwell Davies.* London: Gollancz, 1994.

Smith, Carolyn J., ed. *Peter Maxwell Davies: A Bio-bibliography.* Westport, Conn.: Greenwood Press, 1995.

SEE ALSO

Classical Music; Opera

Del Tredici, David   (b. 1937)

PULITZER PRIZE–WINNING AMERICAN COMPOSER AND pianist David Del Tredici, known for his famous "Alice" works and neo-Romantic style, has also written music concerned with gay experience.

Del Tredici was born on March 16, 1937, in Cloverdale, California. He was a child prodigy at the piano. He made a solo debut with the San Francisco Symphony in 1954, and continued performing as a concert pianist until 1960.

He enrolled as an undergraduate at the University of California, Berkeley, in 1955, initially studying piano. His first composition, *Soliloquy* (1958), written at the summer Aspen Festival, caused Darius Milhaud to encourage him to become a composer. On his return to Berkeley, Del Tredici studied composition, receiving his B.A. in 1959. He went on to Princeton to study with Roger Sessions and Earl Kim, receiving an M.F.A. in 1964.

Del Tredici's compositional ability met with a wealth of early recognition. In 1966, he received a Guggenheim fellowship and spent the summer as composer in residence at the Marlboro Festival. Aaron Copland invited him to composition seminars at Tanglewood.

Del Tredici has taught at a number of institutions, including Harvard (1966–1972), the State University of New York at Buffalo (1972–1973), Boston University (1973–1984), the City University of New York (1984 to the present), and Yale (1999), as well as at the Manhattan School (1991–1993) and Juilliard (1993–1996).

In 1980, Del Tredici was awarded a Pulitzer Prize for *In Memory of a Summer Day*, one of his "Alice" works for soprano and orchestra. He has received commissions from American and European orchestras and from the Koussevitzky and Fromm Foundations, and was composer in residence for the New York Philharmonic (1988–1990).

Until 1967, most of his works were in an atonal style, and many were based on texts by James Joyce. Since then, he has written almost exclusively in tonal styles and has been a strong proponent of tonal music.

For a long time, Del Tredici's fame rested on his series of vocal and instrumental works based on Lewis Carroll's Alice books, notably *Pop-Pourri* (1968, revised 1973), *An Alice Symphony* (1969, revised 1976), the popular Bicentennial commission *Final Alice* (1975), the four-movement *Child Alice* (1981), and his first opera, *Dum Dee Tweedle* (1995). Many of these works are remarkable for their idyllic sensuality, but an overlay of dissonant harmonies and the use of unexpected instruments give the neo-Romantic sound a postmodern edge.

Del Tredici detached himself from Carroll to write three large, dissonant works for orchestra, *March to Tonality* (1985), *Tattoo* (1986), and the threatening *Steps* (1990). However, the real turn in his career came in 1996, when he attended a workshop in gay sexuality and self-acceptance held by Body Electric, a national organization devoted to such workshops.

During that workshop, he set two overtly gay poems for voice and piano. This led to the composition of a number of songs based on gay texts and experiences. For instance, a setting of Paul Monette's "Here" was dedicated to Del Tredici's lover Paul Arcomano, who died of AIDS in 1993; a setting of Allen Ginsberg's "Personals Ad" was dedicated to gay activist Jody Dalton, director of Composers Recordings Inc.; and a setting of Thom Gunn's "Memory Unsettled" was dedicated to Del Tredici's mother, who died in 2000, and who had accepted her son's life choices.

These songs became the core of the cantata *Gay Life* (1996–2001, premiered by the San Francisco Symphony under Michael Tilson Thomas in May 2001). A related collection is *Brother* (1997–2001), a song cycle created with drag performance artist John Kelly, which premiered at P.S. 122 in New York in May 2001.

Since 1996, Del Tredici has made a number of changes in his life, which have been not only discussed in public interviews but also reflected in his compositions. He has written more than fifty songs on texts by American poets, including the monodrama *Dracula* (1999), based on a text by gay poet Alfred Corn.

Del Tredici met his life partner, Ray Warman, in 1999, and the couple held their commitment ceremony in 2000.

—*Paul Attinello*

BIBLIOGRAPHY

Del Tredici, David, et al. "Contemporary Music: Observations from Those Who Create It." *Music and Artists* 3 (1972): 11–23.

Galvin, Peter. "Silent Nights: Renowned Classical Composer David Del Tredici Talks about Life, Loneliness, and Sexual Addiction." *Advocate,* August 22, 1995, 46.

Rockwell, John. "David Del Tredici: The Return of Tonality, the Orchestral Audience and the Danger of Success." *All American Music: Composition in the Late Twentieth Century.* New York: Knopf, 1983. 71–83.

Schwarz, K. Robert. "Composers' Closets Open for All to See." *New York Times,* June 19, 1994.

SEE ALSO

Classical Music; Conductors; Copland, Aaron; Tilson Thomas, Michael

Diaghilev, Sergei   *(1872–1929)*

THE RUSSIAN NOBLEMAN SERGEI (OR SERGE) PAVLOVITCH Diaghilev revolutionized music, the visual arts, theater, and dance, and he set the course of the arts for the twentieth century. He discovered talent and nurtured it to fulfillment in breathtaking productions of art exhibitions, concerts, operas, and, especially, ballets.

Sergei Diaghilev.

Diaghilev brought together the talents of his discoveries—artists such as Vaslav Nijinsky, Igor Stravinsky, Jean Cocteau, Pablo Picasso, Michel Fokine, Léonide Massine, and George Balanchine, to name only a few—to assemble an unsurpassed "total theater."

The ultimate vehicle for his protean genius was the Ballets Russes, the company he created and first presented in Paris in 1909. Although especially noted for superb male dancers, Ballets Russes featured startlingly modern music, innovative choreography, erotic scenarios, and strikingly original scene designs.

Diaghilev's genius and his extraordinary knowledge of all the arts, from painting to music, led him to discover and inspire genius in others and to facilitate the collaboration of his discoveries. Perhaps most important of all, he had an appreciation of the new and distinctly modern and was thus able to help shape a new art for a new century.

Unabashedly homosexual, Diaghilev was a passionate man in all his endeavors. "It is absolutely necessary for me to make love three times a day," he told his friend the composer Lord Berners. Although his homosexuality was frequently noticed unfavorably by officials and rivals, he made no apologies.

Homophobic critics had their revenge after his death in biographies that, while praising him as a creative genius, stressed this "deep flaw" in his character, without recognizing that his homosexuality may have been integral to his creativity.

Most malicious and dishonest of all was a biography of Nijinsky by his wife, Romola Nijinska. From 1909 until 1913, Diaghilev and the dancer had been the most famous gay couple in Europe; though their union could produce no children, it gave birth to masterpieces.

Estranged from Diaghilev after his marriage, Nijinsky became depressed and delusional and was committed to a mental hospital by his wife. To vindicate herself, Romola Nijinska portrayed Diaghilev as a homosexual Svengali whose unwanted sexual advances drove Nijinsky insane, and fashioned herself as the virtuous wife caring for Diaghilev's victim. This scenario titillated a fascinated public and both fed on and contributed to the pervasive prejudices against homosexuals and homosexuality at the time, but it was far from the truth.

Diaghilev's love affairs have sometimes been characterized as exploitative, but a more accurate account would stress the element of pedagogic love that infused them. He was attracted to a series of beautiful young men in whom he saw qualities of genius and with whom he could merge in creative collaboration.

At the age of eighteen, he fell in love with his cousin Dmitri (Dima) Filosofov, also eighteen, with whom he published an influential art journal, *Mir Iskusstva* (*The World of Art*). The relationship lasted fifteen years, until Filosofov left Diaghilev for another man.

Soon after this break, Diaghilev saw the dazzling young Nijinsky dance. He created the Ballets Russes as a showcase for his new lover, and in so doing he brought to fruition both his and Nijinsky's genius. Their affair lasted from 1909 until Nijinsky married in 1913.

Diaghilev's next discovery was an unknown young actor, Léonide Massine, whom he developed into a great dancer and one of the seminal choreographers of the twentieth century. They were together until 1920, when Massine married.

Diaghilev successively fell in love with Boris Kochno, a precocious young poet who eventually became associate director of Ballets Russes; Anton Dolin, a vivacious British dancer; Serge Lifar, a young Russian dancer who traveled to Paris in 1924 determined to seduce Diaghilev and who became the *premier danseur* of Ballets Russes and, later, the director of the Paris Opera Ballet; and Igor Markevitch, a musical prodigy.

Although known for his possessiveness and controlling nature, Diaghilev inspired love and admiration in his partners, as their autobiographies attest. Moreover,

Diaghilev's sexual relationships were integrally related to his artistic achievements. As Markevitch observed, "I would say that the greatest works created by the Ballets Russes were a direct result of love affairs."

With Lifar and Kochno at his bedside—along with his women friends Misia Sert, Coco Chanel, and Baroness Catherine d'Erlanger—Sergei Diaghilev, "the Czar of the Arts," died of complications from diabetes in Venice in 1929.   —*Douglas Blair Turnbaugh*

BIBLIOGRAPHY

Buckle, Richard. *Diaghilev.* London: Weidenfeld and Nicolson, 1979.

Garafola, Lynn. *Diaghilev's Ballets Russes.* New York: Oxford University Press, 1989.

Grigoriev, S. L. *The Diaghilev Ballet 1909–1929.* London: Constable, 1953.

Lifar, Serge. *Diaghilev: His Life, His Work, His Legend. An Intimate Biography.* London: Putnam, 1940.

SEE ALSO

Dance; Ballet; Ballets Russes; Set and Costume Design; Ashton, Sir Frederick; Béjart, Maurice; Berners, Baron Gerald Hugh Tyrwhitt-Wilson; Doone, Rupert; Falla (y Matheu), Manuel de; Kirstein, Lincoln; Lifar, Serge; Nijinsky, Vaslav; Poulenc, Francis; Smyth, Dame Ethel; Szymanowski, Karol Maciej

Dietrich, Marlene   *(1901–1992)*

PROBABLY NO ONE, GAY OR STRAIGHT, OF ANY GENDER, could tear her or his eyes from the sight of Marlene Dietrich, leaning back with lewd abandon, grasping a shapely gartered leg as she growled out her signature song, "Falling in Love Again." That song, and the role of Lola Lola, the sizzling slut with a heart of ice, brought Dietrich to international stardom in Josef von Sternberg's landmark 1930 film, *Der blaue Engel (The Blue Angel).*

Born Maria Magdalene von Losch on December 27, 1901, to a bourgeois family in Berlin, Dietrich had been a promising student of the violin until a hand injury forced her to give up playing. In 1924, she married Rudolf Sieber, a film director who introduced her to acting; but it was Josef von Sternberg who would be the most powerful influence on her career.

In *Der blaue Engel*, von Sternberg created a powerful allegory of German society and spirit in the aftermath of World War I. Within this allegory, Dietrich's character symbolized a harsh and unfeeling decadence that threatened both to captivate and to destroy what was good and innocent in German culture.

Although Dietrich had had several previous film roles, her portrayal of Lola Lola crystallized her stage persona forever. While that persona would be softened and glamorized for her American films, for the rest of her career Marlene Dietrich would be the dangerously sexy femme fatale with the cool and sardonic exterior.

In the early 1930s, both von Sternberg and Dietrich left Germany and its rising Nazi party to settle in the United States. Dietrich soon became a deliciously controversial figure in American cinema. Although she remained married to Rudolf Sieber, the relationship was what would later be called an "open marriage." They remained close, but did not live together, and both had other relationships, often publicly.

Marlene Dietrich.

Dietrich always retained her Continental sophistication, and she scandalized society almost as much by wearing trousers in public as by her numerous love affairs with both men and women. In the 1930 film *Morocco*, audiences were shocked and titillated when Dietrich's character, a nightclub singer in glamorous top-hat-and-tails drag, finishes a number by kissing a female audience member on the lips.

According to Marjorie Rosen, the actress once said, "In Europe it doesn't matter if you're a man or a woman. We make love with anyone we find attractive." Rumors of her numerous affairs with such celebrities as Frank Sinatra, John Kennedy, Edith Piaf, and writer Mercedes de Acosta only added to the Dietrich mystique.

Dietrich became an American citizen in 1937. During World War II, she denounced the German government and, at some risk, entertained Allied troops abroad. After the war, she followed a successful film career with an equally successful cabaret act. Her cool, knowing, self-mocking persona appealed both to gay men and lesbians, who composed a significant portion of her nightclub audiences.

In some ways, however, the actress felt trapped by her own glamorous image; and, as she grew older, she became obsessed with concealing her changing body.

In 1975, the last of several onstage falls resulted in a broken leg, and Dietrich finally retired from performing altogether. She moved to Paris and lived the rest of her life in semiseclusion, surrounded by mementos of her career and her romantic exploits.

Dietrich died in Paris on May 6, 1992. At her request, she was buried beside her mother in Berlin. She was welcomed back to the city of her birth by the tributes of her friends and fans, and over the protests of neo-Nazi groups and others who considered her support for the Allied cause in World War II treasonous.

—*Tina Gianoulis*

BIBLIOGRAPHY

Dietrich, Marlene. *Marlene.* Salvator Attanasio, trans. New York: Grove Press, 1989.

Riva, Maria. *Marlene Dietrich: By her Daughter, Maria Riva.* New York: Knopf, 1993.

Rosen Marjorie. "A Legend's Last Years: To the Very End, Marlene Dietrich Lived Out Her Life a Daring Original." *People,* June 1, 1992, 42.

Schickel, Richard. "The Secret in her Soul." *Time,* May 18, 1992, 72.

Spoto, Donald, *Blue Angel: The Life of Marlene Dietrich.* New York: Doubleday, 1992.

SEE ALSO

Cabarets and Revues; Divas; Set and Costume Design; Drag Shows: Drag Kings and Male Impersonators; Pierce, Charles; Porter, Cole

DiFranco, Ani   *(b. 1970)*

INDEPENDENCE AND INDIVIDUALITY ARE THE HALLMARKS of the life of singer Ani DiFranco. Once called "the thinking person's acoustic punk feminist," she has drawn on an eclectic mixture of musical traditions to create a style distinctly her own. Her music is characterized by an extensive vocal range, percussive guitar technique, and intensely personal lyrics. In order to preserve her artistic freedom, she founded a recording company, Righteous Babe, that has become extremely successful.

DiFranco has never hesitated to defy convention or to speak her mind. She has been forthright in expressing her views on political and social issues and has been candid about her bisexuality.

DiFranco, born September 23, 1970, is a native and lifelong resident of Buffalo, New York.

She got her first guitar at the age of nine and befriended the salesman, a local musician who brought her to his shows. Within about a year, he began including her in them, launching her musical career.

When DiFranco was fifteen, her parents divorced. Not wanting to leave Buffalo, she had herself declared an emancipated minor and supported herself by working at local clubs (though she was under-age) until she graduated from an arts high school.

She moved to New York City to play in clubs, but soon embarked on a nationwide tour, living out of her car as she moved from one gig to the next. Fans clamored for albums of her work. Having recorded none, she borrowed $1,500 to make cassettes and sold them as she toured.

DiFranco put out her first album, *Not So Soft*, on her own label, Righteous Babe, in 1991 (though the company was not officially incorporated until 1993). Righteous Babe, which DiFranco describes as "a people-friendly, sub-corporate, woman-informed, queer-happy, small business that puts music before rock stardom and ideology before profit," has always been based in Buffalo. DiFranco has demonstrated her commitment to her hometown not only by providing jobs but also by contributing to civic projects, including historic preservation.

DiFranco has declined offers to sign with major recording companies in order to maintain artistic control of her career. She credits Scot Fisher, president of the company and her former lover, with building the successful business. By 2004, Righteous Babe had sold more than three million recordings.

For a number of years DiFranco was the label's only artist, but she is a prolific one, having produced over twenty albums by 2004. She has also created a notably diverse body of work.

Originally a solo singer and guitarist, she used an aggressive playing technique to lend force to her performances. Eventually she added a band, but she returned to her roots with *Educated Guess* (2004), which she produced herself and on which she plays all the instruments.

DiFranco has always been open about her bisexuality, stating in a 1994 interview that "in any marginalized community, whether people identify themselves or not affects us all." From the beginning, she has written and sung intensely personal songs about her love for women as well as men. As a result, gay men and, especially, lesbians have been an important segment of her fan base from the start of her career.

Some felt betrayed, however, when she made an opposite-sex relationship the centerpiece of her album *Dilate* (1996) and subsequently married her male lover, her sound engineer, Andrew Gilchrist, in 1998. The couple divorced five years later.

DiFranco has never been loath to tackle political and social issues in her music, addressing such topics as racism, gun violence, domestic abuse, and corporate culture. A self-described "fierce patriot," she has expressed her love for her country in "Grand Canyon" (on *Educated Guess*) and her reaction to the events of September 11, 2001, in "Self Evident" (on *So Much Laughter, So Much Shouting*, 2002). The latter poem, begun in New York on that date, dared to question American foreign policy.

Although DiFranco writes most of her own songs, she also performs those of others. Her rendition of Dusty Springfield's "Wishin' and Hopin'" was featured in the film *My Best Friend's Wedding* (1997), with Julia Roberts and Rupert Everett.

Ani DiFranco, photographed by Danny Clin.

Previously honored with four Grammy nominations, DiFranco won her first award (shared with Brian Grunert) for art direction on *Evolve* (2003).

DiFranco spends considerable time touring, but Buffalo remains her home base. She also maintains apartments in New York and New Orleans, a city she calls "a musical epicenter," adding "I just go there to be fed." She has set up a recording studio there, as a sanctuary where she can develop creative ideas.

That she has become a successful businesswoman seems to have come as a surprise to the antiestablishment DiFranco, who has spurned major record labels and their marketing strategies, such as elaborate videos and expensive advertising campaigns, in favor of a sparer and more intimate operation. Nonetheless, her approach garnered an industry award for Righteous Babe as best mid-sized independent label.

That DiFranco has achieved recognition as an artist, however, comes as no surprise to her loyal fans or to critics. A *Billboard* reviewer called her "one of the smartest lyricists in music today" and "the sexiest voice on the scene," and cited her "typical disregard for expectations or the flavor of the month."

DiFranco has chosen to use her talent to speak for social justice and joyously proclaim her own identity.

—*Linda Rapp*

BIBLIOGRAPHY

Billboard, March 17, 2003, Entertainment News section. Album Review.

"DiFranco, Ani," *Current Biography Yearbook*. Elizabeth A. Shick, ed. New York and Dublin: H. W. Wilson Company, 1997. 141–145.

Goldscheider, Eric. "At Home with Ani DiFranco; At 33, Singer's Finding Her Place in the World." *Boston Globe*, December 4, 2003.

Lloyd, Emily. "Ani DiFranco Has Lots of Luck with Girls." *off our backs* 24 (November 30, 1994): 12.

Navarro, Bruno. "Ani's Solitary Confinement." *Sunday Telegraph* (Sydney), February 22, 2004.

Norman, Michael. "Ani DiFranco a Self-made Star." *Cleveland Plain Dealer*, March 30, 1997.

Saxberg, Lynn. "Righteous Babe Returns; Ani DiFranco Is Touring without Her Band, But with Plenty of Her Trademark Attitude." *Ottawa Citizen*, November 23, 2002.

Sturges, Fiona. "A Singer and Wrong-righter; Ani DiFranco Has Been a Protest Singer since She Was a Child." *Independent* (London), February 6, 2004.

Violanti, Anthony. "A Righteous Guy; Scot Fisher Is Ani DiFranco's Right-hand Man When It Comes to Selling CDs and Making Sure Buffalo Gets Its Due." *Buffalo News*, November 9, 1999.

SEE ALSO

Popular Music; Women's Music; Rock Music

Disco and Dance Music

PERHAPS NO OTHER POPULAR ART FORM IS MORE closely identified with gay culture than disco and dance music. Gay men in particular adopted the intense, loud, throbbing 4/4 beat of the dance music predominating at the bars and discos that were among the few places where they could openly express their sexual identities in the 1970s and 1980s. As the musical backdrop for generations of gay men who came of age and discovered an entirely new gay world in such venues, dance music became inextricably connected with the gay experience.

While dancing to music has, of course, an extraordinarily long history, the contemporary popular genre known as dance music began with the disco craze of the 1970s. Disco, in turn, found its roots in the memorable beats of black funk and rhythm and blues from the late 1960s and early 1970s.

Early Disco

Disco can perhaps be divided into several phases. Early disco (1970–1975) included early 1970s rhythm and blues hits such as "Rock the Boat" by The Hues Corporation (1973). While eminently danceable, early disco often lacked many of the distinguishing features that would later be associated with disco music, such as the clap track (the sound of clapping hands counting the beat) or the soaring choruses of violins.

The success of the 1974 instrumental hit "Love's Theme" by the Love Unlimited Orchestra (led by rhythm and blues great Barry White) and the novelty song "Do the Hustle" (1975) by veteran performer Van McCoy signaled the arrival of a new sound, smooth and frothy, just perfect for the mid-1970s revival of elaborate dance steps. In fact, one of the primary characteristics of disco was just how often the songs themselves were about dancing.

High Disco

High disco (1976–1980) is the sound most often associated with disco by the general public. It reached something of a climax in 1977 with the film *Saturday Night Fever* and its side track full of hits by the Bee Gees (which remains among the best-selling albums of all time). The same year saw the opening of a virtual temple to the disco lifestyle, Studio 54, where gays and straights of all ethnicities danced to the music that had been born in black and gay clubs a few years previously.

For gay audiences, the undisputed queen of disco during these years was Donna Summer. From the highly sexualized moans and groans of "Love to Love You Baby" in 1976 to "On the Radio" in 1980, Summer (in collaboration with the Swiss composer Giorgio

Moroder, who pioneered the use of electronic music in disco as well as the extended remix) had a string of number one hits that made her name synonymous with disco and herself much adored by gay fans.

Postclassic Disco

During disco's postclassic period (1980–1982), its earlier momentum slowed in the face of increasingly violent negative reactions on the part of its foes, who saw disco as shallow, effete, and to a great extent, too queer. Postclassic disco thus went largely undercover and was heard primarily in gay clubs. It nevertheless saw the creation of club hits such as Sharon Redd's "In the Name of Love" (1982).

During the 1980s, disco's detractors celebrated what they deemed "the death of disco." But, in reality, disco never died. Instead, it became absorbed into the broader realm of popular music in the context of the arrival of New Wave and Punk Rock.

Dance Music

By the 1990s, Disco had already returned as a new genre with a new name: dance music. Its survival and triumphant reemergence was ensured by 1980s performers such as Madonna, whose 1983 release "Burning Up" combined a New Wave techno sound with the traditional disco beat; the twelve-inch single, long-play version was a staple in gay bars, and Madonna soon became a gay icon for the 1980s and beyond.

As dance music continued to evolve, by the twenty-first century it split into innumerable subgenres: house, trance, hypno, jungle, and many other subtle combinations and variations. Electronically produced, digitally manipulated sounds predominated.

Disc jockeys became celebrities in the 1990s, selling mixes and remixes of dance songs whose primary attraction was neither the vocalists nor performers, but the mixing talents of the DJs.

And throughout the complex evolution of disco and dance music, gays have remained its most loyal fans.

—*Joe A. Thomas*

BIBLIOGRAPHY

Andriote, John-Manuel. *Hot Stuff: A Brief History of Disco.* New York: Harper-Collins, 2001.

Goldman, Albert. *Disco.* New York: Hawthorn Books, 1978.

SEE ALSO

Dance; Popular Music; Rock Music; Allen, Peter; Boy George (George O'Dowd); Mathis, Johnny; Sylvester

Divas

THE TERM *DIVA* WAS ORIGINALLY AN ITALIAN WORD meaning, quite simply, goddess. Within the culture of Italian opera, the word came to signify a type of mortal female divinity: a soprano (or, in some cases, a mezzo-soprano or contralto) with tremendous musical virtuosity and a flair for the grandiose, a singer who deeply touched her audience's emotions with her performance and thus derived an often fanatic and obsessive admiration from her devotees.

In the twentieth century, particularly in the United States, the concept of the diva has expanded to include popular singers—for example, Judy Garland (1922–1969), Billie Holiday (1915–1959), and Dusty Springfield (1939–1999)—whose emotive qualities and, in many cases, personal sufferings made them objects of admiration and identification for their fans.

More recently, the title *diva* has become rather less meaningful, as it seems now to be bestowed on any female singer who displays extreme emotions or a bad attitude, as evinced by the various "VH1 Divas Live" television concerts.

Still, regardless of how the title is employed, the diva has traditionally played a significant role in both gay and lesbian culture as an object of cult worship with whom those who suffer the heartaches of forbidden love and ostracism from an unaccepting society find solace and identification. In this sense, the diva is, for her queer following, a mortal divinity.

Opera Divas

If opera has long maintained a certain queer appeal, it may well reside in the fact that opera has always provided a space in which, through performance, the boundaries of sex, gender, and sexuality are often blurred.

The *castrati*—that is, castrated male singers who flourished in the eighteenth century and had cult followings to rival those of female divas—played heroic male roles and also female roles in places where women were banned from the stage.

In their wake, female mezzo-sopranos and contraltos assumed the male leads that were once the sole possession of the castrati and, subsequently, performed male romantic roles in many nineteenth- and early-twentieth-century operas. Thus, opera provided a respectable venue for queer expression without naming it as such.

The cult of the diva, however, was not originally a solely gay or lesbian invention. By the nineteenth century, numerous prima donnas had devoted followings similar to those now associated with movie stars and rock stars. The image of the diva as flamboyant, extravagant, and temperamental—altogether larger than life in her demeanor—began to take hold, much as it had for the castrati.

Maria Malibran (1808–1836), her sister Pauline Viardot (1821–1910), Giulia Grisi (1811–1869), and—perhaps most notably—Jenny Lind (1820–1887) all evoked overwhelming emotions in fans of every sexual persuasion and background. This rather universal appeal, though, was probably the result of opera being, to a great extent, still a popular art form in the nineteenth century.

As the twentieth century dawned and other forms of entertainment became more accessible to mainstream audiences, the identification with and admiration of the diva became more clearly identified with gay and lesbian culture, and, indeed, many of the more prominent divas of the period were presumed to be lesbian or bisexual.

Lesbian Diva Worship

Even before the advent of the Hollywood movie star, the operatic prima donna was often the idol of adoring female fans. In the early twentieth century, much of this homoerotic adulation, which Terry Castle calls "lesbian diva worship," was directed toward two figures in particular, the Swedish-born American soprano Olive Fremstad (1871–1951) and the Scottish soprano Mary Garden (1874–1967). Both were women of ambiguous sexuality who specialized in performing provocative, gender-bending roles.

Fremstad was best known for her Wagnerian heroines and seductresses (Brunnhilde, Kundry, Ortrud, Venus) as well as her Carmen, Tosca, and Salome. After her return to the United States in 1903, Fremstad quickly emerged as one of the biggest stars of the Metropolitan Opera, where, in 1907, she starred in the scandalous first Met production of Richard Strauss's *Salome*, based on Oscar Wilde's Decadent play.

Garden was noted for her forward performance style and was the foremost interpreter of many of the amoral female roles of *fin de siècle* French opera, including the leads in Gustave Charpentier's *Louise*, Claude Debussy's *Pelléas et Mélisande*, and Jules Massenet's *Manon*, *Thaïs*, *Sapho*, and *Cléopâtre*.

Garden was celebrated for her trouser roles (that is, male roles sung by a woman). In 1907, she made her American debut (upon which she was hailed as "Mary Garden, Superwoman"); from 1910 until her retirement in the 1930s, she was the leading soprano of the Chicago Opera.

Neither Fremstad nor Garden ever married, and, consequently, both were the focus of much speculative gossip—as well as several *romans à clef*—regarding their sexuality. Fremstad lived for a number of years with her secretary, Mary Watkins Cushing; their relationship is fictionalized—and pathologized—in Marcia Davenport's novel *Of Lena Geyer* (1936). A more heroic portrait of Fremstad can be found in *The Song of*

the Lark (1915), written by that consummate lesbian opera fan Willa Cather. Garden was rumored to have been a lesbian.

The biographical facts about either woman's sexuality remain speculative; what is significant, however, is the role these women played in reaching a vast female audience through their homoerotically charged artistry.

Lesbian diva worship has generally focused on certain singers who have specialized in heroic or gender-bending roles, generally mezzo-sopranos or, in some cases, dramatic sopranos. As such, more recent operatic divas who have had significant lesbian cult followings include the mezzo-sopranos Brigitte Fassbaender (b. 1939) and Tatiana Troyanos (1938–1993) and dramatic soprano Jessye Norman (b. 1945).

Gay Male Diva Worship

It is perhaps too broad a generalization to claim without reservation that while lesbian diva worship is based on desire, gay male diva worship is based on identification. In queer culture, the lines between identification and desire are frequently blurred; critic Stacey DíErasmo, in discussing Dusty Springfield, has observed that the diva almost inevitably raises "that quintessentially queer question: do you want to be her or have her?"

Be that as it may, gay male diva worship, in contrast to the lesbian variety, has traditionally centered on more vulnerable figures, those who might well be described as "tragedy queens." A case in point is the continued gay male adulation paid to the memory of Maria Callas (1923–1977), known to her fans as *la Divina*.

Surely one of the most exciting singing actresses of the twentieth century, Callas specialized in playing the ill-fated and often emotionally fragile heroines of Italian opera who suffer and die for love. This tragic quality carried over into her turbulent personal life as well, in her well-publicized romantic involvements, her heartbreaks, and, ultimately, the loss of her vocal powers.

As Wayne Koestenbaum has explained, this devotion to Callas involves a highly complex system of psychic associations, arising from the conditions informing gay life, particularly social marginalization. Further, as Richard Dyer suggests, minoritized groups tend to exhibit a particularly intense need for cult icons with whom to identify as a response to and enactment of their exclusion from the mainstream.

Thus, as Callas was associated with presumably elitist high culture (and was a controversial figure even within that rarefied realm), devotion to her would mark her fans as different from the ordinary (that is, heterosexual) cultural consumer.

A simpler explanation, though, is that gay and lesbian audiences, given their all too frequent rejection by society, are drawn to divas because these extraordinary, often larger-than-life figures perform a cathartic function by embodying, whether in their performances or in their own lives, all the heartache, grief, humiliation, and suffering that almost inevitably play a large role in queer life.

Expansion of the Cult of the Diva

Accordingly, the cult of the diva, particularly in post–World War II culture, has expanded beyond the realm of opera into popular music as well. Holiday, Garland, and Springfield, for example, all evoked tremendous emotional responses through their performances, suffered publicly from overwhelming personal disaster and substance abuse, and died prematurely—and all had significant gay followings. Springfield, who was herself a lesbian, had a significant lesbian following as well.

As previously suggested, the term *diva* has lost much of its significance in recent years, thanks in great part to the mass media. Attitude or emotionality rather than virtuosity now would seem to be the deciding criteria in bestowing the title. Thus, numerous young female pop singers appropriate the term for themselves. Indeed, it would seem that one need not even be female or, for that matter, a singer in order to call oneself a diva.

This is not to say that there are no longer divas deserving of that distinction. A short list of grand divas among contemporary opera singers would surely include Renée Fleming, Deborah Voigt, Lorraine Hunt Lieberson, Kathleen Battle, Susan Graham, and Jane Eaglen. And there are great living pop divas as well, including Dolly Parton, Barbra Streisand, Bette Midler, Cher, Celine Dion, and Madonna, many of whom have considerable queer followings. For as long as we remain an excluded group, we will need the diva, the cathartic figure who embodies and expresses our joys and sorrows.

—*Patricia Juliana Smith*

BIBLIOGRAPHY

Bronski, Michael. *Culture Clash: The Making of Gay Sensibility*. Boston: South End Press, 1984.

Castle, Terry. "In Praise of Brigitte Fassbaender: Reflections on Diva Worship." *En Travesti: Women, Gender Subversion, Opera*. Corinne E. Blackmer and Patricia Juliana Smith, eds. New York: Columbia University Press, 1995. 20–58.

D'Erasmo, Stacey. "Beginning with Dusty." *Village Voice*, August 19, 1995.

Dyer, Richard. *Heavenly Bodies: Film Stars and Society*. New York: St. Martin's Press, 1987.

———. *Stars*. London: British Film Institute, 1998.

Gallagher, Lowell. "Jenny Lind and the Voice of America." *En Travesti: Women, Gender Subversion, Opera*. Corinne E. Blackmer and Patricia Juliana Smith, eds. New York: Columbia University Press, 1995. 190–215.

Koestenbaum, Wayne. *The Queen's Throat: Opera, Homosexuality, and the Mystery of Desire*. New York: Poseidon, 1993.

Leonardi, Susan J., and Rebecca A. Pope. *The Diva's Mouth: Body, Voice, Prima Donna Politics*. New Brunswick, N.J.: Rutgers University Press, 1996.

Matheopoulos, Helena. *Diva: Great Sopranos and Mezzos Discuss Their Art*. London: Victor Gollancz, 1991.

———. *Diva: The New Generation: The Sopranos and Mezzos of the Decade Discuss Their Roles*. Boston: Northeastern University Press, 1998.

Wood, Elizabeth. "Sapphonics." *Queering the Pitch: The New Gay and Lesbian Musicology*. Philip Brett, Elizabeth Wood, and Gary C. Thomas, eds. New York: Routledge, 1994. 27–66.

SEE ALSO

Opera; Castrati; Classical Music; Popular Music; Disco and Dance Music; Drag Shows: Drag Queens and Female Impersonators; Garland, Judy; Springfield, Dusty

Divine (Harris Glenn Milstead)   *(1945–1988)*

A VERSATILE CHARACTER ACTOR, NIGHTCLUB SINGER, and international cult star who generally performed his stage show and movie roles in drag, Divine first became famous through his appearances in John Waters's films of the late 1960s and early 1970s.

Born Harris Glenn Milstead on October 19, 1945, in Towson, Maryland, the future actor grew up in Baltimore suburbs. His parents, Bernard and Diana Francis Milstead, were generous and indulgent, perhaps because Harris was picked on at school for being plump and effeminate. At the age of twelve, the family moved to Lutherville, another Baltimore suburb. The family lived just six houses from a boy Harris's age named John Waters.

Waters, who became a neighborhood friend, was responsible both for creating Milstead's stage name, supposedly a religious reference, and for crafting a host of outrageous roles for him.

Two scenes in particular from Waters's films contributed to Divine's cult status. In *Pink Flamingos* (1972), Divine eats real dog feces so that her character can prove she is "the filthiest person alive." In *Female Trouble* (1975), the Divine character Dawn Davenport gets sexually attacked by dirty-old-man Earl, also played by Divine (with help from a body double for certain shots).

Other films in which Divine appears include *Polyester* (1981) and *Hairspray* (1988), directed by Waters; *Lust in the Dust* (1984), directed by Paul Bartel; and *Trouble in Mind* (1985), directed by Alan Rudolph.

After beginning in films, Divine gained celebrity in the mid-1970s by performing campy stage plays and disco acts in San Francisco. In the late 1970s and early 1980s, Divine made films and performed in clubs around the world. He became famous in Australia, England, the Netherlands, and Israel, as well as in the United States.

Although Divine often had difficulty releasing records in the United States, his hits such as "Walk Like a Man" and "I'm So Beautiful," both released in 1985, became popular both at home and abroad. During the 1980s, Divine was a frequent guest on talk shows and cable television programs, and often appeared at celebrity events. But a life constantly on the road began to take its toll on the performer.

Professionally, Divine yearned for greater Hollywood stardom and for recognition of his talent, both in and out of drag, as a character actor. In his personal life, Divine faced worry over his romantic involvements, increasing weight, and financial difficulties.

In 1988, when Waters cast him in *Hairspray* as a leading lady—in addition to a cameo as a male character—Divine's personal and professional situations began to improve. With the film's success came publicity and offers for more interesting roles, as well as the possibility of the stardom Divine desired. However, in a sad twist of fate, Milstead died in his sleep on March 7, 1988, soon after the film's opening, the victim of an enlarged heart.

Divine's appeal to audiences springs not only from his innate talent and likeableness, but also from his willingness to do absolutely anything, no matter how bizarre or subversive, in his quest for fame.

As a film actor, Divine constructed serious characterizations even in roles that called for him to perform outlandish actions. On stage and in personal appearances, he exhibited the same measure of control and professionalism. He created a stage persona marked by raunchy humor and sarcastic exchanges with audience members; but he could also moderate this persona by projecting a more subdued appearance and a calm, avuncular demeanor.

Today, with recent video releases and television airings of his films, Divine's wild looks, expressive gestures, strong delivery, and undeniable talent continue to attract new fans.

—*David Aldstadt*

BIBLIOGRAPHY

Bernard, Jay. *Not Simply Divine*. New York: Simon & Schuster, 1993.

Waters, John. *Shock Value*. New York: Thunder's Mouth, 1981.

SEE ALSO

Cabarets and Revues; Drag Shows: Drag Queens and Female Impersonators

Doone, Rupert (1903–1966)

ENGLISH DANCER, CHOREOGRAPHER, PRODUCER, AND teacher of drama Rupert Doone had a varied and distinguished artistic career. He danced the ballet with strength, energy, and originality. His choreography was inventive and often challenging for the performers. With his partner, Robert Medley, he founded the Group Theatre, which in the 1930s produced plays by W. H. Auden and Christopher Isherwood, among others.

In his work with the Group Theatre and at the Morley College School of Drama, where he taught and produced plays, he was known for his imagination and artistic integrity, and for his ability to surround himself with gifted people and nurture their talents.

Doone was born Reginald Ernest Woodfield on August 14, 1903, in Redditch, Worcestershire, where his father was a skilled worker in a needle factory. His mother came from a farming family.

Doone ran away from home to become a dancer. Arriving in London at age sixteen with no money, he led a precarious existence, scraping by on what he earned modeling at the Royal Academy and the Slade School of Fine Art in order to afford lessons at Madame Serafina Astafieva's School of Ballet. He also studied with Margaret Craske, with whom he would perform in 1927 in the Nemchinova-Dolin Ballet in pieces that he choreographed.

Despite a late start in dance, Doone made rapid progress. After only a few years of study, he gave his first professional performance in Basil Dean's production of James Elroy Fleck's play *Hassan*. On that occasion he changed his name to Rupert Doone.

At age nineteen, Doone went to Paris, where he partnered the legendary dancer Cléo de Mérode, who described him as having an "astonishing allure."

Doone was the featured soloist of the Ballet Suédois during the 1923 Paris season but left the company after its American tour as a result of a dispute about costumes.

Soon after arriving in Paris, Doone met and became the lover of Jean Cocteau. In 1924, Doone collaborated with Cocteau on the production of his *Romeo and Juliet* and also danced in the piece.

Through Cocteau, Doone met Sergei Diaghilev, who offered him the opportunity to dance in the *corps de ballet* of the Ballets Russes. Doone declined, feeling that he deserved a more important place in the company.

Doone returned in 1924 to London, where he worked in variety and revue. He understudied Léonide Massine in C. B. Cochran's *Keep on Dancing*. In 1925, he staged and performed in the dances in Nigel Playfair's production of Sheridan's *The Duenna*.

In November 1925, Doone met and fell in love with the painter Robert Medley, with whom he would spend the rest of his life. The following spring, the two went to

Paris. Doone, better known there than in England, hoped for more rewarding professional opportunities. Medley continued his study of painting.

Doone worked with Vera Trefilova and partnered her in her last performances on a tour in Berlin. On his return to Paris, Doone joined Ida Rubenstein's company for the 1928 season. He worked with choreographer Bronislava Nijinska and danced in Ravel's *Boléro*, among other pieces.

Diaghilev, impressed by Doone's performances, again offered him a place in the Ballets Russes—this time as a soloist—and Doone accepted. In July 1930 at Covent Garden, he had solo roles in two ballets: *Cimarosiana*, a work excerpted from Domenico Cimarosa's *L'Astuzie femminili*; and *Aurora's Wedding* (*Le Mariage d'Aurore*), a ballet created by Nijinska from the first and last acts of Tchaikovsky's *Sleeping Beauty* with reorchestration by Igor Stravinsky.

Doone was looking forward to more principal roles and possible opportunities to choreograph for the Ballets Russes, but when Diaghilev died in August 1930, the company lacked direction, and the quality of its work declined. Doone left the company after a tour in Monte Carlo, and he and Medley returned to England.

Doone's departure from the Ballets Russes was a turning point in his career. He did not give up dance entirely, but, believing that he would never again have as important a professional opportunity and fearing that rheumatism might shorten his career, he decided to concentrate his efforts on choreography and theater. His wish was to create "a theatre of all the arts."

In 1930, Doone joined the Festival Theatre in Cambridge, under the direction of Tyrone Guthrie. His first acting role, in Lion Feuchtwanger's *Warren Hastings*, was an important supporting one, but he proved a slow study when it came to memorizing lines, so Guthrie subsequently used him mostly in walk-on parts.

He did, however, have a dancing role in James Bridie's *Tobias and the Angel*. Medley recalled the dance as a "brief but spectacular moment" that earned Doone the enthusiastic approval of audiences and the respect of the other members of the company for his ideas and theatrical discipline.

In 1932, Doone was invited to choreograph a ballet for the recently formed Vic-Wells Ballet. To the music of Ravel's *Le Tombeau de Couperin* he created *The Enchanted Grove*, a work of great originality. Dame Ninette de Valois, one of the principal dancers along with Anton Dolin and Alicia Markova, recalled that she "adored" her role in the ballet and found Doone brilliant but demanding to work with.

Also in 1932, Doone and Medley formed the Group Theatre. Medley described Doone's vision for it as "a creative theatre, in which collaboration [among direc-

tors, actors, designers, musicians and others] would lead to a new sort of expression unknown in English theatre at that time."

They approached the young poet W. H. Auden about providing an original work, and in 1933 he wrote a multimedia piece, *The Dance of Death*. In the 1934 production of the work, Doone appeared as Death the Dancer. The production was enthusiastically received by audiences and recognized, as Medley put it, as "something quite new and vital to the English stage."

Auden subsequently wrote several plays with Christopher Isherwood that were produced at the Group Theatre. Doone directed and produced these works—*The Dog Beneath the Skin* (1936), *The Ascent of F6* (1937), and *On the Frontier* (1939)—and Medley served as the principal set designer.

The Group Theatre also featured the earliest works of Benjamin Britten, T. S. Eliot's *Sweeney Agonistes* (1935), and plays by Stephen Spender and Louis MacNiece. Other contributors to the Group Theatre include William Butler Yeats, Duncan Grant, Havelock Ellis, Richard Masefield, Harold Nicolson, Anton Dolin, and Mary Skeaping.

The beginning of World War II in 1939 brought an end to the heyday of the Group Theatre, which closed down for the duration of the war. Doone stayed in London, contributing to the development of a theater school at Morley College, while Medley volunteered for service in the armed forces, first as an official war artist and later as a member of the Royal Engineers working on camouflage.

The Group Theatre was revived in 1946 and continued productions until 1951, but never regained its former prominence.

Doone continued working at Morley College until 1962. He began suffering from a loss of motor control, which proved to be due to multiple sclerosis. He underwent electrical treatments to try to alleviate the condition, but to no avail.

Medley was frustrated in his efforts to care for Doone by a doctor who "saw no reason to discuss his patient's medical affairs with a person who had no legal rights to information." He was subsequently able to find another doctor, Bevan Pritchard, who respected their relationship.

In 1965, Medley retired from the Camberwell School of Arts and Crafts, where he had taught since 1958, to care for Doone. In the fall of 1965, however, Doone required hospitalization. He died on March 3, 1966.

In his memoir *Drawn from Life* (1983), Medley wrote of Doone, "To all things, personal and professional, Rupert brought an irrepressible enthusiasm for life, and a sense of humour that was positively bucolic, and sometimes rumbustious; for those who knew and loved him best it is the sheer fun of his company that is most immediately remembered. He was the wind that stirred and ruffled the waters."

—*Linda Rapp*

BIBLIOGRAPHY

Medley, Robert. *Drawn from Life*. London: Faber and Faber, 1983.

Morris, Geraldine. "The Story of Rupert Doone." *Dancing Times* 75 (April 1984): 580–582.

Wentinck, A.M. "Doone, Rupert." *Who's Who in Gay & Lesbian History from Antiquity to World War II*. Robert Aldrich and Garry Wotherspoon, eds. London and New York: Routledge, 2001. 132–133.

SEE ALSO

Ballet; Ballets Russes; Britten, Benjamin; Diaghilev, Sergei; Ravel, Maurice; Tchaikovsky, Pyotr Ilich

Drag Shows: Drag Kings and Male Impersonators

A DRAG KING IS ANYONE, REGARDLESS OF GENDER OR sexual preference or orientation, who consciously makes a performance of masculinity. Drag king theater can be raw, raunchy, and confrontational, as well as slick, funny, and entertaining. A recent arrival in the drag arena, drag kings are part of an international drag movement that emerged in London and San Francisco in the mid-1980s.

Del LaGrace Volcano describes seeing her first drag king act in 1985 as part of a strip show for lesbians. Much of the foundational work for drag king culture occurred first in San Francisco, and then in New York and London. There are now drag king performances and competitions in Europe and Australia, as well as in most major cities in North America.

The shifting status of transgender practices within the queer subculture has resulted in a renaissance of drag that has taken it into the mainstream culture of mass media, fine arts, and high fashion. Thus, the actress Demi Moore has been featured in a suit and facial hair in an *Arena* magazine drag spread. Drag kings have also appeared prominently in such varied mainstream publications as *Marie Claire*, the *New York Post*, the London *Times*, *Penthouse* magazine, and *The Face*.

The difference between a male impersonator and a drag king is the latter's ability to make an entertaining show out of male impersonation. Drag kings are also different from other male impersonators who cross-dress in that male clothing is merely a part of their performance of masculinity. They generally do not fetishize male clothing.

The Theatrical Tradition

Although the drag king movement is part of the recent renaissance of drag, it must be seen in the context of the history of cross-dressing and male impersonation. In the simplest terms, cross-dressing occurs when one sex wears the clothes of the other for any reason. The term *drag* is thought to be a colloquialism from the Elizabethan and Jacobean period of English history, when male actors performed female parts in a transvestite theater.

Although this practice ceased after the Restoration of Charles II in 1660, when female actresses were introduced to the English stage, the inversion of roles continued but with a twist. Instead of boys or men playing female roles, women often impersonated men on stage in the "roaring girl" roles that featured the actress in breeches.

Male drag is a staple of theatrical and cinematic tradition. Examples range from the famous stage performances of Sarah Bernhardt as Hamlet and (more recently) Pat Carroll as Falstaff, to the operatic convention of *travesti* or "trouser roles" in which mezzo-sopranos sing male roles, to the memorable presences in male attire of movie actresses as varied as Clara Bow, Greta Garbo, Marlene Dietrich, Katharine Hepburn, and Julie Andrews.

Some entertainers, such as blues singer Gladys Bentley, who sang about "bull-daggers" while dressed in tuxedo and tails, sexualize the cross-dressing.

Although cross-dressing always has a potential to destabilize assumptions about gender and sexuality, the impersonation of men, even by black lesbians, usually has not been seen as threatening when presented as entertainment. Consequently, drag kings usually are greeted with enthusiasm even by predominantly heterosexual audiences.

Cross-Dressing in Real Life

In real life, cross-dressing generally is not accepted with such aplomb, however. Some women, such as the writer George Sand or the painter Rosa Bonheur, successfully created a masculine persona or dressed in male clothes in order to be taken seriously for professional reasons, and their performance of masculinity seems to have had few negative consequences.

Other women have cross-dressed as men throughout their adult lives; and these women—such as the soldier James Taylor (b. 1667), the pirates Anne Bonney and Mary Read (executed in 1720), and the physician James Barry (1799–1865)—have generally found their masquerade stressful. They seem to have spent a great deal of their lives fearful of the ridicule and punishment that they would face were their biological sex revealed.

The horrific example of Brandon Teena, whose life and murder are depicted in Kimberly Peirce's film *Boys Don't Cry* (1999), is instructive as evidence that gender deception is still considered punishable. Because ambiguous gender and sexual identity can incite violent reactions, cross-dressing in real life can be dangerous. Drag kings often report incidents of aggression directed toward them when they are on the streets in their male personas.

Butch/Femme Relationships

Another aspect of the performance of masculinity is found in "butch/femme" lesbian relationships. The subject of butch/femme relationships is complex and not easily summarized. Some lesbians may adopt butch roles in the belief that they are phallic women or men trapped in women's bodies. Radclyffe Hall, author of *The Well of Loneliness* (1928), for example, seems to have adopted this belief, which is now sometimes attacked as essentialist. Hall's ideas reflected the theories of early sexologists and continue to be espoused today by some female transsexuals who choose to become men.

Butch roles are also sometimes adopted as a means of exploring an androgynous ideal, often conceived of as a third sex. This ideal may be best expressed in Virginia Woolf's fictional "biography" *Orlando* (1928), inspired by her notably androgynous lover Vita Sackville-West.

Most women who identify as butch maintain their self-perception continuously and cross-dress in varying degrees because of their belief that many so-called masculine characteristics constitute their core identity.

Drag Kings

Drag kings are mostly lesbians, but also female-to-male transsexuals, as well as androgynous and straight women. Even males may perform as drag kings. However, there are important differences between performing masculinity as a drag king and performing "butchness." The butch lesbians of the 1950s did not dress up as men but as masculine women.

Because of their varied sexual positions and orientations, drag kings exhibit a variety of characteristics, both on- and offstage. Transgender drag kings tend to maintain a male gender identification offstage, while butch lesbians frequently elaborate in their acts their offstage female masculinity.

In contrast, female-identified drag kings, regardless of their sexual orientations, understand themselves to be involved in a parody of masculinity and leave behind their masculine personas after they depart the stage. The many layers of identification and orientation provide some of the richness in drag king performances.

Since drag kings are latecomers to the drag scene, they lack much of the quasi-institutionalized, community tradition that drag queens enjoy as a result of their long connection with gay bar culture. Drag queens have been performing glamorous femininity as part of gay culture since at least the period between the two world wars and probably longer.

Comedy of Cross-Dressing

Peter Ackroyd points out that drag performances partake of the anarchic and festive old English tradition of mumming, where husband and wife swapped roles when visiting friends during the Christmas season. The comedy is part of a vicarious pleasure in the inversion of the sexual and social worlds. Many drag kings return to this practice when they parody masculinity in an overtly comic way and emphasize their enjoyment and sense of fun.

However, there are other explanations for the pleasure of cross-dressing besides inverting and destabilizing gender and sexual conventions. The practice of women dressing as men may provide symbolic compensation for the loss or suppression of "male" aspects of their personalities; cross-dressing may satisfy a longing for asexuality; or the exhibitionistic and fetishistic elements of illusion and fantasy in such performances may give explicit and dramatic form to subversive instincts. Ackroyd notes that while transvestism is often a sexual obsession, during its long history it has also been associated with sacred ritual and social or political dissent.

Cross-Dressing as Parody and Homage

Some lesbians criticize the drag performance phenomenon on the ground that drag kings and queens epitomize only the worst aspects of masculinity and femininity in making fun of the opposite sex. However, the performance of drag kings and queens can be more variable than such criticisms acknowledge.

Judith (Jack) Halberstam observes that in drag king theater it is always interesting to see what part of maleness a king might select to perform. For traditional drag queen acts there are many obvious models to imitate, such as Marilyn Monroe or Cher or Diana Ross: The flamboyance and artificiality of these stars immediately make them available for performance. But comparable male stars such as Paul Newman or Tom Cruise or Mel Gibson strive for an apparent naturalness that makes them difficult to imitate or parody.

The sexist pig or macho figure is much more available for the king to imitate and, in the process, to ridicule exaggerated masculinity. Not all drag kings ridicule masculinity, of course. Many have moved beyond the simple exposure of male violence and gross sexuality to make their acts tributes to male talent and charm and, thus, an expression of their own abilities. Some kings, such as Dred, the Dodge Brothers band, and Elvis Herselvis, enact a range of masculine traits, including some qualities that stem from sincere admiration and respect.

Storme Delaverié, an African American male impersonator of the 1940s, suggested that it is harder to impersonate men than women since the impersonation of femininity entails the addition of elements while the impersonation of masculinity can only be achieved by paring down. This may be why male impersonation often seems less dramatic than drag queen shows.

But contemporary drag kings insist that their masculine personas require both addition and subtraction. The questions remain, however, whether drag king theater depends on parody or imitation or realness, and whether it can continue to provide the element of excess and camp that is the hallmark of drag queen performances.

—*Elizabeth Ashburn*

BIBLIOGRAPHY

Ackroyd, Peter. *Dressing Up: Transvestism and Drag: The History of an Obsession.* London: Thames and Hudson, 1979.

Dickens, Homer. *What a Drag.* London: Angus and Robertson, 1982.

Garber, Marjorie. *Vested Interests: Cross-dressing and Cultural Anxiety.* New York: Routledge, 1992.

Stryker, Susan, and Jim Van Buskirk. *Gay by the Bay: A History of Queer Culture in the San Francisco Bay Area.* San Francisco: Chronicle Books, 1996.

Volcano, Del LaGrace, and Judith "Jack" Halberstam. *The Drag King Book.* London: Serpent's Tail, 1999.

SEE ALSO

Drag Shows: Drag Queens and Female Impersonators; Opera; Bentley, Gladys; Dietrich, Marlene

Drag Shows: Drag Queens and Female Impersonators

FEMALE IMPERSONATION APPEARS TO HAVE EXISTED throughout the length of human civilization and the breadth of its cultures. Ancient Roman literature and history feature a multitude of male cross-dressers, while in numerous Native American cultures, cross-dressing berdaches were respected as prophets and seers who were able to glimpse the world through both masculine and feminine perspectives. In the late nineteenth century, Richard von Krafft-Ebing observed in his *Psychopathia Sexualis* (1887) that the smallest German hamlets often featured drag culture. In contemporary India, men who choose to live and dance as women are sometimes regarded with particular religious reverence.

Female Impersonation and Sexual Identity

Female impersonation need say nothing about sexual identity. For example, many male actors in Elizabethan England and in the classical Chinese theater performed female roles because women were generally banned from the stage. Whether or not these performances blurred the sexual identification of the actors remains a point of debate in social and theater history and a focus of recent films such as *Shakespeare in Love* (1998) and *Farewell My Concubine* (1993).

Although *transvestism,* a term coined by Magnus Hirschfeld in 1910 and derived from the Latin for "across" and "dress," is practiced mostly by heterosexual males, the performance of female impersonation has come to be associated particularly with glbtq culture.

Why this should be so is not altogether clear, but it may be that gender transgression is a component of sexual transgression or at least evokes empathy among those crossing sexual boundaries, particularly when these boundaries seem difficult to define. Certainly, cross-dressing calls into question rigid constructions of sex and gender. In any case, notwithstanding the fact that most transvestites are heterosexual men who fetishize female clothing, drag has for a very long time been almost an institutionalized aspect of gay male culture.

The origin of the term *drag queen* is unclear. It may derive from Elizabethan slang—the term *quean,* referring to a strumpet (or prostitute)—or it may have come to be applied to female impersonators as a consequence of the extravagant drag balls of the earlier twentieth century, a precursor of the drag shows that became associated with gay bars and nightclubs in the period between the world wars.

Why is it that a man performing with over-the-top female clothing and exaggerated mannerisms provokes such fascination among gay men? Kate Millett suggested, in her landmark study *Sexual Politics* (1970), that the thrill produced by a drag queen arises through her denaturalization of gender, her demonstration that femininity is donned like a masquerade and rendered completely irrelevant to biology.

More recently, Wayne Koestenbaum has observed, in *The Queen's Throat* (1993), that drag queens, like opera divas, perform the kind of freedom that most gay men can enjoy only vicariously. Both these explanations may be correct, in view of the multiple manifestations of drag.

Low Camp and High Camp Drag

The drag of low camp, for example, stresses the masquerade itself. In this type of drag, the performer often reclaims fashions and songs that were once serious but that now, many years after their introduction, seem a hysterical failure. The drag queen of low camp evokes this hysteria by emphasizing exactly those features that make the failure all the more obvious and entertaining.

An impersonator of Connie Francis, for example, may exaggerate the singer's famous early-1960s hairstyle or the almost-in-tears quality of her singing in order to stress those features that defined her style. That this style no longer reigns makes its status as a masquerade easier to detect and funnier to witness. Indeed, the fact that a man dons this masquerade as he plaintively sings "Where the Boys Are" makes it all the more obviously, and comically, a construct rather than any genuine expression of femininity.

This is the type of drag whose humor constitutes a gender critique with which gay men can empathetically identify. Performers such as the Kinsey Sicks, Mona Foot, Sherry Vine, The Lady Bunny, and Flotilla de Barge offer good examples of low camp drag.

The drag of high camp, by contrast, takes a far more serious approach. This type of performance tends to idealize rather than criticize, offering the impersonation as an authentic expression delivered anew to an adoring audience.

For example, an impersonation of Judy Garland might stress her exact look at any one point in her career, or the exact quality of voice she would have possessed at that time. The gay male audience enjoying this kind of impersonation tends not to laugh but to attend every note with excitement. Witnessing this type of drag performance, gay men might identify with the diva, allowing her to perform the forceful expressions that they choose to stifle.

Drag Queens and Stonewall

Through the mid-twentieth century, the drag queens of high camp generally took for themselves the right of open self-expression that closeted gay men consistently declined. That may be why a cohort of these high-camp drag queens, having adopted a life of fearless self-expression, were so prominent in the 1969 Stonewall riots that ignited the modern gay liberation movement.

One of the riots' participants, Sylvia Ray Rivera, noted that she rose up at Stonewall not only to protest yet another police raid on her regular bar but also to express anger against all the indignities visited against her because of her open drag identity. She noted further that many drag queens were particularly agitated because their idol, Judy Garland, had been buried the very same day. Such empathetic identification and expression were typical of these rebellious drag queens.

Charles Pierce, Candy Darling, and High Camp Drag

One of the greatest of high camp drag performers was the legendary Charles Pierce (1926–1999), who earned fame even in the homophobic 1950s (when full drag was illegal in most jurisdictions) for his extraordinary impersonations of a host of larger-than-life figures. He was especially known for his renditions of Bette Davis, Joan Crawford, and Tallulah Bankhead, as well as some fictional creations, such as Doris Day's sister "Doo-Dah Day."

Performers of such high camp drag have largely faded from fashion as gay men have claimed the right to speak and act as they please. This type of performance, however, continues to thrive in an area colloquially referred to as the "Drag Belt": the Southern states, where many gay men continue to feel deeply oppressed. Examples of enduring high-camp drag queens are Candy Darling, Jimmy James, and a myriad of local impersonators who enliven small-town bars.

Candy Darling (1946?–1974) probably represents high camp drag's apogee. In the late 1960s, at the age of twenty, she entered Andy Warhol's avant-garde circle and soon became an icon of the Pop Art movement. Born in 1947 in Massapequa Park, Long Island, as James Lawrence Slattery, she came to Warhol's attention because of her convincing female illusion and her uncanny ability to impersonate Hollywood divas.

Darling's skill as a drag queen enabled her to assemble the features of such divas as Marilyn Monroe and Elizabeth Taylor into a striking concoction of high-Hollywood feminine masquerade. The resulting image, augmented by a copious use of hormones, stirred a particular sensation when Darling appeared in Warhol's film *Flesh* (1968).

Her image was further popularized by Lou Reed's song "Walk on the Wild Side," specifically the line "in the back room she was everybody's darlin.'" Although Darling craved the cinematic fame of her idols, her own fame, achieved through small roles in underground films, was more modest. Her death of leukemia while still in her twenties served to engrave her image as a glamorous and tragic figure, forever young, exquisitely beautiful, and of almost beatific sweetness.

Low Camp Drag Performers

As high camp drag has slipped from fashion, low camp drag has gained popularity. And the demands made on drag have shifted, as gay men—at least in big cities—increasingly feel the freedom to express themselves openly. Now, rather than seek the vicarious and reverential experience offered by exacting impersonations, gay men tend to prefer the masquerade and humor of low camp.

This trend is not altogether new. Legendary performers such as Ray Bourbon, for example, specialized in low drag, performing what one audience member described as "doyen drag" when he impersonated a foul-mouthed cleaning woman.

Mona Foot, as an example of a newer generation of low drag performers, always allows her muscular body to show through her skimpy dresses, purposefully impeding any illusion that she may be a true woman. Moreover, like The Lady Bunny and Jackie Beat, she has built a unique drag persona that overwhelms any celebrity she chooses to impersonate.

In fact, many of these contemporary drag queens de-emphasize musical impersonation in favor of spoken comedy, particularly comedy built around the overstatement and failure of their female masquerade. Quite distinct from the reverential aura surrounding high camp drag, this contemporary alternative often makes gay men and even drag queens themselves the butt of humor.

RuPaul

RuPaul is a good, though subtle, example of the recent transformation from high camp drag to low camp drag. Born in 1960 in San Diego, the son of an aeronautics electrician, RuPaul Andre Charles grew up a "sissy." His persistent good nature allowed him to cope with his effeminacy quite well, and this in turn allowed him to become one of the most acclaimed, politically gay-identified drag queens in the United States.

RuPaul got his start in Atlanta's informal Now Explosion drag troupe, which styled itself "punk drag." Like others in this group in the mid-1980s, he combined wigs and wild makeup with clothing that clearly exposed his male body. In the early 1990s, however, he moved into the "glamour drag" for which he is most famous, characterized by enormous blonde wigs, stiletto heels, and tight groin tucks.

Yet, despite this highly worked masquerade so reminiscent of high camp drag, RuPaul normally performs his own songs. When he does sing songs other than his own, he performs them as "covers" of anonymous works to which he applies his own distinct performance styles, as in his "Little Drummer Boy" (1997).

Also, rather than attempting to emulate celebrities, RuPaul, unlike high-camp drag performers, consistently affirms himself, creating a distinctive drag persona of his own. He makes clear that he is a black gay man under the pounds of makeup and costume in which he performs.

This reality check allows him to embrace gay rights and other causes as a black gay male advocate, and he frequently performs at benefits and demonstrations. His musical hits, such as "Supermodel" (1992), have won him a large and devoted following based on his own persona rather than his impersonation of others.

RuPaul's female "realness" and chatty affirmation mildly break the rules of low camp drag where self-deprecating comedy and obvious masquerade have largely become the rule. These components of low camp have not only given drag a new life among gay men, but they have also given the practice a broad appeal well outside its original constituency.

Movies and plays such as Edouard Molinaro's *La Cage aux Folles* (1978), Harvey Fierstein's *Torch Song Trilogy* (1982), Stephan Elliot's *The Adventures of Priscilla, Queen of the Desert* (1994), and Jenny Livingston's *Paris is Burning* (1991); music videos by performers such as RuPaul and Joey Arias; and New York's annual Wigstock festival all demonstrate the increasing popularity of drag for a diverse audience.

The queerness of a gay man offering bitchy banter in a dress has become as acceptably entertaining as an overweight Roseanne Barr telling jokes about her size or comedian Margaret Cho musing on her Korean parents. These various forms of comedy offer a humorous view from outside the confines of normality, even a self-deprecating view to which many in today's audience seem sympathetically inclined.   —*Andres Mario Zervigon*

BIBLIOGRAPHY

Baker, Roger. *Drag: A History of Female Impersonation on the Stage.* London: Cassell, 1994.

Duberman, Martin. *Stonewall.* New York: Penguin Books, 1994.

Garber, Marjorie. *Vested Interests: Cross-Dressing and Cultural Anxiety.* New York: Routledge, 1992.

Koestenbaum, Wayne. *The Queen's Throat: Opera, Homosexuality and the Mystery of Desire.* New York: Poseidon, 1993.

Krafft-Ebing, Richard von. *Psychopathia Sexualis.* Stuttgart: Ferdinand Enke, 1887.

Millett, Kate. *Sexual Politics.* Garden City, N.Y.: Doubleday, 1970.

Woodlawn, Holly, with Jeff Copeland. *A Low Life in High Heels.* New York: St. Martin's Press, 1991.

SEE ALSO

Drag Shows: Drag Kings and Male Impersonators; Divas; Bourbon, Ray; Garland, Judy; Pierce, Charles; Reed, Lou; RuPaul (RuPaul Andre Charles)

Duncan, Isadora   (1878–1927)

FREETHINKING, FREE-SPIRITED, FREE-MOVING ISADORA Duncan brought her bohemian feminist consciousness to the dance stage and changed the art of dance forever. Although some critics ridiculed her flowing, expressive movements and her leftist politics, Duncan brought flexibility and self-expression to the hidebound world of classical dance.

Duncan is known as the "mother of modern dance," but even ballet was influenced by the radical élan of her ideas. In many ways her life was tragic, but she left behind not a sense of despair and loss, but the dynamic imagination of a true original.

Duncan was the child of the radically transformative era at the end of the nineteenth century. Born to free-thinking parents in San Francisco on May 26, 1877, she was mostly raised by her mother, a lover of music, literature, and the arts who earned money teaching piano. It was not long before Isadora, who learned to dance by following the movements of the waves on the beaches near her home, was earning extra cash too, by teaching dance to younger children in the neighborhood.

Duncan's influences were the movements she found in nature and the passion of classical Greek drama. She hated the rigid structures of ballet. She determined to create not only a new form of dance, but also a new outlook on dance, where expressive movement would be an

Isadora Duncan, photographed by Arnold Genthe between 1916 and 1918.

integral part of every child's education, along with the usual academic subjects.

When Duncan was a teenager, she and her mother traveled to Chicago and New York, where she performed in theaters and vaudeville houses to less than enthusiastic audiences. It was not until 1900 when she went to Europe that she began to be taken seriously as a dancer. Although she began by performing at private parties, soon she was touring the major stages of Europe, galvanizing audiences with her "modern" dance.

At the beginning of the twentieth century, ballet had become a voyeuristic art, appealing largely to men who attended to watch women performing in skimpy (for the day) tutus. Isadora Duncan introduced the solo performance to dance audiences. Decrying restrictive women's clothing, she shed her corset and petticoats and danced barefoot in simple, flowing, Grecian-style tunics adorned with long, colorful scarves. Her dances concerned such subjects as motherhood, love, and grief, and her audiences were filled with women.

Almost as titillating as her radical approach to dance was Duncan's bohemian personal life. She was an outspoken socialist and advocate of women's rights who constantly challenged society's rules. Claiming she did not believe in marriage or monogamy, she had two children with two of her many male lovers. (Both children drowned in an accident in 1913.)

She also attended Natalie Barney's Paris salons and had female lovers, among them writer Mercedes de Acosta, about whom she wrote, "My kisses like a swarm of bees / Would find their way between thy knees / And suck the honey from thy lips / Embracing thy too slender hips."

Duncan achieved her dream of creating a new, well-rounded form of education. She established schools of the Duncan method in Berlin, Paris, London, and Moscow. But her life was tragically cut short when, at the age of forty-nine, one of her flamboyant long scarves caught in the wheels of the sports car she was driving and strangled her.

—*Tina Gianoulis*

BIBLIOGRAPHY

Blair, Fredrika. *Isadora: Portrait of the Artist as a Woman.* New York: Harper, 1987.

Daly, Ann. *Done into Dance: Isadora Duncan in America.* Bloomington: Indiana University Press, 1995.

Desti, Mary. *The Untold Story: The Life of Isadora Duncan.* Cambridge, Mass.: Da Capo Press, 1981.

Duncan, Isadora. *My Life.* 1927. New York: Norton, 1996.

"Just Call her Don Juanita." *Advocate,* April 25, 2000, 22.

SEE ALSO

Dance; Ballet; Allan, Maud

Edens, Roger

ROGER EDENS WAS A GIFTED COMPOSER AND ARRANGER who gave a new look to movie musicals through his work with the Arthur Freed unit at the MGM studios. He was mentor and friend to many in the entertainment industry, including Judy Garland.

Edens came from a large family in Hillsboro, Texas. The youngest of eight brothers, he was born Rollins Edens on November 9, 1905. Unlike his rambunctious siblings, Edens was of an artistic and studious nature. His parents, though not well-off, managed to scrape together enough money to finance his education at the University of Texas.

Upon graduation, Edens found work playing piano on a cruise ship. A manager from new York heard him and helped him land a job with a jazz band. Edens, who always enjoyed a close relationship with his family, brought his widowed mother to stay with him on Long Island.

At this time, Edens changed his first name to Roger. The reasons for this are unclear, but William J. Mann suggests that it is "possible he considered 'Rollins' just too precious, too dandy, for the hard-drinking, woman-chasing world of orchestras and musicians."

Edens moved on to a job with the Red Nichols Orchestra, which played at the Alvin Theater on Broadway. In a dramatic turn of events, Edens was called from the orchestra pit to the stage when Ethel Merman's pianist suffered a heart attack before the second performance of George and Ira Gershwin's *Girl Crazy,* in 1932.

Impressed by Edens's work, Merman employed him as her accompanist and arranger for her next show and for her nightclub act. When she headed for Hollywood, she brought along Edens to be music director for Roy Del Ruth's *Kid Millions* (1934), in which she would star.

Also moving to California was Edens's wife, the former Martha LaPrelle, whom he had dated in college. Their marriage was characterized by long periods apart, since her job as a buyer for a fashion house entailed extensive travel. According to Edens's nephew J. C. Edens, his aunt "never cared much for Hollywood." Even Edens's closest friends in California rarely saw her. The couple soon separated and eventually divorced.

Edens meanwhile had attracted the attention of MGM producer Arthur Freed when the latter heard him play at the audition of a singer. Freed was not much impressed by the singer but instantly recognized Edens's skill as a composer and arranger. He quickly hired him as a member of his creative staff.

The Arthur Freed unit was a team of talented composers, arrangers, lyricists, choreographers, and other artisans who set the standard for movie musicals during their golden age, from the late 1930s to the early 1960s. Because so many members were gay, the Freed unit was known in the industry as "Freed's Fairies."

Freed, who was not gay, never intended to create a team of gay artists, nor were all the members of the Arthur Freed unit gay. But Freed wanted a first-rate team, and he hired without regard to sexual orientation. The many gifted and gay members of the team, in addition to Edens, include songwriters Cole Porter and Frederick Loewe, choreographers Robert Alton and Jack Cole, and directors Charles Walters and the closeted Vincente Minnelli.

Edens became the heart and soul of the Freed unit, and Freed had the utmost confidence in him. Production assistant Lela Simone stated that "Freed did not occupy himself with details because he had Roger and he knew that Roger was going to do the best job there is." Freed's reliance on Edens is reflected in his decision to elevate him to the rank of associate producer on a number of films, beginning with Minnelli's *Meet Me in St. Louis* (1944). It was extremely rare in Hollywood to move from a job as a musician to one in production.

Edens's first film with Freed was Victor Fleming's *Reckless* (1935), for which he was musical supervisor. During his career, Edens worked on over forty films as composer, musical director, producer, or a combination of these. His long list of credits includes Robert Z. Leonard's *The Great Ziegfeld* (1936), Fleming's *The Wizard of Oz* (1939), Busby Berkeley's *Babes in Arms* (1939), Minnelli's *Cabin in the Sky* (1943), Charles Walters's *Easter Parade* (1948), Gene Kelly and Stanley Donen's *Singin' in the Rain* (1952), and George Cukor's *A Star Is Born* (1954).

The Freed unit, with Edens at the helm, created a new kind of musical. Whereas, previously, musical movies had been essentially stories interrupted by the occasional song, Edens insisted that "songs in film musicals should be part of the script itself." In the Freed unit, songs fit seamlessly into the plot.

Hollywood honored Edens with three Academy Awards. His first, for *Easter Parade*, was followed in rapid succession by Oscars for Donen's *On the Town* (1949) and George Sidney's *Annie Get Your Gun* (1950).

Edens played an important part in the career of gay icon Judy Garland. The two met in 1935 when Edens was called in to replace Garland's father, Frank Gumm, an amateur pianist, at Garland's audition at MGM. Edens was quick to appreciate her talent and became not only her musical mentor but also a lifelong friend.

Edens wrote a song for Garland to sing at Clark Gable's birthday party in 1937. It not only delighted Gable but also favorably impressed the producer of Del Ruth's *Broadway Melody of 1938* (1937), who had Garland sing it in the film.

After working with Garland on a couple of other projects, Edens served as musical director for *The Wizard of Oz* and also as rehearsal pianist for Garland. Garland's daughter Lorna Luft credits Edens with teaching her mother to have the courage to show her vulnerability in her performances. "Without Roger," she commented,

"we might never have had 'Over the Rainbow,' at least not the way we remember it."

Edens continued to contribute to Garland's professional success. He provided her "Born in a Trunk" number for *A Star Is Born*—uncredited, because he was under exclusive contract to MGM and the film was a Warner Brothers production.

Edens and Charles Walters were also indispensable in arranging Garland's triumphant 1951 vaudeville act at the RKO Palace Theatre, which won rave reviews from the critics.

Edens's professional star continued to rise. Freed chose him as producer of two movies, Donen's *Deep in My Heart* (1954), featuring the music of Sigmund Romberg, and *Funny Face* (1957).

By this time, the heyday of the movie musical was waning, and various members of the Freed unit had moved on. Edens worked on a few more films, notably Walters's *The Unsinkable Molly Brown* (1964) and Kelly's *Hello, Dolly!* (1969), but also pursued other opportunities. During the 1960s, he renewed his professional association with both Garland and Merman, penning material for their nightclub acts. He also coached Katharine Hepburn for her performance in Alan Jay Lerner and André Previn's stage musical *Coco* in 1969.

Edens succumbed to cancer on July 13, 1970, in Hollywood.

Edens's career is a stunning success story, the more remarkable because his achievements came in an era of widespread homophobia. Gay performers sometimes resorted to "lavender marriages" or invented fictitious wives to conceal their sexual orientation. Even working behind the scenes and in the congenial atmosphere of the Freed unit, Edens, according to Mann, kept a photo of his ex-wife on his desk for years though he was living openly with another man.

Mann also recounts a touching recollection of Frank Lysinger, an MGM messenger whom Edens had befriended around 1939. Edens often invited him to dinner along with Lena Horne and musical director Lennie Hayton—a gathering of two "officially unsanctioned" couples, since studio head Louis B. Mayer had forbidden Horne, an African American, and Hayton, who was white, to date each other. Edens, who championed Horne at the studio, also tried to bring happiness to her personal life.

This kindness and compassion was typical of Edens's character. His collaborator and longtime friend Kay Thompson described him as "a darling man," and Michael Morrison, another friend and the business partner of gay actor William Haines, commented that "all sorts of people were drawn to him."

Edens was a model of professional success and personal dignity.

—*Linda Rapp*

BIBLIOGRAPHY

Eder, Bruce. "Roger Edens." http://movies2.nytimes.com/gst/movies/filmography.html?p_id =88652&mod=bio.

Fricke, John. *Judy Garland: The World's Greatest Entertainer.* New York: Henry Holt and Company, 1992.

Kenrick, John. "Edens, Roger." www.musicals101.com/who2d.htm.

Mann, William J. *Behind the Screen: How Gays and Lesbians Shaped Hollywood, 1910–1969.* New York: Viking, 2001.

SEE ALSO

Musical Theater and Film; Cabarets and Revues; Garland, Judy; Minnelli, Vincente; Porter, Cole

Epstein, Brian   (1934–1967)

PERHAPS FEW INDIVIDUALS WERE LESS LIKELY TO create the public image and oversee the career of the world's most famous rock group than Brian Epstein. Born on September 19, 1934, into a family of affluent Jewish furniture merchants in Liverpool, Epstein seemed destined for a career in the family business. He was attracted, however, to such "unmanly" pursuits as fashion design and the stage, which, along with his closeted homosexuality, put him at odds with his family's aspirations.

Epstein left school at sixteen to work at one of his family's stores until he was called up for military service in 1952. After only a year of duty, he was discharged for unspecific psychiatric reasons. Epstein subsequently enrolled at the Royal Academy of Dramatic Arts, but before completing his studies he returned to his family's business, where he became the manager of the store's record department.

It was in this capacity that, in October 1961, he first heard of the Beatles, a Liverpool band whose fans were seeking their recordings. Epstein was unable to locate these records and, intrigued by the mystery, ventured into the Cavern Club, where he encountered John Lennon, Paul McCartney, George Harrison, and drummer Pete Best.

Within two months, although he had no entertainment or managerial background, Epstein had signed the group to a contract. Over the next year, he transformed the group's image from leather-clad ruffians to "Mods" attired in fashionable suits with longish hairstyles, creating, in effect, an androgynous look for his protégés.

Epstein also successfully negotiated the Beatles' first recording contract with EMI Parlophone, replaced Best with Ringo Starr, and became the manager of various other successful Liverpool acts, including Gerry and the Pacemakers, Cilla Black, and Billy J. Kramer with the Dakotas.

By 1964, when the Beatles and his other acts took America by storm, Epstein seemed to personify worldly success. He was, however, living in an almost constant state of anxiety lest his homosexuality—and his attraction to rough and often abusive young men—become public knowledge, as male homosexual acts were still illegal in Britain at the time and any scandal might negatively affect the Beatles' career.

It has often been suggested that Epstein's devotion to the Beatles was based on an unrequited love for John Lennon. Speculation about a possible affair between them has existed since the two vacationed together in Spain in 1963; Christopher Münch's film *The Hours and the Times* (1991) suggests that the two men did share a sexual liaison on this vacation.

In 1966, the Beatles decided to stop performing live and concentrate solely on studio recording. Although this decision resulted in such breakthrough recordings as *Sgt. Pepper's Lonely Hearts Club Band* (1967), Epstein felt that he had effectively lost control of the band and suffered from acute depression, exacerbated by drug and alcohol abuse.

On August 27, 1967, Epstein was found dead in his London home from a barbiturate overdose. Although his death was ruled accidental, many have presumed it was a suicide. Ironically, he died a month to the day after legislation decriminalizing homosexual acts between adult men went into effect in Britain.

For three decades following his death, Epstein was vilified by the popular music world as a controlling figure who tried to suppress the Beatles' creativity—and who was accused, falsely, of having cheated the group out of millions in income. In this, the fact that the world would not have heard of the Beatles had it not been for Epstein's relentless efforts on the group's behalf was heedlessly overlooked.

In recent years, however, his reputation has been reconsidered, and perhaps he will at last receive the honor due to the creator and manager of the group that permanently changed perceptions of popular culture.

—*Patricia Juliana Smith*

BIBLIOGRAPHY

Brown, Peter, and Steven Gaines. *The Love You Make: An Insider's Story of the Beatles.* New York: McGraw-Hill, 1983.

Coleman, Ray. *Brian Epstein: The Man Who Made the Beatles.* London: Viking Penguin, 1989.

Davies, Hunter. *The Beatles.* Second ed., revised. New York: W. W. Norton, 1996.

Epstein, Brian. *A Cellarful of Noise: The Autobiography of the Man Who Made the Beatles.* New York: Pocket Books, 1998.

Geller, Debbie. *The Brian Epstein Story.* London: Faber and Faber, 2000.

Shillinglaw, Ann. "'Give Us a Kiss': Queer Codes, Male Partnering, and the Beatles." *The Queer Sixties.* Patricia Juliana Smith, ed. New York: Routledge, 1999. 127–143.

SEE ALSO

Popular Music; Rock Music

Etheridge, Melissa   (b. 1961)

AWARD-WINNING ROCK SINGER AND SONGWRITER Melissa Etheridge has not only managed to carve out a spectacularly successful career as a popular mainstream performer, but she has also become a lesbian icon and activist for gay and lesbian causes. With a style characterized by intense emotion and unbridled energy, Etheridge has become one of the most distinctive artists in rock music.

Early Years

She was born in Leavenworth, Kansas, on May 29, 1961. Her father, John Etheridge, was a math teacher and athletic director at the local high school, and her mother, Elizabeth Williamson, worked as a computer specialist for the U.S. Army at Fort Leavenworth.

Etheridge's fascination with music began early. When she was eight, her father bought her her first real guitar, a six-string Harmony Stella, and arranged for her to take lessons with Don Raymond, who had been a big-band jazz guitarist. By the age of ten, Etheridge was beginning to write songs.

When she was eleven, "Missy" Etheridge gave her first public performance, singing with two friends at a talent show in Leavenworth. By the age of twelve, she was playing and singing with adult musical groups, doing mostly country and western material. She was also learning to play more instruments—piano, drums, saxophone, and clarinet.

Coming Out and Launching a Career

After high school, Etheridge attended Berklee College of Music in Boston. Her roommate in the dormitory was a lesbian who introduced her to women's bars and afforded her the opportunity to talk freely about her sexuality. Etheridge had realized that she was a lesbian at the age of seventeen but, coming from a family in which emotional matters were not much discussed, had never broached the subject with her parents or publicly acknowledged her homosexuality.

Etheridge did not remain long at Berklee. She began singing in bars and eventually dropped out of college.

Realizing that Boston was not the ideal place to launch a career in rock and roll, she resolved to go to Los Angeles. First, however, she returned home to Kansas to earn money for the trip to California.

Etheridge got a job as music assistant at the Army chapel at Fort Leavenworth. She also began meeting and dating other lesbians in town, on one occasion inviting a woman home to spend the night. The following morning Etheridge found a note from her mother that referred to her "psychological illness" and warned her "not [to] bring that girl over here anymore" if she wanted to continue to live in the house.

Neither Etheridge nor her mother ever mentioned the letter, but Etheridge was deeply disturbed by it and turned to the Army chaplain for guidance. He cautioned her that some people would condemn her but said he could not believe "that God would have invented a love that could be wrong" and urged her to be true to herself. Etheridge called this "one of the most valuable lessons of my life."

By the eve of her twenty-first birthday she had saved enough money for the planned move to Los Angeles. Before leaving for California, she came out to her father, who had already guessed it and who expressed his support.

In Los Angeles Etheridge initially stayed with an aunt. She also made contact with two paternal uncles and learned that they were gay. Etheridge's uncles introduced her to the gay community in Los Angeles.

Etheridge soon found a job playing at a women's bar in Long Beach, where she developed an appreciative following. She worked in other bars as well, including Vermie's in Pasadena, where some loyal fans brought a soccer teammate, Karla Leopold, to a show in the hope that she would persuade her husband, Bill Leopold, a manager in the music business, to represent Etheridge. Bill Leopold was indeed impressed when he heard Etheridge perform. He became her manager, and began attempting to secure a recording contract.

Although several companies expressed some interest, no record deal was immediately forthcoming, but Leopold did get Etheridge a songwriting contract with Almo/Irving Music. Songs by Etheridge eventually became part of the soundtrack of four movies: *Scenes from the Goldmine* (1987, directed by Mark Rocco), *Weeds* (1987, directed by John Hancock), *Welcome Home, Roxy Carmichael* (1990, directed by Jim Abrahams), and *Boys on the Side* (1995, directed by Herbert Ross).

A Record Contract and Success

In 1986, Chris Blackwell, the founder of Island Records, heard Etheridge perform and was eager to sign her for his label. He was less than pleased, however, when he heard the initial version of her first album. Producers had added keyboard tracks that yielded a pop sound completely uncharacteristic of Etheridge.

In hopes of salvaging the project, Etheridge, drummer Craig Krampf, bassist Kevin McCormick, and engineer Niko Bolas rerecorded all the material in just four days. The second version, which captured the energy and spontaneity of Etheridge's live performances, met with Blackwell's approval.

While awaiting the release of the album, Etheridge went on tour in Britain and Europe. In Germany she visited Dachau and was moved by the sight of the uniforms with pink triangles that had been worn by prisoners. She was dismayed that there was no memorial to the homosexual victims of the Holocaust.

In 1988, Etheridge's self-titled debut album was greeted with favorable reviews. Critics praised the vitality of her music and compared her to Janis Joplin, a performer whom Etheridge acknowledges as an important influence on her work.

Love and Honors

While on tour promoting the album, Etheridge made a video of the song "Bring Me Some Water." The associate director of the project was Julie Cypher, who would become Etheridge's longtime partner.

At the time, however, Cypher was married to actor Lou Diamond Phillips. Etheridge and Cypher felt an immediate attraction to each other, but Cypher was still trying to maintain her troubled marriage. Not until January 1990 did she leave Phillips and move in with Etheridge.

Meanwhile, there were important developments in Etheridge's career. "Bring Me Some Water" was nominated for a Grammy in 1989, and Etheridge's second album, *Brave and Crazy*, was released the same year. Etheridge's songs received increasing play on the radio, and her videos appeared frequently on the cable music network VH1. Both of the first two albums eventually went platinum, selling over a million copies each.

Coming Out Publicly

In January 1993, Etheridge, who had performed at some campaign events for Bill Clinton, was invited with Cypher to the president's inauguration. They attended the Triangle Ball, the first inaugural celebration for gay men and lesbians. After her friend k.d. lang introduced her to the crowd, Etheridge declared, "I'm real proud to say I'm a lesbian."

Etheridge's spontaneous decision to come out publicly received press coverage but had no adverse effect on her career. Two months after the announcement, she won her first Grammy for "Ain't It Heavy" from the album *Never Enough*. Her fourth album, *Yes I Am*, released later in the year, was enormously successful. It included the hit song "Come to My Window," which would bring her another Grammy in 1994.

Etheridge was named the *Advocate*'s Person of the Year for 1995. Her fifth album, *Your Little Secret*, debuted in the top ten on the charts. She began publicly addressing social issues such as same-sex marriage, saying that as soon as any state legalized it, she and Cypher would be "first in line."

Motherhood and Activism

In November 1996, Etheridge and Cypher appeared on the cover of an issue of *Newsweek* devoted to gay families. Cypher gave birth to the couple's first child in February 1997 and to their second in November 1998. Etheridge adopted the children in order to secure full parental rights.

Etheridge had not previously used her music as a political vehicle, but the murder of gay student Matthew Shepard in October 1998 led her to write "Scarecrow," a song that decried the homophobia that had caused his death.

In 1999, Etheridge became the host and narrator of a reality-based series on the Lifetime network, "Beyond Chance," a show about improbable reunions, rescues, and paranormal events. Although a rock star seemed an unusual choice for the role, producers felt that the storytelling ability Etheridge had shown as a songwriter suited her well for the job.

In 2000, Etheridge and Cypher broke up. In a creative approach to child custody, they bought houses on back-to-back lots so that their children could go from one to the other at will.

Lesbian Icon

Etheridge has had an extremely successful career as a musician, selling over twenty-five million records worldwide, performing in concert to enthusiastic audiences, and appearing in videos and shows such as MTV's *Unplugged*, where she sang duets with Bruce Springsteen, whose music was an influence on hers.

The passion, intensity, and emotion of Etheridge's performances and the sincerity of her lyrics have won her the admiration of many fans, but lesbians have especially responded to her fearless expression of raw emotion.

Even since coming out publicly, however, Etheridge has not written a specifically lesbian love song. Although her songs have sometimes been interpreted as referring to her lesbianism (as in the title of her album *Yes I Am*), she disavows such interpretations, which she sees as limiting. In her songs, she prefers to use a genderless *you* when referring to her beloved. Explaining this choice in an interview in the *Advocate*, Etheridge said, "I don't want to cut anybody out. I don't want to alienate anyone."

In this aim she has succeeded. As music journalist and Etheridge biographer Chris Nickson notes: "Her songs speak to everybody, showing that whether heterosexual or gay, we share the same emotions—that at the heart of it all, it's passion and love that matter, not sexual orientation."

New Work, New Marriage

In 2002, Etheridge released a DVD entitled *Live...and Alone*. The title refers to the artist's summer 2001 concert tour, on which she performed without any backup musicians.

Happily, however, she is no longer alone in her personal life, having recently acknowledged a relationship with Tammy Lynn Michaels, an actress who appeared on the WB television series *Popular*. Together since 2002, the couple exchanged wedding vows on September 20, 2003, in Malibu, California.

A minister from the nondenominational Agape Church presided at the ceremony. Etheridge and Michaels consider themselves married, though they were not able to get a marriage license in California at the time. Both women were attended by their mothers, who lit candles and held the wedding rings until it was time for the couple to exchange them.

Etheridge released a new album, *Lucky*, in early 2004. Like her 2001 album *Skin*, written in the wake of her breakup with Cypher, *Lucky* is a mirror of her life, but this time reflecting her newfound joy.   —*Linda Rapp*

BIBLIOGRAPHY

Aarons, Leroy. "All Eyes on Us: From Newsweek to Seventeen, Mainstream Magazines Have Begun to See Lesbians and Gays as We Really Are." *Advocate*, January 21, 1997, 76.

Castro, Peter, and John Griffiths. "A House in Harmony." *People*, September 5, 1997, 57.

de Vries, Hilary. "Rock Steady." *InStyle* 8.8 (July 2001): 208–211.

Einhorn, Jennifer H. "Melissa Etheridge: New Queen of Devastation." *Sojourner: The Women's Forum* 14.9 (1989): 34.

Etheridge, Melissa, and Laura Morton. *The Truth Is...My Life in Love and Music*. New York: Villard, 2001.

Hensley, Dennis. "Shedding Her Skin." *Advocate*, May 8, 2001, 30.

Hogan, Steve, and Lee Hudson. "Etheridge, Melissa." *Completely Queer: The Gay and Lesbian Encyclopedia*. New York: Henry Holt, 1998. 204.

Keck, William. "Melissa Etheridge, Making the Most of 'Beyond Chance.'" *Los Angeles Times*, July 22, 2000.

Kelly, Christina. "Melissa Etheridge." *Rolling Stone*, November 13, 1997, 159.

Kurt, Michele. "Melissa Etheridge and Julie Cypher: Proposing Marriage...in Full." *Advocate*, February 28, 2000, 35.

Larkin, Colin, ed. "Etheridge, Melissa." *The Guinness Encyclopedia of Popular Music*. New York: Guinness Publishing, 1995. 1360–1361.

Nash, Alanna. "Rock Mama." *USA Weekend*, November 8, 2002.

Nickson, Chris. *Melissa Etheridge*. New York: St. Martin's Griffin, 1997.

Sculley, Alan. "Melissa Etheridge Feels 'Lucky'; On her New CD, She Dumps the Negativity of the Past and Shares a Sense of Happiness." *Riverside* (Calif.) *Press Enterprise*, February 13, 2004.

Steele, Bruce C. "Melissa & Tammy: A Love Story." *Advocate*, January 20, 2004, 50.

Walters, Barry. "Melissa Etheridge: Rocking the Boat." *Advocate*, September 21, 1993, 50.

"We're a Family and We Have Rights." *Newsweek*, November 4, 1996, 54.

Wieder, Judy. "Melissa Etheridge: The Advocate's Person of the Year on 1995's Battles, Triumphs, and Controversies." *Advocate*, January 23, 1996, 64.

SEE ALSO

Popular Music; Rock Music; Music Video; Women's Music; Indigo Girls; Joplin, Janis; lang, k.d.

Falla (y Matheu), Manuel de (1876–1946)

Mᴀɴᴜᴇʟ ᴅᴇ Fᴀʟʟᴀ ɪs ᴏɴᴇ ᴏꜰ ᴛʜᴇ ᴍᴏsᴛ ɪʟʟᴜsᴛʀɪᴏᴜs of twentieth-century Spanish composers. He contributed important works in a variety of genres, including chamber music, opera, and ballet.

He was born in Cádiz on November 23, 1876, into a prosperous family. His father was Valencian, his mother Catalan. He studied piano and composition with private tutors and then, at age twenty, entered the Real Conservatorio de Música in Madrid. His early compositions were written for small ensembles and were heavily influenced by Spanish folk music. He wrote six *zarzuelas* (a kind of folk operetta), though only one, *Los amores de la Inés,* was staged.

Disappointed with opportunities in Madrid for both composition and the performance of his works, de Falla traveled in 1907 to Paris, where he resided until 1915. In Paris, he met a number of the most important figures in the musical world at that time: Maurice Ravel, Igor Stravinsky, Claude Debussy, Paul Dukas, Ricardo Viñes, and Sergei Diaghilev.

During this time, he composed the well-received *Trois mélodies,* based on texts by the homosexual poet Théophile Gautier, as well as his famous gypsy *gitanería* or ballet *El Amor Brujo* and his "symphonic impressions," the suite for piano and orchestra entitled *Noches en los jardines de España.* He was poised for greater success when the start of World War I forced his return to Spain.

Soon after his return to Madrid, de Falla met Federico García Lorca, the gay poet and a future collaborator, who was to become a close friend. The composer also spent time refining his musical language, which Spanish critics now approvingly discerned as having been purged of foreign, and especially French, mannerisms.

In 1917, Diaghilev and his choreographer Léonide Massine heard de Falla's pantomime *El corregidor y la molinera,* which is loosely based on Alarcón's *El sombrero de tres picos.* They persuaded de Falla to create a version suitable for Diaghilev's Ballets Russes. Completed in 1919, this new ballet, entitled *El sombrero de tres picos,* with sets and costumes designed by Pablo Picasso, opened to rave reviews in London. The ballet, however, was not very well received in Spain a couple of years later.

Madrid's hustle and bustle palled on de Falla, and he retired to Granada for more peace and quiet to compose. Granada did, indeed, prove more conducive to de Falla for composition. He and García Lorca explored several potential collaborations, though only a couple of minor works resulted from their efforts.

Granada also fostered de Falla's innate austerity and religious disposition. At this time, he delved into the historical musical styles of Spain to forge the neoclassical style that defines this period of his life and work. One popular result of this was the chamber opera *El retablo de maese Pedro,* based on an excerpt from Cervantes's *Don Quixote.* This idyllic and productive period was interrupted by the outbreak of the Spanish Civil War in 1936.

De Falla's devout Roman Catholicism led to his cultivation by the Nationalists. However, despite the high esteem he enjoyed in their eyes, the composer was unable to prevent the execution of his friend and collaborator García Lorca.

As the civil war wound down in 1939, de Falla left Spain with his sister for Argentina, where he had been invited to conduct concerts at the Teatro Colón. His decision to leave Spain may have been prompted by the execution of García Lorca and the homophobia of the Franco regime. De Falla remained in Alta Gracia in the Sierra Córdoba of Argentina for the rest of his life, working on a large-scale work, the cantata *La Atlántida*, which remained incomplete at the time of his death on November 14, 1946.

The evidence of de Falla's homosexuality is circumstantial. While he is not known for certain to have had sexual relationships with either men or women, nearly all of his emotional attachments (apart from his close relationships with his sister and the lesbian harpsichordist Wanda Landowska) were with men, especially gay intellectuals and artists.

While the elegance, sensuality, and erotic suggestiveness of his music have sometimes been seen as expressions of the composer's homosexuality, these qualities may have more to do with his Spanish musical formation than with homosexuality *per se*.   —*Mario Champagne*

BIBLIOGRAPHY

Crichton, Ronald. *Falla.* London: British Broadcasting Corporation, 1982.

Hess, Carol. "Falla (y Matheu), Manuel de." *New Grove Dictionary of Music and Musicians.* Stanley Sadie, ed. Second. ed. London: Macmillan, 2001. 8:529–535.

Hoffelé, Jean-Claude. *Manuel de Falla.* Paris: Fayard, 1992.

SEE ALSO

Classical Music; Ballet; Ballets Russes; Diaghilev, Sergei; Landowska, Wanda; Molina, Miguel de; Poulenc, Francis

Faye, Frances   (1912–1991)

IN A LONG CAREER THAT SPANNED MUCH OF THE TWENtieth century, openly bisexual entertainer Frances Faye recorded more than a dozen albums for major record companies, including Verve, Capitol, Bethlehem, and Imperial. She was a gravel-voiced vocalist and pianist whose style and sound evolved over the years to include jazz, pop, Latin, and rock influences; but her unique sense of rhythm and timing remained a strong constant.

In addition to her recording career, Faye was a bright star on New York's 52nd Street during its heyday in the 1930s and 1940s and a fixture in major nightclubs around the world for forty-five years. Her onstage persona was as much a comedienne as it was a musician.

Faye earned a reputation in the press as a social revolutionary because she did not shy away from warmly including references to homosexuals (or "gay kids") in her act and for being publicly known as bisexual at a time when few other performers dared to do so. "Frances Faye, gay, gay, is there another way?" she would burst out singing in every show.

Faye was born in Brooklyn on November 4, 1912, "a Scorpio and Reform Jew...Jewess," as she would proudly tell her audiences. Onstage, she referred to astrology as often as she did to her Jewish heritage.

Faye left school at the age of fifteen after suddenly finding herself in show business. At the last minute she was asked to fill in for an ailing piano player. She did so well that an agent offered her an astounding $120 a week salary.

By the mid-1930s, Faye was a fixture in 52nd Street jazz clubs, and that is when stardom came. The plump young woman was nicknamed "Zazz Zu Zazz," after her trademark scat phrase, and gained notoriety for her enthusiastic piano banging and her screaming vocals.

During the late 1930s and the 1940s, the entertainer toured constantly, lost weight, decreased the volume of her singing and playing, but grew more risqué in her onstage banter. She appeared on Broadway, filmed musical shorts, wrote the hit Andrews Sisters song "Well, All Right," and had two brief marriages.

The 1950s were the period of greatest artistic achievement and productivity for Faye. For most of the decade she sported a parakeet-style crew cut that still has shock value. Her first audience after the severe haircut greeted her in stunned silence, prompting the quick-witted, matronly Faye to joke, "When you're pretty, it doesn't matter how you wear your hair." It would become one of her signature lines.

Faye's masculine appearance in dress and coiffure was so different from the norm and ideal of the day that most articles and reviews mentioned it before her music. Her first two record companies did not feature her photograph on her album covers, but instead opted for cartoons and caricatures.

An increasingly raspy but lively Faye recorded for four different record companies in the 1950s. By the middle of the decade, her unconventional live act had become known for its outrageousness. Songs, hairstyles, and musicians would change, but Faye had found the successful sound, style, and format of jazz comedy, self-deprecating humor, fresh banter, and saucy double entendre that would be her gold mine. She had sold-out performances on the Hollywood Strip and played the major venues in Las Vegas and Miami, earning about $4,000 a week.

At a time when such topics were taboo, Faye parodied her bisexuality onstage. Occasionally, she chose to use same-sex pronouns in her love songs.

In the late 1950s, Faye met a glamorous twenty-two-year-old, Teri Shepherd, who became her lifelong companion and manager. In Shepherd's recollection, "Fran was one big girl, and I was the husband.... Once Fran's conservative mother exclaimed, 'Teri is the best son-in-law I ever had.' Offstage Fran was out there and didn't care what people thought. But backstage, I often overheard people saying the most hateful things out of Fran's earshot; especially from straight men."

Shepherd thought Faye was at her best performing live, so she organized the recording of the *Caught in the Act* album in 1958. It became Faye's biggest-selling record. That electric album was amazing in Eisenhower-era America for its frank embrace of gay people. Faye can be heard joking that she refused to sing "Way Down Yonder in New Orleans" because the "gay kids" do not like the lyric "...with those beautiful queens." Her comic song "Frances and Her Friends" boldly glorified same-sex coupling. She wove Teri Shepherd's name into the lyrics of classic songs, and as she always did onstage, Faye musically proclaimed "Frances Faye, gay, gay, is there another way?"

At a time when there were no sympathetic gay characters in film or television, or any publicly out performers at her level of mainstream success, Faye was quite literally a pioneer.

Suddenly, in 1958, disaster struck. While booked at Las Vegas's Hotel Riviera and playing to capacity crowds, Faye tripped on a bathroom carpet and shattered her hip. For eight years she was in terrible pain and often could not walk. Despite the accident, she still worked hard when she could. She toured and made great albums for Verve in 1961 and 1962. Her energetic nightclub appearances earned her the finest reviews of her career.

Faye was especially well received in Australia, where she made ten tours. In 1962, at Chequers, Sydney's top nightclub, Faye's unconventional act dazzled the young Peter Allen. The seasoned entertainer became a mentor to Allen and taught him about comic timing and how to structure an act and relate to an audience, lessons that he would use for his entire career. In addition, she introduced him to black music and helped him develop his stage persona.

Faye was also an influence on the young Bette Midler. In the early 1970s, funnyman Bruce Vilanch brought the emerging singer to see and learn from Faye's act, which attracted an increasingly large gay following.

In October 1975, Faye returned to New York City after a decade's absence. Her performances at the Spindletop Cabaret received glowing reviews, including one by jazz critic John S. Wilson of the *New York Times*. From the stage she flirted with female members of the audience, joked about marijuana, and comically outed the club's managers, columnist Rex Reed, singers Johnny Mathis and Peter Allen, and writer Noël Coward.

In 1977, Faye had an extended engagement at Studio One in West Hollywood, a cabaret that catered to a large gay and lesbian audience. Part of that show was filmed and worked into a television movie about gay runaways, *Alexander: The Other Side of Dawn*.

Director Louis Malle and screenwriter Polly Platt attended the Studio One show and the next day cast Faye in the film *Pretty Baby* (1977), which starred Brooke Shields as a child prostitute. Faye's riveting performance as the madam of a brothel in New Orleans's Storyville district earned her renewed attention and a wider audience.

In 1978, Faye suffered a heart attack and required a pacemaker; but by autumn she was back on tour. Despite her fragile health, she continued to present shows that were upbeat, energetic, and uninhibited. She performed until 1981, when she finally retired.

Faye died on November 8, 1991, after a series of strokes.

Although cabaret performance is an ephemeral art, Faye's memory has been kept alive, thanks to some high-profile fans. Drag performer Lypsinka (John Epperson), for example, included in his act a rendition of "Frances and Her Friends," the song Faye recorded about same-sex coupling. The same song was the inspiration for the tribute "Blues for Frances Faye" on singer Mark Murphy's album *Lucky To Be Me* (2002).

Photographer Bruce Weber's documentary film *Chop Suey Club* (2001) not only pays warm tribute to Faye and her influence on his early life, but also features an interview with Teri Shepherd about her life with Faye.

Peter Allen described Faye as "truly one of the free people of the world and the wildest woman I ever met," and added: "She was also the first person I ever met who didn't care what other people thought of her." Because Faye was unashamed of her sexuality and of her life, she was able to help pioneer an atmosphere of tolerance and acceptance by publicly embracing her gay and lesbian audience.

Some of Faye's albums, including *Caught in the Act*, have been rereleased on compact disc. —*Tyler Alpern*

BIBLIOGRAPHY

Alpern, Tyler. "Let Me Hear It Now: Biography of Frances Faye." http://hometown.aol.com/trumpdace/myhomepage/tunes.html

Folkart, Burt A. "Frances Faye, Bawdy Nightclub Singer." Obituary. *Los Angeles Times,* November 16, 1991.

MacLean, Stephen. *Peter Allen: The Boy from Oz.* Sydney: Random House Australia, 1996.

Reed, Rex. "Frances Faye Lights a Bonfire." *New York Daily News,* October 17, 1975.

Shaw, Arnold. *The Street That Never Slept.* New York: Coward, McCann & Geoghegan, 1971.

Smith, David, and Neal Peters. *Peter Allen: Between the Moon and New York City.* New York: Putnam Publishing Group, 1983.

Vilanch, Bruce. *Get Bruce.* New York: Miramax Films, 1999.

Weber, Bruce. *Chop Suey Club.* New York: Zeitgeist Films, 2000.

Wilson, John S. "Cabaret: Frances Faye." *New York Times,* November 16, 1978.

———. "Miss Faye Juggles Songs of the Forties at the Spindletop." *New York Times,* October 16, 1975.

See also

Popular Music; Cabarets and Revues; Jazz; Allen, Peter; Coward, Noël; Mathis, Johnny

Feinstein, Michael   *(b. 1956)*

AMERICAN PIANIST AND SINGER MICHAEL FEINSTEIN has had a lifelong fascination with the popular music of the 1920s, 1930s, and 1940s. He cites Al Jolson and Bing Crosby as his earliest musical influences, but among the most important were George and Ira Gershwin. An avid collector of their recordings since he was a boy, Feinstein became an archivist for Ira Gershwin, in which capacity he was able to study rare recordings and unpublished material by the Gershwins.

A popular performer in clubs and on the concert tour, Feinstein has also put out twenty albums, two of which were nominated for Grammy Awards.

Feinstein was born in Columbus, Ohio—"not exactly a hotbed of musical activity, especially for…show music," as he admits—on September 7, 1956, already well after the heyday of the songwriters that he would come to admire.

Music was a part of Feinstein's life from his earliest days. His father, Edward Feinstein, a meat salesman by trade, was a member of the Society for the Preservation and Encouragement of Barber Shop Quartet Singing in America and took his young son along to the meetings. His mother, Florence Mae Cohen Feinstein, an amateur tap dancer, shared his father's "great passion for music," according to Feinstein.

When Feinstein was five, his parents bought a spinet piano. The boy took to it immediately, playing songs by ear. His parents signed him up for music lessons, but he continued to play by ear, imitating what he heard his teacher play. The music lessons were soon abandoned, but Feinstein's fascination with the piano continued, and he became a self-taught musician. He did not learn to read music until he was in his twenties.

Growing up, Feinstein was a rather solitary child. His passion was music, and his musical tastes were distinctly different from those of most of his schoolmates. Intrigued by his parents' old 78-rpm records, he soon began his own collection, going to secondhand stores to buy records by such artists as Al Jolson and Bing Crosby.

At fifteen, he saw a televised movie about the life of George Gershwin. Deeply moved by Gershwin's music, he began scouring the city's thrift stores in search of recordings of his works and books about him.

In high school Feinstein was a member of the choir and the drama club. In his senior year he was voted the best actor in the school.

Never a particularly avid student, Feinstein decided to forgo college but did not have a specific career plan. He was already performing at weddings and bar mitzvahs, and now began to play at clubs as well. He also worked briefly as an accompanist for dance classes at Ohio State University.

When his father received a promotion and transfer to California, Feinstein decided to move there too. He took a job at a piano store, where he proved to be excellent at demonstrating the instruments but, in his own words, was "a lousy salesman."

It was Feinstein's passion for collecting old records that led to an important job opportunity. In a Hollywood record shop, he bought some rare acetate recordings by Oscar Levant, a pianist who had been a close friend of George Gershwin and recorded many of his songs. The shopkeeper told Feinstein that the recordings had come from Levant's estate. Curious about the circumstances of their sale, Feinstein arranged a meeting with the pianist's widow, June Levant.

Levant discovered that the recordings had been included in the estate sale by mistake, and, impressed with Feinstein's knowledge of her husband's career and works, asked him to help her catalog his record collection. In lieu of payment for his work, Feinstein asked Levant to introduce him to Ira Gershwin.

Gershwin, by that time aged and in ill health, received few visitors, but Levant succeeded in arranging for Feinstein to meet him. Once again, Feinstein's extensive knowledge of the music of the era served him. Gershwin was struck by the young man's interest and quickly hired him as an archivist. He worked for Gershwin from 1977 to 1983.

In Gershwin's house, Feinstein found a treasure trove of musical documents—not only commercially released records and sheet music but also privately recorded material and unpublished scores and lyrics. Feinstein catalogued the collection—which grew as Gershwin and his wife acquired more materials at auctions—for eventual donation to the Gershwin Archives in the Library of Congress.

In 1982, when a number of musical manuscripts by George Gershwin, Cole Porter, and other contemporaries were discovered in a warehouse in Secaucus, New Jersey, Feinstein identified eighty-seven written by George Gershwin himself and personally delivered them to the Library of Congress.

While working for Ira Gershwin, Feinstein served as a consultant to the production of the musical *My One and Only* (1982), which was based on George and Ira Gershwin's *Funny Face* (1927–1928).

Feinstein was excited at the prospect of working on a Broadway show but soon became frustrated by the "clash of egos" that he encountered among those involved and by what he saw as a lack of authenticity in various musical selections and arrangements. Although Feinstein was not totally satisfied with the final version, the show, which premiered on Broadway in 1983, was a success.

Feinstein has described his six years with Gershwin as "having lived a dream." The experience was important to him professionally because he learned a great deal about the music and musicians of the Gershwins' era and also, through Gershwin, became acquainted with people in the entertainment industry. In addition, he developed a sincere friendship with Gershwin, whom he admired for his "gentleness of spirit" as well as his talent and knowledge.

Under the terms of Gershwin's will, Feinstein was made one of his literary executors, and so, after Gershwin's death in 1983, he remained at work on various projects, including a book of previously unpublished songs. To Feinstein's disappointment, this work came to a halt when the lyricist's widow, Leonore Gershwin, contested the will. Eventually they were able to come to terms, allowing Feinstein to continue the project.

In the meantime, Feinstein went back to performing in order to earn a living. During the previous six years, his entertaining had been limited to playing and singing at parties given by the Gershwins or their friends.

The contacts that he made there proved valuable. Liza Minnelli became a good friend and called upon him to accompany her when she sang on *The Tonight Show*. This appearance led to other engagements, both at private parties and in clubs.

Critics praised his performances, citing his "personal intimacy" and "sensual involvement with the music." Gerald Nachman, a critic for the *San Francisco Chronicle*, called Feinstein "easily the best there is at what he does."

Feinstein's first album, *Pure Gershwin* (Parnassus Records), was released in 1985. He has since put out nineteen more, including two that received Grammy nominations, *Michael & George: Feinstein Sings Gershwin* (1998, Concord Jazz) and *Romance on Film / Romance on Broadway* (2000, Concord Jazz).

Michael Feinstein, photographed by Randee St. Nicholas in 2003.

Feinstein has performed on a number of television shows including *Cybill, Thirtysomething,* and *Caroline in the City,* as well as in the movie *Get Bruce* (1999, directed by Andrew J. Kuehn), for which he wrote music.

In 1999, he fulfilled a long-held ambition when he opened his own club, Feinstein's, at the Regency Hotel in Manhattan, where he occasionally performs, although much of his time is taken up with concert tours, both in the United States and abroad.

Feinstein's talent has earned him invitations to play for Britain's late Queen Mother and for three American presidents. When he went to the White House during the Clinton administration, he brought a male date.

Feinstein has been open in acknowledging his homosexuality. He has worked with the Human Rights Campaign (HRC), and he wrote a song for the Equality Rocks concert, sponsored by HRC as part of the activities of the Millennium March for gay rights in May 2000. He cited the murder of gay college student Matthew Shepard as a motivation for his participation in the event.

—*Linda Rapp*

BIBLIOGRAPHY

Feinstein, Michael. *Nice Work If You Can Get It: My Life in Rhythm and Rhyme.* New York: Hyperion, 1995.

"Feinstein, Michael." *1998 Current Biography Yearbook.* Charles Moritz, ed. New York: The H. W. Wilson Company, 1989. 157–160.

Malkin, Marc S. "Feinstein's Fine Times: Michael Feinstein is New York's Newest Club Kid—What's More, He Owns the Club." *Advocate,* November 9, 1999, 97.

SEE ALSO

Cabarets and Revues; Pierce, Charles; Porter, Cole

Fernie, Lynne   (b. 1946)

FILMMAKER, LYRICIST, AND EDITOR LYNNE FERNIE, A native of British Columbia, has had a varied career in the arts. Her principal work is the award-winning documentary *Forbidden Love: The Unashamed Stories of Lesbian Lives* (1992), which she codirected with Aerlyn Weissman.

As a young woman, Fernie moved to Toronto, where she became a member of LOOT (Lesbian Organization of Toronto), a lesbian feminist group in existence from 1976 to 1980.

In 1978, Fernie, along with other members of the Women's Writing Collective in Toronto, founded *Fireweed: A Feminist Quarterly of Writing, Politics, Art & Culture.* She coedited that journal's first lesbian issue (Issue 13) in 1983. Later, she worked as coeditor and then editor of *Parallelogramme,* a magazine of Canadian contemporary arts.

Fernie has been the lyricist for various Canadian recording artists, most notably the group The Parachute Club. She won gold records for her work on two of the group's albums and received a Juno award—the Canadian equivalent of a Grammy—for their single "Rise Up" (1983), which became an anthem of the Toronto gay community.

In 1989, Fernie was among a group of Canadian artists who founded the Inside Out Lesbian and Gay Film and Video Festival, held annually in Toronto.

Fernie directed a documentary, *Fiction and Other Truths: A Film about Jane Rule,* for which she won the Academy of Canadian Cinema and Television's Genie Award for short documentary in 1995. She also directed an educational video, *School's Out!* (1996), that places society's views toward homosexuality in a historical context and is intended for use in high schools to promote discussion of homophobia. In 1997, she directed another video for high school students, *Jane Rule...Writing,* in which the lesbian author discusses her writing process.

Fernie is best known as the codirector of *Forbidden Love: The Unashamed Stories of Lesbian Lives,* which won the Genie Award for feature-length documentary in 1993.

Forbidden Love was a product of Studio D of the National Film Board of Canada, the first publicly funded unit for women's films. In 1989, the executive director of Studio D, Rina Fraticelli, brought together Fernie and Aerlyn Weissman, a Vancouver filmmaker, to develop an ambitious project that would survey international lesbian history. Eventually, however, they decided to make a film with a very specific focus, the lesbian bar culture in major Canadian cities during the 1950s and 1960s.

Fernie and Weissman considered it essential to let the women of that milieu speak for themselves. For that reason they eschewed voice-over narration, opting instead for an interview format that allowed the women to tell their own stories of coming out and frequenting the bars, as well as what had happened to them in later years.

Weissman expressed their aim by saying, "Lynne and I felt quite strongly that it was important not to overlay the experiences of these women with a vocabulary of nineties feminist discourse. We really tried to structure the film in a way that would allow the women to speak for themselves, to give their experiences as they lived them, but to provide their contexts as well."

Nine women, ranging in age from approximately forty to eighty, described their experiences. They were a culturally diverse group, including a member of the Haida Nation from British Columbia, a black immigrant from Costa Rica, and a white woman who had been a middle-class Toronto housewife prior to coming out as a lesbian. Archival footage supplements these first-person accounts.

The period depicted in *Forbidden Love* was the heyday of lesbian pulp novels, paperback romances of a formulaic nature generally centered on college sorority members, dissatisfied housewives, or habituées of Greenwich Village bars. Ann Bannon, author of the extremely popular "Beebo Brinker" series of pulp novels, is among the women interviewed in the film.

Bannon's discussion of her experiences as a novelist and also a suburban wife and mother who explored the Greenwich Village lesbian bar scene helps tie together the recollections of the women and the fictional elements in *Forbidden Love.*

Departing from the standard documentary format, Fernie and Weissman interspersed a pulp-style love story with the reminiscences of the interviewees. Using the technique of freeze-frame and dissolve, the film moves from images of covers and illustrations in the style of pulp novels to the film-within-a-film.

The tale recounted in *Forbidden Love* is that of Laura, a country girl who moves to the big city, where, with some trepidation, she goes to a lesbian bar. There she meets and falls in love with Mitch.

The lesbian love affair brings fulfillment to Laura, and her story has a happy—even triumphant—ending. This is at odds with the typical dénouement of the pulp novels, which generally ended with the protagonist going mad or dying. (Bannon's novels were an exception to the pattern.)

It is also inconsistent with some of the stories of the interviewees, whose accounts include discussion of the difficulties and dangers that they faced in trying to create a public lesbian space in a homophobic society. Nevertheless, the women emerge as clever, witty, and courageous. Their stories of survival and endurance can be regarded as a triumph.

Forbidden Love garnered positive reviews in both the gay and mainstream press. In addition to the 1993 Genie, it won awards at the Durban International Film Festival and the International Women's Film Festival in France.

—*Linda Rapp*

BIBLIOGRAPHY

Anderson, Elizabeth. "Studio D's Imagined Community: From Development (1974) to Realignment." *Gendering the Nation: Canadian Women's Cinema.* Kay Armitage, Kass Banning, Brenda Longfellow, and Janine Marchessault, eds. Toronto: University of Toronto Press, 1999. 41–61.

FitzGerald, Maureen. "Fernie, Lynne." *Contemporary Gay and Lesbian History from World War II to the Present Day.* Robert Aldrich and Garry Wotherspoon, eds. London and New York: Routledge, 2001. 133.

Hankin, Kelly. "'Wish We Didn't Have to Meet Secretly?': Negotiating Contemporary Space in the Lesbian-Bar Documentary." *Camera Obscura* 15.3 (2000): 34–69.

McKenty, Margaret. Review of "Forbidden Love." *Herizons* 7 (July 31, 1993): 41.

Rich, B. Ruby. "Making Love." *Village Voice,* August 17, 1993, 58.

Ross, Becki L. *The House That Jill Built: A Lesbian Nation in Formation.* Toronto: University of Toronto Press, 1995.

Tilchen, Maida. "Pre-Stonewall Lesbians Tell All." *Sojourner: The Women's Forum* 19.1 (1993): 33–34.

Wexler, Alice. Review of "Forbidden Love." *American Historical Review* 99.4 (1994): 1270–1272.

Finn, William   (b. 1952)

Playwright and composer William Finn explored the nature of the chosen family with wit and sensitivity, humor and drama in his Tony Award–winning musical *The Falsettos*. Juxtaposing contradictory emotions is typical of his work.

William Alan Finn is the oldest of three children in a family of Russian Jewish descent. Born in Boston on February 28, 1952, he grew up in nearby Natick.

He began composing after receiving a guitar as a bar mitzvah present and subsequently taught himself to play the piano, but did not immediately envision music as his career. Following his graduation from Natick High School, he enrolled at Williams College, where he majored in literature and American civilization.

Finn's interest in music remained lively, however. He participated in musicals at Williams and even penned three of his own. He was awarded the college's Hutchinson Fellowship for Musical Composition, an honor that fellow alumnus Stephen Sondheim had also earned.

After graduating from Williams, Finn spent a year studying music at the University of California at Berkeley, then moved to New York in 1976 to pursue a career in musical theater.

By 1978, Finn had written the book and the songs for *In Trousers,* which was produced off Broadway early the following year, with Finn directing. Richard Eder, then the drama critic for the *New York Times,* wrote a scathing review of the show, which closed quickly. Dispirited, Finn briefly considered giving up music as a vocation and going to medical school.

Fortunately, he abandoned neither music nor Marvin, the central character of *In Trousers,* who reappeared in *March of the Falsettos* in 1980. Frank Rich, who had succeeded Eder at the *New York Times,* gave the show an enthusiastic review, noting that after hearing only a few bars of Finn's music "one feels the unmistakable, revivifying charge of pure talent."

In a 1993 interview, Finn explained the musical allusion in the play's title by saying that the falsetto is a voice outside its normal range and that he "was writing about people outside the normal range of people [he] grew up with in Massachusetts."

March of the Falsettos finds Marvin trying to maintain a close-knit family even though he has just left his wife, Trina, and son, Jason, for a male lover, Whizzer, whereupon Trina begins dating his psychiatrist, Mendel. Critic Rich noted that "the show's hetero- and homosexual couples both suffer from the same anxieties, loneliness, and neuroses" and that the most touching relationship is Marvin's with Jason, whose affection he is afraid of losing.

After *March of the Falsettos* Finn had a fallow musical period during which he wrote articles for airline magazines and also contributed to better-known publications such as *Vogue* and *Harper's Bazaar.*

Finn's return to musical theater was inauspicious; his *Romance in Hard Times* closed after a short run in 1989. The following year, however, he had a hit with *Falsettoland.*

Finn has stated that *Falsettoland* had its genesis at a family Thanksgiving dinner. His family has always been "enormously supportive" of him and has fully accepted Arthur Salvatore, his partner since 1980, as part of the clan. At the fateful Thanksgiving meal Salvatore was helping Finn's little nephew cut his meat when the boy suddenly jumped up in his chair and exclaimed, "I love Uncle Arthur!" This led Finn back to considering the meaning of family and the fate of Marvin.

In *Falsettoland* Trina has married Mendel, and Whizzer, who left Marvin at the end of *March*, returns to him, and the two set up housekeeping next door to a lesbian couple. Whizzer, however, has contracted AIDS, still a nameless disease in the 1981 setting of the piece. Marvin's family—and it is a family—deals simultaneously with the joy of Jason's upcoming bar mitzvah and the pain of Whizzer's inevitable death.

Finn turned the two latter parts of the Marvin story into a single show, called *The Falsettos*, in 1992. The combination was exceptionally powerful; Joe Brown of the *Washington Post* wrote that "the audience, which began the play roaring with laughter, is left in tear-soaked shreds."

The Falsettos was richly honored at the Tony Awards, winning for Best Original Score and Best Musical.

At the moment of triumph when he accepted the statuettes, however, Finn was desperately ill. Having suffered a loss of vision and balance, and even passing out as he tried to walk, Finn was initially diagnosed with a brain tumor, but it was later determined that he had an arteriovenous malformation, a congenital condition.

Conventional surgery being out of the question, Finn underwent radiation Gamma Knife surgery at the University of Virginia hospital, with his family—conventional and unconventional—at his side.

Finn used the experience to create his next and most autobiographical work, *A New Brain* (1998). He managed to create a life-affirming, humor-infused show despite the backdrop of a potentially fatal medical crisis.

The same year saw the premiere of *Love's Fire*, a play that compiles work by seven writers—Tony Kushner, Marsha Norman, Ntozake Shange, Eric Bogosian, John Guare, Wendy Wasserstein, and Finn—each contributing a segment interpreting one of Shakespeare's sonnets. Finn's piece, *Painting You*, based on Sonnet 102, which is almost entirely sung, takes a lighthearted look at a gay artist having trouble capturing his lover on canvas. Perhaps because of its unusual structure, the play has received mixed reviews, ranging from delighted to bewildered.

Finn's most recent venture is *Elegies* (2003), a musical remembrance of loved ones, colleagues, and pets who have died over the past twenty years. Once again Finn takes painful topics, including the loss of his beloved mother and the devastating toll of AIDS among his friends, and creates a celebration of life that critic Stephen Holden calls a "moving and exuberant song suite."

Throughout his career, Finn has been compared to Sondheim because of the wit and urbanity of his writing. He has his own distinctive voice, however, and speaks with understanding about confronting life in all its complexity with sadness and joy, dilemmas and hope intermingled.

—*Linda Rapp*

BIBLIOGRAPHY

Brown, Joe. "The Truth about 'Falsettos'; William Finn and His Coming-Out Tragicomedy." *Washington Post*, May 10, 1992.

Evans, Everett. "'Falsettos' Sings Tradition with a Twist; Tony-winning Musical Depicts Struggle for Love, Support in 'New Family.'" *Houston Chronicle*, December 19, 1993.

Holden, Stephen. "Departed Friends Vibrantly Recalled in Song." *New York Times*, March 28, 2003.

Pall, Ellen. "The Long-running Musical of William Finn's Life." *New York Times*, June 14, 1998.

Rich, Frank. "'March of the Falsettos,' A Musical Find." *New York Times*, April 10, 1981.

Zailian, Marian. "Family Affairs; Tony-winning 'Falsettos' Looks at Changing Relationships." *San Francisco Chronicle*, April 25, 1993.

SEE ALSO

Musical Theater and Film; Sondheim, Stephen

g

Garland, Judy   *(1922–1969)*

To call Judy Garland an icon of the gay community is a massive understatement. Garland's fragile but indomitable persona and emotion-packed singing voice are undeniably linked to modern American gay culture and identity. This is especially true for gay men, but lesbians also are drawn to identify with Garland's plucky toughness and vulnerability.

Garland's signature song, "Over the Rainbow," is the closest thing we have to a gay national anthem, and many have claimed that it was grief over Garland's death from an overdose of drugs in June 1969 that sparked smoldering gay anger into the Stonewall riots and fueled the gay liberation movement. Whether true or not, this story has such poetry that one feels it ought to be true.

After all, in the intensely closeted pre-Stonewall days, gays often identified themselves to each other as "friends of Dorothy," referring to Garland's 1939 role in *The Wizard of Oz*.

Garland was virtually born a performer. Her parents owned a theater in Grand Rapids, Minnesota, where little Frances Gumm was born on June 10, 1922. She began singing and dancing on stage at the age of four. She toured in vaudeville, performing with her sisters, before being discovered in 1935 and signed to a contract with the Metro-Goldwyn-Mayer film studio.

She changed her name to Judy Garland and starred with Mickey Rooney in the *Andy Hardy* film series before being cast in her career-defining role in *The Wizard of Oz*.

Early in her career, studio doctors began giving Garland prescription drugs. The "speed" she took to lose weight made her too nervous to sleep, so she was given tranquilizers and sleeping pills, beginning a destructive cycle that would continue throughout her life and finally kill her.

Garland was painfully insecure; and, unfortunately, she began her career at a time when performers worked under contract to powerful studios and had little control over their careers. Her attempts to take charge of her career caused the studios to reject her as a troublemaker, but Garland's powerful talent and sheer heart propelled her through comeback after comeback.

After Garland's childhood career ended, she wowed audiences in her first adult role in *Meet Me in St. Louis* in 1944. In 1954, after more difficult years, she starred powerfully in *A Star is Born* with James Mason.

When the film roles were not offered, she went back on the concert stage, performing long runs at New York's Palace Theater. Despite an Academy Award nomination for a stunning performance in *Judgment at Nuremberg* (1961) and a brief but memorable television show on CBS (1963–1964), Garland found herself nearly penniless. Near the end of her life, she performed anywhere she could, even in piano bars when she could find no other work.

Garland was adored by gay fans throughout her career, but her connection to the world of homosexuality did not stop with her fans. Her beloved father, Frank Gumm, had

Judy Garland in 1947.

been a closeted gay man, and Roger Edens, her strongest supporter in the early days at MGM, was also gay.

Even two of Garland's husbands, Vincente Minnelli and Mark Herron, were gay, which made possible an intergenerational *ménage* when Herron had an affair with Peter Allen, who was married to Garland's daughter Liza Minnelli.

Garland is surely one of the most memorable and indefatigable performers in the history of American popular entertainment. She made over thirty feature films, received a special Academy Award, and was nominated for two others. She also garnered several Emmy nominations and a special Tony Award.

Garland made numerous recordings, including the Grammy Award–winning *Judy at Carnegie Hall*, which has never been out of print. Her concert appearances became legendary, both for their triumphs and their spectacular failures.

Perhaps the most touching, and telling, image of Judy Garland, embedded in the memories of gay men and lesbians of a certain age, is the way she ended many of her concerts. Dressed in drag as a hobo, her smudged face showing the pathos of the eternal outsider, she approaches the audience and sits on the edge of the stage. Looking far into the distance, she sings "Somewhere Over the Rainbow" with intense, lonely sweetness, longing for that impossible land where dreams come true.   —*Tina Gianoulis*

BIBLIOGRAPHY

Clarke, Gerald. *Get Happy: The Life of Judy Garland.* New York: Random House, 2000.

DiOrio, Al, Jr. *Little Girl Lost: The Life & Hard Times of Judy Garland.* Greenwich, Conn.: Kearny Publishing, 1975.

Gross, Michael Joseph. "The Queen Is Dead." *Atlantic Monthly,* August 2000, 62.

Guly, Christopher. "The Judy Connection." *Advocate,* June 28, 1994, 48.

Vare, Eehlie A. *Rainbow: A Star Studded Tribute to Judy Garland.* New York: Boulevard Books, 1998.

SEE ALSO

Cabarets and Revues; Divas; Popular Music; Musical Theater and Film; Drag Shows: Drag Queens and Female Impersonators; Allen, Peter; Minnelli, Vincente; Porter, Cole

Geffen, David   (b. 1943)

ONE OF THE MOST FEARED AND ADMIRED, REVERED and reviled figures in the entertainment industry, David Geffen succeeded in transforming himself, either through sheer ingenuity or outright guile, from his humble origins in Brooklyn into one of the most important figures in the arenas of corporate rock music, movies, and television.

According to Steve Kurutz, Geffen is responsible for guiding the careers of, and forming lasting (if tumultuous) friendships with, countless big-name musical acts, such as The Eagles, Jackson Browne, Nirvana, Elton John, and Cher.

Geffen's combative style, as well as his forthright honesty and compulsive competitiveness, however, have earned him many detractors and some outright enemies.

For his foes, Geffen exemplifies the greed and excess of the music industry. In their eyes he is a shark who changed the priority from music to money. For others, however, Geffen is regarded as an extraordinarily generous and caring person, one who believes in and passionately supports a diverse array of social and political causes, ranging from homeless shelters to AIDS research.

David Lawrence Geffen was born on February 21, 1943, in Brooklyn, the son of Batya and Abraham Geffen, Russian Jewish immigrants who settled in New York in 1931. While David's older brother Mitchell (b. February 6, 1933) was long considered the family's success story, Abraham and Batya spoiled David, forgoing discipline in favor of extravagant praise, and often referred to him as "King David." Consequently, David struggled in school, barely graduating from New Utrecht (New York) High School in 1960 with a final grade average of 73.59.

Following high school, David shuttled between his home in Brooklyn and Mitchell's apartment at UCLA.

Returning to New York in 1961, he bluffed his way into a mailroom job at the prestigious William Morris Agency by both implying that he was legendary record producer Phil Spector's cousin and padding his résumé with a false degree from UCLA.

At the Morris agency, Geffen set about learning everything about the entertainment industry. After ingratiating himself to agency president Nat Lefkowitz, he began charting his ascendancy. Through Lefkowitz, Geffen became one of the hottest agents in New York, and in 1967 he got his first big break when he signed bisexual songwriter Laura Nyro and, soon afterward, negotiated a lucrative music publishing deal for her that netted them each $3 million plus a substantial share of future royalties.

Geffen's brash style also catapulted him into the executive ranks at Atlantic Records, for which he signed the newly formed supergroup Crosby, Stills, and Nash. Geffen was soon able to bankroll his own label, Asylum Records, which was initially distributed by Atlantic Records but which Geffen quickly sold to Warner Brothers in 1971 for $7 million. Geffen, however, stayed on as head of Asylum.

In 1976, citing burnout and health scares, Geffen retired from the industry; but in 1980, he returned to form Geffen Records, a subsidiary of Warner Brothers. In an attempt to make Geffen Records a viable brand, he quickly snapped up performers such as Elton John and Donna Summer, though both artists, having weathered a shift in musical direction, recorded mediocre material and soon left the label.

In the midst of this early discord at his record label, David Geffen was also maneuvering himself into the arena of movies. In 1982, by parlaying his friendship with Warner Brothers executive Steve Ross, Geffen soon produced several notable movies, including the lesbian-themed *Personal Best* and the teen classic *Risky Business*, which starred Tom Cruise in the memorable role of Joel.

Over the next decade, Geffen went on to produce a mixed array of films, but he leapt at the chance to work again with Cruise in the 1994 *Interview with the Vampire*.

As the 1980s progressed, Geffen also worked diligently to make his record label profitable. By the late 1980s, he had keenly recognized, and subsequently signed, big revenue-producing bands such as Aerosmith and the controversial heavy-metal band Guns N' Roses, weathering controversy over the band's homophobic song "One in a Million." Geffen was also able to resuscitate Cher's career, using his shrewd business acumen and capitalizing on their former romantic attachment.

Although Geffen had been linked romantically to both Cher and actress Marlo Thomas, his homosexuality was an open secret in the entertainment industry. Geffen had already lost several of his close friends to AIDS, but he was particularly affected by the death of his pal and partying companion Steve Rubell, owner of the infamous New York disco Studio 54.

According to Tom King, after Rubell's death, in 1989, Geffen began making large donations to individuals and charities dedicated to helping people with AIDS. His gifts include $2.5 million to AIDS Project Los Angeles, $2.5 million to Gay Men's Health Crisis of New York, and $1.4 million to AIDS Action in Washington, D.C.

Geffen's particular support of AIDS causes roused the attention of queer magazine columnist Michelangelo Signorile, who, in 1990, blasted Geffen as a hypocrite for not coming out as a gay man.

Tom King has noted that Geffen had resisted making an open statement because of a strong belief that his sexual orientation was a private matter. Geffen realized that by virtue of his success, however, he had become a public figure, and at a 1992 benefit for AIDS Project Los Angeles, David Geffen declared that he was a gay man.

Somewhat surprisingly, the disclosure did not detract from Geffen's reputation. In fact, it was viewed by many of his associates as a long-overdue and honest admission that could only increase his stature in the entertainment industry.

In 1990, Geffen again struck gold by signing alternative bands Nirvana and Sonic Youth to his record label. The same year, Geffen decided it was time to sell Geffen Records. After a series of tense negotiations, the label was acquired by MCA for $540 million.

In 1994, Geffen joined with noted movie director Steven Spielberg and former Disney Studios chairman Jeffrey Katzenberg to form the media conglomerate DreamWorks SKG. Continuing to use the skills he had honed successfully over the previous thirty-plus years, Geffen works behind the scenes at DreamWorks, brokering deals, colluding with friends, and antagonizing his enemies.

In May 2002, Geffen donated $200 million to the medical school at UCLA—the largest single donation ever made to an American medical school. The school was renamed the David Geffen School of Medicine at UCLA.   —*Nathan G. Tipton*

BIBLIOGRAPHY

King, Tom. *The Operator: David Geffen Builds, Buys, and Sells the New Hollywood.* New York: Random House, 2000.

Kurutz, Steve. "David Geffen." *All Music Guide.* www.allmusic.com

Singular, Stephen. *The Rise and Rise of David Geffen.* Secaucus, N.J.: Birch Lane Press, 1997.

SEE ALSO

Popular Music; John, Sir Elton

Goode, Joe   (b. 1951)

THE MOST ORIGINAL CONTRIBUTION OF THE WORK OF choreographer Joe Goode is its challenge to traditional assumptions involving gender. Like the dance theater pieces of Bill T. Jones and other openly gay choreographers, Goode's work incorporates spoken word, music, and visual imagery in varying combinations. His dances often tell stories about being gay in the age of AIDS.

Goode was born into a working-class family in Presque Isle, Maine, on March 13, 1951. Depressed and suicidal as a high school student in the 1960s, Goode found solace in the poetry of Allen Ginsberg, which he read as a message from an alternative world where it was possible to be Jewish, intellectual, politically radical, and gay.

"I didn't see how I was going to fit in and have a whole, meaningful life. My sexuality and my sensitivity and my whole being seemed wrong," Goode later told a reporter for the *Washington Blade*.

Goode earned a B.F.A. in drama from Virginia Commonwealth University in 1973, and then studied dance in New York City with Merce Cunningham and Viola Farber.

However, he was unhappy during his years as a young artist in New York City. "All the great choreographers were big old fags," he told the *Blade*, but "their work was dogmatically heterosexual, even in abstraction." The sight of so many male/female, implicitly heterosexual couples, with men lifting and leading the women, impressed Goode as a dishonest spectacle.

Like other maverick spirits before him, Goode went west in search of freedom. In 1979, he left New York for California, where he felt it would be easier to break out of such restrictive roles. The Joe Goode Performance Group, headquartered in San Francisco, was incorporated as a not-for-profit organization in 1986. The company has performed internationally and has been honored with numerous grants and prizes.

One of Goode's most noted pieces, *Deeply There (Stories of a Neighborhood)*, which premiered in 1998, explores the impact of AIDS on San Francisco's Castro district. Another, *The Maverick Strain* (1996), is an examination of the stubbornly individualist streak in American culture; it puts pioneer women and androgynous cowboys on yesterday's range and in today's AIDS wards to make a complex statement about the strengths and weaknesses of the American character.

Other works with significant gay content include *Remembering the Pool at the Best Western* (1990), which meditates on AIDS and life after death, and *Convenience Boy* (1993), which examines the plight of gay and lesbian workers in the sex industry.

The women in Goode's company often lift their male colleagues. In this way and in others, Goode presents images of the softness of men and the strength of women.

"I'm just interested in those images because they're so fearful to our culture," Goode told the *Blade*.

But Goode's creative impulse is not entirely confrontational. The comic performer in him loves to make people laugh. Indeed, humor helps to defuse his risky subject matter, rendering it less threatening to viewers who might otherwise be put off.

Goode's work explores the importance of "inappropriate" behavior. In a mission statement, Goode wrote that he aims to "pierce the veil of toughness that we all have in our lives and to uncover the vulnerable center, the confused, flailing human part of us that we conceal and avoid." Among his goals, he wrote, is "to make the world a more compassionate place."

With his troupe, Goode has done outreach work with various population groups, including gay youth. He has taught at several academic institutions and has received numerous awards, including multiple Isadora Duncan awards and National Endowment for the Arts and Irvine Dance fellowships.

—*Greg Varner*

BIBLIOGRAPHY

Goode, Joe. "Mission Statement." www.joegoode.org

Varner, Greg. "Strong Women, Pretty Men: Maverick Dancer Defies Gender Assumptions." *Washington Blade*, March 20, 1998, 45.

SEE ALSO

Dance; Cunningham, Merce; Jones, Bill T.

Griffes, Charles Tomlinson   (1884–1920)

AMERICAN COMPOSER CHARLES TOMLINSON GRIFFES responded avidly to the emerging musical styles of his day to create works characterized by refined construction, subtle gestures, and rhythmic flexibility.

The third of five children, Griffes was born on September 17, 1884, in Elmira, New York. He grew up in a comfortable middle-class household and took his first piano lessons from his sister, Katharine. At the age of fifteen, he began to study with Mary Selena Broughton, a well-trained English spinster and an instructor at Elmira College, who strongly guided his musical development and financially supported his piano studies in Germany beginning in 1903.

Besides benefiting from some of the best musical instruction available in piano, counterpoint, and composition during his stay in Europe, Griffes also became aware of the emerging homophile movement in Germany and the work of such pioneer figures as Magnus Hirschfeld. He also read the works of Oscar Wilde, André Gide, and Edward Carpenter.

Through exposure to the relatively liberal and nurturing atmosphere of musical circles in Europe, he acquired a sense of comfort with his own sexuality while still young. However, he never divulged his orientation to straight friends or associates.

During his first year abroad, Griffes formed a strong, possibly sexual, attachment to a twenty-eight-year-old fellow student, Emil Joel, who guided his artistic development, procured concert tickets for the young man, and introduced him to such prominent musical figures as Richard Strauss, Enrico Caruso, Ferrucio Busoni, and Engelbert Humperdinck, with whom he briefly studied.

Griffes returned to the United States in 1907 to assume the directorship of music at the Hackley School in Tarrytown, New York, a post he held until his death in 1920 from an abscessed lung. His job held no special prestige, but the school's location just up the Hudson River from New York City gave him opportunities to promote his music there and to pursue an active sexual life in the relative anonymity of Manhattan.

Griffes kept a diary in German in which he reported on his various forays to bathhouses and other favorite gay-friendly haunts. He also enjoyed the company of men outside the public sex spaces and often visited newfound friends in their homes.

New York provided the ideal environment in which to become familiar with the most progressive artistic trends in the country. With his gay companions, Griffes took full advantage of the rich menu of New York's cultural life. He enjoyed not only the city's musical offerings but also its theater and visual art. He was especially interested in watercolors and photography.

Because of his cosmopolitan experience, catholic taste, and solid training, Griffes avidly approached the modern styles of art music emerging in his day more quickly than any other young American except Charles Ives (1874–1954).

While barely out of his teens, he had left the German Romantic sound of his first works to experiment with the Impressionistic techniques now associated with Claude Debussy and Maurice Ravel. *The White Peacock* (1915) is probably Griffes's best-known piano work in this Impressionistic style. (It was later arranged for orchestra.)

Griffes, like Debussy and Gustav Mahler, was struck by the fashion for Asian art subjects, especially those prints and paintings characterized by simple clear lines and empty space. He befriended the Ballets Russes dancer Adolf Bolm, who commissioned a one-act pantomime from him that resulted in *Sho-Jo* (1917), which featured the Japanese dancer Michio Ito accompanied by a spare chamber ensemble of wind and percussion instruments.

Griffes's final pieces, especially his Piano Sonata of 1919, press into even more progressive territory and mark him as a bold experimenter, unafraid to use highly jagged melodies and stinging chord clashes in pursuit of a distinctive individual style.

At the time of his death, he was working on a festival drama based on the poetry of Walt Whitman entitled "Salut au monde."

All told, Griffes composed seven sets of songs, five sets of piano pieces, ten works for orchestra, and a handful of works for chamber ensembles, the latter often written to accompany stage plays. He enjoyed critical success in his lifetime, but evinced almost no interest in the nationalist debates of the day, arguments often characterized by a patriarchal and stridently patriotic tone. He took a thoroughly modern view, free of any nativist sentiment.

Griffes's reportedly modest, shy, unpretentious, and witty personality is mirrored in his music: works recognized for their refined construction, subtle gestures depicting texts and moods, rhythmic sensitivity, and a marked melodic gift.

No man of his time and position could have been completely out without public disgrace, but clearly Griffes was able to express both his art and his sexuality, even if he was not able to integrate them as fully as he might have wished.

—*Thomas L. Riis*

BIBLIOGRAPHY

Anderson, Donna K. *Charles T. Griffes: A Life in Music.* Washington and London: Smithsonian Institution Press, 1993.

Chauncey, George. *Gay New York: Gender, Urban Culture, and the Making of the Gay Male World, 1890–1940.* New York: Basic Books, 1994.

Maisel, Edward. *Charles T. Griffes: The Life of an American Composer.* New York: Alfred A. Knopf, 1943.

Struble, John Warthen. *The History of American Classical Music: MacDowell through Minimalism.* New York: Facts on File, 1995.

SEE ALSO

Classical Music; Ballets Russes; Ravel, Maurice

Handel, George Frideric   *(1685–1759)*

ONE OF THE TOWERING FIGURES OF WESTERN CLASSICAL music, George Frideric Handel was a native German who lived much of his life in England. Unlike his contemporary Johann Sebastian Bach, who never set foot outside Germany, Handel was a cosmopolitan who spent extended periods at aristocratic courts in Germany and Italy before settling into the vibrant urban culture of London.

Handel is widely known for certain of his flashier instrumental pieces such as the *Water Music* (1717) and *Royal Fireworks Music* (1749), as well as the large-scale English oratorios with soloists and chorus, above all *Messiah* (1742). But his prolific output includes many other instrumental works, cantatas, and numerous operas in Italian, some of which, such as *Giulio Cesare* (1724), attract considerable interest today.

Handel was born on February 23, 1685, in Halle, Germany, into a staunchly Lutheran family. His father was a court barber-surgeon. Handel was powerfully drawn to music from an early age, but his father wanted him to study law and he enrolled at the university in Halle in 1702.

However, the composer left home in 1703, at the age of eighteen, in order to pursue a career in music, in which he was largely self-trained. After a brilliantly successful career, he died in London on April 14, 1759.

One of the few composers to enjoy a large measure of fame and mythic stature in his own lifetime, Handel after his death went on to become a British cultural icon. He became the hero of a musical cult (the Handelians), darling of the Christian choral establishment, and, more recently, a lucrative consumer commodity with more than one album of "Greatest Hits" to his credit.

Given Handel's exalted status and the unwritten rule that no star in the classical galaxy may be homosexual, least of all the composer of *Messiah*, it is hardly surprising that scholarly investigation into Handel's personal life, particularly his sexuality, has met with resistance.

In Handel's case, homosexual panic set in early: Even biographers in his own time appear troubled about this celebrity's apparent lack of interest in women, the more so since he never came anywhere close to marriage but did spend a great deal of time in private, all-male social circles.

That Handel himself maintained strict silence about his private life only fueled suspicions of homosexuality, leading scholars and critics over the years to a general "Don't ask, don't tell" policy.

However, neither that policy nor some of the most remarkable feats of invention and denial on record (discovery of "secret" lady friends and lovers, assumptions of chastity on religious grounds or the "holy solitude of the artist," and so on) have allayed the suspicions.

Over two centuries' worth of prevarication—some of it amusing, despite the underlying homophobia—has labored mightily to certify Handel as acceptably straight,

An engraving of George Frideric Handel.

a man of "normal masculine constitution," in the words of one of his nervous biographers, or to embalm him in a state of nonsexual purity.

The attempt has been to remove both the composer and his works from the dross of history in order to canonize them into "timeless universality." Thus, around Handel was constructed the first biographical closet, of many to come, for a major composer in the West.

Whether Handel was in fact homosexual (or its eighteenth-century equivalent; the word itself was not coined until 1869) or had same-sex sexual relations will probably never be known with certainty; such records were compiled only for the hapless victims of criminal arrest.

What we do know is that from the time the composer left provincial Germany, especially during his formative years from age twenty-one to thirty-eight, his social orbit coincided with the most important homosexual venues of the eighteenth-century elites: aristocratic courts and "Arcadian" academies, especially those in Florence and Rome (the latter known colloquially at the time as the "City of Sodom"); the English country retreat; and the London theater and opera scene itself.

In these settings, Handel mingled variously with princes, cardinals, and other aristocratic men of means and influence, as well as with artists, whose homosexuality was known in closed circles or more generally as the "open secret."

From these years the picture of a distinctly "private" Handel emerges with striking clarity, not simply because of all this circumstantial evidence but also on the basis of his work.

Especially important in this regard is a set of cantatas—works for various combinations of solo voices with instrumental accompaniment—written precisely during this time (1706–1730). These largely ignored pieces, written for and in the company of private circles of mainly homosexual men, and which (significantly) Handel never published, give rich expression to the pleasures and dangers of same-sex love.

Standing in opposition to the religious view of homosexuality as sin (sodomy), and the political view of homosexuality as exotic threat to the British nation, these texts connect with the classical pastoral tradition in which male same-sex erotic desire is both idealized and celebrated.

The classical and thus "legitimate" pastoral, with its elaborate system of mythical references and coy Arcadian disguises, functioned in much the same way as the coded references to homosexuality in Hollywood film during its censorship under Will Hays and Joseph Breen—that is, as a screen of metaphorical displacements and double meanings through which what was publicly forbidden could be privately expressed, understood, and enjoyed.

The figure of Orpheus, connoting both "musician" and "homosexual," and with whom Handel was often compared, is one salient example.

It is also significant that when a series of crackdowns on the burgeoning and increasingly open homosexual subculture of London began in the 1730s, Handel reworked many of these texts from which he had borrowed liberally over the years. In so doing, he sanitized them of their more obvious homosexual content.

In light of all this, and in the absence of even a shred of credible evidence to the contrary, we must ask the question on what basis—more to the point, *in whose interests*—can it be argued that Handel was anything other than queer?

Though discomfiting to many, such questions are urgently political, made so not by any "homosexual agenda" but by the persistence of homophobia in our culture. More important, finally, than the question of Handel's sexual identity are the sociocultural contexts and political struggles in which the composer's sexuality was meaningful—for Handel, for his biographers, and for us.

We must take these contexts into account if we are ever to escape the politically suspect myth of "timelessness" and properly appreciate both Handel and his magnificent work.

—Gary C. Thomas

BIBLIOGRAPHY

Brett, Philip. "Musicality, Essentialism, and the Closet." *Queering the Pitch: The New Gay and Lesbian Musicology.* Philip Brett, Elizabeth Wood, and Gary C. Thomas, eds. New York: Routledge, 1994. 9–26.

Harris, Ellen T. *Handel as Orpheus: Voice and Desire in the Chamber Cantatas.* Cambridge, Mass.: Harvard University Press, 2002.

Hogwood, Christopher. *Handel.* London: Thames and Hudson, 1984.

Rousseau, George S. "The Pursuit of Homosexuality: 'Utterly Confused Category' and/or Rich Repository?" *'Tis Nature's Fault: Unauthorized Sexuality during the Enlightenment.* Robert Purks Maccubbin, ed. Cambridge: Cambridge University Press, 1985. 132–168.

Thomas, Gary C. "'Was George Frideric Handel Gay?': On Closet Questions and Cultural Politics." *Queering the Pitch: The New Gay and Lesbian Musicology.* Philip Brett, Elizabeth Wood, and Gary C. Thomas, eds. New York: Routledge, 1994. 155–203.

SEE ALSO

Classical Music; Opera; Castrati; Corelli, Arcangelo

Harrison, Lou (1917–2003)

AMERICAN COMPOSER LOU HARRISON ENJOYED A LONG and distinguished career. He is particularly well known for his use of instruments from the East, especially the Javanese gamelan, and for his melodic and lyrical musical style, despite the fact that he studied composition in the atonal musical style of Arnold Schoenberg.

One of America's most original and articulate composers, Harrison explored a number of interests, including puppetry, Esperanto, tuning systems, the construction of musical instruments, and dance. He was also actively involved in political causes, especially pacifism and gay rights.

He was born Lou Silver Harrison on May 14, 1917, in Portland, Oregon, but his family moved to the San Francisco Bay area when he was a child, and he lived most of his life on the West Coast of the United States. As a child, he was exposed to a wide range of music, including Cantonese operas, Gregorian chants, and Spanish and Mexican music.

Harrison attended San Francisco State University, where he decided on music as his major and his life's work. He studied there with Henry Cowell and quickly became fascinated with melody and its powers, particularly in the music of the Orient. He also developed an interest in the works of American composer Charles Ives, some of whose musical manuscripts he later edited.

Among Harrison's early compositions is a large body of percussion music that reveals Western, Asian, African, and Latin American rhythmic influences.

As a young man, Harrison also worked closely with John Cage, with whom he wrote *Double Music* (1941), for four percussionists, and studied in Los Angeles with Arnold Schoenberg. His early compositions include *Canticles* and *Song of Queztalcoatl,* a reference to the Mexican serpent god.

During World War II, Harrison moved to New York and wrote music criticism for various publications. In the late 1940s in New York, he composed *The Perilous Chapel* and *Solstice,* works that reflect his admiration of Mexican music and culture.

Although Harrison was welcomed into the musical circle surrounding composer Virgil Thomson, who promoted his work, he soon decided that he did not really enjoy living in the crowded and stressful metropolis.

By the early 1950s, Harrison was teaching at Black Mountain College in North Carolina, the experimental arts college where Cage and choreographer Merce Cunningham also taught.

While at Black Mountain, Harrison wrote his chamber opera *Rapunzel* (1951), as well as *Seven Pastorales* (1951) and *Strict Songs* (1955). This latter series of songs was inspired by the music of the Navajo and indicated his continuing interest in native folk cultures of the Americas.

In 1953, Harrison happily returned to the West Coast—specifically, to Aptos, California, near Santa Cruz—and devoted himself to the study of Asian music. In 1961 and 1962, he lived in Korea and Taiwan, where he discovered various Oriental instruments and became particularly fascinated by the gamelan. He began writing his own music for this instrument.

By 1967, he had found his life's partner, William Colvig. Although not a composer, Colvig shared Harrison's passion for music. They collaborated on the construction of a number of instruments, including two American gamelan, one at San Jose State University, the other at Mills College. Colvig's death in 2000 marked the end of a remarkable and productive relationship.

In 1971, Harrison wrote an opera, *Young Caesar,* which relies on a group of Oriental instruments. The work deals with both homosexuality and the confrontations of East and West.

For the gamelan and other instruments, Harrison wrote one of his most famous compositions, *La Koro Sutra* (1972), a work that reflects the East's Buddhist philosophy as well as its musical sounds. He has written three dozen original works for the gamelan, often accompanied by Western instruments.

Harrison taught at various colleges in California, including Stanford University, Cabrillo College, Mills College, and the University of Southern California. From 1968, he maintained an affiliation with San Jose State University.

Harrison's later works include three symphonies and a number of chamber music pieces. His *Suite for Cello and Piano* (1995) is indicative of the continuing quality of his extraordinary productivity. Also in 1995, he wrote "Parade for MTT" for the San Francisco Symphony, to celebrate the inauguration of music director Michael Tilson Thomas.

For many years, Harrison was involved in the movement for gay rights. He also worked on behalf of the ecological movement and the cause of world peace.

Harrison died on February 2, 2003, in Lafayette, Indiana. He was en route to a festival of his music at Ohio State University in Columbus, Ohio. Celebrated as one of America's most accomplished composers, and sometimes dubbed the "Santa Claus" of new music for his white beard, considerable heft, and ready laugh, he was mourned by music lovers throughout the world.

—*John Louis DiGaetani*

BIBLIOGRAPHY

Miller, Leta E. "Lou Harrison." *The New Grove Dictionary of Music and Musicians.* Stanley Sadie, ed. London: Macmillan, 2001. 11:64–67.

———, and Frederic Lieberman. *Lou Harrison: Composing a World.* New York: Oxford University Press, 1998.

Von Gunden, Heidi. *The Music of Lou Harrison.* Metuchen, N.J.: Scarecrow Press, 1995.

SEE ALSO

Classical Music; Conductors; Cage, John; Cowell, Henry; Cunningham, Merce; McPhee, Colin; Thomson, Virgil; Tilson Thomas, Michael

Hart, Lorenz   *(1895–1943)*

BARELY FIVE FEET TALL, BALDING EARLY, AND POSSESS-ing a disproportionately large head, Larry Hart was the first to disparage his own attractiveness. His jokes, however, masked a deeply rooted inability to accept the possibility of romantic happiness or sexual gratification.

Hart impulsively proposed marriage to several women friends, none of whom thought his offer serious. And when he allowed himself to act upon his desire for other men, he seems to have had difficulty performing sexually. (His biographer Frederick Nolan quotes one unidentified male partner's shock at discovering Hart cowering in the bedroom closet after sex, suggesting that the songwriter was unable actively to pursue homosexual pleasure without being overcome by guilt.)

The result of such emotional imbroglio is that, despite having written lyrics as witty as any sung on the Broadway stage before or since, Hart is best remembered for his songs of unfulfilled desire and failed romance.

Born Lorenz Milton Hart on May 2, 1895, to an immigrant Jewish family, Hart learned from his entrepreneur father that self-assertion allows survival. Never without a business venture, many of which were dishonest, Hart's father provided Larry with a lasting model for the cycles of impulsive free-spending and resulting impecuniosity that characterized Hart's own life.

Hart entertained both friends and strangers lavishly, often living far beyond his means, but with a (sometimes unfounded) optimism that something would turn up. And, like his father, Hart was a ball of ferocious energy, both physically and creatively.

As Oscar Hammerstein II, recalls, "In all the time I knew him, I never saw him walk slowly. I never saw his face in repose. I never heard him chuckle quietly. He laughed loudly and easily at other people's jokes and at his own, too. His large eyes danced, and his head would wag. He was alert and dynamic and fun to be with."

As disorganized and undisciplined as he was tirelessly inventive verbally, Hart possessed a nervous energy that could make him an exasperating person to work with. Words poured so easily from him that, increasingly as he aged, he preferred socializing and drinking with hangers-on to working.

And though Hart seems to have inspired genuine affection in everyone he met, no one who knew him was surprised when he died on November 22, 1943, of pneumonia contracted while wandering the streets of Manhattan in a downpour, badly intoxicated.

Composer Richard Rodgers, with whom Hart began an extraordinarily successful collaboration in 1919, recollected that when he met Hart he acquired "in one afternoon a career, a best friend, and a source of permanent irritation." Their early years together, spent writing musical revues and novelty songs for burlesque comedians, culminated in their first Broadway hit, *A Connecticut Yankee*, in 1927.

Finding their chances of continued financial success in New York severely limited by the Great Depression, however, they followed many of their Broadway contemporaries to Hollywood, where, after the initial success of writing the songs for Maurice Chevalier and Jeannette MacDonald in *Love Me Tonight* (1932), they were frustrated by the pedestrian projects the studios assigned them, and by the increasing criticism that Hart's lyrics were too witty and too darkly satiric to succeed on sets decorated with plastic palm trees.

Their return to New York resulted in their final and most fruitful period, which saw the hit productions of *Jumbo* in 1935, *On Your Toes* and *Babes in Arms* in 1936, *The Boys from Syracuse* (a musicalization of Shakespeare's *Comedy of Errors*) in 1938, and the breakthrough musical *Pal Joey* in 1940.

Apart from their polysyllabic rhymes and sophisticated wit (master poet W. H. Auden included Hart's "Take Him, He's Yours" in an anthology of light verse),

Hart's lyrics are remarkable for two reasons. First, they are amazingly frank about sexual matters. In *Pal Joey*, the title character openly boasts of the sexual chase in "Happy Hunting Horn"; his credo is suggested by the double entendre inscribed in the title of another of the play's songs, "Do It the Hard Way."

His inamorata, philandering socialite Vera Simpson, sings of her midlife sexual reawakening in "Bewitched, Bothered, and Bewildered": "I'll sing to him / Each spring to him / And worship the trousers that cling to him."

Far from being taken sexual advantage of, Vera is shrewd about the paradoxical nature of sexual desire. Men, she observes, are stimulants, "Good for the heart / Bad for the nerves," or ornaments, "Useless by day / Handy by night." And if she complains that men are "all alike," she's also honest enough to acknowledge that they're "all I like."

In a double entendre that depends upon the auditor's understanding "on" to refer to the missionary position, she accepts that the socially uncouth Joey is "a laugh, / But I love it / Because the laugh's on me." As she sings elsewhere, "Horizontally speaking, / He's at his very best."

And, after ending their affair, Vera celebrates her relief at being no longer sexually dependent upon Joey— "The ants that invaded my pants, / Finis!"—for she is "Bewitched, bothered, and bewildered no more."

Second, Hart's lyrics are remarkable because they feign indifference to, or casually accept, disappointment. The lyricist is unlike most of his contemporaries who could not imagine a show ending without the boy getting the girl. As songs such as "Blue Moon" and "Lover" evidence, Hart was perfectly capable of writing a traditional love song; likewise, in "My Heart Stood Still" and "With a Song in My Heart" he presents the exhilaration of a love that is freshly, ecstatically, joyously experienced.

But more often—in songs such as "My Romance," "Falling in Love with Love," and "This Can't Be Love"— Hart asserts the reality of a deeply experienced love by mocking the very conventions that other lyricists (and the record-buying public) had grown to rely upon.

Moreover, Hart's most psychologically profound love songs prove to be those in which the speaker laments his or her disappointment. "Spring Is Here," for example, which contrasts the loveless speaker's depression with the natural joy of the season of rejuvenation, might be an Elizabethan complaint.

The speaker in "Glad to Be Unhappy" may well be articulating the fundamental principle of Hart's philosophy of love when he protests that "Unrequited love's a bore, / And I've got it pretty bad. / But for someone you adore, / It's a pleasure to be sad."

Together these reasons explain why, despite one of the most original scores that Broadway theatergoers had yet heard, *Pal Joey*, Hart's greatest play, did not arouse audience enthusiasm when first mounted. The show was a hit, but it inspired little affection in audiences in 1940. Only when it was revived in 1952 did it garner the kind of enthusiasm it deserved.

Joey, more antihero than hero, is a likable cad who exploits women even as he is himself sexually exploited by a supposedly respectable society matron. When Joey and Vera sing of their sexual bliss in the apartment that she has furnished for him ("our little den of iniquity"), they not only challenge the moral standards that the Broadway musical was designed to inculcate, but implicate audience members in their satire of society's hypocrisy.

The audience's appreciation of Joey and Vera's keeping separate bedrooms, "One for play and one for show," for example, reveals audience members' guilty familiarity with the strategy of disguising supposedly immoral private behavior with a carefully crafted public persona; in addition, the line asks audience members to reconsider their impressions of those in society who appear always "*comme il faut.*"

And if the audience is uncomfortable listening to adulterous lovers singing of the salubrious benefits of infidelity, Hart reminds his audience that things have been this way "since antiquity."

Likewise, when the pair boast that "Ravel's Bolero works just great" as background music to their lovemaking, Hart shocks some audience members with the scandalous use to which a piece of classical music is being put, while alerting others to the deeply sensuous nature of a selection they've been trained to think of as sexless (as canonized by the symphony orchestra that they so properly and mechanically patronize). Little wonder that audiences were left cold by the original production.

After Hart's death, Rodgers began a second great collaboration, this one with Oscar Hammerstein II.

Lorenz Hart (standing, right) with Richard Rodgers in 1936.

Together they produced such important but artificially wholesome shows as *Oklahoma*, *The Sound of Music*, and *South Pacific*. Significantly, Rodgers never composed a song of real longing again; without Hart, his music was just too straight.   —*Raymond-Jean Frontain*

BIBLIOGRAPHY

Hart, Dorothy, and Robert Kimball, eds. *The Complete Lyrics of Lorenz Hart*. New York: Knopf, 1986.

Marx, Samuel, and Jan Clayton. *Rodgers and Hart: Bewitched, Bothered and Bedeviled*. New York: Putnam, 1976.

Mordden, Ethan. *Broadway Babies*. New York: Oxford University Press, 1983.

Nolan, Frederick. *Lorenz Hart: A Poet on Broadway*. New York: Oxford University Press, 1994.

Rodgers, Richard, and Oscar Hammerstein II, eds. *The Rodgers and Hart Songbook*. New York: Simon and Schuster, 1951.

SEE ALSO

Musical Theater and Film; Coward, Sir Noël; Porter, Cole; Ravel, Maurice; Sondheim, Stephen

Heath, Gordon   (1918–1991)

AFRICAN AMERICAN ACTOR, DIRECTOR, AND FOLK singer Gordon Heath became a fixture on the Parisian cabaret scene from 1949 until 1976. After an early success on Broadway in the play *Deep Are the Roots* (1945), he went to Europe, where he spent most of the rest of his life. He settled in Paris, where he and his partner Lee Payant owned and entertained at a Left Bank nightclub. Heath performed in theater, film, television, and radio productions and also recorded several albums of folk music.

Heath's father, Cyril Gordon Heath, emigrated from Barbados to the United States. He settled in New York City, where he married Hattie Hooper. Gordon Heath, born on September 20, 1918, was the couple's only child.

Heath's musical education began at age eight, when an aunt gave him violin lessons. He studied other instruments as well, but was most drawn to the guitar, finding it "friendly and sympathetic...to the touch."

As a youngster Heath also showed a talent for drawing, winning prizes for both art and music in high school. He began performing in amateur theater groups and took first prize in a municipal drama competition.

Heath earned scholarships to two music schools and briefly attended the Dalcroze Institute but decided to pursue an acting career instead. He worked on stage and in radio. When he joined radio station WMCA in New York in 1945, he became the first black staff announcer at a major radio station in America.

In 1945, Heath scored a major success on Broadway in the play *Deep Are the Roots*, by Arnaud d'Assue and James Gow. Heath starred as a military hero facing racism when he returns to the Deep South after World War II and falls in love with one of the daughters of a wealthy family for whom his mother works as a housekeeper. Heath's electrifying performance won praise from the critics.

When the play closed on Broadway after a fourteen-month run, Heath went to London and reprised his role in a West End production, again receiving critical acclaim.

When the run in London ended, Heath decided not to return to America. In 1948, he settled in Paris, which he considered more hospitable to blacks and more accepting of his relationship with his white lover, Lee Payant, a fellow actor whom he had met in New York in the early 1940s. Like many other American expatriates fleeing racism and homophobia, Heath found a haven in cosmopolitan Paris.

In 1949, Heath and Payant became co-owners of a Paris club called L'Abbaye, so named because it was behind the abbey church of St Germain des Prés. For nearly thirty years the two entertained appreciative audiences, playing guitar and singing duets of American and French folk songs.

In 1957, Elektra Records released an album of their duets, *An Evening at L'Abbaye*, comprising seventeen songs, five of them in French. Heath and Payant also recorded an album entitled *French Canadian Folk Songs* in 1954, and the same year Heath had a self-titled solo album.

Even after acquiring L'Abbaye, Heath continued to act. He toured in Britain in 1950 as the title character in Shakespeare's *Othello*, a role that he repeated in Tony Richardson's 1955 version of the play on BBC.

Heath appeared in other British television productions, again playing the lead in *Deep Are the Roots* in 1950. He starred in Eugene O'Neill's *The Emperor Jones* in 1953, and appeared in a television adaptation of Alan Paton's novel *Cry, the Beloved Country* in 1958.

Despite the positive reception of his performances on stage and television, Heath did not receive offers for major parts in movies. He narrated John Halas and Joy Batchelor's animated film of George Orwell's *Animal Farm* in 1956, and contributed supporting roles in a number of movies, including *Les héros sont fatigués* (1955, directed by Yves Ciampi), *The Madwoman of Chaillot* (1969, directed by Bryan Forbes), and *L'Africain* (1983, directed by Philippe de Broca). He and Payant also dubbed many films.

In the 1960s, Heath turned his talents to directing, working for a decade with the Studio Theater of Paris, an English-language company that staged plays by Thornton Wilder, Arthur Miller, and Bertolt Brecht, among others. Payant acted in many of the plays.

Payant died of cancer in December 1976 at age fifty-two. Devastated by his loss, Heath could not bear continuing to work at L'Abbaye alone. He returned to the United States, where he spent five years doing some acting and directing.

Eventually, however, he decided to go back to France, and there he found a new partner, Alain Woisson.

Heath died in Paris on August 28, 1991, of an AIDS-related illness.

—*Linda Rapp*

BIBLIOGRAPHY

Blau, Eleanor. "Gordon Heath, 72; Co-Starred in Play 'Deep Are the Roots.' " New York Times, August 31, 1991.

Bourne, Stephen. "Heath, Gordon." Who's Who in Contemporary Gay & Lesbian History from World War II to the Present Day. Robert Aldrich and Garry Wotherspoon, eds. London and New York: Routledge, 2001. 183.

Breman, Paul. "Gordon Heath." Obituary. Independent (London), September 13, 1991.

Heath, Gordon. *Deep Are the Roots: Memoirs of a Black Expatriate.* Amherst: University of Massachusetts Press, 1992.

Shipman, David. "Gordon Heath." Obituary. Independent (London), September 2, 1991.

SEE ALSO

Cabarets and Revues

Henze, Hans Werner (b. 1926)

GERMAN COMPOSER AND CONDUCTOR HANS WERNER Henze is remarkable for his ability to employ a wide range of styles, from those of the avant-garde to opulent neo-Romanticism, especially in his many stage and concert works.

His operas include the lush *König Hirsch* (1955); *Elegy for Young Lovers* (1961) and *The Bassarids* (1965–1966), both to libretti by W. H. Auden and Chester Kallman; the antibourgeois comedies *Der junge Lord* (1964) and *The English Cat* (1980–1982); a political allegory for multiple stages and orchestras, *We Come to the River* (1976); and *Das verratene Meer* (1990), based on a dark tale by Yukio Mishima.

Henze holds strong Marxist convictions, as shown in explicitly political works such as the vituperative *Versuch über Schweine* (1968), the dramatic cantata *Das Floß der Medusa* (1968), the Cuban slave's story *El Cimarrón* (1970), the bizarre "show for 17" *Der langwierige Weg in die Wohnung der Natascha Ungeheuer* (1971), the "anthology" cantata *Voices* (1973), and the ballet *Orpheus* (1978). Most of these works juxtapose downtrodden proletariats and rich oppressors.

Other important works include eight symphonies (1947–1993), five string quartets (1947–1976), the remarkable Piano Concerto no. 2 (1967), and numerous concerti, keyboard works, and chamber works.

Henze was born on July 1, 1926, in the small town of Gütersloh in Westphalia. He studied music in nearby Brunswick, against his parents' wishes, and composed from the age of twelve without formal training; as a teenager he was interested in the modernist music banned by the Nazis.

In 1944, Henze was drafted into the German army. He served in Poland before being transferred to a propaganda film unit. In 1946, he returned to his musical education, studying in Heidelberg with Wolfgang Fortner and writing his first acknowledged compositions.

That year, Fortner brought Henze to the first of the summer music courses in new music in Darmstadt, where the young composer was presented as a star pupil. Over the next fifteen years, as Darmstadt became a center of the avant-garde, Henze's reputation devolved to that of neo-Romantic reactionary.

This ambiguous political and aesthetic position—regarded as avant-garde by the bourgeoisie, but as an Establishment tool or "limousine liberal" by the avant-garde—has haunted Henze's career. It contributed, along with his increasing distaste for Germany, to his decision to establish residence in Italy in 1953.

Henze's career survived detachment from the world of the avant-garde because his theatrical abilities allowed him to become one of the few modernists able to survive as an opera composer.

He was a professor of music in Salzburg from 1962 to 1967 and in Cologne from 1980 to 1991. In 1990, he became the first composer in residence for the Berlin Philharmonic. In 1988, he founded the Munich Biennale, and continues as its director. The Biennale has commissioned many new stage works by young composers.

Henze has been open about being gay for most of his life, as seen in his honest, nonsensational autobiography, *Bohemian Fifths* (1999). Despite his strong leftist convictions, he evidently does not associate sexuality with politics, though much of his work outlines conflicts between sensuality and repression.

Images of and allusions to homosexuality appear in *Heliogabalus Imperator* (1972) and *Le Miracle de la Rose* for clarinet and ensemble (1981), the former a symphonic poem suggesting Roman decadence, the latter an instrumental work that refers to Genet's novel.

—*Paul Attinello*

BIBLIOGRAPHY

Henze, Hans Werner. *Bohemian Fifths: An Autobiography.* Princeton, N.J.: Princeton University Press, 1999.

———. *Music and Politics: Collected Writings 1953–81.* London: Faber & Faber, 1982.

SEE ALSO

Classical Music; Conductors; Opera

Herman, Jerry   (b. 1931)

"I HAVE ALWAYS BEEN DRAWN TO OUTRAGEOUS, LARGER-than-life female characters," Jerry Herman writes in a memoir of his career as a Broadway composer and lyricist. So it is not surprising that, though seemingly retired from the musical comedy stage, he remains the best proponent of the "diva musical," described by theater historian John Clum as a musical comedy "about a woman's escape from the humdrum" and pedestrian life to which social convention would consign her.

As Clum also notes, the diva musical allows a gay theater audience "an escape from the oppressive life into magic" through worship of a female star who has no hesitation—in the words of Herman's Zaza—to "put a little more mascara on" and turn the world into something "ravishing, sensual, fabulous…glamorous, elegant, and beautiful."

Thus, Dolly Levi "puts her hand in" and rearranges everyone's life for the better; Mame Dennis coaxes the blues right out of the horn and teaches everyone to celebrate simply because "it's today"; actress Mabel Normand lights up not only the movie screen but every room she walks into; Mrs. Santa Claus restores childhood innocence, advocates gender equality, and saves Christmas; and transvestite extraordinaire Zaza proudly boasts "I am what I am" while teaching sour moralists that "the best of times is now."

Born on July 10, 1931, to middle-class Jewish parents in Jersey City, New Jersey, Herman was the only child of ardent theatergoers who introduced him to the joys of the Broadway musical at an early age. His family ran a summer camp where Herman worked until he was twenty-one, in the process discovering a talent for producing musical entertainments.

An audition for Frank Loesser (*Guys and Dolls*) encouraged Jerry to work full-time as a composer, and after writing the music for three off-Broadway plays, he scored a major success with *Milk and Honey* (1961). Shortly thereafter, David Merrick hired him to write the music and lyrics for *Hello, Dolly!* (1964; film, 1969), and for the next twenty years Herman was one of the most bankable talents on Broadway.

Megahits such as *Mame* (1966; film, 1974) and *La Cage aux Folles* (1983) alternated with box-office failures such as *Dear World* (1969) and *Mack and Mabel* (1974) that nonetheless quickly attained cult status.

In addition to a revue of songs from his shows (*Jerry's Girls*, 1985), Herman has written the scores for the musically less interesting *The Grand Tour* (1979) and for *Mrs. Santa Claus* (1996), a television musical created for Angela Lansbury that has become a stalwart of the Christmas holiday season.

Despite a highly popular thirtieth-anniversary revival of *Hello, Dolly!* and a much-applauded London concert version of *Mack and Mabel* (1988), Herman laments in his memoirs the end of the era of "upbeat, feel-good" musicals of the sort he enjoys writing. He is no longer creating original work for the theater.

The Three Constants

There are three constant elements in every Herman show:

The Statement Song

First, there is what Herman himself calls the "statement song," in which the heroine delivers her philosophy of life.

For example, Dolly Levi liberates her spiritual nemesis Horace Vandergelder's overworked, underpaid clerks by telling them to "Put on Your Sunday Clothes" and venture from rural Yonkers into Manhattan to discover that "there's lots of world out there."

Mame Dennis throws extravagant parties for no special occasion, insisting simply that "It's Today"; in "Open a New Window," she teaches her nephew Patrick that the only "way to make the bubble stay" is by resisting convention and experiencing something new every day.

Aurelia, the Madwoman of Chaillot, counsels the denizens of her quarter of Paris that hope is reborn "Each Tomorrow Morning," which allows her to go on whenever she feels dejected.

And drag star Zaza teaches her neighbors and audience to "hold this moment fast / And live and love as hard as you know how, / And make this moment last / Because the best of times is now."

Herman's heroines do not hesitate to interfere—always generously, always joyously—in other characters' lives, in particular teaching the younger generation how to live more freely and with greater satisfaction. Their philosophy is clearly Herman's own, and that of the chorus in *Mack and Mabel*, which asserts its refusal to be cowed by disappointment and instructs the audience to "Tap Your Troubles Away."

The Diva's Dramatic Soliloquy

Second, every Herman play allows the diva a musical dramatic soliloquy. The song marks a moment of self-doubt in which she rallies her spirits, even while allowing the audience to see the price that the diva pays for her optimism.

Dolly sings about her loneliness in widowhood and her newfound determination to "raise the roof" and "carry on" as energetically as she can "Before the Parade Passes By."

Stunned when her adult nephew seems to reject all that she taught him in youth, Mame ponders what she would do differently "If He Walked into My Life Today."

Refusing to live in a world without music, laughter, love, or joy, Aurelia passionately asserts that "I Don't Want to Know" that the world has turned ugly.

And Albin, confronted with his lover's son's request that Albin absent himself when the conservative family of the boy's fiancée comes to call, refuses to hide who he is, insisting that "Life's not worth a damn / Till you can say / 'Hey, world, / I am what I am!'"

Such songs are invariably the most dramatic moment in the play, demonstrating the indomitable spirit that makes each Herman protagonist a diva. Similarly, the original actor's extraordinary rendering of them is what made Carol Channing (Dolly), Angela Lansbury (Mame, Aurelia, Mrs. Santa Claus), and George Hearn (Albin) stars, and kept their dangerously over-the-top performances from degenerating into caricature.

While Herman clearly has a particular genius for fashioning such dramatic numbers, it is important to note that he has been ably aided by the directors and set designers of his shows. A semicircular runway extending around the orchestra pit in the original production of *Hello, Dolly!* allowed Channing to sing within a few feet of her audience, winning them over even while towering above them.

The dramatic lighting of Lansbury's soliloquies, especially the amber gel and swirl of falling leaves as she questioned where she went wrong in "If He Walked into My Life Today," transfixed audiences, winning her Tony Awards for both *Mame* and *Dear World*.

And, in a piece of inspired direction, Arthur Laurents had Albin, still in drag after a performance as Zaza, pull off his wig at the conclusion of "I Am What I Am" and proudly exit down the center aisle, to the thrilled applause of the audience, at the close of *La Cage*'s first act.

Herman's directors have created big theatrical gestures that magnify the inner resolve of these larger-than-life women.

The Staircase Number

And, finally, every Herman play offers a "staircase number" in which the assembled company, in a pull-out-all-the-stops fashion, celebrates its transformation by praising the woman who raises the energy level of everyone around her by her mere presence.

Dramatically, there is no reason why the waiters should be so excited about Dolly Levi's anticipated return to the Harmonia Gardens restaurant that they break into a gallop as they serve and bus tables. But theatrically, the title number of *Hello, Dolly!* is the occasion to celebrate Dolly's joy in living, which washes over and renews everyone whom she encounters.

Likewise, the conservative Southern community into which Mame seeks to marry is so impressed by her performance on the fox hunt that crusty old Mother Burnside herself triumphantly asserts that, with Mame in their midst, "This time the South will rise again!"

The chorus of *Mack and Mabel* celebrates Mabel's return to moviemaking in a rousing number that claims every heart beats faster "When Mabel Comes in the Room"; while the chorus of *Dear World* is in effect praising Aurelia in the stirring finale, "One Person."

The message of these songs is that the woman's presence revivifies the stodgy and pedestrian lives of her contemporaries; she brings imagination, magic, and a screwball-comedy madness to their humdrum existence.

But the songs are great theatrical moments as well. Think of Carol Channing's descent of a red-carpeted staircase in a red brocade gown, with red ostrich plumes in her brassy yellow hair, or the jubilant cakewalk on the terrace of an antebellum mansion as the company sings the title song of *Mame*, or *Les Cagelles* in their highest drag forming a sequined constellation around Zaza.

These are moments of glorious, jubilant theatricality that celebrate a woman whose strength of character and comic imagination allow her to resist the pressures of social convention and recreate herself as something bigger, brassier, and livelier than decorum allows. Such moments, like the characters themselves, are a drag queen's dream.

Gay Backlash

While audiences have generally been enthusiastic—often wildly so—in response to Herman's work, a gay backlash emerged in the early 1980s, paradoxically, just as he became most visible in popular gay culture.

In part, the backlash reflects a change in musical tastes that began earlier but was only fully developed in the 1980s. Their very identity as diva musicals puts Herman's plays at odds with the "concept musical," which in Martin Gottfried's definition places greater importance on the weaving of music, lyrics, dance, stage movement and dialogue "in the creation of a tapestry-like theme (rather than in support of a plot)," and so they are less likely to focus upon a single star.

An ensemble ethos marks the groundbreaking musicals of the 1970s, such as *Company* (1970), *Chicago* (1975), and *A Chorus Line* (1975). Indeed, the ensemble number performed by the dancers auditioning for the play-within-the-play of *A Chorus Line* ("One") seems to parody the staircase number that Herman specializes in, the point of *A Chorus Line* being that there is no single star, that everyone contributes to the ensemble.

More problematically, the backlash signaled gay culture's rejection of Herman's basic philosophy. Survival, for Herman, is a question of posture and attitude; one simply has to "put on your Sunday clothes / When you feel down and out," or "put a little more mascara on." But while tapping one's troubles away may have appealed to a generation raised on post-Depression-era Busby Berkeley movie musicals, increased public awareness of the spreading AIDS epidemic gave the lie to *La Cage*'s claim that "The Best of Times Is Now."

Resistance through grand gestures is the pose of both the diva and the drag queen; AIDS required a different theater of resistance, black comedy rather than screwball comedy.

Commenting upon the sudden reversal of opinion concerning *La Cage aux Folles* in the mid-1980s, Mark Steyn—in an aggressively homophobic account of the Broadway musical—notes that "One minute...[it] was the biggest homegrown hit of the day; the next it was gone," largely because as public perception of AIDS grew, "fags weren't funny anymore; fags meant disease and death."

In the 1980s, Sondheim's questioning of his audience's ability to live with ambivalence seemed a braver and more realistic form of engagement than Herman's asking it to choose self-consciously to ignore tragedy and assert joy. As Herman himself observes, "the upbeat, feel-good songs that I write" no longer resonated with audiences.

Criticism of Herman's optimism as escapist is unfair. There is a strong satiric impulse in such songs as "Masculinity," "It Takes a Woman," and "The Spring Next Year" that is every bit as socially engaged as Burton Lane's much-lauded challenge to American racism in *Finian's Rainbow*.

Ironically, then, the moment when Albin, refusing to fashion himself to suit anyone else's expectations, pulls off his wig at the end of "I Am What I Am" was not only the very moment when gays asserted themselves most openly on the Broadway stage; it was also the moment when American gay culture lost its need of a diva to voice its concerns and became free to raise them in its own voice.

Thus, Herman's plays seem dated to newer gay audiences raised on Sondheim's ambivalence and on the openly gay musicals of William Finn, in which characters do not need musicals to feel good about themselves.

Even as *La Cage aux Folles* made homosexuality the undisguised subject of a popular musical, challenged the hypocrisy of the self-proclaimed moral majority empowered by the presidency of Ronald Reagan, and provided gays with a national anthem ("I Am What I Am"), Herman found himself bypassed by the very parade that he had been leading.

—*Raymond-Jean Frontain*

BIBLIOGRAPHY

Clum, John M. *Something for the Boys: Musical Theater and Gay Culture.* New York: St. Martin's Press, 1999.

Herman, Jerry, with Marilyn Stasio. *Showtune: A Memoir.* New York: Donald I. Fine, 1996.

Jordan, Richard Tyler. *"But Darling, I'm Your Auntie Mame!": The Amazing History of the World's Favorite Madcap Aunt.* Santa Barbara: Capra Press, 1998.

Steyn, Mark. *Broadway Babies Say Goodnight: Musicals Then and Now.* New York: Routledge, 1999.

SEE ALSO

Musical Theater and Film; Divas; Finn, William; Laurents, Arthur; Sondheim, Stephen

Hildegard of Bingen   *(1098–1179)*

HILDEGARD OF BINGEN, MYSTIC AND POET, PROPHET and playwright, composer and scientist, lived all but the first few years of her life in the company of women.

Born in 1098 in the Rhineland, Hildegard, the tenth child of a noble family, was offered by her parents at the age of eight to the community of Benedictine nuns in Disobodenberg, where she became abbess in 1136.

Hildegard's spiritual gifts were evident early in her life: At the age of three, as she reveals in her *Vita*, she saw a brightness so great it made her soul tremble. In fact, according to the documents prepared for the process of Hildegard's canonization (a process initiated but never completed, though she has been listed as a saint in the Roman martyrology since the Middle Ages), she had already perceived a vision of the "living Light" while still in her mother's womb.

In 1141, Hildegard experienced a remarkable series of visions, accompanied by a heavenly command to write what she was seeing. Although she initially refused the command, a devastating illness (sent, she believed, from God) persuaded her to begin writing her first visionary text, the *Scivias* (*Know the Ways of the Lord*). Her corpus eventually included two other visionary works, a song collection, a musical drama, and several scientific treatises.

In 1148, anxious to win spiritual and economic independence for her community from the monks of Disobodenberg, Hildegard entered into what was to be a difficult battle to relocate her nuns to the Rupertsberg, on the Rhine near Bingen.

It was about this time, as well, that Hildegard's most difficult personal struggle began. As a spiritual leader and writer, Hildegard necessarily supported the Church's teachings on same-sex desire; nevertheless, her *Vita* and her surviving letters demonstrate a remarkable emotional intensity for the women with whom she came into contact.

In particular, her affection for her disciple and assistant, Richardis von Stade, and the betrayal she felt when Richardis left her, threatened Hildegard's professional credibility and her inner calm.

In 1151, Richardis was offered a position as abbess in a distant convent. Although Hildegard refused permission for her to leave, Richardis did go, and the depth of Hildegard's feeling is revealed in the letters she wrote imploring her young friend to return: "I loved the nobility of your conduct, your wisdom and your chastity, your soul and the whole of your life, so much that many said: What are you doing?"

Hildegard's efforts to force Richardis to return to her included an intense and far-reaching letter campaign, but her efforts was unsuccessful. However, after Richardis's sudden, early death in 1152, her brother revealed in a letter to Hildegard his sister's tears at their separation. He told the abbess, "if death had not prevented her, she would have come to you."

Modern readers of Hildegard's works and her life have delighted in the images of female desire and the positive representations of female sexuality that survive in all aspects of her writing, from her medical texts to her letters. Particularly noteworthy is the homoeroticism of her liturgical cycle, the *Symphoniae,* which expresses physical and spiritual desire for the Virgin Mary.

Hildegard's visionary works are also remarkable for their attention to the feminine aspects of theology. With considerable justification, many contemporary scholars have claimed Hildegard as a premodern instance of a "woman-identified woman."

Since Hildegard's spiritual powers and pronouncements mostly met with approval from the ecclesiastical authorities, and since Hildegard rarely hesitated to exploit either her high social status or her spiritual position as the "Sibyl of the Rhine," she enjoyed a range of possibilities and freedoms unavailable to most medieval women.

—Jacqueline Jenkins

BIBLIOGRAPHY

Cadden, Joan. "It Takes All Kinds: Sexuality and Gender Differences in Hildegard of Bingen's 'Book of Compound Medicine.' " *Traditio* 40 (1984): 149–174.

Dronke, Peter. *Women Writers of the Middle Ages.* Cambridge: Cambridge University Press, 1984.

Holsinger, Bruce Wood. "The Flesh of the Voice: Embodiment and the Homoerotics of Devotion in the Music of Hildegard of Bingen (1098–1179)." *Signs* (1993): 92–123.

Kraft, Kent. "The German Visionary: Hildegard of Bingen." *Medieval Women Writers.* Katharina M. Wilson, ed. Athens, Ga.: University of Georgia Press, 1984. 109–130.

Murray, Jacqueline. "Twice Marginal and Twice Invisible: Lesbians in the Middle Ages." *Handbook of Medieval Sexuality.* Vern L. Bullough and James Brundage, eds. New York: Garland, 1996. 191–222.

Newman, Barbara. *Sister of Wisdom: St. Hildegard's Theology of the Feminine.* Berkeley: University of California Press, 1987.

Wiethaus, Ulrike. "In Search of Medieval Women's Friendships: Hildegard of Bingen's Letters to her Female Contemporaries." *Maps of Flesh and Light: The Religious Experience of Medieval Women Mystics.* Ulrike Wiethaus, ed. Syracuse, N.Y.: Syracuse University Press, 1993. 93–111.

SEE ALSO

Classical Music; Opera; Conductors

Hindle, Annie   *(ca. 1847–19??)*

ANNIE HINDLE WAS THE FIRST WOMAN TO GAIN SIGNIFicant attention as a male impersonator in the United States, and most likely introduced this performance style to the American variety stage. In 1891, the *New York Sun* declared that she was "the first out-and-out 'male impersonator' the New York stage had ever seen."

Born in England in the mid- to late-1840s, and adopted by Mrs. Ann Hindle, Annie Hindle arrived in the United States in late August 1868. According to the *Sun,* Hindle had been active on the provincial English and London music hall stages since the age of five.

Hindle performed on the American variety stage from 1868 to 1886, and during this time she was rarely idle. She was a flexible and resourceful performer who appeared in variety as a solo act and in minstrel shows. On occasion she also took roles in the short dramatic pieces that appeared at the end of each variety bill during that period.

During the 1870s, Hindle worked, very briefly, as the manager of the Grand Central Variety Hall in Cincinnati, Ohio, but poor attendance caused the theater to close. This failure was due in large part to effects of the 1873 financial crash, which lasted into the late 1870s.

Hindle's reviews, and steady bookings, attest to her popularity with American audiences. A reviewer in the *New York Clipper* for December 19, 1868, described one of her early performances at the Metropolitan Music Hall in Washington, D.C.: "Miss Hindle is of medium stature, with a pleasing figure and voice. The Lingard style of business [that is, playing both male and female parts] is the lady's *forte….* The changes were cleverly executed and the songs given with a vim and dash that was really refreshing."

Some eight years later, the great skills of this performer continued to astound her audience. A reviewer of an 1876 performance at the Adelphi Theater in Galveston, Texas (printed in the *New York Clipper* for December 16, 1876), noted: "Annie Hindle has proved a great success. As a male impersonator her sex is so concealed that one is apt to imagine that it is a man who is singing."

Hindle's career began to decline in the early 1880s and ended in 1886, when she married for the third time.

Hindle's first marriage had been to the character and ballad singer Charles Vivian, the founder of the Benevolent Protective Order of Elks in America, which was originally a theatrical fraternity. The couple married in 1868 but after six weeks they parted ways.

Hindle and Vivian did not divorce, and Hindle later claimed he had abused her. In 1878, the *Clipper* reported that she had married the minstrel performer W. W. Long, but no confirmation of this event has been found. If this marriage did occur, it is likely that it was a marriage of convenience for Hindle, as she never performed, lived, or traveled with Long.

Hindle's third marriage took place in Grand Rapids, Michigan, while she was leading her own troupe on a tour through the Midwest. A local Baptist minister married Hindle and her dresser, Annie Ryan, one evening after Hindle's performance. Hindle gave her name as Charles and dressed in male clothing while her bride wore her traveling gown.

Gilbert Sarony, a female impersonator in Hindle's troupe, acted as best man, and a local bank clerk, presumably pulled in off the street, was Hindle's second witness. This marriage, which was discovered almost immediately, caused a stir in Grand Rapids and was also reported in the *Clipper* as well as in the scandal sheet *National Police Gazette.*

Both papers declared that Hindle was really a man and her career as a male impersonator was ended. Upon the collapse of her variety troupe in the wake of the marriage, Hindle and her wife retired to Jersey City, New Jersey. The two women lived there until Ryan's death in late 1891, both dressing in female clothing.

In 1890, Hindle attempted to return to vaudeville. She found small-time bookings and continued to perform into the early twentieth century, though she seems never to have appeared in big-time vaudeville. It is not known when this remarkable woman died.

—Gillian Rodger

BIBLIOGRAPHY

"Man or Woman?" *Grand Rapids Evening Leader,* June 7, 1886.

"Married as a Man." *Grand Rapids Daily Democrat,* June 8, 1886.

"Married Her Maid: The Strange Story of Charles and Annie Hindle, a Man Masquerading as a Woman." *Grand Rapids Telegram-Herald,* June 7, 1886.

Rodger, Gillian. *Male Impersonation on the North American Variety and Vaudeville Stage, 1868–1930.* Ph.D. diss., University of Pittsburgh, 1998.

Senelick, Lawrence. "Male Impersonation." *The Cambridge Guide to Theatre.* Martin Banham, ed. Cambridge: Cambridge University Press, 1995. 674–675.

"Stranger than Fiction: The True Story of Annie Hindle's Two Marriages." *New York Sun,* December 27, 1891.

SEE ALSO

Drag Shows: Drag Kings and Male Impersonators; Variety and Vaudeville; Cabarets and Revues

Hunter, Alberta   *(1895–1984)*

BLUES SINGER, LYRICIST, AND ACTRESS ALBERTA Hunter, a distinctive stylist and one of the top recording artists in the 1920s and 1930s, experienced a dramatic comeback in her old age.

Alberta Hunter was destined to become a legend. Born on April 1, 1895, in Memphis, Tennessee, where she was reared, Hunter left home at age fifteen for Chicago, where, lying about her age, she launched her singing career in the city's nascent saloon and club scene, performing first with King Oliver's legendary Creole Jazz Band.

Possessed of abundant talent and stage presence, Hunter rose quickly to become one of the city's leading attractions in the 1910s and 1920s. Noted for singing the blues over troubled love affairs, she also wrote some of her own material, including "Down Hearted Blues."

Buoyed by her success in the city that had become the premier center for blues entertainers, Hunter began making recordings in 1921. She made more than 100 recordings for numerous labels, occasionally using pseudonyms to record while under contract with rival companies. Among her best-known recordings are "'Tain't Nobody's Business If I Do" and "Aggravatin' Papa."

Having been molested as a child, in disturbing incidents that she would recall later in life, Hunter was largely disdainful of men, particularly those who would control and manipulate her.

In part because she was fiercely independent, rumors began to circulate regarding Hunter's sexuality. In 1919, possibly to quell these stories, Hunter married Willard Townsend. However, the couple never slept together. After the wedding they moved in with Hunter's mother, Miss Laura, and Hunter slept with her instead. But even this degree of marriage was not for her, and Hunter left two months later and obtained a divorce in 1923.

In the days of Prohibition, almost anything went, and in the notorious "buffet flats," where many of the saloon singers also entertained, homosexuality was, if not fully accepted, at least tolerated and acknowledged. Although Hunter never discussed her lesbianism, she also did not keep her relationships hidden.

During her long-term relationship with Lottie Tyler, they shared apartments in New York and traveled to Europe together. Friends later recalled their relationship as volatile. Hunter was notoriously tight with money, while Lottie was something of a dilettante without much income of her own. Eventually, Lottie fell in love with another woman.

Hunter also maintained serious flirtations with men, but none developed into a lasting relationship. During her later years, rather than pursue the company of either men or women, Hunter focused her attention on caring for Miss Laura.

Although her love affairs failed to develop, Hunter's remarkable career flourished from the 1920s through the 1940s. Her recordings and her performances throughout the United States on the black vaudeville circuit and the T.O.B.A. (Theater Owner's Booking Association) made her famous.

Like other African American entertainers, Hunter traveled to Europe, where racism was less oppressive. She performed in London, Paris, Amsterdam, and Copenhagen. In 1928, she was featured opposite Paul Robeson in the London production of *Showboat*. Hunter credited herself as the "first colored girl singing in languages."

During World War II, she led several USO companies on missions to entertain American troops. She even gave a command performance for General Eisenhower at the war's end.

By the 1950s, however, the bookings had dried up, and the ever pragmatic, humanitarian Hunter sought a new career in nursing. She conned her way into a New York hospital's training program for licensed practical nurses by subtracting a dozen years from her age.

Hunter devoted tireless energy to her new profession, which she vigorously pursued for twenty years. No one ever suspected that she had been a star, and she was not one to recall those days.

She broke her vow not to perform only once during her tenure as a nurse, in 1961, to rerecord her signature composition, "Down Hearted Blues," with pianist Lovie Austin, who wrote the music.

Hunter was forced to retire from nursing in 1977; the hospital believed she had reached the mandatory retirement age of seventy. (She was actually eighty-two.) The same year, the indefatigable Hunter embarked upon a remarkable return to performing.

Her voice deepened and enriched by the intervening years, she proved a sensation. She performed regularly at The Cookery in Greenwich Village and was a hit with audiences worldwide. A tiny woman swinging large, dangling earrings that seemed to weigh more than she did, Hunter became the toast of the talk-show circuit as well. She was full of energy, life, and humor.

During the last six years of her life, she recorded two new albums and oversaw the rerelease of her older material. She died on October 17, 1984, at eighty-nine.

—Carla Williams

BIBLIOGRAPHY

Harrison, Daphne Duval. *Black Pearls: Blues Queens of the 1920s*. New Brunswick, N.J.: Rutgers University Press, 1988.

Taylor, Frank C., with Gerald Cook. *Alberta Hunter: A Celebration in Blues*. New York: McGraw-Hill, 1987.

SEE ALSO

Blues Music; Popular Music; Jazz; Cabarets and Revues; Smith, Bessie; Waters, Ethel

Ian, Janis

(b. 1951)

JANIS IAN BURST ONTO THE POP MUSIC SCENE AT THE age of fifteen with her controversial hit tune "Society's Child." After dazzling early success came some fallow years, but she revitalized her career in the early 1990s, when she also came out publicly. Her musical talents have brought her nine Grammy nominations.

Janis Eddy Fink was born in the Bronx, New York, on April 7, 1951, and spent her early years on her parents' chicken farm in southern New Jersey. The family home was filled with folk and classical music and jazz. Ian's interest in music was precocious: She began learning to play the piano at two and a half and later taught herself guitar and French horn.

She wrote her first song, "Hair of Spun Gold," at the age of twelve. Dreaming of a career in show business, she dubbed herself Janis Ian, adopting her brother's middle name as her stage name.

Ian achieved fame with "Society's Child," a song about interracial love, penned when she was fifteen. Because of its controversial topic, some two dozen record companies rejected it before Verve Folkways put out the single, which hit number fourteen on the pop charts despite the fact that many radio stations refused to air it.

The song elicited a certain volume of hate mail, but it also earned Ian many fans, including Leonard Bernstein, who featured her on an April 1967 television special, *Inside Pop: The Rock Revolution.*

Society's Child was on Ian's self-titled first album (1967), for which she received a Grammy nomination for best folk performance.

Although Ian had found artistic success and recognition, her personal life at this time was difficult. She dropped out of New York's High School of Music and Art to pursue a demanding schedule of recording and touring. Ian's parents were divorcing, and she was having problems with her record producer. She had a nervous breakdown and attempted suicide when she was seventeen.

After she recovered from the breakdown, more albums followed. The most successful was *Between the Lines* (1975), on which she sang her biggest hit, "At Seventeen." Described by Timothy Finn of the *Ottawa Citizen* as "a universal ballad for the unwanted," the plaintive yet comforting song spoke of the pain and loneliness of a teenage girl unable to find romance because "love was meant for beauty queens."

"At Seventeen" rose to number three on the pop charts and went platinum, selling over a million copies. The song and album garnered five Grammy nominations in 1975 and won two awards.

Ian stated in a 1995 interview published in the *Advocate* that she realized she was a lesbian at the age of nine. Although she made no public acknowledgment of her sexual orientation, Ian described herself as out in her daily life in the 1970s, often bringing her girlfriend along when she toured. The *Village Voice* publicly outed her in 1976, which caused her considerable anxiety since, like many entertainers, she feared a negative public reaction that could damage her career. At the time, she refused to confirm her lesbianism.

Ian also dated men, and in 1978 she married Portuguese filmmaker Tino Sargo. The union was happy at first, but Sargo reportedly became abusive, and the couple divorced in 1983.

While she was extricating herself from the marriage, Ian also faced emergency abdominal surgery and a long battle with the Internal Revenue Service since the trusted accountant who had been managing her finances from the beginning of her career had failed to pay her income taxes for seven years. She largely dropped out of the music scene, taking time to study dance and acting.

In 1988, Ian, bankrupt after the tax proceedings, moved to Nashville, Tennessee, where the cost of living is lower than in Los Angeles or New York and where music is also a valued part of the life of the community. There she met Patricia Snyder, who was working in the history department at Vanderbilt University and who has subsequently become a criminal defense attorney. Together since 1989, the couple married in Toronto on August 27, 2003.

Ian explains that she and Snyder decided to marry because "as a couple, we wanted the same rights and the same social recognition our heterosexual friends have. We also got married because, just like coming out, public figures need to do that to make the rest of the world aware. I think it's important that people are made aware, because at the end of the day it's a civil rights issue. It's the right to marry who you want to marry regardless of color, regardless of religion, regardless of gender."

In 1993, Ian entered into a new phase of both her personal and professional life. She came out publicly and also released the aptly titled *Breaking Silence*, her first album in over a decade. She was rewarded with a Grammy nomination—her ninth—for best folk album.

Ian had recorded three more albums by 2000, and in 2003 brought out *Working without a Net*, a well-received double CD of concert performances over the course of the previous decade.

Ian's latest album, *Billie's Bones* (2004), pays tribute to singer Billie Holiday with its title cut and memorializes Matthew Shepard, the victim of a vicious homophobic murder, in "Matthew." The album also honors Woody Guthrie with "I Hear You Sing Again," which combines Ian's music with lyrics written by Guthrie and provided to her by his daughter Nora.

Ian's songs have been covered by a long list of artists including Joan Baez, Cher, Bette Midler, Nina Simone, and Dusty Springfield.

In addition to her songwriting, Ian has worked as a writer, contributing a column to the *Advocate* for five years beginning in August 1994.

From the earliest days of her career, Ian has been a voice for tolerance and personal dignity. She continues to use her artistry to further the cause of social justice.

—*Linda Rapp*

BIBLIOGRAPHY

"Celebrity 'I Do.'" *Advocate*, October 14, 2003, 18.

Etheridge, Melissa. "The Best Revenge." *Advocate*, June 13, 1995, 42.

Finn, Timothy. "Ian Helped Others Reveal Sexual Identity." *Ottawa Citizen*, October 2, 1997.

Janis Ian Online. www.janisian.com.

Levinson, Arlene. "Words, Music Help Janis Ian Survive a Turbulent Life." *Albany (N.Y.) Times Union*, July 1, 1999.

McClelland, Eileen. "Janis Ian's Life of Encores." *Houston Chronicle*, March 4, 2004.

Ross, Robert. "Out There and Singing; Happily Married, Folk Legend Janis Ian Is Still Going Strong at 53." *Dallas Voice*. www.dallasvoice.com/articles/dispArticle.cfm?Article_ID=4228.

Snyder, Michael. "Singer Songwriter's New Life; The Rise, Fall and Comeback of Janis Ian." *San Francisco Chronicle*, June 6, 1993.

SEE ALSO

Popular Music; Baez, Joan; Etheridge, Melissa; Springfield, Dusty

Janice Ian in concert.

Indigo Girls

Lesbians Amy Ray and Emily Saliers are Indigo Girls, one of the most successful folk/pop duos in recording history. Ray and Saliers have carved out an enduring career that is due largely to the fierce loyalty of their fans, many of them lesbians.

Ray, a native Atlantan, and Saliers, a transplant from Connecticut, met in elementary school in Atlanta and became friends. They shared a talent for writing and music and began playing together in Ray's parents' basement. During college at Emory University, they played club dates in and around Atlanta as the B Band and later Saliers and Ray, developing their following and reputation as a particularly strong band in live performance.

Beginning in 1981, they released several independent records on tape, and in 1985 released a vinyl single, "Crazy Game." The same year, Ray selected the name Indigo Girls on "sort of a whim," as she explained in an interview years later. "I found it in the dictionary.... It's a deep blue, a root—real earthy."

The duo signed with Epic Records in 1988. Their first record for Epic, the multiplatinum *Indigo Girls,* included their best-known song, "Closer to Fine." That year they were nominated for two Grammy Awards—Best New Artist (narrowly lost to Milli Vanilli) and Best Contemporary Folk Album, which they won.

To date they have released twelve albums that feature original material, including their most recent, *Become You* (2002) and *All That We Let In* (2004). Seven of their records have been certified gold or platinum.

While Indigo Girls never denied their sexuality, early on it was not made explicit in their work because they did not want to be pigeonholed as a "lesbian band." However, they dropped hints to whet the appetites of their large lesbian audience, who were constantly looking for some sense of identity and pride and solidarity.

Rites of Passage (1992) included an impassioned cover of Mark Knopfler's "Romeo and Juliet," sung by Ray in the voice of Juliet's lover. In 1994 and 1995, the women appeared in *Jesus Christ Superstar* in Atlanta, Austin, and Seattle, Ray playing the title role opposite Saliers's Mary Magdelene. Their performances drew the ire of conservative groups that could not abide a female Jesus, let alone a lesbian one.

It was not until *Shaming of the Sun* (1997) that an explicit statement of either woman's homosexuality appeared—in Saliers's "It's Alright," with the line "...and it's alright if you hate that way / hate me cause i'm different / you hate me cause i'm gay...." Also in 1997, Indigo Girls found themselves at the center of controversy when schools throughout the South banned them from appearing on a planned high school tour—because of their homosexuality and because another song on *Shaming of the Sun*, Ray's "Shame on You," includes the word *fucking*.

Nearly as well known for the causes they support as for their music, Indigo Girls have demonstrated an enduring commitment to social and political causes, ranging from Habitat for Humanity and handgun control to gay and lesbian rights and same-sex marriage. Their touring and support for the grassroots environmental organization Honor the Earth has raised hundreds of thousands of dollars for indigenous groups in North America.

To demonstrate her support for independent music, in 1990 Ray founded Daemon Records, a small, not-for-profit independent label based in Atlanta. In 1999, Ray released a solo record on Daemon, *Stag*, backed by The Butchies, a North Carolina–based lesbian punk trio. The record includes "Laramie," a song about the murder of Matthew Shepard, and "Lucystoners," which takes gay *Rolling Stone* publisher Jann Wenner to task for his magazine's lack of coverage of serious women musicians.

Although not as commercially successful or as famous as lesbian singers k.d. lang and Melissa Etheridge, Indigo Girls have nevertheless infiltrated popular culture. An Indigo Girls benefit concert is the recurring backdrop of Stephen King's 1995 novel *Rose Madder*.

They appeared as a bar band in the lesbian-themed film *Boys on the Side* (1995) and as themselves in "Womyn Fest," a 1998 episode of the television show *Ellen* that spoofed women's music festivals.

In late 2001, "Indigo Girls" was the $64,000 answer on a special "supermodel" episode of the popular television program *Who Wants to Be a Millionaire?* (In the show's tradition, the audience had to be polled to help model/actress Carol Alt win.)

Indigo Girls are also the inspiration for the independent feature film *Chasing Indigo* (2001).

—*Carla Williams*

Bibliography

www.lifeblood.net

www.indigogirls.com

www.daemonrecords.com

www.chasingindigo.com/

See also

Popular Music; Music Video; Women's Music; Baez, Joan; Etheridge, Melissa; lang, k.d.

Jazz

THE RELATION OF JAZZ TO HOMOSEXUAL AND TRANS-gendered experience has varied enormously over the course of its history since the beginning of the twentieth century. In the early twentieth century, African American music and dance provided homosexual subcultures with expressive styles and social rituals. In the 1930s, swing and the big bands took jazz out of the speakeasies and small clubs and popularized it with a national American audience.

However, the increased popularity of swing and big band jazz, which introduced jazz to college dances, ballrooms, and the airwaves, and thus into the mainstream, meant that homosexuals became a smaller and less significant group of jazz fans than in the past.

After World War II and the emergence of bebop, jazz lost its connection to the dance hall and ballroom, but without developing a larger gay and lesbian audience.

The postwar jazz scene, dominated by Charlie Parker, Dizzy Gillespie, and Thelonious Monk, also grew increasingly macho and even misogynistic, while the postwar urban gay bar culture created its own style of entertainment around female impersonators and singers such as Judy Garland.

By the end of the twentieth century, jazz and homosexuals seemed to have little in common. In his novel *Significant Others* (1987), Armistead Maupin writes, "Surely there were gay men somewhere who revered jazz, but Michael"—a gay man living in San Francisco—"didn't know any."

Early History

New Orleans, the busy port city near the mouth of the Mississippi River, was probably one of the first places in America where jazz, homosexuals, and transgendered people came together, at the very beginning of the twentieth century. Many of the earliest and most celebrated jazz musicians were born in and around New Orleans. Early jazz grew out of the fusion of disparate sounds in New Orleans—marching bands, ragtime, spirituals, blues, and other forms of African and Anglo-American instrumental and vocal music.

From the beginning, jazz was closely associated with the seamy side of New Orleans nightlife. Early jazz pianists such as Jelly Roll Morton, Eubie Blake, and James P. Johnson were often employed to play in the brothels of Storyville, New Orleans's fabled red-light district.

In Storyville and in the sex districts of many other cities—often located in or near African American neighborhoods—both jazz musicians and homosexuals found niches and a degree of acceptance.

One gay man served as mentor to Jelly Roll Morton. Pianist/singer/songwriter Tony Jackson was probably the most accomplished of all of Storyville's entertainers. He played and sang everything from opera to blues, in their authentic idioms. As Morton recounted to music historian Alan Lomax: "Tony happened to be one those gentlemans that a lot of people call them lady or sissy—I suppose he was either a ferry or a steamboat, one or the other."

Jackson was the author of the classic "Pretty Baby," which was originally about a man. In 1906, Jackson left New Orleans for the relative freedom, as a black gay man, of Chicago. He died from alcoholism at the age of forty-four, sometime during the 1920s.

In addition, the New Orleans tradition of celebrating Mardi Gras provided the opportunity for homosexuals, drag queens, and transgendered people to engage in prohibited sexual activities under the guise of masquerades and cross-dressing.

By the end of World War I, most large cities saw the emergence of annual drag and costume balls where homosexuals danced the cakewalk, two-step, and Charleston—all dance forms that had emerged from and along with African American music.

The 1920s and 1930s

In the 1920s, Harlem was a flourishing enclave of jazz and gay life. The Harlem Renaissance was, according to literary critic Henry Louis Gates Jr., "surely as gay as it was black, not that it was exclusively either of these." Many of the Harlem Renaissance's leading figures were either homosexual or bisexual, including such literary figures as Claude McKay, Countee Cullen, Alain Locke, Wallace Thurman, Richard Bruce Nugent, and Langston Hughes.

Among Harlem's most prominent performers, Bessie Smith, Alberta Hunter, George Hanna, Moms Mabley, Mabel Hampton, Ma Rainey, and Ethel Waters were bisexual or homosexual. They sang songs with sexually explicit lyrics, incorporating homosexual slang terms such as "sissy" and "bull-dagger," as in the lyric "If you can't bring me a woman, bring me a sissy man."

One well-known homosexual haunt in Harlem was the Clam House on the stretch of 133rd Street known as Jungle Alley. There, openly lesbian Gladys Bentley was the headline singer. "If ever there was a gal," noted one journalist, "who would take a popular ditty and put her naughty version to it, La Bentley could do it."

Despite the existence of these overlapping subcultures, however, homosexual life in Harlem remained marginal. As historian Kevin Mumford notes, "The more visible and accessible a Harlem club was the more heterosexual its patrons."

The overlap between homosexual life and jazz survived the repeal of Prohibition and continued into the next decade. According to Kevin Mumford, one University of Chicago sociologist studying homosexuals in the 1930s reported in an unpublished ethnography that at a party the men "played pornographic records sung by Negro entertainers; a homosexual theme ran through all the lyrics." He observed the men at the party "swaying to the music of a colored jazz orchestra...[with] two young men in street clothes dancing together, cheek to cheek."

Jazz Musicians

Once the jazz scene ceased to offer a countercultural haven for homosexuals, the interplay between jazz and homosexual subcultures eventually vanished. In fact, very little is known about the homosexuality or bisexuality of jazz musicians. Whereas blues singing was a predominantly female (and often bisexual or lesbian) musical activity, jazz, like other forms of American musical life, was male dominated from the beginning.

The jazz scene was not hospitable to female instrumentalists or to effeminate or openly homosexual men. Openly lesbian or bisexual women initially fared better as singers. In the jazz subculture, male musical prowess served as an important basis for attracting women. Duke Ellington himself noted that as a young man "I was invited to many parties, where I learned that when you were playing piano there was always a pretty girl standing down at the bass clef end of the piano." To this day, only a few jazz musicians are publicly known to be homosexual.

Billy Strayhorn

The most historically significant known homosexual jazz musician is composer and arranger Billy Strayhorn (1915–1967), who for most of his adult life worked closely with Duke Ellington. For many years, acknowledgment of his work was obscured by his relationship to Ellington, and some of his work was credited to and copyrighted by Ellington.

One of the most accomplished composers in jazz and popular music, Strayhorn is the author of "Take the 'A' Train," "Lush Life," "Chelsea Bridge," and "Something to Live For." From 1937 until his death in 1967, Strayhorn worked for and collaborated with Ellington. He served as Ellington's intimate collaborator in the composition of many of the Ellington band's most important songs and arrangements. They often passed a work back and forth, each contributing phrases and reworking others.

Ellington's support for Strayhorn and his acceptance of Strayhorn's homosexuality was invaluable. David Hajdu, Strayhorn's biographer, shows how Strayhorn was able to choose not to hide his homosexuality because of Ellington's unquestioning acceptance. Ellington's son, Mercer, told David Hajdu in *Vanity Fair* that he always assumed Strayhorn and his father had "experimented" at some point.

Billy Tipton

Jazz musician Billy Tipton (1914–1989) played saxophone and piano from the 1930s until 1958, when he retired from performing and began a career as an entertainment agent in Spokane, Washington.

Born Dorothy Tipton in 1914, Billy lived most of his life as a man. As a young woman, Dorothy first appeared on the jazz scene in Kansas City during the late 1920s. She was moderately talented, but nevertheless after numerous auditions failed to get any bookings in the local clubs, apparently because she was female. Finally, in 1933, with the help of her cousin, she taped her chest, cut her hair, and wore a suit to her next audition. She was immediately hired as Billy Tipton and lived as a man for the rest of her life.

Tipton played saxophone with several well-known bands throughout the late 1930s and 1940s. In the 1950s, he started his own band, The Billy Tipton Trio, and made two recordings. Eventually Tipton's band worked as the house band at a nightclub in Reno, backing such well-known performers as Liberace.

In 1958, Tipton retired from the jazz scene and moved to Spokane, where he married and raised a family. He was revealed to be a female only after his death, when a coroner's autopsy was performed.

The Bebop Revolution

The bebop revolution of the late 1940s and 1950s dramatically affected the relationship of jazz to its audience and players. Bebop's dissonance, complex rhythms, and free solo improvisation created a musical style that dramatically broke with the swing music that had dominated the 1930s and 1940s jazz idiom.

Bebop effectively broke the connection between jazz and dance music. It also reinforced the masculinist sexual attitudes, exacerbating the hostility of an environment already unfriendly to both women and homosexuals.

When Melba Liston, a pianist and arranger, was hired by Dizzy Gillespie, Linda Dahl recounts, the men in his band complained that he had "sent all the way to California for a *bitch*." Gillespie asked one of his men to hand out the music he had written for the band. He said to the man, "Pass it out to these muthafuckas and let me see what a bitch you are…. Play the music, and I don't want to hear no fuckups." As Dahl recalls, "And of course they got about two measures and fell out and got all confused and stuff. And Dizzy said, 'Now who's the bitch?'"

Though Gillespie insisted on hiring Liston, such a hostile atmosphere was not conducive to the open acceptance of men or women who were sexually unconventional.

Post-bebop Jazz

The myth of the macho jazz musician continues to exercise a hold on the world of jazz. Still, several post-bebop musicians have been rumored to be gay, and some have actually come out publicly as homosexual.

Miles Davis (1926–1991), for example, exemplified the masculine self-assurance and "cool" style of post-bebop jazz. He conducted well-known relationships with French singer Juliet Greco and actress Cecily Tyson, but according to his biographer Ian Carr there were also persistent rumors of his bisexuality, and his death of pneumonia, stroke, and heart failure was attributed to AIDS.

Avant-garde jazz pianist Cecil Taylor, born in Boston in 1929, is another post-bebop musician with a very muscular style of playing the piano. John Gill records that, in 1985, Taylor gave an interview to a San Francisco newspaper that stressed the importance to his music of his race and his homosexuality.

Taylor, along with Art Tatum, Earl Hines, Bud Powell, and Thelonious Monk, is one of the five most important jazz pianists to emerge since the end of World War II.

Vibraphonist Gary Burton (b. 1943) is another contemporary jazz musician who has publicly come out of the closet. A prominent composer and bandleader, Burton has had an exemplary career working with many of the leading figures in contemporary jazz, such as Stan Getz, George Shearing, Carla Bley, Keith Jarrett, and Pat Metheny. Although married twice, Burton has said he always knew there was a gay side to his personality. He had gay relationships before and between his marriages.

The 1993 announcement by pianist Fred Hersch (b. 1955) that he was both HIV-positive and gay shocked the jazz community. For years after moving to New York from Cincinnati in the late 1970s, Hersch was so terrified that the celebrated jazz musicians with whom he was working might discover his homosexuality that he felt compelled to suppress his own identity. In order to protect himself from any damaging disclosures, Hersch radically divided his social world between gay friends and fellow musicians.

In 1996, Andy Bey (b. 1939), a suave African American musician who, like his idol Nat King Cole, sings and plays the piano, also came out as an HIV-positive gay man.

Glbtq Audiences

Jazz is one of the America's most significant cultural contributions. Yet homosexual and transgendered audiences in the second half of the twentieth century have expressed little interest in the contemporary developments of this vibrant cultural tradition.

Over the course of the twentieth century, the jazz scene has seemed to become less and less hospitable to gay men, lesbians, bisexuals, and transgendered people. Indeed, in an interview with John Gill, musician Gary Burton has argued that, today, "of all the forms of music, jazz is the least tolerant of homosexuality." Nevertheless, despite a hostile atmosphere, the contributions of gay jazz artists such as Billy Strayhorn, Cecil Taylor, and Gary Burton have been significant.

—*Jeffrey Escoffier*

BIBLIOGRAPHY

Carr, Ian. *Miles Davis: The Definitive Biography*. New York: Thunder's Mouth Press, 1999.

Dahl, Linda. *Stormy Weather: The Music and Lives of a Century of Jazz Women*. New York: Limelight Editions, 1989.

Gill, John. *Queer Noises: Male and Female Homosexuality in Twentieth-Century Music.* Minneapolis: University of Minnesota Press, 1995.

Hajdu, David. "A Jazz of Their Own." *Vanity Fair,* May 1999, 188.

———. *Lush Life: A Biography of Billy Strayhorn.* New York: Farrar, Straus and Giroux, 1996.

Lomax, Alan. *Mister Jelly Roll: The Fortunes of Jelly Roll Morton, New Orleans Creole and the "Inventor of Jazz."* New York: Pantheon, 1950; reprint. Berkeley: University of California Press, 2001.

Middebrook, Diane Wood. *Suits Me: The Double Life of Billy Tipton.* Boston: Houghton Mifflin, 1999.

Mumford, Kevin. *Interzones: Black/White Sex Districts in Chicago and New York in the Early Twentieth Century.* New York: Columbia University Press, 1997.

Watson, Steven. *The Harlem Renaissance: Hub of African American Culture, 1920–1930.* New York: Pantheon, 1995.

SEE ALSO

Popular Music; Blues Music; Bentley, Gladys; Faye, Frances; Hunter, Alberta; Rainey, Gertrude ("Ma"); Smith, Bessie; Strayhorn, William Thomas; Waters, Ethel

Joan Jett.

Jett, Joan   *(b. 1960)*

POP ICON OF THE 1980S TURNED CONTEMPORARY STAR, Joan Jett has long been a part of the rock-and-roll world. Referred to as "the godmother of Riot Grrl" for her emergence as an aggressive, punk-influenced guitarist and singer in a time when most mainstream female musicians performed either bubblegum pop or folk, Jett remains vital as a musician, producer, and actor. Fans admire the fact that, despite her increasing technical proficiency, Jett's music has remained satisfyingly consistent since the outset of her solo career.

Jett was born Joan Larkin in Philadelphia on September 22, 1960. She spent most of her childhood in Baltimore. Her family moved to Los Angeles in 1972, where she became interested in artists such as David Bowie, Suzy Quatro, and Gary Glitter.

Jett's interest in performing rock music was piqued when she received a guitar for Christmas at age thirteen. Only two years later, in 1976, she helped form the Los Angeles–based, all-teen girl band the Runaways. The group made a splash in Europe but was not taken seriously in the United States; largely written off as a novelty act, it disbanded in 1979.

Jett, who had decided early on that she had no interest in prescribed gender roles and simply wanted to succeed in the rock world, went on to establish her musical career without the Runaways. She produced an album for the punk band the Germs and recorded with former members of the Sex Pistols.

After the demise of the Runaways, Jett began looking for a new band; in 1980 she put together the Blackhearts. Their debut album, originally titled *Joan Jett,* was renamed *Bad Reputation* when it was released in the United States in 1981, on Jett and manager Kenny Laguna's own Blackhearts Records label (in conjunction with the now defunct Boardwalk Records). But it was Jett's hugely successful second album, *I Love Rock 'n' Roll,* that—with its number one hit title track in 1982—made her a star.

In the 1980s, Jett had some Top 40 hits and then experienced several ups and downs in her career. She toured frequently in the 1990s and contributed to several sound tracks and compilation albums, in addition to issuing two full-length releases.

Jett's leather-clad, bad-girl image, and her collaboration with seminal Riot Grrl act Bikini Kill as well as with (female) rock groups L7 and Babes in Toyland, helped cement her reputation as a kind of queercore role model despite her lack of a genuine niche. The queercore movement, characterized by hard-core punk music and militant lyrics, embraced Jett, though she had already achieved prominence when queercore came to the fore in the late 1980s.

While she has not issued a public statement regarding her sexuality, Jett has performed publicly with a sticker on her guitar that proclaims "Dykes Rule," and her sizable lesbian following is a formidable presence at her shows. With the Blackhearts, Joan has performed at numerous gay rights events, headlining at St. Louis's Pride Fest in 2001, and she often appears at queer-themed shows and clubs in New York City.

In response to the rumors surrounding her sexuality, Jett has said, "I don't really care what people call me. I think it's important to support people you want to support and not be afraid of being called names."

Jett's acting assignments have included a role in the 1987 feature film *Light of Day* and a successful eight-month stint as Columbia in the 2001 Broadway production of *The Rocky Horror Picture Show*.

Her greatest-hits album, *Fit to be Tied*, came out on Mercury Records—distributing the album for Blackhearts Records—in 1997. Recent albums include *Fetish* (1999), *Unfinished Business* (2001), and *USA: Joan Jett and the Blackhearts* (2002).   —*Teresa Theophano*

BIBLIOGRAPHY

Baird, Kirk. "At 40, rocker Jett still soaring." *Las Vegas Sun,* July 6, 2001. Online interview only: www.lasvegassun.com/sunbin/stories/archives/2001/jul/06/512047894.html?Jett

Joan Jett and the Blackhearts Official Website: www.joanjett.com

Juno, Andrea. "Joan Jett." *Angry Women in Rock Volume One.* Andrea Juno, ed. New York: Juno Books, 1996. 69–81.

SEE ALSO

Popular Music; Rock Music; Bowie, David

Joffrey, Robert   *(1928–1988)*

THE GREAT CONTRIBUTIONS OF ROBERT JOFFREY TO American dance are his creation of a major dance company and his distinguished work as teacher and trainer of dancers. Dedicated to gender parity in ballet, he helped elevate the status of the male dancer, making male virtuosity a priority in his repertoire and in his classroom.

Joffrey was born Anver Bey Abdullah Jaffa Khan Joffrey on December 24, 1928, in Seattle, the only child of a loveless marriage between a Pakhtun Afghani father and an Italian mother. His parents owned a restaurant.

As a small, sickly child, with bowed legs and turned-in feet, Joffrey had to wear casts on his feet and began studying ballet to strengthen his frame. Fortunately, Seattle was blessed with exceptional ballet teachers. He was introduced to the grand tradition of the Ballets Russes by Ivan Novikoff. Later, he studied with Mary Ann Wells, famous for producing professional dancers of note.

When he was sixteen, Joffrey met twenty-two-year-old Gerald Arpino, then serving in the Coast Guard. "It was love at first sight," Aprino later recalled. They became lovers, and Arpino moved into the Joffrey family home. Soon the young men became artistic collaborators as well when Arpino began studying ballet with Novikoff.

Although their sexual intimacy ended soon after 1949, Joffrey and Arpino shared a domestic relationship for forty-three years, one that ended only upon Joffrey's death.

Joffrey later studied at the High School of Performing Arts in New York, and in 1949 and 1950 he danced with Roland Petit's Ballets de Paris. But at 5 feet 4 inches tall, Joffrey realized that his height limited his potential for a career as a dancer. He began to think of choreography and teaching as ways to contribute to dance.

Joffrey began to choreograph his own ballets. He scored an early success with *Persephone* (1952). He also staged dances for musicals, operas, and London's Ballet Rambert.

In 1954, Joffrey formed his own small ensemble troupe, dedicated to presenting his own work and Arpino's. This ensemble gradually grew into a major national company that revolutionized American dance history.

Based in New York City, the Joffrey Ballet distinguished itself in a number of ways. It commissioned the work of modern choreographers (for example, Twyla Tharp's *Deuce Coupe* in 1973), and it revived great ballets of the international repertoire that were neglected by other American companies (for example, work by Tudor, Massine, Nijinsky, and Nijinska, as well as ten ballets by Frederick Ashton and evenings devoted to Diaghilev masterpieces).

Other milestones in the history of the company include Joffrey's multimedia psychedelic ballet *Astarte* (music by Crome Syrcus, 1967) and Arpino's rock ballet *Trinity* (1970).

Joffrey was an unusually gifted teacher. From the beginning, his school, the American Ballet Center, trained many important dancers. Joffrey dancers became known for their youthful sexual vitality and brilliant physical technique.

Joffrey's emphasis on male virtuosity was an attempt to redress the gender imbalance that had developed in ballet, in part as a result of Balanchine's famous dictum that "Ballet is woman." Joffrey's commitment to improving the status of male dancers influenced both his teaching and his and Arpino's choreography.

The Joffrey Ballet Company became popular throughout the United States and abroad. Sometimes criticized for its commercialism, the company made ballet accessible to a large and diverse audience, including people who were not already devotees of the form.

The Joffrey's repertoire contained no overt homosexuality, but there was a great deal of covert male homoeroticism, as a retinue of gorgeous, bare-chested, late-adolescent dancers unfailingly delighted the gay male audience.

Although Arpino has repeatedly denied the presence of homoeroticism in his work, his 1966 all-male ballet, *Olympics*, a tribute to athletics, featured a suggestive pas de deux.

During one curious phase of the Joffrey's development, the men's costumes featured a distracting athletic cup, shaped rather like half a large grapefruit. The cup effectively covered the natural shape of the genitals—previously clearly seen, especially under white or light colored tights—but gave the impression of a giant tumor.

Joffrey produced less choreography as he devoted himself to shaping his company. Arpino became the house choreographer, while Joffrey synthesized his own creative aesthetic with the Diaghilev legacy of nurturing the talents of others.

Joffrey was sexually promiscuous but discreet. His relationship with Arpino provided domestic stability, but he had other romantic attachments and numerous one-night stands.

In 1973, Joffrey fell in love with A. Aladar Marberger, a twenty-six-year-old gay activist and manager of the Fischbach Gallery in Manhattan. At some time during the 1980s, both men contracted AIDS.

While Marberger was outspoken about his illness, Joffrey remained silent. He was ashamed, and wanted his obituary to state that he died of liver disease and asthma. Arpino agreed to his pleas, but the secret could not be maintained: AIDS took a staggering toll on the dance world in general and on Joffrey's company in particular.

Robert Joffrey died on March 25, 1988. Aladar Marberger died on November 1, 1988.

The Joffrey Ballet, now based in Chicago, survives under the direction of Gerald Arpino.

—*Douglas Blair Turnbaugh*

Bibliography

Anawalt, Sasha. *The Joffrey Ballet: Robert Joffrey and the Making of an American Dance Company*. New York: Scribner, 1996.

Solway, Diane. *A Dance against Time: The Brief, Brilliant Life of a Joffrey Dancer*. New York: Pocket Books, 1994.

See also

Dance; Ballet; Ballets Russes; Ashton, Sir Frederick; Diaghilev, Sergei; Nijinsky, Vaslav

John, Sir Elton   (b. 1947)

FOR NEARLY FOUR DECADES, ELTON JOHN HAS ACHIEVED an amazingly successful track record in the music industry. He was not only the biggest-selling pop superstar of the 1970s, but, more surprisingly, he continues to retain popularity among his fans and respect from music critics.

Elton John holds a music industry record for most consecutive singles placing in the Top 40, a string that began in 1970 and was broken only in 2000. Stephen Erlewine has noted that, although Elton John has endured temporary slumps in creativity and sales, he continues to craft contemporary pop standards that showcase his musical versatility.

John's combination of melodic skills, dynamic charisma, and raucous performance style has made him a remarkably popular musical artist.

Elton John was born Reginald Kenneth Dwight in Pinner, Middlesex, England, on March 25, 1947. He began playing piano at age four and at eleven won a scholarship to the Royal Academy of Music in London. After six years at school, he left in order to break into the music business.

In 1961, Dwight joined his first band, Bluesology, but left in 1966 because of creative differences with bandleader Long John Baldry. During this time, Dwight answered a Liberty Records advertisement for songwriters; though he failed the vocal audition, he was given a stack of lyrics written by Bernie Taupin, a young songwriter from Lincolnshire who had also answered the ad.

Dwight wrote music for Taupin's lyrics, and the two young men soon began corresponding. Six months later, after Dwight had changed his name to Elton John (taking his stage name from the first names of Bluesology members Elton Dean and John Baldry), he and Taupin finally met.

The collaboration between John and Taupin would prove to be enduring and lucrative for both men. According to Ed Decker, Taupin would write the lyrics first, and then John would compose music to them with incredible speed, sometimes in less than an hour.

By 1969, John had his first hit album, an eponymous LP that contained the touching ballad "Your Song," which climbed both the American and English record charts. Although John had a retiring personality, he hid his shyness on stage by adopting an outrageous performance style, including wearing outlandish clothes and leaping around as he played the piano.

Throughout the 1970s, John's concert attire would become more and more campy. He pranced across the stage wearing everything from huge feather boas to astronaut suits, almost always highlighted by a selection from his endless collection of bizarre eyeglasses.

From 1972 to 1976, the writing team of John and Taupin scored sixteen Top 20 hits in a row. In 1976, John, citing exhaustion, curtailed his rigorous concert and recording schedule. That year, as Colin Larkin has noted, he entered an uncomfortable phase in his life. John not only acknowledged his bisexuality, but also confessed to personal insecurities about his weight and baldness.

These personal problems affected his working relationship with Bernie Taupin, who broke with John and began working with other musicians. In 1980, however, the pair reunited, and their string of hits resumed unabated. But John's personal life remained in turmoil. According to Erlewine, John had been addicted to cocaine and alcohol since the mid-1970s, and the situation only worsened during the 1980s.

John surprised the media and his fans by marrying Renate Blauel in 1984. The couple remained married for four years, though John later admitted that he had known he was homosexual long before his marriage.

John performed at Wham's farewell concert in 1985 and appeared at the historic Live Aid concert the same year. However, at an Australian concert in 1986, he collapsed onstage and subsequently underwent throat surgery.

During the mid-1980s, John developed a close friendship with Ryan White, a teenage hemophiliac who contracted AIDS through a blood transfusion. White attracted international attention when he was barred from his Kokomo, Indiana, middle school in 1985. John not only befriended the courageous young man but also provided financial help and emotional support for White's family.

Ryan White died on April 8, 1990. John had dedicated "Candle in the Wind," the song he and Taupin had written as an elegy for Marilyn Monroe, to Ryan at the Farm Aid concert in Indianapolis the night before Ryan's death. In a touching performance, he reprised the song at White's funeral.

John, along with talk show host Phil Donahue, was instrumental in helping Ryan's mother, Jeanne White, establish the Ryan White Foundation for the prevention of AIDS. In 1992, John also established his own non-profit group, the Elton John AIDS Foundation, which has contributed more than $25 million to various AIDS causes worldwide. John also announced that all royalties from his singles sales would henceforth go to AIDS research.

Also in 1992, John and Taupin signed a record-breaking publishing deal with Warner/Chappell Music for an estimated $39 million.

In 1994, John collaborated with lyricist Tim Rice on songs for Disney's *The Lion King*, and one of their collaborations, "Can You Feel the Love Tonight?," won an Academy Award for Best Original Song and a Grammy for Best Male Pop Vocal Performance.

In the 1990s, John also made public his relationship with David Furnish, a former advertising executive who has become his longtime companion and life partner. In 1995, Furnish shot a film about John's life, *Tantrums and Tiaras* (1996), which unblinkingly shows the pop

star's most charming and most childish sides. In 1997, Furnish helped form Rocket Films, a film distribution company that shares the same name as John's own record label, Rocket Records.

John had his biggest-selling hit in 1997, though the circumstances behind the song were tragic. Deeply affected by the untimely death of his friend Princess Diana, John rerecorded "Candle in the Wind" with lyrics adapted by Bernie Taupin. "Candle in the Wind 1997," which John performed at Diana's funeral in Westminster Abbey, entered the British and American charts at number one and spent fourteen weeks in the top spot, with all profits going to the Diana, Princess of Wales Memorial Fund.

In 1998, John was honored by the British monarchy when, on the recommendation of Prime Minister Tony Blair, Queen Elizabeth II bestowed on him the title of Knight. Also in 1998, John again collaborated with Tim Rice, this time on a successful Broadway musical adaptation of *Aida*. And in late 2000, John starred in a

Sir Elton John at the GQ Man of the Year Awards in 2004.

television special on CBS in which he performed a selection of his greatest hits at Madison Square Garden.

In 2001, John found himself embroiled in controversy by agreeing to perform on stage with controversial rapper Eminem at the 2001 Grammy Awards. In the face of furious protests from gay and lesbian activists who objected to Eminem's homophobic lyrics, John went ahead with the performance. As Christian Grantham has noted, Elton John is an entertainer who owes creative control to no one but himself. John later explained that music, no matter how controversial, is expression that deserves protection.

Even after more than thirty years as a musical icon, Elton John has proved that he still has a firm claim on the spotlight, though he has moved increasingly from musical arenas to the political arena.

In June 2003, John narrated the critically acclaimed HBO documentary series *Pandemic: Facing AIDS*, while continuing to fund HIV/AIDS education causes through his foundation.

John also announced, in March 2004, that he would marry David Furnish, his partner of eleven years, because "I would like to commit myself to David," but also because of President Bush's proposed constitutional amendment banning gay marriage. As John stated to the *New York Daily News*, Bush's anti–gay marriage stance "gave me the final push down the aisle I needed."

—*Nathan G. Tipton*

BIBLIOGRAPHY

Decker, Ed. "Elton John." *Contemporary Musicians: Profiles of the People in Music.* Stacy A. McConnell, ed. Detroit: Gale Research, 1997. 20:107–111.

Erlewine, Stephen Thomas. "Elton John." www.allmusic.com

Grantham, Christian. "Why Artists Defended Eminem." *The Gay and Lesbian Review* 8.3 (2001): 18.

Larkin, Colin, comp. and ed. "Elton John." *The Encyclopedia of Popular Music*, Third ed. New York: Muze, 1998. 4: 2833–2835.

Shaw, Bill. "Candle In the Wind." *People*, April 23, 1990, 86.

SEE ALSO

Popular Music; Rock Music; Music and AIDS; Musical Theater and Film; Music Video; Geffen, David

Jones, Bill T.   (b. 1951)

O N ST. PATRICK'S DAY, 1971, BILL T. JONES, THEN A freshman at State University of New York–Binghamton, met a twenty-two-year-old photography major named Arnie Zane. Zane soon convinced Jones to leave school and travel with him to Amsterdam to explore Europe and pursue their romance. They shared

their personal and creative lives together for the next seventeen years, forging a relationship and a dance company that made them the most visible gay couple in American dance in the 1980s.

Born on February 15, 1952, in Bunnell, Florida, William Tass Jones was the tenth of twelve children born to Estella and Augustus Jones, African American migrant farm workers. In 1959, the family settled in Wayland, New York, where Jones graduated from high school. He entered SUNY–Binghamton in fall 1970 and soon discovered dance, an experience that transformed his life.

After forming a relationship with Zane, a short Jewish-Italian man to whom he was immediately attracted, Jones began to envision their partnership in dance. Working first in solos and duets based on contact improvisation, the pair made an unlikely but striking couple.

After their return from two years in Amsterdam, they moved to Brockport, New York, where Jones enrolled as a dance major at SUNY–Brockport. They soon followed improvisationist Lois Welk to San Francisco, where she established the American Dance Asylum, a collective of choreographers.

After a year, Welk and Jones and Zane moved back east to Binghamton, relocating the American Dance Asylum to an old Elks Club building. Jones and Zane's performances in such works as *Monkey Run Road*, *Blauvelt Mountain*, and *Valley Cottage* (1979–1980) received positive press attention, which helped generate a financial base to form a company of dancers that they named Bill T. Jones/Arnie Zane & Company.

From its beginning in 1982, the look and choreography of the company set it apart from other modern dance groups: the dancers were a rainbow of races and all sizes; the music was a polyglot of Mendelssohn, gospel, Dada poetry, silence; nudity was as common as clothing; and anger freely mixed with joy. In the Bill T. Jones/Arnie Zane & Company, difference was celebrated, including sexual difference.

The company unabashedly presented the sensual and the erotic, sometimes with an edge. As Jones explained to Henry Louis Gates Jr. in *The New Yorker* in 1994, "My eroticism, my sensuality onstage is always coupled with a wild anger and belligerence."

One of the earliest successes of the company was *Secret Pastures*, which premiered at the Brooklyn Academy of Music's Next Wave Festival in 1984, featuring costumes by Willi Smith, sets by Keith Haring, and music by Peter Gordon.

Other evening-length works include *Last Summer at Uncle Tom's Cabin/The Promised Land* (1990)—a three-hour, four-part fantasia inspired by the Harriet Beecher Stowe novel—and *We Set Out Early...Visibility Was Poor* (1997).

Both Jones and Zane were diagnosed with HIV infection in 1984. In response, Jones went on a two-year trek to eleven cities, interviewing people with life-threatening conditions to create what became his best-known work, *Still/Here* (1994), a piece not about illness or death but about living. It is among the first full-length works to address the subject of living with a terminal illness. Attacked as "victim art" by *New Yorker* dance critic Arlene Croce, who refused to see it, the work has been both damned and (more often) celebrated.

When Zane died of AIDS-related lymphoma in 1988 at the age of 39, Jones made the decision to keep Bill T. Jones/Arnie Zane Dance Company alive as a memorial to his partner of seventeen years.

Jones's works are often more theater than concert dance. Hence, it is not surprising that during the 1990s Jones was hired to direct and choreograph several opera and theater productions. Perhaps the most notable of these is *The Mother of Three Sons* (1991) at New York City Opera, which was conceived and directed by Jones, with music composed by Leroy Jenkins and lyrics by Ann T. Greene.

In 1994, Jones signed a three-year contract as resident choreographer of the Lyons Opera Ballet in France. Yet, as he explained to critic Joseph Mazo, "I don't want—I can't—look to Europe for a place to create. France could not have invented Bill T. Jones."

Like all American modern dance company directors who compete for meager arts funding, Jones depends on international commissions and bookings to keep his company solvent.

In 1994, Jones received a MacArthur "genius" Fellowship. In 1995, he collaborated with author Toni Morrison and drummer Max Roach on *Dega*, and with opera singer Jessye Norman on *How! Do! You! Do!* (1999).

Famously extroverted, Jones is a charismatic performer and gifted choreographer whose autobiographical work often merges the private and the public. At home with the freedom of postmodernism, Jones's choreography often includes spoken text, projections, and videos. His eclectic works range in character from outbursts of emotional agitation to political controversy to formalist abstraction.

After Zane's death, Jones entered into a five-year relationship with company dancer Arthur Aviles, which dissolved in 1993, when he began a relationship with a new companion, Bjorn Amelan.   —*Bud Coleman*

Bibliography

Art Performs Life: Merce Cunningham, Meredith Monk, Bill T. Jones. New York: Distributed Art Publishers, 1998.

Bremser, Martha. *Fifty Contemporary Choreographers.* New York: Routledge, 1999.

Gates, Henry Louis Jr. "The Body Politic." *New Yorker,* November 28, 1994, 112.

Jones, Bill T., with Peggy Gillespie. *Last Night on Earth.* New York: Pantheon Books, 1995.

Mazo, Joseph H. *Prime Movers: The Makers of Modern Dance in America.* Highstown, N.J.: Princeton Book Company, 2000.

Zane, Arnie. *Continuous Replay: The Photographs of Arnie Zane, 1970–1980.* MIT Press, 1999.

Zimmer, Elizabeth, and Susan Quasha, eds. *Body Against Body: The Dance and Other Collaborations of Bill T. Jones and Arnie Zane.* Barrytown, N.Y.: Talman Co., 1989.

See also

Dance; Music and AIDS; Opera; Goode, Joe

Joplin, Janis   *(1943–1970)*

THE NAME JANIS JOPLIN IS PRACTICALLY SYNONYMOUS with the excesses epitomized by the counterculture of the 1960s: sex, drugs, and rock and roll, all of which Joplin took to extreme levels. As troubled as she was talented, Joplin has been portrayed in numerous articles, full-length biographies, and documentaries as everything from a reckless, sex-crazed party animal to a victimized, lost little girl who never believed she was lovable.

The truth is likely somewhere in between, but what is clear is that Joplin's musical legacy lives on and crosses barriers of gender, race, and class.

Joplin was born on January 19, 1943, in small, insular Port Arthur, Texas, where she grew up. She always stood out as a bright, creative misfit in her oil-refinery hometown. She stood out too in her rather conservative family, preferring to pursue visual art and music rather than fulfill her mother's expectations of her becoming a schoolteacher.

Joplin reportedly relished the attention that gossip about her bad-girl image brought, but her status as a social outcast hurt her deeply and would remain with her throughout her short life.

For a while, Joplin attended Lamar State College of Technology and then the University of Texas at Austin, but she decided that school was not for her and never graduated. During her college years she began singing at the hootenannies of the day and at bars in Austin, San Francisco, and Venice, California.

After some time spent traveling and a brief, failed attempt to establish a conventional life back home in Port Arthur, Joplin moved to San Francisco and fully immersed herself in the counterculture there.

Before long, her voice had gained her many followers, and she joined the then unknown group Big Brother and the Holding Company. Joplin scored a major hit at the 1967 Monterey Pop Festival with her smoldering rendition of Big Mama Thornton's blues song "Ball and Chain."

That major "Summer of Love" event heralded her big breakthrough; Big Brother signed a contract with Mainstream Records, and Joplin continued to perform with them for two more years.

Joplin later formed the Kozmic Blues Band, and in 1969 released *I Got Dem Kozmic Blues Again Mama!* When the group fell apart, she spearheaded one last project, the Full Tilt Boogie Band, a more popular-style, professional-sounding group with whom she recorded her third album, *Pearl*. The widely acclaimed record was released posthumously and featured her unforgettable version of the Kris Kristofferson tune "Me and Bobby McGee."

Life was difficult for Joplin. To frame her career in a historical context, one might recall that Joplin's star rose before women's liberation flourished—and prior to the advent of the women's music genre. Her era—despite its proliferation of love children—was not particularly nurturing of a single, enterprising woman in the traditionally male rock and roll world. As her fame grew, so did her alcoholism and drug use; she battled her heroin addiction but never relinquished her Southern Comfort habit.

Joplin's sexuality was expansive and open, encompassing both men and women; but the "freak" circles in which Joplin circulated were generally heterosexual and not immune to sexism. Hippie women, after all, were not supposed to be crass and, as Janis was often described, "ballsy."

In addition, Joplin crossed the race line. Most people had never seen a white woman singing the blues and letting it all hang out the way she did, and perhaps not everyone was ready for her full-on explosion of voice and soul. Citing influences and inspirations such as Billie Holiday, Bessie Smith, and Leadbelly, Janis interpreted the blues in a way that helped break down the old barriers between "black music" and "white music."

Although Joplin took numerous female lovers, she never openly identified as lesbian or bisexual. Instead, she considered herself beyond categorization: she was simply *sexual*.

Her friends mainly referred to her as bisexual, yet the press has long loved to heterosexualize her past, while lesbian culture often claims her as one of its own.

The truth is that Janis maintained long-term relationships with several women, including Peggy Caserta, whose controversial 1973 memoir, *Going Down with Janis*, documented their affair and mutual drug addiction. At the same time, Joplin was also on the lookout for "one good man" with whom to settle down. Twice engaged, she never did marry.

Although she had kicked heroin around the time she formed the Full Tilt Boogie Band, Joplin was tempted again one night when she ran into her former dealer in the lobby of the Landmark Motel in Los Angeles. She died of a heroin overdose, alone in her room at the motel, on October 4, 1970.

Joplin's music continues to flourish. Her *Greatest Hits* album still makes the *Billboard* charts. She was inducted into the Rock and Roll Hall of Fame in 1995.

—*Teresa Theophano*

BIBLIOGRAPHY

Echols, Alice. *Scars of Sweet Paradise: The Life of Janis Joplin*. New York: Metropolitan Books, 1998.

Friedman, Myra. *Buried Alive: The Biography of Janis Joplin*. New York: Harmony Books, 1992.

Janis Joplin Official Website: www.janisjoplin.com

SEE ALSO

Popular Music; Rock Music; Blues Music; Etheridge, Melissa; Russell, Craig; Smith, Bessie

Jorgensen, Christine   (1926–1989)

CHRISTINE JORGENSEN, BORN GEORGE WILLIAM JORgensen Jr., was not the first male-to-female transsexual to undergo a series of sexual reassignment operations, but hers was the first surgical sex change highly publicized in the United States. The publicity surrounding her surgery enabled Jorgensen and medical professionals to educate the larger public about the differences between homosexuality, transvestism, and transsexuality.

A second-generation Danish American, Jorgensen was born on May 30, 1926, to George and Florence Davis Hansen Jorgensen, and raised in the Bronx in a large extended family. In spite of a genuinely happy childhood—Jorgensen's memoir contains numerous lighthearted descriptions of her supportive family environment—her self-described "sissified" and modest ways began making her life miserable by the time she entered puberty.

What can only be called a crush on a male friend during her teenage years disturbed Jorgensen deeply. She had read about but disavowed homosexuality early on, feeling that the term did not apply to her. She later expounded upon gayness as "deeply alien" to her Lutheran religious principles.

Subscribing to the era's "deviation" theories regarding homosexuality, Jorgensen never exactly became a champion of gay rights. She remarks in her autobiography, "I had seen enough to know that homosexuality brought with it social segregation and ostracism that I couldn't add to my own deep feeling of not belonging." She reports that she even became physically ill when a man propositioned her while she was still living as a man.

Jorgensen was drafted into the Army in 1945, after having been rejected twice before when she volunteered for service, but was honorably discharged only a year and a half later, after a bout of illness.

Following her departure from the Army, she made an unsuccessful attempt at a photography career in Hollywood, but returned to the East Coast to study at the Progressive School of Photography in New Haven, Connecticut. While there, Jorgensen read about an endocrinologist doing hormone experiments on animals. Her interest was piqued, and she soon discovered that the solution to her problem could be in Europe.

In 1950, Jorgensen traveled to Copenhagen and met with Dr. Christian Hamburger, the first medical professional to diagnose her as a transsexual rather than a homosexual.

Hamburger began treating Jorgensen with experimental hormone therapy, and the following year, he and Jorgensen's psychiatrist agreed that she was ready to move on to the next step—surgery. After two operations, word of the brand-new Christine Jorgensen leaked to the press.

Thrust into the spotlight while still recuperating in the hospital, Christine became an overnight celebrity: the *New York Daily News* broke the story with the headline "Ex-GI Becomes Blonde Bombshell." Although she spent much time and energy ducking paparazzi and defending herself against slander, Jorgensen met with success as a public figure a short time after her return to the United States.

Jorgensen's name was on everyone's lips, whether they ridiculed her or sympathized with her, and intrigue about her case spread far and wide. She had long dreamed of becoming a photographer, but the relentless glare of publicity made it impossible to pursue a normal life.

After some hesitation, Jorgensen opted for a career as a stage actress and singer. Charismatic and photogenic, she cast herself in the role of the glamorous and gracious, well-coifed and beautifully gowned lady.

During the 1950s and early 1960s, she toured with a nightclub act in which she sang and did impressions. She appeared to capacity crowds at clubs from Havana to Las Vegas, often earning as much as $5,000 per week.

The object of enormous curiosity, she even issued a mildly titillating record, *Christine Jorgensen Revealed*, in which she answered questions about her transformation.

Jorgensen also lectured frequently about transsexuality and used her unsought celebrity as an occasion for educating others. Her book, *Christine Jorgensen: A Personal Autobiography*, was published in 1967, and its film

Christine Jorgensen receives the Woman of the Year award from the Scandinavian Societies of New York in 1953.

adaptation was released in 1970 as *The Christine Jorgensen Story*.

Jorgensen's significance lies in the fact that she ultimately took control of the sensational news of her sex reassignment surgery. The story was at first presented as something titillating and scandalous, but when she presented it as her own story she seized the opportunity to educate the public about transsexuality, especially its status as a phenomenon quite distinct from transvestism and homosexuality.

In addition, the publicity Jorgensen's case attracted served an important function in reassuring other transsexuals both that they were not alone and that sex reassignment surgery might offer hope for them as well. The publicity surrounding Jorgensen's surgery also prompted numerous medical professionals to explain transsexualism and sexual reassignment surgery to an interested public.

Perhaps most importantly, Jorgensen's innate dignity and eloquence helped humanize a phenomenon that has all too often been presented as sensational or risible.

Although she became engaged twice, Jorgensen never married. She lived in Massapequa, Long Island until her parents' deaths in 1967, when she moved to Southern California. She spent her last two years in San Clemente, where she died of bladder and lung cancer on May 3, 1989, at the age of sixty-two.   —*Teresa Theophano*

BIBLIOGRAPHY

Ingrassia, Michele. "In 1952, She Was a Scandal; When George Jorgensen Decided to Change His Name—and His Body—the Nation Wasn't Quite Ready." *Newsday*, May 5, 1989.

Jorgensen, Christine. *Christine Jorgensen: A Personal Autobiography.* New York: Paul S. Eriksson, 1967. Reprint, intro. by Susan Stryker. San Francisco: Cleis Press, 2001.

"Jorgensen, Christine." www.britannica.com

SEE ALSO

Popular Music; Rock Music; Blues Music; Etheridge, Melissa; Russell, Craig

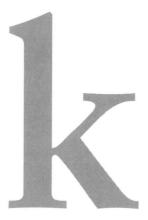

Kabuki

*K*ABUKI, A CLASSIC JAPANESE THEATRICAL FORM USING common or comic themes, with fantastical costumes, stylized gestures, music, and dance, and with all-male casts, is still popular today. Initially, it was a showcase for female and boy prostitutes.

Boy love was a given in ancient Japan. The love of *chigo* (a boy aged ten to seventeen) by Buddhist priests was a tradition, as, in the mode of ancient Greece, was the love of *wakashu* (a youth aged thirteen to twenty) by *samurai* warriors. *Shudo*, the love of young men, became a staple feature of Kabuki literature.

By the early seventeenth century, at the end of a long civil war, the power of the samurai declined and a merchant class emerged. For the merchants' pleasure, dances and dramatic routines, often performed by female prostitutes, began to be performed in Kyoto, Edo, and Osaka. Samurai and court aristocrats were forbidden to attend, but they donned disguises to join the fervid audiences.

This illegal mingling of classes and the deadly violence caused by jealousy over prostitutes disturbed the peace. The response of the alarmed Tokugawa authorities was to ban women from the Kabuki stage in 1629.

This began the era of the Grand Kabuki, or *wakashu kabuki,* where adolescent boys played both the *wakashu-gata* (male roles) and *onnagata* (female roles).

The authorities inadvertently created an ideal vehicle for showcasing the physical charms of beautiful, sexually available youths. These pretty boys, gracefully bending to the dance in long-sleeved kimonos, evoked great enthusiasm. They became the highly sought trophies of their *nouveaux riches* admirers, who were thrilled by the idea that shudo, formerly reserved for the upper classes, was now within their reach.

Many of the merchants were so swept away with passion that they bankrupted themselves over the boys. Thus, the social problems created by the carnal nature of the Kabuki were not solved, but exacerbated, by the decree of 1629. And to the chagrin of the moralistic censors, the situation could be addressed no further, because Iemitsu, the Shogun, was himself a connoisseur of boys.

After the death of Iemitsu in 1651, boys were banned from the stage, but not for long. Kabuki was a large and profitable enterprise, and the owners negotiated to reopen their theaters. They agreed to certain conditions, including the reduction of the repertoire's erotic content.

Moreover, in an attempt to end prostitution, the boy actors were forced to shave their most distinguishing feature, their long forelocks, leaving only sidelocks, in the style of *yaro* (adult men), as men were disqualified from prostitution. This had, however, the effect of extending the age for prostitutes.

As a character in *The Great Mirror of Male Love* (1687) explains: "It used to be that no matter how splendid the boy, it was impossible for him to keep his forelocks and take patrons beyond the age of twenty. Now, since everyone wore the hairstyle of adult men, it was still possible at age thirty-four or thirty-five for youthful actors to get under a man's robe." The new theater form was called *yaro kabuki.*

From 1868 onward, the process of westernization in Japan meant the rapid decline of shudo. By 1910, homosexuality in any form had disappeared from social visibility. Although the all-male Kabuki theater survives, all the shudo plays are excised from its repertoire and long forgotten.

Today, Kabuki presents nonerotic, spectacular musical entertainment. In the mid-twentieth century, novelist Yukio Mishima wrote and directed several Kabuki plays. His involvement with Kabuki reflected his fascination with sadomasochism, but his plays had no lasting effect on the form.

A special fascination for contemporary audiences is to see a man expertly performing as a woman, assuming the onnagata role. Even *geisha,* women trained to please men, attend Kabuki performances to learn from these actors the essence of femininity.

A famous contemporary onnagata, the wildly popular Bando Tamasaburo, has also played such western characters as Ophelia and Camille. Also popular in Japan today are the "male stars" of the all-girl Takarazuka operettas.

As Shakespeare knew, audiences love gender confusion, and in such confusion many gay men, lesbians, and transgendered people have found refuge.

—*Douglas Blair Turnbaugh*

BIBLIOGRAPHY

Gunji, Masakatsu. *Kabuki.* Tokyo: Kodansha International, 1969.

McLelland, Mark J. *Male Homosexuality in Modern Japan.* Richmond, U.K.: Curzon Press, 2000.

Saikaku, Ihara. *The Great Mirror of Male Love.* Paul Gordon Schalow, trans. Stanford, Calif.: Stanford University Press, 1990.

Watanabe, Tsuneo, and Jun'ichi Iwata. *The Love of the Samurai: A Thousand Years of Japanese Homosexuality.* London: GMP Publishers, 1989.

SEE ALSO

Dance; Takarazuka (Japanese All-Female Revues); Kemp, Lindsay; Sondheim, Stephen

The Actor Matsumoto Shigumaki as a Woman, by Torii Kiyumasu (ca. 1715).

Kander, John, and Fred Ebb

*John Kander (b. 1927)
and Fred Ebb (1932?–2004)*

COMPOSER JOHN KANDER AND LYRICIST FRED EBB ARE the musical poets of the polymorphous perverse. The stage (and, in two cases, subsequent film) versions of their commercially successful and critically lauded *Cabaret,* *Chicago,* and *Kiss of the Spider Woman* glorify the creativity inherent in sexual ambivalence and celebrate the social renewal fostered by unorthodox forms of political action.

Surprisingly for many gay fans, however, neither man is willing publicly to discuss his own homosexuality. "I thought they made a spectacle of themselves, frankly," Ebb complained to interviewer Randy Shulman following the nationally broadcast kiss shared by songwriting team and lifelong partners Marc Shaiman and Scott Wittman while accepting a 2003 Tony Award for *Hairspray.* "Your bedroom is not the screen. And it is also not the stage." Instead, Ebb asserts, any statement that he and Kander wish to make about homosexuality has been made through their songs.

Life and Career

Kander was born on March 18, 1927, into a music-loving family in Kansas City, Missouri. After studying music composition at Oberlin College and Columbia University, he settled in New York City, where he worked as an arranger, accompanist, and conductor.

Ebb, a native New Yorker, was probably born on April 8, 1932. Having attended New York University and taken a graduate degree in English from Columbia University, he wrote for nightclub acts, revues, and television (*That Was the Week That Was*) before being introduced to Kander.

In 1965, Kander and Ebb joined forces with the emerging theater powerhouse Harold Prince and the legendary director George Abbott on *Flora, The Red Menace*, which both established their professional reputation as a songwriting team and made a star out of their close friend, nineteen-year-old Liza Minnelli.

A string of huge successes, some near misses, and the occasional flop followed: *Cabaret* (1966), *The Happy Time* (1968), *Zorba* (1968), *70, Girls, 70* (1971), *Chicago* (1975), *The Act* (1977), *Woman of the Year* (1981), *The Rink* (1984), *And the World Goes 'Round* (1991), *Kiss of the Spider Woman* (1993), *Steel Pier* (1997), and *The Visit* (2001). They contributed as well to the film scores of Herb Ross's *Funny Lady* (1975) and Martin Scorsese's *New York, New York* (1977).

In 2003, Kander (who has lived for twenty-six years with one man, a choreographer and teacher) implicitly addressed rumors concerning the nature of his nonprofessional relations with Ebb by describing the latter to interviewer Jeffrey Tallmer as "his 40-year partner in creativity but never in domesticity, much less romance."

Ebb succumbed to a heart attack at his home in New York City on September 11, 2004.

Privileging Alternative Values

Kander and Ebb's songs make a powerful cumulative statement regarding the importance of alternative values, and are the more remarkable for making that statement in a theatrical form more easily given to escapism than to social comment.

"It's refreshing to meet someone odd for a change," Harry sings to Flora in *Flora, The Red Menace*, and Kander and Ebb's musical protagonists include such deviants from the social norm as a group of larcenous septuagenarian former vaudevillians surviving as best they can in a dilapidated residential hotel (*70, Girls*); an indifferently talented cabaret singer whose decadent sexual persona is her most successful performance (*Cabaret*); an effeminate window dresser imprisoned for "corrupting" a male minor (*Kiss of the Spider Woman*); "Chicago's own killer-dillers, those two scintillating sinners," Roxie Hart and Velma Kelly, and the six other "merry murderesses of the Cook County Jail" (*Chicago*); "the lovable

prodigal," Jacques, whose return to his native French Canadian village quickens his family members' hearts with as much anxiety as love (*Happy Time*); and, of course, the title character of *Zorba*, who proclaims in dance and song his freedom from every conventional expectation.

Kander and Ebb write music for characters who, like Flora, have learned, or are in the process of learning, to resist any pressure to conform, particularly when the social system exerting that pressure is itself corrupt ("You Are You").

Kander and Ebb's interest in persons who are barely on the margins of respectability, or who have been left behind entirely by the American Dream, drives them repeatedly to skewer the hypocrisy of social orthodoxy. This is why so many of their plays are set in the Depression era, when, following the widespread collapse of American optimism, those individuals who survived proved themselves by keeping their hearts open and their imaginations alive. In *Flora* and *Steel Pier*, respectively, Kander and Ebb found in that period's breadlines and dance marathons apt metaphors for the indignities heaped upon individuals that shatter their conventional expectations but nonetheless offer them an opportunity to refashion themselves in a nontraditional manner; prison proves a similarly apt metaphor in *Chicago* and *Kiss*.

Protesting Corruption; Seeing Things Differently

The corruption of power is lampooned in such songs as "A Powerful Thing" (*Steel Pier*) and "When You're Good to Mama" (*Chicago*); and the ruthless manipulation of the American legal system by its supposed protectors is satirized in "Razzle Dazzle" (*Chicago*). Social respectability is simply a matter of controlling the spread of gossip, Kander and Ebb chide in "Don't Tell Mama" (*Cabaret*), or of controlling the media ("Jailhouse Rag," *Chicago*).

The exploitation of buzzwords by self-aggrandizing political activists is illustrated in "Sign Here" (*Flora*), where the professed aims of the Communist Party figure also as the American values that Sen. Joseph McCarthy and the House Un-American Activities Committee claimed to be defending through their 1950s witch hunt for suspected communists: "democracy," "the rights of man," "everlasting peace," "milk and cookies for the kids," "a job for everyone," "do away with slums," and "save America." In Kander and Ebb's satire, anyone who sees a big-hearted eccentric like Flora as a "red menace" is as disturbed as the agitator Comrade Ada's much-vaunted acts of disruption are senseless and petty.

Little wonder, then, that when political institutions, the legal profession, the news media, and correction facilities are under the control of self-interested parties, Kander and Ebb's hero is the person who, because of his or her generosity, is relegated to the margins of respectability, if not persecuted outright.

A number of the pair's best songs dramatize different ways of "Seeing Things" (as photographer Jacques sings in *Happy Time*), including several that directly challenge the audience's unthinking acceptance of social stereotypes. "If you want to see old folks / You're in the wrong home tonight," a chorus of rowdy septuagenarians unexpectedly razzes the audience of *70, Girls*. They break into raucous vaudeville routines after first enumerating (and pretending to subscribe to) younger people's stereotypical expectations regarding the aged. And, waltzing genteelly with a tutu-wearing gorilla, the Emcee of the Kit Kat Club in 1930s Berlin (*Cabaret*) complains comically of society's inability to accept his unorthodox love relationship, only to turn to the Nazis scattered among the audience at the song's end and taunt them that "If you could see her through my eyes, / She wouldn't look *Jewish* at all."

Addressing the Darker Aspects of Social Experience

It is their willingness to address directly the darker aspects of social experience that distinguishes Kander and Ebb's music from that of their contemporaries. Jerry Herman's bright optimism easily wears thin, while Stephen Sondheim's wry irony often has the unanticipated effect of making his characters seem cold and distant. The darkness that colors Kander and Ebb's world, however, is tempered by their characters' willingness to make whatever accommodations are necessary for survival without growing bitter in the process.

No other Broadway score confronts the reality of aging and dying with such starkness as *70, Girls* ("The Elephant Song"). Likewise, the chorus's opening song in *Zorba*—"Life is what you do / While you're waiting to die"—proved so troubling to audiences reared on Rodgers and Hammerstein's "cockeyed optimism" that the original production of that show failed. (A successful 1983 revival starring Anthony Quinn carefully altered the line to "Life is what you do / Until the day you die.")

Kander and Ebb parody American audiences' expectation of "Happy Endings" in an extended number by that name that, though filmed, was finally cut from *New York, New York*. More trenchantly, Molina's partnering Aurora with the same casual elegance as Fred Astaire danced with Ginger Rogers ironically figures his death in the aptly titled final number of *Kiss*, "Only in the Movies."

Significantly, Kander and Ebb recognize the appeal of escaping life's difficulties through "too much pills and liquor" (as, for example, in the title song from *Cabaret* or in "The Morphine Tango" from *Kiss*). But ultimately, they insist, immuring oneself from possible adversity only means that one is not living fully. As the protagonist, Ida, instructs her friends in the concluding number of *70, Girls*:

> *There's lots of chaff, but there's lots of wheat:*
> *Say "yes"!*

> *You might get mugged as you walk the street,*
> *But on the other hand you might meet*
> *That handsome stranger that you'd love to greet:*
> *Say "yes"!*

Life must be accepted in all of its weltering ambiguity if any of its possibilities are to be realized.

Similarly, in *Cabaret*, Fraulein Schneider, raised in luxury but reduced during the Depression to renting rooms and emptying chamber pots, sings of the need to lower one's expectations and "learn how to settle for what you get" ("So What?"). Kander and Ebb reject outright the *carpe diem* insistence that one enjoy life's pleasures now because they will end all too soon. Rather, the pair insists, enjoyment of the available light is heightened by one's awareness of shadow.

Thus, while Jerry Herman's Depression-era characters are told to "Tap Your Troubles Away" (*Mack and Mabel*), Kander and Ebb use the 1930s dance marathon as a metaphor for finding joy in the sheer act of survival, no matter how demeaning the circumstances (*Steel Pier*). Herman asks his audience, in the best tradition of the Busby Berkeley musical, to accept that life's problems can be forgotten when one is tap-dancing; Kander and Ebb, on the other hand, show the grimace behind the forced smiles of the marathon dancers.

This may be why audiences rejected Herman's Mack and Mabel for failing to deliver a happy ending, but have less difficulty accepting the tragedy in Kander and Ebb's plays: Mme. Hortense dies and the Widow is killed in *Zorba*; *Kiss* is set in a repressive South American regime's prison for political dissidents and sexual deviants, and concludes with the death of the protagonist; the Nazis gradually take control of Berlin in *Cabaret*.

It is, finally, this insistence that one's full humanity can only be found in the acceptance simultaneously of disappointment *and* success, in the ambivalent mixture of comedy *and* tragedy, that makes Kander and Ebb the premier musical poets of sexual ambiguity and of nonnormative human relationships.

Sexual Ambiguities

Contrary to musical theater convention, the boy rarely gets the girl in a Kander and Ebb show. Cliff abandons Berlin and Sally Bowles in *Cabaret*; Flora discovers herself only after being dismissed by her boyfriend, Harry; Roxie learns that "I am my own best friend" in *Chicago*; a men-less Angel and Anna reconcile in *The Rink*; Rita falls in love with Bill in *Steel Pier*, only to discover that she has been romanced by a ghost and finally must make it on her own; and while three generations of male voices may join in on "A Certain Girl," Jacques and Laurie part over "Seeing Things" in *Happy Time*.

Ironically, Molina's succumbing to the heterosexual allure of the Spider Woman figures death in *Kiss*. And, in *Steel Pier*, Precious McGuire is permitted to perform professionally "Two Little Words," a paean to heterosexual wedded bliss, as payment for betraying her husband sexually with the marathon emcee. *Woman of the Year*, the only one of their plays to deliver a traditional heterosexual romance, is also Kander and Ebb's least distinguished score.

In contrast, Kander and Ebb's scores admit the possibility of homosocial affection, the delights of gender confusion, and (in *Kiss*, at least) the self-sacrificing power of homosexual love.

"I never loved a man as much as I love you," Zorba tells Niko at the conclusion of that play's final number. Likewise, in a poignant moment in *Happy Time*, the first time teenaged Bibi sings that he loves someone, it is to his free-spirited Uncle Jacques. The Emcee includes "boys" among the sexual attractions to be found in *Cabaret*; in the more permissive 1998 revival, the number "Two Ladies," which enacts a *ménage à trois* onstage, is performed not by a male and two females, as in the original production, but by a female and two males.

Extolling to a group of female prisoners the advantages of cooperating with her, Matron Mama Morton sings a song laden with lesbian sexual double entendres in *Chicago*: "Let's all stroke together, / Like a Princeton crew; / When you're stroking Mama, / She'll get hot for you."

In *Kiss*, Molina sings movingly of his love for Valentín in "Anything for Him." Significantly, Kander and Ebb give to a woman the only song in which homosexuality is accepted without reservation or qualification. In "You Could Never Shame Me," Molina's mother assures her imprisoned son, "I know that you're different, / I don't really care. / I would never change a hair."

Sexual Exuberance

This refusal to feel shame in sexual matters extends throughout Kander and Ebb's canon, making them the most sexually exuberant songwriters for the musical theater since Cole Porter. Their music deals frankly with such physiological dynamics of sexual attraction as body odor ("I sniff at a woman," Zorba exults) and crotch watching ("Nowadays you look at bulging trousers, / Some boy with bulging trousers, / And it isn't what you think, / He's got a gun," laments a group of neighbors in a declining neighborhood in *The Rink*).

"Everybody's Girl," which is Shelby's announcement of her sexual availability in *Steel Pier*, contains some of the most risqué lyrics written for the Broadway stage. The lines, "And so to reaffirm my status, / It's absolutely gratis / To use my apparatus," might have been spoken by Chaucer's Wife of Bath, while the asides that she makes during the song ("I could never be a cowhand's girl...I just can't keep my calves together" or "Men and me are like pianos. When they get upright, I feel grand!") are worthy of Mae West or Bette Midler.

Likewise, in "Wet" (also from *Steel Pier*) Rita coaxes Bill to strip to his Skivvies to join her in a late-night swim by cajoling him to "Show your nerve and show your shorts," one of the few times the nude male body has been put on display in the American musical. In *70, Girls*, a pair of physically affectionate septuagenarians musically taunts the audience for its unspoken curiosity: "Do we? / That's what you want to know."

"Nothing need be spoken, / All taboos are broken," Rita promises the sexually reluctant Bill in *Steel Pier*. This holds true for every one of Kander and Ebb's scores. Ultimately in their music, relationships come down to a life-sustaining intimacy.

You and I, love, you and I,
Take each minute for what's in it
As it's spinning by.
Win or lose, love, laugh or cry,
We can weather life together,
You and I. (70, Girls)

It is precisely because life is something to be "weathered"—because the world is a prison, a breadline, or a frenetic dance marathon—that every relationship is valuable, whatever the gender(s) of the persons involved. "Love, give me love, only love," Mme. Hortense sings in *Zorba*; "How good it is to feel, to touch, to care." It is risky to challenge the gender expectations of Broadway musical audiences, which are often composed of socially conservative people, but for Kander and Ebb, as Ida sings at the close of *70, Girls*, one must always say "Yes" to whatever opportunity presents itself, especially "Yes, I'll touch."

Conclusion

Kander and Ebb occupy a curious place in American musical theater. Kander is as great a master of musical idioms as Sondheim, recreating the Kurt Weill–like sound of Depression-era Berlin for *Cabaret*, the 1920s burlesque or vaudeville stage for *Chicago*, an impoverished but lively Greek village for *Zorba*, and 1930s popular dance music for *Steel Pier*. His "The Happy Time" is as perfect a waltz as Richard Rodgers's title theme from *Carousel* or any of the numbers in 3/4 time that Sondheim fashioned for *A Little Night Music*.

Likewise, Ebb can be as tartly sardonic ("Nobody even says oops / When they're passing their gas. / Whatever happened to class?") as he can be lushly romantic ("Walking among my yesterdays"); his line "The hope of summer belies the frost" ("Yes," *70, Girls*) is worthy of the Elizabethan poet Thomas Nashe.

Yet neither "The Happy Time" nor "Yes" has entered the popular musical lexicon, and the pair remains best known to the public ear for "Theme from *New York, New York*," a song that proved far bigger than the film it was created to serve, and for "Cabaret," which, ironically, is a character song during which a woman decides that she will have an abortion, not the hymn to unfettered sensual experience that its numerous popular renditions have mistaken it to be.

Gay theatergoers, however, hold Kander and Ebb in particularly high regard. This is, in part, because the pair has given such divas as Liza Minnelli, Chita Rivera, Gwen Verdon, Lotte Lenya, and Lauren Bacall some of their best stage moments—and the relation of gay audiences to the musical theater depends largely on gay identification with the diva, as John M. Clum observes. More importantly, whatever their restrictions concerning the details of their personal lives, Kander and Ebb have lived their careers in collaboration with other major gay theater talents like A. J. Antoon, Rob Marshall, and Terrence McNally, and have helped realize onstage works by Christopher Isherwood and Manuel Puig that have defined gay sensibility.

But perhaps most important, their songs emphasize the imperative of refusing to accept only those relationships allowed by society, the need to take risks to connect with others, and the value of finding the strength to somehow go on even in the face of rejection ("Maybe This Time," "Somebody Older"). Theirs is a poetry of "You and I" that erases the boundaries of gender and age.

—Raymond-Jean Frontain

BIBLIOGRAPHY

Clum, John M. *Something for the Boys: Musical Theater and Gay Culture.* New York: St. Martin's 1999.

Hirsch, Foster. *Harold Prince and the American Musical Theatre.* Cambridge: Cambridge University Press, 1989.

Kander, John, and Fred Ebb, with Greg Lawrence. *Colored Lights: Forty Years of Words and Music, Show Biz, Collaboration, and All That Jazz.* New York: Faber and Faber, 2003.

Mordden, Ethan. *Open a New Window: The Broadway Musical in the 1960s.* New York: Palgrave, 2001.

———. *One More Kiss: The Broadway Musical in the 1970s.* New York: Palgrave, 2003.

Shulman, Randy. "Ebb's Tide." *Washington (D.C.) Metro Weekly*, June 19, 2003: www.metroweekly.com/arts_entertainment/stage.php?ak=521

Tallmer, Jerry. "Sally Bowles' Muses." *Gay City News*, Oct. 30, 2003: www.gaycitynews.com/gcn_244/sallybowlesmuses.html

SEE ALSO

Musical Theater and Film; Divas; Herman, Jerry; Porter, Cole; Shaiman, Marc, and Scott Wittman; Sondheim, Stephen

Kemp, Lindsay   (b. 1940?)

MIME ARTIST, RENEGADE, AND MAGNETIC STAGE PERformer, Lindsay Kemp has long had a cult status in alternative theater. With its eclectic mix of elements—the commedia dell'arte, burlesque, music hall, ballet, the circus, improvisation, Japanese *Kabuki* and *Noh* theater, travesty, pantomime, and cabaret—his style is difficult to characterize.

In productions that are similar to musical revues—neither complete plays nor ballets, but something in between—Kemp and his company have astonished audiences with intense, erotically suggestive theatrical experiences that blur the line between high and low culture.

Once seen, Kemp's work is rarely forgotten. At its best, it achieves a wordless, resonant fusion of idiosyncratic physical, visual, and aural mime elements that vigorously assert the importance of his homosexuality to his performance ethic.

Stylistic Development

Kemp was born sometime around 1940 in South Shields in the North of England to a mother who encouraged his dramatic interests. His father died at sea when Kemp was three years old. While living in Bradford, he befriended the young artist David Hockney.

Kemp applied for admission to the Royal Ballet, but was rejected. He later studied with Dame Marie Rambert and Marcel Marceau in the late 1950s and early 1960s.

In 1968, Kemp formed a company of his own. His goal, he declared, was to be a Pied Piper, to lure, seduce, and intoxicate an audience with ravishing but emotionally intense gestures and sensations, to fool them into believing that the dream visions and gender illusions he attempts are real.

Kemp's first great success was a celebrated production of *Flowers*—a work that captured the essence of Jean Genet's novel *Our Lady of the Flowers* and eventually had a triumphant run of six months at the Roundhouse, London, in 1974.

Kemp then produced an all-male reinterpretation of Wilde's *Salome* (1976) in which Kemp himself played the young protagonist and performed a seven-veil dance that conjured the ecstasy of a whirling dervish.

Also in the 1970s, he starred as the great Russian dancer in the title role of *Nijinsky*, a work the choreographer Sir Frederick Ashton described as the most thrilling piece of theater he had ever witnessed. Such performances secured Kemp an adoring following, especially in Spain, Italy, and Japan.

Kemp was also invited to work with choreographer Christopher Bruce of the Ballet Rambert in a production called *Cruel Garden* (1977), based on the life of gay icon

Federico García Lorca. He cast a bullfight scene as a dramatic struggle between freedom and the forces of restriction. This work achieved huge popularity and was revived in 1998.

In these productions, Kemp mixed the beautiful and explicitly erotic with utterly grotesque elements of parody and satire. He pushed the boundaries not only of gender but of what was possible in the theater. In doing so, he emulated Antonin Artaud in attempting to achieve an improvised "total theater" that very often perplexed and repelled dance critics who found what they perceived as bathos and lack of discipline distasteful.

Kemp's uniquely mannered, phantasmagoric style has little use for words. His approach is to grab the senses at their most vulnerable, using stark colors and dissonant lighting contrasts. Fragments of poetry or dialogue occur, but the impact derives from gestures and vibrant tableaux. The effect is richly imaginative, layered, evocative, and, ultimately, enchanting.

Kemp's presence as leader and instigator of his own homogeneous and constantly changing company is crucial. He gathers around him loyal performers and musicians dedicated to promoting the Kemp universe. He encourages his actors to live their roles offstage. In Kemp's world, each mimed gesture emerges from within the body, based on a sure belief that the actor *is* a king, a harlot, Garbo, a fairy, a beast, Pavlova, a pimp, Isadora Duncan, or a Pierrot.

Derek Jarman's *Sebastiane*

Film director Derek Jarman used Kemp and his company for the delirious Roman orgy scene that begins his groundbreaking film *Sebastiane* (1976). Kemp appears in the scene nearly naked, splattered in glitter and sperm. According to Jarman, Kemp is "one of the key gay figures of the sixties and seventies."

Actors from Kemp's company, such as David Haughton and The Incredible Orlando, aka blind actor Jack Birkett, have worked closely with Kemp to enhance the company's style. Birkett also appears in other Jarman films, including *The Tempest* (1979) and *Caravaggio* (1989).

A Midsummer Night's Dream

In 1984, Kemp and Celestino Coronado joined forces to make a film of Kemp's idiosyncratic stage production of Shakespeare's *A Midsummer Night's Dream,* which had premiered at London's Sadlers Wells theater a year earlier. Kemp played Puck—a perfect role for him, part Eros, part clown, part satyr—who is seen hovering in the air above the crossed lovers.

Visually eccentric and memorable, this film exemplifies Kemp's ability to reinvent Shakespeare, unearthing the play's haunting, darkly erotic, subconscious allusions.

Fittingly, Kemp even claims to be descended from William Kemp, Shakespeare's clown.

In the film, the changeling boy (François Testory) comes to the fore as a resonant image of the hermaphrodite, lusted after with relish by Oberon (Michael Matou). Thus, the crossed lovers in an enchanted wood are no longer heterosexual, but homosexual. *A Midsummer Night's Dream* may be Kemp's most fully realized work, though it dispensed with much of Shakespeare's text and established its own parameters.

Kemp as Gender Illusionist

In 1991, Kemp performed a rare solo work in a production called *The Onnagata* (Japanese gender illusionists). The title refers to Japanese artists who devote themselves to being perceived as female. Long an admirer of these gender illusionists, Kemp studied the elaborate language of gestures in Japan and devised a "fantasy in kimonos" in which he revisited many of his earlier roles.

Kemp's Influence

Kemp has had a major influence on popular culture even though he has never himself achieved wide fame. For example, Kemp made a decisive mark on David Bowie, who was Kemp's student in the late 1960s. They toured together in a small show called *Pierrot in Turquoise.*

The visual imagery of Bowie's experimental stage persona Ziggy Stardust was given a boost by Kemp, who directed Bowie in his Rainbow Theatre rock concert in 1972. This show incorporated mime and dance in a way not attempted before in rock and roll, but it has since been widely imitated.

The young singer and composer Kate Bush also fell under Kemp's spell. The influence of his gestures and dance style are apparent in her stage and video work. Kemp appeared in her 1994 film *The Line, the Cross, the Curve.*

Elements of Kemp's influence can also be detected in the work of such disparate artists as the British drag theater troupe *Bloolips*, dancer Michael Clark, and even club and performance artist Leigh Bowery.

Contemporary Kemp

Kemp and Company's most recent show, *Dreamdances,* features Kemp and two of his longtime dancer-collaborators, Nuria Moreno and Marco Berriel. A kind of "greatest hits" reconfigured for a company of three, *Dreamdances* presents highlights from some of Kemp's most definitive works, including *Flowers, Salome, Nijinsky,* and *The Onnagata.*

Kemp now lives in Rome, teaching mime and directing operas. He remains the quintessentially outrageous and openly homosexual man of the theater.

—Kieron Devlin

BIBLIOGRAPHY

Burnside, Fiona. "Words Versus Gestures." *Dance Journal* 5.3b (Summer 1987): 16–17.

Kemp, Lindsay. "The Onnagata." *Sunday Telegraph*, April 14, 1991.

Smith, Rupert. "Lindsay Kemp." *Guardian*, January 30, 2002: www.guardian.co.uk/arts/story/0,3604,641424,00.html

Wilms, Anno. *Lindsay Kemp and Company*. Derek Jarman, preface; David Haughton, intro. London: Gay Men's Press, 1987.

SEE ALSO

Dance; Kabuki; Ashton, Sir Frederick; Bowie, David; Duncan, Isadora; Nijinsky, Vaslav

Kirstein, Lincoln   (1907–1996)

BEST KNOWN AS THE LEADING IMPRESARIO OF THE American ballet world, Lincoln Edward Kirstein contributed immensely to the fields of dance, visual arts, and literature. He was a significant influence in the development of twentieth-century American culture.

Born into a wealthy, close-knit Jewish family in Rochester, New York, Kirstein was raised alongside two siblings by his parents, Rose and Louis. His father was chief executive officer of Filene's Department Store in Boston and his mother the daughter of a clothing manufacturer in Rochester.

Kirstein showed artistic leanings from an early age and had his first taste of ballet at age twelve, when he was exposed to Anna Pavlova's performances in Boston.

An unexceptional student, Kirstein was nonetheless accepted to Harvard in 1926. There, in 1927, he founded the influential literary magazine *Hound and Horn*, which he edited until 1934 and for which he reviewed dance and theatrical performances. He also cofounded the Harvard Society for Contemporary Art, a forerunner of the Museum of Modern Art.

After earning a bachelor's degree from Harvard in 1929, and a master's in 1930, Kirstein traveled to Europe, where he saw performances of Diaghilev's Ballets Russes. In London in 1933, he met the choreographer George Balanchine, whose work he admired immensely.

Kirstein persuaded Balanchine to return to the United States with him to establish an American form of classical ballet equal in quality to the Russian tradition. Drawing on his family fortune for funding, Kirstein opened the School of American Ballet in New York City in 1934, with himself as president, an office he would occupy until 1989.

Together, Kirstein and Balanchine founded a series of dance companies. The first troupe they established was the American Ballet Company, which, from 1935 to 1938, served as the Metropolitan Opera's resident ballet troupe. Then, Ballet Caravan was formed in 1936 as a touring company; American Ballet Caravan came next and successfully toured South America in 1941 before it disbanded.

During this period, Kirstein wrote a number of influential (and polemical) books about dance, including *Dance* (1935) and *Blast at Ballet* (1938), in which he articulated his ambitions for creating a grassroots classical dance tradition in America. He also wrote a number of libretti for ballets, including *Billy the Kid* (choreographed by Eugene Loring to music of Aaron Copland, 1938) and *Filling Station* (choreographed by Lew Christensen to music of Virgil Thomson, 1938).

In 1941, Kirstein married Fidelma Cadmus, the beautiful sister of the painter Paul Cadmus, a friend and artistic collaborator. While the marriage was by all accounts a happy one, it did not prevent Kirstein from having a number of homosexual affairs. He maintained liaisons with several male dancers while living with Fidelma, and some of his lovers even shared the couple's living space. In her later years, Fidelma was institutionalized for mental illness, and she died in 1991.

Kirstein joined the army and served as a private first class in Europe during World War II. With the Division of Monuments, Fine Arts, and Archives, he helped to recover stolen artwork from the Nazis and was honorably discharged in 1946.

With Balanchine, Kirstein then founded another dance company called Ballet Society, whose 1948 performance of Stravinsky's *Orpheus* is considered a landmark of modern dance. That year, the troupe, which would become known as the New York City Ballet, was invited to be the resident company of the City Center of Music and Drama.

Kirstein served as director of the New York City Ballet, America's most influential ballet company, from its founding until 1989. With the success of New York City Ballet, Kirstein fulfilled one of his early ambitions—to create a ballet company that could perpetuate a vital tradition of classic dance.

Kirstein was also a prolific writer. He authored many articles and books on various aspects of the arts; wrote criticism, novels, poetry, biographies, and historical works; and founded *Dance Index* magazine, which he edited from 1942 to 1948.

Kirstein received a number of prestigious awards, among them the Medal of Freedom, the National Medal of Arts, the Benjamin Franklin Medal of Britain's Royal Society of Arts, and (with George Balanchine) the National Gold Medal of Merit Award of the National Society of Arts and Letters.

Despite the visibility of his affairs with men, Kirstein did not come out publicly until 1982, when he published an article in *Raritan* about his early-1930s relationship with the writer and merchant seaman Carl Carlsen, a former lover of poet Hart Crane. The essay was republished in both of his memoirs, *By, With, To and From* (1991) and *Mosaic* (1994).

Kirstein died on January 5, 1996, at the age of 88.

—*Teresa Theophano*

BIBLIOGRAPHY

Leddick, David. *Intimate Companions: A Triography of George Platt Lynes, Paul Cadmus, Lincoln Kirstein, and Their Circle.* New York: St. Martin's Press, 2000.

www.nycballet.com

SEE ALSO

Dance; Ballet; Ballets Russes; Set and Costume Design; Barber, Samuel; Copland, Aaron; Diaghilev, Sergei; Thomson, Virgil

Landowska, Wanda   *(1879–1959)*

Wanda Landowska, a member of Natalie Clifford Barney's famed lesbian salon, was almost single-handedly responsible for the revival of the harpsichord as a performance instrument in the twentieth century. In her enthusiastic research to uncover the forgotten music and performance styles of the seventeenth and eighteenth centuries, she paved the way for today's interest in authentic performances of early music on original instruments.

Landowska, born on July 5, 1879, in Warsaw, Poland, was a musical prodigy who began playing the piano at the age of four and from a very young age was trained at the Warsaw Conservatory. At fifteen, she went to Berlin to study composition and, though she was a rather rebellious student, began to win prizes in major competitions for her songs and piano works.

While in Berlin, she met the Polish folklorist Henry Lew, who encouraged her research and performance of early music, and assisted her in writing her book, *Musique ancienne* (1909). In 1900, she married Lew and moved with him to Paris, where she was able to gain a greater audience.

While the relationship was a mostly supportive one, Landowska wished to be relieved of the sexual aspects of marriage. Accordingly, she arranged a *ménage à trois* by hiring a maid who would also function as Lew's mistress. The situation was apparently satisfactory for all involved, and, even after Lew died in 1919, the maid remained in the musician's service until the latter's death.

Landowska's fame grew quickly, and in 1903 she gave her first public performance on the harpsichord, an instrument that, by the nineteenth century, was considered "feeble" in its dynamics and rendered obsolete by the piano. Landowska ferociously championed its use through her performances and writing; she commissioned the construction of new harpsichords; and, in 1913, she returned to Berlin to establish a class devoted to the instrument at the Hochschule für Musik.

In 1920, Landowska settled in Paris, where she became a frequent guest in Barney's circle, often providing musical accompaniment for the various artistic functions of the renowned lesbian salon.

While she toured extensively and recorded during the 1920s, she also began another phase of her career by establishing the École de Musique Ancienne near Paris, which attracted students from many nations. She was recognized as one of the great music teachers of her time, and was rumored to have engaged in a rivalry with Nadia Boulanger, the other great female musical pedagogue, for the romantic affections of a number of young women in their tutelage.

In the 1930s, Landowska met Denise Restout, who became, in turn, her student, her life companion, and the preserver of her artistic legacy.

Landowska's fame and success continued to grow through the 1930s, but, with the Nazi invasion of France in 1940, she lost her school, her property, her extensive library, and all her instruments. She and Restout escaped to southern France and then to Lisbon, and finally arrived in New York as refugees.

Although Landowska had virtually nothing left to her but her talent, she nonetheless reestablished herself in the United States as a performer and teacher. Through the 1940s, she toured extensively and made her landmark recording of Johann Sebastian Bach's *Goldberg* variations, a work she restored to performance on the instrument for which it had been composed.

She continued to work tirelessly until her death on August 16, 1959, at her home in Lakeville, Connecticut. After her death, Restout devotedly edited and translated her writing on music.

Landowska was decorated by the governments of Poland and France, and she was widely respected by her fellow musicians. She thoroughly transformed the performance and reception of early music in the modern period, and, through her pioneering efforts, the harpsichord is frequently heard in many diverse musical genres today.

—*Patricia Juliana Smith*

BIBLIOGRAPHY

Benstock, Shari. *Women of the Left Bank: Paris, 1900–1940.* Austin: University of Texas Press, 1986.

Landowska, Wanda. *Landowska on Music.* Denise Restout, ed. and trans. New York: Stein and Day, 1964.

Sachs, Harvey. *Virtuoso: The Life and Art of Niccolò Paganini, Franz Liszt, Anton Rubinstein, Ignace Jan Paderewski, Fritz Kreisler, Pablo Casals, Wanda Landowska, Vladimir Horowitz, Glenn Gould.* New York: Thames and Hudson, 1982.

SEE ALSO

Classical Music; Boulanger, Nadia

Lane, Nathan   (b. 1956)

A HIGHLY ACCLAIMED ACTOR, NATHAN LANE HAS appeared on stage, screen, and television. He has starred in Broadway productions of *Guys and Dolls, A Funny Thing Happened on the Way to the Forum, Love! Valour! Compassion!,* and *The Producers.* He has received numerous acting honors, including two Tony Awards. Openly gay himself, he has portrayed gay characters in several plays and also on screen in *Frankie and Johnny* and *The Birdcage.*

One of the most accomplished comic actors of his generation, Lane has an appealing presence that has earned him the admiration of legions of fans and critics. Although his métier is that of comedy, he is remarkably versatile. As Alex Witchel has observed, "Lane is an outsize talent who can belt it to the balcony and back,

cajoling and beguiling with song, laughs, a few lumps in the throat. With his classic clown's face, part bulldog, part choirboy, he can be good and evil, smart and stupid, funny and sad, sometimes all in one number."

The youngest of three sons of Daniel Lane, a truck driver, and Nora Lane, a secretary, he was born Joseph Lane on February 3, 1956, in Jersey City, New Jersey. Around the time of his birth, his father's eyesight began to fail. Unemployed, the father fell victim to alcoholism and eleven years later "drank himself to death," according to his son.

When Lane was in his early teens, his mother began to suffer from manic depression severe enough to require occasional hospitalization. Lane's older brother Daniel became a surrogate father to him and encouraged his love of reading and theater.

Lane began acting while attending St. Peter's Preparatory School in Jersey City. He won a drama scholarship to St. Joseph's College in Philadelphia, but even with the award, the family could not afford the expense of college, and so he began working as an actor.

As Lane established himself in the profession by performing in dinner theater and children's productions, he supplemented his income with various jobs, including telemarketing, conducting surveys for the Harris poll, and delivering singing telegrams.

At the age of twenty-two, Lane registered with Actors' Equity. Since there was already a performer listed as Joe Lane, he changed his first name from Joseph to Nathan after the character Nathan Detroit in *Guys and Dolls,* whom he had played in dinner theater the previous year.

With Patrick Stark, Lane formed a comedy team called Stark and Lane. The duo, based in Los Angeles, worked at clubs, opened concerts, and made occasional television appearances. After a couple of years, Lane quit the act, which was not particularly profitable because of the travel expenses involved. In addition, Lane wanted to return to New York.

Before leaving California, Lane auditioned for and won a part in *One of the Boys,* a situation comedy starring Mickey Rooney. The series, which was filmed in New York, ran for only thirteen episodes in 1982, but it brought Lane to the attention of the public.

In the same year, Lane made his Broadway debut, playing Roland Maule in Noël Coward's *Present Laughter,* directed by George C. Scott. His performance met with critical approval, and he went on to appear in a number of plays, including Goldsmith's *She Stoops to Conquer* (1984, directed by Daniel Gerroll), Shakespeare's *Measure for Measure* (1985, directed by Joseph Papp), Simon Gray's *The Common Pursuit* (1986–1987, directed by Simon Gray and Michael McGuire), and August Darnell and Eric Overmyer's *A Pig's Valise* (1989, directed by Graciela Daniele), as well as two unsuccessful musicals, Elmer Bernstein and Don Black's *Merlin* (1982–1983, directed by Frank Dunlop) and William Perry's *Wind in the Willows* (1985–1986, staged by Tony Stevens).

In 1987, Lane made his film debut playing a ghost in Hector Babenco's *Ironweed*, based on the novel by William Kennedy.

In 1989, Lane played his first gay role as Mendy in Terrence McNally's *The Lisbon Traviata*, directed by John Tillinger. His performance earned him the Drama Desk Award for best actor in a play.

Lane's association with McNally has been long and successful. In 1990, he acted in McNally's *Bad Habits* (directed by Paul Benedict), and in 1991, he appeared in the playwright's *Lips Together, Teeth Apart* (directed by Tillinger). In the latter he played a homophobic character.

In the early 1990s, Lane had roles in half a dozen films, including *Frankie and Johnny* (1991, directed by Garry Marshall), which was based on a play by McNally. In it he played the gay friend of Frankie, the female lead.

In 1992, Lane returned to Broadway in a revival of Frank Loesser's *Guys and Dolls*, directed by Jerry Zaks. His performance as Nathan Detroit earned him rave reviews and another Drama Desk Award, this one for best actor in a musical, as well as a Tony nomination. The next year, he was well-received as the star of Neil Simon's *Laughter on the 23d Floor*, also directed by Zaks.

In 1994, Lane supplied the voice of Timon the meerkat in Rob Minkoff's *The Lion King*. Lane teamed with Ernie Sabella, who voiced Pumbaa the warthog, on the movie's extremely popular song "Hakuna Matata." Lane has since been the voice of other animated characters, including a cat in the film *Stuart Little* (1999, directed by Minkoff) and a dog in the Disney cartoon show *Teacher's Pet*, for which he won a Daytime Emmy Award.

In 1994, Lane worked in another play by McNally, *Love! Valour! Compassion!* (directed by Joe Mantello). He earned a Drama Desk Award as best featured actor in a play for his complex and moving portrayal of a gay man with AIDS.

Lane next appeared in a 1996 revival of Stephen Sondheim's *A Funny Thing Happened on the Way to the Forum*, directed by Zaks. Starring as Pseudolus, a Roman slave, Lane garnered enthusiastic reviews and a Tony Award for best performance by a leading actor in a musical.

In 1996, Lane played drag queen Albert opposite Robin Williams's Armand in Mike Nichols's film *The Birdcage*, a remake of Edouard Molinaro's 1978 film based on Jean Poiret's play, *La Cage aux Folles*. The film, with a script by Elaine May and Mike Nichols, was set in Miami's South Beach. Although controversial in a number of quarters, especially for its stereotypical portrait of a gay couple, the film was a commercial success,

and Lane's performance was described as "wide-ranging [and] inventive."

Lane starred in a CBS situation comedy entitled *Encore! Encore!* in 1998–1999. He played a retired opera singer who returns to his home in the Napa Valley to assume management of his family's winery. Lane's original concept for his character was that of a "diva chef in a five-star restaurant" who had come out and was raising his son.

As it turned out, however, his character was entirely heterosexualized and he played an (unlikely) womanizer. Despite his own good acting (and the presence of veteran actress Joan Plowright, who played his mother), the show failed to attract an audience and was soon canceled.

Lane's recent work includes a 2000 production of Moss Hart and George S. Kaufman's *The Man Who Came to Dinner* (directed by Zaks) and, most successfully, a starring role in Mel Brooks's *The Producers* (2001, directed by Susan Stroman), described as "the biggest hit on Broadway in more than a decade." Lane won a Tony Award for best actor in a musical for his hilarious performance as Max Bialystock.

In 2002, Lane appeared as Mr. Crummles in Douglas McGrath's film version of Dickens's *Nicholas Nickleby*. The actor, who has a "talent holding deal" with CBS, also was chosen to star in a comedy series in which he will play a gay congressman. The show has not yet been scheduled.

In 2004, Lane opened to mixed reviews in a musical adaptation of Aristophanes' *The Frogs*, with a book by Bert Shrevelove and music and lyrics by Stephen Sondheim. The show was originally produced in 1974 at the Yale School of Drama; for the 2004 production Lane freely adapted Shrevelove's book and starred as Dionysos, the god of theater.

Lane has never made a secret of his homosexuality. He came out to his family when he was twenty-one and about to move in with a lover. He did not comment publicly on his sexual orientation until 1999, however.

Lane has been criticized by some activists in the gay community for waiting so long to come out publicly. In an interview in the *Advocate* he explained that he "[found] it difficult to discuss [his] personal life with total strangers" but was moved to speak out after the murder of gay college student Matthew Shepard. "At this point it's selfish not to do whatever you can," said Lane. "If I...say I'm a gay person, it might make it easier for somebody else. So it seems stupid not to."

In other interviews Lane has alluded to an "on-again-off-again relationship with an actor who lives in Los Angeles," but has otherwise maintained privacy about his personal relationships.

— *Linda Rapp*

BIBLIOGRAPHY

"Lane, Nathan." *Current Biography Yearbook 1996.* Judith Graham, ed. New York: The H. W. Wilson Company, 1996. 286–289.

"Lane, Nathan." *Contemporary Theatre, Film and Television.* Michael J. Tyrkus, ed. Detroit: Gale Group, 2000. 201–203.

Vilanch, Bruce. "Citizen Lane." *Advocate,* February 2, 1999, 30.

Witchel, Alex. " 'This Is It—As Happy as I Get, Baby.' Nathan Lane." *New York Times,* September 2, 2001.

SEE ALSO

Musical Theater and Film; Coward, Sir Noël; Sondheim, Stephen

lang, k.d.   *(b. 1961)*

k.d. lang, photographed by Jeri Heiden.

LONG BEFORE SHE CAME OUT AS A LESBIAN IN A 1992 interview in the Advocate, and long before she appeared on the 1993 cover of *Vanity Fair* lounging in male drag in a barber's chair with Cindy Crawford hovering teasingly over her, lesbians had made k.d. lang their own. They were drawn not only by her gender-bending hairstyle and clothes, but also by her achingly beautiful voice and her intensely romantic singing style.

A country girl, lang, whose given name is Kathryn Dawn, grew up in the tiny Canadian town of Consort, deep in Alberta's farming territory. She came out as a lesbian while still a teenager and moved to Edmonton, where she joined a performance art group called GOYA, Group of Young Artists.

When she began to sing country music, it was part tribute to her country roots, part performance art, and part camp. But lang's rich voice and deeply felt interpretations gave her legitimacy as a country artist. She released three country albums, *A Truly Western Experience* (1984), *Angel with a Lariat* (1987), and *Absolute Torch and Twang* (1989). She won Grammy Awards for *Absolute Torch and Twang* and for her version of the Roy Orbison classic "Crying."

Although the country music establishment rewarded lang in spite of her eccentricities of dress and identity, the more conservative country audiences had a harder time accepting her, especially after she went public as a vegetarian and made an antimeat television commercial.

The message, "Meat Stinks!," roused anger in the farming communities that love country music. Among the communities responding negatively to the commercial was Consort: In retaliation, her hometown removed the plaque that had identified it as the "Home of k.d. lang."

Lesbians, who had been sure for years that lang was one of them, were pleased when she became one of very few major celebrities to come out openly as gay. However, since lang stood virtually alone on the mainstream stage, her lesbian fans often expected her to represent every aspect of what they considered important about being queer.

lang, who does not view her lesbianism as the central factor of her life, found it difficult and often painful when she was criticized for not living up to the diverse demands of her audience.

However, she does stand up as a lesbian when she feels it is important. She has spoken and performed at gay demonstrations and AIDS benefits. In 1997, she joined another famous lesbian making the transition out of the closet when she guest-starred with Ellen DeGeneres on two episodes of *Ellen.*

Along with her emergence as an out lesbian, lang began to expand and experiment with her musical style. In 1992, the same year that she came out, she released *Ingenue,* a collection of her own compositions in the style of the "torch" ballads of the 1940s. This departure from country would be her most commercially successful album, going double platinum and winning a Grammy for its signature song, "Constant Craving."

lang followed this success with another original album in 1995, *All You Can Eat*; and in 1997, she released *Drag*, a compilation of old songs unified by the common theme of smoking cigarettes.

Between 1997 and 2000, she took a break from recording and performing to relax and gather her forces after her breakneck rise to fame. During this time, she moved from a farm near Vancouver, British Columbia, to a glass-and-wood "cabin" in the woods near Los Angeles. Also during this time, she fell in love with Leisha Hailey of the girl group The Murmurs.

lang's sabbatical and her increasingly solid relationship with Hailey resulted in a newly successful return to music. In the summer of 2000, she released *Invincible Summer*, an album of original love songs with a breezy summery tone, reflecting the influence of Brazilian music and the Beach Boys. The album and its accompanying tour received rave reviews.

lang's most recent albums are *Live by Request* (2002), recorded from the A&E television series of the same name; and, with Tony Bennett, *Wonderful World* (2003), in which the duo sing songs inspired by Louis Armstrong. For the latter work, Bennett and lang received a Grammy Award in the category Best Traditional Pop Album. In *Hymns of the 49th Parallel* (2004), lang performs Canadian songs.

k.d. lang remains an anomalous figure in the music world, both because she is a lesbian and because she refuses to confine herself to a specific genre. Always an experimenter, she resists neat categorization. But her sincerity, charm, and compelling voice continue to attract a wide variety of listeners.

—*Tina Gianoulis*

BIBLIOGRAPHY

Appelo, Tim. "Is k.d. lang Really Patsy Cline?" *Savvy*, July 1988, 18.

Bennetts, Leslie. "k.d. lang Cuts It Close." *Vanity Fair*, August 1993, 94.

Kort, Michele. "k.d.: A Woman in Love." *Advocate*, June 20, 2000, 50.

Robertson, William. *k.d. lang : Carrying the Torch*. Toronto, Ont. and East Haven, Conn.: ECW Press, 1993.

Sischy, Ingrid. "k.d." *Interview*, September 1997, 138.

Starr, Victoria. *k.d. lang : All You Get Is Me*. New York: St. Martin's Press, 1994.

Stein, Arlene. "Androgyny Goes Pop; But Is It Lesbian Music?" *OutLook* No. 12 (Spring 1991): 26–31.

Udovich, Mim. "k.d. lang." *Rolling Stone*, August 5, 1993, 54.

SEE ALSO

Popular Music; Country Music; Music Video; Rock Music; Women's Music; Etheridge, Melissa

Laurents, Arthur (b. 1918)

PLAYWRIGHT, LIBRETTIST, SCREENWRITER, AND DIRECtor, Arthur Laurents brought an independent sensibility to some of the most important works of stage and screen in the post–World War II era.

He dared to live openly with a male lover in Hollywood in a period when the studios insisted upon the appearance of sexual conformity. And, in prime examples of what theorist Wayne Koestenbaum has termed "male double writing," Laurents collaborated with such major gay talents as Stephen Sondheim, Leonard Bernstein, Jerry Herman, Harvey Fierstein, and Jerome Robbins on musicals that challenged audiences to accept an unorthodoxy that goes against the grain of the American success myth.

In Laurents's *The Time of the Cuckoo* (1952), the courtly Renato Di Rossi, asked by a judgmental American spinster to justify the dishonesty required for his extramarital affairs, replies simply, "I am in approval of living." So, apparently, is Laurents.

Laurents was born on July 14, 1918, in the Flatbush section of Brooklyn to middle-class Jewish parents from whom he inherited socialist leanings.

Following graduation from Cornell University, Laurents served during World War II in an army film production unit in Astoria, Queens, where he wrote scripts designed to educate servicemen going overseas, as well as radio plays intended to foster civilian support for the war.

The success of Laurents's first commercially produced play, *Home of the Brave* (1945)—written in nine days and critically applauded for addressing the issue of anti-Semitism in the armed forces—encouraged him to move to Hollywood, then in its heyday.

In the film industry, Laurents quickly became known for his deftness with psychological themes. He wrote the scripts for *The Snake Pit* (1948), the story of a woman's emotional collapse and recovery, set in a mental asylum, with scenes considered shockingly realistic at the time; and Alfred Hitchcock's *Rope* (1948), a psychological thriller with a powerful homosexual subtext, which starred Laurents's then lover, Farley Granger.

Although Laurents was never blacklisted himself, his opposition to the studio heads' support of the communist witch hunts weakened his status in Hollywood.

He returned to New York, where he enjoyed success as a playwright (*Time of the Cuckoo*, 1952; *A Clearing in the Woods*, 1957; *Jolson Sings Again*, 1999), librettist (*West Side Story*, 1957; *Gypsy*, 1959; *Anyone Can Whistle*, 1964; *Do I Hear a Waltz?*, 1965; *Hallelujah, Baby!*, 1967; *Nick and Nora*, 1992), and director (*I Can Get It for You Wholesale*, 1962; the 1973 London premiere and 1989 Broadway revival of *Gypsy*; *La Cage aux Folles*, 1983).

Although he returned to Hollywood to work on the films *The Way We Were* (1973) and *The Turning Point* (1977), he has lived contentedly with his lover, Tom Hatcher, on a beachfront property in Quogue, Long Island, for almost fifty years, since 1955.

Laurents's experience of discrimination as both a Jew and a gay man—intensified by his experience during the Hollywood blacklist period—infuses his work with a strong social conscience.

In *The Way We Were*, Katie Morosky is marginalized both by her Jewish ethnicity and by her unflagging pursuit of social justice; her tragedy is to fall in love with Hubbell Gardner, a WASP who assimilates social norms so effortlessly that, finally, he has no principles.

Laurents also treated the subject of blacklisting in *Jolson Sings Again*, which dramatizes the sacrifices of life and integrity made to the McCarthyite drive to root out possible subversives.

Laurents's musical *Hallelujah, Baby!*, written for his good friend Lena Horne, looks at sixty years of race relations in America and was advertised as a "civil rights musical."

While Laurents followed the basic plot of Shakespeare's *Romeo and Juliet* in his book for *West Side Story*, he made two significant changes in the story. Rather than chance, it is the racial prejudice of the Jets/Montagues that prevents Anita/the messenger from delivering to Tony/Romeo the assurance that Maria/Juliet is still alive; and Maria/Juliet lives to confront the survivors with the evidence of what their hatred has cost the community.

Laurents suggested the "Officer Krupke" scene in *West Side Story*, which comically analyzes society's inability to deal with the juvenile delinquents who have been created by the mainstream's own misguided values.

Laurents's willingness to challenge social conventions makes him particularly interested in the relative values of madness and sanity. The relativity of normalcy is clear in *Time of the Cuckoo*, where Laurents satirizes American tourists in Venice who are unimaginative, insensitive, and self-centered, yet certain of their own superiority to the supposedly childlike, sexually undisciplined, immoral—yet clearly happier—Italians.

More provocatively, one of the settings for *Anyone Can Whistle* is a sanitarium called The Cookie Jar, described as catering to "the socially pressured"; the brilliant "Cookie Chase" scene underscores the contradictions in the American pursuit of success and happiness, which drives social authorities to attempt to destroy any instance of potentially subversive originality. Rose's breakdown in the climactic scene of *Gypsy* dramatizes the consequence of striving for success at any cost.

Laurents is at his best when depicting a female character's search for liberation from the social strictures that demand conformity. In *Gypsy*, Rose angrily protests to her father that her own two daughters will "have a marvelous time! I'll be damned if I'm gonna let them sit away their lives like I did. And like you do—with only the calendar to tell you one day is different from the next!"

Laurents's most daring decision was to focus *Gypsy* not on the title character, on whose memoirs the play was based, but on Gypsy Rose Lee's mother, making the play the portrait of a woman so determined to break free of the humdrum that she is unaware of the moral monster she becomes in the process.

In *The Turning Point*, middle-aged friends Deedee Rogers and Emma Jacklin are forced to confront the choices made earlier in life that led one to leave the ballet stage to marry and raise a family in obscurity, and the other to become an internationally famous ballerina with an unsatisfying private life.

In *A Clearing in the Woods*, Virginia learns that "an end to dreams isn't an end to hope." And in *Time of the Cuckoo*, Leona Samish must let go of her unrealistic romantic expectations and accept the moment as life offers it. As Di Rossi advises Leona, "You are a hungry child to whom someone brings—ravioli. 'But I don't want ravioli, I want beefsteak!' You are hungry, Miss Samish! Eat the ravioli!"

Daring to aspire to a life beyond the humdrum, yet courageous enough to resist the corresponding temptation to be blinded by romantic illusion, Laurents's female characters are portraits of human resilience. They spoke strongly to the pre-Stonewall generation of gay men, themselves experimenting with constructing an alternative, more satisfying existence.

—Raymond-Jean Frontain

Bibliography

Laurents, Arthur. *Original Story by Arthur Laurents: A Memoir of Broadway and Hollywood*. New York: Applause Theatre Books, 2000.

Mann, William J. *Behind the Screen: How Gays and Lesbians Shaped Hollywood, 1910–1969*. New York: Viking Penguin, 2001.

Miller, D. A. "Anal Rope." *Inside/Out: Lesbian Theories, Gay Theories*. Diana Fuss, ed. New York: Routledge, 1991. 119–141.

Mordden, Ethan. *Coming up Roses: The Broadway Musical in the 1950s*. New York: Oxford University Press, 1998.

———. *Open a New Window: The Broadway Musical in the 1960s*. New York: Palgrave, 2001.

See Also

Musical Theater and Film; Bernstein, Leonard; Herman, Jerry; Robbins, Jerome; Sondheim, Stephen

Liberace   *(1919–1987)*

MR. SHOWMANSHIP, THE CANDELABRA KID, GURU OF Glitter, Mr. Smiles, The King of Diamonds, and Mr. Box Office, Wladzui "Walter" Valentino Liberace was for many the epitome of camp, excess, and flamboyance, yet he was also a gay man who steadfastly refused to acknowledge publicly his sexual identity.

Born into a musical family on May 16, 1919, in West Allis, Wisconsin, Liberace learned to play the piano by ear at the age of four. As a teenager, he played popular tunes in local Milwaukee movie theaters and nightclubs as Walter Buster Keys. He also continued his classical training, debuting as a soloist with the Chicago Symphony in 1940.

After a brief stint with the Works Progress Administration Symphony Orchestra, Liberace attended the Wisconsin College of Music on scholarship.

An encore request after a 1939 classical recital altered Liberace's career path. His performance of the popular tune "Three Little Fishes" in a semiclassical style proved an immediate audience favorite.

Soon armed with his trademark candelabra on the piano, Liberace found himself booked into dinner clubs and hotels from coast to coast. Audiences immediately responded to his unique musicianship, which blended classical and popular music with glamour and glitter.

In 1950, Walter Valentino Liberace officially changed his name to Liberace. With an act that now included witty banter and some singing, the performer positioned himself to tackle a new market: television.

Begun in 1952 as a summertime replacement for *The Dinah Shore Show,* within two years *The Liberace Show* was the most watched program in the country. The show was on the air until 1956 and garnered Liberace a huge fan base. By 1954 he was earning over $1 million a year with sixty-seven albums on the market, outselling even pop sensation Eddie Fisher. Although he made several movies, the performer was far more successful on the small screen than on the big one.

Liberace's appearance at the Hollywood Bowl in 1952 was the beginning of another Liberace trademark: elaborate clothes. Fearful he might get lost in the sea of black tuxedos worn by members of the Los Angeles Philharmonic, Liberace wore a custom-made white suit of tails.

Soon Liberace was spending a small fortune on flashy costumes. His elaborate costumes almost killed him in 1963 when he collapsed backstage after inhaling carbon tetrachloride, a cleaning chemical used on his soiled costumes.

Even though Liberace made his Carnegie Hall debut on September 25, 1953, his true home was not the concert hall, but the Las Vegas showroom. He opened the new Riviera Hotel in 1955, becoming the highest-paid entertainer in Vegas, with a weekly salary of $50,000.

Liberace's enormous popularity and exposure made him the object of speculation and interest on the part of gossip columnists, who could hardly fail to note his fey mannerisms and effeminacy.

When he arrived in London for a 1956 appearance at Festival Hall, the *Times* of London noted that he was welcomed by over 3,000 girls and young women and "some ardent young men."

When the London tabloid the *Daily Mirror* called him a "deadly, winking, sniggering, snuggling, chromium-plated, scent-impregnated, luminous, quivering, giggling, fruit-flavored, mincing, ice-covered heap of mother love" and "a sugary mountain of jingling claptrap wrapped in such a preposterous clown," Liberace sued for libel, stating that the tabloid insinuated that he practiced homosexuality, then a criminal offense.

In court, the performer repeatedly lied about his sexual life and thereby won the case. Liberace's lies about his sexual life may have been a calculated response to the virulent homophobia of the 1950s. One can hardly blame him for wanting to strike back at his persecutors.

Still, the lies established a pattern of denial and evasion that Liberace practiced for the rest of his life. In his four autobiographical books there is not a word of his homosexuality, which may suggest not merely discretion, but internalized homophobia.

In the 1960s, Liberace, now a fixture in Las Vegas, made his performances increasingly outrageous. In addition to the fantastic costumes, he made spectacular entrances, sometimes driving onstage in a custom car and then exiting by seeming to fly away.

In 1979, he opened The Liberace Museum in Las Vegas. It soon became the third most popular attraction

Liberace, promoting the *The Liberace Show* in 1969.

in Nevada. It features eighteen of Liberace's thirty-nine pianos, numerous costumes, pieces of jewelry, and many of the performer's one-of-a-kind automobiles, including the "Stars and Stripes," a hand-painted red, white, and blue Rolls-Royce convertible.

All of Liberace's efforts to maintain his closet collapsed when Scott Thorson sued the entertainer for $113 million in palimony in 1982. Dismissing Thorson as a disgruntled employee who was fired for alcohol and drug use, Liberace denied in court that the two had been lovers for five years. Ultimately, the matter was settled out of court for $95,000.

Thorson, whom Liberace sent to a plastic surgeon to have Thorson's face remodeled in the performer's own image, was replaced by eighteen-year-old Cary James, who shared Liberace's life and bed until the performer's death five years later. James and Liberace both tested HIV-positive in 1985; James died in 1997.

In spite of his ill health and having lost fifty pounds, the sixty-seven-year-old Liberace honored his contract to appear at Radio City Music Hall in 1986, his third record-breaking engagement there. Horrified by Rock Hudson's recent outing and death, Liberace steadfastly refused to disclose anything about his sexuality or health. He told close friends, "I don't want to be remembered as an old queen who died of AIDS."

Liberace died at the age of sixty-eight on February 4, 1987. He left the bulk of his estate to the Liberace Foundation for the Performing and Creative Arts.

Despite the railing of critics that he was a failed artist who debased music, Liberace remains popular: As of 1994, thirty-one new editions of his records had been issued since his death only seven years earlier.

Liberace was not only immortalized by a star on the Hollywood Walk of Fame, but by two television biographies: *Liberace* (ABC) and *Liberace: Behind the Music* (CBS), both in 1988.

—*Bud Coleman*

BIBLIOGRAPHY

Faris, Jocelyn. *Liberace: A Bio-Bibliography*. Westport, Conn.: Greenwood Publishing Group, 1995.

Hadleigh, Boze. *Hollywood Gays*. Barricade Books, 1996.

Liberace. *An Autobiography*. New York: G. P. Putnam's Sons, 1973.

———. *Liberace Cooks*. New York: Barricade Books, 1970.

———. *The Things I Love*. New York: Grossett and Dunlap, 1976.

———. *The Wonderful Private World of Liberace*. Tony Palmer, ed. New York: Harper & Row, 1986.

Miller, Harriet H. *I'll Be Seeing You: The Young Liberace*. Las Vegas: Leesson Publishers, 1992.

Mungo, Ray. "Liberace." *Lives of Notable Gay Men and Lesbians*. New York: Chelsea House Publishing, 1995.

Pyron, Darden Asbury. *Liberace: An American Boy*. Chicago: University of Chicago Press, 2000.

Thomas, Bob. *Liberace: The True Story*. New York: St. Martins Press, 1988.

Thorson, Scott, with Alex Thorleifson. *Behind the Candelabra: My Life With Liberace*. New York: Dutton, 1988.

SEE ALSO

Popular Music; Cabarets and Revues

Lifar, Serge   *(1905–1986)*

FROM RATHER UNPROMISING BEGINNINGS, SERGE LIFAR rose to the ranks of leading international ballet dancers and choreographers of the twentieth century. Although often dismissed as a derivative choreographer and a less-than-stellar dancer by his many detractors, he parlayed the talent he possessed into a career that outlasted all his competition.

Fiercely ambitious, with a genius for positioning himself to exploit every opportunity that came his way, he used his extraordinary looks and charismatic personality to attract the attention of powerful supporters such as Sergei Diaghilev, Misia Sert, and Coco Chanel.

Born Sergei Mikhailovich Serdkin in Kiev, Russia, on April 2, 1905, the future dancer seemed to know from an early age that if the front door to the palace was slammed closed in his face, he could find other more welcoming entrances. In Kiev at the age of fifteen, he was rejected by Bronislava Nijinska as a student in her ballet school but persisted in his dream to become a dancer: He enrolled in the Kiev Opera Ballet, where Nijinska taught as well.

In 1923, Diaghilev asked Nijinska to summon five of her best male students from Kiev to join the Ballets Russes. At the last minute one of the five Nijinska choices was unable to make the journey, and Lifar leaped to fill out the quintet. Despite Nijinska's lack of enthusiasm for Lifar, either Diaghilev was helplessly drawn to the handsome eighteen-year-old or Lifar made certain that the master could not take his eyes off him.

Lifar's persistence, charm, and manipulation paid off by 1924, when, following private tutoring by the renowned ballet master Cecchetti, he was enlisted as the latest of Diaghilev's "favorites" (joining the long, distinguished list of dancer-lovers that includes Vaslav Nijinsky, Léonide Massine, and Anton Dolin, among others). As a result, he was cast in attention-getting roles and was groomed as a premier danseur and choreographer.

Despite grumbling in the company, Lifar had very real triumphs in Massine's *Zephyr et Flore* (1924) and Balanchine's *La Chatte* (1926).

Given an inch of acclaim, Lifar kept taking so much that even the world-devouring Diaghilev became exasperated at his extreme ambition and self-promotion. By that point, however, Lifar was indispensable as a star and the only choice for plum roles such as Apollo in Balanchine's history-making *Apollon musagète* (1928) and the title role in Balanchine's *The Prodigal Son* (1929).

Lifar's own first ballet, *Renard* (1929, to a score by Igor Stravinsky), though energetic and athletic, proved to be no masterpiece. His later work, however, demonstrated that he had learned much from Diaghilev, Balanchine, and Stravinsky.

After Diaghilev's death in August 1929, with the Ballets Russes in disarray, Lifar was not at a loss for long. Jacques Rouché of the Paris Opera Ballet invited him to star in a production in the tradition of Diaghilev to be choreographed by Balanchine.

As fortune would have it, Balanchine, ill with tuberculosis, had to withdraw from the project. Stepping in to fill Balanchine's shoes, Lifar established himself with authority as choreographer and star dancer at the premiere of *Prométhée* (choreographed to a score by Beethoven). He was soon engaged as the ballet master and director at the Paris Opera Ballet, where he remained in charge, with one significant interruption, until 1957.

During his tenure at the Paris Opera, Lifar was responsible for reviving the ballet in 1929, carrying on the Diaghilev tradition with productions of Ballets Russes classics, developing a strong presence for male dancers, and employing renowned choreographers such as Balanchine, Massine, and Frederick Ashton.

In his autobiography, Lifar coyly stated that "dance is my mistress" to avoid substantive revelations about his romantic entanglements with men and women of influence. But that statement pales next to his claim that his open socializing with the German High Command during the Occupation of Paris was related to his work as an undercover agent. Although the appearance of collaboration led to Lifar's "banishment for life" from the Paris Opera Ballet in 1944, he was back at work there by 1947.

Despite later upheavals such as his stormy exit from the Opera Ballet in 1957, Lifar's stature as a major force in international dance with a direct link to the great Diaghilev continued undiminished until his death in Lausanne, Switzerland, on December 15, 1986.

—John McFarland

BIBLIOGRAPHY

Buckle, Richard. *Diaghilev.* New York: Atheneum, 1979.

Garafola, Lynn. "Looking back at the Ballets Russes: Rediscovering Serge Lifar." *Dance Magazine,* October 1997, 74.

———. "The Sexual Iconography of the Ballets Russes." *Ballet Review* 28.3 (Fall 2000): 70-77.

Lifar, Serge. *Lifar on Classical Ballet.* Arnold L. Haskell, ed. London: Allan Wingate, 1951.

———. *Ma Vie: from Kiev to Kiev, An Autobiography.* James Holman Mason, trans. Cleveland: World Publishing Company, 1970.

———. *Serge Diaghilev: His Life, His Work, His Legend, An Intimate Biography.* New York: G. P. Putnam's Sons, 1940.

SEE ALSO

Ballet; Ballets Russes; Dance; Ashton, Sir Frederick; Béjart, Maurice; Diaghilev, Sergei; Nijinsky, Vaslav

Little Richard (Richard Penniman) *(b. 1932)*

SINCE ITS INCEPTION IN THE 1950S, ROCK AND ROLL has been considered a primarily white musical form, but one African American performer continues to be cited and, indeed, deferred to as the true architect of rock and roll: Little Richard.

Richie Unterberger has noted that Little Richard merged the fire of gospel with New Orleans rhythm and blues by pounding the piano and wailing with gleeful abandon. The over-the-top electricity of Little Richard's performances were compounded by his outrageous, gender-bending appearance, replete with a six-inch stack of hair, eyeliner, pancake makeup, and flashy, attention-grabbing clothes.

In 1958, however, at the height of his career, Little Richard renounced his rock-and-roll lifestyle in favor of Fundamentalist religion. Since that time, he has continued to vacillate between show business and the church, while never losing sight of his profound influences on countless rock-and-roll performers. Despite his inner conflict, Little Richard has justifiably earned his status as a true musical legend.

Little Richard was born Richard Wayne Penniman on December 5, 1932, in Macon, Georgia, the third oldest of seven boys and five girls. According to Tony Scherman, though Richard's father, Bud, sold bootleg liquor, Bud and his wife, Leva Mae, were high-minded, proper people who were heedful of their children's welfare and hopeful for their future.

The Pennimans also had a family gospel group and Richard grew up steeped in the gospel tradition. At age fourteen, he adopted the stage name Little Richard and ran off to join one of the many itinerant medicine shows (traveling salesmen who plied customers with dubious cure-alls) that performed in small towns around the South.

Richard soon began performing at low-rent rhythm-and-blues revues, where he learned to mix gospel fervor with blues lyrics. In 1951, Richard befriended flamboyant, openly gay R & B singer Esquerita, who taught him the pounding piano style for which he would become famous.

Little Richard attends the 2004 Democratic National Convention Media Party. Photograph by Michael Quan.

By 1955, after seeing his popularity increase dramatically, Little Richard made his way to New Orleans to record a demo tape that he sent to Art Rupe, president of Specialty Records, a small but successful Los Angeles-based rhythm-and-blues and gospel label. The tape ended up on the desk of Rupe's assistant, Bumps Blackwell, who immediately recognized the voice as star material.

Blackwell met Little Richard in New Orleans and, in a break from an otherwise frustrating studio session, watched as Little Richard began fooling around on the studio piano. The result was both electrifying and revolutionary. Little Richard tore into a slightly obscene ditty he had previously penned, and "Tutti Frutti" was born.

By January 1956, "Tutti Frutti" was number seventeen on *Billboard*'s pop chart and number two on the R & B chart. It sold over half a million copies. Perhaps more importantly, it succeeded in bringing the races together, selling to both black and white youth.

Richard observed to his biographer Charles White, "The white kids had to hide my records 'cos they daren't let their parents know they had them in the house. We decided that my image should be crazy and way-out so that the adults would think I was harmless."

Richard quickly followed his initial success with a string of eight Top 40 singles including "Long Tall Sally," "Rip It Up," "Good Golly Miss Molly," and "Lucille," a raucous paean to a female impersonator.

In 1958, however, Little Richard's inner conflict between his sternly religious upbringing and his homosexuality boiled to the surface. According to Scherman, if Richard was a musical rebel, it may indeed have been because of his homosexuality, which he agonized over.

Even in his wildest days he carried a Bible, and read and quoted from it regularly.

On tour in Australia in the autumn of 1958, Little Richard hurled his diamond rings into Sydney Harbor, vowed to quit rock and roll, and on returning to the United States enrolled in Oakwood Bible College in Huntsville, Alabama.

Little Richard staged several comebacks over the years, but he never scored another Top 40 hit after 1958. He continues to seesaw between rock and roll and religion. He occasionally makes appearances on television and in movies, now better known as a colorful figure from the early days of rock and roll than taken seriously as a contemporary performer.

Nevertheless, Little Richard's seminal influence in the arena of rock music cannot be diminished. He remains a legendary and iconic figure in popular music. He continues to perform to appreciative audiences, and he was given further proof of his continued popularity when, in July 2003, he was inducted into the Songwriters Hall of Fame.

—*Nathan G. Tipton*

BIBLIOGRAPHY

Larkin, Colin, comp. and ed. "Little Richard." *The Encyclopedia of Popular Music.* Third ed. New York: Muze, 1998. 4:3270–3271.

Scherman, Tony. "Little Richard's Big Noise." *American Heritage* 46.1 (1995): 554–557.

Unterberger, Richie. "Little Richard." www.allmusic.com/cg/amg.dll?p=amg&uid=UIDSUB040407070 005211809&sql=Bp9508q9tbtm4

Vilanch, Bruce. "The Gay Race Card." *Advocate,* April 1, 1997, 57.

White, Charles. *The Life and Times of Little Richard: The Quasar of Rock.* Rev. ed. New York: Da Capo, 1994.

SEE ALSO

Popular Music; Rock Music; Blues Music; Bowie, David; Sylvester

Lully, Jean-Baptiste   (1632–1687)

JEAN-BAPTISTE LULLY (1632–1687), THOUGH NOT THE first to compose French opera, through his works established its basic principles. His influence on opera throughout Europe was immense, but his career declined as the result of a homosexual scandal.

The son of Italian peasants, Giovanni Battisti Lulli was brought to France in 1646 as an Italian tutor for Louis XIV's cousin Anne-Marie Louise d'Orléans, known to history as "La Grande Mademoiselle." His musical and acting abilities soon distinguished him, and, after the exile of Anne-Marie in 1652, he entered the king's service. He and the king danced in court entertainments, establishing a privileged relationship that led to the musician's quick advancement.

In 1661, Lully became a French citizen and was named Master of the King's Music. The following year, he married the daughter of Michel Lambert, a prominent singer and composer of vocal music at the French court. They had six children (three boys and three girls), and Lully seems to have been a good father and provider in spite of numerous extramarital activities with both men and women.

Lully collaborated with Molière, the greatest French comic dramatist, in creating plays with musical interludes and ballets. The two soon fell out, however, and Lully used his influence to prevent Molière from employing music in his works.

In 1673, Lully staged his first opera, *Cadmus et Hermione*. Fourteen more followed, including such works as *Armide* and *Acis et Galatée*; they established the pattern for French opera for decades to come.

Lully was ruthless in his pursuit of power and used his influence with the king to eliminate potential rivals through the establishment of monopolies over stage music. Perhaps as a result, his enemies spread stories concerning his sexual exploits. Almost certainly many of these stories were true, but Lully was discreet enough that the king could overlook his activities.

However, Lully's influence with the king evaporated in 1685 when he was involved in a scandal that the king could not ignore. The composer conducted an affair with a "music page" being trained in the royal service. This affair with a young man led to the composer's disgrace. Although he was not prosecuted, Lully was forced to break off the relationship and in addition lost his standing at court.

Homosexual activity was a capital offense in seventeenth-century France, but the death penalty was only sporadically imposed. A number of the nobility at Versailles, including the king's brother Philippe, formed a homosexual subculture, and Lully had close ties with them. While the king disapproved of homosexuality, he loved his brother and was unwilling to exile, or otherwise punish, these nobles. At the same time, pressure was exerted by Louis's wife Madame de Maintenon and her priest to rid the court of sodomites.

Lully is said to have died by stabbing himself in the foot with a cane with which he was beating time at a rehearsal. The wound resulted in blood poisoning and gangrene. Beaussaint has argued that the story is apocryphal and that the composer, already in ill health, in effect died as a result of the king's abandonment.   —*Robert A. Green*

BIBLIOGRAPHY

Beaussant, Philippe. *Lully ou Le musicien du Soleil*. Paris: Éditions Gallimard, 1992.

Merrick, Jeffrey, and Bryant T. Ragan Jr., eds. *Homosexuality in Early Modern France. A Documentary Collection*. New York and Oxford: Oxford University Press, 2001.

Prunières, Henry. *La Vie illustre et libertine de Jean-Baptiste Lully*. Paris: Librairie Plon, 1978.

SEE ALSO

Classical Music; Conductors; Opera; Corelli, Arcangelo

Jean-Baptiste Lully.

m

Mathis, Johnny (b. 1935)

WITH MORE THAN SIXTY GOLD AND PLATINUM ALBUMS to his credit, Johnny Mathis is one of the most successful recording artists ever, trailing only Frank Sinatra and Elvis Presley in the number of albums sold. His interpretations of romantic ballads have brought him fame and wealth, but he is notoriously reticent about his own romantic life.

Although he has acknowledged his homosexuality, he has refused to discuss it in any depth, and its effect on his art and life must remain speculative.

Born John Royce Mathis in 1935 in Gilmer, Texas, he grew up in San Francisco. The circumstances of his family were modest. His father, Clem, was a limousine driver and handyman, and his mother, Mildred, a domestic worker. Both parents encouraged him to develop the musical ability that he showed from an early age, but Mathis acknowledges in particular the role of his father.

When Mathis was eight years old, his father bought a used piano for him. The elder Mathis, who had been a vaudevillian in Texas, began to teach his son vaudeville routines, introduced him to the music of such singers as Lena Horne and Ella Fitzgerald, and urged him to participate in church choirs and talent contests.

When Mathis was thirteen, he met Connie Cox, an opera singer and voice teacher, who was so impressed with his singing that she offered to give him free voice lessons. He studied classical technique for six years and credits Cox with teaching him to sing the soft, high notes that are a signature of his style.

After high school, Mathis received an athletic scholarship to San Francisco State College (now San Francisco State University). He competed on the track team, setting a school record in the high jump. His impressive athletic performance earned him an invitation to participate in the 1956 Olympic trials.

The very same week, however, brought the opportunity to sign with a recording company. Mathis decided against trying to make the Olympic team but maintained an interest in his sport. He sponsors the Johnny Mathis Invitational track meet, which has been held annually at his alma mater since 1982. In 1997, SFSU chose him as the Alumnus of the Year.

During his college years, Mathis developed an interest in jazz and began to work in local clubs. When he appeared at the Black Hawk nightclub, Helen Noga, the co-owner of the establishment, quickly recognized his talent. She undertook the management of his career and secured bookings at more clubs in the area.

One such appearance, in 1955, at a San Francisco gay bar called the 440 Club, found George Avakian, a record producer at Columbia, in the audience. Although impressed with Mathis's potential, Avakian did not sign him immediately. He did, however, return to San Francisco the following year, at which time he offered Mathis a contract to record an album.

The debut album, *Johnny Mathis, a New Sound in Popular Song* (1956) did not do particularly well. The "new sound" was flavored with the jazz style of the music that Mathis had been performing in California. But he was soon to discover another sound that would propel him to stardom.

Following the release of the first album, Avakian brought Mathis to New York, where he continued working as a jazz singer, performing at various clubs and concert halls, including the Apollo Theater. But Avakian felt that Mathis needed to take a different direction to achieve greater commercial success. He therefore brought Mathis together with the producer and arranger Mitch Miller.

The pairing proved inspired. In collaboration with Miller, who was known for his lavish string arrangements, Mathis began singing romantic ballads. His first such recording, "Wonderful, Wonderful," was a Top 20 hit in 1957. He released five more extremely successful singles that year alone, including the chart-topping "Chances Are."

In 1958, he released an enormously popular album, *Johnny's Greatest Hits*, which held the number one spot on *Billboard*'s pop chart for three weeks and remained on the chart for a record total of 490 weeks. The album included such standards as "The Twelfth of Never," "It's Not for Me to Say," and "Misty."

Mathis's career skyrocketed in the 1960s. He put out three or four albums a year throughout the decade and was much in demand on the concert tour. His rigorous schedule—with as many as 101 consecutive one-night shows—took a physical toll on him and caused him to become addicted to sleeping pills for a time.

In 1964, Mathis decided to take charge of his own career. He left his previous manager, Helen Noga, and started his own company, Rojon Productions. The break with Noga was rancorous, but they later reconciled their differences.

Mathis's albums of the 1960s and 1970s featured a variety of styles and material. On *Olé* (1965), he sang in Spanish and Portuguese. On albums such as *The Long and Winding Road* (1970), he covered the songs of other pop artists. He also recorded disco music. His albums sold millions of copies.

Singles by Mathis, on the other hand, tended not to make the pop charts. This changed in 1978, when his duet with Deniece Williams, "Too Much, Too Little, Too Late," became his first number one hit since 1957. It also brought Mathis, whose fan base had previously been primarily white adults, to increased attention among African American and younger audiences.

Following the success of his duet with Williams, Mathis recorded duets with several other singers, including Gladys Knight, Dionne Warwick, Natalie Cole, Barbra Streisand, and Nana Mouskouri.

Mathis's enchanting love songs have always appealed to the romantic side of his fans. Their effect on listeners

has given rise to certain waggish comments, such as *People* magazine's "Mathis has often been blamed for the last 10 years of the baby boom." But his work appealed to gay and lesbian couples as well, many of whom may have intuited the singer's homosexuality.

Mathis's own love life, however, remained a mystery. He deflected interviewers' questions about his bachelor state until 1982, when he acknowledged his homosexuality in an interview in *Us* magazine. He spoke of his first love at the age of sixteen and said that being gay was "a way of life that [he had] grown accustomed to."

These disclosures had little if any effect on the public's perception of him; indeed, the public hardly seemed to notice them. In 1992, a group of gay activists attempted to out Mathis, only to discover that his sexual orientation was already on record. Mathis claimed that this had been unintentional. In 1993, he told an interviewer from the *New York Times* that he had intended the information divulged to *Us* magazine to be off the record. He has declined to make any further comments about his sexuality.

Mathis continues to pursue his career as a highly successful vocalist. Indeed, he is one of the most gifted interpreters of romantic ballads in the history of American popular music. After more than four decades in show business, he no longer tours as he once did, though he still gives concerts. He has performed at various charity events and at the White House.

He even had the chance to participate in two Olympic Games—as a singer.

—*Linda Rapp*

BIBLIOGRAPHY

Fitzpatrick, Laurie. "Johnny Mathis." *Gay & Lesbian Biography*. Michael J. Tyrkus, ed. Detroit: St. James Press, 1997. 311–313.

Gavin, James. "A Timeless Reminder of Back Seats in '57 Buicks." *New York Times*, December 19, 1993.

"Mathis, Johnny." *The Guinness Encyclopedia of Popular Music*. Colin Larkin, ed. New York: Stockton Press, 1995. 4:2749–2750.

Petrucelli, Alan W. "Celebrity Q & A," *Us*, June 22, 1982, 58.

SEE ALSO

Popular Music; Jazz; Faye, Frances

McPhee, Colin   (1900–1964)

CANADIAN-BORN COMPOSER COLIN MCPHEE NOT ONLY helped preserve the musical traditions of Bali but also incorporated non-Western musical styles into his own compositions, a practice that influenced other North American composers.

McPhee was born in Montreal on March 15, 1900, but spent most of his youth in Toronto. He received his early musical education in Toronto and at the Peabody Conservatory in Baltimore.

In 1924, McPhee went to Paris to pursue his musical studies and his career as a pianist, but made little headway. After a year and a half he returned to North America to participate in the musical life of New York City—then an exciting center of modern music. Charles Ives, Edgar Varèse, Aaron Copland, Virgil Thomson, and Carlos Chávez were a few of the composers then contributing to the musical life of the city.

Sometime during the late 1920s, "quite by accident," McPhee happened to hear recordings of the gamelan music of Bali. "[A]s I played them over and over," he wrote, "I became more and more enchanted.... I returned the records, but I could not forget them." He decided that he must travel to Bali to see the gamelan for himself.

Around the same time, McPhee met Jane Belo, who had studied anthropology and who was also interested in traveling to Asia. Although he was actively homosexual, McPhee and Belo were soon involved in an intense sexual relationship. They were married in 1930.

Belo was aware of McPhee's homosexuality, but she felt that a relationship with "a feminine man" was an important stage in her emotional development, and that it also revealed "aspects of masculine protest and narcissism" on her part.

In 1931, McPhee and Belo traveled to Bali. Once there, McPhee immersed himself in an exhaustive study of the Balinese gamelan—a percussion orchestra with delicately layered textures and clangorous sounds. He carefully studied how the instruments—gongs and bells, wooden xylophones, skin drums and bamboo flutes—were made as well as how they were played. He also carefully notated the melodic and percussive possibilities of every piece for gamelan he heard.

McPhee's research played a very important role in the preservation of the Balinese gamelan musical tradition, which was slowly dying. His musicological work *Music in Bali* (1966) is still the standard textbook at Bali's Conservatory of Music and Dance.

Since the Balinese were relatively tolerant of homosexuality, soon McPhee also threw himself into the sexual exploration of Balinese men. His sexual involvements with Balinese men led eventually to a separation from Belo.

McPhee wrote to one friend, "I was in love at the time with a Balinese, which she knew, and to have him continually around was too much for her vanity. So it ended as I had foreseen at the beginning...."

McPhee was able to live in Bali only because Belo had the money (which came from her family and her wealthy ex-husband) to do so. They were divorced in 1938, shortly before they both left Bali.

After almost seven years in Bali, McPhee returned to New York in 1939. Even before leaving Bali, he had begun to compose music that was an imaginative hybrid of Balinese and Western traditions.

His most important musical piece in this vein is his orchestral suite, *Tabuh-Tabuhan*. Composed in 1936 as a concerto for two pianos and large orchestra, it combines Balinese and jazz elements in the American style of Copland and Thomson. It premiered in Mexico City in 1936 under the baton of fellow composer Carlos Chávez; it received a standing ovation, but then languished without another performance until thirteen years later.

McPhee's next two decades in New York City were marked by financial hardship and slowly improving fortunes. In 1960, he moved to Los Angeles, and spent the last four years of his life teaching ethnomusicology and composition at UCLA. After two years of steadily deteriorating health from cirrhosis of the liver, he died on January 7, 1964.

McPhee's life is notable for three major achievements. Most important is that his musicological research on the gamelan helped to preserve Bali's musical traditions and contributed to the revival of what had been a dying musical practice.

Second, *Tabuh-Tabuhan*, his great work of musical synthesis, introduced a compositional style that incorporated non-Western musical traditions into Western concert music.

Colin McPhee, photographed by Carl Van Vechten in 1935.

Third, through his writing, his musicological research, and his example as a composer, McPhee helped to shape an entire American musical tradition carried on by composers such as John Cage, Lou Harrison, and Steve Reich.

—Jeffrey Escoffier

BIBLIOGRAPHY

McPhee, Colin. *A House in Bali.* New York: John Day, 1946.

———. *Music in Bali.* New Haven, Conn.: Yale University Press, 1966.

———. *Tabuh-Tabuhan: Music of Colin McPhee.* Sound recording. Toronto: CBC Records, 1997.

Oja, Carol J. *Colin McPhee: Composer in Two Worlds.* Washington, D.C.: Smithsonian Institution Press, 1990.

SEE ALSO

Classical Music; Cage, John; Copland, Aaron; Harrison, Lou; Thomson, Virgil

Menotti, Gian Carlo   (b. 1911)

ONE OF THE LEADING CLASSICAL COMPOSERS OF OUR time, Gian Carlo Menotti not only has had a distinguished career, but also achieved acclaim at a time when his uncloseted homosexuality could have been a major barrier. Amazingly prolific and indefatigable, even in his nineties he continues to be a vital presence in the world of classical music.

Menotti was born in Cadegliano, Italy, on July 7, 1911. Although his family was not especially musical, they recognized their son's prodigious talent. Under the guidance of his mother, Menotti began to compose as a child. He wrote his first opera at the age of eleven.

He began his formal study of music at the Verdi Conservatory in Milan in 1923, but after the death of his father, he and his mother traveled to the United States, where he entered the Curtis Institute of Music in Philadelphia.

Menotti quickly adjusted to American culture and soon mastered the English language. He has spent most of his professional career in the United States and has written most of the libretti to his operas in English.

Among his fellow students at Curtis were composers Leonard Bernstein and Samuel Barber. Barber (1910–1981), with whom he was to share a relationship that endured more than thirty years, soon became his life partner, though Menotti later had a long personal and professional relationship with the conductor Thomas Schippers, as well. Menotti wrote the libretto for Barber's most famous opera, *Vanessa* (1964).

Avoiding the atonalism of the avant-garde school of Schoenberg and Webern, Menotti cast his lot with the popular tonal style of Schubert and Puccini, though he sometime used atonalism for dramatic effect in his operas.

Menotti's first mature work, the one-act opera buffa *Amelia Goes to the Ball* (1936), had its premiere in Philadelphia. It was subsequently staged at the Metropolitan Opera in New York, where it received popular and critical acclaim.

Menotti then wrote a series of operas that were staged very successfully on Broadway. *The Medium* (1945), *The Telephone* (1946), *The Consul* (1949), and *The Saint of Bleecker Street* (1954) established his reputation as the most popular opera composer in America. He received New York Drama Critics' Circle Awards and Pulitzer Prizes for *The Consul* and *The Saint of Bleecker Street*.

Menotti's *Amahl and the Night Visitors* was originally written for television and broadcast in 1951. It has since become a Christmas classic, performed all over the world during the Christmas season.

Most of Menotti's major successes as an opera composer came in the 1940s and 1950s. Since then, he has had a string of operatic failures and modest successes, including such works as *Maria Golovin* (1958), *The Last Savage* (1963), *La Loca* (1979), *Goya* (1986), and *The Singing Child* (1993). Some of these works will undoubtedly be restaged and reevaluated in the future.

Gian Carlo Menotti, photographed by Carl Van Vechten in 1944.

In addition to opera, Menotti has composed orchestral and chamber works in various genres, including several solo concerti (his Piano Concerto is occasionally heard) and three tuneful ballets, of which one, *Sebastian* (1944), has enjoyed an extended life as a ballet suite.

One of Menotti's greatest triumphs has been The Festival of Two Worlds, which he established in Spoleto, Italy, in 1958. The festival, which is devoted to celebrating and encouraging the cultural collaboration of Europe and America, has become one of the most successful ventures of its kind.

In 1977, the Festival literally became "of two worlds" when Menotti founded Spoleto USA in Charleston, South Carolina. He led the Charleston festival until 1993, when he withdrew to become Director of the Rome Opera.

The composer continues to direct opera at Spoleto and elsewhere.

Menotti has sometimes been charged with extending himself too broadly and spreading himself too thin, as he has pursued a notably versatile career—composer of opera, orchestral works, and songs, director of opera, director of the Spoleto Festival, and so on. Still, he has achieved real distinction in many areas.

As a force opposed to the influence of the atonalism of the Vienna School, he has been an important figure in the music of his time. His compositions are written in a traditional tonal style and strive for melodic and harmonic distinction. Moreover, his music is comfortable for singers to sing and for audiences to hear.

Before gay liberation and before gay people could be completely candid about their liaisons, Menotti and Barber proved that gay men could have relationships that did not have to be closeted, though the term *homosexual* was rarely mentioned in public.

During the period of McCarthyism, with its homophobic persecution of queers in America, Menotti made a significant contribution to the cause of human liberation through his vivid example as an accomplished artist who was also an uncloseted homosexual.

Menotti began living in Scotland in the 1970s. He continues to reside there with an adopted son and his family.

—*John Louis DiGaetani*

BIBLIOGRAPHY

Archibald, Bruce, and Jennifer Barnes. "Menotti." *The New Grove Dictionary of Music and Musicians.* Stanley Sadie, ed. London: Macmillan, 2001. 16:432–434.

Ardoin, John. *The Stages of Menotti.* Garden City, N.Y.: Doubleday, 1985.

Gruen, John. *Menotti: A Biography.* New York: Macmillan, 1978.

SEE ALSO

Classical Music; Conductors; Opera; Ballet; Barber, Samuel; Bernstein, Leonard

Mercer, Mabel (1900–1984)

ALTHOUGH SHE NEVER ACHIEVED IN HER LONG LIFEtime the fame she so richly deserved, Mabel Mercer was one of the most respected singers of the mid-twentieth century, a most original stylist, and the toast of the New York cabaret scene.

Her career, which spanned seven decades, brought her to early fame in Paris, where she mingled with some of the most extraordinary gay and lesbian figures of the day, and in her later years she was a much-beloved icon of gay New York.

Mabel Mercer was born on February 3, 1900, in Burton-on-Trent, Staffordshire, England, to an English vaudeville singer and dancer. She was never to meet her father, an African American jazz musician who, according to some sources, died before she was born.

She was at first raised by her grandmother in Liverpool, and later educated at a Catholic convent school in Manchester. She left school at fourteen to join her mother, who had since married another vaudeville performer, as part of a touring company.

After the end of World War I, Mercer settled in Paris, where she met the celebrated Ada "Bricktop" Smith, an American singer and cabaret proprietor whose patrons included Gertrude Stein, Ernest Hemingway, and Zelda and F. Scott Fitzgerald. Mercer based her career at Bricktop's until 1938, when she fled in anticipation of World War II and the feared German invasion.

During her Paris years, Mercer became friends (and possibly more) with the notoriously eccentric lesbian heiress, speedboat racer, and womanizer Marion "Joe" Carstairs. Carstairs, who had settled in her own "kingdom"—Whale Cay, on an island in the Bahamas—paid Mercer's way across the Atlantic, fearing what the Nazis would do to the biracial singer.

Mercer resided in the Bahamas until 1941, when she married Kelsey Pharr, an openly gay African American musician, and obtained an entry visa from the United States government. The marriage was clearly one of convenience, as Mercer and Pharr never lived together and rarely saw each other; however, Mercer, as a devout Catholic, would not divorce Pharr, and they remained legally married, if in no other sense, until his death.

Upon her arrival in New York, Mercer began a series of engagements in some of the city's most elegant supper clubs and cabarets; and, for the rest of her life, the metropolis was her sole venue. Here she became the particular favorite of gay men, who found in her a sympathetic interpreter of their lives and loves, even when those lives and loves had necessarily to remain mostly closeted.

Mercer was a sophisticated interpreter of show tunes and standards, particularly those of Cole Porter and Noël Coward. Although often classified as a jazz singer, her style, which involved movement and gesture along with "proper" English-accented intonations, owed as much to the British music-hall tradition into which she was born as it did to *le jazz hot* of 1920s Paris.

Carstairs admired Mercer for being "ladylike," and this quality, along with her tremendous warmth and sly wit, made Mercer a completely unique talent. She considered each song a story to be narrated, not merely to be sung.

Her interpretations of standard songs, such as Coward's "Sail Away" and "Mad about the Boy," frequently captured qualities within them that other interpreters might have missed, especially the pain and sadness, as well as the pleasures and joy, of the lives of gay men in the 1940s and 1950s.

Mercer's recordings are few, and all date from later in her life. While those fortunate enough to have seen her perform live report that the recordings capture only a fraction of her appeal, much of which involved body language and audience interaction, the recordings nonetheless convey a *joie de vivre* and a personality not to be found elsewhere.

Although Mercer performed well into her seventies, she increasingly preferred the privacy of her country estate in rural New York, where she gardened, created recipes that were often published, and lived with her many pets.

She became an American citizen in 1952, and, in 1983, was awarded the Presidential Medal of Freedom for her contribution to American Culture.

She died quietly on April 20, 1984, in Pittsfield, Massachusetts.

—*Patricia Juliana Smith*

BIBLIOGRAPHY

Cheney, Margaret. *Midnight at Mabel's: The Mabel Mercer Story.* Washington, D.C.: New Voyage, 2000.

Haskins, James. *Mabel Mercer: A Life.* New York : Atheneum, 1987.

SEE ALSO

Cabarets and Revues; Popular Music; Jazz; Coward, Sir Noël; Porter, Cole

Mercury, Freddie   (1946–1991)

FOR TWO DECADES, FREDDIE MERCURY WAS THE FRONT man of one of the world's most popular rock groups, Queen. That he was able to maintain this status in spite of continued critical hostility, his flamboyant gender-bending androgyny, and questions about his sexuality is surely one of the more impressive accomplishments in the history of popular culture. He was also, arguably, the first Indian international rock star.

Freddie Mercury was born Farrokh Bulsara in the British colony of Zanzibar, East Africa (now part of Tanzania), on September 5, 1946. His parents were Parsees (Zoroastrian Indians of Persian descent), and his father was employed in the British civil service.

From the age of six, he attended boarding school near Bombay, India, and showed a considerable aptitude for art and music. It was here that he was first called "Freddie" by his classmates.

In 1964, the Bulsara family moved to England, where Freddie completed his education, graduating in 1969 from the Ealing College of Art with a diploma in art and design. Around this time, he adopted the surname Mercury, naming himself after the Roman messenger of the gods.

After college, he sold second-hand clothes in trendy flea markets, where he met future bandmate Roger Taylor, and joined Ibex, a local London group, as a vocalist and keyboard player.

In 1970, he formed a group with Taylor and Brian May (joined in 1971 by John Deacon), for which he chose the provocative name Queen. Even in its earliest days the band was notable for its stage performances, replete with light shows, flamboyant costumes, theatrics, and very high volume levels.

The group's first album, *Queen* (1973), was greeted with critical hostility, as were its early live performances, a result, no doubt, of the implied queerness of its name and Mercury's effeminate, long-haired, heavily made-up stage persona.

The group's breakthrough came the following year with the album *Queen II*, and the first big hit single, "Killer Queen," a tribute to a fabulous individual "just like Marie Antoinette" who may or may not have been female.

Within a year, Queen was one of the most popular bands in the world and began a series of world tours that drew crowds often in the hundreds of thousands. From 1975 until 1983, Queen enjoyed a long string of successful best-selling recordings.

These include "Bohemian Rhapsody" from the album *A Night at the Opera* (1975), "Somebody to Love" from *A Day at the Races* (1976), "We Will Rock You" and "We Are the Champions" from *News of the World* (1977), "Bicycle Races" and "Fat-Bottomed Girls" from *Jazz* (1978), "Crazy Little Thing Called Love" and "Another One Bites the Dust" from *The Game* (1979), and "Under Pressure" (with David Bowie, 1981).

In 1980, Mercury underwent a drastic image change that demonstrated his talent as a gender shape-shifter. Gone was the flaming, campy, "queeny" persona, replaced by a macho one, mustachioed, muscular, short-haired, and attired in an undershirt and tight-fitting jeans.

The new image was not without its own camp elements, which many fans took at face value. Mercury nevertheless continued to confound gender assumptions, performing with the rest of the band in complete drag in the video "I Want to Break Free" (1984).

By the mid-1980s, Queen's popularity had peaked, and Mercury pursued a number of solo interests. His remake of the Platters' oldie "The Great Pretender" (1987), which suggestively begged the ongoing question of who or what was the "real" Freddie Mercury, proved a success, as did his compelling if unlikely collaboration with Spanish opera diva Montserrat Caballé, which produced the international hit "Barcelona" (1987).

During his lifetime, Mercury made no definitive statements about his private life or sexuality, leaving the interpretation of his public image up to the individual imagination; accordingly, many fans were shocked when events made some sort of revelation inevitable.

In Queen's early years, Mercury lived with a woman, Mary Austin, with whom he subsequently maintained a significant friendship; in 1980, however, they separated, and he lived thereafter until his death with Jim Hutton, supposedly his gardener.

On November 23, 1991, Freddie Mercury released a statement confirming that he suffered from AIDS, as had long been rumored. He died the following day.

Since Mercury's death, many tributes, including an AIDS benefit concert and a ballet choreographed by Maurice Béjart, have honored him. In 2001, he was posthumously inducted as a member of Queen into the Rock and Roll Hall of Fame. He has left a large and devoted following of fans.

—*Patricia Juliana Smith*

BIBLIOGRAPHY

Evans, David, and David Minns. *Freddie Mercury: The Real Life, the Truth Behind the Legend.* London: Antaeus, 1997.

Freestone, Peter. *Freddie Mercury: An Intimate Memoir by the Man Who Knew Him Best.* New York: Music Sales, 2000.

Hodkinson, Mark. *Queen: The Early Years.* New York: Omnibus, 1997.

Hutton, Jim, with Tim Wapshott. *Mercury and Me.* New York: Boulevard Books, 1994.

Jones, Lesley-Ann. *Freddie Mercury: The Definitive Biography.* London: Hodder & Stoughton, 1997.

Smith, Richard. "A Year in the Death of Freddie Mercury: Queen." *Seduced and Abandoned: Essays on Gay Men and Popular Music.* London: Cassell, 1995. 234–239.

SEE ALSO

Popular Music; Rock Music; Music and AIDS; Béjart, Maurice; Bowie, David; Michael, George

Michael, George (b. 1963)

ALTHOUGH POP SINGER/SONGWRITER GEORGE MICHAEL began his musical career in 1980 as half of the queerly inflected pop duo Wham!, Michael's sexual orientation remained elusively undefined until 1998. On April 7, 1998, he was arrested for "lewd behavior" in a park restroom in Beverly Hills, California. Following his conviction, for which he was sentenced to perform community service, Michael confirmed his long-rumored homosexuality.

A week before the 1998 interview in which he formally came out, Michael met with *Advocate* editor Judy Wieder on the set of his music video "Outside." The video explicitly details (and parodies) the events surrounding Michael's arrest, including the resultant media frenzy. In his interview with Wieder, Michael addressed his contentious relationship with the press and the question of why he did not come out sooner.

He remarked, "If you tell me that I have to do something, I'm going to try not to do it. And what people don't understand in the equation of my relationship with the press is that I've had people talking and writing about my sexuality since I was 19 years old."

Born Georgios Kyriakos Panayiotou in London on June 25, 1963, Michael is the son of a Greek Cypriot restaurant owner. His family moved to the affluent London suburb of Bushey and, while in school there, Michael met Andrew Ridgeley, who became the other half of Wham!

In 1982, the duo won a contract with Innervision Records and, in the summer of 1982, released the album *Fantastic*, which became a hit in Britain. Their next album, *Make It Big* (1984), with its infectious single "Wake Me Up Before You Go-Go," exploded worldwide and cemented the pair's success but led to the accusation that Michael and Ridgeley were merely pretty-boy pop stars.

In 1986, at the height of their popularity, Michael and Ridgeley amicably dissolved Wham! and Michael forged ahead as a solo artist. In sharp contrast to Wham!'s "bubblegum pop" sound, Michael's first solo album, the Motown-inspired *Faith* (1987), featured songs with a much more soulful sound.

In addition to topping the pop chart, *Faith* also went to the top of the black album chart, making Michael the first white artist to achieve this honor. The album went on to win American Music Awards for Best Pop Male Vocalist, Best Soul/Rhythm and Blues Vocalist, and Best Soul/Rhythm and Blues Album, as well as the Grammy Award for Album of the Year.

One of the album's singles, "I Want Your Sex," reached number two on the American charts, due in no small part to its controversial content, widely interpreted as encouraging people to have sex in the age of AIDS. Michael, however, explained that the song's message promoted monogamy rather than promiscuity.

In 1992, he appeared at the Concert for Life, a benefit and tribute to Queen singer Freddie Mercury whose purpose was to increase AIDS awareness. The concert led to Michael's involvement in the album *Red, Hot, + Dance*, another project organized to raise funds for AIDS charities. In 1993, Michael released *Five Live*, a five-song EP (extended play, or shorter length LP/CD) featuring his Freddie Mercury tribute. All proceeds from the record went to the Phoenix Trust, an AIDS charity set up in Mercury's memory.

AIDS has been a particularly poignant charitable choice for Michael since the death in 1993 of his first boyfriend, Brazilian designer Anselmo Feleppa. The death spurred Michael to write a coming-out letter to his parents, who, according to him, were more concerned that he had just lost his partner than that he had actually finally said what they already knew.

Michael explained to Judy Wieder that AIDS not only changed his behavior but also helped him along his journey to honest self-discovery. For Michael's life and music, this self-discovery has been liberating and has led to a new sense of joy and triumph.

Michael's popularity seems only to have been enhanced by his coming out, despite the circumstances that forced him to be more honest than he intended. The music video "Outside" was well received and worked to defuse the controversy of his arrest.

Michael's most recent work, however, has not received the acclaim he expected. For example, his single "Freek" (2002) reached only number seven on the charts.

Moreover, in the summer of 2002 Michael found himself at the center of a firestorm prompted by the release in Britain of "Shoot the Dog," a video and song skewering the polices of President George Bush and Prime Minister Tony Blair in the wake of the war on terrorism.

When Americans complained that the song was an insult to the United States, Michael replied, "I am definitely not anti-American, how could I be? I have been in love with a Texan for six years." Michael's partner, Kenny Goss, is from Texas.

A musical artist of notable versatility, Michael emerged from the backlash that "Shoot the Dog" generated, but his vulnerability is indicated by the fact that the *New York Post* headlined its story about the song "Pop Perv's 9/11 Slur," which no doubt alluded to his homosexuality as much as to his arrest.

Despite this setback, two years later Michael once again reclaimed the pop music spotlight with the success of his critically acclaimed album *Patience*. Released by Aegean/Sony Music in March 2004, the album represented what *Billboard* columnist Paul Sexton characterized as a "dramatic rapprochement for Michael and Sony Music," signifying the culmination of a successfully mended relationship between Michael and his record label.

Although immediately before the album's release Michael was quoted as saying that *Patience* would be his last major-label release, Sony executives are already planning Michael's next album, a duet record featuring four new collaborations, plus archived duets with Elton John, Whitney Houston, Queen, and others.

Michael, who was also reported to have said that, after *Patience*, he would quit the music business and release his songs free on the Internet, has apparently discovered that patience is indeed a virtue. His patience was further rewarded when, in May 2004, he was honored by U.K.-based PPL (Phonographic Performance Ltd.) as the most played artist on British radio in the past twenty years. In accepting the honor, Michael paid tribute to his early musical hero Elton John by telling the assembled gathering, "Without Elton John, there is no way I would be standing here. I used to dissect his records and obsess about song after song, and it was the beginning of my love affair with Pop."

After wild successes and equally notable failures, Michael has seemingly and finally found peace with both his homosexuality and his music.   —*Nathan G. Tipton*

BIBLIOGRAPHY

Hay, Carla. "By George, Radio Loves Him." *Billboard*, May 22, 2004, 35.

Larkin, Colin, comp. and ed. *The Encyclopedia of Popular Music*. Third ed. New York: Muze, 1998. 5: 3652–3653.

"The Official George Michael Website." www.aegean.net

Rampson, Nancy. "Michael, George." *Contemporary Musicians: Profiles of the People in Music*. Julia M. Rubiner, ed. Detroit: Gale Research, 1993. 9:169–172.

Sexton, Paul. "Strong Interest Precedes New Michael Album." *Billboard*, March 27, 2004, 9.

Wieder, Judy. "All the Way Out George Michael." *Advocate*, January 19, 1999, 24.

———. "Our Celebrities." *Advocate*, April 30, 2000, 42.

SEE ALSO

Popular Music; Rock Music; Music Video; Music and AIDS; Mercury, Freddie; John, Sir Elton

Minnelli, Vincente   *(1913–1986)*

DAPPER VINCENTE MINNELLI WAS ONE OF HOLLYWOOD'S greatest directors, renowned for his skilled use of color and light and his precise attention to detail. He achieved recognition not only for the new life he injected into movie musicals such as *Meet Me in St. Louis* (1944)

and *Gigi* (1958), but also for emotionally complex comedies such as *Father of the Bride* (1950) and lushly conceived melodramas such as *Lust for Life* (1956).

Minnelli's campy vision and lavish productions were well suited to the 1940s and 1950s, but his style did not long survive the end of Hollywood's structured studio system. Although he continued to make films into the 1970s (such as *A Matter of Time,* with his daughter Liza Minnelli in 1976), his later films did not gain the popularity or acclaim of his earlier work.

Minnelli was born on February 28, 1903, in Delaware, Ohio, into a family of traveling entertainers. Although his early years were spent on the road learning show business, he settled in Chicago at age sixteen.

He took a job as a window decorator for Marshall Field's department store, where he began to develop his sense of design. He soon took his new knowledge back to the theater where he worked as an assistant photographer, costume designer, and set decorator. His originality and sharp eye for the details of design soon took him to the Broadway stage, where he was a successful costume and set designer.

Metro-Goldwyn-Mayer producer Arthur Freed discovered Minnelli on Broadway and brought him back to work his magic designing dance numbers for musicals at MGM. He worked on several films, including *Strike up the Band* (1940) and *Babes on Broadway* (1941) with Judy Garland and Mickey Rooney, before he was given the directorship of an all-black musical entitled *Cabin in the Sky* (1943). The stylish and inventive *Cabin in the Sky* was a success, and the window dresser from Chicago was now a Hollywood director.

Minnelli's next film, *Meet Me in St. Louis,* was a tour de force and a milestone in American filmmaking. Not only was it a textured look at turn-of-the-century Americana that spoke poignantly to a country in the midst of World War II, but it was also a showcase for Minnelli's flamboyant camera techniques and powerful use of color.

Meet Me in St. Louis was child star Judy Garland's first adult film. It led to the star's marriage to her director.

Although he married four times, Minnelli was widely known to be gay. In the deeply closeted world of 1950s Hollywood he kept his sexual orientation quite private, though his gay sensibility is visible in many of his films.

In his 1956 film version of Robert Anderson's exploration of masculinity and homophobia, *Tea and Sympathy,* Minnelli worked around the restrictions of the Motion Picture Association of America's production code to recreate the play's ambiguities without ever using the word *homosexual.*

In the little-noticed *Goodbye Charlie* (1964), Minnelli exploits the lighter side of gender confusion with a frothy comedy about a murdered womanizer who returns to earth in the body of a woman.

With the advent of a harsher realism in the movies in the 1960s and 1970s, Minnelli's dream sequences and fanciful use of color came to seem old-fashioned and out of date. He wrote his memoirs in 1974 and retired after the failure of *A Matter of Time* in 1976.

He died in Beverly Hills on July 26, 1986.

In 1999, Liza Minnelli premiered a tribute to her father called *Minnelli on Minnelli,* in which she performed many of the best-known and most beloved songs from his musicals, some of which had been made famous by her mother, Judy Garland, interspersed with loving reminiscences.

—*Tina Gianoulis*

BIBLIOGRAPHY

Gerstner, David. "Queer Modernism: The Cinematic Aesthetics of Vincente Minnelli." www.eiu.edu/~modernity/gerst—html

———. "The Production and Display of the Closet: Making Minnelli's Tea and Sympathy." *Film Quarterly* 50.3 (Spring 1997):13–27.

Harvey, Stephen. *Directed by Vincente Minnelli.* New York: Harper & Row, 1989.

Minnelli, Vincente, with Hector Arce. *I Remember It Well.* Hollywood, Calif.: Samuel French Trade, 1990.

Naremore, James. *The Films of Vincente Minnelli.* New York: Cambridge University Press, 1993.

SEE ALSO

Musical Theater and Film; Set and Costume Design; Edens, Roger; Garland, Judy

Mitropoulos, Dimitri (*1896–1960*)

IN THE 1950S, AT THE HEIGHT OF HIS SUCCESS AS CONductor of the New York Philharmonic Orchestra, composer Dimitri Mitropoulos became the subject of rumor and innuendo concerning the open secret of his homosexuality, in effect making him yet another victim of McCarthy-era homophobia.

For Mitropoulos, music was a lifelong passion. He delighted in exploring its richness and variety, and never hesitated to stage performances of works that other conductors found too challenging or complex. Twelve-tone music was his specialty.

A native of Athens, Mitropoulos took an interest in music from his earliest years. At around age six he carved himself a little wooden flute to play. A few years later, his parents provided him with piano lessons, at which he quickly excelled. His musical abilities brought him to the attention of a member of the faculty of the Athens Conservatory, who arranged for the boy to audit classes there and, when he was old enough in 1910, to enroll as a regular student.

Although Mitropoulos was devoted to music and had already composed a sonata for violin and piano while in his early teens, he planned on becoming a monk after completing his education. He was particularly drawn to the example of St. Francis of Assisi for his humility, gentleness, generosity, and respect for all others. Indeed, throughout Mitropoulos's life, he had a reputation as a sweet-natured man who shared the characteristics of his revered saint.

Mitropoulos gave up the thought of becoming a monk when his advisor in the Greek Orthodox Church informed him that no musical instruments were allowed in the monastery.

To please his father, who hoped that he would become either a lawyer or a naval officer, he briefly attended the law school of the University of Athens. It rapidly became apparent, however, that his vocation lay elsewhere, and he soon returned to the Conservatory, from which he graduated with highest honors in 1919. In addition, the faculty voted unanimously to award him a special gold medal.

During his last years at the conservatory, Mitropoulos began appearing publicly as a pianist, occasionally as an orchestral soloist. He also composed an opera, *Soeur Béatrice*, based on a play by Maurice Maeterlinck.

Although Mitropoulos had already recognized his homosexuality, he had a brief love affair in 1920 with Katina Paxinou, a drama student at the conservatory. The romance soon faded, but the two remained lifelong friends, exchanging frequent letters.

Paxinou, who came from a prosperous family, helped Mitropoulos stage his opera *Soeur Béatrice* in Athens in 1920. Among those who attended was composer Camille Saint-Saëns, who commented favorably on the work in an article published in a Paris newspaper.

Mitropoulos continued his musical education in Belgium and in Berlin, where he studied with Ferruccio Busoni, who inspired him to concentrate on conducting rather than composition.

On Busoni's recommendation Mitropoulos was chosen as an assistant conductor of the Berlin Staatsoper in 1921. Three years later, he returned to his native city to become the conductor of the Athens Symphony, a post he held for twelve years.

During his tenure in Athens, Mitropoulos was much in demand as a guest conductor and performed with most of the important orchestras of Europe.

His first trip to America came in 1936, when Serge Koussevitzky invited him to conduct the Boston Symphony Orchestra. His appearances there and in Cleveland and Minneapolis were enthusiastically received.

Mitropoulos returned to the United States the following year to become the conductor of the Minneapolis Symphony Orchestra.

Mitropoulos was like nothing the staid midwestern town had ever seen. His vigorous and physical conducting style was uniquely his own. Until the last years of his life he eschewed a baton, instead energetically using his whole body to communicate with the musicians.

Sans baton, Mitropoulos was also usually without a score. His amazing ability to commit every detail of vast numbers of scores to memory was legendary.

Mitropoulos considered himself a missionary of music, and part of his mission was to bring new and challenging works to audiences. Soon after arriving in Minneapolis, he announced that each season would include at least three "intellectual concerts" with programs featuring modern composers such as Arnold Schoenberg, Paul Hindemith, and especially Gustav Mahler, whose music he greatly admired. The public response was wildly positive. Biographer William R. Trotter notes that by 1940 "Minneapolis…officially had the largest per capita concert audience in America."

Mitropoulos left Minneapolis in 1949 to share with Leopold Stokowski the duties of conductor and musical adviser of the New York Philharmonic Orchestra. The next year, Stokowski left, and Mitropoulos was named full musical director, a position widely perceived as the most prestigious in classical music in the United States.

His tenure at the Philharmonic was marked by a number of signal successes, including a concert performance of Richard Strauss's opera *Elektra* during his first season and a presentation of Alban Berg's monumental atonal opera *Wozzeck* in 1950.

As he had in Minneapolis, Mitropoulos lived in modest lodgings in New York and avoided high-society parties. He also continued his habit of following the model of St. Francis when dealing with his musicians, leading through mutual respect and gentle persuasion rather than force and fear. The egos that he confronted at the Philharmonic made this approach problematic, however, and music critics began to carp that he was losing control of his orchestra.

Another element working against Mitropoulos was his sexual orientation, long an open secret in the music community. In the late 1940s and early 1950s, at the height of McCarthyism, it was not a good time to be known as a homosexual. Mitropoulos had always dodged questions about his bachelor status by claiming "I married my art" when queried by the press.

In a 1952 letter to a friend, Mitropoulos wrote, "for me music is another expression of my unlived sexual life." Trotter states that Mitropoulos did indeed lead a celibate life in both Minneapolis and New York, though perhaps "very occasionally" had sex on tour. In general, his "sexual drive [was] sublimated ruthlessly into his music-making."

Although true close friends—including the composers Ned Rorem and David Diamond—viewed Mitropoulos's existence as monkish, rumor and innuendo swirled around him, often fed by orchestra members and contributing to a lack of respect for Mitropoulos on the part of his players. Ironically, among those encouraging the whispers was the closeted Leonard Bernstein, who, since he was married, could present himself as the sort of "family man" that the orchestra wanted in the decade of conformity.

Bernstein got his wish, being named co-conductor with Mitropoulos for the 1957–1958 season and taking over as sole musical director the next. Typically gracious, Mitropoulos bowed out with praise for Bernstein's talent, but the loss of his position as director of this most prestigious American orchestra was deeply hurtful to him and a blow from which he never fully recovered.

He also mentioned his desire to devote more time to "that very tempting mistress, the Metropolitan Opera," which he had been conducting for several years and where he had recently staged a triumphant performance of Tchaikovsky's *Eugene Onegin*.

In the last years of his life, Mitropoulos undertook a demanding tour guest-conducting with European orchestras. The accumulated stress proved too great, however, and he suffered a fatal heart attack on November 2, 1960, while rehearsing Mahler's Third Symphony with the La Scala Opera House Orchestra in Milan.

Tributes poured in for Mitropoulos, not only for his prodigious musical abilities but also for his gentleness and decency as a person. "He was a dear, good man who was always so kind and full of understanding," commented the diva Maria Callas.

Mitropoulos is remembered for his extreme generosity. Throughout his life, he gave away nearly all his money, often to help struggling musicians and orchestras. In addition, during World War II he eschewed the opportunity to supplement his income by going on tour as a guest conductor, choosing instead to volunteer his time coordinating blood drives for the American Red Cross.

After Mitropoulos's death he was largely forgotten in the United States. One can only wonder if the lack of support from the musical community in New York contributed to this. In recent years, however, there has been renewed interest in his work, and many of his recordings have been reissued on CD so that they may be appreciated by new generations of music lovers.

—*Linda Rapp*

BIBLIOGRAPHY

"Maestro Mitropoulos Stricken in Milan, Dies." *Washington Post*, November 3, 1960.

"Mitropoulos, Dimitri." *Current Biography* 1952. Anna Rothe and Evelyn Lohr, eds. New York: The H. W. Wilson Company, 1953. 431–433.

Schonberg, Harold C. "He Lived for Music." *New York Times*, November 6, 1960.

Trotter, William R. "Mitropoulos, Dimitri." *New Grove Dictionary of Music and Musicians*. Second ed. Stanley Sadie, ed. London: Macmillan, 2001. 16: 764–765.

———. *Priest of Music: The Life of Dimitri Mitropoulos*. Portland, Ore.: Amadeus Press, 1995.

SEE ALSO

Classical Music; Conductors; Opera; Bernstein, Leonard; Rorem, Ned; Saint-Saëns, Camille; Tchaikovsky, Pyotr Ilich

Molina, Miguel de   *(1908–1993)*

MIGUEL DE MOLINA ROSE FROM POVERTY TO BECOME one of Spain's most celebrated flamenco singers. His wildly popular performances reinvented a dance and music tradition that had grown stale for lack of innovation and originality. Despite his success, however, Molina's open gayness and gender-bending stage persona provoked hostile reactions that plagued his career.

The naturally effeminate Molina was forced from the stage on numerous occasions and eventually found himself expelled from two countries. Yet, despite this homophobic persecution, Molina never retreated into the closet and refused to alter his feminine stage persona.

Molina's life was as melodramatic as his music. Born Miguel Frías in a small Spanish town near Málaga in 1908, he came from a background of dire poverty.

Expelled from school when a vengeful and sexually abusive priest accused him of "unnatural acts" with other boys, Miguel ran away to Algeciras, where he found employment cleaning a brothel. Because he was only thirteen at the time, the prostitutes cared for him as mothers and even arranged for a schoolteacher client to tutor him.

Moving on at the age of seventeen, Molina found employment on the ship of a Moroccan prince, serving in what was essentially the prince's male harem. The prince soon fell out of political favor, however, and Molina returned to Spain, where he began organizing *Tablas Flamencas*, or flamenco parties, for Granada's Gypsies.

This experience constituted Molina's first full exposure to a musical and dance tradition he already loved. By 1930, Molina arrived in Madrid, where he made increasingly good money organizing *Tablas* in the capital. One year later, he decided the time had come for him to take to the stage rather than to manage it. He appeared in a production of Manuel de Falla's ballet *El amor brujo*, but soon developed his own act, which combined flamenco and cabaret.

Molina's notion was to reinvent flamenco performance by feminizing the usual macho role taken by men. He sewed enormous two-meter-long sleeves, which he called blouses, onto the traditional costume and even sang the type of *coplas*, or popular songs, normally reserved for women.

Although he danced with a female colleague, he nonetheless acquired the name "La Miguela" and immediately met with enormous success. In 1933, he gave himself the name "de Molina."

With the outbreak of the Spanish Civil War in 1936, Molina fled to Valencia and from there entertained Republican troops. Because he and his dance partner Amalia Isaura became near mascots for the Levantine Republicans, both found themselves vulnerable after the Fascist victory in 1939.

Initially, a promoter closely connected to Franco's regime contracted them to tour the country. This arrangement protected the dancers from retribution, but in return they were paid a pitiful wage despite their popularity.

Tired of his status as war booty, Molina decided not to renew his contract once it expired in 1942. Soon thereafter, government thugs kidnapped him from the theater where he was then performing and tortured him, pulling his hair out and beating him with their guns.

Molina survived this abuse, but then suffered sequestration in remote Spanish towns. Unofficially banned from employment in Spain, Molina finally fled to Argentina, where he again met with great success. One year later, however, the machinations of Franco's government forced his expulsion from Argentina. Molina once again found himself in Spain without work.

In 1946, Molina fled to Mexico and soon thereafter settled in Buenos Aires, allegedly under the personal protection of Argentina's most powerful woman, Eva Perón. His customary success soon followed. Although he claimed not to have been political, his identification with Perónism caused many Argentines to despise him. In 1960, he withdrew from the entertainment world with some bitterness.

By the time he died in 1993, Molina had regained some of the esteem in which he had been held earlier, especially in Spain. He had, after all, produced numerous revues, starred in many films, and established two significant signature songs that most Spaniards know by heart, "Ojos Verdes" (Green Eyes) and "La Bien Pagá" (The Woman Well Paid).

According to Molina's not always reliable autobiography, the persecution he experienced at the hands of the Franco government had less to do with hostility from Franco's officials (with whom he enjoyed great popularity) than with the hatred and jealousy of a self-loathing, closeted gay functionary serving under the powerful minister of foreign affairs. Molina concluded that his nemesis begrudged him his openly gay, yet professionally successful life.

Serving Molina best through these tremendous setbacks was his unceasing creativity. By reinventing the role of the male flamenco dancer, feminizing his appearance and sound without rendering either "mannered," Molina attracted audiences well beyond the genre's traditionalists. Clothed in what seemed inverted dresses and singing songs normally reserved for women, he attracted even the roughest of soldiers to his flashy stage and movie persona.

Unfortunately, Molina never returned to live in Spain even after its transition to democracy.

—*Andres Mario Zervigon*

BIBLIOGRAPHY

Molina, Miguel de. *Botín de guera. Autobiografía.* Salvador Valverde, ed. Barcelona: Editorial Planeta, 1998.

SEE ALSO

Dance; Cabarets and Revues; Falla (y Matheu), Manuel de

Morris, Mark   (b. 1956)

MARK MORRIS IS ONE OF THE BEST-KNOWN AND MOST respected leaders in the dance world today. His works typically mix elements of Eastern and Western cultures and of the traditional and the avant-garde; they are set to a wide range of musical styles, from Baroque to rock, and frequently explore sexual ambiguities. No less an authority than Mikhail Baryshnikov has proclaimed Morris one of the greatest choreographers of his time.

Born on August 29, 1956, in Seattle, where he was raised, Mark Morris fell in love with flamenco at the age of eight when he saw a José Greco show. At thirteen, he joined a folk dance group, and later went to Spain intending to become a flamenco dancer. After a brief apprenticeship, Morris realized that flamenco was too limiting for him. He moved to New York when he was nineteen to pursue a career in modern dance.

During the early years of his career in New York, Morris performed with a variety of companies, including the Lar Lubovitch Dance Company, the Hannah Kahn Dance Company, the Laura Dean Dancers and Musicians, the Eliot Feld Ballet, and the Koleda Balkan Dance Ensemble.

Although Morris was primarily a dancer during his tenure with these companies, his ambition to choreograph led him to form the Mark Morris Dance Group in 1980. Founded in collaboration with friends and colleagues, the group had its first performance at the Merce Cunningham Dance Studio in New York.

Mark Morris.

Since then, Morris has created over 100 works for his company, as well as works for the American Ballet Theatre, the San Francisco Ballet, and the Paris Opera Ballet.

During the 1980s, the Mark Morris Dance Group gained increased recognition, performing at the Brooklyn Academy of Music's Next Wave Festival in 1984 and appearing for the first time at the Kennedy Center in 1985.

His works were often unpredictable and irreverent. The provocative program for a 1985 performance in San Francisco included *The Vacant Chair*, in which Morris appeared in his underwear with a brown paper bag over his head; and in *Lovey*, dolls are abused and ripped apart to the accompaniment of recordings by the Violent Femmes.

In 1987, while the Mark Morris Dance Group was working in Europe, choreographer Maurice Béjart retired as Director of Dance at Belgium's state opera house, taking the opera's ballet company with him. The opera's director, Gerard Mortier, recognized the potential of the Mark Morris Dance Group and offered Morris the position.

From 1988 to 1991, Morris served as Director of Dance for the Belgian National Opera in Brussels, bringing to Europe a distinctly American flair with such works as *The Hard Nut* (1988), his witty take on the classic *Nutcracker*, updated to the 1960s and set in a suburban American home, complete with vinyl furniture and a white plastic Christmas tree.

During the same period, Morris choreographed such works as the critically acclaimed *L'Allegro, il Penseroso ed il Moderato* (1988), with music by George Frideric Handel, and *Dido and Aeneas* (1989), a dance set to the baroque opera by English composer Henry Purcell. In the premiere of that work, Morris himself danced the dual roles of Dido, queen of Carthage, and the Sorceress.

When his contract with the Belgian National Opera expired in 1991, Morris and his company returned to the United States. They continue to make regular and frequent appearances throughout the country and in Europe.

Morris has also proved himself an accomplished director and choreographer of opera, most notably *Orfeo ed Euridice* (1996), by Christoph Willibald Gluck, and *Platée* (1997), a comic opera by Jean Philippe Rameau.

In 2001, the Mark Morris Dance Center opened in Brooklyn, New York. The new center provides Morris and his company a permanent space in which to create, rehearse, and teach.   —*Craig Kaczorowski*

BIBLIOGRAPHY

Covington, Richard. "The Dancer and the Dance: The Salon Interview with Mark Morris." *Salon*, September 9, 1996: www.salon.com/weekly/interview960909.html

Gladstone, Valerie. "The Wizard of Dance." *Town and Country*, February 2001, 73.

Mark Morris Dance Company website. www.mmdg.org

Teachout, Terry. "Dance Chronicle: Going a Lot to the Mark Morris Dance Group." *Partisan Review* 67.2 (Spring 2000): 281–285.

Ulrich, Allan. "Mark Morris: 20 years of serious fun." *Dance Magazine*, April 2001, 44.

SEE ALSO

Dance; Ballet; Béjart, Maurice; Cunningham, Merce; Handel, George Frideric

Music and AIDS

A NUMBER OF MUSICAL WORKS IN VARIOUS GENRES have responded directly or indirectly to the AIDS crisis. Many musical works that refer to AIDS are about emotions, thus focusing on expressions of grief, anger, or sympathy, rather than on the personal and social consequences of the disease (as in novels, film, or drama) or on political confrontation (as in many works of visual art).

As a result, music about AIDS sometimes seems less specific than work in other media. Nevertheless, music of all kinds has registered the enormous impact of AIDS.

The earliest works appeared around the same time as the first AIDS plays, including punk songs by Karl Brown and Matthew McQueen for San Francisco's collaborative *The AIDS Show* ("Safe Livin' in Dangerous Times" and "Rimmin' at the Baths," September 1984).

The first commercially distributed music appeared soon after: Frank Zappa's "Thing-Fish" (November 1984), a satire of Broadway where abusive racial and sexual stereotypes people a demented tale of government conspiracy.

Much music about AIDS was written for fundraising purposes. An early and typical success was the vaguely sympathetic "That's What Friends Are For" by Burt Bacharach and Carol Bayer Sager (1985).

The benefit compilation *Red, Hot + Blue* (1990), in which contemporary pop artists cover Cole Porter songs, led to the foundation of the Red Hot Organization, which has since produced numerous CD and video anthologies. Notable Red Hot productions include the alternative rock collection *No Alternative* (1993), the sophisticated jazz/rap *Stolen Moments* (1994), and the hip-hop collection *America Is Dying Slowly* (1996).

Some major popular vocalists have made a point of performing songs about AIDS (usually one each), including Prince ("Sign o' the Times," 1987), James Taylor ("Never Die Young," 1988), Lou Reed ("Halloween Parade," 1989), Linda Ronstadt ("Goodbye My Friend," 1989), Elton John ("The Last Song," 1992), Madonna ("In This Life," 1992), Reba MacEntire ("She Thinks His Name Was John," 1994), Tori Amos ("Not the Red Baron," 1996), Patti Smith ("Death Singing," 1997), and Janet Jackson ("Together Again," 1998).

Most of these are written from the point of view of the survivor remembering a friend or an "outsider" developing sympathy for PWAs. Popular groups sometimes take a more complex approach, including the radical remix of "All You Need Is Love" by The JAMS (1987) or U2's eerie "One" (1992).

Some gay popular artists have not only specifically referred to AIDS but also explored the resultant emotional and social climate, especially Michael Callen and the Flirtations, Marc Almond, Jimmy Somerville, the Communards, and the Pet Shop Boys. The last group is known for songs that present their ironic, oblique view of 1990s gay life, including the discomforts of safe sex.

The most successful musicals that highlight AIDS have been William Finn's *Falsettoland* (1990) and Jonathan Larson's innovative *Rent* (1996), both of which engage gay characters with survivors at various stages of acceptance.

Other stage works, mostly in a soft-rock style, include Brian Gari's *A Hard Time to Be Single* (1991), John Greyson's sloppy but amusing *Zero Patience* (1994), Stephen Dolginoff's *Most Men Are* (1995), James Mellon's *An Unfinished Song* (1995), Cindy O'Connor's family study *All That He Was* (1996), *The Last Session,* by Jim Brochu and Steve Schalchlin (1996), and *Elegies,* by Janet Hood and Bill Russell (1996).

Some films about AIDS have notable music. For example, the soundtrack for *Philadelphia* (1993) included new songs by Bruce Springsteen and Neil Young. Bobby McFerrin created a vocal score for the AIDS Quilt documentary *Common Threads* (1989), and Carter Burwell wrote an orchestral soundtrack for *And the Band Played On* (1993).

The classical music community has produced a number of works, many of them neo-Romantic in style. The most important of these are John Corigliano's Symphony no. 1 (1990) and the ongoing *AIDS Song Quilt* (begun in 1992), created by baritone William Parker (1943–1993), which consists of a series of AIDS poem settings by composers including William Bolcom, Libby Larsen, and Ned Rorem. Younger composers such as Chris DeBlasio and Robert Maggio have made reputations partially on the basis of successful chamber works about AIDS.

Gay and lesbian choruses have performed many apposite works since early in the crisis, including reinterpretations of older songs. New cantatas written for them include *Hidden Legacies,* by Roger Bourland and John Hall (1992) and *Naked Man,* by Robert Seeley (1996).

The most important figure in avant-garde circles—probably the most important figure in music about AIDS—is vocalist/composer/performer Diamanda Galás. She has been creating works about AIDS since before the death of her brother, writer Philip-Dimitri Galás, in 1986. The most important of her works are the *Plague Mass* (1984) and the three-part *Masque of the Red Death* (1986–88), both of which exemplify her combination of savagely visceral texts with extraordinary vocalizations and complex musical textures.

Other women composers who have written avant-garde works include Meredith Monk (*New York Requiem,* 1993), Laurie Anderson (*Love among the Sailors,* 1994), and Pauline Oliveros (*Epigraphs in the Time of AIDS,* 1994).

Works by gay men include Gerhard Stäbler's *Warnung mit Liebeslied* (1986), Robert Moran's minimalist *Requiem: Chant du cygne* (1990), and Bob Ostertag's powerful *All The Rage* (1993), recorded by the Kronos Quartet.

Artist/writer David Wojnarowicz worked on many collaborative pieces, of which one of the most musical was *ITSOFOMO,* written with composer Ben Neill (1989).

The health crisis has directly affected the musical world as much as other areas of the arts. Among many musicians who have died are Klaus Nomi (1944–1983), Calvin Hampton (1938–1984), Sylvester (1947–1988), Freddie Mercury (1946–1991), Michael Callen (1954–1993), and Robert Savage (1951–1993).

Outside the urban West, protest and educational musics referring to AIDS have appeared in Mexico,

South Africa, and (undoubtedly) many other countries. Limited distribution networks and language barriers have kept most from becoming available to English-speaking audiences. An exception is *AIDS: How Could I Know?* (1989), a bilingual recording produced by the Central Australian Aboriginal Media Association.

Despite the range of genres and works, there has been less music written about AIDS than there has been production in other art forms. This fact may be attributable to the strictures of the music industry, or to aspects of the nature of music.

Still, it is perhaps not too much to claim that the evident increase during the 1980s and 1990s in musical works that focused on grief, sympathy, or healing, some of which can be associated with "new age" music, is rooted in cultural changes that came out of the AIDS crisis.

—*Paul Attinello*

BIBLIOGRAPHY

Attinello, Paul. "Music and AIDS: Some Interesting Works." *GLSG Newsletter* 10.1 (Spring 2000): 4–6.

Avena, Thomas, ed. *Life Sentences: Writers, Artists, and AIDS.* San Francisco: Mercury House, 1994.

Baker, Rob. *The Art of AIDS.* New York: Continuum, 1994.

Dellamora, Richard, and Daniel Fischlin, eds. *The Work of Opera: Genre, Nationhood, and Difference.* New York: Columbia University Press, 1997.

Dunbar-Hall, Peter. "Rock Songs as Messages: Issues of Health and Lifestyle in Central Australian Aboriginal Communities." *Popular Music and Society* 20.2 (Summer 1996): 43–67.

Galás, Diamanda. *The Shit of God.* New York: High Risk, 1996.

Hughes, Walter. "In the Empire of the Beat: Discipline and Disco." *Microphone Fiends: Youth Music and Youth Culture.* Andrew Ross and Tricia Rose, eds. New York: Routledge, 1994. 147–157.

Hutcheon, Linda, and Michael Hutcheon. *Opera: Desire, Disease, Death.* Lincoln: University of Nebraska Press, 1996.

Jones, Wendell, and David Stanley. "AIDS! The Musical!" *Sharing the Delirium: Second Generation AIDS Plays and Performances.* Therese Jones, ed. Portsmouth, N.H.: Heinemann, 1994. 207–221.

Lee, Colin. *Music at the Edge: Music Therapy Experiences of a Musician with AIDS.* New York: Routledge, 1996.

McLellan, Jay. *OutLoud!: Encyclopedia of Gay and Lesbian Recordings.* First CD-ROM edition. Amsterdam: OutLoud Press, 1998.

Román, David. *Acts of Intervention: Performance, Gay Culture, and AIDS.* Bloomington: Indiana University Press, 1998.

Ward, Keith. "Musical Responses to HIV and AIDS." *Perspectives on American Music since 1950.* James Heintze, ed. New York: Garland, 1999. 323–351.

SEE ALSO

Musical Theater and Film; Corigliano, John; John, Sir Elton; Mercury, Freddie; Pet Shop Boys; Porter, Cole; Reed, Lou; Rorem, Ned; Somerville, Jimmy; Sylvester

Music Video

MUSIC VIDEO, SINCE ITS MAINSTREAM DEBUT VIA THE cable television network MTV in 1981, has been primarily a Top 40 music format. Gay and lesbian content within the standard three-minute constraint was rare in the early days, but with the advent of more openly gay, lesbian, and bisexual artists, that situation has gradually changed.

MTV and its sister station, VH1, which targets an adult contemporary audience, cater to popular tastes, and the production of music videos, an expensive promotional tool with virtually no other media outlet, has largely remained the reserve of major-label artists.

While the 1980s saw the rise of androgynous artists such as Annie Lennox of the Eurythmics and the openly gay transvestite Boy George of Culture Club, whose images were all over the airwaves, videos with specifically homosexual, nontheatrical characters were scarce.

One notable early exception is the work of heterosexual artist Bruce Springsteen, whose video for "Tougher than the Rest" (ca. 1988) features live concert footage interspersed with vignettes of couples made at venues on his "Tunnel of Love Express" tour. The video includes both gay and lesbian pairs interspersed with heterosexual couples as representatives of the artist's fans. Early on, Springsteen included this explicitly homosexual imagery with neither fanfare nor exploitation.

On the other hand, an ambiguity toward explicit sexual themes marks the content of many early videos produced by gay, lesbian, and bisexual artists. For example, Indigo Girls' first video, "Closer to Fine" (1989), depicts Amy Ray and Emily Saliers performing and singing with little or no interaction.

It was played on MTV (and later VH1), and the Grammy-winning duo became one of the first acts on the channel's emerging *Unplugged* program. At the time, Ray and Saliers were not closeted but neither were they out in the mainstream press.

The 1990s witnessed the beginnings of more deliberateness on the part of artists in depicting their own sexuality in their videos, yet this openness did not always translate into MTV or VH1 airtime, and sometimes led to censorship.

For example, 4 Non Blondes scored a huge radio and video hit with their 1991 song "What's Up," and while promoting the song the lesbian lead singer Linda Perry displayed a "dyke" sticker prominently plastered on her guitar for a performance on "Late Night with David Letterman"; but the group's video was merely a straightforward yet colorful depiction of alternative rock and roll with no reference to homosexuality at all.

Indigo Girls' video for "Joking" (1992), a montage of several sexually ambiguous people interacting and regrouping with one another, received virtually no airplay even though it explicitly deals with, in Ray's words, an "idea about androgyny within relationships and how a relationship is a relationship regardless of what sex you are."

Their 1995 video "Power of Two" opens with an image of male lovers embracing and includes both lesbian and heterosexual pairs throughout, but it received very limited VH1 play.

Lesbian chanteuse k.d. lang, who came out in the *Advocate* in 1992 and more spectacularly in a cover story in *Vanity Fair* in August 1993, has produced numerous videos that have played in heavy rotation on MTV and VH1, yet none include depictions of lesbianism.

Such is also the case with Melissa Etheridge, who came out nationally at an inaugural dinner for President Clinton in 1993. The videos for her blockbuster album *Yes I Am* (1994) include "Come to My Window," featuring actor Juliette Lewis, but none show lesbian relationships.

Tracy Chapman's number one hit "Give Me One Reason" from 1996 subtly implied that the singer was addressing the female bartender depicted in the video, though the narrative was resolved with a straight couple.

Also in 1996, bisexual singer Meshell Ndegéocello's video "Leviticus: Faggot," featuring a butch Ndegéocello (a woman) interacting with black gay men, was immediately banned upon its release, presumably because of its depiction, mirroring the song's lyrics, of parental gay bashing, faith-based opposition to homosexuality, prostitution, and suicide. Despite its initial censorship, the video is now available to view on Ndegéocello's website.

Among openly gay and bisexual male artists, Elton John has persistently adhered to a neutral mainstream aesthetic, a tactic used by many aging yet popular singers in which younger, attractive performers enact the video narrative while the star merely exudes his or her well-honed persona.

George Michael's post–coming out video "Outside" (1998) was an MTV exclusive. The video addresses Michael's homosexuality head-on through a parody of his arrest in a Beverly Hills park restroom on charges of soliciting a male undercover police officer. The video features Michael dancing around, dressed (Village People–style) as a macho cop, plus two other males dressed as cops kissing passionately. MTV played both a censored (blurred kiss) and uncensored (for late-night airings) version.

While the sometimes bisexual singer Madonna receives the most attention for her videos depicting bisexuality and homosexuality—from her cavortings with men and women in "Justify My Love" and "Music" to her remake of Don MacLean's "American Pie," in which gay men and lesbians are depicted kissing in unsensationalized moments—numerous other heterosexual recording artists, including Lenny Kravitz and Aerosmith, have upped the titillation factor in their videos by gratuitously depicting women together in sexual situations.

Singer Marilyn Manson resurrects Boy George by way of "Dope Show" (1999); like Michael's "Outside" video, "Dope Show" features a scene of males dressed as police officers in sexualized couplings while the overall video depicts the heterosexual Manson wearing an androgynous costume that features women's breasts.

As programming on video stations has begun to include fewer videos and more serial programs and films, the message from the video channels, if not from the artists, appears mixed.

In January 2000, MTV introduced its "Fight For Your Rights: Take a Stand Against Discrimination" campaign with the documentary *Anatomy of a Hate Crime— Matthew Shepard*. At the same time, the virulently homophobic rap artist Eminem won the MTV Video Awards Best Video of the Year for his song "The Real Slim Shady," which includes explicit slurs against gay men and lesbians.

—*Carla Williams*

BIBLIOGRAPHY

Cohen, Belissa. "Linda Perry Wants It All." *Lesbian News,* January 1997.

Indigo Girls. *Watershed: 10 Years of Underground Video.* DVD. Sony Music Entertainment, Inc./Epic Music Video, 1995.

John, Richard. "George Michael Video Parodies Arrest." *Jam! Showbiz,* November 2, 1998: www.canoe.ca/JamMusicArtistsM/michael_george.html

lang, k.d. *k.d. lang: Harvest of Seven Years (Cropped and Chronicled).* VHS. Warner Reprise Video, 1991.

Springsteen, Bruce. *Bruce Springsteen: The Complete Video Anthology: 1978–2000.* DVD. Columbia Music Video, 2001.

www.mtv.com

www.vh1.com

www.melissaetheridge.com

www.indigogirls.com. http://lifeblood.net.

www.eltonjohn.com/

www.kdlang.com

www.madonnamusic.com/

www.marilynmanson.com

www.sonymusic.co.uk/georgemichael/

www.lindaperry.com

www.brucespringsteen.net

SEE ALSO

Popular Music; Rock Music; Boy George (George O'Dowd); Etheridge, Melissa; Indigo Girls; John, Sir Elton; lang, k.d.; Michael, George; Village People

Musical Theater and Film

MANY WITHIN AND WITHOUT GAY CULTURE HAVE observed a strong identification on the part of gay men with musical theater. A number of gay writers have seen the musical as a crucial element in their consciousness of their homosexuality.

Alexander, Larry Kramer's alter ego in his play *The Destiny of Me* (1992), sings "I'm Gonna Wash That Man Right Out of My Hair" from *South Pacific* (1949) as a way of drowning out the attacks of his violent, homophobic father.

Queer critics Wayne Koestenbaum (*The Queen's Throat*) and D. A. Miller (*Place for Us*) write of their youthful love of the musical and its relationship to their sense of difference.

At the same time, television situation comedies have used love of musicals or knowledge of show tunes as a definitive sign of homosexuality. Even Kevin Kline's small-town hero in the film *In and Out* (1997) listened to the cast album of *Gypsy* (1959) and worshipped Barbra Streisand.

In reality, such identification is stronger for men who grew up in an age in which musical theater was a more central part of American popular culture than it is now, a time when gay men necessarily had to find ways to sublimate their desires and identity. The flamboyant excess of musical theater, including opera and ballet, offered such outlets.

There are a number of ways to look at the relationship of the musical to gay culture, particularly gay male culture. One can consider the contribution of out or closeted gay composers and lyricists to the musical. Or one can focus on the importance of musicals—and, particularly, the centrality of the women who were its divas—to that group of gay men known as show queens. One could also look at post-Stonewall presentations of openly gay characters and shows written by gay writers primarily for gay audiences.

Composers and Lyricists

It is now common knowledge that some of the most important creators of the American and British musical have been gay men. One has to look only, for instance, at the men who brought *Kiss Me, Kate* to the stage in 1948, at the beginning of the Cold War, when treatment of homosexuals was particularly draconian.

This hit musical was produced by a gay man; written by Cole Porter, a gay man who was married but who rather openly and, for the time, incautiously, conducted his affairs with men; directed by John C. Wilson, who had been, in the 1930s, Noël Coward's lover; and featured among its stars the bisexual Harold Lang, who had affairs with Leonard Bernstein and Gore Vidal, among others.

Of course, none of this was common knowledge (except to people in the theater) at a time when homosexuality dared not speak its name; but it does suggest the ways in which gay men were invested in and responsible for musical theater.

Certainly, not everyone involved in musical theater is or was gay. But a significant number of major gay artists have been involved in musical theater, from composers (Porter, Bernstein, Stephen Sondheim, Coward, Elton John) to lyricists (Lorenz Hart, Porter, Sondheim) to librettists (James Kirkwood, Terrence McNally, among others) to directors and choreographers (Michael Bennett, Tommy Tune, John Dexter, among others) to scene and costume designers, and, of course, performers.

While today the homosexuality of artists involved in musical theater is celebrated in the gay press, during the heyday of musical theater (1920–1960), artists had to be circumspect.

Nonetheless, Cole Porter wrote a number of lyrics that contain homosexual innuendo. Lorenz Hart, half (with composer Richard Rodgers) of one of the most successful songwriting teams of the 1920s and 1930s, penned a number of serious lyrics that can easily be read autobiographically as cries from the heart of an anguished, self-hating homosexual.

Noël Coward and Ivor Novello, the two most successful British musical composers and stars of the period between the world wars (Coward wrote musicals into the 1960s), were both gay men.

In our time, Stephen Sondheim, though never dealing openly with the subject of homosexuality and never offering a gay character (though it is very difficult not to read Robert, the central character in *Company*, 1970, as gay), is something of a gay icon.

Revivals of Sondheim's classic musicals, particularly *Follies* (1971), a hymn to diva worship, and the grand diva classic *Gypsy* (1959, for which Sondheim wrote the lyrics), are quasi-religious events for show queens.

For almost a century, particular show tunes have had special meaning for gay men. From Judy Garland singing "Over the Rainbow" (*The Wizard of Oz*, 1939; Harold Arlen, E. Y. Harburg) to Doris Day celebrating her "Secret Love" (*Calamity Jane*, 1953; Sammy Fain), to the unseen singer in *West Side Story* (1957) reassuring us, in the words of its gay composer and lyricist, Leonard Bernstein and Stephen Sondheim, that there's a place for us "Somewhere," to Albin in Jerry Herman's *La Cage aux Folles* (1983) proudly declaring "I Am What I Am," the Broadway theater and Hollywood musical have provided us with our anthems.

The Broadway Diva

For many gay men, the centerpiece of the musical was the larger-than-life female star, her persona an exaggeration of the femininity that one associates with drag queens. Although there are a number of fine leading men, some of whom do not put much effort into concealing their gayness, show queens have been far more interested in the divas.

The Broadway diva defies conventional notions of gender and plays out the parodic, larger-than-life performance of gender that the musical privileges. For this reason, perhaps, gay men have constituted the core following of a number of leading ladies.

From the devoted following of Judy Garland's stage appearances to the fans of Garland's daughter, Liza Minnelli, to the admirers of Elaine Stritch, Barbra Streisand, Angela Lansbury, Bette Midler, Barbara Cook, and, more recently, Betty Buckley, gay men have made adulation of the leading lady part of the gay theatrical experience.

Now, when fewer musicals are being written for star turns—because of the long runs necessary for musicals to be profitable, musicals are usually written with leading roles that can easily be played by a succession of lesser-known performers—many divas have been required to build their careers on concert and cabaret appearances, and many show queens have turned their attention to cabaret.

Particularly in the pre-Stonewall days of the closet, the diva was part of the camp appeal of the musical. Camp allowed gay spectators to find gayness in shows that were ostensibly heterosexual and heterosexist. The artificiality of the musical reinforced gay men's sense of the artificiality of the gender order that excluded them. While the content may not have been transgressive, the form and the style were. Excess is at the heart of the traditional musical.

Representations of Gay Characters

Since Stonewall and gay liberation, a large number of gay men are no longer satisfied with queering ostensibly heterosexual musicals, but want to see themselves on stage. Over the past three decades, mainstream Broadway musicals have acknowledged their gay audience, though often by trotting out tired stereotypes.

Lauren Bacall's diva vehicle *Applause* (1970, book by Betty Comden & Adolph Green, music and lyrics by Charles Strouse and Lee Adams), an adaptation of the camp film classic *All About Eve* (1950), featured as Margo Channing's sidekick a flamboyant gay hairdresser who early in the show takes her to a gay bar, where she is worshipped by show queens, a unique acknowledgment of a large segment of the show's audience.

Since Tommy Tune played a gay choreographer in *Seesaw* (1973, book by Michael Bennett and Michael Stewart, music by Cy Coleman, lyrics by Dorothy Fields), show-business musicals have acknowledged the role of gay men in their creation.

However, Bennett's next musical, *A Chorus Line* (1975), rather incredibly had only two gay men in the show's group of eager candidates, neither of whom was good enough actually to be cast as a member of the chorus for which the show presented a fictional audition.

Set in a Saint Tropez gay nightclub, *La Cage aux Folles* (1983, book by Harvey Fierstein, music and lyrics by Jerry Herman) offered a chorus of drag performers and a drag diva and her "husband" of twenty years as the leading characters in a saga of middle-aged gay marriage. Presenting a cartoon version of gay couples acceptable to heterosexuals, the show ran for four years and has since become a staple of amateur theater groups.

One element of the crossover success of *La Cage aux Folles* is its dependence on traditional stereotypes of drag, effeminacy, and the notion that a gay couple has to parody the gender politics of a heterosexual couple. Nonetheless, the musical had a large gay following, in part because its writers and director were openly gay.

The same kind of stereotyping is apparent in subsequent musicals. For example, *Kiss of the Spider Woman* (London 1992, New York, 1993; book by Terrence McNally, music and lyrics by John Kander and Fred Ebb) removed the irony and complexity of Manuel Puig's novel to present a nelly mama's boy's love for a macho straight man and his worship of a flamboyant diva, played by musical veteran Chita Rivera.

For all its vaunted hipness, Jonathan Larson's *Rent* (1996), which includes among its couples a black man and a Puerto Rican drag queen, builds on the same stereotypes.

At least the megahit *The Producers* (2001, book, music, and lyrics by Mel Brooks) is aware of the outrageousness of its cartoons of gay stereotypes, who at one point sing a number aptly titled "Keep It Gay." Brooks's gay caricatures, an essential element of a musical in which everything is over-the-top parody, mock traditional stereotypes more than they mock lesbians and gay men.

The irony of casting openly gay Nathan Lane as the ostensibly straight leading man adds to the possibilities of gender and sexuality bending.

The more realistic musical comedy *The Full Monty* (2000, book by Terrence McNally, music and lyrics by David Yazbek) has a gay couple among the unemployed steel workers who have taken up stripping to gain cash and regain their self respect. Here gayness is not exoticized in any way, though it is presented rather cautiously; and the gay couple develop one of the show's least problematic, most loving relationships.

Musicals Written for Gay Audiences

There have been gay-themed musicals since gay culture in American cities became open in the late 1960s. These shows see their primary audience as gay men and seldom attract a large number of heterosexual theatergoers.

From early low-budget works such as *Boy Meets Boy* (1975, music and lyrics by Bill Solly) to recent works such as *Hedwig and the Angry Inch* (1998, book by John Cameron Mitchell, music and lyrics by Stephen Trask), *Closer to Heaven* (2001, book by Jonathan Harvey, music and lyrics by the Pet Shop Boys), and *Mother Clap's Molly House* (2001, book and lyrics by Mark Ravenhill, music by Matthew Scott), there have been musicals that speak directly and powerfully to a predominantly gay audience.

These works demonstrate the variety of approaches to gay musical theater. Moreover, many of them share the diva worship that has been an essential element of gay men's relationship to musical comedy.

For example, *Hedwig and the Angry Inch*, with its brilliant, hard-driving rock score, is a contemporary gay version of the traditional diva musical. A rock concert *cum* autobiography, *Hedwig* tells the story of a German transsexual who aspires to being a rock diva.

A more conventional book musical, *Closer to Heaven* combines several aspects of musical theater popular with gay men. In essence a show-business biography, the musical tells the story of Straight Dave, a young man from Ireland, who gets a job as a dancer in a London gay club whose shows are presided over by a hilarious larger-than-life transsexual diva. Straight Dave discovers he is not as straight as he thought, comes out, and becomes a successful singer.

Amid the powerful songs and humor, *Closer to Heaven* is a hard-hitting look at the sometimes destructive marriage of drugs and club culture for young gay men. The musical posits the possibility of a gay male star to rival, and perhaps transcend, the appeal of the traditional musical diva. However, the most theatrically powerful character is the transsexual diva, who has the best lines and the most enjoyable musical numbers.

Although mostly set in eighteenth-century London's gay male culture, *Mother Clap's Molly House* features another diva role, a shrewd London woman who gains wealth and personal empowerment from running a "molly house," a gay club. Mother Clap, brilliantly portrayed in the original production by Deborah Findlay, is a direct descendant of Angela Lansbury's Mrs. Lovett in *Sweeney Todd* and Carol Channing's Dolly Levi in *Hello, Dolly!*

Closer to Heaven did not find an audience beyond its core gay constituency, and gay men in London do not seem as invested in musical theater as gay men in American cities. *Mother Clap's Molly House* had a successful though limited run in repertory at London's Royal National Theatre.

The Revue

Musicals whose primary appeal is to a gay audience tend to be intimate productions. The revue, a satirical mix of comedy and song, once a mainstay of the larger commercial theater, has proven to be a viable form for gay audiences.

Robert Schrock's *Naked Boys Singing* (1998), for example, is a small-scaled revue, representing the popularity of cabaret with gay audiences. As in many gay-themed revues (such as the compilation show *The Gay Nineties*, 1995, and Eric Lane Barnes's *Fairy Tales*, 1997), the songs in *Naked Boys Singing* satirize aspects of urban gay life. The "Gratuitous Nudity" celebrated in the title and opening song is a popular, some would say essential (for box office success), aspect of gay theater.

Among successful gay revues, the wittiest have been the work of the late Howard Crabtree, whose outlandish costume designs inspired *Whoop-Dee-Doo* (1993) and *When Pigs Fly* (1996).

Musical Films

For many gay men during the golden age of the musical, Broadway was out of reach geographically and economically, but from the early 1930s until the mid-1960s, Hollywood offered a steady stream of musical films, some of which have been particularly susceptible to gay readings.

In his enormously successful series of films with Ginger Rogers in the 1930s, which boast superb scores by Irving Berlin, Jerome Kern, and George Gershwin, Fred Astaire was surrounded by a group of supporting players who certainly could be read as gay: Eric Blore's eyeball-rolling, lisping queens, Edward Everett Horton's prissy milquetoasts, Erik Rhodes's flamboyant portrayals of men who never get the girl and do not seem to care, and Helen Broderick's butch sidekicks.

Of course, the classic 1939 film *The Wizard of Oz* has played a special role in gay culture: For years, gay men referred to each other in code as "friends of Dorothy."

During the 1940s, the unit at MGM that produced *The Wizard of Oz* and followed it with a string of outstanding musicals was known as "Freed's Fairies," because producer Arthur Freed had gathered such an array of talented gay men as directors, choreographers, composers, arrangers, and designers.

In the 1950s and 1960s, wide-screen epic musicals offered audiences classic diva turns by Judy Garland (*A Star Is Born*, 1954) Gwen Verdon (*Damn Yankees*, 1958), and Barbra Streisand (*Funny Girl*, 1968).

In 2000, *The Sound of Music* (1965), hardly a film that could be considered gay, was resurrected as a camp classic and, with the lyrics superimposed on the print, became for the London gay community the sort of costume party/audience participation event *The Rocky Horror Picture Show* had been for teenagers twenty years before.

Although the film musical seems to be a dead genre and musical theater no longer holds a central position in popular culture and popular music, the musical nevertheless holds an important place in the history of gay men.

It may be no accident that the recent film of the Kander and Ebb musical *Chicago* (2002), which has been acclaimed as the best film musical in years, is the product of the collaboration of several out gay men, including director Rob Marshall, screenwriter Bill Condon, and executive producers Neil Meron and Craig Zadan. All four have spoken of the crucial significance of musicals in their own lives from an early age, almost in the same terms in which gay men and lesbians frequently speak of their early awareness of their sexual difference.

—*John M. Clum*

Bibliography

Clum, John M. *Something for the Boys: Musical Theater and Gay Culture.* New York: St. Martin's 1999.

———. *Still Acting Gay: Male Homosexuality and Modern Drama.* New York: Palgrave, 2000.

Giltz, Michael. "Confessions of Chicago's Gay Mafia." www.advocate.com/html/stories/879/879_chicago.asp

Koestenbaum, Wayne. *The Queen's Throat: Opera, Homosexuality, and the Mystery of Desire.* New York: Poseidon Press, 1993.

Miller, D. A. *Place for Us: Essay on the Broadway Musical.* Cambridge, Mass.: Harvard University Press, 1998.

Mordden, Ethan. *Beautiful Mornin': The Broadway Musical in the 1940s.* New York: Oxford University Press, 1999.

———. *Broadway Babies: The People Who Made the Broadway Musical.* New York: Oxford University Press, 1988.

———. *Coming up Roses: The Broadway Musical in the 1950s.* New York: Oxford University Press, 1998.

———. *Make Believe: The Broadway Musical in the 1920s.* New York: Oxford University Press, 1997.

———. *Open a New Window: The Broadway Musical in the 1960s.* New York: Palgrave, 2001.

See also

Divas; Cabarets and Revues; Ashman, Howard; Bennett, Michael; Bernstein, Leonard; Coward, Sir Noël; Edens, Roger; Finn, William; Garland, Judy; Hart, Lorenz; Herman, Jerry; Kander, John, and Fred Ebb; Lane, Nathan; Novello, Ivor; Porter, Cole; Shaiman, Marc, and Scott Wittman; Sondheim, Stephen; Tune, Tommy; Wright, Robert, and George "Chet" Forrest

n

Near, Holly   (b. 1949)

THE ACTIVIST, SINGER, AND SONGWRITER HOLLY NEAR has been a tremendous influence in the formation and promotion of the women's music movement. Popular among lesbian feminists in the 1970s and still changing and growing today, the prolific Near founded the alternative record label Redwood Records in 1972 to promote music from feminist and politically conscious artists worldwide. To date, she has released twenty albums of her own.

Born to political activist parents in rural Ukiah, California, Near grew up with two sisters in a supportive, liberal family environment. She demonstrated an early proclivity for performance and began singing publicly at the age of eight, going on to act in local talent shows and, later, theater productions.

In her early adulthood she broke into film and television, appearing on such shows as *All in the Family*, *Mod Squad*, and *The Partridge Family*. Her film credits include *Cult of the Damned* (1969), the John Cassavetes film *Minnie and Moskowitz* (1971), and *Slaughterhouse Five* (1972).

She also appeared on Broadway in the original production of *Hair* (1969) and toured the Pacific with Jane Fonda, Donald Sutherland, and other performers in an anti–Vietnam War show called *FTA (Free the Army)* in 1971.

Near's passionate commitment to social change was truly awakened at UCLA, where she enrolled in 1967. This commitment led her to focus her artistic talents primarily on politically themed music.

Near began writing music, and soon formed her label Redwood Records, which was created specifically to release her first album, *Hang in There* (1973). Redwood came into existence because major labels told Near that her lyrics were simply too political. From the start, her folksy songwriting straightforwardly addressed such issues as gay rights, feminism, pacifism, and racism.

Near's pioneering work in helping to create the women's music genre distinguishes her from other political singers. She toured continually in support of the peace movement and other causes, but soon became especially associated with the women's movement and with women's music. She performed at the first Michigan Womyn's Music Festival in 1976; and there she outed herself as a lesbian.

One of the consequences of Near's coming out was that Redwood became a lesbian feminist label. Near's parents had been helping to run Redwood, but they turned it over to Holly and the women who would become her business partners, and the company took its place alongside the legendary Olivia Records as one of the most important alternative record labels.

However, Near's lesbian identification veered toward the political rather than the wholly personal, and she never felt entirely comfortable with lesbian feminist separatism. She had had heterosexual relationships in the past, and when she became involved with men again she was initially met with distrust by many in the women's music community.

Despite Near's reluctance to label her sexual orientation at all, she worked to regain the trust of the women's music community by her unflagging commitment to lesbian issues and the ongoing use of lesbian themes in her work. "Except for the purpose of inviting people out of isolation or for the purpose of defense," Near said in a recent interview, "I try to avoid self-definition through group identity."

In her autobiography, Near comments that her idea of lesbianism is not a narrow one defined simply by sexual experience or preference. "My lesbianism is not linked to sexual preference," she writes. "For me, it is part of my world view, part of my passion for women and central in my objection to male domination."

Whatever her views on self-definition, Near's adamantly feminist views, along with her continual promotion of gay and lesbian rights and culture, make her an important and accepted part of the movement.

Although many of her songs use genderless lyrics in an attempt to appeal broadly across all sexual and gender barriers, Near also writes songs that specifically celebrate lesbian love (perhaps most famously, "Simply Love") and lesbianism itself (as in "She").

Holly Near, photographed in concert by Mike Rogers.

But it is probably no accident that her best-known song is the inclusive anthem "Singing for Our Lives," with the moving refrain "We are Gay and Straight together... / We are old and young together... / We are a gentle loving people / And we are singing, singing for our lives."

Near's recent albums include a compilation called *Simply Love: The Women's Music Collection*—which features selections from her work over the last twenty-five years as well as that of other classic women's music artists such as Alix Dobkin, Meg Christian, and Cris Williamson—and her solo record *Edge* (2000). Both were released on Near's own Calico Tracks music label, established after the demise of Redwood Records in 1993.

In addition to her musical accomplishments, Near is the author of a children's book entitled *The Great Peace March* (1997). Her autobiography was published in 1990.

Near's awards and honors are numerous: She has been recognized by the ACLU, the National Lawyers Guild, and the National Organization for Women, and was chosen as *Ms.* magazine's 1985 Woman of the Year. Her pioneering work with lesbian and feminist music earned her the 2000 Legends of Women's Music Award.

Near continues to tour extensively and to teach performance and songwriting classes.

—Teresa Theophano

BIBLIOGRAPHY

Cannon, Liz. "Holly Near." *Gay & Lesbian Biography.* Michael J. Tyrkus, ed. Detroit: St. James, 1997. 337–340.

Near, Holly, with Derk Richardson. *Singer in the Storm...Fire in the Rain.* New York: William Morrow, 1990.

Wentworth, Shannon. "Holly Near shares her wisdom on marriage, music and aging." http://content.gay.com/channels/arts/musiccorner/010420_near_holly.html

www.hollynear.com

SEE ALSO

Women's Music; Popular Music; Women's Music Festivals; Choruses and Bands; Christian, Meg; Sweet Honey in the Rock; Williamson, Cris

Nijinsky, Vaslav   (1890–1950)

ONE OF THE GREATEST DANCERS IN THE HISTORY OF ballet, Vaslav Fomich Nijinsky almost single-handedly reasserted the primacy of male dancers in ballet after a long period of decline. A radically innovative choreographer, the full extent of whose genius is only now being recognized, he embodied the sensuality and sexual ambiguity associated with the distinctive new art of the twentieth century.

Nijinsky was born on March 12, 1890, in the Russian city of Kiev, the son of Polish dancers who toured Russia as guest artists. He had already performed on stage with his parents when, at the age of ten, he was admitted to the St. Petersburg Imperial School of Ballet. There, as a ward of the Czar, he also received an excellent academic education.

Sexually precocious, he was reprimanded for masturbating, thus presaging his amazing autoerotic performance onstage in his ballet *L'Après-midi d'un faune* (1912).

Nijinsky was a brilliant ballet student; in 1907, after his graduation, he joined the Imperial ballet as a soloist, a rare achievement. He also fell in love with Prince Pavel Dimitrievitch Lvov, a wealthy nobleman in his early forties and himself an athlete.

The prince provided Nijinsky with an apartment, a splendid wardrobe, and a magnificent diamond ring; and he also assisted Nijinsky's mother, who had been living in marginal poverty.

When the Prince cooled toward him, Nijinsky had a brief liaison with another nobleman, Count Tishkievitch, but, he wrote, "I loved the prince, not the count."

Nijinsky then met his match in the dynamic, thirty-five-year-old Sergei Diaghilev and joined the ballet company Diaghilev was preparing to take to Paris in 1909, the Ballets Russes. Nijinsky was the star attraction of their sensational success and was soon dubbed *"le dieu de la danse."*

Nijinsky and Diaghilev became lovers, and Diaghilev used all his resources to create ballets designed to highlight Nijinsky's phenomenal artistry and sexual magnetism. For example, his roles as the Golden Slave in *Schéhérazade* (1910) and as the androgynous scent of the rose in *Le Spectre de la rose* (1911) displayed the dancer's talent and charisma.

Diaghilev also encouraged Nijinsky to choreograph ballets, giving him the finest dancers to work with and unprecedented amounts of rehearsal time. The four ballets that Nijinsky created for Diaghilev, *L'Après-midi d'un faune* (1912), *Le Sacre du printemps* (1913), *Jeux* (1913), and *Till Eulenspiegel* (1916), were box-office failures but are now considered, by virtue of their technical innovations, to be the foundation of modern dance.

Nijinsky's ballets and the roles he danced are especially notable for their exploration of sexuality. Indeed, they were as scandalous for their sexual themes as for their radical balletic experimentations. Voyeurism, sexual primitivism, bisexuality, autoeroticism, and sexual ambiguity are all features of his work. Moreover, Nijinsky's own sexual charisma, and poetic acting, contributed powerfully to the erotic resonances of his performances.

In 1913, while on a tour to South America, Nijinsky impulsively married a young Hungarian woman, Romola Pulsky, who had pursued him throughout Europe. The marriage ended his relationship with Diaghilev, who was outraged by the betrayal.

Vaslav Nijinsky.

At that time, there were no companies remotely comparable to Diaghilev's, so the split with his former lover left the dancer, soon encumbered by a child as well as a wife, with no way to pursue his career. The stress was intensified by the outbreak of World War I, which found him in Budapest. As a Russian citizen in Hungary, and therefore an enemy alien and prisoner of war, Nijinsky was unable to dance at all.

Despite the war, Diaghilev arranged a tour of the Ballets Russes to the United States. He was also able to effect Nijinsky's release from Hungary to rejoin the company. Diaghilev met the dancer, his wife, and baby daughter upon their arrival in New York City.

The two men kissed, and Nijinsky thrust his baby daughter into Diaghilev's arms, an action that infuriated his wife, who proceeded to make life unbearable for both men. As a result, Diaghilev returned to Europe, leaving the company to struggle across North America under Nijinsky's reluctant and inept management.

Later in Spain, Diaghilev again invited Nijinsky to rejoin the company, but again Romola thwarted any reconciliation. The strain on Nijinsky was intense. His career in ruins, he recognized that his marriage had been a grave error. He was also depressed by the war and began to sympathize with revolutionaries in their loathing of materialism.

Nijinsky may at this time have receded into delusion. Romola committed him to a mental institution, where drugs and experimental shock treatments (perhaps administered in an attempt to "cure" his homosexuality as well as his depression) effectively destroyed him.

He lived, like a melancholy ghost, shuttled between private homes and institutions, until April 8, 1950, when he died of renal failure in London.

—Douglas Blair Turnbaugh

Bibliography

Buckle, Richard. *Nijinsky*. London: Weidenfeld and Nicolson, 1971.

Nijinska, Bronislava. *Early Memoirs*. New York: Holt, Rinehart and Winston, 1981.

Nijinsky, Vaslav. *The Diary of Vaslav Nijinsky*. New York: Farrar, Straus and Giroux, 1995.

Ostwald, Peter. *Vaslav Nijinsky: A Leap into Madness*. New York: Carol Publishing, 1991.

See also

Dance; Ballet; Ballets Russes; Béjart, Maurice; Diaghilev, Sergei

Novello, Ivor   (1893–1951)

Show-business renaissance man extraordinaire, Ivor Novello not only composed the scores of musical comedies but also acted in films, while dominating the London stage as a playwright and handsome romantic leading man for three decades.

He was born David Ivor Novello Davies in Cardiff, Wales, on January 15, 1893. His mother was a choir director and celebrated vocal coach. Through her, young Novello developed his deep interest in music and by age fifteen had published his first song.

He attended Magdalen College, Oxford, where he was a chorister. He served in World War I, first as an entertainer in France, then as a pilot in the Royal Naval Air Service. During the war, he composed scores for several musical comedies, but his biggest hit came with the patriotic song "Keep the Home Fires Burning" (1914).

Novello's persona was that of a handsome bachelor made for romantic melodrama and adventure. As such, he dominated the English stage from the 1920s until his death in 1951, rivaled only by another notably versatile actor/writer/composer, Noël Coward.

The lesbian writer and socialite Mercedes de Acosta, in her memoir *Here Lies the Heart* (1960), described

Novello's beauty and élan: "A uniquely handsome man, his sensitive face had perfectly balanced features, the dark eyes beautifully cut into it and set off by black and shining hair. He wore his uniform with style and dash and altogether looked enchanting."

Novello made his film acting debut in *The Call of the Blood* (*L'Appel du Sang*, 1919), followed by *Miarka: the Daughter of the Bear* (*Miarka, Fille de L'Ourse*, 1920), both produced in France.

Novello debuted on stage in London in *Deburau* (1921). He then starred on-screen in *Carnival* (1921), *The Bohemian Girl* (1922), *The Man Without Desire* (1923), and D. W. Griffith's *The White Rose* (1923).

A homosexual with no desire to become a family man, Novello thrived professionally in multiple careers. His stint as playwright, and frequent actor of his own words, took off in 1924 when he wrote and performed in *The Rat*. Back on-screen, he acted against type, playing a psychopath in Alfred Hitchcock's *The Lodger* (1926).

Other screen credits include *The Vortex* (1927), from a Noël Coward play; *Downhill* (1927), again for Hitchcock; and *The Constant Nymph* (1928). These were followed by stage runs of *Symphony in Two Flats* (1930), *The Truth Game* (1930), and *I Lived with You* (1932).

The press linked him romantically to *Bohemian Girl* costar Gladys Cooper, but the real love of his life was actor Robert Andrews, with whom he lived from 1917 until his death in 1951.

Novello never hid his homosexuality through marriage or denial, but his women fans adored him anyway, primarily for his striking good looks and remarkable stage presence.

His sophisticated and urbane social circle was peopled with leading homosexuals in the arts, including Noël Coward, Clifton Webb, and Somerset Maugham.

It is likely that the open secret of Novello's homosexuality played a part when a notoriously homophobic judge sentenced him to a month's imprisonment during World War II for evading wartime restrictions on the use of gasoline.

In 1931, Novello went to Hollywood and cowrote several film scripts, including *Mata Hari* (1931) and *Tarzan, the Ape Man* (1932), but he preferred the theater to movies.

In addition to tackling Shakespeare with *Henry V* in 1938, he wrote, composed, and starred in four successful musicals at Drury Lane: *Glamorous Night* (1935), *Careless Rapture* (1936), *Crest of the Wave* (1937), and *The Dancing Years* (1939).

In the late 1930s, British theater critic W. A. Darlington remarked that "without Mr. Novello, Drury Lane is a white elephant; with him it is a gold mine. He writes plays, composes music and acts the principal male parts. Anybody who can do this successfully is a craftsman of the highest order."

Novello's work is rarely revived, as his unashamedly romantic style is far out of fashion. Perhaps it is time for rediscovery. He was amazingly prolific, publishing 250 songs, fourteen plays and eight musicals, in addition to maintaining an active career as an actor.

Ivor Novello died in London on March 6, 1951, from a coronary thrombosis, just four hours after appearing in a performance of *The King's Rhapsody*, a play he wrote. He was fifty-eight.   —*Matthew Kennedy*

BIBLIOGRAPHY

Harding, James. *Ivor Novello*. London: W. H. Allen, 1987.

Macqueen-Pope, Walter James. *Ivor, The Story of an Achievement: A Biography of Ivor Novello*. London: Allen, 1951.

Noble, Peter. *Ivor Novello: Man of the Theatre*. London: Falcon Press, 1951.

Rose, Richard. *Perchance to Dream: The World of Ivor Novello*. London: Leslie Frewin, 1974.

Wilson, Sandy. *Ivor Novello*. London: Michael Joseph, 1975.

SEE ALSO

Musical Theater and Film; Coward, Sir Noël

Nureyev, Rudolf   (1938–1993)

*E*NFANT TERRIBLE, MONSTRE SACRÉ, AND *DIEU DE la danse* are just some of the terms that have been used to describe the incomparable dancer, choreographer, and ballet director Rudolf Nureyev.

Rudolf Hametovich Nureyev was born on a train somewhere in Siberia, about 1,900 miles from Vladivostock, on March 17, 1938. The son of Muslim peasants, he was a small, malnourished, and highly sensitive child, bullied and tormented by other children.

The young Rudolf's proficiency at folk-dancing brought him to the attention of two exiled ballerinas living in Ufa. They gave him classes and introduced him to the opera ballet company there.

When Rudolf's father returned from service in World War II, he regularly beat his son for studying dance. The child dreamed of "a savior who would come, take me by the hand and rescue me from that mediocre life." However, he was rescued not by some prince but by his own protean talent, supported by unyielding willpower.

What seemed an impossible dream of studying ballet at the fabled Kirov school in Leningrad came true. At age seventeen, he enrolled in the Leningrad Ballet School, where he was an outstanding dancer but a rebellious student. He refused to join the Communist youth league, and he studied English privately. After graduation in 1958, he became a soloist with the Kirov Ballet.

Three years later, while on tour with the Kirov Ballet in Paris, he learned that he was to be sent back to the USSR for flouting Soviet security regulations. As a consequence, he sought political asylum in France, making what came to be known as his great "leap to freedom."

He was subsequently convicted of treason in absentia by a secret Soviet trial. He lived most of the rest of his life at risk of being kidnapped or assassinated.

Nureyev's defection made headlines throughout the world. Overnight, he became a superstar. His physical beauty and sexual magnetism, coupled with his athletic ability, excited men and women alike. His seductive personality made him the darling of international society.

Moreover, his bravura dancing, especially his stupendous jumps with multiple turns in the air, and his great risk taking changed the way male ballet dancers danced. His fame and charisma attracted new audiences to the ballet.

Nureyev made his American debut in 1962, appearing to great acclaim on television and with Ruth Page's Chicago Opera Ballet. Later in 1962, he joined London's Royal Ballet as permanent guest artist. In so doing, he revitalized the company. Partnered with Margot Fonteyn, he gave new life to such classics as *Giselle* and *Swan Lake* and introduced contemporary ballets such as Sir Frederick Ashton's *Marguerite and Armand* (1963).

As artistic director, he formed his own touring companies and transformed the national ballet companies of Australia and Canada from provincial to world class.

In 1983, he found the artistic base for which he longed when he became artistic director of the Paris Opera Ballet. He remained in this position until 1989, when he resigned. However, he served as premier choreographer of the Paris Opera Ballet until his death.

Among his most successful works of choreography are his stagings of *Romeo and Juliet*, *Manfred*, and *The Nutcracker*.

Nureyev also choreographed (and codirected) a lavish film ballet of *Don Quixote* (1973). This work has recently been restored and presented as part of PBS's "Great Performances" series.

An indefatigable performer, Nureyev for many years danced almost every day, sometimes with performances back to back. He appeared in cities throughout the world and attracted a large and diverse audience. As a result, he amassed a fortune, which he invested shrewdly, but also spent lavishly on houses and works of art.

One of Nureyev's great contributions to ballet had to do with his sexual openness. Completely comfortable with his own sexuality, Nureyev expended no effort in presenting a heterosexual image onstage or off. Hence, he was able to concentrate on expressing music and choreography as it seemed appropriate to him. His openness helped liberate other male dancers from the obsession with maintaining a heterosexual image.

Nureyev's sex life was as legendary—and frenetic—as his dancing. His sexual partners ranged from hustlers to the rich and famous. The large size of his penis was not only the subject of gossip, but was also confirmed by photographs taken by Richard Avedon.

Nureyev's most intense affair was with the Danish dancer Erik Bruhn (1928–1986). Bruhn possessed an elegant, refined, classical style, quite different from Nureyev's feral qualities. Yet, in 1961, Nureyev felt that Bruhn was the only living dancer who had anything to teach him.

He sought out the older dancer and fell in love with him. Although the dour Bruhn responded physically to Nureyev, the intense and turbulent relationship that ensued was not a happy one, perhaps because Bruhn suffered from professional jealousy and anxiety. As Nureyev's star rose, Bruhn became reclusive and alcoholic.

The dancers' physical relationship ended in the mid-1960s, but Nureyev never ceased loving Bruhn.

Nureyev also had a long-term relationship with director and archivist Wallace Potts in the 1970s. In 1978, Nureyev was briefly infatuated with a young dancer, Robert Tracy. Tracy moved into Nureyev's New York apartment, where he stayed until evicted thirteen years later, treated, as he said, "like a lackey."

Nureyev and Tracy were both diagnosed with the AIDS virus in 1983. When he learned that the dancer had left him nothing in his will, Tracy filed a palimony suit against Nureyev's estate and received a settlement of about $600 thousand.

Nureyev died in Paris of AIDS-related complications on January 6, 1993. He left the bulk of his fortune to establish foundations to promote dance and medical research.

The greatest dancer of his time, Nureyev thrilled millions of people with his artistry. He also gave the world a new and glamorous image of a sexually active gay man.

—*Douglas Blair Turnbaugh*

BIBLIOGRAPHY

Bland, Alexander. *The Nureyev Image*. London: Studio Vista, 1977.

Boris, Mario. *Rudolf Nooreev*. Paris: Editions Plume, 1993.

Nureyev, Rudolf. *An Autobiography*. London: Holder and Stoughton, 1962.

Solway, Diane. *Nureyev: His Life*. New York: William Morrow, 1998.

Watson, Peter. *Nureyev: A Biography*. London: Hodder and Stoughton, 1994.

SEE ALSO

Dance; Ballet; Ashton, Sir Frederick; Bruhn, Erik; Van Dantzig, Rudi

Opera

OPERA, AN ECLECTIC SYNTHESIS OF VOICE, DRAMA, music, costume, visual arts, and spectacle, has played an integral role in queer culture since its development in seventeenth-century Venice.

As opera intermingles the sublime and the absurd, and has unabashedly embraced high artifice, unfettered emotion, melodrama, and improbable, convoluted plots, it shares many of the qualities that define queer sensibility, through a combination of idealistic romantic identification and camp travesty.

Holding up an allegorical and larger-than-life mirror to the incongruous experience of many gay men and lesbians, opera revels in cross-dressing, illicit romance, intrigue, gender-bending, despair and triumph, passion and death, and the cult of the diva.

The Origins of Opera

Opera, or *dramma per musica*, developed in early-seventeenth-century Venice, where a combination of Renaissance humanism, anticlericalism, and, perhaps most important, a large, mixed public audience willing to pay for entertainments that appealed to popular tastes sustained and informed this new genre. Hence, opera could exercise some autonomy from Church censorship and aristocratic patronage, resulting in plots that celebrated the human rather than the divine and that punctured caste hierarchies.

Typically, these operatic plots, replete with intrigue, reversals of fortune, Byzantine complication, and masquerade, valorized human passion and created an idealized form of romantic heroism. While many of the plots featured contemporary characters and subjects, most were based on Greco-Roman sources, given a popular, deflationary, or erotic twist. For instance, Pier Francesco Cavalli's *La Callisto* (1651), Giacomo Castoreo's *Pericle Effeminato* (*Effeminate Pericles*, 1653), and Aurelio Aureli's *Alcibiade* (1680) utilized ancient Greco-Roman figures or plots to legitimize representations of male and female homoeroticism, though numerous detractors deemed them "immoral."

Claudio Monteverdi (1567–1643), the most renowned composer of early Venetian opera, developed stylistic conventions to express "affections," particularly desire, rage, madness, grief, and despair, in female and male characters alike. The individual, and her overpowering personal emotions and conflicts, was thus culturally valorized through the aesthetic vehicle of musical virtuosity, which could transform madness into sublime or quasi-divine possession.

Such artistically controlled loss of control was featured in operas such as Monteverdi's *La Finta Pazza* (*The Feigned Madness of Licori*, 1627), Francesco Manelli's *La Maga Fulminata* (*The Raging Sorceress*, 1638),

Cavalli's *Ercole Amante* (*Hercules in Love*, 1662), and Antonio Vivaldi's *Orlando Furioso* (*Orlando Enraged*, 1713), to cite but a few.

That emotion could overwhelm both female and male characters in this new art form contributed to the gender-bending characteristic of opera in the following centuries.

Gender-Bending and Cross-Dressing

From its beginnings, opera has not merely allowed but also in many instances encouraged cross-gendered casting. Although most operatic gender-bending involves women playing male roles, in the earliest operas male singers also at times performed female roles for various reasons, including legal strictures against women performing in public and the vocal ranges of available performers.

For example, in Monteverdi's best-known opera, *La Favola d'Orfeo* (*The Fable of Orpheus*, 1607), the role of Orpheus, the mythological poet and musician, has been sung by either a soprano or tenor. His later opera *L'incoronazione di Poppea* (*The Coronation of Poppea*, 1643), which narrates the rise of Poppea from Roman courtesan to empress, features numerous roles that have been sung by either male or female performers.

Poppea's lovers, Ottone and Nero, have been sung by female contraltos, male castrati, or male tenors, as has suited the custom or taste of the time. The comic role of her nurse, Arnalta, conversely, has been more frequently performed by a tenor. The one decidedly male voice in this opera, the philosopher Seneca, is condemned to death, to the great rejoicing of the other characters. (Indeed, opera is antithetical to the stoical self-restraint Seneca championed.)

Such artistically self-conscious gender play also informs the works of eighteenth-century opera composers—for example, George Frideric Handel (1685–1759) and Christoph Wilibald Gluck (1714–1787).

This period also witnessed the zenith of the castrati, male singers who were castrated before puberty to retain their high tessitura, or vocal range. Possessing voices of fabled power and angelic purity, such legendary castrati as Senesino, Farinelli, and Caffarelli enthralled audiences and were the eighteenth-century equivalent of international superstars.

However paradoxically, castrati usually played heroic and "masculine" roles as generals, gods, and emperors, though their capacity to transcend conventional gender assignment through their vocal prowess associated the most powerful human beings with the androgynous and quasi-divine.

Handel, himself probably gay, remains best known for his *Messiah* (1741), but he concentrated much of his artistic energy on distinctly profane operas that took gender-bending and cross-dressing to new heights of confusion.

For instance, the lead role of his *Serse* (*Xerxes*, 1738) was originally written for the castrato Caffarelli, while two of the other male characters were played by female mezzo-sopranos. With the eclipse of the castrati, female mezzo-sopranos now play the roles originally written for castrati, which means that modern productions of *Serse* and many other Baroque operas have become, for visual and aural purposes, lesbian romantic and political melodramas.

Even before the practice of castrating prepubescent male singers was gradually abolished toward the end of the eighteenth century, composers such as Wolfgang Amadeus Mozart (1756–1791) created so-called "trouser" or *en travesti* roles specifically for female mezzo-sopranos and contraltos, who usually played adolescent males. This new role remained popular from the late eighteenth through the early twentieth century.

Mozart's most notable trouser role, Cherubino in *Le Nozze di Figaro* (*The Marriage of Figaro*, 1786), worships Countess Almaviva but also seduces Barbarina, the gardener's daughter. Mozart thus uses gender play in his comic political assault on aristocratic privilege.

The nineteenth century witnessed an increasing number of female singers in male roles—the heroic "armor roles" once the province of castrati or young romantic heroes.

Gioacchino Antonio Rossini (1792–1868) made spectacular developments in the "armor roles" in works such as *Tancredi* (1813), *La Donna del Lago* (*The Lady of the Lake*, 1819), and *Semiramide* (1823). In the latter, Semiramide, Queen of Babylon, falls in love with the mezzo-soprano Arsace, commander of her army and also, indeed, her long-lost son by Nino, the husband she had conspired to murder. In the meantime, Arsace becomes enamored of the Indian Princess Azema, and seeks vengeance for the murder of "his" father.

While nominally representing heterosexual intrigue, *Semiramide* marks the moment in the history of opera when elaborate gender-bending devolves into the incoherent, unconsciously camp, or kitsch spectacle of an adulterous and murderous woman falling in love with a girl in armor who is not only her actual son but also in love with another woman and out to avenge "his" father's murder by killing Semiramide's former paramour.

Although Rossini's operas fell out of fashion by the mid-nineteenth century, the use of female singers in the roles of young male lovers continued even into the early twentieth century in many notable operas from Vicenzo Bellini's *I Capuletti ed I Montecchi* (1830) to Richard Strauss's *Der Rosenkavalier* (1911), perhaps the first opera to present an explicit love scene performed by two women.

Over the course of the nineteenth century, opera became increasingly concerned with political themes of nationalism, often resulting in heterosexual romance plots functioning as microcosmic representation of political struggles. This is not to say that there were no homoerotic aspects in nineteenth-century opera; love between two men or two women is a crucial factor in such operas as Bellini's *Norma* (1831), Giuseppe Verdi's *Don Carlo* (1867), Georges Bizet's *Les Pêcheurs de Perles* (1863), and Richard Wagner's *Tannhäuser* (1845) and *Parsifal* (1882).

Twentieth-Century Opera

The twentieth century witnessed three major developments in opera relevant to gay men and lesbians: the representation of open gay and lesbian operatic characters, the cult of the diva, and camp treatments of traditional operatic plots and themes. Moreover, antibourgeois works such as Strauss's *Salome* (1905, based on the Wilde play) and *Elektra* (1909) early in the century signaled a new openness in dealing with sex and sexuality.

Also of significance, gay modernist composers such as Maurice Ravel (1875–1937) and Virgil Thomson (1896–1989) typically abandoned traditional heterosexual plots in favor of modes that explore the psychological, metaphysical, and social parameters of individuality and community, often emphasizing themes that are at least implicitly relevant to the gay and lesbian experience.

For example, Ravel's *L'Enfant et les Sortilèges* (*The Child and the Enchantments*, 1925), with libretto by Colette and set in a magical child's world in which injured animals and objects become speaking subjects, considers the relationships among mother identification, destructiveness, creativity, and ethical responsibility. Thomson collaborated with Gertrude Stein to produce two highly original works, *Four Saints in Three Acts* (1934) and *The Mother of Us All* (1947), the latter presenting the struggles of the feminist movement in America.

Implicitly gay and lesbian concerns also surface in the work of Francis Poulenc. In his compelling *Dialogues des Carmélites* (1957), Poulenc returns to the scene of the French Revolution to explore how a community of women, the Carmelite nuns of Compiègne, respond to their scapegoating and martyrdom at the hands of the all-male revolutionary authorities.

Gay and Lesbian Characters in Opera

Alban Berg's *Lulu* (1937) presents the first self-identified queer character in opera, the Countess Martha Geschwitz. Lulu, an attractive if amoral femme fatale, has many suitors, but only the noble and self-sacrificial Geschwitz seems genuinely to love her, and emerges as the only admirable character in an otherwise selfish and brutal social realm.

The gay composer Benjamin Britten (1913–1976) wrote three operas that, like *Lulu*, deal with the social exclusion, scapegoating, and death of characters who either are or are perceived to be gay.

Peter Grimes (1945) concerns a misanthropic fisherman suspected of murder and pederasty. *Billy Budd* (1951)—with libretto by E. M. Forster and Eric Crozier, after Herman Melville's novella—presents a beautiful sailor who is sacrificed, in Christlike fashion, because his evil superior, Claggart, cannot tolerate his romantic and sexual longings for the boy. *Death in Venice* (1973), based on Thomas Mann's novella, sustains Britten's interest in the relationships among youth, gay desire, and death, as the dying writer Aschenbach becomes hopelessly infatuated with the beautiful if ever inaccessible adolescent Tadzio.

In contrast to such modernist queer tragedies, Leonard Bernstein's *A Quiet Place* (1983) makes a bisexual male character the symbol of social mediation and conflict resolution, while Libby Larsen and Bonnie Grice's *Mrs. Dalloway* (1993), based on Virginia Woolf's novel of repressed homoerotic desire, reinvokes queer modernist concerns.

In the recent opera *Harvey Milk* (1995), composer Stewart Wallace pays tribute to a heroic pioneer who, in 1977, became the first openly gay man to win elected office in the United States. Milk was assassinated the following year, along with San Francisco Mayor George Moscone, by Dan White, a former police officer and city supervisor. White, in his infamous "Twinkie defense," claimed that junk food had undermined his reason, and his seven-year sentence was widely perceived as reflecting societal homophobia. (White committed suicide after his release.) Wallace's opera is perhaps the first operatic representation of a historical gay tragic hero.

The increasing visibility of gay and lesbian artists and audiences in recent years has also affected the world of opera. Not only have earlier Baroque works been revived, but productions of mainstream operas have explored the homoerotic possibilities of familiar and ostensibly heterosexual plots. Newer compositions, such as John Corigliano's *The Ghosts of Versailles* (1991), combine the pleasures of camp masquerade with serious considerations of issues of personal liberty, sexuality, scapegoating, and misogyny.

Diva Worship and Camp Opera

While queers, like opera fans in general, have probably worshipped the larger-than-life figure of the diva since opera's emergence as a popular art form, in the twentieth century gay and lesbian identification with or adulation of such figures was documented for the first time and became an explicit feature of queer culture.

For various reasons, early-twentieth-century lesbian opera fans adulated Emma Calve, Mary Garden, Olive Fremstad, Geraldine Farrar, and Kathleen Ferrier.

The lesbian novelist Willa Cather saw in Fremstad, the renowned Wagnerian soprano who had also dared to play the title role in the American premiere of Richard

Strauss's *Salome,* the embodiment of the serious woman artist "married" to her art and to artistic perfection. Mary Garden, who became the "directa" of the Chicago Lyric Opera, specialized in *en travesti* roles and, for decades, exerted considerable power in the operatic world.

Gay male culture has produced the "opera queen," a fan notable for his fetishistic, indeed perhaps obsessive, knowledge of opera plots, productions, and recordings, along with an equally extensive lore of gossip and speculation about the scandals, rivalries, romances, breakdowns, and triumphs in the personal lives of operatic divas.

Onstage and offstage converge in this extravagant figuration of the diva, who is perceived by her devotees as a quasi-divine mediatrix, both redeemed and imperiled by the extremities of her existence. Maria Callas (1923–1977), the Greek American dramatic coloratura soprano, became perhaps the most magnetic object of such worship in the twentieth century and, to a great extent, remains so, even more than a quarter century after her death.

The extraordinary artistic virtuosity required to sing opera, on the one hand, coupled with the high artifice, emotional extravagance, and melodrama of this art form on the other, produces a genre that veers between aesthetic sublimity and camp absurdity. For modern audiences, the ornate plots and elaborate gender-bendings of Baroque opera, for example, can provide as much camp pleasure as parodic treatments of nineteenth-century "serious" opera.

The all–gay male La Gran Scena opera company, founded in 1981 by artistic director Ira Siff, presents hilarious camp renditions of famous operas but, in keeping with opera's profound commitment to the beauties of the rigorously trained human voice, insists on quality singing. Siff, as a member of the company, has adopted the camp stage name Vera Galup-Borszkh, and other members bear names such as Fodor Szedan and Kavatina Turner. Also known to his audiences as the "traumatic soprano" or "La Dementia," Siff has poked affectionate fun at the long-suffering heroines of many nineteenth-century operas in his aria "La suicidio."

Although La Gran Scena recently disbanded because, according to Siff, contemporary opera divas no longer display the kind of extravagant excess that enables camp appropriation, queers' long involvement with this art form promises to continue, taking new directions in the ongoing revival of Baroque operas and the creation of new operas with specifically gay and lesbian plots and characters.

—*Corinne E. Blackmer*
—*Patricia Juliana Smith*

BIBLIOGRAPHY

Blackmer, Corinne E., and Patricia Juliana Smith, eds. *En Travesti: Women, Gender Subversion, Opera.* New York and London: Columbia University Press, 1995.

Brett, Philip, Elizabeth Wood, and Gary C. Thomas, eds. *Queering the Pitch: The New Gay and Lesbian Musicology.* New York and London: Routledge, 1994.

Clement, Catherine. *Opera, or the Undoing of Women.* Minneapolis: University of Minnesota Press, 1988.

Dellamora, Richard, and Daniel Fischlin, eds. *The Work of Opera: Genre, Nationhood, and Sexual Difference.* New York: Columbia University Press, 1997.

Heriot, Angus. *The Castrati in Opera.* New York: Da Capo Press, 1974.

Koestenbaum, Wayne. *The Queen's Throat: Opera, Homosexuality, and the Mystery of Desire.* New York: Poseidon Press, 1993.

Leonardi, Susan J., and Rebecca A. Pope. *The Diva's Mouth: Body, Voice, Prima Donna Politics.* New Brunswick, N.J.: Rutgers University Press, 1996.

McClary, Susan. *Feminine Endings: Music, Gender, and Sexuality.* Minneapolis: University of Minnesota Press, 1991.

Mohr, Richard D. *Gay Ideas: Outing and Other Controversies.* Boston: Beacon Press, 1992.

Robinson, Paul A. *Opera, Sex and Other Vital Matters.* Chicago: University of Chicago Press, 2002.

Rosand, Ellen. *Opera in Seventeenth Century Venice: The Creation of a Genre.* Berkeley: University of California Press, 1991.

Solie, Ruth A., ed. *Musicology and Difference: Gender and Sexuality in Music Scholarship.* Berkeley: University of California Press, 1995.

SEE ALSO

Classical Music; Castrati; Divas; Wagnerism; Bernstein, Leonard; Britten, Benjamin; Corigliano, John; Handel, George Frideric; Poulenc, Francis; Ravel, Maurice; Thomson, Virgil

Pansy Division

SAN FRANCISCO–BASED PANSY DIVISION, NOW CONSISTing of Christopher Freeman (b. 1961), Jon Ginoli (b. 1959), Patrick Goodwin (b. 1973), and Luis Illades (b. 1974), was the first rock band entirely composed of gay musicians who sang frankly gay-themed tunes. After a productive period of recording and touring, they had a fallow spell, but have recently reemerged with a new album and a more mature sound.

Guitarist Jon Ginoli and bassist Chris Freeman started the band in 1991. They were accompanied by a drummer, but for the first five years the percussionists came and went with regularity.

Ginoli and Freeman felt doubly marginalized: the rock world was not particularly welcoming to gays, and many in the gay community were less than enthusiastic about punk rock music. They rose to the challenge by writing music that was unabashedly gay and punk and that also showed a sense of humor.

Pansy Division's first album, *Undressed*, which featured titles such as "Fem in a Black Leather Jacket" and "Boyfriend Wanted," appeared in 1993. Thereafter, they put out an album a year until 1998.

The debut album caught the attention of another Bay Area band, Green Day, who signed them as the opening act for their concerts.

The Green Day band members were not gay, but they strongly supported Pansy Division and brought them along on tour for five years. Concert audiences were sometimes hostile to the gay band, however. On several occasions Pansy Division found themselves pelted with objects thrown by the crowd.

Despite the adverse incidents, Pansy Division began winning a devoted fan following with their songs frankly celebrating gay sexuality. They were particularly gratified to receive letters from gay teenagers who had felt isolated or even suicidal but found hope and solace in Pansy Division's positive messages. "Those letters alone make me feel like what we did was worthwhile," Ginoli commented.

One of Pansy Division's constant messages was the importance of practicing safe sex. They not only sang about it but also included information on proper condom use in the materials accompanying their CDs. Ginoli stated, "While our HIV-positive fans loved the fact that we were so life-affirming, we wanted to make sure our HIV-negative listeners stayed negative."

Pansy Division gained a permanent drummer in 1996 when Luis Illades joined the group. Born in Tijuana, Mexico, Illades left home and moved to San Diego at sixteen to escape the homophobia of his homeland (though he says that his own family is supportive of him). He subsequently settled in San Francisco.

Guitarist Patrick Goodwin joined the group in 1997. The two new band members made the group more solid musically, and Pansy Division's 1998 album, *Absurd Pop Song Romance*, moved the band in a new direction—

away from the in-your-face punk style toward a more lyrical Pop sound—while retaining a gay-positive message.

Instead of gaining them new fans, however, the album proved their least successful commercially, and their tour of North America and Europe was fraught with problems. Upon their return to California the discouraged group broke up. The members drifted off to join other bands.

Pansy Division's record label, the independent Lookout! Records, asked the group to reunite and play at a college music festival in late 1999. Although the members were reluctant, they consented and were rewarded with an enthusiastic reception from the audience.

Buoyed by the experience, Pansy Division began practicing and performing together again, sometimes with understudy guitarist Bernard Yin (b. 1964) sitting in for Goodwin, who was also working with another band, Dirty Power.

Their concerts, in which they played both their old standards and new material, drew a mixed response from fans, many of whom came for the classic numbers and were less interested in the band's more mature work. Gay British rocker Tom Robinson, who faced a similar situation, said of Pansy Division's dilemma, "I have a theory that every band fortunate enough to write the songs that become the soundtrack for other people's lives ceases in time to own those songs. They have a responsibility to act as caretakers for that heritage." And they have a responsibility to move on musically as well.

Pansy Division's latest album, *Total Entertainment!*, came out in 2003. The reviewer Nate Cavalieri called their sound "straight-ahead power pop" that departed from both "the simplistic punches of their early days and the power balladeering" of their previous effort. Echoing Robinson, he stated that "diehard queercore fans may bemoan the change," but also noted that "without Pansy Division, those fans wouldn't exist in the first place."

— *Linda Rapp*

BIBLIOGRAPHY

Brown, G. "They Were Gay Before It Was Cool; Pansy Division Broke Barriers 12 Years Ago." *Denver Post*, September 5, 2003.

Cavalieri, Nate. "Pansy Division." *Dallas Observer*, November 27, 2003.

Engardio, Joel P. "Boys' Band: Pansy Division's All-Gay Punk Was a Shocking First. Will Fans Let the Group Escape Its Pioneering Role and Just Make Music?" *SF Weekly*, August 15, 2001.

Pansy Division. www.pansydivision.com

SEE ALSO

Popular Music; Rock Music; Robinson, Tom

Pears, Peter   *(1910–1986)*

THE BRITISH TENOR SIR PETER NEVILLE LUARD PEARS was a highly respected vocalist in opera as well as lieder and choral music whose long and productive career spanned nearly half a century. For forty years he was the life partner of the composer Benjamin Britten, who wrote the leading roles in many of his operas and a number of song cycles with Pears as their intended interpreter.

Their partnership is noteworthy not only for the vast body of music and recordings it produced, but also for the extent to which homosexual subjects figured in their work.

Pears was born in Farnham, Surrey, on June 22, 1910, and studied organ at Hertford College, Oxford. From 1933 to 1934, he attended the Royal College of Music as a voice student, and while there he joined the BBC Singers, with whom he remained until 1938. It was as a member of the BBC Singers that he met Britten in 1936; within the year their relationship and artistic collaboration had begun.

In 1939, as World War II began, Britten and Pears, both of whom declared themselves conscientious objectors, left England for the United States. While there, Britten composed the song cycles *Les Illuminations* (1939), a setting of poems by Arthur Rimbaud; and *Michelangelo Sonnets* (1942), a setting of homoerotic verse by the Renaissance artist. These works were premiered after Britten and Pears returned to England in 1942.

In the same year, Pears made his debut as an operatic singer as Hoffmann in a London production of Offenbach's *Les contes d'Hoffmann*. His popularity grew, and in 1943 he became a leading lyric tenor of the Sadler's Wells Opera, where he developed an extensive repertoire, including the roles of Almaviva in Rossini's *Il barbiere di Siviglia*, Rodolfo in Puccini's *La Bohème*, the Duke in Verdi's *Rigoletto*, Tamino in Mozart's *Die Zauberflöte*, and Ferrando in Mozart's *Così fan tutte*.

Pears's greatest triumph at Sadler's Wells, however, was his creation of the title role of the tortured and possibly homosexual outcast in Britten's *Peter Grimes* (1945).

In 1946, Pears cofounded the English Opera Group with Britten. Within a year the company—and the couple—found a home in Aldeburgh, a small fishing town in Suffolk, where they would subsequently found the Aldeburgh Festival and, in 1972, the Britten-Pears School for the training of young musicians.

Over the next three decades, Pears created many operatic roles that Britten wrote for him, including the title role in *Albert Herring* (1947), Captain Vere in *Billy Budd* (1951), Essex in *Gloriana* (1953), Peter Quint in *The Turn of the Screw* (1954), Flute in *A Midsummer Night's Dream* (1960), the Madwoman in *Curlew River*

(1964), Nebuchadnezzar in *The Burning Fiery Furnace* (1966), the Tempter in *The Prodigal Son* (1968), Sir Philip Wingrave in *Owen Wingrave* (1971), and Aschenbach in *Death in Venice* (1973).

Pears's career after 1946 was not exclusively devoted to Britten's music, however. From 1948 onward, he sang many roles at the Royal Opera House, Covent Garden, and was noted for his performances of songs and choral music by such diverse composers as Bach, Schütz, Purcell, Handel, Mahler, Schubert, and Schumann.

In 1974, Pears made a much-belated debut at the Metropolitan Opera Company, New York, in the first American performance of *Death in Venice*.

Even after Britten's death in 1976, Pears continued his singing career until nearly the age of seventy. He spent the remainder of his life teaching and administering the Britten-Pears School.

Pears was knighted by Queen Elizabeth II in 1977, and died in Aldeburgh on April 3, 1986. He is buried there, next to Britten. —*Patricia Juliana Smith*

BIBLIOGRAPHY

Headington, Christopher. *Peter Pears: A Biography*. London: Faber and Faber, 1992.

Pears, Peter. *The Travel Diaries of Peter Pears: 1936–1978*. Philip Reed, ed. Rochester, N.Y.: Boydell and Brewer, 1999.

SEE ALSO

Classical Music; Opera; Britten, Benjamin; Handel, George Frideric; Poulenc, Francis; Schubert, Franz

Pet Shop Boys

A FORTUITOUS MEETING BETWEEN NEIL FRANCIS Tennant (b. 1954) and Christopher Sean Lowe (b. 1959) in August 1981 led to the formation of the Pet Shop Boys. With Tennant's distinctly British and somewhat effete vocals and Lowe's deft synthesizer-based pop compositions, their creative partnership has given rise to a significant body of work, one central to the field of popular music of the 1980s and 1990s.

The Pet Shop Boys are at once a very fine example and a result of the various experimentations that emerged in the wake of the early 1980s New Wave movement. Moreover, two of their albums, *Disco* (1986) and *Disco 2* (1994), pay homage to a musical genre that is meaningful in terms of gay history and bar culture.

Their entire oeuvre may be seen as a personal documentation and reaction to events that stirred the British gay community in the last two decades of the twentieth century.

The Pet Shop Boys' music engages both traditional themes, such as love and relationships, and socially conscious subjects, such as AIDS and opposition to the notorious Section 28 bill that prohibited the promotion of homosexuality by government bodies in the United Kingdom.

Their first album, *Please* (1986), with its wistful melodies and overarching themes of love, relationships, and unrequited desire, is a pastiche of longing, irony, and camp familiar to all, but perhaps especially to gay, lesbian, and transgender people.

"It's a Sin" (1987) makes a deeply poignant and forceful statement about the Catholic Church's sexual prohibitions and its power to regulate desire.

The duo's music has also brought to the fore issues relating to AIDS. For example, their 1993 album, *Very*, contains two tracks, "Dreaming of the Queen" and "Go West," that confront the loss and despair occasioned by AIDS.

Interestingly, the musical arrangement of "Go West" may be understood as a synecdoche of the effects of AIDS on gay communities. For the first five minutes, Tennant and Lowe cover the Village People's gay anthem in a relentless though somewhat reflective mood, which is followed by two minutes of silence. The pause is broken by a "Postscript," whose tone is utterly somber.

Tennant and Lowe's contribution extends beyond music into the important cultural phenomena of music videos. Some of their music videos are notably homoerotic, as, for example, "Domino Dancing" (1988).

Often they have collaborated with important figures from the visual and performing arts, particularly with fellow gay artists. For example, the late filmmaker Derek Jarman produced the video for "It's a Sin" (1987), as well as other songs. The photographer Bruce Weber created a dramatization of "Being Boring" (1991), while actor and gay rights activist Ian McKellen was prominently featured in the visualization of "Heart" (1988).

Further, the Pet Shop Boys have supported the theme of transgenderism by producing, with vocals from Boy George, a cover of Dave Berry's 1964 ballad "The Crying Game," from Neil Jordan's 1992 film of the same title.

In 1994, Tennant agreed to an interview with the British lifestyle magazine *Attitude*. Without trepidation he revealed what his creative work stated unequivocally: "I could spend several pages discussing 'gay culture,' but for the sake of argument we have contributed a lot. And the simple reason for this is that I have written songs from that point of view. What I'm saying is that I'm gay, and I have written songs from that point of view. So, I mean, I'm being completely honest with you here, but those are the facts of the matter."

—*Eugenio Filice*

BIBLIOGRAPHY

Attig, R. Brian. "The Gay Voice in Popular Music." *Journal of Homosexuality* 21.1 (1991): 185–201.

Burston, P. "Honestly." *Attitude,* August 1994, 62.

Frith, S. *Performing Rites.* Cambridge, Mass.: Harvard University Press, 1996.

Gill, John. *Queer Noises: Male and Female Homosexuality in Twentieth-Century Music.* Minneapolis: University of Minnesota Press, 1995.

Pet Shop Boys. "PSB Chronology": www.petshopboys.co.uk

Robertson, Textor A. "A Close Listening of the Pet Shop Boys' 'Go West.' Review Essay. *Popular Music and Society* 18.4 (Winter 1994): 91–96.

SEE ALSO

Popular Music; Music Video; Musical Theater and Film; Disco and Dance Music; Music and AIDS; Boy George (George O'Dowd); Springfield, Dusty; Village People

Pierce, Charles   (1926–1999)

"**Y**OU CAN CALL ME AN IMPERSONATOR, AN IMPRESsionist, a mimic, or a comic in a dress. But not a drag queen! A drag queen is someone who dresses up and goes to a ball! I'm an entertainer," Charles Pierce told the *New York Post*'s Bob Harrington in 1988.

Before gay culture became more visible in the 1970s, this self-proclaimed male actress was a courageous pioneer. In the clubs where he played (beginning in the 1950s), Pierce took a public, aggressive stance against homophobia in the conviction that lightening-fast wit, a serious attitude, and consummate acting skill could vanquish oppression.

While this camp vaudevillian's repertoire of jokes often seemed between 2,000 and 3,000 years old, his brilliant delivery and dead-on impressions made his act a non-stop laugh fest.

Often veering unexpectedly into lengthy serious monologues by Katharine Hepburn from *Lion in Winter* or *Coco,* or into a stirring rendition of Dietrich's "Illusion," Pierce gave his act a humanity and poignancy often absent in other drag acts. Pierce revered the timing of Jack Benny and Bea Arthur; and many in his audience recognized that beneath the dresses, wigs, and lipstick was a comic mastermind.

As a drag artist, Pierce never aimed for complete illusion in his impersonation of his female icons. Audiences were always aware of the man in Pierce's gallery of women.

In 1990, he called his show "The Legendary Ladies of the Silver Screen: All Talking, All Singing, All Dancing …All Dead." His targets/homages included "turban ladies" such as Norma Shearer, Maria Montez, Gloria Swanson, and Maria Ouspenskaya, with stopover zings at Mae West, Carol Channing, and Barbara Stanwyck.

Born in Watertown, New York, on July 14, 1926, Pierce started his acting training at the legendary Pasadena Playhouse, then split his time between a radio job at home and summer stock in Newport, Rhode Island.

When Arthur Blake (who did impressions of Bette Davis, Charles Laughton, and Tallulah Bankhead) rejected material submitted to him by Pierce, the latter decided to perform the act himself, initially at parties.

His first paying gig was at Altadena, California's, Café La Vie in 1954. Because of laws against crossdressing, Pierce performed in a tux with accessories such as a boa, hats, and pocketbooks. Ann Dee, of Ann's 440 Club in San Francisco, saw Pierce and got him started on the cabaret circuit.

In Florida, at Miami Beach's Red Carpet, Pierce met his future show-biz partner, Rio Dante. With Dante as the "straight man," their act consisted of some lip sync and puppets (the Moppettes—headless puppets that Pierce would put up to his own face and then perform outrageous dialogue). In 1962, the duo opened at San Francisco's Gilded Cage, where they played a record six years.

Other legendary gigs included "saving" the Plush Room in San Francisco's York Hotel in the early 1980s, and lengthy engagements at the Venetian Room of the San Francisco Fairmont Hotel and New York's Top of the Gate and The Ballroom.

Dante was dropped from the act, and for the rest of his career Pierce performed solo—dubbing himself "La Suberba of Transvestivania"—frequently joined by the best musical directors/accompanists in the country: Michael Biagi, Michael Ashton, and Joan Edgar, among others. Michael Feinstein accompanied him at the Studio One Backlot in West Hollywood in 1981.

Pierce not only had difficulty with strict cross-dressing ordinances around the country, but he was sometimes attacked by members of the gay community. In 1980, all sixty members of the San Francisco Lesbian Chorus walked out of a benefit at the Castro Theater when Pierce performed. They demanded a public apology for jokes such as "Liz Taylor has more chins than a Chinese phone book" and an analysis of why Pierce's show was "racist, sexist, classist, and women-hating."

When Pierce "abdicated" from the stage in the mid-1990s, he no doubt sensed that the audience that would recognize his cast of the stars of yesterday was dying out. He introduced an impersonation of Joan Collins into his act, but admitted he could find nothing comic about younger female performers.

He appeared on numerous television shows (not always in drag), including *Fame, Laverne and Shirley, Designing Women, Starsky & Hutch,* and *Love, American Style.*

His films include *Rabbit Test* (1978), *Torch Song Trilogy* (1988), and *Nerds of a Feather* (1990).

He also issued several recordings, including *Live at Bimbo's* (ca. 1972) on the Blue Thumb label, and a video, *Charles Pierce at The Ballroom* (1988).

Pierce also created a successful line of comic greeting cards that featured him in various drag-star personas accompanied by witty one-liners.

"The Master and Mistress of Surprise and Disguise," as he was billed, died of cancer on May 31, 1999, having been weakened by an earlier stroke. He was 72.

Charles Pierce wanted to be remembered as an actor who made his living doing "some really good impressions." His pioneering work as a camp gender illusionist paved the way for Charles Busch, RuPaul, and Lady Bunny, among many others.

—*Bud Coleman*

BIBLIOGRAPHY

"Charles Pierce, 72, Impersonator of Screen Divas." Obituary. *New York Times*, June 3, 1999.

Harrington, Bob. "King of Queens Abdicates." *New York Post*, September 27, 1988.

Mintun, Peter. "Charles Pierce dies at 76 [sic]." *Bay Area Reporter*, June 3, 1999.

Wetzsteon, R. "Private Wives: The Disguises of Sex." *Village Voice*, April 28, 1975, 90.

SEE ALSO

Cabarets and Revues; Drag Shows: Drag Queens and Female Impersonators; Dietrich, Marlene; Feinstein, Michael; RuPaul (RuPaul Andre Charles); Russell, Craig

Popular Music

GAY, LESBIAN, BISEXUAL, AND TRANSGENDERED PERSONS have had tremendous influence on popular music. As artists, muses, producers, composers, publishers, and every role in between, gay men and lesbians have left an indelible impression on the popular consciousness through their contributions to music. Their presence can be found everywhere, from out lesbian Vicki Randle playing percussion and singing in the *Tonight Show* band to two men dressed as cops and kissing in a Marilyn Manson music video.

Popular music has always had a gay and lesbian presence, but it has not always been out in the open. Nor has there been an entirely linear progression from total repression to today's relative openness. For example, several well-known gay men, bisexuals, and lesbians of the 1920s who lived their lives openly were forced back into the closet when social mores shifted. For decades, their sexuality was obscured and hidden.

In the music industry, it is not only the "talent" who are homosexual: David Geffen, founder of Geffen Records, is one of the most successful producers in recording history and one of the wealthiest men in entertainment. Similarly, Jann Wenner, founder of *Rolling Stone* magazine, long considered the rock and roll bible, is now involved in a homosexual relationship.

Nonetheless, popular music remains largely a heterosexual world, and some artists, such as 1970s rocker Joan Jett and late-1980s sensation Neneh Cherry, waited until they were well beyond the height of their popularity before revealing their sexuality to fans.

In recent years, however, musicians such as Michael Stipe of R.E.M., Rob Halford of Judas Priest, Pete Townshend of The Who, and Chuck Panozzo of Styx have come out as gay or bisexual (and, in Panozzo's case, as HIV-positive).

Although many younger artists feel at ease simply to be themselves from the outset of their careers, the biggest stars in popular music are still packaged as heterosexual idols.

Homophobia is stronger in certain musical genres than in others. Country western and rhythm and blues, for example, have had very few gay and lesbian personalities; and in those camps there have been career-ending scandals that centered on rumors of homosexual activity.

Some popular music genres, such as folk and disco, and heterosexual performers, such as Bette Midler and Diana Ross, are associated with gay and lesbian culture because of their popularity with that core audience rather than the sexuality of the performer or the content of the music.

Larger-than-life musical divas—the sobriquet *diva*, meaning goddess, derives from opera, a genre that is also popular with gay men—have a certain over-the-top theatrical appeal that is manifested in another product of gay culture, drag performance. Divas such as Midler, Ross, and Cher are popular objects of imitation and adulation by drag queens.

Numerous heterosexual artists, such as David Bowie and Madonna, have vaguely flirted with androgyny or homosexuality, only to back away when it seemed no longer chic or advantageous for them to bend genders. Others, such as Prince, parlayed sexually ambiguous personas into a heterosexual taboo fantasy while staunchly maintaining their own exaggeratedly "straight" orientation.

Still, some heterosexual performers sympathetic to their gay audiences have pushed boundaries with no explanation or defensiveness. An example is onetime *Advocate* cover boy Bruce Springsteen in his sensitive, ambiguous song "My Lover Man" (recorded in 1990, released in 1998). And occasionally there is simply confusion—in 2001, Irish singer Sinéad O'Connor declared her lesbianism (not bisexuality), only to marry a male reporter by the end of the year.

Blues

In 1920, Mamie Smith's "Crazy Blues," written by Perry Bradford, became the first vocal blues record, selling more than 100 thousand copies in its first month of release. Publishers rushed to capitalize on the market, employing popular club singers such as lesbian thrush Alberta Hunter to make recordings to meet the burgeoning demand for blues music.

The success of the blues also introduced to the public a genre with often frankly sexual lyrics, as well as a group of lesbian and bisexual performers who lived their lives freely and often flamboyantly.

Gertrude "Ma" Rainey and Bessie Smith, both openly bisexual, were among the biggest stars of the day. In their lyrics sexual double entendres abounded. References to "jelly rolls" and "handy men" were understood by the initiated, though probably not by the millions who bought their records but knew nothing about living "in the life."

Sometimes, the lesbian content was stated more plainly—Rainey's 1928 lesbian blues classic "Prove It On Me Blues" contains these unequivocal lines:

> *They said I do it, ain't nobody caught me*
> *Sure got to prove it on me*
> *Went out last night with a crowd of my friends*
> *They must've been women, 'cause I don't like no men.*
> *It's true I wear a collar and a tie...*
> *Talk to the gals just like any old man....*

Similarly, Lucille Bogan, also known as Bessie Jackson, recorded "B.D. [Bull-Dykers] Woman's Blues" in 1935.

However, as the popularity of the blues waned in the 1940s and 1950s, the gay and lesbian content in popular music disappeared.

Still, as blues gave way to rock and roll, lesbian singers such as Big Mama Thornton kept the tradition alive. Thornton, a powerful performer who frequently dressed in masculine clothing, released the classic "Hound Dog" in 1953, three years before Elvis Presley.

The tradition of blues women continues in contemporary performers such as lesbian Gaye Adegbalola, one-third of the blues group Saffire: Uppity Blues Women, which she cofounded in 1984. In 1999, Adegbalola released her solo album *Bitter Sweet Blues*, on which she covers Ma Rainey's "Prove It On Me Blues."

The record also includes the original composition "Front Door Blues," with the lyrical refrain "all of her stuff is out of the closet / but she can't walk through that front door," of which Agdebalola says: "This gay little ditty is an ode to courage."

Candye Kane is a swing, rockabilly, and blues singer from San Diego whose shows have been described as like "a revival meeting in the parking lot of an X-rated bookstore." A bisexual, sex-positive former porn actress

turned singer, Kane has a big voice and larger-than-life persona. Her record *The Toughest Girl Alive* (2000) features the number "(Hey Mister!) She Was My Baby Last Night."

Jazz and Cabaret

From the 1920s through the 1950s, gay composer Cole Porter wrote dozens of unforgettable songs such as "Let's Do It (Let's Fall in Love)," "I Get a Kick out of You," and "Don't Fence Me In." Many of them became standards of the American songbook.

Educated at Yale, where he composed more than 300 songs, including fight songs and musical productions, before he graduated, Porter was expected to become a lawyer but instead pursued his true love, music. Although Porter married in 1919, the marriage was not a traditional union and did little to interfere with his pursuit of homosexual affairs.

The 1945 film *Night and Day*, starring Cary Grant, was loosely based on Porter's life, but contained no reference to his homosexuality. Because of his marriage and his inarguable importance in American musical history, many biographers still downplay if not actually deny his homosexuality.

Although everyone from Ella Fitzgerald to Johnny Mathis covered his tunes, Porter's music fell out of fashion with the advent of rock and roll. Recently, however, it has experienced a resurgence in popularity. *Red Hot & Blue*, a 1990 tribute album featuring covers of Porter's songs by Neneh Cherry, k.d. lang, Erasure, and Jimmy Somerville, was a benefit for AIDS research and relief. And in 2004, a second Cole Porter biopic, Irwin Winkler's *De-Lovely*, appeared, this time taking a more honest view of the composer's sexuality.

The pianist Liberace was a fixture in Las Vegas and on television beginning in the 1950s. He made his Hollywood debut in 1950 and began starring in his own television show two years later. He earned two Emmy Awards, but never gave up his concert career.

Liberace played to capacity crowds from Madison Square Garden to the Hollywood Bowl to Soldier Field in Chicago, where in 1955 he performed for an astonishing 110 thousand people. In his flamboyant, diamond-and-rhinestone-encrusted costumes, with his signature candelabra atop his grand piano, "Mr. Showmanship" brought a delightfully campy aesthetic and staggering talent to the interpretation of old standards.

When he opened in Las Vegas in 1955, Liberace became the highest-paid performer in the town's history. The author of four autobiographical books, none of which mention his homosexuality, he is better remembered for his outrageous style than for his music.

Frances Faye was a Los Angeles–based vocalist and lesbian. She began a 1976 performance with "My name is

Frances Faye—I'm very gay, gay, gay." Faye performed on television and in movies for nearly fifty years, including a role as the madam in Louis Malle's *Pretty Baby* (1978). She is best known for her rendition of "Bewitched, Bothered, and Bewildered." Faye had a loyal gay and lesbian following until her death in 1991.

Australian Peter Allen, cabaret singer, composer, and ex-husband of Liza Minnelli, had his biggest hit with "I Go to Rio" (1977), though he penned hits for other artists, including "I Honestly Love You" for Olivia Newton-John and "Don't Cry Out Loud" for Melissa Manchester.

Allen won an Oscar in 1982 for cowriting "Arthur's Theme (Best That You Can Do)" from Minnelli's film *Arthur*. Allen was an exuberant entertainer, known for leaping atop his piano during a performance.

Carrying on the cabaret torch, Rufus Wainwright is an openly gay singer/songwriter whose style owes more of a debt to Cole Porter than to any of his contemporaries. The son of folksingers Loudon Wainwright III and Kate McGarrigle, his repertoire has been described as updated American standards and is critically lauded.

More experimental jazz and vocal artists include Milwaukee-based Mrs. Fun, a keyboard and drum duo, and BETTY, a theatrical New York–based band fronted by a trio of women—Alyson Palmer and sisters Amy and Elizabeth Ziff, both lesbians—who began performing together in the 1980s.

Active on behalf of gay and lesbian causes, BETTY contributed to the *Out Loud CD*, a benefit for human rights and freedom for lesbians and gay men, and appeared in the gender identity film *It's Pat* (1994) and the lesbian love story *The Incredibly True Adventure of Two Girls in Love* (1995).

The Billy Tipton Memorial Saxophone Quartet is a Seattle-based all-woman band named for Billy Tipton, a jazz musician who lived her life as a man for more than fifty years, in part to be able to pursue a career in music, then a man's domain.

Pop

Pop music has been filled with gay and lesbian personalities. Johnny Mathis, a sweet-faced, honey-voiced singer from Gilmer, Texas, by way of San Francisco, rose to fame in the 1950s, singing ballads such as "Chances Are" (his first number one single), "Misty," and "Wonderful, Wonderful." He scored Top 40 hits in each of the next four decades, and his *Greatest Hits* (1958) compilation stayed an astonishing 490 continuous weeks—nearly ten years— on the *Billboard* top albums chart.

Mathis has been a figure in the recording business for more than forty years. It was not until 1982, however, in an *Us* magazine article, that Mathis publicly came out as gay to his long-suspecting fans, stating, "Homosexuality

is a way of life that I've grown accustomed to." The revelation did not appear to affect his record sales.

British singer Dusty Springfield was the powerhouse voice behind such hits as "Wishin' and Hopin' " (1964, covered by Ani DiFranco in 1997 for the soundtrack to *My Best Friend's Wedding*) and "Son of a Preacher Man" (1968).

Regarding her sexuality, Springfield stated: "Look, let's say I've experimented with most things in life. And in sex. I suppose you can sum it up that I remain right down the middle." An icon for gay and lesbian fans, Springfield teamed up in 1989 with Pet Shop Boys for "What Have I Done to Deserve This."

Singer/songwriter Laura Nyro (1947–1997) began writing as a teenager. She released her first album in 1968 at age nineteen. Performers as diverse as Three Dog Night and Barbra Streisand covered her songs "Stoney End," "Eli's Coming," and "Stone Soul Picnic."

Elton John is a pop chameleon known as much for his ever-changing appearance as for his music. The writer of such pop/rock classics as "Bennie and the Jets," "Goodbye Yellow Brick Road," and "Candle in the Wind," he came out to *Rolling Stone* as bisexual in 1976, then surprised fans by marrying a woman in 1984, and later stunned gays and lesbians when he performed a duet with rabidly homophobic rapper Eminem at the 2001 Grammy Awards.

An enduring presence in pop music, John is arguably the most successful and prominent gay performer today. He is now refreshingly open about his long-running relationship with his life partner, David Furnish.

The 1980s New Wave era saw a number of gay musicians find success in the mainstream. Boy George, the cross-dressing lead singer of Culture Club, burst onto the scene with the band's hit "Do You Really Want to Hurt Me?" (1982). Plagued by drug problems, George later embarked on a solo career as a singer and more recently as a DJ.

George Michael, who became a best-selling artist with the 1980s pop duo Wham! and later a successful solo artist, came out in 1998 following his arrest in a Beverly Hills park restroom on charges of soliciting an undercover male police officer. He seems not only to have survived the scandal, but also to have been liberated by it.

Pet Shop Boys, Erasure, The Smiths (with singer Morrissey, who has said, "I refuse to recognize the terms hetero-, bi-, and homo-sexual. Everybody has exactly the same sexual needs. People are just sexual, the prefix is immaterial"), Bronski Beat and The Communards (both led by mellifluous singer Jimmy Somerville, now a solo act), Frankie Goes to Hollywood, Soft Cell, and the B-52s all included gay members.

Although his own sexuality has been hotly contested, pop/jazz singer Joe Jackson perhaps best represents the gay Zeitgeist of the New Wave era in his 1982 song "Real Men":

> See the nice boys—dancing in pairs
> Golden earring golden tan
> Blow-wave in the hair
> Sure they're all straight—straight as a line
> All the gays are macho
> Can't you see their leather shine
> You don't want to sound dumb—don't want to offend
> So don't call me a faggot
> Not unless you are a friend
> Then if you're tall and handsome and strong
> You can wear the uniform and I could play along
> And so it goes—go round again
> But now and then we wonder who the real men are.

Bisexual singer Jill Sobule's 1996 hit song "I Kissed a Girl" is one of the few explicitly lesbian-themed hit songs in recording history. Its happy, bouncy message is unequivocally celebratory of a moment of revelation as a young woman—fed up with her dumb, handsome, "hairy behemoth" boyfriend—explores her sexuality with a friend who is equally unimpressed with her own fiancé.

The title of Sobule's album *Pink Pearl* (2000) is an obvious wink toward female genitalia, recalling the refrain from "I Kissed A Girl": "they can have their diamonds / and we'll have our pearls...." Sobule's oeuvre is filled with such wry, humorous songs; many casually refer to lesbian characters.

Country Western
Although Canadian chanteuse k.d. lang started out as an alternative country singer, mainstream country music never fully embraced her. Despite her early "torch and twang" sound, lang found commercial success as a pop singer because she had one of the richest, lushest voices to be heard in popular music in years.

lang came out in the *Advocate* in 1992 and, more spectacularly, in a cover story in *Vanity Fair* in August of the following year. In so doing, she became the first lesbian celebrity to so openly celebrate—and be celebrated for—her sexuality. An actress as well as a singer, lang thrilled her lesbian fans when she briefly appeared nude in the 1991 independent film *Salmonberries* in a role written for her by director Percy Adlon.

In contrast, mainstream country music has not produced any out stars. In 1995, singer Ty Herndon was arrested for drug possession and allegedly exposing himself to a male undercover officer in a Fort Worth, Texas, park, but the career-threatening charge was dismissed and buried.

More positively, in 1992, best-selling heterosexual singer Garth Brooks recorded "We Shall Be Free," a song that espouses tolerance and acceptance. He has publicly stated his support for gay marriage. His lesbian sister, Betsy Smittle, plays in his band.

Folk
The singer/songwriter dominates folk music, and no other musical genre is as well suited to exploring gay and lesbian lives in all their complexity, beauty, and, often, pain. Among the most famous folk legends is Joan Baez, who came out as bisexual following the dissolution of her marriage in 1972.

Janis Ian, whose "At Seventeen" (1975) was the theme song of every awkward adolescent girl, freely discusses her sexuality on her website, www.janisian.com. Lesser-known but no less talented lesbian folksingers emerged in the early 1970s, including Ferron, Cris Williamson, Linda Tillery, and Holly Near. These singers have been in the forefront of women's music.

The all-women a cappella group Sweet Honey in the Rock was founded in 1973 by Bernice Johnson Reagon. While only one member of Sweet Honey was self-identified as a lesbian (Evelyn Maria Harris, who sang with the group for eighteen years), their experience touring and working with and performing for political lesbians led Reagon to write songs specifically about women loving women.

As Reagon explained, their exposure to the lesbian community led them to "sing about oppression of every kind, including the oppression experienced by the homosexual community."

Like Sweet Honey in the Rock, lesbian vocalist, percussionist, and historian Linda Tillery explores the roots of African American music and storytelling. In 1992, she formed the Cultural Heritage Choir to preserve this history and to perform traditional folk music such as slave field hollers, work and play songs, and spirituals.

Grammy-winning lesbian singer/songwriters Amy Ray and Emily Saliers, the Indigo Girls, have become one of the most successful folk/pop duos in recent history. Their success is in large measure due to the fierce loyalty of their fans, many of them lesbians.

The Atlanta-based duo's first album, the multiplatinum *Indigo Girls* (1989), included their best-known song, "Closer to Fine." *Rites of Passage* (1992) featured an impassioned cover of Mark Knopfler's "Romeo and Juliet." Sung by Ray in the voice of Juliet's lover, it quickly became a lesbian classic.

However, it was not until *Shaming of the Sun* (1997) that an explicit statement of either woman's homosexuality appeared—in Saliers's "It's Alright," with the line "...and it's alright if you hate that way / hate me cause I'm different / you hate me cause I'm gay...."

Over the years, Indigo Girls have been an integral part of a strong musical scene in Atlanta that has included lesbian singer/songwriters Michelle Malone, Kristen Hall, and Wendy Bucklew.

About the same time that Indigo Girls were making their first record, Tracy Chapman came seemingly out of nowhere with the spare, haunting single "Fast Car" from her eponymous 1988 debut album. Along with Indigo Girls, Chapman led the pack of socially conscious singer/songwriters whose voices emerged in the late 1980s.

In the 1990s, Lilith Fair, Sarah McLachlan's all-woman tour—dubbed "Lesbopalooza" because of the number of lesbian acts and its popularity among lesbian fans (though there is a real Lesbopalooza music festival)—provided a high-profile venue for Indigo Girls, Chapman, and other like-minded acts. Melissa Ferrick, disappear fear (founding member Sonia is now a solo act), Catie Curtis, Nedra Johnson, and Toshi Reagon continue in this folk genre.

Bisexual singer Ani DiFranco became a poster girl for dykes in the early 1990s with her shaved head, combat boots, and the take-no-prisoners approach of her raw, honest lyrics about relationships and politics.

A self-described "freak," DiFranco sings about relationships with both men and women; her song "In or Out" defies the persistent desire to label her as either straight or gay: "some days the line I walk / turns out to be straight / other days the line tends to deviate / I've got no criteria for sex or race / I just want to hear your voice / I just want to see your face."

DiFranco has released all her records on the label she founded in 1990, Righteous Babe Records, which is also home to the eclectic lesbian and transgendered performance band Bitch and Animal.

In a genre all her own is Los Angeles–based "all-American Jewish lesbian folksinger," performance artist, and Tupperware lady Phranc. Her eclectic oeuvre includes the recordings—and personalities—of "Hot August Phranc," "Surferdyke Pal," "Cardboard Cobbler," and "Milkman." Not surprisingly, humor is an integral part of her work.

Rock

In the late 1950s, Little Richard, born Richard Wayne Penniman in Macon, Georgia, brought a shockingly fey, shrieking style to rock-and-roll music with his smash hits "Lucille," "Tutti Frutti," "Long Tall Sally," and "Good Golly Miss Molly." Richard, an androgynous black man sporting a pompadour hairstyle, eyeliner, and tight pants, was unlike anything American culture had ever seen, yet he never altered his outrageous style to suit prevailing tastes.

In 1996, Little Richard was inducted into the Rock and Roll Hall of Fame. In 2000, NBC produced *The Little Richard Story*, a drama based on his life. Despite the obvious, Richard has never explicitly come out as a homosexual.

In the early 1970s, bisexual British rocker David Bowie, a pioneer of "glam rock," would eventually take androgyny to a new level in his incarnation as Ziggy Stardust.

Freddie Mercury was the flamboyantly gay lead singer of the British band Queen. Anchored by his soaring voice, Queen had a string of hits throughout the 1970s and 1980s, including "Bohemian Rhapsody" and "Another One Bites the Dust." Mercury died of AIDS in 1991, just one day after publicly announcing that he was gay and infected with the disease.

Rock and roll has produced several classic songs about transvestites. Bisexual Lou Reed's seminal "Walk on the Wild Side" (1972) is an ode to the homosexual, transvestite hustlers Holly, Candy, Little Joe, Sugar Plum Fairy, and Jackie. Like Bowie, Reed was part of the glam rock movement as a member of Andy Warhol's Velvet Underground.

The Kinks' "Lola" (1970) is also about a young man's sexual awakening with a transsexual: "I'm not the world's most masculine [alternately "passionate"] man / But I know what I am, and I'm glad I'm a man / And so is Lola."

The soundtrack for *The Rocky Horror Picture Show* (1977) includes the song "Sweet Transvestite," performed by the actor and singer Tim Curry.

Rocker Janis Joplin was a hard-living, wildly talented bisexual woman from Port Arthur, Texas, who redefined rock and roll. With her first band, Big Brother and the Holding Company, Joplin helped define the look and sound of Bay Area hippie rock music in the 1960s. Her hits include "Me and Bobby McGee" and "Piece of My Heart."

In a gesture of musical and sapphic continuity, Joplin, along with Juanita Green, a Philadelphia woman, bought a tombstone to mark the unmarked grave of pioneer blues singer Bessie Smith, who died prematurely from injuries sustained in an automobile accident. Joplin herself died too young, of a heroin overdose at age twenty-seven.

Lesbians have had a significant impact in rock as well. Joan Jett rose to fame in the 1970s all-girl rock band The Runaways. Her cover of "I Love Rock and Roll" was a number one hit in 1982; "Crimson and Clover" was another hit for her. Jett came out as a lesbian in the 1990s, and has appeared as Columbia in the Broadway production of *The Rocky Horror Picture Show*.

The group 4 Non Blondes, with lesbian lead singer Linda Perry, scored a huge radio hit with their 1991 song "What's Up."

Grammy Award–winner Melissa Etheridge, long a staple on the lesbian club scene in Long Beach, California, had a string of successful albums before she came out nationally in 1993 at an inaugural ball for President Clinton. The same year, her breakthrough best-selling album, *Yes, I Am*, featured the hit "Come To My Window," with the lyrics "I don't care what they think /

I don't care what they say / What do they know about this love anyway?"

Etheridge and her then partner Julie Cypher set tongues wagging when they posed nude for a PETA (People for the Ethical Treatment of Animals) campaign in 1995, but it was nothing compared to the media coverage surrounding their revelation in January 2000 that rocker David Crosby was the biological father of their two children, conceived through artificial insemination.

Sophie B. Hawkins, whose hits include "Damn, I Wish I Was Your Lover" and "As I Lay Me Down," and who was the subject of the biographical documentary *The Cream Will Rise*, prefers the term *omnisexual* to describe her sexuality.

The fiercely independent bisexual singer Meshell Ndegéocello became the first woman artist signed to Madonna's Maverick Records. Her first album, *Plantation Lullabies* (1994), featured the hit "If That's Your Boyfriend (He Wasn't Last Night)."

The Murmurs, the solo artist Skin (vocalist of the late band Skunk Anansie), and Kate Schellenbach (drummer of the late band Luscious Jackson) are also lesbian rock and rollers.

Punk

Punk music, dominated by angry young men in the 1970s, reemerged in the 1980s and 1990s with several lesbian bands at the forefront, including L7, Sleater-Kinney, Tribe 8 (a play on an old term for lesbians, *tribade),* the Butchies, and Le Tigre.

Both the Butchies (Alison Martlew, Kaia Wilson, and Melissa York, the latter two formerly of the all-dyke punk-rock band Team Dresch) and Le Tigre (Kathleen Hanna, formerly of Bikini Kill, Johanna Fateman, and JD Samson) are on Mr. Lady Records, an independent label run by Wilson and her partner, Tammy Rae Carland, that also distributes lesbian videos and films.

Le Tigre combines a fiercely feminist take on art, culture, and politics with witty, high-energy pop/punk performances. A former member and founder of Le Tigre, Sadie Benning, is a lesbian video art pioneer.

Disco

The advent of disco in the early 1970s provided perhaps the watershed moment in gay music. The disco scene, centered largely in urban areas, provided an atmosphere of tolerance and release that dovetailed with the gay and lesbian rights movement born of the Stonewall Rebellion in 1969.

Much disco music focused on themes of sex, freedom, and dancing as means of escape from the pressures and injustices of life. A memorable example is "It's Raining Men" (1983) by the Weather Girls (formerly Two Tons of Fun and Sylvester's backup singers), Martha Wash and Izora Rhodes (Armstead).

At the same time, hits such as Machine's "There But for the Grace of God (There Go I)" (1979) addressed issues of social exclusion and discrimination. The song includes the lines "now they gotta split 'cause the Bronx ain't fit / for a kid to grow up in / 'Let's find a place' they say / somewhere far away / with no blacks, no Jews, and no gays."

The Village People, a six-man band dressed as gay male stereotypes or objects of desire—biker/leatherman, GI, construction worker, cop, cowboy, and Native American—is probably the best known gay-themed band of the disco era. The group sold more than 65 million records. Their hit anthems "Y.M.C.A." and "Macho Man" are tongue-in-cheek odes to male bonding.

The Village People even starred in their own feature film, *Can't Stop the Music* (1980). Although founding member and original biker/leatherman Glenn Hughes died in 2001, the band continues to perform together.

As in rock, androgyny figured prominently in disco music. Among the most popular gay disco singers was bisexual Grace Jones, the Jamaican-born model, singer, and performance artist whose hits include "I Need a Man" (1977) and "Pull Up to the Bumper" (1981), a thinly veiled paean to anal sex.

One of the distinguishing aspects of Jones's persona was her androgynous image, which she explained in this way:

"I always liked to wear my hair very short, and my voice was deep. So even before creating that [androgynous image] for the public, I used to go in to buy bread and they would say 'Bonjour, monsieur,' and I would try and say 'No, I am a mademoiselle,' and forget it, they'd say 'Bonjour, monsieur' again. I think I have the features of an African man.... When I put a wig on with long hair, I look like a hooker or a drag queen. So I look actually more feminine when I'm dressed as a man."

Sylvester James, who came to fame as Sylvester, was born in 1946 in Los Angeles. Encouraged in music early on by his aunt, a jazz singer, he became an openly gay, cross-dressing performer, beginning his career in San Francisco performing with the Cockettes, an androgynous musical revue. His big hits were "You Make Me Feel (Mighty Real)" (1978), which both Jimmy Somerville and comedian/singer Sandra Bernhard later remade, and "Dance (Disco Heat)" (1978).

Sylvester made his film debut opposite gay icon Bette Midler in *The Rose*, loosely based on the life and career of Janis Joplin. He died of AIDS in 1988.

When disco, or dance music, experienced a rebirth in the 1990s, campy, gorgeous gay drag queen RuPaul scored big with his 1992 hit "Supermodel" and went on to host *The RuPaul Show* on VH1. As the first "face" of M.A.C. Cosmetics, he helped raise more than $22 million for AIDS research.

R & B, Hip-Hop, and Reggae

Like country western music, R & B (rhythm and blues) has remained a bastion of heterosexuality in popular music. As in country, scandals involving alleged homosexual activities have plagued some of R & B's biggest male singers.

In 1976, lead singer Teddy Pendergrass left the popular group Harold Melvin & The Blue Notes to pursue a solo career. By 1982, he was the reigning R & B sex symbol, giving women-only concerts for his adoring fans. That year, however, Pendergrass's career came to a screeching halt following an automobile accident that left him paralyzed from the chest down and his passenger, a transsexual male, dead.

Formerly a heartthrob, Pendergrass was unable to regain his popularity. His career could not transcend his paralysis or his companion's sexuality (and its implications for his own sexuality).

Years later, actor and onetime recording artist Eddie Murphy found himself in a similar situation when he was caught with a transvestite prostitute in Hollywood; Murphy insisted he was merely giving her a ride. Murphy's singing career had already run its course on the limits of his talents; though he became the butt of late-night jokes, the incident did not seem to affect his acting success.

In the 1980s, singer Luther Vandross seemed to take over Pendergrass's crown, only to be dogged from the beginning of his career about rumors of his own homosexuality, which he has never acknowledged. However, a 1990s *Ebony* magazine feature article begins with Vandross proudly showing the reporter his David Hockney drawing of a male nude. Informed readers might draw their own conclusions.

Hip-hop, rap music, and reggae are perhaps the most homophobic of popular music genres, and the lyrics have traditionally been laced with hatred and violence. Ice Cube, in "Horny Lil' Devil" (1991), brazenly states, "But horny little devil true niggaz aren't gay / And you can't play with my Yo-Yo / and definitely can't play with me you fuckin' homo."

The white rapper Eminem drew the ire of gay and lesbian groups in 1999 over the violent, homophobic lyrics on his album *The Marshall Mathers LP*. Although he performed a duet of the song "Stan" with Elton John at the 2001 Grammys, Eminem later claimed to have no idea that John is gay.

However, numerous female rappers—including Queen Latifah, M. C. Lyte, Da Brat, and Eve—have been presumed or rumored to be lesbians, though none of these artists has ever come out.

Perhaps the only explicit, positive reference to lesbianism in rap is in bisexual rapper Queen Pen's "Girlfriend" (1997), a reworking of Meshell Ndegéocello's "If That's Your Boyfriend (He Wasn't Last Night)," featuring a cameo by Ndegéocello.

A more recent phenomenon, hip-hop lesbians and homo thugs, has garnered mainstream press in publications such as *VIBE* and *XXL*. Brooklyn-based Caushun (Jason Herndon), who has been spotlighted in these articles, bills himself as "The Gay Rapper." He has had success on New York radio and has been featured on MTV's program *The 10 Spot*.

The lyrics of reggae songs frequently advocate gay bashing and even murder. Four Jamaican reggae singers, Beenie Man, Bounty Killer, Elephant Man, and Buju Banton, have been the objects of protest in the United States and Europe over their homophobic lyrics.

Banton's "Boom Bye Bye" urges listeners to shoot gay men in the head, pour acid over them, and burn them alive, while Beenie Man's "Bad Man Chi Chi Man" (Bad Man Queer Man) includes these lyrics:

> *"If yuh nuh chi chi (queer) man wave yuh right hand and (NO!!!)*
> *If yuh nuh lesbian wave yuh right hand and (NO!!!)*
> *Some bwoy will go a jail fi kill man tun bad man chi chi man!!!*
> *Tell mi, sumfest it should a be a showdown*
> *Yuh seem to run off a stage like a clown (Kill Dem DJ!!!)"*

In the summer of 2004, British police opened a probe into whether these songs violate British hate laws, and protests and threats of boycotts led to the cancellation of concert appearances in the United States and Europe by Beenie Man and other reggae singers.   —*Carla Williams*

Bibliography

Bashir, Samiya A. "Strictly for the Ladies." *XXL*, July 2001, 116.

Davis, Angela Y. *Blues Legacies and Black Feminism: Gertrude 'Ma' Rainey, Bessie Smith and Billie Holiday.* New York: Pantheon Books, 1998.

Faris, Jocelyn. *Liberace: A Bio-Bibliography.* Westport, Conn.: Greenwood Press, 1995.

Hardy, James Earl. *B-Boy Blues: A Seriously Sexy, Fiercely Funny, Black-On-Black Love Story.* Los Angeles: Alyson Publications, 1994.

Jackson, Joe. *A Cure for Gravity.* New York: Public Affairs, 1999.

Jasper, Tony. *Johnny: The Authorised Biography of Johnny Mathis.* London: W. H. Allen, 1983.

Liberace. *An Autobiography.* New York: G. P. Putnam's Sons, 1973.

———. *The Things I Love: America's Greatest Showman Invites You on an Intimate Tour through His Homes and Shares the Treasures of His Fabulous World.* New York: Grossett & Dunlap, 1976.

MacLean, Stephen. *Peter Allen: The Boy from Oz.* Milsons Point, Australia: Random House Australia, 1996.

McDonnell, Evelyn, and Ann Powers, eds. *Rock She Wrote: Women Write About Rock, Pop, and Rap.* New York: Delta Books, 1995.

Middlebrook, Diane. *Suits Me: The Double Life of Billy Tipton.* New York: Mariner Books, 1999.

Moore, Peter. "Outcry Grows Against Anti-Gay Singers." www.365gay.com (August 19, 2004): www.365gay.com/newscon04/08/081904ukBeenie.htm

Thomas, Bob. *Liberace: The True Story.* New York: St. Martin's Press, 1987.

Venable, Malcolm. "A Question of Identity." *VIBE,* July 2001, 98.

White, Charles. *The Life and Times of Little Richard: The Quasar of Rock.* New York: Harmony Books, 1984.

Artist Home Pages:

www.lauranyro.com/

www.adegbalola.com/

www.rufuswainwright.com/

www.bitchandanimal.com

www.melissaetheridge.com

www.johnnymathis.com/

www.kdlang.com

www.joanjett.com/

www.sonymusic.co.uk/georgemichael/

www.hollynear.com/

www.thebutchies.com/

www.letigreworld.com

www.hellobetty.com/

www.righteousbabe.com

www.candyekane.com/

www.coleporter.org/

www.liberace.org/

www.dustyspringfield.co.uk/

www.eltonjohn.com/

www.joejackson.com/

www.smoe.org/soniadf/ (Sonia and disappear fear)

http://thecreamwillrise.com/ (Sophie B. Hawkins page)

www.smelll7.com/main.html

www.jimmysomerville.co.uk/

www.rupaul.com/

www.indigogirls.com

www.michellemalone.com/

www.wendybucklew.com/

www.kristenhall.com/

www.vickirandle.com

www.culturalheritagechoir.com

www.skunkanansie.com

www.criswilliamson.com

Additional Pages:

Frances Faye fan page: http://hometown.aol.com/tyjonal/myhomepage/fan.html

Indigo Girls: http://lifeblood.net. Contains an extensive database of articles relevant to almost all the artists discussed in this essay.

Lgbtq hip-hop: www.phatfamily.org

Little Richard fan page: www.kolumbus.fi/timrei/lre.htm

Gertrude ("Ma") Rainey: Sullivan, Tom. "Remember Ma Rainey": www.lambda.net/~maximum/rainey.html

www.andwedanced.com/artists/sylvest.htm

www.soulwalking.co.uk/Sylvester.html

www.mrlady.com/

www.killrockstars.com/

www.mrsfun.com/

SEE ALSO

Blues Music; Country Music; Disco and Dance Music; Divas; Rock Music; Women's Music; Allen, Peter; Baez, Joan; Bowie, David; Boy George (George O'Dowd); Cheung, Leslie; DiFranco, Ani; Etheridge, Melissa; Faye, Frances; Geffen, David; Hunter, Alberta; Ian, Janis; Indigo Girls; John, Sir Elton; Joplin, Janis; lang, k.d.; Liberace; Little Richard (Richard Penniman); Mathis, Johnny; Mercury, Freddie; Michael, George; Near, Holly; Porter, Cole; Rainey, Gertrude ("Ma"); RuPaul (RuPaul Andre Charles); Smith, Bessie; Smiths, The, and Morrissey; Somerville, Jimmy; Springfield, Dusty; Sweet Honey in the Rock; Sylvester; Wainwright, Rufus; Williamson, Cris; Bell, Andy; Pansy Division; Robinson, Tom; Stipe, Michael

Porter, Cole   *(1891–1964)*

FOR MORE THAN THIRTY YEARS, COLE PORTER WAS AS well known for the (often scandalously) witty and urbane music that he crafted for Broadway musicals and Hollywood films as for being one of the leaders of international cafe society. Because he feared that the music-buying public would not take seriously love songs written by a homosexual, he lived the paradoxical life of an openly closeted gay man.

Married to socialite Linda Lee Thomas, one of the most beautiful women of her generation (but variously reported as from eight to fourteen years Porter's senior), he publicly maintained a heterosexual facade while privately indulging in weekend all-male gatherings that included chorus boys, wartime servicemen, and Hollywood bit players, in addition to conducting intense, short-lived love affairs with Ballets Russes designer Boris Kochno, architect Eddy Tauch, dancer/choreographer Nelson Barclift, and actor Robert Bray, among others.

Thus, even while giving, as the author of some of the most popular love songs of the day, deeply memorable voice to his culture's romantic longing, Porter was repeatedly forced to obscure his own.

Porter's Life

Porter was born on June 9, 1891, the only child among three to survive infancy. His maternal grandfather was the wealthiest man in Peru, Indiana, which both fostered in Porter a sense of entitlement and guaranteed his financial independence in early adulthood. At age fourteen, he was sent east to boarding school, and from there to Yale University, where he distinguished himself in the Glee Club and dramatic society.

In 1917, Porter escaped the embarrassing failure of his first professionally staged musical revue, *See America First*, by departing for Paris, purportedly to volunteer as a wartime ambulance driver. He quickly fell in with the smart set, marrying the beautiful and socially well-connected divorcee Linda Lee Thomas in 1919. He remained at the center of international society for the rest of his life.

Porter's love of travel and of urban life is suggested by the titles of many of his songs ("You Don't Know Paree," "I Love Paris," "I Happen to Like New York," "Take Me Back to Manhattan," "Please Don't Monkey with Broadway," "A Stroll on the Plaza Sant'Ana," "Martinique," "Come to the Supermarket in Old Peking," and "Siberia," not to mention the witty rondel of Italian cities mentioned in "We Open in Venice").

Porter's life was severely circumscribed in 1937, however, by a horseback-riding accident that crushed both his legs; a resulting bone-marrow infection only complicated his recovery. Despite an eventual thirty-four operations, he suffered severe pain much of the remainder of his life, walking only with the help of a cane or crutches and requiring permanent assistance. One leg was eventually amputated, which caused him—following the deaths of his mother and wife—to sink into a depression exacerbated by alcoholism.

He died on October 15, 1964, following an emergency surgery, when the attending physician, unfamiliar with Porter's personal circumstances, mistook the symptoms of alcohol withdrawal for Parkinson's disease and failed to prescribe a necessary medication.

Porter's Plays and Films

For nearly thirty years—from his first success with *Paris* (1928) until his last show, *Silk Stockings* (1955)—Porter was one of the most successful composer/lyricists on Broadway. The greatest stars of his generation, and not a few of the next—among them, Franny Brice, Fred Astaire, Ethel Merman, Jimmy Durante, Clifton Webb, Gertrude Lawrence, Mary Martin, Sophie Tucker, Beatrice Lillie, Bert Lahr, and Gwen Verdon—scored personal triumphs in his plays or in the films subsequently made of many of them.

Those films adaptations include *Fifty Million Frenchmen* (1929), *The New Yorkers* (1930), *The Gay Divorcee* (1932), *Anything Goes* (1934), *Jubilee* (1935), *Red, Hot,* *and Blue* (1936), *Leave It to Me* (1938), *DuBarry Was a Lady* (1939), *Panama Hattie* (1940), *Something for the Boys* (1942), *Mexican Hayride* (1944), *Kiss Me, Kate* (1948), *Out of This World* (1950), and *Can-Can* (1953).

In addition, Porter wrote original scores for such Hollywood successes as *The Pirate* (1947), in which Gene Kelly and Judy Garland introduced "Be a Clown"; and *High Society* (1956), in which Bing Crosby crooned "True Love" to Grace Kelly.

As a result, Porter's name became synonymous with songs that were as linguistically sophisticated as they were musically rich. Indeed, discussing the popular songs that tuned his own ear as he was growing up in the 1930s and 1940s, the Pulitzer Prize–winning composer Ned Rorem praised Porter's songs for being "equal in vocal arch and harmonic ingenuity to the songs of Monteverdi and Schumann."

Challenging Accepted Social Values

Despite the heterosexual facade he carefully maintained in public, Porter delighted in challenging accepted social values and moral opinions. The haunting ballad "Love for Sale" was banned from radio play because it offered a sympathetic, rather than a properly censorious, appreciation of a prostitute's life. Conversely, "Miss Otis Regrets" narrates the tragic misalliance contracted by a Southern town's best-mannered lady.

The largest number of Porter's songs offer a knowing, witty, even comically exuberant hedonism. "Let's Do It" (the ambiguity of whose antecedent for "it" is clarified only at the end of each chorus, "Let's fall in love"), offers a Chaucerian world in which every animal species is copulating ("Birds do it, / Bees do it, / Even educated fleas do it"), rendering unnatural any human reluctance to do the same.

Similarly, advancing the argument that "bears / Have love affairs, / And even camels," the song "Let's Misbehave" concludes that since humans are "merely mammals," it is only logical that the couple likewise "misbehave."

And while human mothers may caution their daughters to preserve their virginity until marriage, the would-be seducer in "It's De-Lovely" attends to a higher maternal authority: "You can tell at a glance / What a swell night this is for romance, / You can hear dear Mother Nature murmuring low, / 'Let yourself go.'" For Porter, natural law, which makes sexual *jouissance* a universal right, invariably trumps any moral law prescribing caution and abstinence.

While often risqué, Porter is never vulgar. The wit of his lyrics and the musical sophistication of his melodies prevent his songs from ever being in poor taste. Marlene Dietrich's lethargic delivery in her cabaret act of "The Laziest Girl in Town" left little doubt as to what the speaker could, should, and would indeed do if only she found the needed energy.

But in "You Do Something to Me," Porter's speaker never specifies what effect the person in question has on him, although clearly sexual arousal is one of the possibilities.

Nor does another speaker, in "You've Got That Thing," explain exactly what "Adam craved when he / With love for Eve was tortured," simply that the lover being addressed possesses the same indefinable attraction.

Even while delighting in the physical sensations of life—as, for example, in "I Get a Kick out of You" or "I've Got You under My Skin"—Porter prided himself on being a gentleman. And, when risking indecency, Porter invariably lapsed into French, a language so formal that it makes even the basest desire sound elegant to American ears ("Si Vous Aimez les Poitrines").

"Anything Goes," the title song of one of his most successful plays, celebrates a modern world in which individuals are free to enjoy themselves however they please: "If old hymns you like, / If bare limbs you like, / If Mae West you like, / Or me undressed you like, / Why, nobody will oppose."

Throughout his career, Porter delighted in opposing anyone who dared to "oppose" another person's private pleasure. As a challenge to Prohibition, for example, he composed the "Lost Liberty Blues," a theatrically outrageous lament for the loss of personal freedoms in the United States sung by an actress dressed as the Statue of Liberty.

Pleasure overcomes puritanism in *Silk Stockings*, in which a female Soviet military officer is seduced by the sensual and romantic delights of the West. And *Can-Can*, which deals with a Paris magistrate's attempt to close the late-nineteenth-century club where the scandalous title dance originated, was conceived as a comment on censorship. Its song "Live and Let Live" might well have been Porter's personal theme.

Circumventing Censorship

The master of the seemingly innocent double entendre, Porter reveled in finding ways to circumvent Hollywood's Hays Code and the censor in Boston, where many of his plays were first tried out.

For example, in *Kiss Me, Kate*, the irrepressibly promiscuous Lois explains to her boyfriend that while she is willing to date wealthy men in exchange for gifts, she is "Always True to You in My Fashion."

While she sees nothing wrong in earning "a Paris hat" by allowing "Mr. Harris, plutocrat" to "give my cheek a pat," the auditor alert to Porter's ambiguity wonders which pair of "cheeks" is being patted, making the gesture in question either a grandfatherly chuck under the chin or an energetic game of grab-ass.

Even some of Porter's performers did not fully understand the significance of the words they sang. Mary Martin was famously reported to be so naive that when she introduced the following stanza in the wonderfully suggestive "My Heart Belongs to Daddy," she had no idea of its import:

If I invite
A boy, some night
To dine on my fine finnan haddie,
I just adore
His asking for more,
But my heart belongs to Daddy.

She reportedly did not understand that the meal she offers her suitor is sexual and that the reason she gives for imposing limits on their congress (because "My Daddy treats me so well") suggests that she is a kept woman.

Censors frustrated to have unintentionally let one of Porter's sexual double entendres slip by in the past could render themselves ridiculous in their zeal to suppress any potentially inflammatory meaning in a new work.

Thus, even though the song "All of You" was one of the most popular love songs of the early 1960s and had been adopted by numerous major recording stars before *Can-Can* was translated into film, Hollywood producers insisted that Porter alter the final phrase of this quatrain: "I like the looks of you, the lure of you, / I'd love to make a tour of you. / The eyes, the arms, the mouth of you, / The east, west, north, and the south of you."

"South," they were certain, was a covert reference to the beloved's genitalia and, thus, suggested cunnilingus or fellatio. Ironically, their anxiety may have been fully justified, the upbeat tempo of the song having prevented the majority of its performers and listeners from recognizing Porter's devilry.

As Ethan Mordden observes, "What makes Porter the utter one is his disdain for the received values, the morality of a national culture. He didn't care, and he didn't care who knew it. Yet he was working in a medium most intent on preserving those values. It makes for an interesting set of internal contradictions."

Queering the Popular American Song

More than any other composer of his century, Porter "queered" the popular American song, introducing nonnormative values and risqué double entendres into what was one of the most pedestrian and hackneyed of cultural forms. This was true, in large part, because Porter's own philosophy of love was nonnormative. Most important, he was willing to accept sex, with all its vagaries, as the essential component of romance.

In "Night and Day," for example, the exclamation *oh* disrupts the long line "There's an, oh, such a hungry yearning burning inside of me," miming musically how passion involuntarily shatters the speaker's composure. And while the speaker of "What Is This Thing Called Love?" can easily dismiss love as "a funny thing," he also admits how, inexplicably, it has been able to "make a fool of me."

For Porter, love is a mysterious attraction, invariably sexual, which bewilders and unsettles the speaker. It is so illogical that in "It's All Right with Me" the speaker accepts what can only be termed "compensation sex":

> It's the wrong time and the wrong place,
> Though your face is charming, it's the wrong face,
> It's not her face but such a charming face
> That it's all right with me.

The speaker, devastated by the failure of another relationship, should by his own admission be impervious to this sudden attraction to somebody new; the attraction, however, is so powerful that it reverses the values of "right" and "wrong."

Cole Porter in 1942.

Contrary to the assertions of the more idealistic Rodgers and Hammerstein, love for Porter is gloriously amoral, and it is hypocritical to pretend otherwise.

Celebrating Betrayal and Disappointment

Having founded love on the ephemeral experience of sexual attraction, Porter was willing not simply to accept, but even to celebrate, betrayal and disappointment. In *Kiss Me, Kate*, Lilli (who is still in love with her wayward ex-husband) sings the emotionally dark lines "So taunt me and hurt me, / Deceive me, desert me" just before her voice soars in exultation: "I'm yours till I die, / So in love with you, my love, am I."

Similarly, despite having crafted the image of an insouciant man-about-town, Porter wrote a surprising number of songs about the inability to protect oneself from heartache.

In "Down in the Depths (on the Ninetieth Floor)," for example, the speaker complains of her inability to transcend emotional pain even though she is immured in the "regal eagle nest" of her Manhattan penthouse. The sophisticated urban life of the speaker is no compensation for the sorrows of disappointment in love but, as the juxtaposition of height and depth in the refrain suggests, the speaker's pose of stylish aloofness is the only way to combat depression in Porter's world.

Porter wrote of both painful sexual yearning and heartache in a mannered, sophisticated way. Little wonder that Fred Astaire, who could dance seduction with an equally mannered elegance, was Porter's favored interpreter.

Porter's World of Style and Wit

For radio listeners and movie- and theatergoers in Depression-era and Eisenhower-era America, Porter's name was synonymous with "fashionable" and "debonair," summoning images of art deco sleekness, tuxedoed elegance, and chilled martinis served on the Lido.

In his songs Porter fashioned a world of style, wit, and refinement that seemed to exist in inverse proportion to the reduction-to-least-common-denominator democratic emphases of the period's political demagoguery.

In contrast to the quotidian world, Porter's was a world composed of superlatives ("You're the Top"), a world as mysterious as the chords of "In the Still of the Night," and one as surprising and intoxicating as "a sip of sparkling Burgundy brew" ("You Go to My Head").

Through his music, as well as through his much photographed and reported-upon social life, he offered middle-class America the thrill of something so sophisticated as to be faintly scandalous and, so, all the more fascinating.

The "Otherness" that he represented was understood by the shrewd to include homosexuality.

The playwright and scenarist Leonard Spielglass recalls that even while homosexuality was disparaged among the population at large, Porter's behavior placed him in "the most exclusive club in New York. That's terribly important to realize—that it was a club into which... [the average person] couldn't get.... I mean, no ordinary certified public accountant could get in the Larry Hart,... [Noël Coward], George Cukor world. That was the world.... that was Cole Porter.... On the one hand you said, 'They were homosexual—oh, my, isn't that terrible!' On the other hand you said, 'My God, the other night I was at dinner with Cole Porter!' "

Porter's greatest achievement may have been to make straight, middle-class America secretly crave what it publicly despised.

—*Raymond-Jean Frontain*

BIBLIOGRAPHY

Citron, Stephen. *Noel and Cole: The Sophisticates.* New York: Oxford University Press, 1993.

Kimball, Robert, ed. *The Complete Lyrics of Cole Porter.* New York: Alfred A. Knopf, 1983.

McBrien, William. *Cole Porter: A Biography.* New York: Alfred A. Knopf, 1998.

Mordden, Ethan. *Broadway Babies: The People Who Made the Broadway Musical.* New York: Oxford University Press, 1983.

SEE ALSO

Musical Theater and Film; Popular Music; Music and AIDS; Coward, Sir Noël; Dietrich, Marlene; Feinstein, Michael; Garland, Judy; Hart, Lorenz; Mercer, Mabel; Rorem, Ned; Sondheim, Stephen

Poulenc, Francis   *(1899–1963)*

ONE OF THE FIRST OPENLY GAY COMPOSERS, FRANCIS Poulenc wrote concerti, chamber music, choral and vocal works, and operas. His diverse compositions are characterized by bright colors, strong rhythms, and novel harmonies. Although his early music is light, he ultimately became one of the most thoughtful composers of serious music in the twentieth century.

Poulenc was born on January 7, 1899, into a well-off Parisian family. His father, a devout Roman Catholic, directed the pharmaceutical company that became Rhône-Poulenc; his mother, a free-thinker, was a talented amateur pianist. He began studying the piano at five and was following a promising path leading to admission to the Conservatoire when his life was altered by the untimely death of his parents. Although he did not attend the Conservatoire, he did study music and composition privately.

At the death of his parents, Poulenc inherited Noizay, a country estate near his grandparents' home, which would be an important retreat for him as he gained fame. It was also the source of several men in his life, including his second lover, the bisexual Raymond Destouches, a chauffeur who was the dedicatee of the surrealistic opera *Les mamelles de Tirésias* (1944) and the World War II Resistance cantata *La figure humaine* (1943).

From 1914 to 1917, Poulenc studied with the Spanish pianist Ricardo Viñes, through whom he met other musicians, especially Georges Auric, Erik Satie, and Manuel de Falla. It was also during this period that, through his friend Raymonde Linossier, he met a number of leading writers and poets, including Guillaume Apollinaire, André Gide, Paul Valéry, and Paul Claudel.

Conscripted into the military in 1918, he continued to compose and, in 1920, became a member of a group of young composers dubbed "Les Six"; the others were Darius Milhaud, Arthur Honegger, Auric, Germaine Tailleferre, and Louis Durey.

In 1921, Poulenc approached Charles Kœchlin, the noted teacher, for composition lessons; in the same year, he received a commission from dance impresario Sergei Diaghilev for his Ballets Russes, which resulted in the ballet *Les biches* (1924).

His first great popular success, *Les biches* opened many doors for Poulenc in the circles of Parisian society; for example, Princesse Edmond de Polignac (the lesbian American expatriate Winnaretta Singer) commissioned his Concerto for Two Pianos (1932) and the Organ Concerto (1938).

During the late 1920s, Poulenc came to realize his homosexuality and met his first lover, the painter Richard Chanlaire. This realization resulted in his first serious period of depression, heightened in 1930 by the death of Raymonde Linossier, the only woman Poulenc seriously considered marrying. (He would later have a brief affair with a woman known only as Frédérique and have a daughter, Marie-Ange, by her in 1946.) Linossier's death affected Poulenc deeply and may have led him to return to Roman Catholicism for solace.

The death in 1936 of a rival composer, Pierre-Octave Ferroud, prompted Poulenc to undertake a religious pilgrimage to Notre Dame de Rocamadour, near Noizay. This pilgrimage in particular seems to have confirmed the revival of his Roman Catholicism, for he began to compose sacred works thereafter, beginning with *Litanies à la Vierge noire* (1936) and continuing with some of his most popular works: the *Stabat Mater* (1950) and the *Gloria* (1959).

Poulenc never entirely abandoned the light gracefulness of his earlier music, but many of the later compositions are notably deeper and more serious.

Poulenc was a very productive composer. During the period from 1934 to 1959, he composed some ninety songs for the recitals that he gave with the noted singer Pierre Bernac, many of them based on texts by Apollinaire.

The composer's particular melodic gift seems to have been strongest in setting French poets, especially Apollinaire or Paul Eluard. His *Trois Chansons de García Lorca* (1944), which, given Federico García Lorca's homosexuality, would have appeared congenial, are disappointing and were not well received.

Poulenc toured widely, mostly as a means of raising money, but did not enjoy traveling beyond the confines of the comfortable and familiar parts of Europe. He made one tour of the United States, where he met a friendly gay couple, Arthur Gold and Robert Fizdale, the accomplished duo pianists who commissioned the Sonata for Two Pianos (1953).

Poulenc found the tours difficult, for they separated him from his lover of the time, Lucien Roubert. Roubert died of pleurisy in 1955, just after Poulenc completed one of his masterpieces, the opera *Les dialogues des Carmélites*.

After the *Dialogues*, Poulenc found it difficult to compose, but in 1957 he met his last significant lover, Louis Gautier, who helped to revive his spirits. In that year, Poulenc produced his Flute Sonata.

La voix humaine, a one-act lyric tragedy based on a libretto by Jean Cocteau, one of the icons of French homosexuality and a friend of Poulenc's for more than fifty years, followed in 1958. This was also the time that he renewed his acquaintance with Benjamin Britten and Peter Pears.

Two more important works were to be written before Poulenc's death: the *Gloria* and, at the commission of Leonard Bernstein for the opening of the Philharmonic Hall of Lincoln Center, the *Sept répons des ténèbres* (1961).

Poulenc died suddenly of a heart attack in his home on January 30, 1963. One of the most honored composers of his time, he left an enduring legacy.

—*Mario Champagne*

BIBLIOGRAPHY

Buckland, Sidney, and Myriam Chimènes. *Francis Poulenc: Music, Art and Literature.* Aldershot, England: Ashgate Press, 1999.

Chimènes, Myriam, and Roger Nichols. "Poulenc, Francis." *New Grove Dictionary of Music and Musicians.* Second ed. Stanley Sadie, ed. New York: Macmillan, 2001. 20:227–35.

Hell, Henri. *Francis Poulenc: Musicien français.* Paris: Fayard, 1978.

Ivry, Benjamin. *Francis Poulenc.* London: Phaidon, 1996.

Machart, Renaud. *Poulenc.* Paris: Éditions du Seuil, 1995.

SEE ALSO

Classical Music; Opera; Ballets Russes; Bernstein, Leonard; Britten, Benjamin; Diaghilev, Sergei; Falla (y Matheu), Manuel de; Pears, Peter

Rainey, Gertrude ("Ma")   *(1886–1939)*

SHORT, FAT, AND COUNTRY TO THE CORE, MA RAINEY may not have appeared very impressive to someone passing her on the street. However, when she took the stage, dressed in one of her trademark sequined gowns and her necklace of gold coins, and began to belt out a song such as "See See Rider," Rainey captivated every audience that heard her.

In the process, she introduced audiences to one of the most powerful forces in American music—the blues.

Born Gertrude Pridgett in Columbus, Georgia, on April 26, 1886, Rainey was initiated into show business by her family, who performed in minstrel shows. She first sang and danced for an audience when she was fourteen years old.

Two years later, in 1902, she heard her first blues song, in St. Louis, and made the warm, earthy rhythms a part of her style. In 1904, she married the comedian and song-and-dance man Will Rainey. Since Will had long been billed as "Pa" Rainey in his act, it was only natural that Gertrude would be called "Ma" when she joined him, and the name stuck throughout her career.

Billed as "Ma and Pa Rainey and the Assassinators of the Blues," the Raineys played the Southern minstrel circuit for two decades with a show called the Rabbit Foot Minstrels.

Ma Rainey not only sang the blues, but also actually created them, blending the raw country sound of her youth with the more sophisticated urban music she heard on the circuit.

When Paramount Records signed her to a recording contract in 1923, she became virtually the first artist to record the blues, and the sound became identified with the powerful, gutsy voice of Ma Rainey.

Variously nicknamed "the Mother of the Blues," "the Paramount Wildcat," and "Madame Rainey," Rainey recorded over 100 songs for Paramount between 1923 and 1928. Her music, beloved for years across the South, had finally come North.

Accompanied by her "Georgia Band," which included such jazz greats as Louis Armstrong, Thomas Dorsey, and Coleman Hawkins, she belted out song after song with titles like "Rough and Tumble Blues," "Jealous Hearted Blues," and "Ma Rainey's Black Bottom Blues."

In spite of her marriage to "Pa," Rainey made no secret of her relationships with women. Indeed, her famous "Prove It on Me Blues," recorded in 1928, sounds more like the testimony of a lesbian than that of a bisexual:

Went out last night with a crowd of my friends,
They must have been women, 'cause I don't like no men.
Wear my clothes just like a fan,
Talk to gals just like any old man
'Cause they say I do it, ain't nobody caught me,
Sure got to prove it on me.

Rainey was a close friend (and a friendly rival) of another bisexual blues singer, Bessie Smith. The Raineys had "discovered" Smith when their minstrel show passed through Smith's home state of Tennessee. Smith had joined the show, and many credit Ma Rainey as a major influence on Smith's career.

In fact, Smith bailed Rainey out of a Chicago jail in 1925, after police raided a women's party hosted by Rainey. There is no proof, but much suspicion, that Rainey and Smith were lovers.

Ma Rainey retired from performing in 1935 and moved back to Columbus. Unlike many of her contemporaries, Rainey had maintained control of her own career and her own money (the famous necklace of gold coins was one of her "savings accounts"); and when she retired, she owned her own house as well as two theaters, the Airdrome in Columbus and the Lyric in Rome, Georgia.

She operated the theaters herself until her death on December 22, 1939, from a heart attack.

—*Tina Gianoulis*

BIBLIOGRAPHY

Baxter, Derrick S. *Ma Rainey & the Classic Blues Singers*. Lanham, Md.: Madison Books, 1970.

Davis, Angela Y. *Blues Legacies & Black Feminism*. New York, Pantheon Books, 1998.

Lieb, Sandra. *Mother of the Blues: A Study of Ma Rainey*. Amherst: University of Massachusetts Press, 1981.

Sullivan, Tom. "Mother of the Blues." The Ma Rainey Page: www.lambda.net/~maximum/rainey.html

SEE ALSO

Blues Music; Popular Music; Jazz; Cabarets and Revues; Smith, Bessie;

Maurice Ravel ca. 1915.

Ravel, Maurice   *(1875–1937)*

ONE OF FRANCE'S MOST DISTINGUISHED COMPOSERS, Maurice Ravel was a prolific and versatile artist who worked in several musical genres, creating stage music (two operas and several ballets), orchestral music, vocal music, chamber music, and piano music. His unique musical language, employing harmonies that are at once ravishing and subtle, made him one of the most influential composers of the twentieth century.

Ravel's sexuality has been the subject of considerable speculation. Although it is not certain that he was gay, he was rumored to be so. Fiercely protective of his privacy, his most significant emotional relationship seems to have been with his mother. At the same time, however, he embraced a public identity as a cultured dandy, a dapper man-about-town of refined taste and sensibility.

A lifelong bachelor, Ravel had several significant relationships with men, including the pianist Ricardo Viñes, a fellow dandy and bachelor, but it is not certain whether these friendships were sexual.

He was born Joseph Maurice Ravel on March 7, 1875, at Ciboure, France, near St. Jean de Luz, Basses-Pyrénées, a village close to the French-Spanish border, to a Swiss father and a Basque mother.

Ravel's father, who was talented musically, was an engineer. The composer may have inherited from his father the devotion to craftsmanship and meticulous detail that led Igor Stravinsky to describe him as the "Swiss watch-maker of music."

Although he was raised in Paris, Ravel was very conscious of his Basque heritage. He always felt a special affinity with Spanish and Basque culture.

Ravel studied music at the Conservatoire de Paris with Emile Decombes, Charles-Wilfrid Beriot, Emile Pessard, and Gabriel Fauré. An accomplished pianist, he took courses at the Conservatoire in both piano and composition.

As a young man, Ravel joined a circle of avant-garde writers and composers called Les Apaches. This group included Viñes and the composers Manuel de Falla, Florent Schmitt, and Stravinsky. Several members of the circle, including Ravel, developed an interest in the new American form of music, jazz. Not surprisingly, jazz rhythms entered some of Ravel's compositions, such as his late Sonata for Violin and Piano, which includes a jazzy movement called "The Blues."

Ravel's career and life can be divided into two parts, separated by World War I, which had a traumatic effect on him. Before the war, he was an important presence in French musical circles, often conducting his own works, giving piano concerts, and collaborating with Sergei Diaghilev on commissions for the Ballets Russes. After the war, however, the composer's physical and emotional health deteriorated. He retreated from Paris and spent the last decade of his life in semiretirement.

Ravel is most famous for instrumental works that capture the music and culture of Spain. His interesting uses of harmony and subtle orchestration have added to the distinctive quality of his highly sophisticated music. His music also often refers back to earlier French composers such as Couperin and Rameau. In addition, it reflects Ravel's enduring fascination with the East and its cultures and music.

Among Ravel's earliest compositions are *Schéhérazade* (1898) and the *Rapsodie espagnole* (1908), both of which are distinguished by exotic settings. His stately *Pavane pour une infante défunte* (1910) also grows out of his interest in Spanish history and culture.

Perhaps Ravel's most famous early composition is *Daphnis et Chloë* (1912), a ballet originally commissioned by Diaghilev and choreographed by Michel Fokine for the Ballets Russes. The music for *Daphnis et Chloë* is particularly noteworthy for its eroticism and mystery, including a rhapsodic part for wordless chorus.

Ravel's *Le Tombeau de Couperin* (1914–1917) beautifully indicates his interest in French music of the Neoclassical period, while the ballet *La Valse* (1919), originally choreographed by Bronislava Nijinska, reflects his enduring desire to create music for the dance.

Ravel's most familiar work to contemporary audiences is the *Boléro* of 1928, which he considered something of a well-orchestrated joke because of its constant repetition of the same melody. Commissioned by the dancer Ida Rubenstein for a ballet choreographed by Nijinska, *Boléro* is a bravura work built on a relentless rhythm that culminates in the wild abandon of Dionysian revels. It is certainly one of the most widely performed and recognized pieces of classical music.

In 1930, Ravel wrote his Piano Concerto for the Left Hand at the request of pianist Paul Wittgenstein, who had lost his right arm in World War I.

Ravel also wrote two appealing operas. Although they are minor works, they continue to please contemporary audiences. *L'Heure espagnole*, which premiered in Paris in 1911 at the Opéra Comique, tries to capture a day in the life of the bored, unfaithful wife of a clockmaker in eighteenth-century Spain. *L'Enfant et les sortilèges*, with a libretto by Colette, had its first performance at the Monte Carlo Opera in 1925 and explores a child's relationship with his mother, his environment, and his fantasies.

Near the end of his life, Ravel received numerous accolades. The French government planned to award him the Légion d'Honneur. Unfortunately, the honor was announced publicly before Ravel had been informed of the decision. Infuriated, the composer declined to accept the award. In 1931, however, he accepted an honorary doctorate from Oxford University.

In 1928, Ravel made a triumphant four-month tour of the United States, where he met many musical notables, including George Gershwin, whom he admired greatly.

In his final years, Ravel suffered a series of health problems and gradually lost the ability to communicate with others. He died in Paris on December 28, 1937, after a series of strokes and an unsuccessful brain operation.

—*John Louis DiGaetani*

BIBLIOGRAPHY

Kelly, Barbara A. "Maurice Ravel." *The New Grove Dictionary of Music and Musicians*. Stanley Sadie, ed. London: Macmillan, 2001.

Laloy, Louis. *Louis Laloy on Debussy, Ravel, and Stravinsky*. Aldershot, England: Ashgate, 1999.

Mawer, Deborah, ed. *The Cambridge Companion to Ravel*. New York: Cambridge University Press, 2000.

SEE ALSO

Classical Music; Opera; Ballets Russes; Béjart, Maurice; Diaghilev, Sergei; Falla (y Matheu), Manuel de; Griffes, Charles Tomlinson

Reed, Lou   (b. 1942)

IN THE 1960S, 1970S, AND 1980S, THE ROCK MUSICIAN Lou Reed, pencil-thin, craggy, and dressed in tough leather or androgynous glitz, came to symbolize the rebellious outsider. Reed produced a gritty urban rock and roll that made even the protest and acid rock of the 1970s seem tame in comparison.

Beatniks listened to Pete Seeger and the Weavers. Hippies listened to the Doors and Jimi Hendrix. The real freaks listened to Reed's Velvet Underground.

A rebel from an early age, Reed horrified his parents on Long Island with his effeminacy and his violently loud rock music. Hoping to curb his homosexuality, they sent him to a mental hospital for electroshock treatments. Although the treatments were painful and damaging, Reed emerged with his antisocial impulses (and bisexuality) more or less intact.

He moved to New York City, where he met Andy Warhol, the experimental artist who made a cult of both the decadent and the mundane. In 1965, Reed—as part of Warhol's studio, The Factory—joined fellow musicians John Cale, Sterling Morrison, and Maureen Tucker to form the Velvet Underground. Andy Warhol managed the band, which supplied the music for his Exploding Plastic Inevitable art shows in 1966.

Although Velvet Underground sold few albums and disbanded after only five years, the group had an impact that lasted for decades. Taking rock back to its rawest form—a few simple chords played very loudly—Velvet Underground's urban decadence was the opposite of the visionary dreaminess of much of the music of the era.

Their songs were about drugs and junkies, hustlers and drag queens, all sung with a bare-bones intensity that made them appealingly taboo. The 1980s alternative rock scene would honor the music of Velvet Underground as an influential forerunner of punk.

After the breakup of Velvet Underground, Reed continued to violate taboos as a solo artist. Bisexual in his private life, Reed linked up with another allegedly bisexual rocker, David Bowie, who in 1972 produced Reed's first solo album, *Transformer.*

On *Transformer,* Reed changed his look from urban tough to glam-rock flash. He also introduced his most famous signature song, "Walk on the Wild Side," the story of a transgendered hooker's odyssey from Los Angeles to the hard streets of New York, told with an understated, ironic affection and a catchy backbeat.

Reed has continued his solo career, producing well-reviewed albums every few years and frequently touring Europe and the United States. His work retains an honesty and clarity of poetic lyric that often makes him seem a more mature performer than many other aging rock stars.

His 2000 album *Ecstasy* is a powerful work with an unusual theme for a rock album—the celebration of a long-term relationship. Inspired by his association with the experimental rock musician Laurie Anderson, Reed explores the issues of partnership with a hard-edged depth and complexity.

Reed's brutally romantic lyrics can also stand on their own, as, for example, in his artistically designed books: *Between Thought & Expression* (1995) and *Pass Thru Fire* (1999).
—*Tina Gianoulis*

Bibliography

Bockris, Victor. *Transformer: The Lou Reed Story.* New York: Simon & Schuster, 1994.

Browne, David. "Lou Reed: Too Legit to Quit." *Entertainment Weekly,* February 21, 1992, 28.

"Lou Reed." *Current Biography* 50.7 (July 1989): 28–33.

Rogers, Ray. "Lou Reed." *Interview,* March 1996, 86.

Sischy, Ingrid. "Focus, Thy Name is Lou." *Interview,* May 1998, 90.

See also

Popular Music; Rock Music; Music and AIDS; Drag Shows: Drag Queens and Female Impersonators; Bowie, David

Robbins, Jerome   (1918–1998)

THE BISEXUAL CHOREOGRAPHER AND DIRECTOR JEROME Robbins was both a great choreographer of classical ballet and a Broadway innovator. But he was fearful that he might be outed, and his reputation was tarnished when—during the height of McCarthyism—he "named names" during a meeting of the House Un-American Activities Committee.

According to the critic Clive Barnes, Jerome Robbins "was an extremely demanding man, not always popular with his dancers, although always respected. He was a perfectionist who sometimes, very quietly, reached perfection."

From 1944 to 1997, Robbins choreographed sixty-six ballets and choreographed (and often also directed) fifteen Broadway musicals. During his extraordinarily prolific career he not only excelled in two different fields of dance, but he also worked with chameleon-like versatility, never seeming to repeat himself.

Born Jerome Rabinowitz to Harry and Lena Rabinowitz on October 11, 1918, in New York City, he and his family soon moved to Weehawken, New Jersey. His father's corset business allowed young Robbins to attend New York University for one year, where he majored in chemistry, before a slump in business forced him to withdraw.

Robbins had already started accompanying his sister to dance classes, which led to his professional debut in a Yiddish Art Theater production in 1937.

For five summers Robbins choreographed and performed at the famous Poconos resort Lake Tamiment, in between dancing in four Broadway musicals, one choreographed by George Balanchine.

Robbins was hired as a choreographer for the second season of Ballet Theatre (1940–1941). His meteoric career took off with his first ballet, *Fancy Free* (1944), to an original score by Leonard Bernstein.

The ballet was an instant hit; and the composer and choreographer, both twenty-five years old, joined forces with lyricists Betty Comden and Adolph Green to create a musical out of Robbins's comic ballet of three sailors on leave in New York City: *On the Town.* The success of *On the Town* made Robbins the boy genius of two worlds: musical theater and concert dance.

In the 1950s, Robbins began to direct as well as choreograph, creating such masterpieces as *The King and I* (1951), *Bells Are Ringing* (1956), *Gypsy* (1959), *Fiddler on the Roof* (1964), and, most notably, *West Side Story* (1957).

Robbins's darkest hour occurred at the height of McCarthyism. In 1953, he named eight colleagues as members of the Communist Party during a House Un-American Activities Committee hearing.

Robbins never explained or defended his motives for naming names. He may have testified to avoid being blacklisted on Broadway or out of fear of being outed as a homosexual. Many colleagues and others considered his behavior a betrayal and never forgave him for it.

Unlike other directors of musicals, Robbins demanded that his actors dance as well as sing. His high expectations of the cast of *West Side Story*, for example, created the triple-threat performer: the actor/singer/dancer. This landmark production in the history of musical theater was also the beginning of a new genre: musical tragedy.

While the librettist Arthur Laurents felt that the shared Jewishness of its collaborators was the greatest influence on the creation of *West Side Story*, surely the show was also influenced by the fact that seven members of the creative team were gay: Robbins, Laurents, composer Leonard Bernstein, lyricist Stephen Sondheim, set designer Oliver Smith, lighting designer Jean Rosenthal, and costume designer Irene Sharaff, in addition to the first actor to play Tony, Larry Kert.

One result of the homosexuality of most of the creative team is that, despite the heterosexual plot line, *West Side Story* is nevertheless intensely homoerotic. The male characters are eroticized as much as the female characters, if not more so; and Riff seems to love Tony as much as Tony loves Maria.

At the invitation of Balanchine, Robbins joined New York City Ballet as a dancer, choreographer, and Associate Director from 1949 through 1959. He returned to New York City Ballet as Ballet Master in 1969.

For the next twenty years, the former king of Broadway choreographed numerous masterpieces of ballet, including *Dances at a Gathering* (1969), *The Goldberg Variations* (1971), *Glass Pieces* (1983), *Ives, Songs* (1988), and *2 & 3 Part Inventions* (1994). There is little doubt that his ballets would have been more highly regarded, then and now, had they not been created in Balanchine's shadow.

Robbins's classicism was not as dedicated to a strictly codified idiom as Balanchine's; rather, it was infused with theatricality and emotional expressiveness. Many of Robbins's ballets have a naturalness, a democratic air, because they translate (and transform) European (especially Russian) ballet conventions into a more familiar vernacular. Robbins's ballets are not about Americana, yet they are very American.

Shortly before the death of Balanchine in 1983, Robbins and Peter Martins were named codirectors of New York City Ballet, a post Robbins held until 1990.

Robbins took a leave from New York City Ballet in 1988 to stage *Jerome Robbins' Broadway* (1989), an anthology of dances and scenes from eleven of his Broadway shows. It won the Tony Award for Best Musical and ran for 624 performances.

Robbins the perfectionist was often his own worst enemy. He was savagely demanding of his performers and unrelenting in his demands on himself. High expectations ruled his personal life as well, as Robbins pursued both men and women, but formed no permanent relationship.

Robbins's ballet *Facsimile* (1946) reflects his bisexuality, as two men and one woman vie for one another's affections.

The ballet dancer Nora Kaye told reporters that she and Robbins were to be wed in 1951; at the same time, Robbins was in the midst of a five-year live-in relationship (1950–1955) with the Broadway dancer Buzz Miller. Robbins also had romantic affairs with the actor Montgomery Clift, the writer Christine Conrad, the photographer Jesse Gerstein, and the filmmaker Warren Sonbert.

On July 29, 1998, Robbins died of a stroke at the age of seventy-nine. His numerous awards include one Emmy (*Peter Pan*), two Oscars (*West Side Story*), four Tony Awards, the Kennedy Center Honors (1981), and a National Medal of the Arts (1988).

The greatest classical choreographer born in this country, and a Broadway innovator, Robbins took millions of people to a new place—a world, as he once said, "where things are not named."

—*Bud Coleman*

Jerome Robbins in "Three Virgins and a Devil,"
photographed by Carl van Vechten in 1941.

BIBLIOGRAPHY

Conrad, Christine. *Jerome Robbins: The Broadway Man, That Ballet Man.* London: Booth-Clibborn Editions, 2000.

Kisselgoff, Anna. "Jerome Robbins, 79, Is Dead; Giant of Ballet and Broadway." *New York Times,* July 30, 1998.

Lawrence, Greg. *Dance With Demons: The Life of Jerome Robbins.* New York: G. T. Putnam's Sons, 2001.

SEE ALSO

Dance; Ballet; Musical Theater and Film; Ailey, Alvin; Bennett, Michael; Bernstein, Leonard; Laurents, Arthur; Sondheim, Stephen; Tune, Tommy

Robinson, Tom   (b. 1950)

ROCK MUSICIAN TOM ROBINSON WAS EMBRACED BY the gay rights movement when he sang "Glad to Be Gay" in the late 1970s, but found himself the subject of controversy in the 1990s when he chose to live with a woman and become a father.

Robinson was born into a middle-class family in Cambridge, England, on June 1, 1950. His first musical experience was as a choirboy.

Robinson realized at the age of thirteen that he was gay, a frightening thought for the boy given that penalties in England for same-sex sexual activity included prison terms at the time. He had a nervous breakdown and attempted suicide when he was sixteen and spent the next six years in a therapeutic community facility.

Robinson moved to London in 1973 and founded the trio Café Society. The group recorded an album, but it sold only 600 copies.

In London Robinson became involved in the gay rights movement and in combating sexism and racism, causes that he continues to champion.

He left Café Society in 1976 and founded the more political Tom Robinson Band. The following year, the group put out the hit single "2-4-6-8 Motorway," which alludes obliquely to a gay truck driver, and "Glad to Be Gay," which was embraced by gay audiences and banned by the BBC.

The band recorded an extremely successful first album, *Power in the Darkness* (1978), but the follow-up was a failure, and the group soon broke up.

Robinson organized a new band, Sector 27, that produced a well-reviewed but not particularly successful album. The band nevertheless received an enthusiastic reception at a Madison Square Garden concert with The Police. In short order, however, their management company went bankrupt, the band disintegrated, and Robinson suffered another nervous breakdown. Desolate and in debt, Robinson moved to Germany, cadging music work in East Berlin.

In 1982, Robinson penned the song "War Baby," about divisions between East and West. It spent nine weeks on the Top 10 charts in the United Kingdom and revived his career.

Upon returning to the British Isles, Robinson began performing in cabarets in Scotland. A producer from the BBC soon tapped him to become the host of a BBC World Service radio show. He continues to host music programs and occasional special features, including *Surviving Suicide,* which he wrote and presented in 1994.

Robinson, a longtime supporter of and former volunteer for London's Gay Switchboard help line, was attending a 1982 benefit for the organization when he met the woman with whom he would eventually live and have two children.

In the mid-1990s, when Robinson became a father, the tabloid press had a field day, blaring the news with the headline "Britain's Number One Gay in Love with Girl Biker!" The gay press reviled him, but Robinson continued to identify as a gay man, telling an interviewer for the *Manchester Guardian,* "I have much more sympathy with bisexuals now, but I am absolutely not one." He added that "our enemies do not draw the distinction between gay and bisexual."

Tom Robinson.

In a 1994 interview with the *Boston Globe,* Robinson asserted, "We've been fighting for tolerance for the last 20 years, and I've campaigned for people to be able to love whoever the hell they want. That's what we're talking about: tolerance and freedom and liberty—life, liberty, and the pursuit of happiness. So if somebody won't grant me the same tolerance I've been fighting for for them, hey, they've got a problem, not me."

Robinson has indeed been a strong advocate of liberty for all. He is a steadfast supporter of Amnesty International and Peter Tatchell's human rights organization Outrage!, and is a leader in the Rock Against Racism campaign in England.

Over his career, Robinson has put out more than twenty albums either as a solo performer or as a member of a group. Among the best known are *Love over Rage* (1994) and *Having It Both Ways* (1996).

In addition to doing radio work, he continues to tour. He has moved to a more mellow sound, playing acoustic guitar in his concerts, and even includes some spoken-word pieces in his performances. He knows, however, that his fans turn out to hear his classic songs, and so his signature tune, "Glad to Be Gay," remains in his repertoire, although he updates it to reflect current events.

— *Linda Rapp*

BIBLIOGRAPHY

Fanshawe, Simon. "The War Baby at Peace: He Was Glad to Be Gay, and He Became the Spokesperson for a Generation. Then It All Went Wrong and He Fled the Country with a Nervous Breakdown. Now, Tom Robinson Is Back." *Manchester* (England) *Guardian,* May 27, 1994.

Fowler, Rebecca. "National Music Festival: 2-4-6-8, It's Never Too Late; He Went in and out of Fashion, but Tom Robinson Is Still Driven by Music." *Independent* (London), June 4, 1996.

Graustark, Barbara. "Rock 'N' Wrath." Newsweek, July 30, 1978, 72.

Robinson, Tom. www.tomrobinson.com

Sullivan, Jim. "Robinson Returns; After 15 Years, the Angry Young Revolutionary Has a New Record Deal and the Same High Ideals." *Boston Globe,* August 12, 1994.

SEE ALSO

Popular Music; Rock Music; Bowie, David; Pansy Division

Rock Music

ROCK MUSIC REFERS TO AN ARRAY OF RELATED MUSIcal styles that have come to dominate popular music in the West since about 1955. Originating in the United States, rock music was initially influenced by the black rhythm-and-blues (R & B) music of the American South.

Over the last five decades, rock music has been shaped by, and in turn has been an influential force on, a broad range of cultures and musical traditions, including country western, folk, gospel, blues, electronic, dance, and the popular music of Asia, Africa, and Latin America. The genre also encompasses a wide range of substyles, such as heavy metal, punk, alternative, world beat, rap, and techno.

Rock music has become closely associated with freedom of expression, symbolized especially by the rebellious rock star. As such, rock music and musicians have helped to establish new fashions, forms of language, attitudes, and political views.

Surprisingly, however, homosexuality is still generally considered a stigma in the world of rock music. Despite the large number of gay and lesbian people working behind the scenes in the industry, mainstream gay and lesbian rock artists are often discouraged by their corporate record companies from being publicly open about their sexual orientation.

Little Richard to Wayne/Jayne County

In the late 1950s, Little Richard (born Richard Wayne Penniman) brought a flamboyantly theatrical style to early rock music with his sequined vests, tight trousers, eyeliner, and pompadour hairstyle. His shouted vocals and frantic piano playing defined the dynamic sound of rock and roll and led to an uninterrupted run of smash hits— "Tutti Frutti," "Long Tall Sally," "Rip It Up," "Lucille," "Keep A Knockin," and "Good Golly Miss Molly." Little Richard was inducted into the Rock and Roll Hall of Fame in 1986. He has, however, never explicitly come out as gay.

Flamboyant theatrics reemerged in the early 1970s with the flourishing of glitter and glam rock, a fusion of feminized—or at best androgynous—images and virile rock anthems.

Glitter or glam rock groups include, most notably, the New York Dolls, T. Rex, Mott The Hoople, and Alice Cooper. Despite their image as sexual outlaws, these rock performers were, nevertheless, firmly ensconced in the world of heterosexuality. Even such rock luminaries as Lou Reed and David Bowie flirted with glam rock and cultivated fashionably gay or bisexual personae; they later married, however, and claimed they had been straight all along.

The one openly gay performer in the era of glam rock was Jobriath, born Bruce Wayne Campbell in 1946. "I'm a true fairy," the renamed Jobriath Boone proclaimed to the press when his eponymous debut album was released in October 1973. The release of that album was followed by a colossal media blitz. Full-page ads appeared in *Vogue, Penthouse, Rolling Stone,* and the *New York Times,* with an image of Jobriath as a discreetly nude statue crawling on smashed legs. The image was even reproduced on a Times Square billboard and splashed across hundreds of New York City buses.

Jobriath's first album was quickly followed up with the release of a second one, *Creatures of the Street*, a mere six months later. Although the albums, especially the first, received a few respectable reviews, the extensive media hype did not help to sell records. Drug and alcohol addiction also hastened the rapid descent of Jobriath's music career; he was abandoned by his manager and record company halfway through his first U.S. tour.

Jobriath promptly announced his retirement from the music industry and moved to New York, where he pursued an acting career with little success. Jobriath died of an AIDS-related illness in 1983.

Perhaps rock's most prominent transgendered performer is Wayne/Jayne County, born Wayne Rogers in 1947. A performance artist as much as a rock musician, he began his career in the late 1960s as Wayne County in New York's underground theater world. In the early 1970s, County formed his first band, Queen Elizabeth. The band recorded several music demos, most notably a song titled "Max's Kansas City," celebrating the legendary New York club of the same name, where County had begun performing in drag. County subsequently formed another group, Wayne and The Back Street Boys, which became part of New York's burgeoning punk scene. The group's first album, recorded in 1976, was never released.

Unsuccessful in finding an American label interested in his brand of rock music, County moved to England. There he formed yet another group, The Electric Chairs; they were signed by the independent label Safari Records, which issued his 1978 debut album, *The Electric Chairs*. Soon after came the release of the most renowned of County's songs, "Fuck Off," which Safari chose to release under a pseudonymous label. Further albums include *Storm the Gates of Heaven* (1978), the group's most commercially successful work, and *Things Your Mother Never Told You* (1979).

In 1979, Wayne County moved to Berlin and later that year reemerged as Jayne County. A live album titled *Rock 'N' Roll Resurrection*, County's first recording as Jayne, was released in 1980. Her next album was the self-produced *Private Oyster,* released in 1986. Periodic releases followed in the 1990s, some featuring new songs, others featuring reworked versions of past material. County published her autobiography, *Man Enough to be a Woman*, in 1996. Her most recent album is *So New York* (2003).

Freddie Mercury to Melissa Etheridge

The 1970s disco scene saw the emergence of such gay, or at least gay-friendly, performers as Sylvester, the Village People, and Grace Jones, and in the 1980s, dance and techno groups such as Bronski Beat, Frankie Goes to Hollywood, and the Pet Shop Boys. The world of adult contemporary music has also seen several openly gay—and best-selling—artists, such as Boy George, Elton John, George Michael, Rufus Wainwright, and k.d. lang.

However, within the realm of rock music, a world dominated by swaggering men with electric guitars and their mostly straight male audiences, there have been, until quite recently, few openly gay musicians whose music also reflects their sexuality.

For example, Freddie Mercury, the gay rock icon and former front man for the British power-rock group Queen, only publicly declared his homosexuality one day before his death of AIDS-related illnesses in 1991.

Likewise, Morrissey (born Steven Patrick Morrissey), lead singer of the British rock band The Smiths from 1984 to 1988, who has been embraced by many in the gay community as one of their own, has never publicly come out and has contradicted himself repeatedly on the subject of his sexuality.

There have, nevertheless, been a few exceptions. The British rocker Tom Robinson broke political ground in the late 1970s with his song "Glad To Be Gay." Although Robinson subsequently married and fathered two children, he continues to define himself in the media as either queer or bisexual. And his music continues to reflect his sexuality. He cleverly titled his 1996 album *Having It Both Ways*, and the bisexual-themed "Blood Brother" won him Best Song at the 1998 Gay/Lesbian American Music Awards.

Joan Jett rose to fame in the 1970s all-girl rock band the Runaways. Her cover of "I Love Rock 'N' Roll," with her band the Blackhearts, was a number one hit in 1982; "Crimson and Clover" was another hit. Jett, however, did not come out as a lesbian until the 1990s.

One of the most successful gay rock artists today is the award-winning singer/songwriter Melissa Etheridge, who began recording in 1988. Etheridge's sensual, blues-based, and autobiographical songs became even more deeply personal and confessional after she publicly came out as a lesbian in 1993. Moreover, her coming out caused her career no harm; her album *Yes I Am*—released in the year of her coming out—became her biggest seller to date.

Although Melissa Etheridge has a strong lesbian following, she has also become a crossover success; among her ardent fans are men and women of all sexual orientations.

Queercore

Angered by the homophobia and sexism within much of the rock and punk music scenes, a group of young, militant gay musicians started a movement that has been dubbed *queercore*. It is characterized by hard-core punk music and frank lyrics that address such issues as queer desire and societal prejudice.

Queercore gained notoriety in the late 1980s through such underground zines as *Homocore*, *JD's*, and *Chainsaw* and in the art of Bruce La Bruce and G. B. Jones. Later, throughout the 1990s, queercore was most visibly exemplified by the raw music, political rage, and social commentary of such groups as Pansy Division, Fifth Column, Team Dresch, and God Is My Co-Pilot.

At the same time, the Riot Grrl movement started to take off. Riot Grrl was a grassroots feminist movement with several lesbian bands in the forefront, including Bikini Kill, L7, Tribe 8, and the Butchies. As the Riot Grrl movement gathered steam, queercore participants (both men and women) started to take notice, and the two movements began to feed off each other, leading to a diverse assortment of music and ideas.

Although queercore has a small but passionate group of supporters, it is perhaps too raw and controversial to move beyond the fringes of the music industry. Few radio stations are willing to play queercore music, and the independent labels that support queercore bands rarely have the resources to market them sufficiently.

As more musicians publicly declare their homosexuality, being gay in the world of rock music may become less of an issue or a perceived detriment to a mainstream career. In recent years, for example, such rock musicians as singer/songwriter Ani DiFranco; Kathleen Hanna of the bands Bikini Kill and Le Tigre; Corrin Tucker and Carrie Brownstein of Sleater-Kinney; Michael Stipe, the lead singer for R.E.M.; Jonsi Thór Birgisson, the front man for the Icelandic techno-rock group Sigur Rós; Chuck Panozzo, the longtime bassist and cofounder of the arena-rock band Styx; and Rob Halford, vocalist of the heavy-metal British band Judas Priest, have all come out publicly as gay or bisexual.   —*Craig Kaczorowski*

BIBLIOGRAPHY

Collum, Danny Duncan. "Rock's Little Secret." *Sojourners* 30.5 (September–October 2001): 52.

County, Jayne, with Rupert Smith. *Man Enough to be a Woman.* New York: Serpent's Tail, 1996.

Dickinson, Chris. "The Music Is the Message: Some Radical Gay Bands Put Their Sexuality Way Up Front." *St. Louis Post-Dispatch,* April 21, 1996.

McDonnell, Evelyn, and Ann Powers, eds. *Rock She Wrote: Women Write About Rock, Pop, and Rap.* New York: Delta Books, 1995.

Sullivan, Caroline. "Queer to the Core." *Guardian,* December 17, 1993.

ARTIST HOME PAGES:

www.thebutchies.com

www.eltonjohn.com

www.sonymusic.co.uk/georgemichael

www.jaynecounty.com

www.joanjett.com

www.jobriath.org

www.kdlang.com

www.melissaetheridge.com

www.morrissey-solo.com

www.pansydivision.com

www.petshopboys.co.uk

www.rufuswainwright.com

www.letigreworld.com

www.tomrobinson.com

SEE ALSO

Popular Music; Country Music; Bowie, David; Boy George (George O'Dowd); DiFranco, Ani; Etheridge, Melissa; John, Sir Elton; lang, k.d.; Little Richard (Richard Penniman); Mercury, Freddie; Michael, George; Reed, Lou; Smiths, The, and Morrissey; Somerville, Jimmy; Wainwright, Rufus; Bell, Andy; Pansy Division; Robinson, Tom; Stipe, Michael

Rorem, Ned   *(b. 1923)*

NED ROREM IS ONE OF THE MOST ACCOMPLISHED AND prolific composers of art songs in the world, but his musical and literary endeavors extend far beyond this specialized field. Rorem has also composed symphonies, piano concerti, operas, chamber music, ballets, and music for the theater. In addition, he is the author of thirteen books, including five volumes of diaries and collections of lectures and criticism.

Born in Richmond, Indiana, on October 23, 1923, to Quaker parents, Rorem was raised in Chicago, where he demonstrated an early interest in composition and piano. At seventeen, Rorem entered the Music School of Northwestern University, where he pursued advanced musical studies.

Two years later, he received a scholarship to the Curtis Institute in Philadelphia. He then studied composition under Bernard Wagenaar at Juilliard, where he received his master's degree in 1948. While at Juilliard, Rorem also worked privately with Aaron Copland at Tanglewood and Virgil Thomson in New York.

Additionally, in 1948 the Music Library Association voted his song *The Lordly Hudson* (based on a poem by Paul Goodman) the best published song of that year.

Upon graduating from Juilliard, Rorem traveled to Morocco, and in 1950 to Paris, where he remained for seven years, achieving international recognition for his compositions and recording his experiences in a diary published to literary acclaim.

His years as a young composer among the leading figures of the artistic and social milieu of postwar Europe are portrayed in *The Paris Diary of Ned Rorem*

Ned Rorem, photographed by Marc Geller in 1995.

(1966). His subsequent diaries and essays offer elegant and erudite analyses of aesthetic questions and candidly detail his life in the gay cultural fast lane.

Since his return to the United States in 1957, Rorem has divided his time between Manhattan and Nantucket, continuing to add to his extensive catalog of over 400 art songs. His individual settings and cycles draw their texts from a wide range of poetry and prose. Among his favorite sources have been works by W. H. Auden, Paul Goodman, Frank O'Hara, Theodore Roethke, and Walt Whitman.

In addition to his art songs, Rorem has composed three operas, most notably *Miss Julie*, based on the play by August Strindberg, which premiered at the New York City Opera in 1965; three symphonies; three piano concerti; several large-scale choral works, including the powerful *Whitman Cantata* (1983); as well as smaller-scale keyboard and chamber pieces.

Among the distinguished conductors who have performed his music are Leonard Bernstein, Eugene Ormandy, Kurt Masur, Thomas Schippers, and Robert Shaw.

In 1976, Rorem received the Pulitzer Prize in Music for his orchestral work *Air Music*.

Rorem continues to write and compose, and he enjoys a steady stream of commissions and performances. He has steadfastly remained faithful to tonality and the song; his compositions are musically rich and exquisitely fashioned. Above all, there is an emotional generosity that pervades much of his work, together with his unique brand of soaring lyricism that has attracted some of the twentieth century's most distinguished interpreters.

Recent recordings of Rorem's work include *Evidence of Things Not Seen* (1998), a thirty-six-song cycle based on disparate texts ranging from works about youth's unbounded hope to the losses and hard-won faith of old age; *Songs of Ned Rorem* (2000), a collection of thirty-two songs sung by lyric mezzo Susan Graham; and *More Than A Day* (2000), a song cycle sung by the countertenor Brian Asawa and based on poems by actor and writer Jack Larson to his late lover, the film director James Bridges, both of whom Rorem first met in the early 1960s.

Rorem's own lover of over thirty years, Jim Holmes, died in 1999. *Another Sleep* (2002), a cycle of nineteen songs based on texts by such authors as Milton, Shakespeare, and Sappho, is a memorial to Holmes.

—*Craig Kaczorowski*

BIBLIOGRAPHY

Goldstein, Richard. "AIDS Culture: The Next Wave." *Village Voice*, April 13, 2001, 50.

Philbrook, Erik. "Words' Worth." *Playback* 5.4 (1998): 6–8.

Smith, Patrick. "Diamond Ned Rorem." *Opera News*, March 28, 1998, 4.

The Official Ned Rorem Web Site. http://nedrorem.com

SEE ALSO

Classical Music; Conductors; Opera; Music and AIDS; Choruses and Bands; Bernstein, Leonard; Copland, Aaron; Porter, Cole; Thomson, Virgil

Rosenmüller, Johann   (1619–1684)

ONE OF THE MOST IMPORTANT COMPOSERS OF INSTRU-mental music and sacred vocal music in Germany in the middle of the seventeenth century, Johann Rosenmüller survived a homosexual scandal in Leipzig and reconstituted his career in Venice.

At age twenty-one, Rosenmüller entered the University of Leipzig and became the assistant of the Thomasschule Cantor (or director of music). In 1651, he was appointed organist at the Nicolaikirche, one of the three important churches in the city. Two years later, the town council promised him the position of Cantor at the Thomasschule on the demise or resignation of the current holder. This was the same position that Johann Sebastian Bach would assume in 1723.

In 1655, however, Rosenmüller's career was abruptly derailed when he and several choirboys were arrested on charges of homosexuality. He managed to escape prosecution and fled to Venice, where presumably a less restrictive environment existed.

Nothing else is known of Rosenmüller's personal life, but the arrest has led, perhaps unjustifiably, to the assumption that he was a pedophile.

In Venice in 1658, Rosenmüller became a trombone player at St. Mark's, the most prestigious musical establishment in the city. A few years later, he attained a position as *maestro di coro*, or Master of the Chorus, at the Pio Ospedale della Pietà, a school for illegitimate girls that specialized in musical training. As late as 1682, he was being paid by the school as a composer.

In Venice, Rosenmüller also continued to compose music (primarily masses, psalms, Magnificats, and motets, as well as instrumental sonatas), which reflected Italian influence and which circulated in Germany. Moreover, he attracted students who came to study with him from Germany. Thus, as a result of his disgrace, he helped disseminate Italian musical idioms in Germany.

None of his music sets homoerotic texts, but some of his music for solo voices adopts an arguably eroticized approach to the setting of sacred texts.

In 1682, he finally returned to his homeland to become the court composer at Wolfenbüttel in Saxony, where he died in 1684.

At his death, Rosenmüller was described as "the Amphion of his age." In the late eighteenth century, he was praised by Goethe. Recent recordings of Rosenmüller's sacred music have reestablished him as a significant composer.   —*Robert A. Green*

BIBLIOGRAPHY

Skinner, Graeme. "Rosenmüller, Johann." *Who's Who in Gay and Lesbian History from Antiquity to World War II.* Robert Aldrich and Garry Wotherspoon, eds. London: Routledge, 2001. 382–383.

SEE ALSO

Classical Music

RuPaul (RuPaul Andre Charles)   *(b. 1960)*

ASIX-FOOT-FIVE-INCH-TALL AFRICAN AMERICAN DRAG queen who usually performs in a blonde wig, RuPaul has been responsible for giving drag a new visibility in American popular culture. He is one of the most famous drag queens in mainstream media history. RuPaul is credited with the statement "We're born naked, and the rest is drag."

RuPaul conveys a gentleness and an almost wholesome warmth that have made drag far less threatening to mainstream audiences. As a result, he has had not only a successful recording career as a disco diva, but also a wide variety of film roles, both in and out of drag, and has hosted a popular VH1 talk show.

In perhaps his most appropriate gender-bending career, he has been the "Face of M.A.C. Cosmetics": spokesmodel for the Canadian cosmetics company and chairperson of the M.A.C. AIDS charity fund.

The concept of drag is all about manipulating surface images, and RuPaul's life has given him an intimate understanding of the ways in which the surface can be deceptive.

Born into a working-class family in San Diego on November 17, 1960, RuPaul Andre Charles had an early fascination with things feminine. By the age of four, he was already an effeminate boy, imitating Diana Ross and Jane Fonda and beginning to be labeled a sissy.

His parents divorced when he was seven, and RuPaul was raised from then on in a household of strong women, consisting of his adored twin sisters, seven years older than he, and his mother, whom he describes in his autobiography as "the fiercest drag queen I've ever known."

By the time he was fifteen, RuPaul was ready to come out as a gay man, and he chafed under his mother's iron rule. He moved into his sister's house, then moved with her to Atlanta.

There, free from parental constraints, he threw himself into the gay life, performing in drag clubs, and, briefly, with his own band, RuPaul and the U-Hauls.

In 1987, he relocated to New York and began the move into the big time. He landed roles in such films as Spike Lee's *Crooklyn* (1993), Betty Thomas's *The Brady*

RuPaul performs a tribute to Diana Ross at VH1 Divas 2000. Photograph by Nancy Kaszerman.

Bunch Movie (1995), Barry Shils's *Wigstock: The Movie* (1995), Wayne Wang's *Blue In The Face* (1995), Beeban Kidron's *To Wong Foo, Thanks For Everything, Julie Newmar* (1996), and Jamie Babbit's *But I'm a Cheerleader* (2000). In the latter film he appears sans drag, playing the part of a male, ex-gay camp counselor.

His albums, such as *Supermodel of the World* (1993) and *Foxy Lady* (1996), have received respectable reviews; and, from 1996 until September 1998, *The RuPaul Show* aired six days a week on VH1, featuring such guests as Cher, k.d. lang, Eartha Kitt, and Dennis Rodman.

In 2000, he narrated the acclaimed documentary *The Eyes of Tammy Faye*, about the evangelist Tammy Faye Bakker. His presence in the film is a poignant irony for those who recognize the clownishly made-up right-wing Christian Bakker as an unintentional drag icon herself.

RuPaul enjoys playing with the contradictions of drag. As a black man, he is very conscious that most white people are much less threatened by him when he is dressed as a woman, even a six-foot-five woman.

However, though he cheerfully bends gender and challenges assumptions wherever possible, he is clear and irrepressible about his identity as a gay man. As he said to Maria Speidel in *People* magazine, "I never feel that I dress as a woman. I dress as a drag queen because, you know, women don't dress the way I dress. It's too uncomfortable."

—*Tina Gianoulis*

BIBLIOGRAPHY

Charles, RuPaul Andre. *Lettin' It All Hang Out*. New York: Hyperion, 1995.

Feinberg, Leslie. *Transgender Warriors: Making History from Joan of Arc to Ru Paul*. Boston, Beacon Press, 1997.

Motsch, Sallie. "Dude Looks Like a Lady." *GQ*, June 1997, 198.

Speidel, Maria. "Happy Camper." *People*, September 23, 1996, 148.

Trebay, Guy. "Cross-dresser Dreams: Female Impersonator RuPaul Andre Charles." *New Yorker*, March 22, 1993, 49.

Yarbrough Jeff. "RuPaul: The Man Behind the Mask." *Advocate*, August 23, 1994, 64.

SEE ALSO

Popular Music; Drag Shows: Drag Queens and Female Impersonators; Disco and Dance Music; Divas; lang, k.d.; Pierce, Charles; Sylvester

Russell, Craig   (1948–1990)

CRAIG RUSSELL WAS ONE OF THE MAJOR FEMALE impersonators of the 1970s and 1980s. He was one of the last of the school that actually sang or spoke in the voices of the ladies he impersonated. He was also an accomplished actor.

Born Russell Craig Eadie in Toronto on January 10, 1948, he began mimicking people at age five to amuse his family. His parents divorced when he was nine. As an adolescent, he suffered from skin problems and therefore wore makeup to school and was all too predictably picked on.

As a teenager, he became president of the Mae West International Fan Club and soon moved to Los Angeles to work for West as her secretary/companion. He returned to Toronto to complete high school, but quickly dropped out. He worked as a typist and, from 1969 until 1971, as a hairdresser.

By 1971, he had adopted the name Craig Russell and began performing at gay clubs in Toronto. He soon became a popular attraction at drag venues across the continent, acclaimed especially for his impersonations, which comprised a remarkable range of characters. His ladies included Bette Davis, Carol Channing, Janis Joplin, Judy Garland, Marlene Dietrich, Peggy Lee, and Mae West.

Equally remarkable was Russell's three-octave vocal range, which allowed him to impersonate Barbra Streisand in her own key. He could perform a duet between Ella Fitzgerald and Louis Armstrong. For his act's finale, he frequently performed a rundown of all the ladies who had performed in *Hello, Dolly!*

Another favorite impersonation, sure to whip up the audience in the late 1970s, was his Anita Bryant singing "The Battle Hymn of the Republic." Russell's satirical impersonation of the antigay crusader indicated an astute political awareness and commitment on his part.

As a female impersonator, Russell attempted genuine verisimilitude, but he also added a great deal of his own personality and comic sensibility. His approach lies somewhere between the sharp-witted performances of drag comedians such as Charles Pierce or Lynne Carter and the dead-on likenesses of impersonators such as Jim Bailey or Jimmy James.

Russell became famous as a result of his starring role in the Canadian feature film *Outrageous!* (1977), directed by Richard Benner, one of the first North American films with a gay theme to receive widespread distribution. In it, Russell played Robin Turner, a gay hairdresser who wants to be a drag queen.

The film is based on Margaret Gibson's novel *Making It*, a chronicle of the author's life as Russell's roommate. Russell was awarded Best Actor by the 1978 Berlin Film Festival for his work in the film.

After Russell's success in *Outrageous*, he was able to play much larger and more prestigious venues. He performed in Las Vegas, Hollywood, Berlin, London, and Paris. He even had a one-man, off-Broadway show entitled *A Man and His Women* (1977).

But at the peak of his success, Russell became unable to cope with the pressures of fame. His substance abuse and psychological problems increasingly affected his performances, and his career suffered.

In 1986, Russell returned to Toronto to film a sequel to *Outrageous*. Entitled *Too Outrageous!* and also directed by Benner, the sequel follows Russell's life as a female impersonator in New York City. It was released in 1987 to mixed reviews and failed to find an audience.

Although he never made a secret of his homosexuality, Russell married Lori Jenkins, one of his female fans, in 1982.

During the final years of his life, Russell battled AIDS. He died from an AIDS-related stroke on October 30, 1990.

—*Joe E. Jeffreys*

BIBLIOGRAPHY

Senelick, Laurence. *The Changing Room: Sex, Drag and Theatre.* New York: Routledge, 2000.

Slide, Anthony. *Great Pretenders: A History of Female and Male Impersonation in the Performing Arts.* Lombard, Ill.: Wallace-Homestead, 1986.

Street, David. *Craig Russell and His Ladies.* Toronto: Gage Publishing, 1979.

SEE ALSO

Cabarets and Revues; Divas; Drag Shows: Drag Queens and Female Impersonators; Dietrich, Marlene; Garland, Judy; Joplin, Janis; Pierce, Charles

S

Saint-Saëns, Camille *(1835–1921)*

ALTHOUGH NOW CONSIDERED A RATHER CONSERVATIVE composer and one of the last proponents of nineteenth-century French musical Romanticism, Camille Saint-Saëns was widely regarded as a virtuoso by his peers and contemporaries, and he was one of the most highly honored French artistic figures of his day.

His personal life was both dramatic and glamorous, and he traveled in circles that included many of the most prominent homosexual figures of the *fin de siècle*.

Charles Camille Saint-Saëns was born on October 9, 1835, in Paris. His father, an official of the Ministry of Interior, died of tuberculosis when the boy was three months old. He was subsequently raised by his mother, with whom he lived until her death in 1888, and his great-aunt, Charlotte Masson.

Saint-Saëns early demonstrated musical gifts. Madame Masson began teaching him piano before he was three years old, and he was able to play difficult pieces within a year; by the age of five he was composing songs. He began his formal musical training in 1842 and made his debut as a concert pianist in 1846, before his eleventh birthday.

After graduating from the Paris Conservatory in 1853, Saint-Saëns gained recognition among his peers as an organ virtuoso and thus won the coveted position of chief organist at the Madeleine Church in Paris, a post he held from 1858 to 1877.

Simultaneously, he pursued a career as a pianist and conductor, taught at L'École Niedermeyer in Paris (where

Camille Saint-Saëns (right) with John Philip Sousa.

his students included Gabriel Fauré and André Messager), and composed a prodigious number of musical works of various genres.

Among Saint-Saëns's best-known compositions are his Second Piano Concerto, in G minor (1868), the tone poems *Le Rouet d'Omphale* (1868) and *Danse macabre* (1875), the First Cello Concerto, in A Minor (1873), the opera *Samson et Dalilah* (1875), the Third Violin Concerto, in G minor (1881), and the Third Symphony, in C minor, with organ (1886).

His body of works includes chamber music, masses and other choral compositions, a dozen operas, a wide variety of orchestral music, numerous songs, and solo pieces for organ and piano.

His unique and now familiar *Le Carnaval des animaux* (*The Carnival of the Animals*, 1886), for two pianos and orchestra, was intended as a private entertainment for his friends, and he forbade its public performance during his lifetime. The part of the narrator, now usually included, was added by others after his death.

During his lifetime, Saint-Saëns's private life gave rise to many rumors and much speculation, and it continues to do so even now. In some ways he was a solitary, even secretive, individual, prone to "disappearing" for weeks. At the same time, he was a remarkable host who entertained lavishly at his Paris home, where his performances in drag (particularly his impersonation of Marguerite, the female lead in Charles Gounod's opera *Faust*) were well known among his circle.

He is said to have danced in ballerina attire for the benefit of his fellow gay composer, Pyotr Ilich Tchaikovsky.

Although he is reputed to have stated—perhaps sardonically—that he was not a homosexual but rather a pederast, Saint-Saëns's homosexuality is now, for the most part, taken for granted. Nevertheless, at least one recent biographer, Stephen Studd, has attempted to claim him as a heterosexual.

Long a bachelor, Saint-Saëns married, at forty, a woman less than half his age. Although the marriage quickly produced two sons, it was nonetheless an unhappy one from the beginning. In 1878, both children died (from a fall from a fourth-floor window and of illness, respectively) within a six week period. His wife's purported negligence became a pretext for his deserting her in 1881.

After vanishing while on vacation, he wrote to advise her that he was simply no longer able to live with her, and afterward never saw or communicated with her again.

Thereafter, the composer traveled extensively, and spent his winters in Algeria, which, while still a French colony, became a favored holiday spot for European homosexuals who enjoyed the adolescent male companionship offered there.

He died of pneumonia in Algiers, at the age of eighty-six, on December 16, 1921.   —*Patricia Juliana Smith*

BIBLIOGRAPHY

Harding, James. *Saint-Saëns and His Circle*. London: Chapman & Hall, 1965.

Rees, Brian. *Camille Saint-Saëns: A Life*. London: Chatto & Windus, 1999.

Saint-Saëns, Camille. *Musical Memories*. Edwin Gile Rich, trans. New York: Da Capo Press, 1969.

Studd, Stephen. *Saint-Saëns: A Critical Biography*. Madison, N.J.: Fairleigh Dickinson University Press, 1999.

SEE ALSO

Classical Music; Tchaikovsky, Pyotr Ilich

Schlesinger, John   (1926–2003)

A DIRECTOR OF NUMEROUS FILMS, STAGE PRODUCTIONS, television programs, and operas, John Schlesinger was one of the most influential figures in the post–World War II British entertainment industry. Always a daring innovator, Schlesinger was a significant force in introducing homosexual themes into mainstream British and American films.

Born on February 16, 1926, in London, Schlesinger attended Balliol College, Oxford, where he first became involved with acting and filmmaking. He directed a short film, *Black Legend* (1948), while a student.

During the late 1940s and early 1950s, Schlesinger acted a number of small roles in films. His first significant success, however, came in television; between 1956 and 1961, he directed documentary films for the British Broadcasting Corporation.

His work for the BBC led to his first feature film, *Terminus* (1961), a documentary set in a London train station. Subsequently, he was selected by the producer Joseph Janni to direct a series of films that focused on the restlessness of young people coming of age at the beginning of the "swinging sixties."

Notable for their empathetic treatment of their youthful protagonists, these films featured such rising stars as Alan Bates, Tom Courtenay, and Julie Christie, and include *A Kind of Loving* (1962), *Billy Liar* (1963), and *Darling* (1965).

The latter film, although ostensibly concerned with the heterosexual adventures of its antiheroine Diana Scott, a model who sleeps her way to wealth and fame but fails to find love or happiness, is informed by gay sensibilities, not only through the introduction of a sympathetic minor character who is unambiguously homosexual, but also in its casting of the two male leads, Dirk Bogarde and Laurence Harvey.

Darling, which garnered a Best Actress Academy Award for Christie and a nomination for its director, established

Schlesinger's international reputation. His newfound prestige allowed him to explore controversial themes, including homosexuality, more directly in his films.

Schlesinger's first American film, *Midnight Cowboy* (1969), which won the Academy Award for Best Picture despite an "X" rating, focuses on a relationship between two men, a male hustler (Jon Voigt) and an ailing con artist (Dustin Hoffman). It also features a disturbing scene in which the hustler beats up a client.

Released in 1971, only four years after homosexual acts between male adults in private were decriminalized in Britain, *Sunday Bloody Sunday* explores a romantic triangle with a different twist: an older gay man (Peter Finch) and a divorcee (Glenda Jackson) become rivals for the sexual attention of a younger man (Murray Head).

Schlesinger later directed numerous feature films, including *The Day of the Locust* (1975), *Marathon Man* (1976), *Yanks* (1979), *Honky Tonk Freeway* (1980), *The Falcon and the Snowman* (1985), *Madame Sousatzka* (1988), and *Pacific Heights* (1990).

A recent film, *The Next Best Thing* (1999), takes a wry look at a one-night stand (and an ensuing pregnancy) between a gay man (Rupert Everett) and a straight woman (Madonna).

Even as he continued his prodigious output as a director, Schlesinger also served, from 1973, as an associate director of the National Theatre, London, and was responsible for a number of opera productions at the Royal Opera House, Covent Garden, where his spectacular rendering of Jacques Offenbach's *The Tales of Hoffman*, first staged and televised in 1980, was revived once again in 2000.

Schlesinger never made a secret of his homosexuality, and he lived quite openly with his partner, Michael Childers, from the late 1960s until the end of his life in 2003.

He became publicly out, however, when, in 1991, Sir Ian McKellen, the first openly gay individual to be knighted by the British monarchy, was attacked in a public letter from filmmaker Derek Jarman for accepting the honor. Schlesinger was one of the dozen British gay and lesbian artists who signed a respectful response in McKellen's defense.

Schlesinger died on July 25, 2003, in Palm Springs, California, following a prolonged illness.

—*Patricia Juliana Smith*

BIBLIOGRAPHY

Brooker, Nancy. *John Schlesinger: A Guide to References and Resources.* Boston: G. K. Hall, 1978.

Philips, Gene. *John Schlesinger.* Boston: Twayne, 1981.

SEE ALSO

Opera

Schubert, Franz (1797–1828)

FRANZ PETER SCHUBERT IS OFTEN REGARDED AS THE consummate tragic artist: sickly, poor, prolific, and unappreciated during his lifetime. This view is only partially true, however. Although he remained relatively unknown outside of his native Vienna, Schubert did achieve substantial popular success, particularly for his songs (*lieder*).

Still, the depth of Schubert's talent remained unknown until after his death because many of his orchestral works, including his symphonies and operas, were unperformed and unpublished during his lifetime. Only when these works came to light following his death—through the help of friends and of composers such as Liszt, Schumann, and Brahms—did his reputation grow.

Schubert's music bridges the classical and romantic styles and is known for its simplicity and depth of feeling. He often juxtaposes moods within a piece, evoking, for example, both sadness and conviviality.

In its supposedly "feminine" character, Schubert's music was long regarded as the antithesis of Beethoven's. In the words of the nineteenth-century composer and critic Robert Schumann, who first articulated the opposition, the feminine Schubert "pleads and persuades where the man [Beethoven] commands."

Born to Franz Theodor Schubert, a schoolmaster, and his wife Elisabeth, a domestic servant, Franz was their fourth son. A respected middle-class family, the Schuberts were cultivated and musical. Franz received his earliest musical education from his father and played the viola in a string quartet with his older brothers Ignaz, Karl, and Ferdinand.

In 1808, Schubert won a scholarship that included a place in the imperial court chapel choir and an education at the Stadtkonvikt, the principal boarding school for commoners in Vienna, where his tutors were Wenzel Ruzicka, the imperial court organist, and, later, the composer Antonio Salieri.

When his voice broke in 1812 and he left the school, Schubert continued to study privately with Salieri. During this time, he entered a teachers' training college in Vienna and in the autumn of 1814 became assistant in his father's school. While composing vigorously, Schubert worked as a schoolmaster until 1818.

Schubert's harmonic ingenuity and skillful blending of piano and voice transformed the *lied* into a respected genre. The composer's first undisputed masterpiece in this genre, *Gretchen am Spinnrade* (1814), is set to a poem by Goethe. In 1815, he composed more than 140 songs; and in total he wrote more than 600.

Schubert's unfinished Symphony in B Minor (1822) is noted for its haunting quality and harmonic daring. It was his last major work before he contracted syphilis in late 1822.

After 1822, his works reveal an increasing seriousness and despair. While in the hospital in 1823, he composed *Die schöne Müllerin*, considered the epitome of his lyrical art, in which the sexual passion of the protagonist leads to his suicide. In the Quartet in D Minor, known as *Death and the Maiden* (1824), death offers comfort to an innocent youth.

On March 26, 1827, the death of Beethoven, who influenced his compositional style greatly, added to Schubert's despair. But Beethoven's death undoubtedly contributed to a deepening in Schubert's music, as for example in the Piano Trio in E-Flat, composed several months later, which explores a cyclical structure similar to that of Beethoven's Fifth Symphony. It was performed on the first anniversary of Beethoven's death.

The last year of Schubert's all too brief life, 1828, was filled with masterpieces. He completed his Symphony in C Major (The *Great*) in March of that year. Performed for the first time twelve years after his death, it is considered one of the summits of his musical achievement.

A string of works for piano, four hands also date from 1828, including the masterful F Minor Fantasy, which evokes both a disturbing violence and lyrical beauty.

In September and early October of 1828, Schubert composed his last three piano sonatas, in C minor, A major, and B flat major, successfully synthesizing many of his stylistic features. The String Quintet in C Major was the last instrumental piece he completed before his death on November 19, 1828.

Schubert is buried in Vienna's Wahring cemetery, practically adjacent to Beethoven.

Schubert was significantly influenced by his close-knit group of male friends, known as the Schubert Circle. His relationships with an older school friend, Joseph von Spaun, the young poet Johann Mayrhofer, and the wealthy young sensualist Franz von Schober were the most important of his life. He and Schober often lived together for extended periods.

Although Schubert's homosexuality had long been rumored in gay musical circles, it was not explicitly argued in print until 1981, when Maynard Solomon published an article in *American Imago*, later expanded in *19th Century Music*.

Citing the composer's dissipation, his lack of female love interests, his passionate male friendships, and several oblique references in his surviving correspondence, Solomon argued that Schubert's primary erotic orientation was homosexual.

The reaction on the part of many musicologists and music critics, who often simply refused to consider the evidence, revealed a deep-seated homophobia among many specialists in classical music.

In recent years, however, the notion of a gay Schubert has become, if not commonplace, at least much less con-troversial. Schubert's alleged homosexuality and its effect on his music are subjects of continuing debate among music historians and critics.

—*Julia Pastore*

BIBLIOGRAPHY

Brett, Philip. "Piano Four Hands: Schubert and the Performance of Gay Male Desire." *19th Century Music* 21 (1997): 149–176.

Brown, Maurice. *Schubert: A Critical Biography*. New York: St. Martin's Press, 1958.

Gibbs, Christopher. *The Life of Schubert*. Cambridge: Cambridge University Press, 2000.

Kramer, Lawrence, ed. "Schubert: Music, Sexuality, Culture." *19th Century Music* 17 (1993).

Newbould, Brian. *Schubert: The Music and the Man*. Berkeley: University of California Press, 1997.

Solomon, Maynard. "Franz Schubert and the Peacocks of Benvenuto Cellini." *19th Century Music* 12 (1989): 193–206.

SEE ALSO

Classical Music; Menotti, Gian Carlo

Franz Schubert.

Set and Costume Design

SET AND COSTUME DESIGN AND PROPERTIES FOR STAGE and film are fields that have attracted many talented people, a large percentage of whom have been gay men. In fact, this field in the entertainment industry has often been identified specifically as "queer work."

While many heterosexuals have also been successful in the area of art direction, set design and decoration for stage and film have a distinctly gay cachet. Perhaps an even "gayer" field is that of costume design.

As William Mann has recently documented, even during the worst periods of repression, Hollywood offered opportunities of creative expression for gay men and lesbians, many of whom were open about their sexual orientation.

Opera and ballet also offered opportunities for gifted homosexuals. The trend here has been for painters to cross over from the fine arts to the applied arts, adding stage design to their range. For many notable stage designers working in this field, their sexual orientation was never an issue in their professional lives.

Among the most significant gay and lesbian artists who are distinguished for their work as set designers are Charles Ricketts, Duncan Grant, Erté (Romain de Tirtoff), Pavel Tchelitchew, Oliver Messel, Cecil Beaton, Léonor Fini, George James Hopkins, Robert Colquhoun, Robert MacBryde, Franco Zeffirelli, David Hockney, Derek Jarman, and Keith Haring.

Many gay artists of Hollywood's golden age were extremely versatile, but openly gay men became especially associated with costume design. In some cases, Hollywood costume designers were considered on a par with world-class couturiers and fashion designers and had a palpable influence on public taste. Among these designers, Howard Greer, Travis Banton, Adrian (Adrian Adolph Greenberg), Orry Kelly, and Walter Plunkett are best known.

Set Designers

In the first decades of the twentieth century, two significant factors influenced the development of stage and set design, making it central rather than peripheral. The first was the massive impact of Sergei Diaghilev's lavish productions for the Ballets Russes. In particular, Leon Bakst's bold designs helped audiences appreciate the way color could be used to integrate an entire production.

The second factor that altered the development of stage and set design was the impact of Robert Wiene's German Expressionist film The Cabinet of Dr. Caligari (1919), which set a precedent for using sets to express mood and theme. The film employs fantastic, stylized sets to capture the subjective perceptions of the main character. This cinematic innovation raised the status of sets to an importance comparable to that of characterization and narrative. Hence, it gave set designers a new prestige as significant collaborators in film and stage productions.

Charles Ricketts

Although more famous as creator/owner of the Vale Press and as a book illustrator, Charles Ricketts (1866–1931) also designed abstract, nonrealistic sets for the London stage. He designed costumes for George Bernard Shaw's early comedies.

Ricketts first made a name as a set designer with Herbert Trench's production of King Lear (1909). He designed Shaw's St. Joan (1924) and Gilbert and Sullivan's The Mikado (1926) and The Gondoliers (1929). As a specialist in Japanese art, he was the perfect choice to design The Mikado, while his knowledge of Venetian art allowed him to give a distinctly authentic flavor to The Gondoliers.

Duncan Grant

The Bloomsbury artist Duncan Grant (1885–1978) was probably the most famous British painter in the 1920s and 1930s. Although mainly preoccupied with painting and interior decor, Grant often designed for the theater.

He was invited to Paris to design an adaptation of Twelfth Night, La nuit des rois (1913), by Theodore Lascaris. His abilities as a costume designer were also in evidence in Pelléas et Mélisande (1917) for Jacques Copeau, cofounder with André Gide of the journal la Nouvelle Revue Française.

During the 1920s, he designed for C. B. Cochran Revues, including The Pleasure Garden (1924). He also designed a ballet, The Enchanted Grove, for Rupert Doone, with music by Ravel. He regretted that he never had the opportunity to design a ballet for his idol, Vaslav Nijinsky.

Erté

One of the most innovative and enduring designers of the twentieth century, Erté, or Romain de Tirtoff (1892–1990), earned fame for his sinuous and sophisticated Art Deco fashion designs, frequently featured on the covers of Harper's Bazaar; but he also designed sets and costumes for opera, theater, and ballet productions.

Among these were the 1947 Paris production of Francis Poulenc's opera Les mamelles de Tirésias and the production of La Traviata for the Paris Opera celebration of the Verdi centenary in 1951. He also designed costumes for the ballerina Anna Pavlova and the American opera singer Mary Garden.

In 1925, Erté was transported from France by Louis B. Mayer to lend even more elegance and glamour to films at the MGM studios. Erté arrived in Hollywood with his lover Nicholas Ourousoff, under the lavish sponsorship of Mayer and in a blaze of publicity. He contributed work to *Ben Hur* (1925) and *La Bohème* (1926), but his stay in Hollywood ended after only a few months. He returned to Paris to design for the Music Hall.

Erté's drawings are intricate and highly detailed, creating an extravagant, exotic world of women dripping in pearls, covered in plumes, and wearing low-cut back lines. Erté treated costume design as a fine art, and his numerous designs, though often whimsical, were also slyly erotic and technically perfect.

Pavel Tchelitchew

Pavel Tchelitchew (1898–1957) was a theater designer and painter of homoerotic images quite daring for their time. The son of a Russian family who fled their homeland after the 1918 revolution, he first gained artistic recognition in Berlin, where he designed sets for Rimsky-Korsakov's *The Wedding Feast of the Boyar* (1922) and met Diaghilev.

He settled in Paris, where he became a member of the Gertrude Stein circle. In 1928, he designed a minimal but magical ballet, *Ode*, which had stark lighting and was well in advance of its time.

An accomplished portraitist, Tchelitchew often painted his lover Charles Henri Ford, a novelist, filmmaker, and critic. After his emigration to the United States, he became part of the Paul Cadmus–Lincoln Kirstein circle in New York.

In 1936, Tchelitchew designed Gluck's *Orfeo ed Euridice* at the Metropolitan Opera House. The long-remembered sets had gauzelike graves and ladders leading nowhere.

Tchelitchew's design for *Hide and Seek* (1942) for New York City Ballet, the theme of which was children at play, was rumored to have included a disguised rendition of dancer Nicholas Magallanes's penis. His painting *Hide and Seek* is one of the treasures of New York's Museum of Modern Art.

Léonor Fini

Argentinean Léonor Fini (1908–1996) was often associated with the Surrealist movement, yet developed her own distinctive style. Her work has a strange and visionary cast reminiscent of the Symbolists.

Among her other design work, Fini did costumes for her close friend Jean Genet's only ballet, *Adam Miroir*, which premiered in Paris in 1947. This ballet, danced to music by Darius Milhaud, highlighted the doubling themes of Genet's novel *Querelle*. The Surrealist Paul Delvaux did the sets.

Christian Bérard

Genet himself was very much influenced by Jean Cocteau's circle, which included the designer Christian Bérard (1902–1947), known simply as *Bébé*. Although Bérard

was not immediately taken up by Diaghilev for the Ballets Russes, he made a name for himself in the French theater.

He was particularly known for his subtle, nostalgic use of color in designs for such works as *Cotillion* (1930) for George Balanchine and Molière's *Les fourberies de Scapin* (1947).

Bérard and his lover Boris Kochno (1904–1990), who directed the Ballets Russes and was cofounder of the Ballet des Champs Elysées, were the most prominent openly gay couple in French theater during the 1930s and 1940s. Perhaps Bérard's greatest achievement was his lustrous, magical designs for Jean Cocteau's film *Beauty and the Beast* (1946).

Oliver Messel

For almost three decades, Oliver Messel (1904–1978) was Britain's most celebrated theatrical designer. He created lavish costumes and sets for ballet and stage productions in the country's most prestigious venues.

Messel first started out under the tutelage of the homosexual English painter and portraitist Glyn Philpot. He was then taken under the wing of French designer Christian Bérard, with whom he shared a similar sense of color and unerring use of fabrics.

Messel's first commission was to design the masks for a London production of Diaghilev's ballet *Zephyr et Flore* (1925). He then achieved great acclaim with his white-on-white set for Offenbach's comic opera *Helen* (1932). He won a Tony Award for *House of Flowers* (1935) on Broadway and received acclaim for the elaborate royal box decorations for the premiere of Benjamin Britten's opera *Gloriana* (1953), presented in the presence of the new queen, Elizabeth II.

Messel also designed the Royal Ballet's 1959 production of *The Sleeping Beauty*. In this work, which borrowed subtle nuances from the paintings of Antoine Watteau, the designer's innate sense of pomp and grandeur is evident. His work in opera at Glyndebourne and the Met was also notable.

In 1935, the gay film director George Cukor invited Messel to design the sets for *Romeo and Juliet*. Although Messel did not regard these designs as entirely successful, he subsequently designed numerous other Hollywood films, including *The Thief of Baghdad* (1940) and *Suddenly, Last Summer* (1959).

Cecil Beaton

Cecil Beaton (1904–1980) was Messel's principal rival as leading British designer. Although he is best known as a society photographer, after World War II Beaton designed extravagant stage sets and costumes for Broadway and London theater as well as opera and film.

Beaton loved the simplicity of ballet, and his design for *Apparitions* (1947) for the Royal Ballet bore the hallmarks of Tchelitchew's influence, containing as it did symbolic lamps, harps, and chandeliers.

Beaton's design for Lawrence Olivier's production of *The School for Scandal* (1947) was also notable. He won a Tony Award (1957) for his costumes for the Broadway production of *My Fair Lady*, and an Academy Award (1958) for sets and costumes for the film *Gigi*.

George James Hopkins

In 1916, the young George James Hopkins (1896–1988) was hired to do costumes for Theda Bara and set designs for her films. His set designs helped elevate the status of the profession in Hollywood, raising design beyond what was previously regarded as "glorified carpentry."

Hopkins executed a striking peacock throne for Bara's infamous film *Salome* (1919). *The Soul of Youth* (1920) included scenes set in a male whorehouse. *The Furnace* (1920) included an elaborate nude scene in hell.

But Hopkins's career was stalled for a while by an unresolved scandal involving his lover William Desmond Taylor, who died in 1922. In 1935, Hopkins joined Warner Brothers studios and went on to do the set designs for *Casablanca* (1942) and *Mildred Pierce* (1945), among others. He won awards for *A Streetcar Named Desire* (1951), *My Fair Lady* (1964), and *Hello, Dolly!* (1969).

Robert Colquhoun and Robert MacBryde

Scottish artists Robert Colquhoun (1914–1962) and Robert MacBryde (1913–1966), a gay couple known as "the two Roberts," lived and worked together after meeting at the Glasgow School of Art in 1932.

Colquhoun's work was the stronger of the two, being influenced by Wyndham Lewis and having an identifiable existentialist tone. They were close contemporaries of Francis Bacon, but were associated with the neo-Romantic movement in England. They designed frequently for the stage and the lyric theater. Ken Russell made a short film for British television, "Two Painters" (1959), about their work.

Franco Zeffirelli

The Italian designer and director Franco Zeffirelli (b. 1923) studied architecture and acting as a young man. Under the tutelage of director Luchino Visconti, for whom he did set and costume designs, he gradually made the transition from protégé to hugely successful film and opera director.

His *La Traviata* (1958) in Dallas is remembered largely because it featured a definitive Violetta in Maria Callas—the production's sole *raison d'être*. He also directed Joan Sutherland in a memorable *Lucia di Lammermoor* (1959).

Zeffirelli was nominated for a Tony Award for his scenic designs for the *Lady of the Camellias* (1963). His film *Romeo and Juliet* (1968) is remembered for its casting of unknown young actors to give authenticity and a fresh view to the production, as well as for its lush sets. His film and opera work, usually characterized by lavish and beautiful designs, still gains international attention, though he is sometimes criticized for allowing his designs to overpower other aspects of the productions.

Derek Jarman

Derek Jarman (1942–1994) was such a versatile artist that his work straddles many media, including gardening and political activism. However, he started out as a set designer at the Slade school of Art. His first break came when he was invited by Sir Frederick Ashton to design for the ballet *Jazz Calendar* (1968).

In the same year, Sir John Gielgud asked him to design *Don Giovanni* for the English National Opera. Jarman then met the director Ken Russell and designed the monstrous set for *The Devils* (1970). He also worked on Russell's *Savage Messiah* (1971).

Jarman's fruitful association with Russell included a joint project, *The Rake's Progress*, at the Pergola Theatre during the Florence festival in 1982. Even during his career as a provocative film director in the 1970s and 1980s, Jarman continued to design for ballets, the English National Opera, and plays, including a memorable 1988 production of *Waiting for Godot*.

David Hockney

David Hockney (b. 1937) was lured into opera only in the 1970s when he was asked by John Cox of Glyndebourne Opera to do set designs for a new production of *The Rake's Progress* (1974). Hockney was particularly interested in the subject, for he identified the Rake's progress with the homosexual's plight in society, and he had given the Rake a gay slant in a series of paintings completed in 1961.

He also welcomed the assignment because he had reached an impasse in his painting and hoped that designing for the theater would free his imagination. Hockney based his designs on the 1735 engravings by William Hogarth and playfully emphasized the graphic effects of cross-hatching in red, blue, and green.

Hockney was later invited to design *The Magic Flute* (1977). These designs were immensely popular and distinguished by their vivid sense of color and realistic detail, drawn from sketches that the artist made on trips to Egypt.

Keith Haring

Keith Haring (1958–1990) had a characteristic Day-Glo linear style influenced by subway graffiti, but he was very much the public artist who worked in multiple media. He did installations, children's books, and large-scale murals. He even body-painted gay icon Grace Jones for her 1984 appearance at Paradise Garage.

Less known is his work for the theater and ballet, especially at the Brooklyn Academy of Music. He designed such productions as *Secret Pastures* (1984), *Sweet Saturday Night* (1984), *Rodhessa Jones* (1986), and *Interrupted River* (1986). He also designed for Munich's Body and Soul Ballet in 1988.

Other Theater and Ballet Designers

The British designers Sir Francis Rose (1909–1976), Christopher Wood (1901–1930), and Rex Whistler (1905–1944) were known in homosexual circles but were either bisexual or never disclosed their sexuality.

The French painter Marie Laurencin (1885–1956) was also noted as a stage designer for her lyrical depictions of young girls in the ballet *Les Biches* (1924), commissioned by Diaghilev to music by Francis Poulenc.

Artists not noted primarily for being designers but who nevertheless did sets and costumes include the film directors James Whale (1896–1957) and Vincente Minnelli (1910–1986).

One of the most productive art directors in Hollywood, Cedric Gibbons (1893–1960), was rumored to be homosexual. He won an academy Award for *An American in Paris* (1951).

Even Pop artist Andy Warhol (1930–1987) designed dangling silver pillows filled with helium for Merce Cunningham's ballet *Rainforest* (1968).

Robert Rauschenberg (b. 1925) is another artist who designed for ballet and modern dance productions. He collaborated on several works choreographed by Paul Taylor.

Costume Designers

Costume design for stage and film has generally attracted a different kind of artist, designers often without a specific fine arts background. Nevertheless, their work has frequently reached pinnacles of stylishness and had a huge impact on the public taste and imagination.

Howard Greer

Howard Greer (1886–1964) started as a costume designer on Broadway and was one of the first to be appointed head of wardrobe at a major Hollywood studio. He worked on *Greenwich Village Follies* (1922) and *Jack and Jill* (1923) before moving to Hollywood to do set designs for Paramount Pictures. There he was responsible for such movies as *Bringing Up Baby* (1938).

Travis Banton

The most sought-after Hollywood costume designer of the 1930s and 1940s was Travis Banton (1894–1948). He is best remembered for creating the style of such actresses as Carole Lombard, Lilyan Tashman, Marlene Dietrich, and Mae West. His trademarks were understated elegance and luxurious fabrics.

Banton served as head designer at Paramount Studios for many years, but also designed for Fox and Universal Studios as well. Perhaps his most successful creations were the angled hat and veiled look that helped establish the onscreen charisma and mystery of Dietrich in such films as *Dishonored* (1931), *Shanghai Express* (1932), and *The Devil Is a Woman* (1935).

Orry Kelly

Australian-born Orry Kelly (1897–1964) emigrated to the United States as a young man. He found success as a costume and scene designer on Broadway before going to Hollywood during the Great Depression. His friend Cary Grant introduced him to the head of Warner Brothers' wardrobe department, where he stayed for eleven years.

Primarily associated with Warner Brothers, he designed costumes for a broad range of films in the 1930s, 1940s, and 1950s, including Busby Berkeley extravaganzas as well as gangster films and costume dramas. Near the end of his career he was especially associated with Hollywood musicals.

He designed for stars as various as Ingrid Bergman and Marilyn Monroe, but was especially close to Bette Davis. He won Academy Awards for his designs for *An American in Paris* (shared with Walter Plunkett and Irene Sharaff, 1951), *Les Girls* (1957), *Some Like It Hot* (1959), and *Gypsy* (1962).

Walter Plunkett

Walter Plunkett (1902–1982) is best known for his costume designs for *Gone With the Wind* (1939), but his long and distinguished career included many other triumphs. He came to Hollywood to become an actor, but gained an interest in costume design when he was invited to design costumes for the dancer Ruth St. Denis.

Plunkett worked for RKO from the late 1920s to the late 1930s, earning a reputation for the authenticity of his period costumes. He later worked primarily for MGM and designed for stars such as Irene Dunne, Judy Garland, Fred Astaire, Ginger Rogers, and Katharine Hepburn.

Although he did not receive an Academy Award for his designs for *Gone With the Wind*, he received numerous nominations and shared an Oscar with Orry Kelly and Irene Sharaff for their work on *An American in Paris* (1953).

Adrian

Adrian Adolph Greenburg (1903–1959) was one of the most flamboyant and successful costume designers of Hollywood's golden age. His first films were with Rudolph

Valentino; then he moved to MGM, where he had the opportunity to design for some of Hollywood's biggest female stars, including Greta Garbo, Jean Harlow, Joan Crawford, and Norma Shearer.

Among the films for which he designed costumes are *The Wizard of Oz* (1939), *The Women* (1939), and *The Philadelphia Story* (1940). His work had an enormous influence not only on other designers, but also on the fashion world in general, as fans attempted to duplicate the glamorous style he created for Hollywood divas.

Arthur Freed and Roger Edens

Primarily a lyricist, choreographer, and producer, Arthur Freed (1894–1973) nevertheless exerted a massive influence on the design of some of Hollywood's most glamorous musicals. He, along with his assistant Roger Edens (1905–1970), reshaped this genre, taking it to new heights by unifying the designs of all the artists involved.

Freed himself was not gay, but his unit at MGM was known as "Freed's Fairies" because he had gathered so many talented gay designers, costumers, and other artists, including Roger Edens, whom he trusted implicitly. Among their most notable work are such classic film musicals as *The Wizard of Oz* (1939), *Meet Me in St. Louis* (1944), *Easter Parade* (1948), *Singin' in the Rain* (1952), and *Kismet* (1955).

Irene Sharaff

One of the few costume designers to have worked both on Broadway productions and on their film adaptations, Irene Sharaff (1910–1993) first developed a reputation in New York and then joined "Freed's Fairies" at MGM in 1942, an association that did not prevent her from continuing to design for Broadway.

Among the shows that she designed both for Broadway and for film are *The King and I* (1951/1956), *West Side Story* (1957/1961), *Flower Drum Song* (1958/1961), and *Funny Girl* (1964/1968).

She was nominated for Academy Awards nine times and won Oscars for five films: *An American in Paris* (1951), *The King and I* (1956), *West Side Story* (1961), *Cleopatra* (1962), and *Who's Afraid of Virginia Woolf?* (1966).

Equally adept at period or contemporary costume, Sharaff earned distinction for her attention to detail and for the elegance of her creations.

Although several other women achieved distinction in the fields of set and costume design—Edith Head, for example, who apprenticed with Howard Greer—openly lesbian women seem not to have found the same degree of success as gay men.

—*Kieron Devlin*

BIBLIOGRAPHY

Bottomley, George. "Charles Ricketts." *The Durham University Journal* 23.3 (1940): 169–184.

Castle, Charles. *Oliver Messel.* New York: Thames and Hudson, 1986.

Celant, Germano, ed. *Keith Haring.* Munich: Prestel Verlag, 1997.

Leddick, David. *Intimate Companions: a Triography of George Platt Lynes, Paul Cadmus and Lincoln Kirstein.* New York: Stonewall Inn Editions, 2000.

Lewis, Wyndham. "Round the London Art Galleries." *Listener,* November 30, 1950, 650.

Livingstone, Marco. *David Hockney.* London: Thames and Hudson, 1996.

Mann, William J. *Behind the Scenes: How Lesbians and Gays Shaped Hollywood, 1910–1969.* New York: Viking, 2001.

Pierpoint, Claudia Roth. "Bébé." *Ballet Review* 18.2 (1990): 23–27.

Saslow, James M. *Pictures and Passions: A History of Homosexuality in the Visual Arts.* New York: Viking, 1999.

Snow, Peter. "Designing for the Theatre and Cinema." *Derek Jarman: A Portrait.* Roger Wollen, intro. London: Thames and Hudson, 1996. 81–88.

Spencer, Charles. *Erté.* New York: Clarkson N. Potter, 1970.

Watney, Simon. *The Art of Duncan Grant.* London: John Murray, 1990.

SEE ALSO

Ballet; Dance; Musical Theater and Film; Opera; Ballets Russes; Ashton, Sir Frederick; Britten, Benjamin; Cunningham, Merce; Diaghilev, Sergei; Dietrich, Marlene; Doone, Rupert; Edens, Roger; Garland, Judy; Kirstein, Lincoln; Minnelli, Vincente; Nijinsky, Vaslav; Poulenc, Francis; Taylor, Paul; Zeffirelli, Franco

Shaiman, Marc, and Scott Wittman

Marc Shaiman (b. 1959)
and Scott Wittman (b. 1955)

THE COMPOSER MARC SHAIMAN AND THE LYRICIST AND director Scott Wittman, partners in life and collaborators in theater, film, and television projects, have a long list of credits in the entertainment industry. Their work on the musical version of John Waters's *Hairspray* earned Tony and Grammy Awards in 2003.

Both Shaiman and Wittman grew up in the vicinity of New York City, the former in Scotch Plains, New Jersey, and the latter in Nyack, New York. Both were fascinated with musical theater from an early age and dreamed of careers on Broadway.

Shaiman played piano with local community theater groups from the time he was twelve, and Wittman apprenticed in summer stock in his hometown. Such was their love for the stage that they both cut high school classes to travel into New York for matinees.

Wittman attended Emerson College in Boston but left after two years to pursue a career as a writer and director in musical theater in New York. In the city's East Village he crossed paths with Shaiman, who had quit high school at sixteen to join the New York musical scene. Wittman was directing a show at a club in Greenwich Village when Shaiman came in and started playing the piano. Wittman promptly hired him. They subsequently fell in love and have been a couple since 1979.

The two soon began collaborating professionally, writing songs that Shaiman describes as "full of anarchy and joy." In the 1980s, at off-Broadway venues such as Club 57, they produced quirky musicals including *Livin' Dolls*, a story about the Barbie and Ken figures, which was, in the words of Jesse Green of the *New York Times*, "a cult success downtown but ran afoul of [toy company] Mattel on the eve of its uptown transfer."

Both Shaiman and Wittman explored other professional avenues. Shaiman, a longtime fan of Bette Midler, parlayed the fortuitous circumstance of Wittman's being the neighbor of one of her backup singers into becoming her arranger and producer for albums and concert appearances.

Shaiman also wrote for television shows including *Saturday Night Live*, on which he began working in 1975. Through that job he met Billy Crystal, with whom he would work frequently over the years in film as well as television. Since 1997, Shaiman and Wittman have contributed and directed music for the Academy Awards presentation show, often hosted by Crystal.

At the same time, Wittman, who humorously calls himself "a great diva wrangler," was directing concerts. In addition to working with Midler, he has had a long association with Patti LuPone and has worked with Christine Ebersole, Raquel Welch, Dame Edna Everage (Barry Humphries), and Lypsinka, among many others. He also directed Bruce Vilanch's one-man show *Almost Famous* in 2000.

In the late 1980s, Shaiman and Wittman went to California so that Shaiman could begin writing for films. He has over fifty credits as a music writer, arranger, and producer. The couple now have homes in both New York and Los Angeles.

The first film on which Shaiman worked was Rob Reiner's *Misery*, released in 1990. Among others to which he contributed are *When Harry Met Sally* (1989, also directed by Reiner), Nora Ephron's *Sleepless in Seattle* (1993), and Hugh Wilson's *The First Wives Club* (1996). In addition to his other work, Shaiman has appeared in around a dozen films, often as a piano player.

One of Shaiman's best-known projects is the score for Trey Parker's *South Park: Bigger, Longer & Uncut* (1999), particularly the hilarious march, "Blame Canada," for which he received one of his five Academy Award nominations.

Shaiman and Wittman's greatest triumph thus far is *Hairspray*, an adaptation of the 1988 John Waters movie for the musical stage. Shaiman and Wittman wrote the music, and Mark O'Donnell and Thomas Meehan wrote the book for the play.

Shaiman and Wittman, both avid Waters fans, were excited to have the chance to work on *Hairspray*, the story of a chubby Baltimore high schooler who goes from being an outsider and a nobody to a heroine when her love of pop music sets her on a course that leads to the desegregation of a television dance show in 1962.

After a nationwide tour, *Hairspray*, featuring Harvey Fierstein in the role played by Divine in the movie, took Broadway by storm in August 2002, quickly becoming one of the hottest tickets in the city. The show dominated the 2003 Tony Awards, winning eight, including best musical and best score.

At the end of their acceptance speeches, Shaiman declared to Wittman, "I love you, and I'd like to spend the rest of my life with you." The couple then embraced and shared a long and tender kiss. News outlets around the world took note of this affecting moment.

Because of the success of the play, which has already grossed over $76 million, New Line Cinema is bringing the musical to the big screen. Shaiman and Wittman are the executive producers, and Shaiman will also be the music producer.

In addition to that project, Shaiman and Wittman are working on the score for a musical stage version of Stephen Spielberg's 2002 film *Catch Me If You Can*.

Shaiman and Wittman have been very generous in contributing their time and talent to fundraisers for AIDS charities, participating in numerous concerts and other benefits to support research and treatment.

—*Linda Rapp*

BIBLIOGRAPHY

Cagle, Jess. "Hollywood's Best Kept Secret." *Entertainment Weekly*, July 30, 1993, 36.

Green, Jesse. "The Pop Alchemist." *New York Times*, July 21, 2002.

Isherwood, Charles. "Risky Gamble Scores Marriage Made in Heaven." *Variety*, April 21, 2003.

Langton, James. "A Gay Kiss Breaks TV Taboo." *Evening Standard* (London), June 9, 2003.

Ouzanian, Richard. "Beyond Hairspray's Joyous Hold." *Toronto Star*, March 14, 2004.

Posner, Michael. "A Match Made in Musical Heaven." *Globe and Mail* (Toronto), March 17, 2004.

"The Musical Mind of Marc Shaiman." http://shaiman.filmmusic.com

SEE ALSO

Musical Theater and Film; Divine; Kander, John, and Fred Ebb

Smith, Bessie (1894–1937)

"**E**MPRESS OF THE BLUES" IS THE REGAL TITLE RIGHTLY bestowed upon Bessie Smith, whose history has been filled with persistent, colorful legends. Gifted with a powerful voice and sophisticated musical artistry, she conducted her life by her own set of rules and had affairs with both men and women.

Born in severe poverty, probably on April 15, 1894, in Chattanooga, Tennessee, Smith became the undisputed favorite blues singer of ticket and record buyers alike throughout the 1920s and 1930s. Specializing in songs of heartbreak, violence, and longing, her vocalization is characterized by haunting expressivity, perfect phrasing, and a superb sense of timing.

Smith was reared by a sister, Viola, but her oldest brother, Clarence, had the greatest influence on her. He encouraged Bessie to learn how to sing and dance. By the time she was nine years old, she was singing on Chattanooga street corners; and by the time she was a teenager, she had joined veteran blues singer Gertrude "Ma" Rainey in the Moses Stokes traveling show, which operated in tent shows throughout the South.

Smith made her first recordings in 1923, including her rendition of Alberta Hunter's "Down-Hearted Blues," which sold 780 thousand copies in less than six months, solidifying the regal status that she had earned through performing.

Smith mostly performed for all-black audiences and occasionally all-white audiences in the South, but her 160 known recordings reached fans all over the world and eventually made her wealthy. Although her career began to wane somewhat during the Great Depression and her longtime contract with Columbia records was terminated in 1931, Smith never lost her fame or her loyal following on the road.

Even though she was born a black woman in the Jim Crow South, Smith managed to conduct her life on her own terms. By nearly all accounts, she was violent, foul-mouthed, a heavy drinker, and sexually promiscuous. However, her extraordinary talent and subsequent wealth afforded her some latitude in these regards. She was also notoriously stingy with her touring company, often leaving them stranded without pay in the midst of a tour.

Like several notable women blues singers, Smith often preferred the company of women. Her relationships include a volatile, near-fatal affair in 1926 with a chorus girl, Lillian Simpson.

Smith was said to have a voracious appetite for both sex and alcohol that she regularly and openly indulged. Although homosexuality is often referred to in blues lyrics and is a recognizable theme for many listeners, Smith's most explicit reference to homosexuality is in her composition "Foolish Man Blues." Somewhat surprisingly, it is rather condemning:

*There's two things got me puzzled, there's two
things I can't understand
That's a mannish actin' woman and a skippin,'
twistin' woman acting man.*

Despite her numerous affairs with both men and women, Smith married Jack Gee in June 1923. Theirs was a tumultuous union rife with abuse and infidelity; and although they adopted a son three years later, Gee forced his separation from Smith, and his identity was unknown to her biographers until the 1970s.

Smith and Gee finally separated in 1929 but never divorced. Thus, Gee was able to claim sole rights to Smith's considerable estate following her untimely death on September 26, 1937, as a result of injuries sustained in a car accident on a lonely Southern highway.

Mystery and legend surround Smith's death. The often-repeated story, based on an article by John Hammond in *Downbeat* magazine and perpetuated in Edward Albee's play *The Death of Bessie Smith* (1960), is that she was denied care because she was black and subsequently died from non-life-threatening injuries.

Bessie Smith, photographed by Carl Van Vechten in 1936.

This account is untrue and was almost immediately corrected. Yet it persists because the aura of racial injustice surrounding the accident is entirely believable and the story is as suitably tragic as Smith's premature death.

Smith's funeral was attended by thousands of mourners paying their respects, yet her grave remained unmarked from 1937 until 1970, when Juanita Green, a Philadelphia woman, aided by a donation from singer Janis Joplin, paid for a gravestone.

(As a footnote, the former emergency room of the colored hospital in Clarksdale, Mississippi, where Smith is believed to have died, is now Room 2 of the Riverside Hotel; guests may request to sleep in Smith's room, though for no more than one night.)   —*Carla Williams*

BIBLIOGRAPHY

Albertson, Chris. *Bessie.* New York: Stein and Day, 1972.

———. *Bessie Smith: Empress of the Blues.* New York: Schirmer Books, 1975.

Davis, Angela Y. *Blues Legacies and Black Feminism: Gertrude 'Ma' Rainey, Bessie Smith and Billie Holiday.* New York: Pantheon Books, 1998.

Kay, Jackie. *Bessie Smith.* Bath, England: Absolute Press, 1997.

Oliver, Paul. *Bessie Smith.* New York: A. S. Barnes, 1959.

SEE ALSO

Popular Music; Blues Music; Jazz; Cabarets and Revues; Hunter, Alberta; Joplin, Janis; Rainey, Gertrude ("Ma"); Waters, Ethel

Smiths, The, and Morrissey

THE SHORT-LIVED, BUT INTENSE, CREATIVE UNION OF singer and lyricist Stephen Patrick Morrissey (b. 1959), guitarist Johnny Marr (b. John Martin Maher, 1963), drummer Michael Joyce (b. 1963), and bassist Andrew Rourke (b. 1964) began in 1982, when they formed the Manchester pop group The Smiths.

By positioning themselves in opposition to the new romantic groups of the early 1980s, represented by such bands as Duran Duran (formed 1978) and Spandau Ballet (formed 1979), The Smiths brought to the British pop scene a refreshing class of independent, punk-inspired music.

The Smiths reacted against mainstream pop by reverting to a quasi-conservative and old-fashioned style of musicmaking, based on 1960s pop. They refused to employ machine-generated sound, such as the synthesizer, and were reluctant to nourish a burgeoning music video industry.

When The Smiths disbanded in 1987, they had produced seven albums: *The Smiths* (1984), *Hatful of Hollow* (1984), *Meat is Murder* (1985), *The Queen is Dead* (1986), *The World Won't Listen* (1987), *Louder Than Bombs* (1987), and *Strangeways, Here We Come* (1987).

After the group's demise, Morrissey began a solo career that has been mixed, yielding both successes and failures. His solo albums include *Viva Hate* (1988), *Bona Drag* (1990), *Kill Uncle* (1991), *Your Arsenal* (1992), *Beethoven Was Deaf* (1993), *Vauxhall and I* (1994), *Southpaw Grammar* (1995), and *Maladjusted* (1997).

Although The Smiths are now defunct, their astonishing, intellectual, and highly original body of work endures. The energy and verve of the music was the outcome of an impassioned and direct presentation of vocals and sound.

The Smiths expressed bravura by steadfastly avoiding trite and stereotypical lyrics. Even when Morrissey wrote about a common subject matter such as love, he stated unconventional ideas in surprising ways. In "Is It Really So Strange?" for example, he uses surprising images such as the murder of a horse and a nun to prove that he is in love.

Morrissey also animated his lyrics by drawing upon tortured personal experiences, for instance, his acknowledged alienation from others, as highlighted in the immensely popular ballad, "How Soon Is Now?" Moreover, as one commentator has observed, their music "archly expressed" queer subtexts.

Provocative hints of transvestism may be found in such songs as "Sheila Take A Bow," "Vicar in a Tutu," and "The Queen Is Dead." Morrissey also often broached the subject of masculinity, a theme exceedingly relevant to gay men.

Images of rough boys, such as James Dean and those populating the "sex and violence" books by Richard Allen (b. James Moffat, 1922), may be observed in such titles as "Rusholme Ruffians," "Sweet and Tender Hooligan," and "Suedehead" (found on Morrissey's solo recording *Viva Hate*). Also from his solo career is "Piccadilly Palare," which recovers *polari*, a form of "gay speak" used by rent boys in the 1960s.

A certain degree of homoeroticism also permeated The Smiths' album covers, as well as their concerts. The album covers frequently featured single portraits, often of brawny men, such as porn actor Joe Dallesandro on *The Smiths* and an unidentified Jean Cocteau model on *Hatful of Hollow*.

Inspired perhaps by Oscar Wilde, whom the lyricist avidly read and studied, The Smiths at their early concerts showered fans with gladioli from the stage. In turn, The Smiths' disciples exhibited great loyalty and admiration. They returned the symbolic gesture of camaraderie and tenderness by thrusting flowers at Morrissey's feet. Numerous men attempted to cross stage barriers (and often succeeded), in order to hug or kiss the "unloved," apparently miserable singer.

Morrissey has fiercely cultivated what some observers have called an androgynous persona. His appeal to gender rather than to sexual orientation has allowed him to manifest an emotional and sensitive demeanor while maintaining a largely heterosexual following.

Although he has been featured in countless publicity photographs as though he were a pornographic pinup boy/sex symbol, Morrissey has resolutely professed celibacy.

Morrissey has also always deflected questions regarding his alleged homosexuality. He once remarked, "I don't recognise such terms as heterosexual, homosexual, bisexual, and I think it's important that there's someone in pop music who's like that. These words do great damage, they confuse people and they make people feel unhappy, so I want to do away with them."

—*Eugenio Filice*

BIBLIOGRAPHY

Kent, Nick. "Dreamer in the Real World: Morrissey and Marr Interviewed." *The Face* No. 61 (May 1985).

Kopf, Biba. "A Suitable Case for Treatment: Morrissey and Johnny Marr Interviewed." *New Musical Express,* December 22–29, 1984, 6.

"Morrissey Answers Twenty Questions." *Star Hits,* September 1985.

Stringer, Julian. "The Smiths: Repressed (But Remarkably Dressed)." *Popular Music,* January 1992, 15.

Young, Russell. "Morrissey's Year." *Jamming!* No. 23 (November 1984).

SEE ALSO

Popular Music; Rock Music

Smyth, Dame Ethel   *(1858–1944)*

ETHEL (OR ETHYL) SMYTH WAS THE MOST IMPORTANT female composer in early-twentieth-century English music and one of the few significant English composers of opera of either sex. In addition to six operas, composed between 1894 and 1925, she also wrote chamber ensemble works and a Mass in D (1891).

Thomas Beecham thought *The Wreckers* (1904) "one of the three or four English operas of real musical merit and vitality"; and Queen Victoria invited Smyth to perform at Balmoral. She was created Dame Commander of the Order of the British Empire in 1922.

Born on April 23, 1858, into a military family, Smyth grew up as a tomboy. Her family traveled back and forth from England to India during her childhood, an experience that developed her love of travel and adventure.

In defiance of her father's wishes, at age nineteen, Smyth fought to be allowed to study music at Leipzig, where she became friends with Tchaikovsky, Brahms, Clara Schumann, and Grieg.

Women musicians were subject to such discrimination that she was forced to rely on influential patrons, such as the Empress Eugénie, to get her music performed. "Let it be pointed out," she wrote, "that very few girls happen to live next door to rich empresses of pronounced feministic sympathies."

Smyth's class privilege made it easy for her to be an unapologetic lesbian. At the end of the nineteenth century and early in the twentieth, the cult of the creative artist was very much alive in European culture, and sexual flamboyance was tolerated, or even expected of such sensitive souls.

Smyth considered herself part of an informal queer freemasonry of artists, writers, and musicians, including Proust, Cocteau, Romaine Brooks, Sergei Diaghilev, Violet Trefussis, Radclyffe Hall, and Oscar Wilde (to whose brother she became briefly engaged during a railway journey).

Smyth's love life was a series of grand lesbian passions. Many were fully reciprocated, while others—such as the deep crush she developed in her seventies on a much younger Virginia Woolf—probably were not.

She spent ten strange years with Harry Brewster, brother-in-law of her then lover, Lisl von Herzogenberg, but this seems to have been her single anomalous heterosexual affair. She wrote to him, "I wonder why it is so much easier for me to love my own sex passionately, rather than yours? ...I am a very healthy-minded person, and it is an everlasting puzzle."

Smyth's passion fueled a determined feminism. She fought tirelessly for women in music, urging female musicians and composers to "swear that unless women are given equal chances with men in the orchestra and unless women's work features in your programmes, *you will make things very disagreeable indeed.*"

She became a key figure in the fight for women's suffrage, composing music for *The March of Women,* the anthem of the Women's Social and Political Union.

Smyth spent two months in Holloway Prison for smashing the window of the Colonial Secretary during a suffragist demonstration. Thomas Beecham recounted seeing "the noble company of martyrs" marching around the prison courtyard singing Smyth's *March,* while she conducted them with a toothbrush from her cell window.

Typically, she fell passionately in love with suffragist leader Emmeline Pankhurst, and there is some evidence that this love was reciprocated.

Smyth's love for women was integral to her passion for female equality, and both her political work and lesbian desire are reflected in her operas and other compositions. She wrote, "I want women to turn their minds to big and difficult jobs; not just to go on hugging the shore, afraid to put to sea."

Smyth died on May 8, 1944, having become an inspirational figure in feminist and lesbian history. —*Tamsin Wilton*

BIBLIOGRAPHY

Collis, Rose. *Portraits to the Wall: Historic Lesbian Lives Unveiled.* London: Cassell, 1994.

Crichton, Ronald, ed. *The Memoirs of Ethyl Smyth* (abridged). London: Viking, 1987.

Smyth, Ethel. *Impressions That Remained.* 2 vols. London: Longman, 1919.

———. *Mass in D and Other Works.* Sound recording. The Plymouth Music Series conducted by Philip Brunelle. London: Virgin Classics, 1991.

Wood, Elizabeth. "Sapphonics." *Queering the Pitch: The New Gay and Lesbian Musicology.* Philip Brett, Elizabeth Wood, and Gary Thomas, eds. New York: Routledge, 1994. 27–66.

SEE ALSO

Classical Music; Conductors; Diaghilev, Sergei; Tchaikovsky, Pyotr Ilich

Somerville, Jimmy   *(b. 1961)*

NOTED FOR HIS DIMINUTIVE SIZE AND AMAZING VOICE, Jimmy Somerville first shot to fame in the mid-1980s as the lead singer with the openly gay pop group Bronski Beat.

Bronski Beat's first single, "Small Town Boy," which, along with its video, dealt with the problems of being gay in provincial Britain, was an instant success (reaching number three in the UK pop charts) and quickly established the group's reputation.

Born in Glasgow on June 22, 1961, Somerville was twenty-three when he formed Bronski Beat in 1984 as a collaboration with Steve Bronski and Larry Stenbachek. The three musicians met while they were working on a video by young gay men and lesbians entitled *Famed Youth.* It was during this project that Somerville realized he could sing.

Bronski Beat's debut album, *Age of Consent* (1984), included a pink triangle on the cover and listed the age of consent for gay sex in European countries on the inside sleeve, as a means of calling attention to the disparity between British and Continental laws at that time.

Consisting of a series of songs dealing with various aspects of gay life, the album sold more than a million copies. In 1985, Bronski Beat teamed up with another gay singer, Marc Almond, to record a version of Donna Summer's "I Feel Love," which was also a hit.

After a series of disagreements over politics, Somerville left Bronski Beat in April 1985 and formed another group, The Communards, with another gay musician, Richard Coles.

The music of The Communards was also politically tinged. It featured songs dealing with issues such as gay relationships ("There's More to Love than Boy Meets Girl," 1987) and the loss of friends to AIDS ("For a Friend," 1987). Other hits of The Communards include "You Are My World" (1986), "Don't Leave Me This Way" (1986), and a cover of Gloria Gaynor's "Never Can Say Goodbye" (1987).

Always up-front about his sexuality and political affiliations, Somerville made no secret of the fact that he was an active member of the Labour Party Young Socialists and the Anti-Nazi League. It was no surprise that The Communards took part in a left-wing collaboration, The Red Wedge tour, which actively supported the miners' strike against the closure of coal mines in the mid-1980s.

When The Communards disbanded in 1988, Somerville spent some time in Los Angeles, where he channeled his political activities toward the fight against AIDS. He became an active member of the direct-action organization ACT UP (AIDS Coalition to Unleash Power).

On his return to Britain, Somerville continued to work with ACT UP, using his celebrity status to highlight the AIDS epidemic and the plight of people with HIV. As a result of his activities with ACT UP, he was arrested in 1990.

In 1989, Somerville released his first solo album, entitled *Read My Lips.* The title referred to then U.S. president George Bush's electoral promise not to raise taxes, which he subsequently broke. Not surprisingly, many of the songs on the album are overtly political.

Commenting on the title song for an interview published in the program for his 1990 ACT UP tour of Britain, Somerville said, "It's a song with a really potent message and it's emotional and angry at the same time. I'm really proud of it because I've done this disco anthem that has taken elements that have made dance music what it is today.... It's so difficult to get across politics, emotion and anger in a four-minute pop record and I think I've managed to achieve that."

With his strong tenor voice and ringing falsetto, Somerville appeared as an Elizabethan castrato singer in Sally Potter's 1992 film adaptation of Virginia Woolf's *Orlando.*

Among Somerville's recent solo albums are *Something to Live For* (1999) and *Manage the Damage* (1999), both dominated by disco and dance music. "Lay Down," a track on the former album, is a paean to fellatio, while the title track of the latter album is dedicated to Matthew Shepard, the young American college student who was killed in a homophobic murder.

                                                                    —*Shaun Cole*

BIBLIOGRAPHY

Bernard, Edwin J. "An Interview with Jimmy Somerville." The ACT UP Tour Program, 1990.

Clements, Paul. "Don't Leave Me This Way." *The Pink Paper,* May 28, 1999, 20.

Smith, Richard. "The Happy Wanderer: Jimmy Somerville." *Seduced and Abandoned: Essays on Gay Men and Popular Music.* New York: Cassell, 1995. 77–82.

Who?, Stuart. "Jimmy Somerville." *qx international,* May 26, 1999, 18.

SEE ALSO

Popular Music; Disco and Dance Music; Rock Music; Music and AIDS

Sondheim, Stephen   *(b. 1930)*

STEPHEN SONDHEIM'S SEVENTIETH BIRTHDAY, ON March 22, 2000, was marked by a gala fete at the Library of Congress and proved the occasion for numerous retrospectives of his remarkable career.

The only child of a mother who designed clothing for his father's company, Sondheim grew up in an environment of wealth, talent, and refined sensibility. His parents divorced when he was ten years old. When his mother moved to Bucks County, Pennsylvania, Stephen became a friend of a neighbor boy, Jimmy Hammerstein, son of the presiding Broadway genius, Oscar Hammerstein II, who encouraged Sondheim in his earliest efforts.

Sondheim studied music at Williams College with the avant-garde composer Milton Babbitt. After graduating, he wrote scripts for the television series *Topper.*

One of the most innovative careers in Broadway history was launched when, at age twenty-six, Sondheim was asked to write the lyrics for Leonard Bernstein's *West Side Story* and, the following year, for Jule Styne's songs for *Gypsy.* His first score as composer/lyricist was *A Funny Thing Happened on the Way to the Forum* (1962)—one of the few successful musical farces.

Multiple Tony Awards, an Academy Award, and a Pulitzer Prize followed, as well as the bestowal of Kennedy Center for the Performing Arts honors by President Clinton in 1993.

A Paradoxical Place in Gay Culture

Sondheim's musicals occupy a paradoxical place in gay culture. A gay creative artist who has never created an explicitly gay character and who, according to his biographer Meryle Secrest, did not come out until his early forties or allow himself to fall in love with another man until age sixty-one, Sondheim has nevertheless attained gay cult status.

He is recognized both as the most intelligent, witty, and musically audacious of composers and as a brilliantly ironic lyricist in the tradition of his gay predecessors Lorenz Hart, Noël Coward, and Cole Porter.

He incarnates the paradox of a highly intellectualized gay perspective that prizes ambivalence, undercuts

traditional American progressivism, and rejects the musical's historically idealistic view of sex, romance, and the family; but that at the same time eschews camp, deconstructs the diva, and is apparently oblivious to AIDS, the post-Stonewall struggle for civil equality, and other sociopolitical issues that concern most gay men of his generation.

Sondheim's Remarkable Range

At first glance, Sondheim is uncategorizable. His aesthetic mirrors that of painter Georges Seurat, the subject of Sondheim's Pulitzer Prize–winning *Sunday in the Park with George* (1984): "If you know where you're going, / You've gone. / Just keep moving on."

In each of his projects, Sondheim moves on, addressing a new creative challenge and in the process stretching the limits of one of America's most conventional dramatic forms.

His subjects or sources alone give a cursory sense of his extraordinary range: memoirs of the stripper Gypsy Rose Lee (*Gypsy,* 1959), a film by Ingmar Bergman (*A Little*

Stephen Sondheim receives an award in 2003.
Photograph by Ronald Asadorian/Splash.

Night Music, 1973), and a painting by pointillist painter Georges Seurat (*Sunday*); plays by dramatists as diverse as Kaufman and Hart (*Merrily We Roll Along*, 1981), Arthur Laurents (*Do I Hear a Waltz?*, 1965), William Shakespeare (*West Side Story*, 1957), and Plautus (*A Funny Thing Happened on the Way to the Forum*); nineteenth-century British grand guignol (*Sweeney Todd*, 1979) and biting sketches of contemporary American domestic life (*Company*, 1970); Grimm's fairy tales (*Into the Woods*, 1987) and a nineteenth-century Italian novel of tormented passion (*Passion*, 1994); a history of American imperialism (*Pacific Overtures*, 1976), a sociology of American political assassinations (*Assassins*, 1991), and the psychological complexities of the murder mystery (*Getting Away with Murder*, 1996).

Follies (1971), which remains Sondheim's most brilliant effort to date, was actually inspired by a 1960s newspaper photograph of the silent-film star Gloria Swanson standing triumphantly amid the ruins of the demolished Roxy movie palace.

Progressing musically from show to show, Sondheim has mastered the idiom of folk music, the Strauss waltz, nineteenth-century light opera, the British music hall, every prerock twentieth-century American popular style, and Japanese Kabuki. His music has become standard repertoire in both cabarets and opera houses. Sondheim has proved relentless in his need to move on.

Queering the American Dream

Rejecting the conventional and "pretty" (which, his Georges Seurat explains, is subject to time and change; beauty is, rather, "what the eye arranges"), Sondheim's plays represent a queering of the American dream that is traditionally inscribed in the Broadway musical.

While Rose disdainfully dismisses the passivity of "Some People" who "thrive and bloom, / Living life in a living room," her vibrant assertion that "Everything's Coming Up Roses" is shown by the conclusion of *Gypsy* to be as delusional as Willy Loman's dreams of success in *Death of a Salesman*.

Pursuit of the American dream invariably involves people selling out what they value most. The accomplishments of "Franklin Shepard, Inc." as a Hollywood producer are deconstructed in *Merrily*, the play moving backward from his most recent moment of public success to the recognition of the creative potential and the friendships that he betrayed along the way.

Juxtaposing the ghosts of hopeful young people with the middle-aged persons they have become in the reunion of Weissman Girls in *Follies*, Sondheim anatomizes the disintegration of pre–World War II American optimism into late-century cynicism and emotional emptiness.

The ultimate result of Admiral Perry's "gunboat diplomacy" in the 1850s, *Pacific Overtures* shrewdly demonstrates, is Japan's learning only too well the lessons of American economic imperialism and undercutting the American economy in the 1980s.

Joanne's toast to "The Ladies Who Lunch" in *Company* is a stinging analysis of the emptiness of their seemingly prosperous lives.

Consequences of Exclusion

There is a consistent concern in Sondheim's plays with the individual or group excluded from the mainstream, and what the consequences of that exclusion are for the community as a whole.

For example, Benjamin Barker revenges himself upon the Victorian sentimentality and hypocrisy that allowed him to be falsely imprisoned and his family destroyed in *Sweeney Todd*; and *Assassins* dramatizes the devastating social consequences of the American system's exclusionary politics.

Ironically, the most rousing number in *West Side Story* is the Puerto Ricans' celebration of the "America" into which they will never be assimilated: "Life is all right in America / If you're all white in America."

The theatrically brilliant "Cookie" sequence of *Anyone Can Whistle* questions whether the self-appointed guardians of the American dream are not more insane than those who, emotionally broken by their pursuit of it, have withdrawn to the margins of society.

Interpersonal Relationships

As pervasive an impulse in Sondheim's canon as the queering of the American dream is his queering of interpersonal relationships.

The men in *Company* recognize that in marriage one is "always sorry, always grateful," just as Bobby eventually accepts that "Being Alive" demands going beyond the isolation of the self even while accepting the ambivalences and compromises of a relationship.

"Send in the Clowns," like the "Soon/Now/Later" trio earlier in *A Little Night Music*, dramatizes the comedy that results because one's desires never coincide with those of one's partner.

The extraordinary "Loveland" sequence of *Follies* shows the two principal couples forced by experience to alter their naive concept of love.

And the play *Passion* functions as alchemically as a John Donne lyric, inviting the audience initially to identify with Giorgio and Clara's soaring celebration of the happiness they've discovered in love, only to betray those assumptions by revealing the passion "implacable as stone" that the sickly and unappealing Fosca arouses in the romantic hero.

There are no absolutes and, thus, no "happily ever after" in Sondheim's world, only the struggle to live humanely after breaking through the prison of one's romantic illusions.

Sondheim and Popular Culture

"I'm telling you, the only times I really feel the presence of God are when I'm having sex, and during a great Broadway musical!" the rambunctious Father Dan tells the title character in Paul Rudnick's *Jeffrey* (1994). "*Phantom. Starlight Express. Miss Saigon!* Know ye the signs of the devil: overmiking, smoke machines, trouble with Equity."

Sondheim delivers to Broadway musical queens like Father Dan what the musicals of the Antichrist, Andrew Lloyd Webber, cannot: psychological depth rather than special effects; witty and insightful lyrics rather than clichéd expressions; and complex, often atonal music rather than vapidly hummable melodies.

Thus, Sondheim has been absorbed by gay popular culture in the most unusual ways: The line "add 'em up, Bobby," from *Company*, is used as a refrain in James Kirkwood's *P. S. Your Cat Is Dead* (1972); the William Higgins porn star Ben Barker fixes the Sondheimian dimension of his *nom de porn* by wearing a Sweeney Todd T-shirt in the opening scene of *The Boys of San Francisco* (1980); and the songs "Somewhere" from *West Side Story* and "Being Alive" from *Company* became the anthems of two very different generations of gay men.

Moreover, the Sondheim revue became a staple of AIDS fund-raising on both coasts in the 1990s. As Father Dan understands, the lyrics and music of Sondheim allow the heightened perception and intense feeling of being alive that are usually associated only with religious experience and sexual orgasm. —*Raymond-Jean Frontain*

Bibliography

Banfield, Stephen. *Sondheim's Broadway Musicals*. Ann Arbor: University of Michigan Press, 1993.

Clum, John M. *Something for the Boys: Musical Theater and Gay Culture*. New York: St. Martin's Press, 1999.

Goodhart, Sandor, ed. *Reading Stephen Sondheim: A Collection of Critical Essays*. New York: Garland, 2000.

Gordon, Joanne. *Art Isn't Easy: The Theater of Stephen Sondheim*. Updated ed. New York: Da Capo Press, 1992.

———, ed. *Stephen Sondheim: A Casebook*. New York: Garland, 1997.

Miller, D. A. *Place for Us: Essay on the Broadway Musical*. Cambridge, Mass.: Harvard University Press, 1998.

Secrest, Meryle. *Stephen Sondheim: A Life*. New York: Knopf, 1998.

Zadan, Craig. *Sondheim & Co.* Second ed., updated. New York: DaCapo Press, 1994.

See also

Musical Theater and Film; Cabarets and Revues; Classical Music; Bennett, Michael; Bernstein, Leonard; Blitzstein, Marc; Coward, Sir Noël; Finn, William; Hart, Lorenz; Herman, Jerry; Kander, John, and Fred Ebb; Lane, Nathan; Laurents, Arthur; Porter, Cole; Robbins, Jerome

Springfield, Dusty (1939–1999)

DUSTY SPRINGFIELD BECAME THE MOST POPULAR British female rock star of the 1960s, one of the most prominent white soul singers ever, and a major influence on subsequent generations of singers. Now widely acclaimed as one of the greatest voices of popular music, she was long an icon of gay and lesbian culture.

Born Mary Isobel Catherine Bernadette O'Brien in London on April 16, 1939, she was educated in Roman Catholic convent schools. As an adolescent, Springfield was a bespectacled "ugly duckling."

She joined her brother Tom in a folk combo, the Springfields. They became the most popular group in England prior to the advent of the Beatles. In 1962, with "Silver Threads and Golden Needles," the Springfields became the first British group to have a Top 20 hit in the United States.

In 1963, inspired by the music of American girl groups, Dusty left the Springfields and embarked on a solo career. She changed from the "wholesome" Springfields style to a more trendy "Queen of the Mods" image, with fashionable clothing, excessive bouffant hairstyles, and heavy black mascara.

In 1964, her first solo recording, "I Only Want to Be with You," made her the first "British Invasion" artist to enter the American charts in the wake of the Beatles.

Springfield gained a wider audience by mixing American soul and British standards on her second album, *Ev'rything's Coming Up Dusty* (1965).

Her biggest hit, the melodramatic "You Don't Have to Say You Love Me" (1966), was a major success on both sides of the Atlantic. But by this time she was shifting from Queen of the Mods to female drag queen. She claimed she learned her makeup techniques from female impersonators—as her hair and dresses became increasingly over-the-top.

While her campy image and emotionally overwrought recordings of Italian ballads (refitted with English lyrics) made her a cult figure among gay fans, Springfield seemed adrift stylistically until she issued her 1968 album *Dusty in Memphis*, recorded with the Atlantic Records session musicians who played on many of the soul music hits of the decade.

Although it featured the hit single "Son of a Preacher Man" and has long been considered her masterpiece, this sophisticated and finely wrought album was ahead of its time and was, at the time of its release, a commercial failure.

In 1971, frustrated and depressed by the direction of her career and hounded by the press, Springfield took the amazingly courageous if self-destructive step of coming out publicly as "bisexual," though, as recent biographies have detailed, she was in fact a lesbian.

She moved to Los Angeles and basically dropped out of sight, her career and personal life in shambles. She performed little over the next fifteen years.

In 1986, at the insistence of the Pet Shop Boys, she resumed recording, teaming with them on their worldwide hit "What Have I Done to Deserve This?"

With her comeback she returned to England, where she was venerated as a pop heroine, and made a moderately successful album, *Reputation* (1990), produced by the Pet Shop Boys.

In 1995, while recording what would be her final album, *A Very Fine Love*, she was stricken with breast cancer.

Shortly before her death on March 2, 1999, Dusty Springfield was inducted, however belatedly, into the Rock and Roll Hall of Fame and awarded the Order of the British Empire by Queen Elizabeth II.

At her funeral, Pet Shop Boy Neil Tennant summed up her life and career aptly: "She was fab and, because of her music, she always will be."

—*Patricia Juliana Smith*

The Springfields band members (left to right) Mike Pickworth, Dusty Springfield, and Tom O'Brien.

BIBLIOGRAPHY

O'Brien, Lucy. *Dusty*. Rev. ed. London: Sidgwick & Jackson, 2000.

Smith, Patricia Juliana. "'You Don't Have to Say You Love Me': The Camp Masquerades of Dusty Springfield." *The Queer Sixties*. Patricia Juliana Smith, ed. New York: Routledge, 1999. 105–126.

Valentine, Penny, and Vicki Wickham. *Dancing with Demons: The Authorized Biography of Dusty Springfield*. London: Hodder & Stoughton, 2000.

SEE ALSO

Popular Music; Divas; Pet Shop Boys

Stipe, Michael   (b. 1960)

MICHAEL STIPE HAS BEEN THE LEAD SINGER, LYRICIST, and composer for the successful rock band R.E.M. for over two decades. Among his best-known songs is "Losing My Religion," which rose to number four on the U.S. rock charts in 1991. He has also become involved in film and now has his own production companies.

As is typical for the child of a career military officer, John Michael Stipe had a peripatetic childhood. Born on January 4, 1960, in Decatur, Georgia, he grew up on bases around the United States and also in Germany, and spent his high-school years in Illinois.

Stipe returned to his native state for college, enrolling as an art student at the University of Georgia in 1978. There he met fellow alternative music fans Peter Buck, Mike Mills, and Bill Berry. Within a year, all four had dropped out of college to forge a career as a rock band, R.E.M.

They went on a concert tour, and in 1980 put out their first single, "Radio Free Europe." Its success, particularly on college radio stations, won them a recording contract. Their first full-length album, *Murmur* (1983), was chosen as Album of the Year by *Rolling Stone* magazine.

Stipe's vigor onstage contributed to the success of R.E.M.'s concerts. He interacted with the audience and charged about with boundless energy. He blasted his often dark and brooding lyrics into the microphone with such force that they were frequently barely intelligible.

In addition to composing and performing, Stipe has also directed several of R.E.M.'s music videos and oversees the creation of their album covers.

R.E.M. has enjoyed unusual longevity for a rock band. They have evolved over the years, using horns, strings, and electronics to back up their music at various times.

By 2003, the band had recorded nearly twenty albums with collective sales of almost fifty million copies worldwide, making it one of the most successful in the history of rock music. Another album is scheduled for release in the fall of 2004.

Stipe has received consistent praise for his lyrics, which Christopher John Farley of *Time* magazine describes as "erudite and elusive." Some of Stipe's compositions reflect his concerns with social, political, ethical, and environmental issues. Fiona Sturges of the *Independent* calls him "arguably the most important and influential rock icon of his generation."

Stipe's brash persona onstage contrasts markedly with his demeanor offstage. He does not like to discuss his private life with the media, and long declined to comment on speculation about his sexual orientation. He did dispel rumors in the early 1990s that he had AIDS. A few years later, he commented that he had been attracted to both men and women. By 2001, Stipe was identifying himself as a "queer artist," and in a *Time* magazine interview said that he was "in a relationship with an amazing man" whose name he did not reveal.

Stipe has founded two film companies, C-Hundred, based in New York, and Single Cell Productions in Los Angeles, which make low-budget films. Since 1997, Stipe has been producer or executive producer of a dozen films, some for television. By far the most successful was Spike Jonze's *Being John Malkovich* (1999), which was nominated for an Oscar.

One of Stipe's recent movies is Brian Dannelly's *Saved!* (2004), a comedy set in a Christian high school in which a girl questions her beliefs when her "perfect Christian boyfriend" reveals that he may be gay. The Reverend Jerry Falwell condemned the film—without having seen it—but film critic Phoebe Flowers wrote that "*Saved!* is actually a fairly balanced portrayal of the faith, ultimately preaching tolerance and kindness." This assessment fits well with the philosophy that Stipe expressed in a 2003 interview: "Idealism has been the springboard for almost everything I've ever done."   — *Linda Rapp*

BIBLIOGRAPHY

Browne, David. "Stipe's Rich Pageant: R.E.M.'s Main Man Riffs on Sex, Music, and Big-screen Dreams." *Entertainment Weekly*, July 14, 1995, 16.

Farley, Christopher John. "The Group's Gone Electronic. The Singer's Gone Hollywood. Is This the Band's End? Nah, It's a New Beginning." *Time*, May 21, 2001, 84.

Flowers, Phoebe. "As Producer of 'Saved!,' R.E.M.'s Stipe Returns to Religious Themes." *Boston Globe*, June 18, 2004.

Sturges, Fiona. "Who Are You Calling an Elder Statesman?" *Independent* (London), October 20, 2003.

SEE ALSO

Popular Music; Rock Music; Music Videos

Strayhorn, William Thomas   (1915-1967)

DESPITE HIS INDISPUTABLE MUSICAL GENIUS, THE PROlific composer, arranger, and performing musician Billy Strayhorn spent much of his life in near anonymity. Best known for his collaborations with Duke Ellington over a span of nearly thirty years, Strayhorn was the writer and arranger behind the famous Ellington Orchestra theme "Take the 'A' Train," as well as the creator of such classics as "Lush Life," "Satin Doll," and "Johnny Come Lately."

Yet the small, bespectacled, openly gay Strayhorn—by all accounts a quiet and extraordinarily refined man—lived behind the scenes of jazz glory for most of his life. He released only one solo album during his lifetime, and until the mid-1990s not a single biography had been written about him.

The first of five surviving children born to a softspoken, ladylike mother and a brutish father in Dayton, Ohio, Strayhorn was raised in the Homewood area of Pittsburgh. The town never much suited Billy, a classical music enthusiast whose sophistication from an early age far exceeded that of his surroundings.

Because Strayhorn's family did not have sufficient money to buy Billy a piano, he worked and saved up during high school to buy himself one.

Although his grandmother, who played the piano for the choir of her church, encouraged his musical interests, Strayhorn never received much formal musical instruction. Racism was certainly a contributing factor: He was discouraged from applying to colleges because he was black—and black concert pianists were practically nonexistent at the time.

When Strayhorn heard a jazz record for the first time, his musical focus began to shift. While his work would always show classical influences, he had discovered a world of innovative musicians who were serious, successful—and black.

He began to compose in the jazz idiom, including an early composition that would be his signature song, "Lush Life." In 1937, Strayhorn formed his first jazz group, eventually called The Mad Hatters. Although they achieved moderate local success, Strayhorn continued to earn most of his money working at a drugstore.

All of that changed when, in 1938, Strayhorn was introduced to Duke Ellington, already a successful orchestra leader. Ellington, instantly and thoroughly impressed with Strayhorn's obvious talent, quickly took him on as a protégé, even moving Strayhorn into his Harlem home in 1939 to live with other members of the Ellington family.

By the end of his first year in New York, Strayhorn had arranged a new living situation, moving in with a musician named Aaron Bridgers. Strayhorn and Bridgers

Billy Strayhorn, photographed by Carl Van Vechten in 1958.

were anything but secretive about their relationship, and Strayhorn's homosexuality became well known in the black musical community.

As an out gay black man in the first half of the twentieth century, Strayhorn was unusual indeed—especially considering that no other jazzmen were openly gay. But unconcerned about appearances, Strayhorn refused to don a facade of heterosexuality.

Most of his time was spent out of the spotlight, so his sexuality simply was not an issue in his career or in his relationship with Ellington. It may, however, explain why he seemed to avoid the spotlight and let Ellington receive credit for their collaborative work.

In 1942, Strayhorn began an intimate friendship with the singer Lena Horne, who memorably described him in her 1965 autobiography as her "alter ego": "A pixie, brown color, horn-rimmed glasses, beautifully cut suit, beautifully modulated speaking voice, appeared as if by magic and said 'I'm Billy Strayhorn—Swee Pea.' We looked at each other, clasped hands...and I loved him."

During her career, Horne recorded many of his compositions, including "Maybe," "Something to Live For," "A Flower Is a Lovesome Thing," and "Love Like This Can't Last."

Although Strayhorn did a great deal of the composing for Ellington's bands, he was credited infrequently, and remained fairly invisible to the public.

Upon learning that their published collaborative works were all copyrighted by Ellington, who received the royalties, Strayhorn became understandably dismayed—though it was really the lack of independence in his own career, rather than the money, that bothered him.

It was not until mid-1957, when an effort entitled "Drum Is a Woman" was broadcast for the first time, that Ellington and Strayhorn were credited equally.

While Strayhorn refused to pity himself or complain to friends and family, it was clear that he was often unhappy with his failure to receive credit for work that had helped make Ellington rich and famous.

His drinking, friends noticed, escalated considerably as the years passed. Consequently, his health began to deteriorate, which affected his work and activities. Although Strayhorn, a civil rights advocate, attended the 1963 March on Washington with Martin Luther King Jr., an acquaintance of his, he did not feel well enough actually to march.

The reason for his physical decline soon became clear. In early 1964, he was diagnosed with esophageal cancer—a type of cancer usually stemming from use of alcohol and tobacco, both of which Strayhorn indulged in heavily.

The following year, Strayhorn played the only concert showcasing him without Ellington's presence, name, or influence. The concert at the New School in New York City completely sold out. It was, alas, one of Strayhorn's final accomplishments.

After a tracheostomy and the subsequent removal of his esophagus, Strayhorn finally succumbed to the disease. He died prematurely on May 31, 1967, at the age of fifty-three, leaving behind a legacy deserving of far more recognition for decades to come than it had garnered during his lifetime.

Happily, he is now recognized as a major figure in American music, one who immensely enriched jazz music by investing it with complexly orchestrated form.

—*Teresa Theophano*

Bibliography

Hajdu, David. *Lush Life: A Biography of Billy Strayhorn*. New York: Farrar Straus and Giroux, 1996.

See also

Popular Music; Jazz

Susa, Conrad   (b. 1935)

AMERICAN COMPOSER CONRAD SUSA IS BEST KNOWN for his operas and choral music, some of which is informed by his experience as a gay man.

Conrad Stephen Susa was born in Springdale, Pennsylvania, near Pittsburgh, on April 26, 1935. His family was Slovak, and there was a great deal of amateur music making at home, especially choral music. He studied music at Carnegie Institute of Technology (now Carnegie Mellon University) and at Juilliard, where his teachers included William Bergsma and Vincent Persichetti.

From the beginning of his career, Susa has been involved with dramatic music, as indicated by his work as composer in residence of the Old Globe Theater in San Diego (1959–1994), music director of the APA-Phoenix Repertory Company in New York (1961–1968), and music director of the American Shakespeare Festival in Stratford, Connecticut (1969–1971). He has also been dramaturge for the Eugene O'Neill Memorial Theater Center in Waterford, Connecticut (1986–ca. 1990).

Susa has won various prizes, including a George Gershwin Memorial Scholarship, two Ford Foundation Fellowships, a Gretchaninoff Prize, and a National Endowment for the Arts grant.

In 1972, he moved from New York to San Francisco. In 1988, he joined the composition department at the San Francisco Conservatory, becoming Chair in 2000.

Susa's compositions are mainly tonal, and reflect a love of Baroque counterpoint and a joy in the polyphony of voices. In addition to many film and television scores and instrumental works, Susa has written a number of vocal works, both stage and choral.

Susa is the first composer ever commissioned by a gay men's chorus. The New York Gay Men's Chorus (together with Susa's publisher, G. Schirmer) commissioned *Chanticleer's Carol* (1982), an antiphonal work whose cries of "Awake!" are accompanied by brass, including an offstage trumpet.

He has since had numerous commissions by the Gay and Lesbian Association of Choruses (GALA) and its members, including the San Francisco, Boston, Minneapolis, and San Diego choruses.

Susa's first opera, *Transformations* (1973), was among the most famous commissions by the theatrically innovative Minnesota Opera, and has become one of the most widely performed American operas.

Its staging of Anne Sexton's radical reinterpretations of fairy tales expands the gender roles of the originals, including cross-gender casting (approved by Sexton) and a lesbian seduction. The composer's libretto works in a story of Sexton's creative and personal growth as a subplot, and the musical numbers parody a range of popular-music styles.

Two of Susa's operas, *Black River* (1975, revised 1981) and *The Love of Don Perlimplin* (1984), were written to libretti by the composer's then partner Richard Street; the latter is based on a text by Federico García Lorca.

Two later operas, *The Wise Woman* (1994) and *The Dangerous Liaisons* (1994, revised 1996–1997, after the Laclos novel), use libretti by gay songwriter Philip Littell; the former was commissioned by the American Guild of Organists, the latter by the San Francisco Opera.

Dirge from Cymbeline (1991), for men's chorus with offstage trumpet, was written in memory of Susa's lover Nikos, who died of AIDS.

Susa has written other pieces occasioned by gay deaths. The first song of *The Cricket Sings* (1985), a GALA commission for the Seattle Men's Chorus, is a memorial for a young man who died of cancer.

—*Paul Attinello*

BIBLIOGRAPHY

Adams, Byron. "Susa, Conrad." *Gay Histories and Cultures: An Encyclopedia.* George E. Haggerty, ed. New York: Garland, 2000. 851.

———. "Susa, Conrad." *Revised New Grove Dictionary of Music and Musicians.* Stanley Sadie, ed. London: Macmillan, 2000. 729–730.

Jackson, Gilbert. *The Choral Music of Conrad Susa.* Ph.D. diss., Michigan State University, 1984.

SEE ALSO

Classical Music; Opera; Choruses and Bands

Sweet Honey in the Rock

"AN ENSEMBLE OF BLACK WOMEN SINGERS" IS HOW Sweet Honey in the Rock defines itself. A group of cultural and political activists, whose repertoire includes everything from Negro spirituals to civil-rights-movement freedom songs to a feminist anthem by lesbian folksinger Ferron ("Testimony," 1983) to their own original compositions, Sweet Honey has included in its roster, to date, some twenty-two women.

Early on, founder Bernice Johnson Reagon realized that, because the group defined itself as professional but part-time, it was best to keep membership open, allowing members to come and go depending upon the demands of their lives.

Born in 1973 in Washington, D.C., out of a vocal workshop led by Reagon, whose own roots were in the church and the Student Nonviolent Coordinating Committee Freedom Singers, Sweet Honey is currently composed of founding members Reagon and Carol Maillard, Nitanju Bolade Casel (joined 1985), Aisha Kahlil (joined 1981), Ysaye Maria Barnwell (joined 1979), and sign-language interpreter Shirley Childress Saxton (joined 1980).

Although an early member of Sweet Honey, Dianaruthe Wharton, played piano and the performers do use hand percussion instruments, Sweet Honey remains an a cappella vocal group.

A Grammy-winning ensemble with an international following, Sweet Honey in the Rock incorporates spiritual, gospel, blues, jazz, folk, African, and rap musical styles to sing about the political as well as the personal.

Sweet Honey in the Rock's enduring connection with the gay and lesbian community dates back to a 1977 California tour arranged by feminist activist Amy Horowitz. Through Horowitz, the group was also invited to perform on a record by Meg Christian, who self-identified as a "political lesbian."

According to Reagon, on that tour their audience went from "Black people, churches, schools, theaters, folk festivals, and political rallies, to the radical, separatist, White-women-dominated, lesbian cultural network in California."

While only one member of Sweet Honey was self-identified as a lesbian (Evelyn Maria Harris, who sang with the group for eighteen years), the experience of working with and performing for political lesbians led Reagon to write songs specifically about women loving women and to reevaluate the group's overall political mission.

That first song included the powerful lyric: "Every woman who ever loved a woman / You ought to stand up and call her name / Mama, sister, daughter, lover." As Reagon explains, the group's exposure to the lesbian community led them from that point forth to "sing about oppression of every kind, including the oppression experienced by the homosexual community."

From songs specifically about lesbianism to the simple but defiant act of not switching genders in songs sung from the point of view of a male, such as "I'm Going to Get My Baby Out of Jail" (1993), Sweet Honey in the Rock has embraced homosexuality as a life force that deserves a voice.

In 1981, Reagon and Harris helped Horowitz and her organization Roadwork to found Sisterfire, a "women's cultural day" that eventually became a two-day, multistage festival. In its six years, Sisterfire hosted many lesbian artists, including Reagon's folksinger daughter, Toshi Reagon, June Jordan, Holly Near, Cris Williamson, Ferron, and Kate Clinton, among many others.

Solidifying their relationship with the lesbian community, Sweet Honey has also performed at the Michigan Womyn's Music Festival, the legendary annual women-only music festival.

—*Carla Williams*

BIBLIOGRAPHY

Bessman, Jim. *Sweet Honey in the Rock.* www.pressnetwork.com/sweet.htm

Reagon, Bernice Johnson, et al. *We Who Believe in Freedom: Sweet Honey in the Rock...Still on the Journey.* New York: Anchor Books, 1993.

SEE ALSO

Popular Music; Women's Music; Women's Music Festivals; Near, Holly; Williamson, Cris

Sylvester (Sylvester James)   *(1946?–1988)*

BY THE TIME SYLVESTER DIED ON DECEMBER 16, 1988, from AIDS-related complications, he had firmly cemented his reputation as one of the most original and talented musicians to come out of the disco arena.

According to Anthony Lamar Rucker, while Sylvester represented to mainstream America the black and gay cultural origins of disco music, his body of work included not only crucial contributions to the disco songbook, but also ballads that proved he was a versatile stylist who brought a realness and depth to all his material.

Inspired by the flamboyant musical icon Little Richard (Richard Penniman), Sylvester's own wild and outrageous personality influenced contemporaries such as Bette Midler and the Village People and paved the way for gender-bending performers such as Prince and RuPaul.

In tandem with his brazenly showy onstage personality, Sylvester's unique voice and skilled musical arrangements made a lasting impression, and his work remains a landmark of disco and dance music.

Sylvester was born Sylvester James into a middle-class family in Los Angeles, probably in 1946, though his birth year is sometimes given as 1944 or 1947. He was raised by his grandmother, the blues singer Julia Morgan, who taught him to sing and exposed him to a wide variety of music, including blues, jazz, and gospel.

At age eight, he entered the gospel circuit and began building a career as a gospel singer, but as he entered adolescence he found it increasingly difficult to hide his burgeoning homosexuality.

In 1967, Sylvester moved to San Francisco and joined the Cockettes, the androgynous experimental theater troupe, with whom he made his debut on New Year's Eve 1970. As a member of the Cockettes, Sylvester took the persona "Ruby Blue" and soon embarked on a solo career.

In 1973, Sylvester helped form the group the Hot Band, signing with Blue Thumb Records.

Over the next few years, the Hot Band underwent several lineup changes, including the important addition of two backup vocalists, Izora Rhodes and Martha Wash, who would later become world famous, first as Two Tons of Fun and later as the Weather Girls. Sylvester and the Hot Band, aided by an outrageous live show, secured their local reputation in San Francisco.

However, a chance discovery by former Motown producer Harvey Fuqua, who recognized Sylvester's stage presence and obvious talent, led to Sylvester's exposure to a much wider audience. In 1977, Sylvester once again went solo and, aided by Fuqua, signed with Fantasy Records.

Although his self-titled Fantasy debut album appeared in 1977 with little fanfare, a particular track, Sylvester's remake of Ashford and Simpson's "Over and Over," garnered critical and popular admiration.

The next year, Fantasy released *Step II*, an album marked by fierce performances showcasing what Colin Larkin calls Sylvester's unswerving urgency, as well as his soaring falsetto.

Supported by synthesizer overlays provided by remixer Patrick Cowley, two particular songs from *Step II*, "You Make Me Feel (Mighty Real)" and "Dance (Disco Heat)" became instant disco classics. The standout track "You Make Me Feel" was originally a gospel song but, after being given the "disco treatment," grew into a worldwide club hit and an eventual gay anthem. *Step II* garnered three *Billboard* Disco Forum Awards and, in 1979, coinciding with his all-disco release *Stars*, *Disco International Magazine* crowned Sylvester Best Male Disco Act.

By 1980, however, disco's influence had waned severely, and Fuqua urged Sylvester to tone down his outrageousness and branch out into other, ostensibly "straighter" musical styles.

After releasing three more albums that included torchy covers of "Ooh Baby Baby" and "Cry Me a River," Sylvester, citing creative differences, split from Harvey Fuqua and joined Patrick Cowley's fledgling record label, Megatone, in 1981.

Produced by Cowley, *All I Need*, Sylvester's Megatone debut, featured another high-energy dance classic, "Do You Wanna Funk?," which was released to thundering acclaim.

Cowley died in 1982, soon after the record appeared. He was one of the first celebrities to die of AIDS.

Although Sylvester subsequently released albums solidly produced by Ken Kessie and Morey Goldstein, and replete with hit singles such as "Take Me To Heaven," "Sex," and a classic cover of Freda Payne's "Band of Gold," the songs did not compare to those produced by Cowley.

By 1986, however, Sylvester's work had attracted major-label attention, and he soon found himself at Warner Brothers, recording *Mutual Attraction*. That same year he also realized an early dream by singing backup on Aretha Franklin's album *Who's Zoomin' Who?*, including the hit single "Freeway of Love."

Also in 1986, Sylvester was diagnosed with AIDS.

In the summer of 1987, he made his final public appearance, as part of the San Francisco Gay Pride parade.

Sylvester died from AIDS-related complications on December 16, 1988, and was eulogized by San Francisco writer Armistead Maupin as "one of the few truly gay celebrities to have never renounced their gayness along the ladder to success."

—*Nathan G. Tipton*

BIBLIOGRAPHY

Austen, Jake. "Sylvester." *Roctober* 19 (1997): www.roctober.com/roctober/greatness/sylvester.html

Huey, Steve. "Sylvester." www.allmusic.com/cg/amg.dll?p=amg&token=&sql=11:sex1z88ajyv6

Lamb, William. "Dance Superstar Sylvester." www.andwedanced.com/1980/sylves.htm

Larkin, Colin, comp. and ed. "Sylvester." *The Encyclopedia of Popular Music*. Third ed. New York: Muze, 1998. 7:5270–5271.

Rucker, Anthony Lamar, and B. Graff. "Sylvester." *Deep Groove Online Encyclopedia*. www.allthingsdeep.com/dge/Sylvester.htm

SEE ALSO

Popular Music; Disco and Dance Music; Music and AIDS; Little Richard (Richard Penniman); RuPaul (RuPaul Andre Charles); Village People

Szymanowski, Karol Maciej   (1882–1937)

REVERED AS THE FATHER OF POLISH CONTEMPORARY classical music, Karol Szymanowski unequivocally expresses homoeroticism in his music.

He was born at Timoshovska, Ukraine, on October 3, 1882. Although born in Russian territory, Szymanowski was of a noble Polish family.

The family estate was a center of musical activity, and, with his father as his teacher, Szymanowski's musical education began at an early age. A masterly pianist, he later studied privately in Warsaw, but was an autodidact in composition. His earliest work, influenced by Chopin and Scriabin, is lyrical, but dominated by sentimental melancholy.

In 1905, Szymanowski began to live abroad, as he continued his self-education. The rich, talented, handsome young aristocrat was an ornament in the stupendous social whirl of pre–World War I Berlin, Leipzig, and Vienna.

With his friend Stefan Spiess, he visited Sicily in 1911 and Algiers and Tunis in 1914. Szymanowski, not unlike other European gay artists such as Baron von Gloeden, Oscar Wilde, and André Gide, found the spectacle of unabashed boy love in the less-inhibited southern climate to be psychologically liberating and, thereby, an inspiration to his art.

Szymanowski celebrated his newly liberated sexuality in his music. After the Sicilian visit, the melancholy of his earlier work was vanquished by the joy that would be present throughout the rest of his creative life.

Homoeroticism is discernible in much of his music, especially in such works as *Love Songs of Hafiz* and Symphony no. 3 (*Song of the Night*), for tenor solo, mixed chorus, and orchestra, a setting of a poem by the thirteenth-century Persian poet Rumi. Krysinski and de la Motte-Sherman declare that Szymanowski's music is "unrivalled as a lyric song of a soul in love."

Szymanowski lived on his family's estate from 1914 until it was destroyed by the Bolsheviks in 1917. He then moved to Warsaw. He traveled in Europe and twice visited the United States.

Also a writer, between 1917 and 1919 Szymanowski devoted himself to composing his legendary novel "Efebos," of which only one chapter survives. Then, in 1919, he met his fantasy Ganymede in the person of a fifteen-year-old refugee from Moscow, Boris Kochno.

Kochno was a precocious boy from a noble Russian family and a budding poet. Szymanowski fell deeply in love and wrote poems to him. His passion was for a time reciprocated.

However, unknown to Szymanowski, Kochno also became the lover of the redoubtable Sergei Diaghilev. The pianist Artur Rubinstein, a friend of Szymanowski, describes in his memoirs a chance meeting of the trio in Paris—Szymanowski's pain, Kochno's chagrin, and Diaghilev's jealousy.

After the war, with the pianist Ignace Paderewski as Prime Minister of a free Poland, Polish folk music became a factor in Szymanowski's music. The composer spent much of his time in the Podhale region, where a large community of friends, musicians, and artists was devoted to him.

He dealt with his spirituality—the guilt-inducing Catholic attitude toward homosexuality during his youth now mitigated by a Dionysian concept of Christianity—in his *Stabat Mater* (1928).

He was appointed rector of the Academy of Music in Warsaw in 1927, but intrigues, fueled by homophobia, caused him to resign in 1932.

In failing health, in 1934 Karol Szymanowski declared that there was one thing in his life he did not regret: He had loved many. He had been loved, too.

He died on March 29, 1937, at Lausanne, Switzerland.

UNESCO declared 1982 the International Year of Karol Szymanowski.   *—Douglas Blair Turnbaugh*

Bibliography

Krysinski, Lech, and Colin de la Motte-Sherman. "A Heart in Flames—Karol Szymanowski." *Erato—Journal of the International Lesbian and Gay Cultural Network* No. 17 (Autumn 2000): 3–4.

Maciejewski, B. M. *Karol Szymanowski: His Life and Music.* London: Poets' and Painters' Press, 1967.

Scholes, Percy A. "Szymanowski, Karol." *The Oxford Companion to Music.* John Owen Ward, ed. London: Oxford University Press, 1970. 1003.

Szymanowski, Karol. *Das Gastmahl: Ein Kapital aus dem Roman "Ephebos."* Berlin: Bibliothek Rosa Winkel, 1993.

See also

Classical Music; Diaghilev, Sergei

Takarazuka (Japanese All-Female Revues)

DURING THE TWENTIETH CENTURY IN JAPAN, Takarazuka, all-female musical and theater companies in which women play all roles, have thrived; and actresses playing males have generated large female fan clubs.

The revues are elaborately costumed, flamboyant, and extravagant in execution. These commercially successful and mainstream theatrical enterprises generally present plays with safe, middle-of-the-road topics. During World War II, for example, the productions emphasized patriotic themes and the liberation of other Asians from European exploitation.

Despite the mainstream subjects of Takarazuka, the revues have nonetheless spawned fringe activities that are gender transgressive and that tellingly illustrate the construction and deconstruction of gender roles.

It is important not to put a Euro-American imprint on Takarazuka. This is a Japanese theater in a Japanese context. It does not map well onto Euro-American concepts of desire, gender, and sexuality.

Theater in Japan became monosexual in 1629, when the Tokugawa regime banned women (and later boys) from Kabuki. Men playing women (*onnagata*) in Kabuki are said to "embody" the ideal of femininity, while women playing men (*otokoyaku*) in Takarazuka only "represent" masculinity.

The oldest and most successful of the all-women groups is the Takarazuka Revue, founded in a hot-springs resort near Osaka in 1913 by Kobayashi Ichizo (1873–1957), a male industrialist, impresario, and politician. He called it "New Citizens' Theater" in contrast to the old and elitist Kabuki. He conceived Takarazuka as a mass theater for families.

The 3,000-seat theater near Osaka sells out regularly during the performing season year after year. The Tokyo troupe is planning a new and larger theater complex near the Tokyo Disneyland. Its most prominent rival, Tokyo's Shochiku Revue, opened in 1928 and ceased regular productions in 1990.

The performers for the three Takarazuka troupes have all been educated and trained in the two-year Takarazuka Music Academy. Entrance to the Academy is highly competitive, and well-off families train their daughters for years to enhance their chances for admission.

The students (and later the performers) are subject to tight discipline and regimes designed to maintain their respectability. Nonetheless, gossip about the performers is intense (and marketed in both official and unofficial venues), and scandals—including lesbian scandals—have occurred. Students are assigned their gender identity after they are accepted, on the basis of appearance (and, to a certain extent, on personal preference). The roles are based on contrasting gender stereotypes.

Thus, the women (*musumeyaku*) and the men (*otokoyaku*) are both examples of constructed gender. The *otokoyaku*'s hair is cut short. Following the Stanislavsky method of acting, which Takarazuka directors have used from the beginning, the actors not only create the internal lives of the characters but also physically embody them. The *musumeyaku* are used theatrically to define and enhance the masculinity of the *otokoyaku*.

Most Takarazuka fans are as respectable and mainstream as the performers—housewives, industrialists, politicians, and teenagers. But the intense fan response (from both women and men) indicates that more is going on than the official ideologies of theatrical gender acknowledge.

Women fans' passions for *otokoyaku* are multifaceted. Heterosexual women may feel an attraction for a "romantic" man that they do not experience in their own lives: a man who is "sensitive" because he is a woman. For some women, the *otokoyaku* expresses a freedom that is not available to them as housewives or secretaries.

There are undeniable lesbian and homoerotic components to some of the fan relationships. Everything is framed within the complex transgression of a woman being a man while still being a woman. Some fans are crushed when an *otokoyaku* later in life leaves Takarazuka and becomes an actress. *Otokoyaku* often maintain their "masculinity" offstage as well as on. The official reason for this is that they do it out of respect for their fans, but it seems apparent that, as with the fans' reactions, something more complex goes on here as well.

—*Laurie Toby Edison*

Bibliography

Garber, Marjorie. *Vested Interests: Cross Dressing and Cultural Anxiety.* New York: Harper Perennial, 1992.

Robertson, Jennifer. *Takarazuka: Sexual Politics and Popular Culture in Modern Japan.* Berkeley: University of California Press, 1998.

Sievers, Sharon. *Flowers in Salt: The Beginnings of Feminist Consciousness in Modern Japan.* Stanford, Calif.: Stanford University Press, 1983.

See Also

Kabuki; Drag Shows: Drag Kings and Male Impersonators

Taylor, Paul   (b. 1930)

ONE OF THE MOST INFLUENTIAL DANCERS AND CHOREOgraphers of the twentieth century, Paul Taylor has been an important presence in American dance since the 1950s.

When he wrote his autobiography at the age of fifty-seven, Taylor revealed his ambivalence about sex and gender in dance and life, remarking that to "pick partners of consistent gender would've run against an arbitrary streak" that he considers one of his strengths.

He was born Paul Belleville Taylor Jr. on July 29, 1930, in Allegheny County, Pennsylvania. After his parents divorced, he was shuttled between various friends and relatives as his mother worked full-time in a restaurant.

Taylor attended Syracuse University on an athletic scholarship as a swimmer and majored in sculpture and painting. He left school during his junior year to study with Martha Graham, Antony Tudor, and José Limón, among others.

He then danced with the Merce Cunningham Dance Company (1953–1954), Pearl Lang (1955), and the Martha Graham Dance Company (1955–1962).

Taylor established his own company in 1964. After appearing at the Festival of Two Worlds in Spoleto, Italy, the company began to tour all over the world. Several of his company's tours have been sponsored by the U.S. State Department.

At six feet three inches, Taylor is a large man for a dancer, but he danced with a startlingly fluid movement. His lyrical approach gave barefoot modern dance a neoclassic style with a virtuosic edge.

When Taylor retired from dancing in 1974 at the age of forty-four, many felt that this very good choreographer was on his way to becoming a great one.

Many of his dances, especially *Aureole* (1962), *Esplanade* (1975), *Airs* (1978), and *Arden Court* (1981), have been performed by major ballet and modern companies around the world. No other modern dance choreographer is so popular with ballet companies and their audiences: Over fifty ballet troupes have performed his pieces.

Taylor's fertile imagination has created over 100 dances. Perhaps most impressive is the expressive range of his work, which extends from the despairing *Last Look* (1985) to the critical social commentary of *Cloven Kingdom* (1976) and *Big Bertha* (1971) to the exuberant comedy of *Ab Ovo Usque Ad Mala* (1986).

While Taylor has collaborated with such established visual artists as Robert Rauschenberg, Gene Moore, John Rawlings, and Alex Katz, another designer of his dances, identified as "George Tacet," is Taylor himself. Since the 1960s, Jennifer Tipton has lit almost all of Taylor's dances.

From its beginning, the Paul Taylor Dance Company was distinguished by the look of its male dancers. Typically, they are larger than men in other companies. Their size gives Taylor's choreography a muscular weight.

With rare exceptions, Taylor has treated his company as a true ensemble, equally distributing solo roles among his dancers.

Several former members of the Paul Taylor Dance Company have gone on to establish their own companies, which is another indication of Taylor's influence on the shape of twentieth-century modern dance. Among

Paul Taylor, photographed by Carl Van Vechten in 1960.

them are Laura Dean, Pina Bausch, Daniel Ezralow, David Parsons, Twyla Tharp, and Dan Wagoner.

The dancer and budding choreographer Christopher Gillis (1951–1993) had been designated Taylor's heir apparent. However, he died from AIDS-related complications, and the company's future leadership is now uncertain.

In 1987, the company's concerts began to include work by choreographers other than Taylor; and in 1992 Taylor established a junior company, Taylor 2.

In his chatty autobiography, *Private Domain* (1987), Taylor mentions sexual encounters with both men and women, yet concludes, "As far as romance goes, I can forget it." He seems to find his responsibility for his "family" of dancers a satisfying substitute.

Same-sex partnering appears in works such as *Esplanade* (1975), *Kith and Kin* (1987), *Company B* (1991), and *Piazzolla Caldera* (1997). Still, these works may not indicate much about Taylor's private life. As he has warned many interviewers during his career, "I'm not trying to do autobiographical dances, that's not my thing."

Among Taylor's honors are a Guggenheim Fellowship (1961), an Emmy Award (*Speaking in Tongues,* 1991), a Kennedy Center Award (1992), and a National Medal of Arts (1993).
                                                      —*Bud Coleman*

BIBLIOGRAPHY

Bremser, Martha. *Fifty Contemporary Choreographers.* New York: Routledge, 1999.

Diamond, Matthew, dir. *Dancemaker.* Videocassette. New Video, 1998.

Mazo, Joseph H. *Prime Movers: The Makers of Modern Dance in America.* Highstown, N.J.: Princeton Book Company, 2000.

Taylor, Paul. *Private Domain.* New York: Alfred A. Knopf, 1987.

———, and Matthew Diamond. "Training Cameras on Every Step a Troupe Takes." *New York Times,* February 28, 1999.

SEE ALSO

Ballet; Dance; Cunningham, Merce

Tchaikovsky, Pyotr Ilich   *(1840–1893)*

PYOTR ILICH TCHAIKOVSKY WAS THE LEADING COMposer of late-nineteenth-century Russia, beloved for his ballet scores, symphonic poems, concerti, symphonies, operas, songs, piano music, and chamber works. He became one of the most famous composers in history, inspiring a cult of gay admirers who detected in his work themes of forbidden love.

Until recently, knowledge of Tchaikovsky's life as a homosexual was far less accessible than his music. Although some of his letters and diaries survive, many of his personal papers were suppressed, destroyed, or altered, especially during the Soviet period.

Today, most musicologists acknowledge the composer's homosexuality, but opinion concerning its importance and its relationship to his musical life varies widely.

Early Life

Tchaikovsky was born on May 7, 1840, to Ilya Petrovich Tchaikovsky and his second wife, Aleksandra, in Votinsk, in the Ural Mountains. Sensitive and deeply devoted to his mother and family, Tchaikovsky was no musical prodigy as a child, despite his family's love of music and his own obvious talent. He was a high-strung but charming and attractive child.

A career in civil service was planned for him, so in 1850 Tchaikovsky entered the Imperial School of Jurisprudence in St. Petersburg, where he received both his secondary and higher education. Departing home for school was very difficult for him because of his extreme attachment to his mother. Her death of cholera in 1854 affected him deeply.

At school Tchaikovsky formed several close relationships with other male students, some of which may have been sexual or at least romantic. Numerous memoirs depict him as an angelic beauty surrounded by ardent admirers.

Tchaikovsky left the School of Jurisprudence in 1859. He accepted a position with the Department of Justice in St. Petersburg, but his civil service career ended abruptly in 1862 when he was passed over for a promotion.

Musical Education and Early Compositions

In September of 1862, Tchaikovsky matriculated at the new St. Petersburg Conservatory, where he matured as a composer astonishingly quickly. Upon completing his course of study in 1866, he began teaching at the new Moscow Conservatory, directed by Nikolay Rubinstein.

Tchaikovsky had the first of several nervous breakdowns in July 1866, brought on by the strain of teaching while working on his first critical success, the Symphony no. 1, in G Minor ("*Winter Dreams*"). In his earliest major composition, Tchaikovsky's originality and inventiveness are already apparent.

Scholars disagree as to what to make of the young composer's sexuality during this early period. He certainly took seriously the negative social implications of being a known homosexual and he may have worried about the rumors of his homosexuality that flourished in the musical circles of St. Petersburg and Moscow, but such concerns did not stop him from moving in homosexual circles.

It has been suggested that in 1867 Tchaikovsky began a relationship with his private pupil Vladimir Shilovsky (who would later marry, in 1877), a rich and temperamental young man, but he was also briefly involved with the Belgian soprano Désirée Artôt. The relationship with Artôt ended abruptly, perhaps terminated by the soprano's mother, who may have heard rumors of the composer's unorthodox sexual practices.

In 1871, Tchaikovsky took on a twelve-year-old servant, Aleksey Sofronov, who became his traveling companion and eventually his lover. Sofronov, affectionately called "Aloysha," remained Tchaikovsky's servant, even after his own marriage, until his master's death.

Throughout this early and productive period of his career, Tchaikovsky lived in Moscow and produced many works: two more symphonies, three string quartets; various tone poems such as *Romeo and Juliet*, *The Tempest* (both 1873), and *Francesca da Rimini* (1876); piano music, songs, and early operas; the incidental music for *The Snow Maiden* (1873) and the ballet *Swan Lake* (1875–1876).

Two Women

At this point, two women figure prominently in Tchaikovsky's adult life: his patron, Nadezhda von Meck, and his wife, Antonina Mulykova.

He received an admiring letter from the rich widow von Meck in 1877, which began a deep personal relationship conducted entirely by correspondence. In fact, the two

agreed never to meet. Von Meck proved an invaluable ally to him in the years ahead.

Also in 1877, Tchaikovsky entered into a disastrous marriage with Mulykova, a conservatory student who also wrote him admiring letters. He apparently hoped that his marriage would "cure" his homosexuality or at least dispel the rumors of his homosexuality. No doubt, the fact that Mulykova was wealthy also contributed to his decision to marry, for he was unhappy having to support himself by teaching.

The marriage was not successful. Tchaikovsky found his pretty bride utterly unattractive and he was unable to consummate the union. Wracked with guilt over his deception of his wife, he began drinking heavily and may have attempted suicide. He suffered another nervous breakdown.

Two months after the wedding, while the composer recuperated in Switzerland, a separation was announced. Mulykova never divorced Tchaikovsky, and she demanded money from him thereafter. In 1896, after Tchaikovsky's death, having borne three illegitimate children, she was confined to an insane asylum.

From the trauma of 1877 came the great Fourth Symphony, as well as the opera *Eugene Onegin*, whose plot—a worldly young man spurning a girl who declares her love in a letter—has parallels in his own life. Several scholars have argued that the anguish expressed in the autobiographical Fourth Symphony reflects the composer's despair at his homosexuality. It may additionally (or alternatively) express his despair at the complications of his ill-advised marriage.

The Middle Period

In 1878, with the financial patronage of von Meck, Tchaikovsky left teaching to devote more time to composition. The works that followed include his major sacred works, the *1812 Overture* and the *Serenade for Strings* (1880), the *Manfred* symphony (1885), and various orchestral suites. His final operas include *The Maid of Orleans* (1878–1879), whose story of Joan of Arc had fascinated him since childhood, and *Mazeppa* (1881–1883).

Accolades came late to Tchaikovsky. He received recognition in 1881 from the new Czar, Alexander II, who ascended the throne that year. In 1888, his successor, Alexander III, for whom Tchaikovsky wrote the *Coronation March*, awarded the composer a generous lifetime pension.

Freed from teaching, Tchaikovsky traveled extensively. He undertook a series of European tours in the late 1880s and an even more successful American tour in 1891, where he conducted his own work at the opening of New York's Carnegie Hall.

In the 1890s, Tchaikovsky's works began being performed regularly at home and abroad. Indeed, he became a cult figure, especially among homosexuals, who discerned in his music a tragic yearning that they found particularly resonant.

The Final Works

Tchaikovsky's final works were composed abroad, among them orchestral suites, the magnificent Fifth Symphony (1888), the ballet *The Sleeping Beauty* and the opera *The Queen of Spades* (1890), the ballet *The Nutcracker* (1891), and his last symphony, the Sixth (*Pathétique*, 1893), lovingly dedicated to his gay nephew, Vladimir ("Bob") Davidov, with whom he was extremely close.

The *Pathétique* almost immediately became the subject of intense speculation, especially among homosexuals, who felt that this mysterious work depicts a homosexual's search for love. It has been suggested that the symphony was inspired by Tchaikovsky's passion for Davidov.

His Final Years and Death

After years of travel, Tchaikovsky returned to Russia. He first rented various houses around Kiln, near Moscow. His final year was spent in St. Petersburg, where he died in 1893, a victim of a cholera epidemic that swept the city. He was surrounded by Davidov, his servant "Aloysha," his bother Modest, and a retinue of young men.

Although Tchaikovsky's death of cholera is well documented, some biographers—largely on the basis of scurrilous rumors—have suggested that the composer was forced to commit suicide rather than be exposed in a sex scandal involving a member of the Imperial family. The biographical works by Alexander Poznansky have attempted to rescue Tchaikovsky from such sensational scandal, but the circumstances of the composer's death continue to be debated.

Sexuality and Music

The importance of Tchaikovsky's sexuality to his music is also a matter of considerable debate. In general, heterosexual musicologists tend to downplay or deny its importance, while queer historians and biographers highlight it in two ways. They argue that events in the composer's life are reflected in his music and that specific musical elements found in his scores are typically "gay."

Because music is perhaps the most purely objective of the arts, the level to which a composer casts his own life into his compositions is very much a matter of subjective opinion. However, it is certainly true that many gay men and lesbians have found in Tchaikovsky's music emotions that seemed to speak directly to their own experience. Hence, he has been an important presence in gay and lesbian history and culture.

While discussion continues as to the significance of Tchaikovsky's homosexuality to his music, there is now general agreement that he was in fact homosexual. This

Pyotr Ilich Tchaikovsky photographed in the 1880s.

itself represents an enormous change in musicological scholarship, which has tended to be cautious and conservative in matters of sexuality, especially when it comes to composers as important as Handel and Tchaikovsky, whose achievements are central to classical music and to the Western cultural tradition.

—Robert Kellerman

BIBLIOGRAPHY

Henry, Seán. "Peter Ilich Tchaikovsky." *Gay and Lesbian Biography.* Michael J. Tyrkus, ed. Detroit: St. James Press, 1997. 427–429.

Holden, Anthony. *Tchaikovsky: A Biography.* New York: Random House, 1995.

Jackson, Timothy L. "Aspects of Sexuality and Structure in the Later Symphonies of Tchaikovsky." *Music Analysis* 14.1 (March 1995): 3–25.

McClary, Susan. *Feminine Endings: Music, Gender, and Sexuality.* Minneapolis: University of Minnesota Press, 1991.

Karlinsky, Simon. "Tchaikovsky, Pyotr Ilich." *Gay Histories and Cultures.* George Haggerty, ed. New York: Garland, 2000. 865–866.

Poznansky, Alexandre. *Tchaikovsky's Last Days: A Documentary Study.* Oxford: Clarendon Press, 1996.

———. *Tchaikovsky: The Quest for the Inner Man.* New York: Schirmer, 1991.

Wiley, John Roland. "Tchaikovsky, Pyotr Ilyich." *The New Grove Dictionary of Music and Musicians.* Stanley Sadie, ed. London: Macmillan, 2001. 25:144–183.

See Also

Classical Music; Ballet; Opera; Cliburn, Van; Handel, George Frideric;

Thomson, Virgil   *(1896–1989)*

THE CRITIC AND COMPOSER VIRGIL THOMSON WAS A pioneer in creating a specifically American form of classical music that is at once "serious" yet whimsically sardonic. He is best known as Gertrude Stein's collaborator in two operas, *Four Saints in Three Acts* (1934) and *The Mother of Us All* (1947).

The hymn melodies that shape the score of *Four Saints* are an echo of Thomson's earliest musical career, that of an organist in a Baptist church in Kansas City, Missouri, where he was born on November 25, 1896, into a tolerant, middle-class family. His mother especially encouraged his musical and artistic talents, which were obvious very early.

Thomson joined the U.S. Army in 1917 and served during World War I. After the war, he studied music at Harvard University, where he discovered *Tender Buttons* (1914), Stein's playful and elaborately encoded poetic work of lesbian eroticism.

He subsequently studied composition in Paris under Nadia Boulanger, the mentor of at least two generations of modern composers. In 1925, he finally met Stein, whose works he had begun to set to music. In Paris, he also met Jean Cocteau, Igor Stravinsky, and Erik Satie. Satie in particular influenced his music greatly.

There he also cemented a relationship with the painter Maurice Grosser, who was to become his life partner and frequent collaborator; Grosser directed *Four Saints in Three Acts* and devised the scenario for *The Mother of Us All.*

On February 8, 1934, Hartford, Connecticut saw the premiere of what is surely one of the strangest—indeed, queerest—works ever composed for the operatic stage, *Four Saints in Three Acts*, the product of the collaboration between the closeted gay composer and the extroverted lesbian poet.

With a minimal plot (focusing on the Spanish Catholic saints Teresa of Avila and Ignatius Loyola) and a score based, in great part, on Protestant hymns, the opera debuted with an all-black cast under the auspices of the sardonically named Friends and Enemies of Modern Music, having, as might be expected, few others willing to back the production.

The work (which, in spite of its title, features a cast of numerous real and imaginary saints and four acts with a prologue) has never quite become part of the standard operatic repertory; it has nevertheless achieved a certain quirky longevity and stands today as its composer's best-known work.

More than a decade later, after the end of World War II and only months before Stein's death in July 1946, the pair collaborated on a second opera, *The Mother of Us All* (1947). While a more accessible work than *Four Saints*, Stein's apotheosis of suffragist leader Susan B. Anthony combines with Thomson's pastiche of nineteenth-century American popular and sentimental musical styles to create yet another unconventional piece of musical theater.

Thomson was not, however, merely the man who set Gertrude Stein to music. From 1940 to 1954, he was the music critic of the *New York Herald Tribune*. In that

Virgil Thomson, photographed by Carl Van Vechten in 1947.

role, he was noted for his stylish, opinionated, and at times acerbic essays on twentieth-century music, later collected in three volumes, *The Musical Scene* (1945), *The Art of Judging Music* (1948), and *Music, Right and Left* (1951).

Thomson continued to write and compose prolifically for the rest of his long life. He wrote more than 150 compositions in all, including scores for a number of plays and films. His score for the film *Louisiana Story* won the 1948 Pulitzer Prize for music.

Thomson's music is characterized by wit and playfulness and is rooted in American speech rhythms and hymnbook harmony. It partakes of Satie's ideals of clarity, simplicity, irony, and humor. Thomson's music influenced a number of his contemporaries, including most notably Aaron Copland, who always acknowledged his debt to Thomson.

Despite his association with noted lesbian figures, Thomson remained cautiously closeted for most of his life—at times problematically so. For many years—especially during the McCarthy era—he lived in fear that he might be outed and that such a revelation would have a detrimental effect on his career. It has been suggested—perhaps unfairly—that his friendships with women were motivated by a need to mask his homosexuality.

But in many ways Thomson lived an openly gay life. He and Grosser lived at the Hotel Chelsea, where he presided over a largely gay salon that attracted many of the leading figures in music and art and theater, including Leonard Bernstein and Tennessee Williams. He also encouraged many younger composers and literary figures such as Ned Rorem, Lou Harrison, John Cage, Frank O'Hara, and Paul Bowles.

Thomson played a crucial role in shaping twentieth-century American music, not only through his compositions and criticism but also through his incorporation of gay and lesbian icons as points of reference in his works.

A final opera, *Lord Byron* (1972), was commissioned by the Metropolitan Opera but never staged by the company, apparently because of its then taboo subject matter, the poet's incestuous relationship with his sister.

Thomson died on September 30, 1989, only a year after the death of Grosser.

—*Patricia Juliana Smith*

BIBLIOGRAPHY

Blackmer, Corinne E. "The Ecstasies of Saint Teresa: The Saint as Queer Diva from Crashaw to Four Saints in Three Acts." *En Travesti: Women, Gender Subversion, Opera.* Corinne E. Blackmer and Patricia Juliana Smith, eds. New York: Columbia University Press, 1995. 306–347.

Hoover, Kathleen O'Donnell, and John Cage. *Virgil Thomson: His Life and Work.* New York: T. Yoseloff, 1959.

Thomson, Virgil. *Music with Words: A Composer's View.* New Haven, Conn.: Yale University Press, 1989.

———. *Virgil Thomson.* New York: E. P. Dutton, 1985.

Tommasini, Anthony. *Virgil Thomson: Composer on the Aisle.* New York: Norton, 1998.

Watson, Steven. *Prepare for Saints: Gertrude Stein, Virgil Thomson, and the Mainstreaming of American Modernism.* Berkeley: University of California Press, 1995.

Wittke, Paul. "Virgil Thomson: Vignettes of His Life and Times." http://www.schirmer.com/composers/thomson_bio.html

SEE ALSO

Classical Music; Opera; Ballet; Ashton, Sir Frederick; Barber, Samuel; Bernstein, Leonard; Boulanger, Nadia; Cage, John; Copland, Aaron; Harrison, Lou; Rorem, Ned

Tilson Thomas, Michael (b. 1944)

THE CONDUCTOR, PIANIST, AND COMPOSER MICHAEL Tilson Thomas has become in a relatively short time one of the most prominent American conductors of his generation. Perhaps most significantly, he is the first gay conductor to achieve such prominence without masking or hiding his sexuality.

Tilson Thomas does not discuss his homosexuality or his personal life with the public, but his dedication to creating and presenting music that explores the gay experience confirms his importance as a gay conductor.

Born on December 21, 1944, Tilson Thomas grew up in an artistic family—his grandparents, the Tomashevskys, were well known in Yiddish theater. He attended the University of Southern California, where he studied composition, conducting, piano, and harpsichord.

After winning the Koussevitzky Prize at the Berkshire Music Center at Tanglewood in the summer of 1968, Tilson Thomas became the youngest assistant conductor in the history of the Boston Symphony Orchestra. In 1969, he garnered great critical praise by conducting the second half of the symphony's New York concert after its musical director, William Steinberg, became ill.

From that point on, Tilson Thomas steadily rose in the world of classical music. He served as conductor of a number of prestigious orchestras, including as associate and principal guest conductor of the Boston Symphony Orchestra (1970–1974), music director of the Buffalo Symphony Orchestra (1971–1979), and principal guest conductor of the Los Angeles Philharmonic (1981–1985). In 1988, he became principal conductor of the London Symphony Orchestra.

In 1995, Tilson Thomas stepped down from his position at the L.S.O. to become the music director of the San Francisco Symphony Orchestra. Not only has he impressed audiences with his musical vision, talented conducting, and a prolific output of recordings, but he has also used his position to commission works by gay composers that use the medium of classical music to represent gay life and gay history.

Tilson Thomas has acknowledged that he is something of a maverick in the music world. Known for his dedication to innovative and inventive composers, he has persistently performed their works in the hope that he might expose his audiences to the wonderful diversity of classical music in the United States.

To this end, he organized the American Mavericks music festival in San Francisco in June 2000. The festival highlighted the works of such composers as Lou Harrison, Lukas Foss, Earle Brown, Steve Reich, David Del Tredici, and Meredith Monk.

Tilson Thomas has similarly pushed audiences to rethink the relationship between classical music and homosexuality by celebrating openly gay composers such as Harrison and by commissioning works from Del Tredici and others that explicitly explore the experiences of gay men and lesbians.

Although gay men and lesbians have long been present in the world of classical music, both as performers and as audience members, they have often remained invisible. Tilson Thomas has taken bold steps to change this.

In May 2001, Tilson Thomas conducted the premiere of Del Tredici's *Gay Life*, a series of pieces based on poems by Allen Ginsberg, Thom Gunn, and Paul Monette. The work, commissioned by Tilson Thomas, both explores the experiences of gay men in America and delves into the challenges that gay men have faced in their struggle to survive the AIDS epidemic.

In addition, two of Tilson Thomas's own compositions have added to the small but growing classical music repertoire focused on gay subjects. *Three Poems by Walt Whitman*, for baritone and orchestra, and *We Two Boys Together Clinging*, for baritone and piano, use Whitman's poetry to explore intimacy between men.

As a prominent American conductor, Tilson Thomas has displayed his mastery of tradition and his sense of musical adventure. His decision to live openly and his support of other gay musicians have enhanced his stature, both professionally and morally.

—*Geoffrey W. Bateman*

BIBLIOGRAPHY

Barber, Charles. "Michael Tilson Thomas." *The New Grove Dictionary of Music and Musicians of the Twentieth Century*. Second ed. Stanley Sadie, ed. New York: Macmillan, 2001. 25:413.

Fries, Kenny. "It's a Classically 'Gay Life.'" *Advocate* (May 2001). www.advocate.com/html/stories/838/838_del_tredici.asp

Key, Susan, and Larry Rothe, eds. *American Mavericks*. Berkeley: University of California Press, 2001.

Schwarz, K. Robert. "Cracking the Classical Closet." *Advocate*, May 11, 1999, 48.

Tilson Thomas, Michael. *Viva Voce: Conversations with Edward Seckerson*. Boston: Faber and Faber, 1994.

Walsh, Michael. "Hitting the High Notes." *Time*, April 1, 1996, 74.

SEE ALSO

Classical Music; Conductors; Del Tredici, David; Harrison, Lou

Tippett, Sir Michael   (1905–1998)

OVER THE COURSE OF A LIFETIME THAT VIRTUALLY spanned the twentieth century, Sir Michael Tippett, a most unlikely composer and musician, progressed from being the great enigma of British classical music to being one of its most respected and influential figures.

His visionary, idealistic humanism informed his compositions, which, while firmly grounded in the traditions of European music, embraced contemporary and popular forms as well.

Tippett was, in the words of his partner Meirion Bowen, an "unabashed homosexual," and he defied the social taboos of his time by incorporating homoerotic themes in his operas.

Michael Kemp Tippett was born in London on January 2, 1905, and raised in Surrey, where he lived most of his life. Unlike many composers, he was not a child prodigy, and, aside from piano lessons, he had little early involvement with music. In his teens, however, he attended concert performances of Beethoven's symphonies, and as a result of this experience he realized his desire to become a composer.

Consequently, he persuaded his parents to support his studies at the Royal College of Music, from which he graduated in 1928. For several years, he taught French in a preparatory school and conducted local musical ensembles. In 1940, he was appointed Director of Music at Morley College in London, a post he retained until 1951.

Although Tippett's early compositions had their first public performance in 1930, the work that brought him widespread recognition came a decade later. The oratorio *A Child of Our Time* (1939–1941) was inspired by Tippett's concern for the oppressed and his outrage over Nazi persecution of the Jews.

The work is dedicated to Hershel Grynzpan, a gay Jewish youth who, in 1937, assassinated a Nazi official in a Paris club frequented by homosexuals, an act that the Nazis used as a pretext for the acts of anti-Semitic terror known as Kristallnacht.

Tippett wrote the libretto for this oratorio, as he would subsequently do for all his vocal compositions. It demonstrates not only his concern for the outcast, but also his interest in Jungian archetypes, two elements that would recur in many of his later works.

Tippett composed in all genres of classical music, including symphonies, string quartets, piano sonatas, choral works, concerti, and songs, as well as a variety of unique pieces that would seem to defy categorization. Aside from *A Child of Our Time*, he is perhaps best known, however, for his operas.

Tippett's first opera, *The Midsummer Marriage* (1955), was first staged at Covent Garden with a young Joan Sutherland, then beginning her stellar career, in the lead role. Although the opera has endured the test of time, the plot, which incorporates Jungian archetypes and shows the influence of both T. S. Eliot's poetry and Mozart's *The Magic Flute*, at first bewildered audiences used to more traditional opera fare.

King Priam (1962) retells the ancient story of the siege of Troy and, in one scene, presents the homoerotic attachment between Achilles and Patroclus.

More daring is *The Knot Garden* (1970), an examination of the dynamics of contemporary relationships. Among the main characters are Mel and Dov, an unambiguously gay, mixed-race couple.

The Icebreak (1977), which includes elements of psychedelic rock and African music in its contextual synthesis, is likewise controversial, addressing issues of racial prejudice and the plight of refugees.

Tippett's final major work was the opera *New Year* (1989), written by the octogenarian composer as a sort of postscript to his long career. In keeping with Tippett's ongoing interest in contemporary currents in music and culture, this late piece is perhaps the first opera to include a "rap" vocal.

Tippett was a lifelong humanist and pacifist who stood by his beliefs, even when they were out of step with the rest of society. In 1943, he was incarcerated for three months in London's notorious Wormwood Scrubs prison for refusing to do the civil defense duty expected of conscientious objectors; he responded to his conditions by organizing and conducting the prison orchestra.

Tippett was, moreover, openly gay at a time when male homosexual acts were criminal in Britain. Yet despite his "outlaw" history, he was knighted by Queen Elizabeth II in 1966, made a Companion of Honour in 1979, and granted the Order of Merit in 1983.

Tippett remained active through his eighties, and only declined at the very end of his life. His autobiography, *Those Twentieth Century Blues*, was published in 1991. In November, 1997, while attending a retrospective celebration of his music in Stockholm, he was stricken with pneumonia. He died of the illness in his London home on January 8, 1998, days after his ninety-third birthday.

—*Patricia Juliana Smith*

BIBLIOGRAPHY

Bowen, Meirion. *Michael Tippett*. Second ed. London: Robson Books, 1997.

Clarke, David, ed. *Tippett Studies*. Cambridge: Cambridge University Press, 1999.

Gloag, Kenneth. *Tippett, A Child of Our Time*. Cambridge: Cambridge University Press, 1999.

Hurd, Michael. *Tippett*. Sevenoaks, Kent, U.K.: Novello, 1978.

Jones, Richard Elfyn. *The Early Operas of Michael Tippett: A Study of The Midsummer Marriage, King Priam, and The Knot Garden*. Lewiston, Me.: Mellen, 1996.

Kemp, Ian. *Tippett: The Composer and His Music*. Oxford: Oxford University Press, 1987.

Matthews, David. *Michael Tippett: An Introductory Study*. London: Faber, 1980.

Tippett, Michael. *Abundance of Creation: An Artist's Vision of Creative Peace*. London: Housmans, 1975.

———. *Those Twentieth Century Blues: An Autobiography*. London: Hutchinson, 1991.

White, Eric Walter. *Tippett and His Operas*. London: Barrie and Jenkins, 1979.

Whittall, Arnold. *The Music of Britten and Tippett: Studies in Themes and Techniques*. Second ed. Cambridge: Cambridge University Press, 1990.

SEE ALSO

Classical Music; Opera

Tune, Tommy (b. 1939)

AT SIX FEET SIX AND A HALF INCHES, TOMMY TUNE cast a long shadow over Broadway for many years, accumulating nine Tony Awards in eighteen years. Tune is the first person to have won Tonys in four different categories: Best Director, Best Choreographer, Best Featured Actor in a Musical, and Best Actor in a Musical. (The only other person to accomplish this feat is Harvey Fierstein.)

Since making his Broadway debut dancing in the chorus of *Baker Street* in 1964, Tune was almost synonymous with the Great White Way until 1999, when he departed to star in the Las Vegas spectacle *EFX*.

An only son, Thomas J. Tune was born in Wichita Falls, Texas, on February 28, 1939. He started his dance training as a five-year-old. He ultimately received a B.F.A. in drama from the University of Texas at Austin and an M.F.A. in directing from the University of Houston.

After ten years of being a very tall chorus boy in many Broadway productions, Tune played David, a gay choreographer, in *Seesaw* (1973), stopping the show (and winning his first Tony) with "It's Not Where You Start,

It's Where You Finish." Although *Seesaw* was directed and choreographed by Michael Bennett, Tune collaborated with Bennett on his own choreography.

Onstage, Tune was usually cast to showcase his fresh-faced sweetness and infectious enthusiasm.

While appearing in the chorus of *How Now, Dow Jones,* Tune was spotted and whisked off to Hollywood. A seven-year contract with Twentieth Century Fox resulted in Tune's appearance in one of the last of the film musicals, Gene Kelly's *Hello, Dolly!,* starring Barbra Streisand. Tune also served as the assistant choreographer on the television variety program *The Dean Martin Show* during its last years on the air.

Tune received Obie Awards for his direction of the off-Broadway hits *The Club* (1976) and *Cloud Nine* (1981). As director or choreographer (and frequently performer as well), his Broadway successes include *The Best Little Whorehouse in Texas* (1977), *A Day in Hollywood / A Night in the Ukraine* (1980), *Nine* (1982), *My One and Only* (1983), *Grand Hotel* (1989), and *The Will Rogers Follies* (1991).

Tune's star seemed to tarnish with the quick closings or bad reviews that met *Stepping Out* (director, 1987), *The Best Little Whorehouse Goes Public* (codirector and choreographer, 1994), and *Grease* (creative consultant, 1994). After breaking his right foot in 1995 during the final out-of-town tryout performance of *Busker's Alley* in Florida, he has not returned to Broadway.

Tune's trademark style is infused with a respect for and knowledge of old-fashioned musical theater, but staged with state-of-the-art savvy. While other choreographers such as Jerome Robbins and Agnes de Mille individuated members of the ensemble, Tune celebrates the chorus line.

A choreographic sense of humor also distinguishes Tune from his peers; his dancing dolls in *The Best Little Whorehouse in Texas* and his staging of the Hollywood Production Code as a tap dance in *A Day in Hollywood / A Night in the Ukraine* remain comedic classics.

Normally reticent about his personal life, Tune shocked many by discussing his bisexuality in his autobiography, *Footnotes* (1998). "What I arrived at in my 59th year is that I just want to walk in truth and live by my own time." The book contains moving passages about his lover of almost ten years, stage manager David Wolfe, who died of AIDS in 1994, and about actor and costumer Michael Stuart (1943–1997), with whom Tune lived for seven years.

AIDS also robbed Tune of his longtime agent and close friend, Eric Shepard. Indeed, Tune notes in his autobiography, "Since AIDS claimed his [Shepard's] life I've won nothing. My career has floundered. The man behind the man. Gone."

In late 2002, Tune returned to New York for an off-Broadway "all-singing-all-dancing tuneful big band show" entitled *Tommy Tune: White Tie and Tails.* In this revue, Tune, backed by the Manhattan Rhythm Kings, performed song and dance numbers set to the music of such composers as Peter Allen, George Gershwin, and Cole Porter.

—*Bud Coleman*

BIBLIOGRAPHY

Tune, Tommy. *Footnotes.* New York: Simon and Schuster, 1998.

SEE ALSO

Musical Theater and Film; Dance; Allen, Peter; Bennett, Michael; Porter, Cole; Robbins, Jerome; Wright, Robert, and George "Chet" Forrest

Van Dantzig, Rudi (b. 1933)

AS ARTISTIC DIRECTOR AND RESIDENT CHOREOGRAPHER of the Dutch National Ballet from 1971 to 1991, Rudi van Dantzig brought his company to international attention with a repertory that embraced works of both classical elegance and modern energy. He has created a body of choreographic work that explores liberation, hope, and the place of homosexuality in our time, as well as such controversial issues as abuses of power.

Born in Amsterdam on August 4, 1933, van Dantzig was six years old when the German Army invaded the Netherlands. During the following five years, van Dantzig grew up under the Nazi Occupation, and for a particularly formative period was separated from his parents when he was sent to stay in the countryside, which presumably was safer from combat and bombing.

In his prize-winning autobiographical novel *For a Lost Soldier* (1991), van Dantzig recounts the harsh experiences of wartime from a child's perspective, including the story of a post-Liberation love affair between twelve-year-old Jeroen (the character standing in for van Dantzig) and a young (though significantly older than twelve) Canadian soldier who arrives with the Allied troops in 1945.

Running through the novel are themes of the loss of youthful innocence and the complexity of relationships in an atmosphere of aggression and fear. Not surprisingly, the same themes recur time and again in van Dantzig's choreography. (*For a Lost Soldier* was adapted in 1994 as a film of the same title, written and directed by Roeland Kerbosch.)

Classic adolescent problems, complicated by his wartime memories and premature introduction to adult sexuality, emerged after van Dantzig's return to Amsterdam. Uninterested in most of his schoolwork, he was a troubled student and dreamed of becoming a painter.

Then, one day, when he was fifteen, he wandered into a movie theater to be swept away by the film on view. The movie was not about a painter he might wish to become, however; the movie was *The Red Shoes*, Michael Powell's 1948 dance-filled masterpiece about a ballerina torn between a diabolical impresario and a struggling composer.

From that moment on, van Dantzig's sole obsession was to become a dancer. He studied first with Anna Sybranda before finding his way to the studio of Sonia Gaskell, a former Ballets Russes dancer who ran a small company and school in Amsterdam at that time.

By his own admission, van Dantzig was at a severe disadvantage since he had had no dance experience and was starting late. He was fortunate, however, as Gaskell overlooked his deficiencies and focused on his zeal and intelligence. Once he slipped into Gaskell's realm, van Dantzig worked hard, became a company member, and by 1955 had choreographed his first dance, *Nachteiland* (to a score by Claude Debussy).

Because Gaskell and her dance companies were dedicated to a classical and Diaghilev-style ballet repertory, he was not prepared for the impact that modern dance would have on him. Seeing his first Martha Graham performance hit van Dantzig like a bombshell. With a larger choreographic world opened to him by Graham's expressiveness and power, he traveled to New York to study her technique.

Upon returning to Amsterdam, the intense and mercurial van Dantzig became embroiled in disagreements with Gaskell and eventually decided to join ranks with Hans van Manen and Benjamin Harkarvy in 1959 to found The Netherlands Dance Theatre.

After a year with the new group, however, van Dantzig found himself dissatisfied and drifted back to Gaskell (whose company combined in 1961 with the Amsterdam Ballet to become the Dutch National Ballet). Upon Gaskell's retirement in 1968, he and another dancer, Robert Kaesen, took over the reins of the Dutch National Ballet; van Dantzig assumed the sole directorship in 1971.

Being in charge of the company suited van Dantzig. He possessed the rare combination of administrative ability and an unwavering drive to create powerful dances, such as *Monument to a Dead Boy* (1965, to a score by Jan Boerman), which created a sensation at its premiere.

Choreographed before van Dantzig shouldered administrative responsibilities, that piece explored innocence and corruption in homoerotic desire and offered the ballet superstar Rudolf Nureyev his first role in a modern work.

Critics may question the edgy elements of homoerotic tension and existential malaise that recur in van Dantzig's work, but they also appreciate the vigor with which he places his politics front and center without diminishing the theatricality of the dance.

Sans Armes, Citoyens (1987, to a score by Hector Berlioz) is one example of van Dantzig drawing inspiration from his complex personal life and extending it to address social issues through movement. Requiring ensemble dancing that demands great virtuosity, this piece is a virtual manifesto urging the ideals of Liberty, Equality, and Fraternity without resort to violence.

In its political and artistic vision, *Sans Armes, Citoyens* is emblematic of the more than fifty provocative works van Dantzig created before leaving the Dutch National Ballet in 1991. Since that time, he has devoted himself to writing and to staging his work with other companies.

—*John McFarland*

BIBLIOGRAPHY

Campbell, R. M. "On Stage at PNB Dance: Work from a Dutch Master." *Seattle Post-Intelligencer*, January 27, 1998.

Dantzig, Rudi van. *For a Lost Soldier.* Arnold J. Pomerans, trans. London: Bodley Head, 1991.

Klooss, Helma. "Dostoyevski of the Dance." *Dance Magazine* 67.11 (November 1993): 92.

Loney, Glenn. "Evolution of an Ensemble: Rudi van Dantzig on the National Ballet of Holland." *Dance Magazine* 48.3 (March 1974): 34–39.

Perceval, John. "The Voice of the People." *Dance and Dancers* 448 (May–June 1987): 32–34.

Utrecht, Luuk. "Rudi van Dantzig." *International Encyclopedia of Dance.* Selma Jeanne Cohen, ed. New York: Oxford University Press, 1998. 2:346–348.

———. *Rudi van Dantzig: A Controversial Idealist in Ballet.* Nicoline Gatehouse, trans. Zutphen, Netherlands: Walburg Press, 1993.

SEE ALSO

Ballet; Ballet Russes; Dance; Diaghilev, Sergei; Nureyev, Rudolf

Vargas, Chavela   *(b. 1919)*

THE ACCLAIMED COSTA RICAN-MEXICAN PERFORMER and singer Chavela Vargas became notorious for the eroticism of her performances and for her open expression of lesbian desire.

Vargas was born Isabel ("Chavela") Vargas Lizano to Herminia Lizano and Francisco Vargas on April 19, 1919, in the province of Santa Bárbara de Heredia, Costa Rica, which is nestled between Nicaragua and Panama.

She grew up in Mexico, in exile, where she associated with leading intellectuals such as Frida Kahlo, with whom she had an affair, Diego Rivera, Agustín Lara, and Juan Rulfo, and even befriended political leaders such as Luis Echeverría, who served as President of Mexico from 1970 to 1976.

Vargas's career as a singer commenced in the mid-1950s, under the direction of José Alfredo Jiménez, her producer. Her first recording came a decade later, in 1961.

Chavela Vargas performs in the Port of Veracruz, Mexico, in 2003. Photograph by Luis Monroy.

Vargas became famous in the mid-1960s for her hallmark interpretations, frequently melodramatic and heartwrenching, of sentimental Mexican songs. The originality of her style and the deep pain she was able to communicate marked her as a singular talent.

At the same time, however, she became infamous for her outlandish behavior, which violated a number of Mexican taboos. Not only did she wear trousers and dress as a man, but she also smoked cigars, carried a gun in her pocket, and sported a red poncho in her celebration and vindication of folklore.

A crucial element of her radical performance art was her seduction of women in the audience and her singing *rancheras* written to be sung by a man to a woman.

Vargas has come to be known as "the woman with the red poncho," as the Spanish singer Joaquín Sabina dubbed her, as well as "the queen of Mexican song." She shares this latter accolade with Mexico's greatest popular singers: Lola Beltrán, Angélica María, Juan Gabriel, Lucha Reyes, and Rocío Durcal.

For those intimately acquainted with her performances, Vargas is known simply as "La Doña" or "La Chabela." These epithets are signs of respect and reverence, which are extended to her despite her "black legend," which included a devastating bout with alcoholism as well as overt lesbianism.

Vargas's life has been dedicated to ritual performance that transgresses social, gender, and cultural borders through song. Perhaps because she was afflicted with illness in childhood—including polio and blindness that she declares were cured by shamans—she claims that she shares the stage with her own gods.

Through her long life, she has expressed a bold faith in spirituality and artistic expression—a faith that she has relied upon time and time again, especially when she has been labeled "other," "queer," and "strange."

After gaining fame in the 1960s, Vargas fell into alcoholism in the 1970s. She retreated from the public sphere for about twelve years. She attempted comebacks with only modest success, though she did sing in local cabarets, especially those frequented by gay men, who continue to constitute a large fraction of her admirers.

In 1981, however, she made a major comeback with stellar performances at the Olympia Theatre of Paris, Carnegie Hall in New York, the Palacio de Bellas Artes in Mexico, and the Palau de la Música in Barcelona.

In the early 1990s, she experienced another revival. The gay filmmaker Pedro Almodóvar helped bring her a new audience by incorporating her bold, expressive, and seductive music into his films.

Vargas has recorded over eighty albums. Among her most notable and cherished titles and interpretations are "Macorina," "La China," "La Llorona," "Luz de Luna," "Toda una Vida," "Corazón Corazón," "Quisiera Amarte Menos," and "Volver Volver."

In November of 2000, the President of the Spanish government presented Vargas with "la Cruz de la Orden Isabel Católica," one of the most prestigious awards for artistic production.

This award, the singer declares, is a testament to her vexed legacy, one that includes her unapologetic persona and creative lesbian aesthetic.

—*Miguel A. Segovia*

BIBLIOGRAPHY

De Alba, Rebecca. "La 'leyenda negra' de Chabela Vargas." *Diario Noroeste de Mazatlán,* November 1, 2000.

EFE. "Chavela Vargas Clama Bienestar Social." *Terra: arte y cultura,* May 17, 2002.

Yarbro-Bejarano, Yvonne. "Crossing the Border with Chabela Vargas: A Chicana Femme's Tribute." *Sex and Sexuality in Latin America.* Daniel Balderston and Donna J. Guy, eds. New York: New York University Press, 2001. 33–43.

SEE ALSO

Cabarets and Revues

Variety and Vaudeville

FROM THE MID-NINETEENTH CENTURY ONWARD, A number of popular theatrical forms that included play on gender flourished in Britain, Europe, and the United States. The best known among these styles of theater, and the ones that flourished most in the United States, were minstrelsy, vaudeville (and its precursor, variety), and burlesque. All of these forms featured cross-dressed acts, as well as routines that challenged prevailing gender constructions.

In addition, certain performance specialties featured in some of these theatrical forms were known to attract homosexual performers. One of the difficulties in discussing sexual orientation in reference to performers of this period, however, is that the identity "homosexual" was relatively new and may well have been rejected by those whom we would now identify with this term.

On the other hand, there was a clear recognition by theater folks of this period that some performers were in same-sex or untraditional relationships. This recognition can be seen in snippets of gossip columns in theatrical newspapers that make oblique, usually snide, references to performers' private lives.

Many popular theater forms of the nineteenth century relied heavily on parody, stereotype, and novelty. Crossgender casting was one way in which serious drama or opera could be parodied. In all-male minstrel companies, cross-dressing was a necessity if female characters were to be included. And in forms such as British pantomime, which relied heavily on illusion and transformation, certain roles were purposely cast cross-gender.

Minstrelsy, burlesque, vaudeville, and variety were highly complex theatrical forms, and they all contained social commentary in addition to parodies of gender and gender constructions, but these parodies were a significant part of their appeal.

Minstrelsy

Minstrelsy emerged in the northeastern United States during the 1840s and flourished until almost the end of the century. After the Civil War, minstrelsy began to face competition from other popular forms such as burlesque, variety, and musical comedy. As Robert Toll notes, in order to compete with these rival forms a new role emerged within the all-male minstrel company—that of the glamorous female impersonator.

Indeed, in the United States minstrelsy can properly be regarded as the origin of glamour drag, and a number of prominent female impersonators of the earlier twentieth century—Karyl Norman and Julian Eltinge, for example—began their careers in minstrelsy.

Probably the best known of the early minstrel female impersonators was Francis Leon. Leon billed himself as "The Great Leon" and was featured in burlesque operettas staged by the Leon and Kelly Minstrel Company. Leon and his business partner, Kelly, maintained their troupe for five years, leasing a theater in New York City. Toll notes that by 1882 Leon was the highest paid minstrel performer and one of the most praised.

There were a number of other very successful female impersonators active in minstrelsy in the period, and reviews note that they sang in a believably female range.

The "prima donna" or "wench" role was not the only female role available to male minstrel performers. There was also a comic female role, the "Funny Old Gal," which was often performed by a large actor dressed in old and mismatched clothes.

This role was not unlike the comic cross-dressed roles for men found in burlesque, and similar characters were also found in the Irish comedies of Harrigan and Hart in the 1880s and later. This comic role was essentially parodic and relied on low comedy; these characters could be used to make fun of old women, unattractive women, unmarried women, and women advocating suffrage.

Burlesque

Burlesque is now most often associated with seedy strip shows and low comedy, but in the mid-nineteenth century this theatrical form was associated primarily with parody of high culture through puns, word play, and nonsense.

Burlesque in the United States was transformed by the tour of Lydia Thompson's British Blondes in the late 1860s. This troupe continued to use the standard formulae of burlesque, but they infused the form with sex. The actresses in this predominantly female troupe dressed in scanty costumes that showed their legs to the audience.

Burlesque always included cross-dressed roles, in keeping with the topsy-turvy world of this form. The "dame" role of burlesque was not unlike the "Funny Old Gal" role of minstrelsy, except that the costume was less ridiculous. Like the "Funny Old Gal," this role was also often played by a large actor who looked ridiculous in female attire.

One actor who won some fame in these roles was George Fortescue, who weighed well over 200 pounds. British pantomime provided similar comic female roles for men dressed as women—for example, the ugly sisters and the stepmother in the story of Cinderella.

Burlesque and also pantomime provided women with opportunities to play a number of male roles. Known as the "principal boy" and "second boy" roles, these characters were usually gallant young men who were still innocent to the ways of the world. The actresses who played these roles dressed in short tunics or pants, but retained their feminine curves and exposed the full length of their legs. There was no attempt to be realistically masculine.

Burlesque as it was performed by Lydia Thompson's troupe met fierce opposition in the United States, particularly from moral reformers. The feminist actress Olive Logan was horrified by the form, feeling that burlesque performances degraded theater as a whole. She described burlesque actresses as nude women and likened the troupe managers to pimps.

The role that excited the most opposition was that of the principal boy. Critics were disturbed by watching a woman who was clearly identifiable as such striding, swearing, spitting, and otherwise acting like a man.

Female Minstrel Companies

During the 1880s, burlesque and minstrelsy united in the form of female minstrel companies. This hybrid form consisted of a minstrel opening act performed by the women of the troupe, sometimes in blackface, sometimes not. A series of variety acts followed, and the entertainment was concluded with a burlesque.

With the advent of female minstrelsy, the emphasis shifted even more toward sexual display. Companies featured dozens of female performers who provided the audience with a mass display of scantily clad femininity. In most cases these women took nonspeaking roles, performing in the "Amazon chorus" or as a corps de ballet for suggestive dances such as the cancan.

Female minstrel companies were the forerunners of modern burlesque, with its heavy reliance on the female body and sexually suggestive performance.

Variety and Vaudeville

Variety first emerged in northeastern cities of the United States in the 1850s as formal and informal entertainment provided in bars. In its earliest days, this entertainment consisted mostly of singers hired to entertain the patrons and to lead sing-alongs.

By 1860, it had grown quite elaborate, and large concert saloons provided stage reenactments of current events as well as a succession of singers, dancers, and comedians. Patrons were also plied with drinks by "pretty waiter girls" who were hired to serve alcohol.

Authorities, alarmed by the rising number of these establishments, began to enact laws designed to put concert saloons out of business. As a response to changes in the law, and to ongoing harassment by the police, managers began to present what came to be known as variety in theaters rather than bars.

Variety was a theatrical form that could and did include almost any kind of act from performing animals to comedians to singers and dancers to one-act plays. It consisted of a series of acts unconnected by a narrative structure and concluded with a one-act play, usually a melodrama or burlesque.

It was considered the lowest class of popular forms, and individual acts rarely attracted much attention from the authorities or moral reformers unless they too obviously transgressed moral standards. Olive Logan considered variety to be a low and vile form of theater, but saw it as less of a threat to decency than burlesque because no one type of act dominated the stage.

A number of the kinds of acts featured on variety bills did challenge gender norms of the period, however. Female impersonators were present on the variety stage, though they were less common here than in minstrelsy or burlesque until the 1890s, when variety had come to be known as vaudeville.

Glamorous female impersonators appeared as solo acts, while the comic "Funny Old Gal" appeared in a number of variations. Comic depictions of women, often spinsters or widows, were common, as was the depiction of ethnic female types. The Russell Brothers, for example, performed a comedy routine as Irish cleaning women, and Harrigan and Hart performed an Irish act in which Tony Hart appeared as a woman.

A number of glamorous female impersonators won fame in vaudeville in the early twentieth century. Among these were Julian Eltinge, Bothwell Browne, Karyl Norman, and Barbette.

Barbette performed an acrobatic and wire-walking act in female costume. It was not at all uncommon in the late nineteenth century for young male acrobats to perform dressed as girls—the audience was apparently more appreciative of feats of daring from young women. Barbette was widely known as homosexual, and such was reputed to be the case with many circus acrobats.

Julian Eltinge and Karyl Norman both began their careers in minstrelsy and later moved to vaudeville. Although their sexual orientations are not known, neither man was married.

In nineteenth-century variety there were also acts featuring women dressed in male costume. Sister acts featuring one sister dressed as a girl and the other as a boy were common into the twentieth century. Acts such as the Foy Sisters or the Richmond Sisters sang light sentimental songs in duet. This style of male impersonation was closest to that found in burlesque, with less emphasis on sex appeal and more on sentiment.

Variety also featured realistic male impersonators who sang in a believably male range. These were women who were masculine in appearance and dressed in the height of male fashion. They shared their repertoire and performance style with male performers. Among the most successful of these women were Annie Hindle, Ella Wesner, and Blanche Selwyn.

While these women had largely been forgotten by the end of the century, they were among the highest-paid variety performers of the 1870s and 1880s, earning as much as $200 a week. They depicted a wide range of masculinity in their acts and were extremely popular with all-male working-class audiences because their acts mercilessly parodied middle-class values, while glorying in the excesses of leisure—alcohol, women, and fine fashion.

By the beginning of the twentieth century, this style of male impersonation had disappeared and male impersonators were more feminine in appearance and were generally sopranos.

Other kinds of acts in variety also challenged prevailing gender constructions. Among these were acts such as the "double-voiced vocalist," which could be performed by either a man or a woman. The performer was often dressed in a costume that combined male and female clothing—one half male, one half female.

One performer active in the 1870s was Dora Dawron, who sang both soprano and baritone and turned the appropriate side to the audience as she sang. Karyl Norman also performed a double-voiced act, alternating between male and female characters and changing costume between songs.

Female strongwomen were also featured on the stage, and the audience delighted in watching women do the impossible—lifting weights and furniture and even people. Female multi-instrumentalists also challenged gender norms, as young women played instruments usually reserved for men, such as trumpet and saxophone and banjo. Because variety relied heavily on novelty, women performing such unfeminine feats of strength and skill were often very popular.

—*Gillian Rodger*

BIBLIOGRAPHY

Allen, Robert. C. *Horrible Prettiness: Burlesque and American Culture.* Chapel Hill: University of North Carolina Press, 1991.

Bean, Annemarie, James V. Hatch, and Brooks McNamara, eds. *Inside the Minstrel Masks: Readings in Nineteenth-Century Blackface Minstrelsy.* Hanover, N.H.: University Press of New England for Wesleyan University Press, 1996.

Kibler, M. Alison. *Rank Ladies: Gender and Cultural Hierarchy in American Vaudeville.* Chapel Hill: University of North Carolina Press, 1999.

Logan, Olive. "About the Leg Business" and "About Nudity in Theatres." *Apropos of Women and Theatres, With a Paper or Two on Parisian Topics.* New York: Carleton, 1869. 110–153.

Lott, Eric. *Love and Theft: Blackface Minstrelsy and the American Working Class.* New York: Oxford University Press, 1993.

Rodger, Gillian. *Male Impersonation on the North American Variety and Vaudeville Stage, 1868–1930.* Ph.D. diss., University of Pittsburgh, 1998.

Snyder, Robert. *The Voice of the City: Vaudeville and Popular Culture in New York.* New York and Oxford: Oxford University Press, 1989.

Toll, Robert C. *Blacking Up: The Minstrel Show in Nineteenth-Century America.* New York: Oxford University Press, 1974.

SEE ALSO

Cabarets and Revues; Drag Shows: Drag Queens and Female Impersonators; Drag Shows: Drag Kings and Male Impersonators; Hindle, Annie

Village People

The Village People were a disco-era singing group formed in the late 1970s. Although the group never identified itself as gay, its primary appeal was clearly to a gay male audience. It successfully translated the interests, coded language, and iconography of the gay male subculture into music that crossed over into mainstream pop.

Because the general public was largely unaware of the meanings and suggestiveness of the lyrics or the costumes associated with the group, the gay audience not only enjoyed the music on its own terms, but also relished the irony of a mainstream audience unknowingly embracing subculture values and images.

The Village People were formed in 1977 by French record producer Jacques Morali, who was inspired to create the group after seeing performer Felipe Rose, dressed as a Native American, singing and dancing in the streets of Greenwich Village. Hence the group's name.

Morali approached Rose about forming a group and then, with his partner Henri Belelo, auditioned other singers by advertising in trade publications for "singers with mustaches."

All members of the group performed in costume to represent masculine (and, not coincidentally, gay male

fantasy) archetypes: the Native American Rose, construction worker David Hodo, policeman Victor Willis, soldier Alex Briley, cowboy Randy Jones, and biker/leatherman Glenn Hughes. Rose was openly gay, but the other singers never discussed their sexual orientation.

Regardless, the Village People's core audience was undeniably gay men, and their most popular hits were overtly homoerotic.

"YMCA" (1978), for example, told its presumably male audience about the delights of staying at the YMCA with other young men; "In the Navy" (1979) sang the joys of being in the Navy with other young men; and so on.

The group's other major hits included "Macho Man" (1978), "Fire Island" (1977), and "Go West" (1979). Three of their albums went gold (selling more than 500 thousand albums) and four went platinum (selling more than one million).

The Village People starred in a largely fictionalized film version of their origins, Allan Carr's *Can't Stop the Music* (1980), which featured blatantly homoerotic production numbers. One of the most memorable took place in a gym and involved a large number of muscular men going through Busby Berkeley routines to the tune of "YMCA." Although critics savaged the film, it has gone on to achieve a certain status as a camp classic.

Several of the Village People's albums were released only in Europe, where they had a large and faithful following. Their third album released in America, *Renaissance* (1981), was their attempt to reinvent themselves as a New Wave 1980s group, after the decline of disco. The album was a commercial flop, and the Village People disbanded from touring in 1986. Morali, the group's founder and creative director, died of AIDS-related illnesses in 1991.

Never taken particularly seriously (musically or otherwise), the Village People nevertheless remain one of the enduring legacies of 1970s gay male popular culture. They regrouped in 1998, with three of the original singers and three replacements (Jeff Olson as the cowboy, Ray Simpson as the cop, and Eric Anzalone as the biker/leatherman). They continue to tour, performing both their early hits and new material as well.

—*Robert Kellerman*

BIBLIOGRAPHY

"A Straight Road to Gay Stardom." *Maclean's*, April 24, 2000, 9.

"With a Bump, a Grind and a Wink, Disco's Macho Men are Time-Warp Wonders." *People*, June 17, 1996, 60.

SEE ALSO

Popular Music; Disco and Dance Music; Pet Shop Boys; Sylvester

The Village People, photographed by Alecsey Boldeskul/NY Photo Press in 2003.

Wagnerism

WAGNERISM ESSENTIALLY HAS TO DO WITH THE music, theoretical writings, political ideas, and aesthetics of the German composer, conductor, and essayist Richard Wagner (1813–1883). One of the most influential cultural figures of the nineteenth century, Wagner has had both swooning admirers and rabid detractors.

For some, Wagnerism was above all a political rallying call, at first appealing to class consciousness and then degenerating into proto-Fascism. For others, it nurtured the most diverse idealistic beliefs and Romantic sensibilities. Wagner's operatic works brought together mythology and philosophy in a way that was radically different from any opera that had come before.

Simultaneously erotic, death-obsessed, and spiritual, Wagner's music dramas (his preferred term for his art) suggested both sin and redemption, an ideal atmosphere in which nineteenth-century aesthetes could immerse themselves.

It is primarily in this realm that Wagnerism influenced and inspired the so-called Decadents and Symbolists, who were largely concerned with nonconformist sensibility and sexuality, including same-sex desire.

Influence on Nineteenth-Century Art and Culture

Adherents of the Symbolist movement in art and literature championed Wagner during the second half of the nineteenth century. One of Wagner's early admirers was the French poet and art critic Charles Baudelaire. Inspired by the concert overtures of *Tannhäuser*, *Lohengrin,* and *Der Fliegende Holländer* performed at the Paris Opera, Baudelaire wrote enthusiastically of the composer's idea of *Gesamtkunstwerk* (a unification of all art forms into a single event), linking it to his own aesthetic of synesthesia (basically, the commingling of the senses).

According to Baudelaire, Wagner's music promoted a dreamlike reverie and suggested more than it explained. Wagner's theory of the unity of the arts and Baudelaire's idea of correspondences gave the Symbolists a rough framework from which to champion their movement.

Very little of late-nineteenth-century European culture was untouched by Wagnerism. A Symbolist periodical, *La Revue Wagnérienne*, was founded in 1885 to promote the cause of Wagner. Contributors to this journal included J. K. Huysmans, Paul Verlaine, and Stéphane Mallarmé.

Wagnerism was by no means limited to French authors and artists. Oscar Wilde included a characteristic comment about Wagner in his novel *The Picture of Dorian Gray* ("I like Wagner's music better than anybody's. It is so loud that one can talk the whole time without other people hearing what one says").

Aubrey Beardsley's illustrations for the *Ring* cycle (Wagner's magnum opus, *Der Ring des Nibelungen*) and his sexually explicit farce "The Story of Venus and Tannhauser" (also published as "Under the Hill"), complete with his erotic illustrations, also indicate the scope of Wagnerian influence among the *fin de siècle* Decadents.

The philosopher Friedrich Nietzsche, once a friend and admirer of Wagner, denounced what he perceived as Wagner's decadent aspects: "How closely related Wagner must be to the whole of European decadence to avoid being experienced by them as a decadent. He belongs to it: he is its protagonist, its greatest name." What Nietzsche probably did not intend is that his essay managed to make Wagner's decadence seem downright attractive.

For many, Wagner's music took on quasi-religious overtones, and followers of his music were referred to as "disciples" who "made the pilgrimage" to the Festival Hall in Bayreuth. Concertgoers were reported to have fainted at the performances as if under the influence of some religious fervor or ecstasy.

The Swan King

In spite of his early poverty, Wagner insisted on living in luxurious surroundings and wearing silk and velvet-lined clothing. "I am a different kind of organism," Wagner said, by way of justification. "My nerves are hypersensitive, I must have beauty, splendor and light."

Given these declarations, it is no wonder that Wagner appealed to nineteenth-century French dandies. When Wagner sent a seamstress to obtain specially ordered dressing gowns, silk underclothes, and perfumes, she told the customs officials that they were for a countess in Berlin!

Wagner needed much money to settle his debts, build his dream theater in Bayreuth, and live in a style he felt was owed to him. Luckily for him, a dreamy eighteen-year-old Bavarian prince who identified himself with the swan-knight Lohengrin was about to become King Ludwig II of Bavaria.

Ludwig had grown up among paintings and tapestries of the same Teutonic legends Wagner employed in his operas. Attending his first Wagner opera was a deeply moving dream come true for the young prince; and upon ascending to the throne, Ludwig immediately requested that Wagner come to Bavaria.

After accepting Ludwig's ring and portrait, Wagner soon enjoyed the royal patronage of the king. "My only one! My godlike friend!" wrote the monarch to Wagner. Wagner could hardly believe his good fortune and responded in kind: "O my King! You are divine!"

Because of Ludwig's homosexuality, the passionate letters exchanged between these two have led to some speculation that there was a homosexual relationship between the king and the composer. But Ludwig was evidently attracted to Wagner's artistic visions and accomplishments rather than to Wagner the man. (Wagner's physical appearance was undoubtedly a disappointment to the beauty-worshipping king.)

Still, Wagner knew how to manipulate Ludwig on his own terms and was not above encouraging the monarch's fantasies (and generosity). Thus, he responded to Ludwig's

Richard Wagner.

purple prose in kind. Thanks to the royal coffers, Wagner was able to mount productions of *Tristan und Isolde* and *Die Meistersinger* while finishing the score of the *Ring* cycle.

But not everyone among Ludwig's cabinet was as enamored of Wagner as the king. Because of Wagner's drain on the treasury, his participation in the Dresden uprising in 1849 (an act of treason), and his liaison with Cosima von Bülow, the wife of Wagner's own concert-master, Ludwig's aides urged the king to sever his relationship with the composer.

Reluctantly, Ludwig sent word to Wagner that he would have to leave Munich. But he continued to help Wagner financially throughout the rest of his life. It is probably not an exaggeration to say that without King Ludwig II's great admiration and financial support, there would be fewer complete Wagner operas today and certainly no Festival Hall at Bayreuth for their performances.

Parsifal: The Restoration of Male Society

Wagner's last music drama, *Parsifal*, was admired by the Symbolists especially because of its themes of sin and redemption. Many Symbolists viewed Christianity as a mystical inward quest and displayed a morbid fascination with the suffering of Christ. While *Parsifal* is Wagner's most Christian opera, it also turns out to be the opera with the clearest homosexual overtones.

Parsifal is an "innocent fool" whose task is to restore the sacred male society that is in charge of protecting the Holy Grail. The Brotherhood has fallen into decline because of the loss of the spear that pierced Christ's side and the illness that the Grail King Amfortas suffers as a result. It was while engaging in sexual relations with the witch Kundry that Amfortas lost the spear that had been his charge.

A queer reading of *Parsifal* notes that the masculine order of the Grail considers intercourse with a woman a sin, a fall from grace, or a crime against the knights. The chaste Parsifal refuses the temptations of the flower maidens, and, upon Kundry's attempted kiss, pulls away from her and shouts "Amfortas!"—thereby declaring his loyalty to the male order.

By refusing Kundry's seduction, Parsifal regains the sacred spear that will heal Amfortas. In a gesture that suggests both physical and spiritual union, Parsifal touches Amfortas's wound with the spear and the king is healed and redeemed. At the end of the opera, Kundry, the lone female character in the opera, is dead and the Grail Brotherhood is restored.

These aspects of *Parsifal* were not lost on the poet Paul Verlaine, who struggled with his own religious and sexual conflicts; in 1886, he composed a poem of the same name.

An interpretation of the opera in keeping with this reading is a 1983 film version by Hans-Jürgen Syberberg. Emphasizing Parsifal's androgyny, it has the young boy become a woman at the point of Kundry's kiss in Act II. In a nod to Baudelaire's *Les Fleurs du mal*, Syberberg portrays the flower maidens as deformed and ugly, suggesting that any sort of union with these women will result in sickness and death.

It is to Wagner's credit as a composer that the complex themes and interpretations of *Parsifal* are realized by some of the most beautiful music he ever wrote.

—*Robin Imhof*

BIBLIOGRAPHY

Hanson, Ellis. "The Dialectic of Shame and Grace: Perfect Wagnerites." *Decadence and Catholicism*. Cambridge, Mass.: Harvard University Press, 1997. 27–43.

King, Greg. *The Mad King: The Life and Times of Ludwig II of Bavaria*. Secaucus, N.J.: Carol Publishing Group, 1996.

Large, David C., and William Weber, eds. *Wagnerism in European Culture and Politics*. Ithaca, N.Y.: Cornell University Press, 1984.

Millington, Barry. *Wagner*. London: Dent, 1984.

Magee, Bryan. *Aspects of Wagner*. Oxford: Oxford University Press, 1988.

Nietzsche, Friedrich. *The Birth of Tragedy and The Case of Wagner*. Walter Kaufmann, trans. New York: Vintage, 1967.

Panizza, Oskar. "Bayreuth and Homosexuality." *Wagner* 9.2 (1988): 71–75.

Peyre, Henri, ed. *Baudelaire: A Collection of Critical Essays*. Englewood Cliffs, N.J.: Prentice Hall, 1962.

SEE ALSO

Classical Music; Opera

Wainwright, Rufus   (b. 1973)

THE SINGER AND SONGWRITER RUFUS WAINWRIGHT has built a successful career with witty lyrics and rich melodies that have earned him comparisons to Cole Porter and George Gershwin. Wainwright cites Al Jolson, Edith Piaf, and Nina Simone as artists who were among his early inspirations.

Both music critics and Wainwright's loyal fans appreciate the structural complexity and lush orchestrations of his works. Described by *Advocate* reviewer Anderson Jones as "the thinking gay man's sex symbol," Wainwright composes and performs songs marked by intelligence, humor, and pathos. In his rendition, his songs are at once achingly plaintive and hip, their frank romanticism only barely mediated by a light dose of irony.

Wainwright comes from a distinctly musical family. His father is the American folksinger and humorist Loudon Wainwright III, and his mother is the Canadian folksinger and songwriter Kate McGarrigle. Born on July 22, 1973, in Rhinebeck, New York, Rufus Wainwright grew up in Montreal, where his mother made her home after his parents separated when he was three and subsequently divorced.

Music has always been at the center of Wainwright's life. He began learning to play the piano at six and by his early teens was performing on tour with his mother, his aunt Anna McGarrigle, and his sister Martha Wainwright as the McGarrigle Sisters and Family.

Wainwright wrote his first song, "I'm A-Runnin'," for the children's film *Tommy Tricker and the Stamp Traveller* (1988, directed by Michael Rubbo), for which his mother and aunt had been engaged to provide the music. He was rewarded with nominations for a Juno Award (the Canadian equivalent of a Grammy) and a Genie Award (the Canadian version of an Emmy) for his performance of the song in the television movie.

Wainwright spent his high school years at Millbrook, a boarding school in upstate New York. While in his early teens, he discovered opera. This taste not only gave him his own musical niche in the family but also led him to incorporate classical elements in his songs, creating

Rufus Wainwright.

a texture and sophistication that sets them apart from ordinary pop fare.

At the age of fourteen, Wainwright also discovered that he was gay and came out publicly. He has consistently been forthright about his sexual orientation.

After high school, Wainwright briefly attended McGill University in Montreal, studying piano and composition, but left to write music and perform in clubs in Quebec.

He made a demo tape of his songs, which his father gave to producers at the fledgling Dreamworks Records. Impressed, they quickly signed Wainwright to a contract.

Two years in the making, his self-titled first album came out in 1998 and was an immediate success. His sophisticated tunes were compared to the work of Harry Nilsson and George Gershwin. *Rolling Stone* magazine named Wainwright the best new artist of the year.

As the album was set for release, some advisers at the record company suggested excising references to Wainwright's sexual orientation from the press kit, but Wainwright refused. His candor earned him a special place in the hearts of gay fans.

Wainwright's second album, *Poses* (2001), showed him maturing as a musician and was well received by both critics and his fans, among whom are many teenage girls who enjoy his romantic love songs, as well as gay men, who are attracted to his boyish good looks and who flock to his concerts.

In the same year that *Poses* appeared, Wainwright contributed songs to the soundtracks of three films, Baz Luhrmann's *Moulin Rouge*, Jessie Nelson's *I Am Sam*, and Andrew Adamson, Vicky Jensen, and Scott Marshall's *Shrek*.

While Wainwright's career was flourishing in the new millennium, his personal life was troubled. He became addicted to alcohol and drugs, including methamphetamines. In addition, he suffered from depression. Without a steady love in his life, he took to meeting men over the Internet and engaging in loveless affairs.

To break this dangerous pattern Wainwright underwent a month of rehabilitation and therapy at the Hazelden Clinic in Minnesota. Upon completing the program, he plunged back into his work, creating new material for the albums *Want One*, released in 2003, and *Want Two*, scheduled for release in 2004. Elizabeth Weinstein of the *Columbus Dispatch* called *Want One* "at once heartbreaking and heartening" with "lyrics [that] are emotionally charged and revealing."

Wainwright will soon appear on the big screen, playing a nightclub singer in Martin Scorsese's *The Aviator*, which is set to premiere in late 2004. He also has a speaking role in an upcoming Merchant-Ivory film entitled *Heights*.

The singer maintains a busy concert schedule, appearing frequently in Canadian, English, and American cities. In a recent concert in Los Angeles, Wainwright was joined onstage by Elton John, with whom he sang a duet of "Greek Song."

Wainwright has expressed an interest in doing more acting work while pursuing his career in singing and songwriting. He also aspires to write a Broadway musical and perhaps even an opera.

Wainwright has participated in benefits for AIDS charities in both the United States and Canada. As he has matured, he has become more politically aware and has stated that he feels "it's almost irresponsible of artists not to be socially conscious these days." Although his songs are not generally political, he hopes to be able to reach out to his fan base, particularly glbtq people and youth, to encourage them to stand up for individual rights.

—*Linda Rapp*

BIBLIOGRAPHY

Empire, Kitty. "Nowt Queer as Folk: Raffish of Look and Forthright of Speech, Singer Rufus Wainwright Tells Kitty Empire about the Legacy of His Famous Parents, a Past Penchant for Crystal Meth and His Self-Inflicted 'Gay Hell.'" *Observer* (London), October 12, 2003.

Ganahl, Jane. "From Rehab to a New Album, He's Walked through Fire and Come out Singing." *San Francisco Chronicle,* January 9, 2004.

Jones, Anderson. "Romantic for Rufus." www.advocate.com/html/stories/910/910_wainwright.asp

Mitchell, Rick. "Wainwright Propelled by Offbeat Melodies." *Record* (Kitchener-Waterloo, Ontario), April 7, 1999.

Orlov, Piotr. "Shining Son; Rufus Wainwright Is on the Verge of Greatness—And He Knows It." *Miami New Times*, May 2, 2002.

Patterson, Rob. "Strings Attached." *Houston Press*, March 11, 2004.

Powers, Ann. "Embracing Gay Identity with Candor and Pride." *New York Times*, July 1, 2001.

www.rufuswainwright.com

SEE ALSO

Popular Music; John, Sir Elton; Porter, Cole

Waters, Ethel (1896–1977)

ETHEL WATERS IS PERHAPS BEST REMEMBERED FOR THE depth and acuity she brought to her fat "mammy" roles in plays and films such as Carson McCullers's *Member of the Wedding* (1950, 1952) and television shows such as *Beulah* (1950), in the title role of which she replaced the redoubtable Hattie McDaniel. However, Waters had a long, varied, and colorful career.

She began as "Sweet Mama Stringbean," a slender and glamorous blues singer whose technical and emotional agility made her one of the major stars of the Harlem nightclubs of the 1920s.

Her ability to infuse dramatic meaning and intensity into her music made her a natural in musical theater as well, and for a time in the 1930s she was the highest-paid performer on Broadway, winning rave reviews for her roles in such plays as *Blackbirds* (1930) and *Mamba's Daughters* (1938).

She earned an Academy Award nomination for her supporting performance in the film *Pinky* (1949) and a New York Drama Critics' Circle Award as Best Actress of 1950 for her luminous performance on Broadway as the maid in *Member of the Wedding*, a role she reprised on film to further acclaim two years later.

Waters climbed to stardom from a childhood of crushing deprivation. Born on October 31, 1896, in Chester, Pennsylvania, the daughter of a twelve-year-old rape victim, Waters herself was married to her first husband by the age of twelve and divorced by fourteen.

In her autobiography, *His Eye Is on the Sparrow* (1950), she described her rough upbringing: "I never was a child...I just ran wild as a little girl. I was bad, always a leader of the street gang in stealing and general hellraising. By the time I was seven I knew all about sex and life in the raw. I could out-curse any stevedore and took a sadistic pleasure in shocking people."

As a teenager, while working as a chambermaid in a Philadelphia hotel, Waters gathered her courage one Halloween and sang for the first time on a nightclub stage—behind a mask. Heartened by her success, she began to sing professionally in Philadelphia and Baltimore. Then she moved to New York to join the dynamic explosion of African American creativity that was the Harlem Renaissance.

Singing such trademark blues songs as "Dinah," "Heat Wave," and "Stormy Weather," Waters quickly became a star in the Harlem clubs, and she also traveled a nightclub circuit from Chicago to St. Louis and throughout the South.

Marked by a vitality that gloried not only in black artistic achievement but also in black identity, the Harlem Renaissance also celebrated sexuality with a remarkable lack of censure. Like most blues singers of the time, Waters sang her share of raunchy, openly suggestive songs, such as "Organ Grinder Blues" and "Do What You Did Last Night."

Ethel Waters.

And, like many other women blues singers of the day, such as Bessie Smith, Ma Rainey, and Alberta Hunter, she was known to have sexual relationships with other women.

Although she was not as open as Rainey about her same-sex relationships, Waters had at least one quite public affair with a dancer named Ethel Williams, with whom she flirted from the stage and had notorious lovers' spats. She is also rumored to have had a brief liaison with the British novelist Radclyffe Hall, whom she mentions in her autobiography.

In the late 1920s and early 1930s, Waters was able to remake herself as an actress. She first appeared in several Broadway revues, then gradually garnered nonsinging dramatic roles on both stage and screen.

During her later years, Waters considerably toned down her "red hot mama" image and redefined herself as an evangelical Christian. Her last performances were as a member of Billy Graham's crusade. She died on September 1, 1977.   —*Tina Gianoulis*

BIBLIOGRAPHY

Antelyes, Peter. "Red Hot Mamas." *Embodied Voices: Representing Female Vocality in Western Culture.* Leslie C. Dunn and Nancy A. Jones, eds. Cambridge: Cambridge University Press, 1994. 212–229.

Garber, Eric. "A Spectacle in Color: The Lesbian and Gay Subculture of Jazz Age Harlem." *Hidden from History: Reclaiming the Gay and Lesbian Past.* Martin Baum Duberman, Martha Vicinus, and George Chauncey Jr., eds. New York: NAL Books, 1989. 318–331.

McCorkle, Susannah. "The Mother of Us All." *American Heritage* 45.1 (1994): 60–72.

Stryker, Susan. "Lesbian Blues Singers." www.planetout.com/news/history/archive/gladys.html

Waters, Ethel, with Charles Samuels. *His Eye Is on the Sparrow.* New York: Doubleday, 1950.

SEE ALSO

Popular Music; Blues Music; Cabarets and Revues; Jazz; Hunter, Alberta; Rainey, Gertrude ("Ma"); Smith, Bessie

Williamson, Cris   (*b. 1948*)

A PIONEERING SINGER, SONGWRITER, ACTIVIST, AND teacher, Cris Williamson has been at the forefront of the women's music movement—and a major presence in the lesbian community—for decades.

Like other women's music innovators in a time when such a genre was truly "alternative," Williamson, while not widely recognized by the mainstream, has met with large and appreciative audiences since the 1970s. Her fans admire her honesty; while her lyrics cross lines of gender,

age, and sexual preference, they are also intensely personal, and she has been out as a lesbian throughout her career.

Born in South Dakota and raised in Colorado and Wyoming, Williamson released her first album, *The Artistry of Cris Williamson* (1964), at the tender age of sixteen. That record, along with two more LPs she recorded in the following two years, became a hit in her hometown. She later attended the University of Denver and began to foster a musical style very similar to that of her idol Judy Collins.

Knowing that it would be difficult to get a record deal because she was a woman—and also because she was commonly regarded as a "Judy Junior"—Williamson began networking with other women artists such as Meg Christian, Margie Adams, and Holly Near. Shortly thereafter, in 1971, she cofounded Olivia Records.

Olivia, the first record label created and run entirely by women—mostly lesbians—in a time when independent labels were scarce and women's labels were unheard of, released Williamson's landmark 1975 album, *The Changer and the Changed.* That album, only the label's second

Cris Williamson, photographed by Irene Young.

release, openly explored themes of love among women, making it a breakthrough and instant classic for both Williamson and the women's music genre.

Even with no hit single and zero radio airplay, 100 thousand copies of the record were sold in its first year of circulation, through mail order and word of mouth alone. *The Changer and the Changed* has subsequently sold more than 500 thousand copies, making it one of the best-selling independent albums ever. Williamson went on to release two more albums in 1978.

Williamson's life began to take a new turn when she started recording *Lumière*, a children's album that won a 1982 Parent's Choice Award, with the help of performer and recording engineer Tret Fure. The two women went on to form a professional and personal relationship that would last for almost twenty years.

Fure had signed on to Olivia as well, and when Olivia changed from a record label to a women's travel company, Williamson and Fure founded another label, called Wolf Moon, in 1996.

Williamson and Fure each recorded their own albums on Olivia and then on Wolf Moon, collaborating on duet records such as *Postcards from Paradise* (1993) and *A Peek between the Covers* (1997). Their relationship was nearly as important as their music itself to their devoted fans, many of whom recall coming out to the sounds of Williamson's records. When the duo broke up in early 2000, many fans reported feeling a sense of loss and near abandonment.

Despite the setback, Williamson continues to record on her own; *Ashes*, her latest album, was released on Wolf Moon in September 2001.

In 1995, she received the first annual Michael Callen Award at the Gay and Lesbian American Music Awards, for her services to the gay and lesbian community.

—*Teresa Theophano*

BIBLIOGRAPHY

Pomeroy, Margaret L. "The Song and Soul of the Changer." *Left Bank Review/Echo Magazine.* www.leftbankreview.com/echo

www.criswilliamson.com

SEE ALSO

Popular Music; Women's Music; Women's Music Festivals; Christian, Meg; Near, Holly; Sweet Honey in the Rock

Wolfe, George C.   (b. 1954)

THE DIRECTOR, WRITER, AND PRODUCER GEORGE C. Wolfe has had a distinguished career in the theater. Among the numerous awards and prizes that he has garnered are two Tony Awards.

In addition to directing such important works as Tony Kushner's *Angels in America,* Wolfe has also written a number of plays and musicals, several of which have had successful runs on Broadway.

Since 1993, he has been the producer and artistic director of the New York Shakespeare Festival and the Joseph Papp Public Theater, positions that give him one of the most influential voices in American theater.

Origins in Kentucky

Wolfe was born on September 23, 1954, in Frankfort, Kentucky, a segregated city at the time. He recalls the "very tight black community" in which he grew up as nurturing. As a child, he says, he "was told that [he] was magical...special and extraordinary," and he "grew up with no concept of racial inferiority."

He did, however, encounter racism. He experienced what he called a "defining event" when, at age seven, he could not get into Frankfort's Capitol Theater to see the animated Disney film *101 Dalmations* because he was black.

He used his altogether justified outrage in a positive manner. He determined to strive for excellence in everything he did so that he could get "into any place [he] wanted to get into." He adds that "it was also a given that once I got into the room, I was supposed to open the windows and doors and let in other people."

As a young child, Wolfe attended the private all-black school where his mother taught and later was principal. Eventually, when the family moved and Wolfe began going to an integrated school, he felt rather isolated until he started directing plays in high school.

Wolfe says that he was "obsessed with theater." Beginning at an early age, he wrote his own plays. At twelve, he saw his first Broadway shows, including a particularly memorable production of Jerry Herman's *Hello, Dolly!* starring Pearl Bailey.

After high school, Wolfe enrolled at historically black Kentucky State University, the alma mater of his parents, Costello and Anna Lindsey Wolfe. Following his first year, he transferred to Pomona College in California, where he studied theater.

Move to California

In 1975, Wolfe's play *Up for Grabs* was performed at Pomona College, and was chosen as the Pacific Southern Regional winner at the American College Theater Festival (ACTF). The following year, the college staged his *Block Party*, which earned Wolfe a second ACTF award.

After his graduation in 1976, Wolfe remained in California, teaching at the Inner City Cultural Center in Los Angeles, where his plays *Tribal Rites* and *Back Alley Tales* were staged in the 1978–1979 season.

Wolfe's experience in Los Angeles taught him the uses of theater as a political and social force. It also brought him into contact with communities that he had not encountered back in Frankfort—Hispanics, Asians, and gays. In this setting, he began coming out publicly.

Move to New York

Wolfe achieved something of a cult following in Los Angeles, but in 1979 he moved to New York, where he taught at City College and the Richard Allen Center for Cultural Art while studying at New York University, from which he received a master's degree in dramatic writing in 1983.

Wolfe's musical *Paradise*, produced off Broadway in 1985, turned out to be a critical failure, but his next play, *The Colored Museum*, won the admiration of Joseph Papp, the director of the New York Shakespeare Festival, who included it in the program at the festival's Public Theater in 1986.

One of the play's eleven vignettes, "The Gospel According to Miss Roj," features a feisty drag queen character, a fierce black snap queen who rages against exploitation and indifference.

The satirical *Colored Museum* was not universally hailed. Some African Americans viewed the play as anti-black. It was a success with the critics, however, and Wolfe won the Dramatists' Guild's Elizabeth Hull–Kate Warriner Award for the best play dealing with a controversial social, political, or religious topic.

Three years later, Wolfe received critical acclaim for his play *Spunk*, an adaptation of three stories by Zora Neale Hurston. He also won an Obie as best director of an off-Broadway production.

Papp selected Wolfe, clearly a rising star in the theater world, to be a resident director at the Public Theater in early 1990. Wolfe's play *Blackout* was included among the theater's offerings in the next season.

Success on Broadway

At the same time that he was directing at the Public Theater, Wolfe, renowned for his seemingly boundless energy, was bringing to fruition a project on which he had been working for four years, a musical about the life of jazz musician Jelly Roll Morton.

Jelly's Last Jam opened in Los Angeles in 1991, and the next year moved to Broadway, where it garnered eleven Tony nominations, including best book of a musical and best director.

Up to this point, Wolfe had directed plays with mostly African American characters and themes. This changed in 1993, when Tony Kushner asked him to direct the Broadway production of his much-acclaimed AIDS drama, *Angels in America: The Millennium Approaches*.

When Wolfe's direction—which *New York Times* critic Frank Rich described as being of "crystalline lucidity"—earned him a Tony, he became the first person of color to win the award for directing a "white" play.

The production earned three other Tony Awards, five Drama Desk Awards—including one for Wolfe as best director—and the New York Drama Critics Award. Wolfe went on to direct the second part of *Angels*, *Perestroika*, the following year.

Artistic Director and Producer

Meanwhile, Wolfe had taken on a new and daunting task as artistic director and producer of the New York Shakespeare Festival and the Joseph Papp Public Theater.

Following the death of its founder, Papp, in 1991, the institution was administered by artistic director JoAnne Akalaitis and producing director Jason Steven Cohen. Dissension was rife within the organization, however, particularly with regard to the work of Akalaitis. In 1993, the board of directors decided to relieve her of her duties and give the artistic direction role to Wolfe, who would also serve as producer, thus making him the principal administrator of the enterprise.

Wolfe's mission was twofold: He was responsible for the budget and organizational structure and also for the artistic vision of the theater.

Wolfe was able to increase the theater's endowment considerably and to balance its budget. In the wake of the economic downturn and the events of September 11, 2001, funding has fallen off, but Wolfe remains optimistic about the institution's future.

As artistic director, Wolfe wanted to "create a theater that looks, feels and smells like America." Accordingly, he has sought to reach beyond the Public Theater's traditional clientele group—"uptown white"—and attract black, Asian, and Hispanic spectators as well.

Commitment to Diversity

Early on, he introduced a community affairs department to attract new theatergoers, including inner-city children, to the Public. In the effort to promote such diversity, Wolfe chose plays such as Oliver Mayer's *Blade to the Heat*, about black and Latino boxers and a homophobic murder, and Chay Yew's *A Language of Their Own*, about four gay men, two of them Chinese.

Wolfe speaks of hoping to create positive "cultural collisions" among members of the audience at the Public by offering plays that will appeal to different segments of society.

Wolfe's own musical *Bring in 'Da Noise, Bring in 'Da Funk* was presented at the Public, and then moved to Broadway, where it earned Wolfe his second Tony Award in 1996. The Public Theater then sponsored a national tour for the play. Taking a show on the road was a new and controversial move for the organization, but the gamble paid off when the production was well received around the country.

In the late 1990s, Wolfe faced a serious health problem caused by kidney failure. After a year on dialysis, he had an organ transplant. His older brother, William Wolfe, was the donor. With characteristic energy, Wolfe kept working throughout the health crisis, citing the ethic instilled in him by his family: "keep delivering."

Recent Projects

Among Wolfe's recent projects have been three musicals, *The Wild Party*; *Harlem Song*; *Caroline, or Change*, and an acclaimed drama.

The Wild Party is based on a 1928 poem by Joseph Moncure March. Wolfe wrote the book for the musical in collaboration with Michael John LaChiusa, who also provided the music and lyrics.

The piece, which "evoke[s] the racial, sexual, and intellectual ferment of New York in the 1920s," features "a parade of bizarre characters," including a "sexually ambitious" vaudeville actress, an "ambisextrous" playboy, a lesbian stripper, and two gay, black, incestuous songwriter brothers.

Although described by one reviewer as "easily the most fascinating Broadway show of the year," *The Wild Party* received mixed reviews and closed after a short run.

Harlem Song—"a combination Broadway-style musical and Harlem history lesson"—is a multimedia show featuring photographs and newsreel footage from the 1930s through the 1960s as well as musical numbers from the various periods. Wolfe wrote the piece for the reopening of the refurbished Apollo Theater in 2002.

In 2003, Wolfe directed the acclaimed and unusual musical *Caroline, or Change,* by Tony Kushner and Jeanine Tesori. Set in Civil Rights–era Louisiana, the story focuses on a black maid who works for a Jewish family at a time of profound social change. In May 2004, the musical moved to Broadway, where it is expected to enjoy a long run.

Wolfe also recently directed Suzan-Lori Parks's *Topdog/Underdog*, which won the 2002 Pulitzer Prize for Drama. The play, about two black brothers, has been widely praised for its insights into family dynamics and competitiveness. After its run at the Public, it was moved to Broadway.

"Democratic Fascist"

As a director, Wolfe calls himself "the most democratic fascist you'll ever meet," listening to all opinions before handing down a final decision—one consistent with his own vision of a project.

Joe Mantello, directed by Wolfe in *Angels* and himself the director of Terrence McNally's *Love! Valour! Compassion!*, echoes this assessment, calling Wolfe "a patient tyrant...[who] sees very clearly what he wants, and you

end up there—but feeling that you've done it all on your own." *Blade* playwright Oliver Mayer says that Wolfe encouraged him "to push the envelope, to be brave."

Wolfe is widely admired for his exuberance and energy, his strong work ethic, and his abiding commitment to bringing cultural diversity to the stage and a culturally diverse audience to the theater.

Wolfe recently announced that he plans to leave his position at the Public in order to devote more time to his own writing.

—*Linda Rapp*

BIBLIOGRAPHY

Barbour, David. "Night People: Surreal Illumination Fuels The Wild Party." *Lighting Dimensions*, July 2000.

Bay, Willow. "Profile of George C. Wolfe, Producer of Joseph Papp Theater." *CNN Pinnacle*, July 13, 2002: Transcript #071300CN.V39.

Dominguez, Robert. "Years Swing by in Lively Revue; Harlem History on Parade at Apollo." *New York Daily News*, July 11, 2002.

McNeil, Donald G. Jr. "George Wolfe and His Theater of Inclusion." *New York Times*, April 23, 1995.

Pacheco, Patrick. "Forget Jelly, George Is Jammin'." *Los Angeles Times*, November 20, 1994.

———. "Rap, Tap and...'Macbeth'?" *Los Angeles Times*, March 1, 1998.

———. "Wolfe Is Opening Doors to Theater of a New Century." *Baltimore Sun*, March 7, 1995.

Thelen, Lawrence. "George C. Wolfe." *The Show Makers: Great Directors of American Musical Theater.* New York and London: Routledge, 2000. 209–225.

"Wolfe, George C." *Current Biography Yearbook 1994.* Judith Graham, ed. New York: The H. W. Wilson Company, 1994. 622–626.

SEE ALSO

Musical Theater and Film; Herman, Jerry

Women's Music

Since its emergence in the 1970s as an outgrowth of what was then called the "women's liberation" movement, women's music has remained a phenomenally popular genre among feminists—especially lesbian feminists.

Women's music, loosely and logically defined as music made specifically by and for women, has always been stylistically diverse, incorporating elements of folk, acoustic pop, blues, jazz, and rock. The genre has broadened musically over time, and modern-day feminist and openly queer female performers have expanded upon the artistic freedoms established by pioneering acts.

The women's music boom of the 1970s set the precedent for later forms of DIY (do-it-yourself) and even less conventional types of music such as Riot Grrl and queer punk.

By encouraging women to get involved in all stages of the production of music as well as in venues such as festivals, cabarets, and coffeehouses, the initial phase of the movement helped launch a tradition of women creating their own underground media networks.

While contemporary lesbian feminism and its musical manifestations may not embody the separatism embraced by 1970s women's music culture, early separatist collectives were fundamental in providing women with a starting point to create a cottage industry within the music world.

1972 and the Birth of Women's Music

Among the first performers of what would be considered women's music was Holly Near, a folk musician and civil rights activist. Because most labels would not produce music with lesbian-themed subject material such as Near's, she founded her own label, Redwood Records, in 1972. Redwood released albums from such feminist acts as Ferron, Sweet Honey in the Rock, Teresa Trull, Ronnie Gilbert, and Faith Nolan.

Around the same time, another folksinger, Alix Dobkin, formed her all-lesbian group Lavender Jane. Their album *Lavender Jane Loves Women* was released and distributed under a label run by Dobkin and flautist Kay Gardner, Women Wax Works, and made history as the first album to be created, start to finish, by lesbians.

In 1973, Maxine Feldman recorded her song "Angry Atthis," a coming-out ode that expressed Atthis's frustration at not being able to hold the hand of her girlfriend Sappho in public. The single circulated widely in the gay community.

The following year marked the founding of feminist label Olivia Records. Originating from members of a Washington, D.C., separatist collective (musician Cris Williamson was a cofounder), Olivia debuted with a split single featuring Meg Christian's "Lady" and Williamson's "If It Wasn't for the Music." Later that year, Christian's "I Know You Know" was Olivia's first full-length offering.

Williamson's landmark album *The Changer and the Changed* appeared in 1975; to date, the record has sold approximately 500 thousand copies, making it one of the best-selling independent albums ever.

By 1975, Olivia and Redwood were both producing numerous albums annually. The following year heralded the startup of Lady Slipper, a mail-order women's music distribution company operated out of North Carolina.

Around the same time these groundbreaking records and labels began to gain popularity, women's festivals commenced as a venue for bringing the music and musicians to a large audience of lesbians. The National Women's Music Festival and the Amazon Music Project were two of the first weekend festivals to emerge, in 1974, followed by Womansphere in Maryland.

The largest and most popular festival of them all, the Michigan Womyn's Music Festival, was inaugurated in 1976. Now dozens of other music festivals are held around the country every year.

Other 1970s performers to become standards among women are Deadly Nightshade, Margie Adams, Robin Flower, Mary Watkins, and Linda Tillery. Urana, Pleiades, Lima Bean, Leonarda, and Goldenrod—the latter also a women's music distributor—were among the independent women's labels of the time.

Women's Music: The 1980s and 1990s

By the end of the 1970s, approximately twenty recording companies, forty-five production companies, and twenty-five independent distributors were promoting the work of about forty performers of women's music.

As the 1980s began, profit became more of a goal even for the grassroots music industry, and men became more involved in the songwriting and production segments of the movement. After the steps forward taken by grassroots performers, mainstream acts began to join the music festival circuit.

Meanwhile, newer female musicians such as the Indigo Girls, Melissa Etheridge, and Tracy Chapman broke out into the pop world of radio play. Singer/songwriter Phranc, who self-identifies as an "all-American Jewish lesbian folksinger," was signed to a major label, Island, a first for an out female performer. This kind of crossover would probably not have been possible without earlier independent female artists paving the way.

Along with the developments among traditional women's music figures, many of whom were still recording, the early 1990s brought the Riot Grrl movement into existence. Riot Grrl, a youth-based feminist culture that first developed in West Coast towns such as Olympia, Washington—a hotbed of independent music—laid claim to girl-produced zines and bands with an adamantly anticorporate ethic.

Bands such as Bikini Kill, Heavens to Betsy, and Bratmobile screamed lyrics that, along with the women who penned them, were unapologetically feminist and often queer; they captured the spirit of true "girl power" long before the Spice Girls co-opted it.

Also in the 1990s, queercore became established as a movement linked to, yet distinct from, traditional punk rock; bands such as Tribe 8, Team Dresch, and The Need sang about overt dyke desire and attracted fans of punk who never felt entirely happy about the male-dominated mosh pits.

Mr. Lady records, run by video artist Tammy Rae Carland and musician Kaia Wilson (formerly of Team Dresch and currently vocalist/guitarist of the dyke trio The Butchies), was launched in 1996 to promote queer recording artists. Albums from Sarah Dougher, The

Haggard, and Le Tigre, featuring Kathleen Hanna from the seminal Riot Grrl band Bikini Kill, have since been released. The company recently ended its operations.

On the folk-inspired front, the prolific and openly bisexual Ani DiFranco, with her folksinger-meets-punk-girl style, began playing at college campuses nationwide. In 1990, she started her own label called Righteous Babe Records, and began producing almost an album a year throughout the decade. Out lesbian Melissa Ferrick incorporated a similar confessional style of songwriting, accompanying herself on acoustic guitar, and developed a following as well. Both DiFranco and Ferrick continue to promote current albums today.

The New Millennium

Olivia Records became Olivia Cruises, a lesbian cruise company, some time ago; and Redwood ceased to exist in the early 1990s. But Lady Slipper is still in operation as both a distributor and a small record label, issuing albums from artists such as Kay Gardner, Ubaka Hill, and Rhiannon.

Holly Near recently released an album on her new label, Calico Tracks Records. And other record labels such as Kill Rock Stars, Chainsaw Records, and similar independents have picked up where Olivia and Redwood left off, though with a flair all their own.

Many old-school women's music artists such as Cris Williamson, Ferron, and Tret Fure are alive and well, making regular appearances at music festivals and producing new recordings. And new queercore groups like Tracy and the Plastics and the dyke-fronted The Gossip are emerging all the time, earning steady followings at live shows as well as praise in alternative publications.

In today's women's music there is often more room for the expression of third-wave feminist principles such as gender fluidity and raw sexuality, but the message is still a political one.

Crucial to women's music of both the old school and the new is the visibility of feminism and lesbianism both within and outside the music industry.

—*Teresa Theophano*

BIBLIOGRAPHY

Hogan, Steve, and Lee Hudson, eds. *Completely Queer*. New York: Henry Holt & Co., 1998.

Witt, Lynn, Sherry Thomas, and Eric Marcus. *Out in All Directions*. New York: Warner Books, 1995.

RECORD LABEL AND ARTIST WEBSITES:

www.mrlady.com

www.chainsaw.com

www.righteousbabe.com

www.killrockstars.com

www.hollynear.com

www.criswilliamson.com

www.lesbianation.com

SEE ALSO

Popular Music; Women's Music Festivals; Christian, Meg; DiFranco, Ani; Etheridge, Melissa; Indigo Girls; Near, Holly; Sweet Honey in the Rock; Williamson, Cris

Women's Music Festivals

A CULTURAL INSTITUTION AMONG LESBIANS FOR THE last quarter century, women's music festivals are eagerly anticipated community-based events that celebrate women's space as much as their music.

Dozens currently take place every year in the United States alone, and unlike the highly publicized Lilith Fair—a traveling tour with corporate sponsorship and an emphasis on mainstream female performers—grassroots festivals can provide satisfyingly intimate environments even with thousands of women in attendance.

Moreover, because "safe space" and "women's space" are often stressed at these festivals, the experience differs greatly from attending concerts in the everyday "real world." While some festivals such as the National Women's Music Festival welcome male attendees, others like the Michigan Womyn's Music Festival were founded on the separatist tenets that led to the initial development of women's music, and remain strictly women-only to this day.

Early Festivals and the Michigan Womyn's Music Festival

The first women's music festivals—the National Women's Music Festival, which is still held annually, the Amazon Music Festival in Santa Cruz, California, and Womansphere, near Washington, D.C.—took place in 1974.

But the best-known festival now, and one of the oldest, is the legendary Michigan Womyn's Music Festival, which was launched in 1976. The Michigan Womyn's Music Festival takes place in the second week of August each year and is among the largest of all women's festivals. Held on 650 acres of privately owned women's land in remote Hart, Michigan, the event is currently produced by Lisa Vogel, a former member of the founding collective.

Like most women's festivals, the Michigan Womyn's Music Festival features much more than just musical performances. Myriad workshops, athletic events, nature activities, and meetings are held alongside an array of exhibits and services provided by female vendors.

The weeklong festival, whose ticket price includes camping accommodations, vegetarian meals, bathing facilities, and all other activities, attracts around 10,000 attendees each year, all of whom participate in rotating work shifts.

Performers' musical styles vary greatly, and past headliners include prominent women's music figures such as Alix Dobkin, Ferron, and Teresa Trull, as well as newer queer female performers such as Melissa Ferrick, Kinnie Starr, the spoken-word troupe Sister Spit, and the Butchies.

The festival prides itself on the notion that its grounds are "safe space" for women, but over the years many of its policies have proven controversial, for example, its "womyn-born womyn only" rule, which specifies that no transgendered or transsexual women are welcome on the land.

In response to this policy, the activist group Transsexual Menace began organizing protests in 1994 and set up Camp Trans to establish visibility and distribute information just outside the festival entrance.

Other debates have developed over issues such as the presence of women involved in S/M and the performance of dyke-punk group Tribe 8, whose unconventional stage act led numerous women wrongly to accuse them of promoting violence against women.

The admission of male children has been another point of contention. Currently, the Michigan Womyn's Music Festival permits males under five years of age onto the land, while older boys are housed at the nearby camp Brother Sun.

The National Women's Music Festival

First held in Champaign–Urbana, Illinois, the National Women's Music Festival does not seem to stand out in festival history the way the Michigan Womyn's Music Festival does, despite being the first women's music festival in the United States.

Now held annually on the campus of Ball State University in Muncie, Indiana, the festival is a four-day celebration that attracts a mostly female crowd, though men are permitted to attend as well. Concerts are staged by such legendary women's music performers as Cris Williamson, Holly Near, Heather Bishop, and Lucie Blue Tremblay.

Other entertainment encompasses coffeehouses, workshops, a crafts marketplace, films and videos, and even a shopping mall. The indoor environment creates a very different feel from the campsites of Michigan, and attendees are responsible for securing their accommodations in the university's dormitories.

Wiminfest

Established in 1985 in Albuquerque, New Mexico, Wiminfest remains an annual three-day celebration of lesbian culture and women's music and art, with an emphasis on diversity among both performers and attendees. The festival is run by the nonprofit organization Women in Movement in New Mexico (WIMIN) and is held indoors at Albuquerque's historic KiMo Theatre.

Performers from years past include Catie Curtis, Ubaka Hill, and Linda Tillery; activities available include women-only dances (all other parts of the festival are open to everyone), arts and crafts, storytelling, open microphones, and athletic events.

Ladyfest

A six-day women-produced festival based in Olympia, Washington, the first Ladyfest was held in 2000. Some events at the fest were for women only; and while some bands performing had male members, no all-male bands were invited.

No future Ladyfests are planned for Olympia, but spinoff events were held in other locations in 2001: Ladyfest Midwest in Chicago; Ladyfest Scotland in Glasgow; and Ladyfest East in Boston.

The first Ladyfest was a nonprofit event featuring bands popular in the independent music scene—such as Bratmobile, The Need, The Gossip, Cat Power, and the Butchies—as well as spoken word performances, visual art, workshops, panels, and dance parties. On the whole, it is fair to say that Ladyfest attracts a younger crowd than many other festivals, as its performers and organizers are more deeply rooted in independent music and third-wave feminism.

Local and International Women's Music Festivals

Varying considerably in size as well as in the types of performers featured, many local women's music events are held around the United States. Locales include Iowa, Alaska, Hawaii (Hawaiifest), Missouri (St. Louis Women's Music Festival), Texas (which has two festivals, FriendsFest and the Houston Women's Music Festival), New Hampshire, North Carolina (Spring Fling and Starfest), Virginia (CampOut Virginia Women's Music Festival), and West Virginia (Sistah Summerfest).

In addition, some other countries also hold women's music festivals. Among these are Australia's Venus Rising festival in Melbourne and the Sistajive Women's Music Festival in Illawarra; Canada's Southern Ontario Womyn's Drum Camp and the Rock City Women's Fest, both in Ontario, as well as the Woman's Voices Festival in Quebec; and England's Coventry Woman's Festival and Chard Festival of Women in Music.

—Teresa Theophano

BIBLIOGRAPHY

Hogan, Steve, and Hudson, Lee, eds. *Completely Queer*. New York: Henry Holt & Co., 1998.

Witt, Lynn, Sherry Thomas, and Eric Marcus. *Out in All Directions*. New York: Warner Books, 1995.

www.wiaonline.org/nwmf

www.ladyfest.org

www.michfest.com

www.wiminfest.org

www.womensfestival.com

SEE ALSO

Women's Music; Popular Music; Christian, Meg; Near, Holly; Williamson, Cris

Wright, Robert, and George "Chet" Forrest
Robert Wright (b. 1914)
and George Forrest (1915–1999)

FOR OVER SEVENTY YEARS, ROBERT WRIGHT AND George Forrest were partners in life and art. Together they wrote music and lyrics for film, stage, and club acts. They specialized in adapting themes from classical music into engaging tunes for movie scores and stage musicals.

George Forrest Chichester Jr., later to be known professionally as Chet Forrest, was born in Brooklyn, New York, on July 31, 1915. A musical prodigy, despite scant formal training he was playing the piano masterfully before he even started school.

In the early 1920s, the Chichester family moved to Florida. By the age of thirteen, Forrest had launched his musical career, playing in clubs in Miami.

He was also a member of the Miami High School glee club, through which he met his future life partner, Robert Wright, who was the club's pianist.

Wright, born on September 25, 1914, in Daytona Beach, Florida, had also taken early to music. By the time he met Forrest, he was the conductor of a radio show.

Brought together by their shared love of music, Wright and Forrest soon began collaborating.

In 1934, Forrest, who was working at a Miami nightclub, played for an audition by drag entertainer Ray Bourbon. Forrest and Wright soon began writing material for Bourbon, who the following year took them on a nationwide tour ending in California, where he helped them pursue their career in music.

At their audition for Metro-Goldwyn-Mayer, Forrest and Wright played a dozen of the approximately eighty songs that they had written during the tour. Impressed with their work, studio executives signed them to a seven-year contract.

Wright and Forrest had already written songs or lyrics for several films when they were called upon to provide music for Robert Z. Leonard's *Maytime* (1937), which starred Jeanette MacDonald and Nelson Eddy. When the producer Hunt Stromberg suggested that Wright and Forrest rework material in the public domain, they used musical themes from operas and from Tchaikovsky's Fifth Symphony to create new songs.

Throughout their career they were known for their refashioning of classical works as well as for their original compositions. They used themes from Rudolf Friml in Leonard's *The Firefly* (1937) and songs by Victor Herbert in the scores for W. S. Van Dyke's *Sweethearts* (1938) and Reinhold Schunzel's *Balalaika* (1939).

During their years at MGM, Wright and Forrest were thrice nominated for Academy Awards—in 1938 for "Always and Always" (for which they wrote the lyrics and Edward Ward the music) from Frank Borzage's *Mannequin*; in 1940 for "It's a Blue World" from Joseph Santley's *Music in My Heart*; and in 1942 for "Pennies for Peppino" from George Archinbaud's *Flying with Music*.

Cole Porter, who was working for MGM at the same time, became a great admirer of the pair. When the studio wanted additional lyrics for Van Dyke's *Rosalie* (1937), he suggested that they "get the boys" to write them. Wright and Forrest willingly provided uncredited lyrics to the film.

The two wrote music and lyrics for dozens of films and shorts at MGM, the last being Van Dyke's *I Married an Angel* (1942), the movie version of the Richard Rodgers and Lorenz Hart musical, for which the studio wanted new lyrics to replace some by Hart that they deemed too risqué.

When their MGM contract ended, Wright and Forrest, who had already done some theater work, gave up writing for movies to devote themselves to the musical stage.

They soon had a hit on their hands with *Song of Norway* (1944, book by Milton Lazarus), a fictionalized biography of Edvard Grieg, whose music they adapted for the score. *Song of Norway*, which featured dance performances by the Ballet Russe de Monte Carlo and choreography of George Balanchine, had a run of 860 performances on Broadway, the longest ever for an operetta in New York. The show also had a very successful two-year run in London beginning in 1946.

Wright and Forrest are probably best known for the score of *Kismet* (book by Charles Lederer and Luther Davis), which was based on the music of Alexander Borodin and won a Tony Award in 1953. Immensely popular on Broadway, the show also had great success in London. A film version, directed by Vincente Minnelli, came out in 1955. The most popular song from the show, "Stranger in Paradise," has been recorded by many artists, perhaps most notably Johnny Mathis.

Not all of Wright and Forrest's works were box-office hits. *Magdalena* (1948, book by Frederick Hazlitt Brennan and Homer Curran), based on music by Heitor Villa-Lobos, was, in Wright's opinion, one of their finest efforts, and the music and lyrics garnered favorable reviews, but the show closed after only eleven weeks on Broadway. *Anya* (1965, book by George Abbott and Guy Bolton), a retelling of the story of the czarina Anastasia set to music based on the work of Sergei Rachmaninoff, also closed quickly.

Timbuktu (1978, book by Luther Davis), a reworking of *Kismet* with an all-black cast, including Eartha Kitt, enjoyed a modest run in New York.

Wright and Forrest's adaptation of Vicki Baum's novel *Grand Hotel*, called *At the Grand* (book by Luther Davis), closed out of town in 1957, but a revised version, *Grand Hotel* (1989, book again by Davis), directed on Broadway by Tommy Tune, was a great success, winning five Tony Awards. Wright and Forrest's "Let's Take a Glass Together" is a show-stopper and was a highlight of the year's Tony Awards show. The critic Ed Real called *Grand Hotel* "one of the great musicals of the past decade—a complex and compelling work of theater."

During the 1990s, Wright and Forrest returned to a work they had begun three decades earlier with P. G. Wodehouse, *Betting on Bertie*, a musical about the Bertie Wooster character from Wodehouse's "Jeeves" stories.

The project ended when Forrest died in Miami on October 10, 1999.

Forrest's passing brought to an end a loving and creative partnership of over seven decades. Wright and Forrest's professional career included work in film, television, radio, the cabaret circuit, and most notably the stage, rightfully acknowledged when they were given the 1995 ASCAP/Richard Rodgers Award for their contributions to American musical theater.

—Linda Rapp

Bibliography

Block, Geoffrey. "Wright, Robert." *The New Grove Dictionary of Music and Musicians.* Second ed. Stanley Sadie, ed. London: Macmillan, 2001. 27: 579.

Chute, James. "The Men behind It Spin Popular Shows from Classical Works." *Orange County* (Calif.) *Register,* February 5, 1988.

Hanley, Robert. "George Forrest, 84, Songwriter for Broadway, Films and Clubs." Obituary. *New York Times,* October 12, 1999.

Real, Ed. "Grand 'Hotel' Open for Business at Le Petit." *New Orleans Times-Picayune,* September 17, 1999.

Vallance, Tom. "George Forrest." Obituary. *Independent* (London), October 14, 1999.

See also

Musical Theater and Film; Cabarets and Revues; Classical Music; Popular Music; Bourbon, Ray; Edens, Roger; Hart, Lorenz; Mathis, Johnny; Minnelli, Vincente; Porter, Cole; Tchaikovsky, Pyotr Ilich; Tune, Tommy

Z

Zeffirelli, Franco   (b. 1923)

FOR NEARLY HALF A CENTURY, FRANCO ZEFFIRELLI HAS been in the spotlight for his visually extravagant opera, stage, and film productions. While his self-proclaimed "crusade against boredom" in the dramatic arts and his emphasis on spectacle have brought him considerable acclaim, they have also been the target of significant critical derision.

The controversial Italian director has been lambasted by religious groups for his supposedly blasphemous representation of biblical figures, yet he has also provoked the ire of many gay men and lesbians for siding publicly with the Roman Catholic Church on homosexual issues.

Zeffirelli was born on February 12, 1923, in Florence, the son of Ottorino Corsi, a wealthy businessman, and his mistress Adelaide Garosi, a fashion designer. Through his father, Zeffirelli was related to the family that centuries before had produced Leonardo da Vinci.

He was originally Gianfranco Corsi, but his mother subsequently followed the Florentine tradition of naming a child born out of wedlock with a created name beginning with the letter Z. After his mother's death, he was placed in the care of an English governess, from whom he learned the English language and its literature.

Zeffirelli graduated from art school in 1941 and, following his father's plan, became an architecture student at the University of Florence. While at the university, he became active in directing student theatrical productions, including stagings of operas under the tutelage of his aunt Ines Alfani Tellini, a retired soprano.

In 1943, he left college to join the Partisans and fight against the Nazi occupation of Italy. Subsequently, he became an interpreter for the British Army after the Allied invasion.

As a result of meeting British troops who shared his dramatic interests, Zeffirelli abandoned his plans for a career in architecture and, after the war, became a theatrical set and costume designer.

During the late 1940s, he worked as an assistant to director Luchino Visconti, whose attention to realistic detail and action profoundly influenced the young apprentice's own work.

Through the 1950s and 1960s, Zeffirelli firmly established his reputation as a drama and opera director. In the former capacity, he presented highly naturalistic stagings of Shakespeare at London's Old Vic.

Simultaneously, he was responsible for noted productions at Milan's La Scala, London's Covent Garden, and New York's Metropolitan Opera, starring the leading divas of the period, particularly Maria Callas, Joan Sutherland, and Leontyne Price.

His lavish visual appeal created greater mainstream interest in legitimate theater and opera, but Zeffirelli's characteristic style—which he likened to that of the Hollywood epics of Cecil B. De Mille, "but in good taste"—did not meet with universal acclaim.

Many found his productions overdone to the extent that the sets and stage action drew attention away from the actual performance. Indeed, this was the case with the 1966 world premiere of Samuel Barber's *Antony and Cleopatra*, which was commissioned for the opening of the new Metropolitan Opera House in Lincoln Center. The technology operating the prodigious stage machinery malfunctioned, the spectacle was almost unanimously panned, and Barber's career was effectively ended.

His detractors notwithstanding, Zeffirelli continued to expand his audience during the mid-1960s with his debut as a film director. His first feature film, *The Taming of the Shrew* (1967), featured the most discussed theatrical couple of the day, Elizabeth Taylor and Richard Burton. As a cinematic rendering of a traditional work of English literature, it set the tone for many of his subsequent screen productions.

His best-known film, *Romeo and Juliet* (1968), soon followed. It was controversial for his casting of unknown and inexperienced (if highly attractive) teenaged actors in the title roles. He would again present such adolescent sensuality and sexual awakening in *Endless Love* (1981), which tells the story of an obsessive teen romance set against the backdrop of parental prohibition.

Zeffirelli's later films have received widely mixed reviews and are generally regarded as uneven in quality. These include *Brother Sun, Sister Moon* (1973), *Jesus of Nazareth* (television miniseries, 1977), film versions of Verdi's operas *La Traviata* (1982) and *Otello* (1986), *Hamlet* (with Mel Gibson and Glenn Close, 1990), *Jane Eyre* (1996), the autobiographical *Tea with Mussolini* (1999), and *Callas Forever* (2001).

Although Zeffirelli is openly gay and has frankly discussed his sexuality in his autobiography, he is nonetheless somewhat paradoxical in this regard. Some critics have noted a "homosexual gaze" in his films, particularly in their lingering and erotically tinged close-up shots of the seminude male body. In *Tea with Mussolini*, moreover, he cast Lily Tomlin as an unambiguously lesbian character.

At the same time, however, his advocacy of Catholic dogma in opposition to gay activism has not gone unnoticed, particularly his backing of Vatican efforts to thwart the inception of a Gay Pride parade in Rome.

Yet this seeming contradiction is, perhaps, characteristic of Zeffirelli's career and work, for which he has long been regarded with extreme degrees of reverence and revilement, in almost equal measure.

—*Patricia Juliana Smith*

BIBLIOGRAPHY

Zeffirelli, Franco. *Zeffirelli: The Autobiography of Franco Zeffirelli*. New York: Weidenfeld & Nicolson, 1986.

SEE ALSO

Opera; Set and Costume Design; Divas; Barber, Samuel

notes on contributors

DAVID ALDSTADT is a doctoral candidate in French cinema, modern French literature, and French culture at Ohio State University. His dissertation examines cinematic collaboration, authorship, and star personae in films by Marcel Carné with Arletty and by Jean Cocteau with Jean Marais. Entry: Divine

TYLER ALPERN is a painter. He teaches art at the University of Colorado at Boulder and other schools. Music and film studies are a consuming interest for him. Entry: Faye, Frances

ELIZABETH ASHBURN, Professor and Head of the School of Art in the College of Fine Arts at the University of New South Wales, Australia, is author of *Lesbian Art: An Encounter with Power* and numerous articles. She is copresident of the Australian Center for Gay and Lesbian Research. Entry: Drag Shows: Drag Kings and Male Impersonators

PAUL ATTINELLO teaches in the Department of Music at the University of Newcastle upon Tyne; he formerly taught at the University of Hong Kong. He has published in a number of journals, anthologies, and encyclopedias, including *Queering the Pitch,* the first collection of gay and lesbian musicology. He established and edited the Newsletter of the Gay & Lesbian Study Group of the American Musicological Society, and was also cofounder of the Society of Gay & Lesbian Composers in San Francisco. Entries: Bussotti, Sylvano; Choruses and Bands;

Del Tredici, David; Henze, Hans Werner; Music and AIDS; Susa, Conrad

GEOFFREY W. BATEMAN is the Assistant Director of the Center for the Study of Sexual Minorities in the Military, a research center based at the University of California, Santa Barbara, that promotes the study of gay men and lesbians in the military. He is coeditor of *Don't Ask, Don't Tell: Debating the Gay Ban in the Military,* as well as author of a study on gay personnel and multinational units. He earned his M.A. in English literature at the University of California, Santa Barbara, in eighteenth-century British literature and theories of genders and sexuality, but now lives in Denver, Colorado, where he is coparenting two sons with his partner and a lesbian couple. Entries: Conductors; Tilson Thomas, Michael

CORINNE E. BLACKMER is Associate Professor of English at Southern Connecticut State University. With Patricia Juliana Smith, she has edited a collection of essays on opera. Entry: Opera

JEFFERY BYRD, Professor of Art at the University of Northern Iowa, is a performance artist and photographer whose work has been featured in numerous solo exhibitions and journals. He has performed at New York City's Lincoln Center and Alternative Museum, Boston's Institute of Contemporary Art, Chicago's N.A.M.E. Gallery, and Cleveland's Performance Festival. Entries: Cage, John; Cunningham, Merce

ALBERT J. CAREY is a lifelong resident of New Orleans. An architect by profession, he was one of the designers of the St. Bernard Auditorium, where most of the gay Mardi Gras balls are held. He is an avid fan of musical theater. Entry: Coward, Sir Noël

MARIO CHAMPAGNE, Administrative Director of the Department of Music at Stanford University, holds a Ph.D. in Musicology from the University of North Carolina at Chapel Hill. He has been a member of the Gay and Lesbian Studies Group of the American Musicological Society since its inception in 1985. Entries: Falla (y Matheu), Manuel de; Classical Music; Poulenc, Francis

JOHN M. CLUM is Professor of English and Professor of the Practice of Theater at Duke University. Among his books are *Still Acting Gay: Male Homosexuality in Modern Drama; Something for the Boys: Musical Theater and Gay Culture*; and *He's All Man: Learning Masculinity, Gayness and Love from American Movies.* Entry: Musical Theater and Film

SHAUN COLE is Curator of Designs at the Victoria and Albert Museum, London. He is author of *"Don We Now Our Gay Apparel": Gay Men's Dress in the Twentieth Century* and has curated numerous exhibitions, including Graphic Responses to AIDS (1996), Fashion on Paper (1997), and Dressing the Male (1999), as well as two innovative "Days of Record" to document Tattooing (2000) and Black British Hairstyles and Nail Art (2001). Entries: Bowery, Leigh; Somerville, Jimmy

BUD COLEMAN, Associate Professor in the Department of Theater and Dance at the University of Colorado at Boulder, is a former dancer with Les Ballets Trockadero de Monte Carlo (as Natasha Notgoudenuff), Fort Worth Ballet, Kinesis, and Ballet Austin. He has directed and choreographed numerous productions and published in several journals and encyclopedias. Entries: Ballets Trockadero de Monte Carlo; Bennett, Michael; Cabarets and Revues; Jones, Bill T.; Liberace; Pierce, Charles; Robbins, Jerome; Taylor, Paul; Tune, Tommy

KIERON DEVLIN studied Art & Design at Manchester Art School, England. He holds a Master's degree from Leicester University and an M.F.A. in Creative Writing from New York City's New School. He is working on a novel and a collection of short stories. Entries: Corelli, Arcangelo; Kemp, Lindsay; Set and Costume Design

JOHN LOUIS DIGAETANI is Professor of English at Hofstra University, where he specializes in modern literature and its connections with music. He is author of *Richard Wagner and the Modern British Novel; An Invitation to the Opera; Puccini the Thinker*; and *A Search for a Postmodern Theater: Interviews with Contemporary Playwrights,* as well as numerous essays. Entries: Harrison, Lou; Menotti, Gian Carlo; Ravel, Maurice

LAURIE TOBY EDISON is an internationally exhibited photographer based in San Francisco. Her work includes *Women En Large: Images of Fat Nudes; Familiar Men: A Book of Nudes*; "Women of Japan"; and "Double Visions." The mother of two daughters, she is a member of the Gay & Lesbian History Project, Queer Nation, and other queer activist groups. Entry: Takarazuka (Japanese All-Female Revues)

JEFFREY ESCOFFIER writes on glbtq history, politics, culture, sexuality, music, and dance. One of the founders of OUT/LOOK: National Lesbian and Gay Quarterly, he has published widely. Among his books are *American Homo: Community and Perversity* and a biography of John Maynard Keynes in the Chelsea House series on the Lives of Notable Gay Men and Lesbians. He coedited (with Matthew Lore) Mark Morris's *L'Allegro, il Penseroso ed il Moderato: A Celebration.* His most recent book is *Sexual Revolution,* an anthology of writing on sex from the 1960s and 1970s. He is currently working on a book on sexual politics and writing about the production of pornography. Entries: Jazz; McPhee, Colin

EUGENIO FILICE is a doctoral student in art history at McGill University. He is currently preparing a dissertation on the representation of gay men in contemporary Canadian art, and on the revival of figurative painting that occurred during the late 1970s and 1980s. Entries: Pet Shop Boys; Smiths, The, and Morrissey

RAYMOND-JEAN FRONTAIN is Professor of English at the University of Central Arkansas. He has published widely on seventeenth-century English literature and on English adaptations of biblical literature. He is editor of *Reclaiming the Sacred: The Bible in Gay and Lesbian Culture.* He is engaged in a study of the David figure in homoerotic art and literature. Entries: Hart, Lorenz; Herman, Jerry; Laurents, Arthur; Kander, John, and Fred Ebb; Porter, Cole; Sondheim, Stephen

TINA GIANOULIS is an essayist and freelance writer who has contributed to a number of encyclopedias and anthologies, as well as to journals such as *Sinister Wisdom.* Entries: Allen, Peter; Boulanger, Nadia; Boy George (George O'Dowd); Country Music; Dietrich, Marlene; Duncan, Isadora; Garland, Judy; lang, k.d.; Minnelli, Vincente; Rainey, Gertrude ("Ma"); Reed, Lou; RuPaul (RuPaul Andre Charles); Waters, Ethel

ROBERT A. GREEN, Professor in the School of Music at Northern Illinois University, is author of *The Hurdy-Gurdy in Eighteenth-Century France* and of several articles in *The New Grove* and in journals such as *Early Music* and the *Haydn Yearbook*. Entries: Lully, Jean-Baptiste; Rosenmüller, Johann

ROBIN IMHOF is a Reference Librarian at San Francisco State University. She specializes in nineteenth-century Symbolist and Decadent literature. Entry: Wagnerism

JOE E. JEFFREYS lives in New York City. His writing has appeared in publications from the *Village Voice* to the *Dallas Voice*, from *blue* to *Blueboy*, and from *Bay Windows* to the *Bay Area Reporter*. Entry: Russell, Craig

JACQUELINE JENKINS teaches Medieval Literature and Culture as well as Film and Gender Studies at the University of Calgary. Her research interests include vernacular book production and the reading habits of late medieval lay-women; women's spirituality and late medieval religiosity; Saints' legends and performance; medieval and contemporary popular culture. Entry: Hildegard of Bingen

CRAIG KACZOROWSKI writes extensively on media, culture, and the arts. He holds an M.A. in English Language and Literature, with a focus on contemporary critical theory, from the University of Chicago. He comments on national media trends for two newspaper-industry magazines. Entries: Morris, Mark; Rock Music; Rorem, Ned

ROBERT KELLERMAN holds a doctorate in English literature from Michigan State University. Entries: Blitzstein, Marc; Corigliano, John; Tchaikovsky, Pyotr Ilich; Village People

MATTHEW KENNEDY teaches anthropology at City College of San Francisco and film history at the San Francisco Conservatory of Music. A film critic for the *Bay Area Reporter,* he has also written for such publications as *Performing Arts*, the *San Francisco Chronicle*, and *Bright Lights Film Journal*. He is author of *Marie Dressler* and a biography of film director Edmund Goulding. Entry: Novello, Ivor

CHARLES KRINSKY teaches in the Liberal Studies and Ethnic and Women's Studies Departments of California State Polytechnic University, Pomona. His research focuses on the construction of masculinity and male sexuality in post–World War II American films and culture. Entry: Cowell, Henry

JOHN MCFARLAND is a Seattle-based critic, essayist, and short story writer. He is author of the award-winning

picture book *The Exploding Frog and Other Fables from Aesop*. He has contributed to such anthologies as *Letters to Our Children: Lesbian and Gay Adults Speak to the New Generation; The Book Club Book; The Isherwood Century;* and *Letters to J. D. Salinger*. Entries: Béjart, Maurice; Bruhn, Erik; Lifar, Serge; Van Dantzig, Rudi

JULIA PASTORE is a New York–based freelance writer who works in book publishing. Entry: Schubert, Franz

LINDA RAPP teaches French and Spanish at the University of Michigan–Dearborn. She freelances as a writer, tutor, and translator. She is Assistant to the General Editor of www.glbtq.com. Entries: Allan, Maud; Ashman, Howard; Bell, Andy; Cheung, Leslie; Christian, Meg; Cliburn, Van; Curry, John; DiFranco, Ani; Doone, Rupert; Edens, Roger; Etheridge, Melissa; Feinstein, Michael; Fernie, Lynne; Finn, William; Heath, Gordon; Ian, Janis; Mathis, Johnny; Mitropoulos, Dimitri; Pansy Division; Robinson, Tom; Shaiman, Marc, and Scott Wittman; Stipe, Michael; Wainwright, Rufus; Wolfe, George C.; Wright, Robert, and George "Chet" Forrest

THOMAS L. RIIS is Director of the American Music Research Center and Professor of Music at the College of Music at the University of Colorado–Boulder. A specialist in American musical theater, Riis's interests are wide-ranging, including medieval song, historical performance practice, and African American music. Entry: Griffes, Charles Tomlinson

GILLIAN RODGER, Assistant Professor of Musicology at the University of Wisconsin–Milwaukee, completed her Ph.D. from the University of Pittsburgh with a dissertation entitled "Male Impersonation on the North American Variety and Vaudeville Stage, 1868–1939," which received the 1998 Philip Brett Award for exceptional work in the field of queer musicology. Her current work focuses on American popular music and musical theater from the mid-nineteenth century and on gender representation in contemporary popular music and music videos. Entries: Bentley, Gladys; Hindle, Annie; Variety and Vaudeville

MIGUEL A. SEGOVIA was born in Monterrey, Mexico, and raised in Houston, Texas. He is a doctoral student in Religious Studies at Brown University. Entry: Vargas, Chavela

PATRICIA JULIANA SMITH is Assistant Professor of English at Hofstra University. With Corinne Blackmer, she has edited a collection of essays, *En Travesti: Women, Gender Subversion, Opera*. She is also author of *Lesbian Panic: Homoeroticism in Modern British Women's*

Fiction and editor of *The Queer Sixties* and *The Gay and Lesbian Book of Quotations*. She serves on the editorial advisory board of www.glbtq.com. Entries: Barber, Samuel; Berners, Baron Gerald Hugh Tyrwhitt-Wilson; Bernstein, Leonard; Britten, Benjamin; Castrati; Copland, Aaron; Davies, Sir Peter Maxwell; Divas; Epstein, Brian; Landowska, Wanda; Mercer, Mabel; Mercury, Freddie; Pears, Peter; Saint-Saëns, Camille; Schlesinger, John; Springfield, Dusty; Thomson, Virgil; Tippett, Sir Michael; Zeffirelli, Franco

CLAUDE J. SUMMERS is William E. Stirton Professor Emeritus in the Humanities and Professor Emeritus of English at the University of Michigan–Dearborn. He has published widely on seventeenth- and twentieth-century English literature, including book-length studies of E. M. Forster and Christopher Isherwood, as well as *Gay Fictions: Wilde to Stonewall* and *Homosexuality in Renaissance and Enlightenment England: Literary Representations in Historical Context*. He is General Editor of www.glbtq.com. Entries: Bourbon, Ray; Coward, Sir Noël

TERESA THEOPHANO, a freelance writer, is a social worker who specializes in community organizing with glbtq populations. She is also the editor of *Queer Quotes*. Entries: Baez, Joan; Jett, Joan; Joplin, Janis; Jorgensen, Christine; Kirstein, Lincoln; Women's Music Festivals; Women's Music; Near, Holly; Strayhorn, William Thomas; Williamson, Cris

GARY C. THOMAS is Morse–Alumni Distinguished Teaching Professor in Cultural Studies and Comparative Literature at the University of Minnesota. Among his published works are a historical edition of Constantin Christian Dedekind's *Aelbianische Musen-Lust* and, coedited with Philip Brett and Elizabeth Wood, *Queering the Pitch: The New Gay and Lesbian Musicology*. Entry: Handel, George Frideric

JOE A. THOMAS is Associate Professor and Chair of the Art Department at Clarion University of Pennsylvania. His research focuses primarily on issues of sexuality and representation, but also digresses into American Pop Art and Italian Mannerism. Entry: Disco and Dance Music

NATHAN G. TIPTON is a Ph.D. student in Textual Studies at the University of Memphis. He has published essays in a number of periodicals and scholarly journals. His dissertation focuses on couples and coupling in Shakespeare's problem plays, but he has "queered"

everything from Robert Penn Warren to Martha Stewart to Cartoon Network's "Cow and Chicken." Entries: Geffen, David; John, Sir Elton; Little Richard (Richard Penniman); Michael, George; Sylvester

DOUGLAS BLAIR TURNBAUGH is Representative to the U.S.A. and Membre Conseiller of the Conseil International de la Danse/UNESCO. A contributor to *New York Magazine*, the *Atlantic, Playbill*, the *Advocate, RFD, James White Review, New York Native, Performing Arts Journal, Ecrits sur Nijinsky*, among others, he is author of *Duncan Grant and the Bloomsbury Group; Private: The Erotic Art of Duncan Grant; Strip Show: Paintings by Patrick Angus*; and *Beat It: 28 Drawings*. He has been awarded the Nijinsky medal (Poland) and the Diaghilev medal (Russia). His *Serge Diaghilev* is forthcoming. Entries: Ailey, Alvin; Ashton, Sir Frederick; Ballet; Ballets Russes; Dance; Diaghilev, Sergei; Joffrey, Robert; Kabuki; Nijinsky, Vaslav; Nureyev, Rudolf; Szymanowski, Karol Maciej

GREG VARNER was arts editor of the *Washington Blade* from October 1997 until September 2001. He earned an undergraduate degree in writing at Oberlin College, and a master's degree at the University of Virginia. He lives in Washington, D.C. Entry: Goode, Joe

CARLA WILLIAMS is a writer and photographer from Los Angeles who lives and works in Santa Fe. Her writings and images can be found on her website at www.carlagirl.net. Entries: Blues Music; Hunter, Alberta; Indigo Girls; Popular Music; Music Video; Smith, Bessie; Sweet Honey in the Rock

TAMSIN WILTON is Reader in Sociology at the University of the West of England, Bristol. She has published widely on lesbian and gay issues since 1988, and has visited many countries to lecture on lesbian studies and on the sociology of HIV/AIDS. Her books include *Lesbian Studies: Setting an Agenda; Immortal, Invisible: Lesbians and the Moving Image*; and *Sexualities in Health and Social Care*. Entries: Bowie, David; Smyth, Dame Ethel

ANDRES MARIO ZERVIGON earned his Ph.D. from Harvard University and is now Associate Professor of Art History at California's University of La Verne. He specializes in the art and design of Germany's Weimar period and in the painting of Britain's post–World War II era. Entries: Drag Shows: Drag Queens and Female Impersonators; Molina, Miguel de

index of names